The Interpretation of
the Epistle to the Hebrews
and the Epistle of James

R. C. H. LENSKI

Augsburg Fortress
Minneapolis

THE INTERPRETATION OF THE EPISTLE TO THE HEBREWS
AND THE EPISTLE OF JAMES
Commentary on the New Testament series

First paperback edition 2008

Copyright ©1946, 2008 Augsburg Fortress. All rights reserved. Except for brief quotations in critical articles or reviews, no part of this book may be reproduced in any manner without prior written permission from the publisher. Visit http://www.augsburgfortress.org/copyrights/contact.asp or write to Permissions, Augsburg Fortress, Box 1209, Minneapolis, MN 55440.

Richard C. H. Lenski's commentaries on the New Testament were published in the 1940s after the author's death. This volume was copyrighted in 1938 by the Lutheran Book Concern, published in 1946 by the Wartburg Press, and assigned in 1961 to the Augsburg Publishing House.

ISBN 978-0-8066-9010-0

The paper used in this publication meets the minimum requirements of American National Standard for Information Sciences—Permanence of Paper for Printed Library Materials, ANSI Z329.48-1984.

Manufactured in the U.S.A.

ABBREVIATIONS

R. = A Grammar of the Greek New Testament in the Light of Historical Research, by A. T. Robertson, 4th ed.

B.-D. = Friedrich Blass' Grammatik des neutestamentlichen Griechisch, vierte, voellig neugearbeitete Auflage, besorgt von Albert Debrunner.

C.-K. = Biblisch-theologisches Woerterbuch der Neutestamentlichen Graezitaet von D. D. Hermann Cremer, zehnte, etc., Auflage, herausgegeben von D. Dr. Julius Koegel.

T. = Synonyms of the New Testament, by Richard Chevenix Trench, D. D.

C. Tr. = Concordia Triglotta. The Symbolical Books of the Ev. Lutheran Church, German-Latin-English. St. Louis, Mo., Concordia Publishing House.

NOTE. The translation is intended only as an aid in understanding the Greek.

The Epistle
To the Hebrews

INTRODUCTION

Τίς δὲ ὁ γράψας τὴν ἐπιστολήν, τὸ μὲν ἀληθὲς Θεὸς οἶδεν. Origen. "Who wrote the epistle in truth God alone knows." Riggenbach, in Zahn's commentary: "This admonishes us to exert ourselves less about the solution of at present insoluble problems and more about the attainable goal, a thorough understanding of the letter." The older Origen and the recent Riggenbach are discouraged, yet the case is not hopeless by any means. The trouble has been that students have not used the data that are available in the New Testament itself.

Differences of opinion about New Testament writings are for the most part of recent origin. A number of doubts and denials is the product of modern, hypercritical minds. The uncertainty regarding Hebrews extends back to the end of the first century. It involves not only the question of authorship, of the people addressed, of the time of composition, but also the grave question regarding its right to a place in the canon. More than two centuries passed before Hebrews was authoritatively accepted as a part of the New Testament canon. However, since that time Hebrews has kept that sacred place on the strength of the quality and the character of its contents, which the great body of the church has recognized as bearing the stamp of inspiration despite the fact that the identity of the writer has not been determined during all these centuries.

The older uncertainties led Luther to place Hebrews after the Third Epistle of St. John in his German translation of the Bible. For him as the translator and for the scholars of his time all the old questions about Hebrews were raised anew. Luther accepted the book as deutero-canonical, as one of the antilegomena, which are a part of the canon; because they were not universally accepted during the first centuries they are to be considered as being on a lower level than the proto-canonical books, the homologoumena. Those who are interested in the question may consult Zahn, *Geschichte des Neutestamentlichen Kanons*, 300, etc., where they will find a sketch of the attitude regarding Hebrews during the early centuries. Chemnitz wanted all the deutero-canonical books removed from the New Testament canon. On the other hand, many now want the distinction between the deutero-canonical and the proto-canonical books wiped out. Both are extreme positions. The history of Hebrews in the early church remains what it is. It cannot be wiped out to please some, nevertheless this history does not warrant a rejection of this book from the canon.

Hebrews attests itself as being an inspired writing. It is and must remain a part of the canon. The warrant for classing Hebrews as deutero-canonical does not lie in its contents — there lies its invincible strength; this warrant lies only in the early uncertainty regarding the writer of Hebrews, an uncertainty which still perplexes the scholars.

* * *

Paul did not write Hebrews.

The early Alexandrians thought that Paul was the author of this epistle. The Synod of Hippo in 393 and the Synods of Carthage in 397 and 419 definitely placed Hebrews into the canon, the former two adding Hebrews to the thirteen Pauline letters with *ejusdem ad Hebraeos una*, the latter counting fourteen Pauline letters. In spite of these decisions the use made of

Hebrews declined in the fifth century, and in the middle of the sixth century Cassiodorus states that as yet no Latin commentary on Hebrews had been written. The Council of Trent decreed that Hebrews is one of the fourteen letters of Paul; yet ardent Romanists like Bellarmine, Este, and recent Catholic scholars hold other views.

An older opinion maintained that Luke translated a Hebrew original from the pen of Paul into Greek. This supposition aimed to explain the great difference in style between Hebrews and Paul's acknowledged letters. Yet Hebrews cannot be regarded as a translation from the Aramaic. The difference in style is decisive against Pauline authorship. This includes far more than formal style; it refers to the whole manner of thought and to its mode of presentation. An appeal to the great versatility of Paul is not a satisfactory answer. Paul is as versatile in Greek as he is in Aramaic, and he would write a Greek letter without thought of employing a translator. But it is inexplicable that he should use the most perfect Greek when he is writing to readers, all of whom were former Jews and inclined to return to Judaism, and never write such Greek in any other of his letters when he is addressing readers who were for the most part Gentiles. As for Luke, who is, indeed, skilled in Greek, whenever he reproduces Aramaic originals he allows it to remain evident that his sources are Aramaic.

The mention of Timothy in 13:23 has caused some to think of Paul. But this has too little weight to offset all that speaks so decisively against Pauline authorship. The incorrect reading τοῖς δέσμοις μου in 13:3, "my bonds," has been referred to in order to make Hebrews one of Paul's letters that was written while he was in prison. The correct reading is τοῖς δεσμίοις, "those that were in bonds," "the prisoners," see the exposition of 13:3. Much more may be added, yet not a single thing that points to Paul as being the author.

* * *

In the ancient church Barnabas was regarded as a possible author of this epistle. Riggenbach, in Zahn's commentary, advocates this possibility and locates the readers of Hebrews in Cyprus where Paul and Barnabas began their missionary labors, whither Barnabas and Mark returned for further missionary work (Acts 15:39), where there were many Jews. Judging from the first missionary journey of Paul and Barnabas, during which Sergius Paulus, a pagan of Cyprus, was impressed by the gospel, during which the Galatian churches, all of which were predominantly Gentile, were founded, it cannot be assumed that in his further labors in Cyprus Barnabas built up purely Jewish Christian congregations and that he now addresses them as such. Yet, if these congregations in Cyprus were made up of both Jewish and Gentile Christians, as they must have been, it would be impossible for Barnabas to write a letter only to the Jewish membership without addressing a single word to the Gentile portion of these churches.

Stress is laid on the fact that Barnabas had been a Levite and was thus fully acquainted with the entire Temple ritual. The writer of Hebrews, however, does not refer to the Temple ritual but only to the Tabernacle and to its ritual as these are recorded in the Pentateuch because he has divine Scripture for this material; he does not refer even to the Solomonic Temple, to say nothing of Ezra's or Herod's temples. All who knew the Law, the Pentateuch, also all the Hebrews addressed in this letter, even if they had never been to Jerusalem and had never seen the Temple, knew all about the Tabernacle in the wilderness and its ritual, knew it from their sacred LXX.

A Levite with a knowledge of the Jerusalem Temple, which he had gained by personal service in Jerusalem, was not needed to write this letter or to read it with perfect understanding. It is strange that Riggenbach sees so clearly that Hebrews deals only with the Tabernacle and with the Scripture about the Tabernacle and yet lays emphasis on a Levite's experience in the Temple.

Barnabas was, indeed, a man of power. So was John, so was Peter. But grant all the power desired, this does not explain the quality of the Greek used in Hebrews. It is not credible that Barnabas wrote Greek that is finer than that of even Luke.

The writer of Hebrews speaks to his readers with great authority and at times severity. One might think that this is fitting in a man of power such as Barnabas was when he writes to Jewish Christians, say in Cyprus. But the writer of Hebrews never speaks as though he were the founder of the congregations to whom he writes; on the contrary, he speaks of their leaders as being already dead (13:7) and distinguishes these from their present leaders (13:17). Even if we accept the view that this letter was addressed to Christians who were living in Cyprus, Barnabas could not very well have been the author of Hebrews, for Barnabas was the founder of these congregations. The impossibility of accepting Cyprus as the destination of this epistle is intensified by 10:32-34 and 12:4 unless we imagine situations in Cyprus to fit these two references to the persecutions suffered by the readers.

To escape these insuperable difficulties regarding Cyprus the readers have been located in Jerusalem or in Palestine in general. Thus some hope to retain either Paul or Barnabas as the author; Delitzsch decides for Paul. Now we do find Barnabas in Jerusalem in Acts 4:36; 9:27; 11:22, yet he has no authoritative standing. Barnabas rose to prominence only after he left Jerusalem, only in Antioch (Acts 11:22, 25; 11:30; 12:25; 13:1) and not in connection with Jewish but with Gentile missionary endeavor, first in connection with Gentile missions right in Antioch and then in company with Paul on the first great missionary journey especially in founding the Gentile Galatian churches. It is quite impossible to assume that Barnabas was many years later again connected with Jerusalem and with the Jewish work in Palestine so that he could have written Hebrews to the Jewish Christians in Jerusalem or in Palestine. The probability is that Barnabas was dead when Hebrews was written. The limited tradition regarding Barnabas as the writer of Hebrews is too slender to support itself. All the known facts contradict this tradition.

It is equally impossible that Paul should have written Hebrews to Christians in Jerusalem or in Palestine. As was the case with Barnabas, the course of his life and labors took him into other directions. The readers of Hebrews, all of whom were former Jews, were inclined to revert to Judaism; the purpose of the letter is to prevent this apostasy. If these people lived in Jerusalem or in Palestine in general, who would be the man to step in to show them the folly of this their intention or inclination? Men like Barnabas or like Paul who were far from the Holy Land and its capital? Was there no one nearer to them, in closer contact with them personally, no one right on the ground, who did not need to write and to send them a letter? The question answers itself.

Jerusalem had James the Just, the brother of the Lord, a mighty leader to the very time of his martyrdom, which is by Josephus dated in the year 63, by Zahn in 66, by Hegesippus as late as 68. We need not trouble about the exact date of his death. For in addition to James the Just, Jerusalem and Palestine had the apostle John until the time of the Jewish war.

Introduction 13

When he could remain no longer he transferred his headquarters to Ephesus. Then also the Christians evacuated Jerusalem and fled to Pella. *If* a desire to return to Judaism had become evident among these people, there was James until the time of his martyrdom, and there was John himself to take the necessary measures, and not by means of a letter sent from afar — James never travelled far from Jerusalem, and John had his headquarters in the mother church. *If*, however, a letter had to be written, let us say after the death of James, not Paul or Barnabas but John would have written that letter.

Much more must be said. When Jerusalem's doom was sealed, we find the Christians safe in Pella. The very idea that these Jewish Christians in Jerusalem or in Palestine could at any time during this period have entertained the thought of reverting to Judaism is impossible. Read Josephus! For years the conditions in the capital and in the land generally had grown desperate. As a nation the Jews were disintegrating. The city and especially the Temple became the stage for the most horrible scenes, assassinations and massacres. Fanatical factions sought to exterminate each other. The Romans were literally forced to step in. The story is too long to be even sketched here. It is impossible to imagine that any Christian in Palestine should think of going back to these Jews, to such high priests as they had, and to a Judaism that was in such a state. No matter who wrote Hebrews, the people to whom this letter was sent cannot have lived in Jerusalem or in Palestine during this entire period.

The main question is in regard to the people to whom Hebrews is addressed. The entire epistle reveals them as being a body of Jewish Christians, some of whom were minded to apostatize and to revert to Judaism. These people did not live in Jerusalem or in Palestine, no matter what date we assign to the epistle.

Introduction

Other names have been suggested. Mark is one of these; but his Greek is inferior even to that of Matthew. Ad. Harnack offers Aquila and Priscilla as joint writers; no refutation of this view is needed.

* * *

The recipients of this epistle were not Gentiles although such a view has been advocated. Nor were they a mixed group, partly Jewish, partly Gentile. Hebrews nowhere deals with or addresses Gentile Christian readers; and it is impossible to assume that Hebrews is addressed only to the Jewish members of a mixed group to the exclusion of the Gentile members. Hebrews is addressed exclusively to Jewish Christians. Yet this letter is not a general or catholic epistle that is addressed to any and to all Jewish Christians who were living in the world at the time of its writing. It is addressed to a specific group of Jewish Christians who live in the same city or locality, whom the writer intends to visit as soon as possible in company with Timothy (13:23), some of whose noble leaders are dead (13:7), whose living leaders the writer bids the readers obey (13:17), and whom he also salutes (13:24).

In this body of Jewish Christians a movement is under way to give up Christianity and to go back to their former Judaism. This movement has as yet not gained much momentum, no members have actually apostatized, the leaders still stand firm. This body of Jewish Christians has suffered some persecution for sympathizing with brethren who are of their own body but were imprisoned (10:32-34), yet none of the readers were themselves imprisoned at that time, and none of them had lost their lives by martyrdom (12:4). This entire body of Jewish Christians had remained true during the trying times of the past; but something had now occurred which led a number of them to think that it would be a great advantage to them to go back

Introduction 15

to their old Judaism. It is this incipient defection which calls forth this letter. Its one object is to counteract this dangerous movement. This letter is convincing in the attainment of this object. Every paragraph strikes home.

These are the data that are embodied in the letter itself. The great question for us to decide is: "Where do we at the time this letter was written find such a body of unmixed Jewish Christians?" There is only one answer: "Not in Palestine, not in Cyprus, as we have already shown; nor in Alexandria, in Berea, or in any similar place." This body of purely Jewish Christians lived *in Rome*. The salutation of "those from Italy" in 13:24 points almost directly to Rome.

A number of investigators are agreed that the readers of Hebrews were located in Rome and cannot be found in any other place. Zahn is one of them. Yet none of them has seen how complete and how convincing the evidence is. They fail especially in one point. They think that the Jews whom Paul converted during his first imprisonment in Rome joined the original congregation which had existed in Rome for something like twenty years and included a considerable proportion of Gentile Christians. In order to establish this point let us review the story that is presented in Acts.

* * *

The night after the centurion Lysias had placed Paul before the Sanhedrin the Lord appeared to Paul and said to him: "Be of good cheer, Paul, for as thou hast testified of me *in Jerusalem,* so must thou testify *also in Rome.*" A remarkable statement! Paul's great work of testifying had been done in *pagan* lands, among Gentiles; he had done very little "in Jerusalem." Yet the Lord himself says: "As in Jerusalem, so also in Rome," and not: "As in the Roman provinces, so also in Rome itself." The Lord himself is sending Paul to Rome to do a great piece of *Jewish* mission work in Rome that is to be far greater than the bit of Jewish mission work he had been able to do in that other capital, Jerusalem.

The implication lies on the surface: no *Jewish* mission work had as yet been done in Rome. Here was a rich field, hitherto untouched, into which the Lord himself sends Paul. A Christian congregation had existed in Rome for some time. Before Paul's journey to take the collection of the Gentile churches to Jerusalem, Paul had written to this Roman congregation from Corinth and had told of his plans to visit them when he would be going westward to work in the great province of Spain. Paul had not intended to stop in Rome for a long time, had not thought of doing much work there, especially not among the Jews in Rome. The Lord's plan was that Paul should first do this great Jewish work in Rome and after that the work in Spain. The Lord intended to retain Paul in Rome for two years in order to have this Jewish work thoroughly done.

At this time Rome had seven large synagogues. There was a considerable number of Jews in Rome. Imperial decrees accorded them and their religious customs many special privileges. Claudius had been their very good friend. Only because they grew too turbulent in the city did he feel compelled to expel them, Acts 18:2; they returned after his death. The Christian congregation in Rome had ever let the Jews in Rome severely alone. The remark made by Tacitus that the disturbance at the time of Claudius was instigated by a man named Christus is wrongly referred to Christ. The Christian congregation in Rome was in no way involved in this Jewish episode even as the Christians were not ordered to vacate the city. The commentators on Romans have ever disputed about the complexion of this original congregation and have asked to what extent it was composed of former Jews and to what extent of former Gentiles. Rom. 16:3-16 furnishes the direct answer to this question. Paul salutes the *entire* congregation and names all its prominent members, and tells us who of them were Jewish. He even indicates who of them had been converted to Christ prior to his own conversion. We find Romans (Acts 2:10) in Jerusalem already at the time of Pentecost.

It is not difficult to discover why this original congregation in Rome, despite the fact that there were converted Jews in its membership, despite the fact that some of these converts were themselves Romans at the time of their conversion, never attempted any work among the large Jewish population in Rome. A number of these Jewish Christians of the original congregation had passed through the direst experience in Jerusalem a brief time after their conversion, during the persecution that began with Stephen's martyrdom, from which the Christians in the Holy City fled in dismay. They had had enough of the murderous Sanhedrin and of the Jews in general, whom even their friend Claudius had to drive out of Rome. Thus, when they fled Jerusalem and Palestine and came to live in Rome, which for some of them was their former home, they kept aloof from all contact with the seven Jewish synagogues in Rome.

This was the situation when Paul arrived in Rome as a prisoner. Paul, however, has the Lord's own orders to testify to the Jews in Rome, Acts 23:11. He proceeds to do so at once. As soon as he is established in his rented house he invites the head men of the Jews, their rabbis and their leaders, to come to him. Remarkable! How could Paul hope to have his invitation accepted if the Jews in Rome had already clashed with the original Christian congregation in

Rome? Not only is Paul's invitation promptly accepted, but when Paul explains how he has come to Rome as a prisoner, these leading Jews state that they have heard nothing whatever against Paul and know only that "this sect" (the Christians) is everywhere spoken against, i. e., they themselves have never had any personal contact with Christians although Rome itself has had a Christian congregation for years. This statement cannot be called a "diplomatic" remark. These leading Roman Jews state the facts.

That is why they gladly appoint a day for a special conference with Paul when he may present the whole account of the gospel at length. Luke tells us that, when the day came, even more (πλείονες) of the Jewish πρῶτοι or chief men attended the conference and remained with Paul the livelong day. Think of it: so many of the rabbis and prominent men from the seven synagogues all day with Paul, listening to his testifying (σε δεῖ μαρτυρῆσαι, Acts 23:11)! What was the result? On that day about half of all these Jewish leaders were brought to faith. Luke writes, Acts 28:24: οἱ μέν . . . οἱ δέ: fifty . . . fifty. In my opinion it was the greatest success Paul had ever scored in one day's work. This was only the beginning. Paul continued this work for two years. He may, of course, have done considerable work also among the Gentiles, but he certainly energetically followed up his great success among the Jews, for which he had the Lord's own special order. See the full exposition of Acts 28:16-31.

Since so many leaders were converted on that one day, it is easy to surmise what followed. These leaders carried Christ into their synagogues. There the work went forward. It surely was not long until the separation between believing Jews and unbelieving Jews became fixed and permanent. The assumption that the converts left the seven synagogues and became members of the original mixed congregation cannot be correct. No; several of the seven synagogues in Rome, shall we say at least three or four, became Christian congregations. Those members of the synagogue that refused to accept the gospel left and went over to the synagogues that remained unbelieving.

The important point when one is considering Hebrews is the fact that we here have the compact body of entirely unmixed Jewish Christians to whom this epistle was written. It was formed by Paul during his first imprisonment in 61-63.

* * *

Let us continue. Paul left Rome in 63. Early in 64 Paul returned from Nicopolis to Rome on his way to Spain. Peter had come to Rome. It is agreed that Peter's stay in Rome was about a year in duration. Thus Paul met Peter in Rome in the spring of 64. Paul hastened on to Spain and left Peter in Rome, who certainly also taught in the Christianized synagogues in Rome. In this same year, in July, 64, Rome went up in flames. The rumor spread that Nero himself had fired the city. To avert this suspicion Nero and his adherents accused the Christians in Rome of this incendiarism. By October, 64, many had been crucified, thrown to wild dogs, daubed with pitch, tied to stakes, and converted into torches in Nero's gardens while he drove by in his chariot and enjoyed the evening. Peter himself was crucified. Still worse, Christianity, which was now clearly distinguished from Jewry, became a *religio illicita* in Rome and then in the provinces. To be a Christian became a capital crime. Paul was in Spain. When Peter, who was in Rome, saw what was coming he wrote his first epistle to all the churches in the provinces mentioned in I Pet. 1:1. He acted for Paul in this capacity. On the data involved see the introduction to Paul's letters to Timothy and to Titus and to Peter's first letter.

At this point some are confused in regard to Hebrews. They place all of Paul's Jewish converts in Rome into the old, original congregation and thus have difficulty in explaining 10:32-34 and 12:4. Paul's converts, this entire body of Jewish Christians in Rome, remained in their own synagogues. They remained a body apart The authorities in Rome and the general populace still considered the people in these Christianized synagogues as Jews. Nero's blow fell only on the old, original congregation, a number of whose members belonged to Nero's own household; see the exposition of Rom. 16:10b, 11b, and of Phil. 4:22. The martyrs came from this old congregation; the Jewish Christians escaped.

We may now read 10:32-34 and 12:4 with a fuller understanding. The Jewish Christians, who were unaccused by Nero, sympathized with their brethren of the old congregation who were thrown into dungeons to be made martyrs by terrible deaths. They sought to help these poor victims. For this effort they, too, had to suffer. The populace resented this sympathy and this help. Rowdies, hoodlums attacked the bazars and the homes of the Jewish Christians, wrecked and looted these places, and attacked the owners. Yet none were arrested by the authorities, none suffered martyrdom (12:4). The persecutions instigated by Nero finally died down. One bad effect remained: Christianity had become and remained an illicit, criminal religion. This entire body of Jewish Christians in Rome remained under this black pall.

Then Paul, the spiritual father of this Jewish missionary work in Rome, returned from Spain, was arrested, was thrown into a vile dungeon, and was executed. Like Peter, being a chief exponent of this hateful *religio illicita*, his case was hopeless from the beginning. Paul perished late in 66 or early in 67.

We are now able to understand Hebrews. The Jewish Christians stood unshaken during the terror of 64 — see the exposition of 10:32-34. But now, since Peter was dead, since even Paul, their spiritual father, had been removed, since Christianity was permanently branded as criminal, since there was no other apostle to stiffen their courage, some of these Jewish Christians began to weaken. Voices were raised which advocated a return to Jewry. If their synagogues became Jewish as they had been a few years ago they would be safe like the other Jewish synagogues, for Judaism continued to remain a religion that was legally approved in Rome and in the empire. Arguments were put forward that were derogatory to Christ and to Christianity — our epistle treats them in detail — arguments extolling Judaism — our epistle answers them in detail. Thus the entire epistle becomes lucid. There is no difficulty in regard to a single point. All the data fall into proper relation; we need no hypotheses whatever.

* * *

This leaves the question: "Who, then, wrote Hebrews?" Since we know who received this letter we are greatly aided in deciding who wrote the letter. The answer to this second question ties into the answer to the main question.

It is Luther who suggests Apollos as the writer of Hebrews: *"Dieser Apollo ist ein hochverstaendiger Mann gewest, die Epistel Hebraeorum ist freilich sein."* Erlangen ed. 18, 38. "This Apollos was a man of high understanding, the Epistle of the Hebrews is indeed his." Luther's remark is only incidental; it is made in his sermon on the party divisions in Corinth, I Cor.

3:4, etc. We are thus unable to say to what extent Luther had investigated this question. His conviction disregards all the names that are mentioned in the old tradition.

Luther's conviction will be rejected by men who do not correlate the data which we have presented in regard to the identity of the readers for whom Hebrews was intended. Even Zahn, who agrees with Luther, does not note how strong the support for Apollos is. Zahn also thinks that the original congregation in Rome was mainly Jewish; he does not regard Paul's Jewish converts in Rome as a separate body that retained its synagogues as its houses of worship. Zahn is right in regard to Apollos and in regard to Rome as being the home of the readers of Hebrews but does not realize how completely right he is. He sums up his opinion: "Luther's hypothesis has a twofold advantage over all others: 1) among the teachers of the apostolic time, so far as we are able to form a conception of them, there is no one whom our impression of the author of Hebrews suits better than Apollos; 2) in the little that we know of his history there is nothing directly opposed to the hypothesis." The case is much stronger. Luther does not advocate a "hypothesis," nor is the evidence for Apollos entirely negative as Zahn words it. Zahn's date for Hebrews, about the year 80, is entirely too late and overlooks the assured historical data which we possess.

The evidence we possess fully warrants the conclusion that Apollos wrote Hebrews to the body of Jewish Christians at Rome after the martyrdom of Paul and before the destruction of Jerusalem, between the years 67 and 70, probably in 68 or 69.

Let us review the story of Apollos. As the New Testament presents it, only one gap occurs, which needs to be bridged when we accept him as the writer of Hebrews.

His first appearance, recorded in Acts 18:24-28, presents him as an Alexandrine scholar, a Jew, an ἀνὴρ λόγιος who was trained in one of the great universities of Alexandria, this ancient seat of learning, a man δυνατὸς ἐν ταῖς γραφαῖς, "powerful in the Scriptures." Fully instructed in the gospel of Christ by Priscilla and Aquila, he goes to Corinth, one of Paul's main congregations, and greatly assists the Corinthian believers by mightily and publicly convincing the Jews in Corinth by means of the Scriptures "that Jesus is the Christ."

Hebrews shows the fine Greek scholar who is mighty in the Old Testament Scriptures, who supports the work of Paul just as he did in Corinth, who is mighty to convince Jewish minds "that Jesus is the Christ" just as he was in Corinth. If we should make an inventory of the qualifications of the writer of Hebrews and did not have Acts 18:24-28, our inventory would contain the features which Luke records about Apollos.

We note next Apollos' connection with Paul and Paul's work. In Corinth he strongly aids the congregation that had been established by Paul. We see him next with Paul in Ephesus. The Corinthians wanted Apollos back in their midst, so did Paul himself; Apollos agrees to go at a somewhat later time (I Cor. 16:12). Timothy was already on his way to Corinth (I Cor. 16:10). We note that Apollos continues to support Paul's work, and that already here Apollos and Timothy are connected with this work. This agrees with Heb. 13:23, where Apollos states that he is waiting for Timothy so that the two may go to Rome together.

As late as Titus 3:13 we meet Apollos in connection with the work of Paul. The apostle writes from Macedonia. He expects to winter in Nicopolis (Titus 3:12) and to go to Spain as early as possible the following spring (in 64). He is sending Apollos and Zenas on a mission which takes them through Crete and asks Titus to help to expedite them on their way. Thus all the data we possess regarding Apollos connect him with Paul, and do this for years. The Jewish Christians to whom Hebrews is addressed are also converts of Paul's. All these data are positive facts that are recorded in the New Testament itself; their weight is according.

The statement made in Titus 3:13 is the last that we possess. Now there follows the gap to which we have referred. In Heb. 13:19, 24 a previous connection of the writer of Hebrews with his readers is implied. The writer has been in Rome, his readers know him well, he is able to deal with them as he does in his letter. What we lack in regard to Apollos is a direct statement in the New Testament that he has been in Rome with Paul. A last link that would connect Apollos with Rome would be valuable indeed. It is wanting. Did Apollos rejoin Paul at Nicopolis and go to Rome with Paul when Paul went on to Spain? This would supply the missing item, which happens to be a necessary one.

To sum up: we have so much that speaks for Apollos as being the writer of Hebrews. This considerable amount of evidence is circumstantial and as such not quite complete. To this positive amount of evidence we add, with Zahn, the negative item: beyond the one man Apollos we know of no other man among all the prominent workers in the church after the death of Paul who could have written Hebrews to Paul's Jewish converts in Rome. We thus join Luther in his conviction: *Die Epistel Hebraeorum ist freilich sein.*

* * *

The ancient caption Πρὸς Ἑβραίους was not put there by the pen of the writer but was affixed to the manuscript rolls by the scribes when copies were made for publication. Written on the outside of the roll, the caption merely identified the document. All Jews were "Hebrews" in distinction from Gentiles and were proud to be known as "Hebrews" as also II Cor. 11:22 indicates, where Paul himself boasts of being a "Hebrew." Ὁ Ἑβραῖος (LXX) = *der Jenseitige*, "one from beyond," i. e., from the Euphrates, was a designation for the Israelite which other peoples gave him and was then adopted by the Israelites themselves to distinguish themselves from other peoples (Koenig, *Woerterbuch*, 312). It was also a linguistic distinction: the Hebrews spoke Hebrew as their native tongue (in later times Aramaic).

The title of the epistle is to be understood in this general sense and not in the narrow sense, in which certain Jews who retained their native tongue were distinguished as "Hebrews" from other Jews who were termed "Hellenists" because they adopted the Greek language. See the two types of Jewish Christians in Acts 6:1. The letter itself shows that the readers were Hellenists, for it is written in elegant Greek. If it had been intended for Hebraistic readers it would have been composed in Aramaic. The term "Hebrews" does not occur in the letter itself. The caption of the manuscripts was sometimes slightly expanded yet conveys no more than is obvious from the letter itself.

CHAPTER I

The First Main Part

The Incarnate Son Supreme
1:1 to 2:4

Incomparably Supreme in His Being, Work, and Position, v. 1-3

Incomparably Supreme over All Angels in His Exaltation, v. 4-14

The Warning: How Shall We Escape if We Neglect so Great Salvation? 2:1-4

The Incarnate Son, Incomparably Supreme in His Being, Work, and Position, v. 1-3

1) Chapter one is a connected unit. When we divide it at v. 3, this is done because the rest of the chapter is attached as a special elaboration. Διὰ τοῦτο, "for this reason," adds the warning voiced in 2:1-4 to chapter one. This forms the first part of the letter which is an independent unit. Some include more, but a second great unit begins at 2:5. Throughout the letter the expository or didactic sections are followed by specific hortations.

Hebrews resembles the First Epistle of St. John by dispensing with a greeting. John, however, begins with the personal "we" and "you" (1:1-5) while Hebrews begins with a majestic objective statement and does not reach the personal note until 2:1, etc., where the writer then includes himself with the readers in "we." This is most impressive. The bearer of the letter named its sender when he delivered it. When it was first read in public, the assembly was told whose letter this was.

The ancients supposed that Hebrews originally had a greeting, and that this was omitted when copies of the letter were made. They naturally tried to explain the excision but did not do so in a convincing way. Following the same supposition, other and more recent explanations for the excision are equally unconvincing. It is better to suppose that Hebrews never began with a greeting from the writer to his readers. The opening sentence makes that impression.

This leaves us the equally difficult question as to why the writer begins as he does. We are told that some letters were written in this way; some perhaps were, yet this was never the custom. All that we are able to say is what we see and feel — a powerful impression which is increased by the omission of even the briefest greeting.

When the letter was later copied and published for other Christians, this omission robbed them and us of the name of the writer and the identity of the original recipients so that the long search for both began with the uncertain results discussed in our introduction. This letter won its place among the inspired writings of the canon by its own inherent inspired quality.

The perfect form of the first sentence strikes the grammarians; R. 422 notes the balance and the rhythm, B.-D. 464 the two members forming a period and also the eight additions with the rhetorical asyndetic anaphora (B.-D. 489) plus the *wirklich rednerische, gewaehlte Wortstellung* (473, 2). Luke 1:1-4 is comparable, but Hebrews is full of such noble sentences and such fine rhetoric, all of which were written without special effort by one who was able and eloquent.

Effortless alliteration meets us again and again, for instance, the opening words: Πολυμερῶς καὶ πολυτρόπως πάλαι, three adverbs at that.

In many portions and in many ways in olden times God, having spoken to the fathers in the person of the prophets, at the end, during these days, spoke to us in the person of (his) Son, whom he placed as heir of all things, through whom he made the eons; who, as being his glory's effulgence and his being's impress, and as bearing all the (existing) things by means of the uttered word of his power, after having wrought for himself cleansing from the sins, sat down at the right hand of the majesty on high; etc.

The master organist strikes the fundamental chords of his entire composition. Their grandeur falls upon the ears and the heart of the reader and the hearers. This must have had a powerful effect. These former Jews who were now half-inclined to revert to their former Judaism because they were discouraged by persecution and by the difficulties of the Christian life, in the very first solemn clause hear an acknowledgment and a confession of the whole inspired Old Testament, which no Jew could outdo. Every Jewish heart must give unconditional consent: God did speak in content and in a manner so manifold to the Israelite fathers in the person of the prophets in those olden times!

The Old Testament is no less than the voice of God himself. The fathers heard that voice of God, among whom were all the greatest Old Testament saints. The present sons of those fathers still hear that voice in every line that is read to them from the sacred Old Testament scrolls.

God spoke in the person of the prophets (ἐν used with persons, R. 587), Moses, the greatest of them all, Samuel, and all the other mighty names down to Malachi.

So richly and abundantly, so variously God spoke in those olden times by the pens of all the ancient holy writers in order to preserve all that future generations were to know, all that the readers of this very letter know so well. It sounds as though Paul's voice, Peter's voice were again speaking to them with the old convincing power in new eloquence.

We have no discounting of the Old Testament here. The two adverbs "in many portions and in many ways" have been understood to mean "in many parts" but only in fragments and not in completeness; "in many ways" but all of them inferior. But these adverbs convey the opposite sense: the first refers to quantity — so rich the varied contents; the second to quality — so rich the variety of form.

The Old Testament is *history* that covers ages, but history as God wanted it written with true, spiritual intent for our learning (Rom. 15:4), God's voice speaking in every historical line. The Old Testament is *revelation* which makes known the thoughts, plans, and purposes of God. It is *prophecy* in the narrow sense, promises yet to be fulfilled, judgments yet to come, which unveil the future to the very end of the world. It tells of the *Messiah* and of his reign of grace and glory in an everlasting kingdom. It contains the *experience of the saints* in psalms of praise, prayers, agonies, and exaltation, yet as God wants all this for our hearts. Here is simple prose beside supreme poetry (none grander than Isa. 40-66). Here is type, symbol, literalness, apocalypsis.

As to completeness, this is present at every stage from Adam to Malachi. God spoke to every generation what each needed to know. First the bud, then the gradual increase step by step with the promise of the coming full flower — no imperfection at any stage save that the stages advanced.

The one point to be noted is the fact that this clause is participial: λαλήσας ("God having spoken"), pointing forward to the main verb with its aorist of finality: ἐλάλησεν, "God spoke." The Old Testament itself speaks in the same way. God spoke in Moses who wrote the first part of the Old Testament, yet God promised to send another Prophet like unto Moses but one who was to be vastly greater than even Moses, the greatest of all the prophets: "I will put my words in his mouth, and he shall speak unto them all that I shall command him; and it shall come to pass that whosoever will not hearken unto my words which he shall speak in my name, I will require it of him," Deut. 18:18, 19; compare John 8:28; 12:49, 50; 17:8. There is no danger of placing the Old Testament on too high a level or of making it seem too grand; for the more it is exalted, the more it itself is made to exalt the Son and all that God spoke in the person of the Son, the whole New Testament.

2) In perfect balance with πάλαι, "in olden times," there follows ἐπ' (temporal, B.-P. 445) ἐσχάτου τῶν ἡμερῶν τούτων, which does not mean "at the end of these days" and is not the same as the expressions used in I Pet. 1:20; II Pet. 3:3; Jude 18, for which days are "these days," and what would be their "end"? We have a double designation of time, the second being an apposition of time within: "at the end — during (within) these days," i. e., at the end of the Old Testament period, during the recent past. After speaking so fully and so wondrously in the distant and the extended past God recently finished his speaking: "he spoke to us in the person of his Son" — once "to the fathers," now "to us" — to them "in the person of the prophets," to us "in the person of (his) Son." This latter speaking crowns the former even as Deut. 18:18 foretold. The R. V. margin, which has the Greek ἐν υἱῷ = "a

Son," is inadequate. The article is omitted in order to indicate the quality expressed in "Son," yet "Son" is most definite in the Greek, it is made so by the relative clauses. We cannot duplicate this in English, especially not the qualitativeness. The point is that "the prophets," exalted though they were, are not the limit for God who finally used his "Son."

Ἐν is not instrumental, not = διά (Luther and others) — where the latter is the thought διά is used (second relative clause; 2:2; etc.); not a Hebraism, but when it is used with persons means "in the case of," or "in the person of," R. 587. Διά would make "the prophets" and the "Son" God's means or instruments. It is often used thus: "that spoken by the Lord *through* the prophet, saying," etc. (Matt. 1:22). Ἐν is only a variation of this conception: "in" the speaking of those named *God* spoke, and they who heard them heard *God*. Deut. 18:18: "I (*Yahweh*) will put my words in his (the Prophet-Messiah's) mouth." Compare Matt. 10:20; also and notably Luke 10:16.

Here we have the fact of inspiration: God spoke in the person of the prophets — God spoke in the person of his Son: *God* was the real speaker, the prophets and the Son were the persons employed by God; what these uttered *God* uttered. Add the apostles. The Son wrote nothing, the prophets, the apostles wrote down what they spoke orally. *How* God inspired them is not told us, *that* he did this is a fact. The result lies before us today. There is no theory of inspiration, can be none; it is wrong to theorize — the Germans have removed *the great fact* by theorizing about it, and many have followed them. This has left us mere human words that are errant, unreliable, with which liberties have then been taken. See the interpretation of II Tim. 3:16.

The remarkable fact is the statement that the Son himself is said to have been inspired of God. Yet this is what Deuteronomy states, what Jesus himself restates in John 8:28; 12:49, 50; 17:8; Rev. 1:1. The Son spoke on earth "as man" (Phil. 2:8); his disciples and men generally heard him. The writer of Hebrews says: "God spoke in the person of (his) Son *to us*." Yet he and the readers of this letter did not hear Jesus' voice; "to us" is nevertheless correct — read 2:3, 4. The great point to be noted is the way in which "the prophets" and the "Son" are paralleled. This is not the Son ἄσαρκος but ἔνσαρκος, the Logos who became flesh (John 1:14). This is so important because all the relative clauses that follow are predicated of the incarnate Son in whose person, while he was here on earth, God spoke "to us."

One additional thought should not be overlooked. There is no one beyond the incarnate Son whom God might use for his speaking to us. This means that now, having spoken in the person of his Son, we have the ultimate Word and revelation of God. No more and nothing further will God ever say to men. They who look for more and for new revelation will never find it; 2:3 is God's answer to them; likewise Deut. 18:19. This is certain also because the Old Testament promises of redemption have been fulfilled by the incarnate Son. Only one thing will yet follow, namely the judgment, Rev. 1:7.

Yes, the Jewish Christians to whom this is written have all the Old Testament prophets, all that the fathers had and heard, but they have also all the blessedness which many prophets and righteous have desired to see and to hear and did not get to see and to hear (Matt. 13:17), namely the incarnate Son's own work and word.

The incomparable greatness, power, and majesty of this incarnate Son are now set forth in relative clauses. The first two clauses are brief, preliminary to the third which is fully elaborated. This "Son" is he "whom

God placed as heir of all things, through whom God also made the eons." Note the asyndeton in the three relative clauses. Yet καί, "also," indicates a special relation between the first two. Because God made his Son "heir of all things" he "also" made the eons as he did, namely "through the Son," διά to indicate the personal medium.

It is essential to understand that the incarnate Son is referred to; we shall otherwise not grasp how he could be set or placed as "heir of all things." It makes no difference whether we date the historical aorist in eternity or in time. Ἔθηκε is the proper word, for "to place" as an heir involves a testament, a διαθήκη (which is derived from this very verb τίθημι). From all eternity and thus at the very creation when the eons of time began God made his Son the heir of all things, not according to his deity which could inherit nothing, but according to his humanity which could and did inherit all things. When the Son in his human nature came to earth incarnate and as a man completed his great saving work, then this mighty inheritance was paid out to him, the inheritance now being in the hands of the heir.

Here belong all those great passages like Dan. 7:13, 14: "There was given to him dominion, and glory, and a kingdom," etc.; Matt. 11:27: "All things are delivered unto me of my Father"; 28:18: "All power is given unto me in heaven and in earth"; Luke 1:32: "The Lord God shall give unto him the throne of his father David, and he shall reign over the house of Jacob forever, and of his kingdom there shall be no end"; so also 10:22; John 3:35; 5:22; 13:3; 17:2; Rom. 14:9; I Cor. 15:27; Eph. 1:10, 21; Phil. 2:9, 10; Heb. 2:8; I Pet. 2:22. Given to him, delivered unto him, etc., refer to the Son's human nature. "This is the heir" (Matt. 17:38); we are joint heirs with this heir (Rom. 8:17); he inherits from the Father (John

Hebrews 1:2

3:38); he is the seed and thus the heir (Gal. 3:16). Heir "of all things" is without restriction or limitation. The church is his, but all other things are likewise his, for he governs these in the interest of his church. The fact that the human nature of the Son could have and could administer this vast inheritance is possible only in virtue of its personal union with the divine.

Thus already at the beginning God made the eons "through him," namely with a view to the Son's being the heir in the fulness of time to have the vast inheritance as a man. Ποιεῖν is the same as *barah* (Gen. 1:1), to bring into being. "All things δι' αὐτοῦ (the same phrase) ἐγένετο, through him came into existence; and without him there came into existence not a single thing that has come into existence (and thus exists)," John 1:3. The eternal deity of the Son is fully revealed. As God's creative act is beyond all human powers of comprehension, so also is this διά, this working of the one person "through" the other. Δι' οὗ is not the same as ἐν υἱῷ; we could not exchange the prepositions. The point is not our comprehension of the divine act of creation but an apprehension of the true nature of the Son, who is one in essence, omnipotence, and glory with the Father, and thus his Sonship, partnership, and heirship that were involved at creation.

The statement is not that through the Son God made πάντα or τὰ πάντα (v. 3), which repeats heir "of all things"; it is τοὺς αἰῶνας, "the eons." "The worlds" used in our versions would lead us to think of many worlds or heavenly bodies. G. K. 204 wants *"Welten, Weltraeume* to be spacially conceived"; he regards them as a substitute for κόσμος. C.-K. retains the temporal conception. Like the later Hebrew plural *'olamim,* "the eons" are used metonymically in the Greek and mean, not merely vast periods of time as mere time, but "eons" with all that exists as well as all that transpires in them, *complexus eorum quae temporibus continenter.* We have no multiplicity of worlds or world spaces but the cosmos in its entire time-extent with all that fills and forms one eon after another; in brief: heaven and earth and all that has its being in them.

3) A third relative clause, which is built more grandly because it contains three participial elaborations, reveals still more: not only the infinite exaltation and the incomparable glory of the Son but, woven into this, the blessedness of the redemptive work which makes him more than the supreme Prophet (Deut. 18:18), namely our eternal High Priest and King. The structure is beautiful: three relatives and three participles in the third. The first two participles are closely connected with τε, the third stands out by itself.

It is still the incarnate Son "who as being his glory's effulgence and his (God's) being's impress and as bearing all the (existing) things by means of the uttered word of his power," etc. This is the Son in whose person God eventually spoke to us. The first two participles are durative presents and denote continuous condition and action.

'Απαύγασμα is the result of ἀπαυγάζειν, the result of sending out the αὐγή. The word occurs only here in the New Testament. Chrysostom defines it as φῶς ἐκ φωτός, "light out of light," a sun shining out from the original light but participating in its essence and viewed by itself. The eternal, timeless generation of the Son lies back of this word. Some of Philo's uses of the word might make us think of "reflex," light that falls on a medium and is reflected from it as the light of the sun is reflected from the moon; yet no reflecting medium is conceivable. Hence the active meaning *Ausstrahlung*, "effulgence," is best. The inscrutable glory of God streams forth in the Son who is the effulgence of that glory.

Δόξα is not merely the shining forth of one of the divine attributes but the shining forth of all of them; αὐτοῦ, which is placed after ὑποστάσεως, belongs also to δόξης: "the effulgence of his (God's) glory"; the genitive makes "effulgence" definite. As the effulgence of God's glory the Son is God in essence and has every divine attribute, yet not in the light to which no man can approach, which no man hath seen nor can see (I Tim. 6:16), but in the light we are to see (John 1:4, 5). As we cannot see the sun without the light and the radiance which it sends forth, so God is hidden from us without the Son, the effulgence of his glory (John 14:9; 12:45; Col. 1:15, "the image of the invisible God").

The second predicate advances the description of the deity of the Son in his relation to God. Not a temporary, passing effulgence of God's glory is the Son, in whose person God spoke to us, but "his being's impress." We note that "effulgence" and "impress" correspond save that the former blazes forth from God, the latter terminates in the Son himself. "His glory" and his "being" also correspond, but again God's glory is the shining forth of the effulgence of his attributes while his being is God himself, of whom the Son is the very counterpart. Thus the first predicate rests on the second.

Ὑπόστασις is used in a variety of meanings, but since it is here predicated of God it denotes the reality or actuality of his being. To "his glory," which is the revelation of his being, it adds the *Wirklichkeit*, the existence, the being itself (compare C.-K. 540). The English has no comparable term, hence the A. V. uses "person," the R. V., "substance," both of which only approach the Greek term. The philosophical use of *hypostasis* is foreign to our passage; also Philo's nonpersonal use of the word. The theological idea of *hypostasis*: that which exists in and by itself whether it be a person or not originated much later although the word was then applied to the three persons in the Trinity. See the uses of the word in 3:14 and 11:1.

Χαρακτήρ, from χαράσσειν, "to engrave or inscribe," means both the tool for such work and the impress or image made by the tool. Note that the word is not χάραγμα, the result of an impression, which is used with reference to a sign or a symbol and is thus an unsuitable word. The word used means *Gepraege, Auspraegung* (C.-K. 1131), not what Christ has received from God, but what he is for us and for the world as the expression of the very being, essence, reality of God. Language fairly groans with the weight of meaning. Our poor human tongue and mind, which are occupied so much with the things that are beneath us, strain to rise to the heights of the divine persons. But these mighty expressions form the rock bottom of our Christian faith, the essence of the sweet gospel realities. If the Son in whose person God drew nigh to us were less than is said here, in Col. 1:15; Phil. 2:6; John 14:9; 20:28; etc., our faith and our hope would be vain indeed.

Τέ, like the Latin *-que,* connects closely and adds something that is self-evident: "and as bearing all the (existing) things by means of the uttered word of his power." The incarnate Son's relation to God involves his relation to the world. He was placed as the heir of all things, the very eons were created through him, the Son, the effulgence of glory and the impress of God's being; he, indeed, bears τὰ πάντα (here with the article), "all the things which exist," all these eons in their course with all that they contain. Not, however, as an Atlas with the world or the universe as a dead weight upon his shoulders, who merely keeps all things from sinking into nothingness; he bears all things so that his will and his purpose are fulfilled.

We need not argue as to whether φέρων means only "sustaining" ("upholding," our versions), the *conservatio*, or "bearing" in the sense of administering or ruling, for there is no reason for restricting the term. Jewish theology combined the thought of resisting disruptive forces with bringing to the designed goal, and both are included here.

All that the Son needs for this is "the ῥῆμα of his power" (which is stronger than "his powerful word"), the mere "utterance" of his will. This is not his gospel word but the utterance of his omnipotence. He commands, and it stands fast (Col. 1:17). During the days of his humiliation he uttered many words of omnipotent power when he was working his miracles.

The third participle is an aorist to denote one past historical act; it is introduced without a connective and thus stands out by itself: "after having wrought for himself cleansing from the sins." The A. V. retains δι' ἑαυτοῦ, "by himself" purged, etc., which the best texts and the R. V. omit. When he was dealing with the world the Son encountered "the sins" of the world. What did he do? This terse statement answers: "He wrought for himself cleansing from sins." The middle voice implies that the act was in some way reflected on himself; we know how — by his sacrificial death. The genitive after καθαρισμός is not unusual, especially since καθαρός and its derivatives are followed by the objective genitive about as often as by the preposition ἀπό.

This expression recalls the work of the Jewish high priest on the great Day of Atonement. "On that day shall the priest make an atonement for you, to cleanse you, that you may be clean from all your sins before the Lord," Lev. 17:30. The expression speaks of the Son as the High Priest, and the rest of this epistle will speak of him in this function at length. This statement takes the incarnation for granted; in fact, its real purpose is here brought out: to enable the Son to accomplish this purification by his blood and sacrifice. The cleansing here referred to is the objective atonement for sin, which was made once for all on Calvary, which each individual sinner must now appropriate unto himself by faith.

The Son, having effected the cleansing, "sat down at the right hand of the majesty on high" in one formal, all-glorious act. The ascension was visible to the disciples until a cloud hid the Savior's form. In that instant he was transferred timelessly into the heavenly world where God, the angels, and the saints dwell, to the *sessio ad dextram*. Ἐν δεξιᾷ (feminine: χειρί) is not a circumscribed locality in heaven as Zwingli, Calvin, and others think when they deny the possibility of Christ's bestowing his body and his blood in, with, and under the bread and the wine in the Sacrament. We dismiss all ideas of time and of space and of limitations when we are thinking of the heavenly world; they do not apply there, nor does an argument that is based on such ideas. What timelessness (eternity) and spacelessness are no human mind is able to conceive.

Instead of saying only "at the right (hand) of God," we have the grander expression "at the right (hand) of the majesty." This abstract term "the majesty" denotes the omnipotent glory of God, and it is folly to imagine that it has either a right or a left side. The term "majesty" makes this the clearest of the pertinent passages: Ps. 77:10; 118:16; Exod. 15:6; Isa. 48:13; Matt. 26:64; etc. "The majesty" or "greatness" is infinite; to sit down at its right is taken from Ps. 110:1: "Sit thou at my right hand until I make thine enemies thy footstool." The Biblical description is found in Eph. 1:20-22. To be seated thus is to exercise "the majesty" and to do this in all its infinitude.

Hebrews 1:3

We do not construe ἐν ὑψηλοῖς with "the majesty" as naming the place where it exists but with the verb: "he sat down in the high places" (= ἐν τοῖς οὐρανοῖς, "in the heavens"), far above all the earthly regions (compare Ps. 93:3; 113:5; Isa. 57:15). Angels and men stand before the throne, the Son sits, not in idleness, but in active power and rule. Riggenbach notes that Ps. 110 was interpreted with reference to the Messiah by the ancient Jews; that traces of this interpretation are still left after Judaism rejected Christianity; that Jesus significantly employed this psalm (Matt. 22:44; 26:64); that a number of thoughts that are developed in Hebrews are expositions of this psalm, the first thought being found here; in 1:13; in 8:1; the fourth in 5:6, 10; 6:20; 7:1-25.

Our Confessions note that this exaltation refers to Christ's *human* nature. "God's right hand is everywhere, at which Christ is placed in deed and in truth according to his human nature, being present, rules, and has in his hands and beneath his feet everything that is in heaven and on earth, where no man else, nor angels, but only the Son is placed." *C. Tr.* 811. The reason is stated in 821: "Hence we believe, teach, and confess that the Son of man is *realiter,* that is in deed and truth, exalted according to his human nature to the right hand of the almighty majesty and power of God, because he (that man) was assumed into God when he was conceived of the Holy Ghost in his mother's womb, and his human nature was personally united with the Son of the Highest." This includes the fact that the human nature of Christ "did receive, apart from, and over and above its natural, essential, permanent properties, also special, high, great, supernatural, inscrutable, ineffable, heavenly, *praerogativas* and excellencies in majesty, glory, power, and might above everything that can be named, not only in this world, but also in that which is to come" (1033, 51). Hence, "that also according to his assumed human nature and with the same, he can be, and also is, present where he will, and especially that in his Church and congregation on earth he is present as Mediator, Head, King, and High Priest, not in part or one-half of him only, but the entire person of Christ is present, to which both natures belong, the divine and the human . . . . Even as he instituted his Holy Supper for the certain assurance and confirmation of this, that also according to that nature according to which he has flesh and blood he will be with us, and dwell, work, and be efficacious in us" (1043, etc., 78).

The Incarnate Son Incomparably Supreme Over All Angels in His Exaltation, v. 4-14

4) We make a division at this point because of the thought, which makes a comparison with the angels, and not because of the construction, for this continues with another aorist participle which is followed by elucidations.

Addressed to Jewish Christians who are inclined to drop back into Judaism, the first three verses are sure of producing a tremendous effect, something like that which was produced on Saul when Jesus appeared to him in all his glory on the road near Damascus. These three verses concentrate the great glory rays upon the Jewish readers in one mighty focus. That is why so many terse clauses are brought together in a unit statement and end with the exaltation: "he sat down at the right of the majesty on high." Verses 1-3 are certainly a unit.

When eleven verses follow, all of which contain a comparison with the angels although they are participially attached to v. 1-3, it should be obvious that we now come to a specific subject, the supreme exaltation of Jesus above all the angels. In other words, from the concentrated thematic statement made in v. 1-3 one specific line of thought is singled out and elaborated in detail, at the end of which 2:1-4 brings an effective warning.

That raises the question as to why this section on the Son and the angels has been introduced in writing to these Jewish Christians. No polemical intent is evident as though the readers held false views about the angels, as though they were to be worshipped. The Jews never worshipped angels. These eleven verses are not placing angels beside "the prophets" mentioned in v. 1. Our question is answered in v. 7 and at the end of the section in v. 14. Among the agents and ministrants whom God employs the heavenly angels, pure spirit beings, rank highest in every way. Yet incomparably higher stands Jesus.

Since they are thoroughly versed in Scripture, which is also the ultimate authority for both the writer and the readers, God's own Word (v. 1) is allowed to speak. No reader would think of contradicting or raising objection. We should see the force of the participle: it indicates that what follows is not independent but is subjoined as elaborating one line of thought contained in v. 1-3. Thus, letting the thought speak for itself in its connection with the foregoing, the writer continues: **having gotten to be by so much better than the angels by how much more superior a name than they he has inherited.** His very name expresses his infinite superiority in comparison with the angels. Ὄνομα is not a mere designation to distinguish one individual from others who are like him but a name that reveals what this person really is. The revealing effect of ὄνομα should not be overlooked.

Τοσούτῳ . . . ὅσῳ, which is never used by Paul, occurs several times in Hebrews; κρείττων, which is rarely used by Paul and then only in the neuter and in an adverbial sense, appears thirteen times in Hebrews and also in Peter. "BETTER, BETTER!" together with other great comparatives rings through Hebrews as its keynote. None of the excellence of the others is denied; yea, their very excellence shows how much better Christ is. Διάφορος implies comparison, the comparative διαφορώτερος intensifies this. Originally meaning "different," the word indicates a difference that marks superiority; the comparative denotes: different from the angels because of an altogether greater superiority. Παρά after the comparative, which is frequently found in Hebrews = beside or in comparison with.

The supreme "name" referred to is not the one mentioned in Rev. 19:12, which no man's tongue can utter but, as the following shows, the name "Son" which was mentioned already in v. 2. But the aorist participle states that he who is named here "got" or "got to be" as much better than the angels as he "has inherited" a name that is more superior than theirs, namely the name "Son." There is no reference in these tenses to the Son's deity, which is eternal. The perfect tense "has inherited" explains the aorist "got to be." In the incarnation the human nature of Jesus inherited the name "Son," (Luke 1:32) which belonged to his person from all eternity, which, in reference to his human nature, was given to him already in the Old Testament; the perfect tense implies that what he inherited remains his ever since. The incarnation ushered him into this world for his great work. This work Jesus wrought through his human nature and in accomplishing his work proved himself vastly superior to the angels. They, indeed, also do God's will and may thus be compared with Jesus; but none of them could possibly have done this work that Jesus did and hence could possibly ever have inherited the name "Son." Compare 10:5-9a: Jesus carried out God's will by means of the sacrifice of his body; add Mark 14:42; John 4:34; 5:30; Matt. 3:17: "This is my Son," etc.

When the angels are called "sons of God" in the Old Testament, this is done only in a generic way; so Israel, too, is called a son (Exod. 4:22; Deut. 14:1; Hos. 11:1), Solomon likewise (II Sam. 7:12-14), and we are "all sons of God, through faith in Christ Jesus," Gal. 3:27. But the name "Son" belongs to Jesus in a way that is different from and altogether superior to that of any creature, namely by an inheritance (compare "heir" in v. 2), i. e., by virtue of the personal union of his human nature to the divine, and by virtue of the work he did in and through his human nature in this union. The only-begotten Son was the "Son" also in his human nature which is now exalted at the right hand of the majesty.

5) "For" substantiates the fact that this inheritance of the name "Son" has taken place. **For to whom of the angels did he ever say:**

> **Son of mine art thou!**
> **I on my part have begotten thee?**

And again:
> **I on my part will be to him Father,**
> **And he will be to me Son?**

The rhetorical questions call for the answer: "Never did God say such a thing to any angel." He spoke thus only to this one person. Not merely once did God call him "Son" in the most exalted sense but many times. Not only in one way but in more than one. All that lies in God's calling him "Son" has already been made manifest, and what remains will yet be manifested.

The first quotation is taken from Ps. 2:7, and in answer to the critics we note that Peter attributes this psalm to David (Acts 4:25). The Hebrew and the LXX agree. The reference is to II Sam. 7, especially to 7:14, 16, to the seed of David who should reign in the Davidic kingdom and on the Davidic throne forever. It is this everlasting King himself who in the psalm quotes Yahweh as having said to him: "Son of mine art thou!" etc. This word is echoed in the New Testament when at Jesus' baptism God said to him: "Thou art my beloved Son!" Luke 3:22. That was the time when Jesus assumed his great office. This declaration was repeated at the transfiguration of Jesus, Luke 9:35.

Although these two declarations are verbally almost identical with the one found in Ps. 2, they are quite often overlooked in the interpretation of this passage and of Acts 13:33. We take this statement prophetically — David was one of "the prophets" mentioned in v. 1, in whose person God spoke of old — that God spoke thus already in the Old Testament. "I myself have begotten thee" is figurative for God's placing David's Son, the heir of all things (v. 2), on his everlasting throne in the eternal kingdom. The inauguration of such a King is for Yahweh the begetting of a Son who rules like Yahweh himself. This inauguration is attested throughout the Old Testament and culminates, as Paul says in Acts 13:33, in the resurrection of Jesus.

The passage quoted from the psalm does not speak of the *generatio aeterna;* not of the inner Trinitarian relation of the two persons although this is involved; not of σήμερον, "today," as eternity but as time, and involves the incarnation, the human nature, and the redemptive work of Jesus, who purged away the sins of the world (v. 3). The idea is not that we may restrict "have begotten thee" to the incarnation, or to the baptism, or to the transfiguration. Even the resurrection must include all that preceded as well as the exaltation at the right hand of the majesty.

The question continues: To whom of the angels did God ever say what he said in II Sam. 7:14: "I on my part will be to him Father" in the supreme sense, "and he shall be to me Son"? As in the psalm the Messianic statement pertained to David, so this second Messianic statement pertained to Solomon. In both Yahweh looked far beyond both men to the eternal Solomon, the ultimate heir (v. 2), in whom alone II Sam. 7:16 could be fulfilled: "And thine house and thy kingdom shall be established forever before thee; thy throne shall be established forever." See Luke 1:33.

In both quotations ἐγώ is emphatic: "I myself" or "I on my part." After "I shall be," "he shall be" the predicate nominative is expressed by εἰς with the accusative (so in the LXX), B.-D. 145, 1; R. 481. But we do not translate: "I shall be *a* Father, he shall be *a* Son"; but simply "Father — Son." This passage doubles the idea of "Son" by adding that of "Father." All that lies in "I have begotten thee" for the exaltation of the Son, who became incarnate for his work and his office, appears in the addition of "Father" to "Son."

In brief, (1) the Son in his deity, one in essence with the Father, (2) is the Son through whom and for whom in the eternal counsel of the Trinity as the heir of all things the eons were to be and then actually were created, (3) he to be the incarnate Savior to cleanse, the incarnate King to rule at his Father's side. All this is present to the writer's mind; his careful Jewish Christian readers felt and perceived it all.

6) Moreover, when he shall again bring in the First-begotten into the inhabited earth he declares:

And let all God's angels worship him!

Δέ adds this somewhat different point. Ps. 2:7 and II Sam. 7:14 show what Yahweh called Jesus, namely "Son," he himself being this Son's "Father," and the writer notes the important fact that Yahweh never did such a thing for any angel. This third quotation brings out the fact as to what the position of the angels really is in respect to the Son. Yahweh himself demands that all the angels prostrate themselves in worship (προσκυνέω) before the Son.

The point of this would amount to very little if it meant no more than that the angels are called upon to bow in worship before the deity of the Son. The fact that all creatures must bow before the persons of the Godhead was a truism to all Jews. Moreover, we should know that all Jews of Old Testament times and of apostolic times were Trinitarians; Jewish unitarianism developed later as a result of Jewish hostility to Christianity. In order to bring out the real point of this third quotation the writer of Hebrews prefaces Yahweh's word with the clause: "when he shall again bring in the First-begotten into the inhabited earth he says," etc. *Then*, when Yahweh brings him in again, he demands that all the angels cast themselves down in worship before the Son as the First-begotten. Once before Yahweh has brought the First-begotten into the οἰκουμένη (sc. γῆ), into the earth that is inhabited by men. That was at the time of the incarnation and in the redemptive mission of the incarnate Son, when he wrought the cleansing of the world from its sins (v. 3). Then, too, God's angels worshipped him (over Bethlehem's fields, at the end of the forty days of the temptation, etc.) although this worship is not mentioned here. He who was brought in once shall be brought in again, which must occur at the end of the world, when he will execute the final judgment. Then all the angels of God shall accompany him, and then they shall worship him, and not only in his deity, but equally as the Son of man in his humanity, in which the heavenly host worshipped him already at his incarnation.

That is why the writer calls the incarnate Son "the First-born." So much lies in this term. For one thing, the very Sonship of which the writer speaks — the First-born is the supreme Son. For another, he is the heir of all things (v. 2). For a third, the thought already expressed in "I have begotten thee" as explained in v. 5. The main point in the term "the First-born" is the human nature of the Son; he is "the Son of man" who shall come again for the final judgment (Matt. 25:31), he who on the cross cleansed the world from the sins (v. 3), he shall return in glory, him all God's angels will worship, before him every knee must bow (Phil. 2:10).

Jesus is called "the First-born of all creation" in Col. 1:15; "the First-born from the dead" in Col. 1:18 and Rev. 1:5; "the First-born among many brethren" in Rom. 8:29; these brethren are called "the church of the first-born" in Heb. 12:23. "First-born" does not refer to time but to dignity, to "pre-eminence in all respects" (Col. 1:18: "get to be first ἐν πᾶσιν, in all respects," adverbial). In our passage we have "the First-born" without modification. This surely means that the term is to be taken in the broadest sense, so as to include the four parallel passages. Some exclude Col. 1:15; but is this First-born not the heir of all things? They restrict it to Rom. 8:29 and let "First-born" in our passage imply that there are others who were born later; but the term is not temporal — it refers to dignity. See the exegesis of Col. 1:15. "First-born" covers all the eons (v. 2), all creation from its beginning to its end in time, from eternity to eternity — and this for the Incarnate One, the Son of man, through whom the eons were wrought, who bears all that exists, who wrought the redemptive cleansing, who shall judge all things at his Parousia. Him all God's angels must worship.

Πάλιν is not "carelessly placed." We translate "when he shall again bring in" and not "and again . . . he says" (A. V. and R. V. margin), which would require the reading πάλιν δὲ ὅταν κτλ. The aorist subjunctive = "shall again bring in," the aorist is used because a single act is referred to; not: "shall again have brought in" as some translate. Πάντες is at times used without the article (R. 773); here, however, Θεοῦ makes ἄγγελοι definite. It is noted that "he says" (present tense) does not agree with "shall bring in" (the subjunctive referring to the future); but this only seems so. Yahweh said this about his angels in the distant past, yet not as something that applied to the moment of his speaking only but as something that we may quote at any time with the verb λέγει, "he says," since it applies to any time. We use "God says" in the same way.

The words quoted do not appear in the Hebrew Masoretic text, of which our versions are a translation. In the Song of Moses (Deut. 32:1-43) the LXX amplified v. 43. The LXX Vaticanus has the wording found in Hebrews; the Alexandrinus has "sons of God" in Deut. 32:43 but in the Song of Moses, which appears again at the close of the Psalms, it has πάντες οἱ ἄγγελοι Θεοῦ. This addition found in Deuteronomy is apparently borrowed from Ps. 97:7, where, however, we have "all (ye) gods," kol-'elohim, although the words refer to angels. Since Hebrews retains καί in the quotation it quotes from Deuteronomy, where this connective appears; it is absent in Ps. 97. Delitzsch thinks that the addition to the Song of Moses was made when it came into liturgical use among the ancient Jews. The fact that Yahweh said what this quotation contains is above doubt. In Ps. 97:7 these words follow the confounding of the idolaters; in the Song of Moses they likewise follow the vengeance upon

Yahweh's adversaries. So in Hebrews they are also referred to the final judgment of the last day.

Regarding this whole subject of the quotations found in Hebrews it must be said that, while the LXX is used, we never find the Jewish rabbinical manipulations of Scripture words; never is a foreign meaning introduced. But there is a penetration into the full depth and the bearing of the Old Testament words. This is due to the original inspiration of the Old Testament prophets and their words (v. 1) and to the inspiration of the writer of Hebrews, who is led and guided by the Holy Spirit to see God's intention in the Old Testament utterances. Thus the quotations are neither made in a mechanical and slavish manner, as some critics think they are made, nor are they used in a mechanical manner. The Spirit guided the writer in using the words that were originally written under his (the Spirit's) divine guidance; he directed the way in which he wished them to be quoted, what combination of passages to make, what interpretative restatements to employ, and the true interpretations he desired to be recorded for the New Testament readers. The Holy Spirit is his own interpreter despite those who deny inspiration or those who fail to adopt his interpretation.

7) The writer continues with a second comparison: what God says "in regard to the angels" and what he says in contrast "in regard to the Son." In v. 4-6 he alone is God's Son and not the angels, they must bow in the dust before him. Now in v. 7-14, which starts with a chiasm and ends with another, the incomparable supremacy of the Son is shown by comparing the height to which the angels attain with the height which belongs to the Son — they are λειτουργοί, God's ministrants and no more, the Son is the everlasting King. We cannot agree with the view that in v. 7-12 there is a comparison

regarding the *Wesen,* nature or being, of the angels and of the Son; this is the point of comparison in v. 4-6. **And in regard, on the one hand, to the angels he says:**

**The One making his messengers winds,
And his officials fire-flame.**

They are able to attain to no greater height. Note the correlation of μέν with the δέ used in v. 8. The two πρός phrases occurring in v. 7 and 8 = "in regard to" (R. 626), for in v. 7 the psalmist is not speaking "to" the angels.

The correctness of the Greek translation of the Hebrew of Ps. 104:4 has been challenged on the basis of the claim that this must be: "The One making winds his messengers and fire-flame his officials" — these poetic lines do not speak of angels at all. Delitzsch (*Die Psalmen,* 4th ed.) says that this rendering is possible but that the one given here has equal right. Even a third is possible: "The One making his messengers out of winds," etc. We certainly do not hesitate a moment to accept the rendering of the LXX which is quoted by the writer of Hebrews, who himself states that these lines speak of the angels. An inspired Hebrew poet wrote Ps. 104, the great Creation Hymn, yet here λέγει makes God the speaker who says this about the angels. The solution is found in v. 1: God spoke in the person of the prophets.

In the line quoted from the psalm τοὺς ἀγγέλους αὐτοῦ has its original Greek meaning "his messengers," and it should not be translated "his angels" (our versions) although the psalmist himself says that "the angels" are referred to. Our word "angel" is merely an adoption of the Greek word, but we have lost the idea of a messenger. So we should not translate the predicative πνεύματα "spirits" (A. V. and R. V. margin); the word means "winds," which is the original sense of the word; its parallel in the next line is "flame of fire" (a singular because the Hebrew '*esh*, "flame," has no plural).

The psalmist says that God makes his angel-messengers fleet as winds, his angel-officials destructive as the consuming flame of fire. The point is not merely the predicate accusatives "winds" and "flame" but still more the designations "messengers" and "officials." To be this is to attain the greatest height and function to which angels may rise, for which God makes them swift in the one function, destructive in the other. They carry God's messages as Gabriel did when he was sent from God to Mary (Luke 1:26) — these are errands for a good purpose. Again they function as God's λειτουργοί, "officials," to execute his judgments (the word means those who function in an office) like the angel mentioned in Exod. 12:29 who slew the first-born in Egypt, the angel mentioned in II Kings 19:35 who smote the camp of the Assyrians, the angel referred to in Acts 12:23 who smote Herod. All these were acts of consuming destruction.

The interpretation which considers only the predicates "winds" and "flame of fire" and then claims that the angels are variable in their being, at one time being this, again that, cannot be accepted. No angel ever became a wind or a flame. Neither did God in the fiery bush become fire or flame. Jewish views are sometimes introduced to the effect that the Jews saw angel powers in all the phenomena of nature: "the angels of the spirit of the winds, and the angels of the spirit of the clouds, and of darkness, and of snow, and of hail, and of hoar frost, and the angels of the voices of the thunder and of the lightning, and the angels of the spirits of cold and of heat, and of winter, and of spring," etc. *Book of Jubilees*, 2:2. But such fictions do not illumine the truth.

8) **In regard, on the other hand, to the Son** (he says):

*Thy throne, God, (is) for the eon of the eon,
And the scepter of straightforwardness
    scepter of thy royal rule.
Thou didst love righteousness and didst hate
    lawlessness.
For this reason, God, thy God, did anoint thee
With oil of gladness beyond thy associates.*

We cannot reproduce the delicate μέν and δέ save by the bulky "on the one hand — on the other hand." Ps. 45:6, 7 pictures the height on which the Son moves. The Messianic character of the whole psalm lies on the surface; the writer of Hebrews quotes these lines as being spoken "in regard to the Son." Λέγει is omitted, yet here, too, as v. 1 shows, God speaks in the singer's person who addresses the Son as follows: "Thy throne, O God, for the eon of the eon!" Here we have a vocative even in the Hebrew as well as in the LXX and in Hebrews, and only the unwillingness of commentators to have the Son addressed so directly as *'Elohim*, ὁ Θεός (the article with the nominative is used as a vocative), "God," causes the search for a different construction.

When in his *Psalmen* Delitzsch justifies this *'Elohim* he reduces its meaning by pointing to governmental authorities who are also called *'Elohim* (he might have pointed to Ps. 97:7 which is discussed under v. 6 where the word is applied to angels) and by pointing to "God, *thy* God," in the following lines as if this placed "God" when it is applied to the Son beneath "his God." But such interpretations are inadequate: the Son is "God" in the fullest sense of the word.

Yet the point to be emphasized here is not essence and being in contrast to the angels who are creatures

Hebrews 1:8

but position, office, function, and what a height angels have in this respect as compared with the supreme height of the Son in the corresponding respect. The Son occupies his throne for the eon of the eon, the Greek expression meaning "for all eternity" (the plural is sometimes used: "for the eon of the eons"). "Thy throne" implies that the Son is King. In v. 3 he sat down at the right of the majesty on high as a king also in his human nature. Luke 1:32, 33. See also v. 13 below. The angels are messengers, officers who have wondrous power, but never is one of them "God" who has a throne eternal. Jesus is this.

The second line adds the scepter to the throne: "and the scepter of straightforwardness scepter of thy royal rule." The LXX construes the article with the second ῥάβδος: "a scepter of straightforwardness thy scepter of thy royal rule," which appears also as a variant reading in Hebrews but with αὐτοῦ in place of σου. The difference is immaterial: either may be subject, either predicate, the meaning is the same. For the point is that with "thy throne" there goes this "scepter" and this βασιλεία, "kingdom," not territory, not subjects, but "royal rule," *Koenigsherrschaft*. Unlike earthly kingdoms which make and also unmake their kings, this King makes his kingdom: wherever he wields his scepter, there is his *Basileia*.

Since this second line, like the rest of the quotation, only amplifies the incomparably high royal position of the Son, the great point in this line is not the quality of the scepter as being straightforward (A. V. margin "rightness," "straightness"; R. V., "uprightness"), for this King could not have a scepter of any other kind. The Hebrew word, too, means "straightness"; it is not deflected from the true, level line by either partiality or prejudice as is many a scepter of earthly kings. Such kings debase their royal authority; the straight scepter of this eternal King ever keeps the exalted height of his royal authority. So this line, too, describes his absolute and unvarying exaltation. The whole Old Testament proclaims this fact. Jer. 23:5; Ps. 72:1, 2; also Rev. 15:3.

9) The next line corroborates this by stating what has been in this King's heart: "Thou didst love righteousness and didst hate lawlessness"; his whole reign proclaims this love of his and its corresponding hate.

Therefore, because he is the King that he is, "God, thy God, did anoint thee with the oil of gladness beyond thy associates." One may hesitate between this rendering and the one which has a vocative as was the case in the first line in v. 8: "there did anoint thee, God, thy God with the oil," etc. In this alternative translation the Son would again be addressed as "God." But the main point is the fact that in this anointing the human nature of the King is stressed, wherefore also "thy associates" are mentioned. As the Son of man he sat down at the right of the majesty after effecting the world's cleansing from sins (v. 3). The verb "to anoint" has two accusatives, one of the person and another of the oil. "Oil" is the symbol of gladness. Thus this expression is figurative: gladness, delight, bliss were poured out upon the head of this King.

This does not refer to the anointing with the Holy Spirit at the time of Christ's baptism, nor to the anointing for his office of King; for the psalm deals with the King's wedding. These μέτοχοι are not angels who have already been described as being only God's messengers and officials. These "associates" of the King are the saints: he is the heir (v. 2), they his joint heirs (Rom. 8:17); he is on the throne, they sit with him in his throne (Rev. 3:21). They share his gladness. For he did not take on the nature of angels, but he did take on that of the seed of Abraham (2:16).

"God, thy God," in no way lessens the deity of the Son who is addressed as God in v. 8. We have John 20:17, a statement from Jesus' own lips. We have already stated that the human nature is in the mind of the writer from v. 2 onward, and for this human nature God was the God of Christ, our King, and will ever remain so. Those who have an unclear understanding of the union of the two natures will always offer hesitating or inadequate or even wrong comment. But when clarity is attained, the tremendous effect of this writer's quotations upon the Jewish Christians he addresses appears at once. This Jesus is the Lord and King of whom God spoke so fully and so clearly of old in the person of the ancient prophets — how can their faith possibly decline?

10) Ps. 102:25-27 is added with a simple "and." It describes the Son still further, namely as to his eternal unchangeableness. Calvin stated that only by means of *pia deflectione* could the writer of Hebrews make this psalm speak of the Messiah, and others speak of "an audacious innovation"; but these views have been fully answered, especially by those who note that the whole psalm applies to Yahweh, the Immutable, as the Coming One, and that especially in the lines quoted, which speak of the final consummation when heaven and earth shall be changed, the Messianic meaning is as clear as a Jew or a Christian could wish it. Of necessity, however, if the Son is immutable, his immutability must extend back before even creation. As for the slight textual changes, these are negligible, for "thou" is placed first instead of fifth because for clearness' sake Κύριε is inserted from the preceding, the psalm being addressed throughout to *Yahweh*.

And:
Thou, down in the beginning, Lord, didst found the earth,

> And works of thy hands are the heavens.
> They shall perish, but thou, thou dost continue on;
> And all they as a robe shall grow old,
> And as a mantle thou wilt roll them up;
> As a robe also they shall be exchanged.
> But thou, the same art thou;
> And thy years shall not fail.

The psalmist uses thoughts and expressions that he has learned from the prophets; Delitzsch has traced them in his *Psalmen*. The first two lines, which describe the creation of the earth and the heavens, only expand the clause occurring in v. 2: "through whom also he made the eons." "Thou didst found the earth" is poetic to express the solidity of the earth, a vast mass resting on a mighty foundation. Poetic also is the statement that the heavens are "works of thy hands," as if the Lord's hands had fashioned them and put them in place.

The Incarnate Son is the Creator. All that we said about the relative clauses used in v. 2 belongs also here. Certainly, the incarnation occurred historically in time, long after the creation; but God is beyond and above time and dates; Rev. 13:8 affords us a glimpse of this. Only mechanical thinking will cling to dates and seek to subject the Eternal One to this limitation. Realizing that we are on the brink of the humanly conceivable every time we touch eternity, omnipotence, etc., we shall go as far as Scripture actually goes but shall never venture a step farther. In heaven we may be granted the privilege of seeing more of this connection between the creation and the incarnation of the heir of all things, the Changeless One.

11, 12) One leap takes us from the creation of the earth and the heavens to their destruction: *"They* (αὐτοί, emphatic) *shall perish."* This is not speculation, philosophic deduction, or "the assured results of science." It is revelation, the same revelation which records the creation in Gen. 1. Speculation has never found a beginning, likewise never an end. When scientists say that they are not obliged to do this they seek to excuse themselves from the main thing they must do to be true "knowers" (scientists), for unless they truly know the beginning and the end and him who fixes both, how can they truly know what lies between? The humble Christian, who knows this main thing, is far, far in advance of all the learned men, who in spite of all that they learn lack the absolute essentials.

"They — but *thou"* are in sharp contrast: "but thou, thou dost continue on" — a simple, human way of stating the Son's eternity. "Continue on" is an expression of time; human thought and language have no other expressions for what by another word of time we call "eternity." He who was *before* creation will be the same *after* heaven and earth perish.

Καί is explicative: "And all they (the heavens) as a robe shall grow old." Surely, the heavens seem permanently changeless, but they are like a robe that is presently worn out and must be discarded. "And as a mantle thou wilt roll them up," a variant reading is "thou wilt exchange them" for a better mantle. Isa. 34:4; 51:6; Matt. 24:35; II Pet. 3:7, 10; Rev. 21:1. "As a robe also shall they be exchanged" is what Rev. 21:1 describes when it speaks of "a heaven new, an earth new."

Again we have the contrast: "But *thou,* the same art thou; and thy years shall not fail." The Son is the Immutable One; his eternity is expressed once more in a human way with terms of time.

13) Δέ adds. **Moreover, to whom of the angels has he ever said:**

Sit at my right
Until I place thine enemies as a footstool for thy feet?

This is the climax just as it is in v. 3. We see that v. 4-14 are the Old Testament exposition and elaboration of v. 1-3. These are the prophetic voices of the Old Testament by which God spoke in olden times. To believe in Jesus means only to believe the Old Testament prophecies, believe God who spoke about Jesus in the person of the Old Testament prophets (v. 1).

Ps. 110 was composed by David. That point is vital for an understanding of Matt. 22:41-46; Mark 12:35-37; Luke 20:41, 44. The first line of the psalm: "The Lord (*Yahweh*) said to my Lord (*'Adonai*)," is omitted and only the command is quoted: "Sit at my right," etc., present imperative: "be sitting and so continue," etc. The phrase ἐκ δεξιῶν is the Greek idiom which looks "out from" a place toward the speaker and uses the neuter plural as if the right consisted of parts. What sitting at God's right means, and how this applies to the human nature of the Son we have discussed in v. 3.

Spurgeon misunderstands when he regards this sitting as being otiose: "His work is done, and he may sit . . . he may therefore quietly wait. . . . In his sitting he is our representative. . . . While we see our Lord and representative sitting in quiet expectancy, we, too, may sit in the attitude of peaceful assurance." Yahweh, Spurgeon thinks, will subdue the enemies while Christ merely sits and waits. But read Ps. 2:9. This is not quiet waiting. We know that the *opera ad extra sunt indivisa;* all the persons of the Godhead join in them. The Father may, indeed, be said to lay the enemies of the Son at his feet, but this does not exclude the fact that the Son smashes his foes with the rod of iron. God, too, sits and laughs at the raging kings of earth and at the violent hosts of men and of devils that assail his Son's kingdom. This sitting is the *exercise* of power and majesty.

This expression is anthropomorphitic: "till I place thine enemies as a footstool for thy feet" (compare Josh. 10:24). Conquering kings emphasized their triumph by placing a foot upon the neck of some conquered king. The figure is extended so as to include all the incarnate Son's enemies, and it is in accord with the idea of a "footstool" to match the sitting and at the same time conveys the idea of permanent triumph by means of "footstool." So Delitzsch writes: "Temporal history shall end with the triumph of good over evil, yet not with the annihilation of evil but with its subjugation. To this it will come when absolute omnipotence for and through the exalted Christ shows its effectiveness."

The question asked in v. 13 is like that asked in v. 5. The answer is: "To no angel has God ever said such a thing."

14) The answer to the second question indicates the reason God could never have said and never did say anything like this to even the highest angel. The interrogatory form implies that no reader of this epistle will think of dissenting. **Are they not all** (only) **officiating spirits commissioned** (again and again, iterative present) **for ministry for the sake of those about to inherit salvation?** Yes, that is what they are, no more than that is possible for them. They fit into the incarnate Son's royal rule of grace, none of them could ever act as the King himself.

Οὐχί is the strengthened οὐ. "All" becomes emphatic because of "to whom" in v. 13 which implies "to none"; "all" are only what is here said of them. The adjective λειτουργικά recalls the noun used in v. 7 and has the corresponding meaning: "officiating" spirits. They may officiate in God's acts of judgment (v. 7) but also in God's grace (here) as being "commissioned" on all sorts of errands "for ministry" (or service), commissioned thus "for the sake of (διά with the accusative) those about to inherit salvation." It is the angels' delight to do this service for Christ's saints. To act as Christ's officiating ministrants in saving us poor mortals is the height of their joy. It is also the limit of their activity. They cannot make us heirs of salvation, only the heir (v. 2) can do this, who alone has the inheritance to share with us as joint heirs (Rom. 8:17). Μέλλω with the present infinitive paraphrases the future tense. "Salvation" refers to our deliverance at the time of death (Luke 16:22) and in the final judgment.

For one service, however, angels are never employed; they are never sent out to preach the gospel. That service Christ reserves for the church and its ministry. Through both Testaments there runs the story of the angels and of the missions they perform. It is most entrancing in the New Testament. Shall the angels be for the readers of this epistle a consuming "flame of fire" (v. 7), or shall they be what v. 14 says? Are the readers among "those about to inherit salvation," or are they among the enemies to be laid low as Jesus' "footstool" (v. 13)? These and similar questions are involved in this wonderful presentation of the incarnate Son's incomparable exaltation.

The writer, we may note, proceeds as Jesus does in Luke 24:25-27: he expounds the Scriptures in order to remove all doubts.

Again we note that, all denials to the contrary, the Old Testament is full of the revelation of the Trinity and of the Son and his incarnation and human exaltation. This chapter is the evidence.

CHAPTER II

The Warning:
How Shall We Escape if We Neglect so
Great Salvation? 2:1-4

1) The writer lets the facts concerning the incomparable greatness of the Son (chapter 1) merge into a strong warning for his readers. This is a warning and not merely an admonition. His word grips the hearts with the same firmness with which he grips the facts. The warning is only somewhat softened by the inclusion of himself, for the readers and not he are showing signs of defection.

For this reason (presented at length in chapter 1) **it is necessary the more earnestly to give heed to the things that were heard** (by us) **lest we ever get to be drifted past** (them). This danger calls for the warning. "The more earnestly" (abundantly) = because these things were spoken to us by God, not only in the person of his prophets, but also in the person of his Son (1:1, 2), and because the danger of drifting past them has already appeared. With προσέχειν we supply νοῦν: "to keep holding the mind to something," "to give heed," here: "to continue to heed the things that we were made to hear" (the neuter plural aorist passive participle implying an agent who made them hear: God speaking in the prophets and in his Son and in the New Testament heralds). Δεῖ indicates any kind of necessity, here the one arising from what God made them get to hear (aorist ἀκουσθεῖσι); it is our "must."

The verb παραρρέω = to flow or drift aside; the second aorist passive subjunctive means "get to be drifted past" like a ship that a contrary wind causes to drift past its harbor so that it is prevented from reaching its destination — a calamity, indeed. The passive veils the agent. In Eph. 4:14 Paul has a similar figure: "carried about with every wind of doctrine." A strong current or wind was threatening to make these Jewish Christians drift away from the harbor of "salvation" (1:14; 2:2).

Since in the classics προσέχειν is used in connection with ships with the meaning "to turn or bring to their moorings," it may be that the verb "drifting past" is chosen to match this thought. While the aorist is effective: "actually caused to drift past," the indefinite μή ποτε, "lest ever or at any time," warns against its becoming actuality at any time; for this danger is not one of the present moment only. The way to overcome it is ever to keep the mind on the things heard, to tie fast to them ever more abundantly, with ever stronger cords.

2) This warning injunction is strongly fortified by a question which contains a deduction *a minori ad majus* or *a fortiori*, and this is made doubly strong by a repetition of the major premise. The argument thus becomes unanswerable. The only escape open is that of desperation, unreasonable refusal to yield, deliberate challenge of God and his Word and of the just judgments he has already executed. It will pay to let the mind dwell on this. Unbelief claims to be reasonable, rational; it is, in fact, the height of irrationality. It claims to act with sanity; it is wholly devoid of sanity. It puts up arguments; its arguments do not rest on premises of facts; the towering facts demand the one, true, opposite conclusion. Unbelief damns itself by its own utterances, deliberately challenges God and Christ to its own doom in spite of the doom that all past unbelief has already met.

For if the word that was (once) spoken by means of angels became firm, and every transgression and refusal to hear received just payment in

full, how shall we on our part escape on having neglected so great salvation, such as, after having received a start in being spoken through the Lord, was made firm for us by those who heard it, God supporting them with additional testimony by means of both signs and wonders and by means of manifold powers and apportionings of the Holy Spirit in accord with his volition?

"The *logos* spoken by means of angels," historical aorist, is the law which was given by God on Sinai. It was first spoken by God (Exod. 20:1; Deut. 5:22) and was then given to Moses on tablets of stone. The law was not spoken by the angels. Just what their function was in this connection beyond causing the thunders, the lightnings, the terrible trumpetings, we do not know. Gal. 3:19 speaks of their participation as showing the law to be inferior to the gospel; while Acts 7:35, 53 speak of their participation as making God's law more glorious than any other law. The angels are mentioned here because of 1:4-14. They are only what 1:7, 14 state them to be. Angels participated in the giving of the law, in the utterance of the New Testament gospel the Lord himself was concerned (v. 3). God was, indeed, back of both; but the employment of angels indicates that the law was far inferior to the New Testament gospel of salvation. In fact, the law came in 430 years after the covenant that was made with Abraham, and that covenant God made directly, in person, without angels.

Even so, this law-word "became firm," its threats went into effect, not one of them proved empty. Explicative καί states this fact: "and every transgression (stepping aside from the law) and refusal to hear (turning the hearing aside from it and listening to something else) received just payment in full" as the long history of the Jews proves. In Acts 7 Stephen reviews it. The last noun refers to the gift of pay or wages ἀπό, in full, all that was coming to the transgressors. "Recompense of reward" in our versions is not so clear.

3) If this is fact — and what Jew or former Jew would dare to deny it? — "how shall we on our part escape on having neglected so great salvation?" The question is far more effective than the declaration "we shall not escape" would be. "How shall we escape?" you, my readers, and I — tell me if you can, for I do not see how we possibly can. Note the mastery of the question and also the doubling of the question. The law demanded obedience, "salvation" was an unspeakably great gift. Yes, it was obedience to accept the gift, God asks it and wants to create it by his gift; but here is "so great salvation," this wondrous gospel content with only the obedience of receptive faith needed to make it our own. The expression is not: "on rejecting so great salvation" it is: "on neglecting," *sich nicht bekuemmern*, just letting it lie, remaining indifferent to salvation, the one supreme thing that every sinner needs. The aorist participle indicates the completion of the act: "after we have neglected"; it is usually called conditional: "if we neglect" (our versions).

The qualitative relative clause with all its modifications drives in the unanswerable question to its deepest depth: so great salvation, "of such a kind as (ἥτις), after having received a start in being spoken through the Lord, was made firm for us by those who heard it," etc. This qualitative clause contains three considerations regarding the great salvation, all three of which intensify the conviction that we certainly shall not escape after having neglected salvation of this kind. The view that the relative applies only to the noun "salvation" and not also to the adjective "so great" is untenable, for the noun and the adjective go together.

The quality of this salvation is not described according to its substance, to what it contains and brings to us, all of that lies in the very idea of σωτηρία: rescue from mortal danger and safety here and hereafter; its divine quality is described according to the divine way in which it was confirmed for us, according to the stamps and seals God placed upon it. The fact that these seals are greater than those which the law of Moses received is beyond question; 1:1-3 have already stated this fact, only the details are brought out here, but in all their greatness.

The first great point is subsidiary to the second and is hence expressed by the participial phrase, literally, "having received (or taken) a start of being spoken through the Lord." Ἔχω or λαμβάνω are used thus with ἀρχήν; the aorist participle marks the moment when the beginning was made while the present infinitive describes the Lord's speaking in its progress. The Lord himself started to proclaim the New Testament salvation. We have his entire prophetic ministry; see Deut. 18:18, 19.

The δι' ἀγγέλων used in v. 2 and διὰ τοῦ Κυρίου are undoubtedly to match; in the same way the passive λαληθείς used in v. 2 and the passive λαλεῖσθαι match although the one is aorist to indicate the past fact and the other a descriptive present to indicate the Lord's speaking. The fact that "so great salvation" received a start in "being spoken" is not an incongruity in terms, it is compactness of expression. The readers know that the Lord offered and conveyed the salvation by word of mouth; it is still so conveyed. The infinitive depends on ἀρχήν; R. 1075 calls such infinitives complementary.

This statement is placed first because it is fundamental as far as making Christ's salvation firm for us is concerned. Who this "Lord" is chapter 1 has verified from the Old Testament; his eternal superiority over the angels has been fully presented. The fact that the angels did not personally speak the word of the law the readers know; that the Lord did speak the salvation they also know since 1:2 has restated that fact. While the two διά differ they are, nevertheless, alike as far as expressing mediation is concerned. If it was fatal to disregard the law which God mediated by means of angels, who does not see that it would be even more fatal to disregard the actual salvation which God mediated by the Lord? This title "the Lord" instead of "our Lord Jesus Christ" is the more impressive.

The main point is found in the main clause: "was made firm for us by those who heard it"; the English is compelled to reverse the word order. Neither the writer nor his readers heard the Lord himself but got their hearing from those who did hear the Lord at firsthand. The fact that "the Lord," being what he is according to chapter 1, would know how to transmit his salvation beyond these first hearers is beyond question. "Those who heard" does not refer to any and all of the first hearers but only to the chosen apostles.

According to Gal. 1:12 Paul cannot be included among those who obtained the Word from the apostles, which is one of the reasons he cannot have written Hebrews. The ὑπό and these apostolic first hearers extend the speaking done by the Lord to the writer and to the readers of this epistle: this so great salvation "was made firm (sure, solid, admitting of no doubt)" for them by the apostles. If we are correct in surmising that the readers were the Roman Jewish Christians, then Paul converted them, then they had heard also Peter, then this ὑπό phrase becomes vivid indeed. See the introduction.

The whole statement says nothing about faith; it is entirely objective; the basis of faith is firm. This is what the readers, who, like the writer, have believed but, unlike him, have begun to doubt, must see fully anew. This firm basis stands, will stand even though they should leave it. Yet, realizing its firmness, their faith, too, will cease to hesitate. Εἰς ἡμᾶς is not "in us" but "for, in regard to us."

4) Added to these two considerations is the third which again presents a great fact: "God supporting them with additional testimony by means of both signs and wonders," etc. In the double compound σύν is associative but, as so often, with the idea of support and help; ἐπί, "upon," adds the thought of adding God's own testimony to that of these apostles. God gave his testimony in three ways: 1) by means of both signs and wonders; 2) by means of manifold powers; 3) by means of apportionings of the Holy Spirit, all three "in accord with his (God's) volition," θέλησις, the act of willing (θέλημα = what is willed).

First, the Lord attested and sealed the great salvation; next, he attested the apostles whom the Lord made hearers and thus witnesses; finally, God used three different seals in this attestation. In this way was this salvation made firm and placed beyond doubt "for us."

"Signs and wonders" refer to the apostolic miracles which were great and glorious indeed. Others, too, like Stephen, were given this grace. "Signs" is the greater word because it is ethical and designates the miracles as signifying something; "wonders" or portents indicates only their astonishing character so that the New Testament never uses this word alone as it does "signs." The latter is broader; a sign does not always need to be a wonder. Moreover, pagan religion had wonders and portents which, however, were never true signs. The term δυνάμεις sometimes means "power works," which is another term for miracles that is derived from the omnipotence involved. Here, because of the adjective "manifold powers," the word seems to refer only to the many powers which God bestowed upon the apostles as Stephen was "full of faith and power" (Acts 6:8). The next term is allied: "apportionings of the Holy Spirit," among them being powers but also other charismatic gifts.

More than the plural "apportionings" and the absence of the Greek article with "Holy Spirit" are required to regard this as an objective genitive which divides the Holy Spirit into "portions" that God distributes. "Words in -$\mu o \varsigma$ expressing action" (R. 151) make it obvious that this is not an objective but a subjective genitive: the Holy Spirit makes the apportionings exactly as I Cor. 12:11 states: "dividing to every man severally as he wills"; B.-P. 795 interprets: "the different gifts proceeding from the Spirit." Those who divide the Spirit have this alone done "in accord with his (God's) volition" and not the bestowal of miracles and of powers.

This final phrase modifies the participle of the genitive absolute and thus applies to all the datives. We submit that it cannot modify $\mu\epsilon\rho\iota\sigma\mu o\tilde{\iota}\varsigma$ because one word expressing action ("apportionings") cannot be modified by another word expressing action (in accord with his "willing," $\theta\epsilon\lambda\eta\sigma\iota\varsigma$). It seems that this is why the writer used these words expressing action and not $\mu\epsilon\rho\eta$ and $\theta\epsilon\lambda\eta\mu\alpha$. As to the miracles of the apostles, they never wrought these at will but only as, when, where, and how God willed; see the exposition of Acts 3:4 for the details.

Powerful as this warning is for us today, it must have been even more powerful for its first readers; especially also if our conclusion is correct that they were the great body of Jews that had been converted by Paul in Rome, who had also witnessed Peter's and Paul's death by martyrdom.

THE SECOND MAIN PART

The Incarnate Son's Suffering
2:5-4:13

*It Behooved Him to Partake of Our Flesh
and Blood to Deliver Us, 2:5-18*

Preliminary: To Man, not to Angels, God Subjected All Things, v. 5-8.

5) While γάρ connects this section with the preceding, the whole thought is a new subject which is followed by its own warning and hortation in 3:7-4:13. We do not agree with those who extend the first main part of the letter to 4:13 because they feel that the idea of the supremacy of the Son continues to that point. Supremacy is concluded at 2:4; with 2:5 humiliation begins, the humiliation of Christ's suffering.

For not to angels did he subject the inhabited earth that is to come, concerning which we are speaking.

Much has already been said about "the angels," their high position and office (1:7), to show how infinitely higher are the position and the royal rule of the incarnate Son. This presentation was concluded with the statement that all the angels are only officiating spirits for the sake of those who are to inherit salvation (1:14). "For" connects with this statement and means: "to explain still further," yet this explanation is not with reference to the incarnate Son as it was in chapter 1 but with reference to us who are to inherit the world to come with its salvation, who are to be joint heirs (Rom. 8:17) together with "the (supreme) heir of all things" (1:2).

The great fact is that "not to angels did God subject the inhabited earth which is about to come," the new earth (Rev. 21:1). Angels are not joint heirs with the supreme heir; angels are not to sit on the throne with this heir and to reign with him in the new heaven and earth (Rev. 3:21; Matt. 19:28; II Tim. 2:12); not with angels did the Son become associated but only with the seed of Abraham by assuming, not the nature of angels, but the human nature of Abraham's seed.

Although angels seem to be so far above us, we have already been told that they are only officiating spirits who are commissioned to service for our sake (1:14). We are the royal heirs of the world to come and not they; to us and not to them has God subjected (literally, ranged in order under) "the inhabited earth, the one about to come" for us. "Concerning which," the writer says, "we are speaking," namely you, my readers, and I, in the discussion of this letter (this is not a majestic or an editorial plural). Have we not said διὰ τοὺς μέλλοντας κτλ., in 1:14, "*the ones coming* to inherit," just as we are now saying τὴν (γῆν) μέλλουσαν, "the inhabited earth, *the one coming*"? What *we* shall then be, and what *it* shall then be, is our real subject.

To call this new earth the *oikoumene* is striking since this participial term is usually used with reference to the present inhabited earth; yet this term may well be used, as is done here, with reference to the new, the coming earth in which there shall dwell salvation, righteousness, peace, glory, etc. Men strive to rule big areas of this sinful earth, wage bloody wars to this end, and in the end get only a few feet of it for their grave, their bones not resting safely even there (think of the Egyptian royal mummies). Our inheritance is the earth to come, where we shall reign with Christ on his throne forever, a boon that is not accorded even to the angels.

6) **Now one has somewhere solemnly testified, saying:**

**What is man that thou art remembering him,
Or man's son that thou art looking in upon him?
Thou didst make him a little lower than angels;
With glory and honor thou didst crown him
And didst set him over the works of thy hands.
All things didst thou subject under his feet.**

Ps. 8:4-6 is introduced by δέ, but only in a general way even as "one somewhere" is quite indefinite. The readers know that David wrote these lines; their importance is indicated only by the verb "did solemnly testify," which is quite sufficient. No "but" and not even "moreover" are suggested by the connective. The first two questions express well-grounded surprise because of the fact that God remembers man and keeps looking in upon him, namely with his constant care for him.

The two ὅτι are consecutive: "so that thou," etc. (R. 1001; B.-P. 938). Modern skepticism, especially Deism and philosophy, observing man's insignificance, imagine that, if there is a God at all, he certainly cannot bother with us little creatures. Like Paul in Acts 14:15-17, David sees that God ever remembers man and looks in upon him to supply his needs and thus to attest himself to man in a thousand ways. The fact that he also sends calamities, etc., is no upsetting mystery to them, for they know man's sin and God's judgments that would lead sinners to repentance.

7) As if giving an answer to his own questions David continues: "Thou didst make him (only) a little lower than angels," literally, "thou didst lower him (only) a little as compared with angels," those beings who appear so exalted to us in their heavenly powers

and glories. Man, too, has an immortal spirit, personality, reason, will although these are found in a human body. Βραχύ τι might mean "a little while" (temporal) instead of "a little" (degree); but the latter is the sense of the psalm, and this quotation nowhere indicates that it is intended as a modification of the original. This creature, man, does not belong in the same class with the brutes and the lower creation but rather with angels.

The next lines show where God ranks man and why he remembers and looks in upon him: "With glory and honor thou didst crown him," which explicative καί explains: "and didst set him over the works of thy hands" (a line which some texts omit, yet for no sound reason since it is so necessary to the picture of man's high place in the creature world).

8) The final line makes this still plainer: "All things didst thou subject under his feet." This verb ὑπέταξας significantly repeats the ὑπέταξε occurring in v. 5 and thus, as in a flash, reveals the connection between David's description of man and the opening statement of v. 5 that God "did *not* subject" the world to come to angels. God "*did* subject" all things beneath the feet of man. What, then, *is* the place of man? With a few simple, exegetical strokes the writer makes the whole matter plain: **In that he (God) subjected all the things to him** (man) **he left nothing unsubjected to him.** That last line quoted from the psalm should not be disregarded; in that line πάντα means just what it says, what the writer of Hebrews, who repeats it with the article of previous reference, τὰ πάντα, likewise says, namely that God excluded nothing in his act of subjecting "all things" (aorist) to man. This is the first point.

Now, however, not yet do we observe all the things subjected to him (perfect participle with its connotation of durative present). The fact is that so many things on this present earth are still far beyond man's control. As far as the inhabited earth to come (v. 5) is concerned, this, as the writer himself says, is yet to come, and we ourselves are called "they who are to come to inherit salvation" in the new earth (Rev. 21:1). So much for the second point when we place v. 5 alongside of the lines quoted from David's psalm, especially the last line. What, then, clears up this matter? The fact that the incarnate Son who suffered and was glorified tasted death for the benefit of every man. There is no need to go into the whole story of man's sin and its consequences. The presentation selects one brief, direct line of thought and counts on the intelligence of the readers to supply the obvious additional thoughts that are implied. That coming world is one of completed "salvation," of which we believers are the heirs (1:2, 14).

Before we go on we may note that some commentators refer the quotation, Ps. 8:4-6, to Christ. Insert "Christ" in v. 6 and note the sense of the passage; but in the rest of the quotation, in fact, through v. 8 the pronouns refer to "man" and "son of man" without change. The whole ancient Jewish exegetical tradition understood David to refer to "man" and not to the Messiah. It would have been extremely hazardous for a writer to Jewish Christians to insert the Messiah into a passage which does not speak of the Messiah in the original; faith cannot be confirmed by such methods. If we keep to what David said and to what the writer of Hebrews adds, all remains both clear and sure.

Elucidation: The Suffering Jesus Brings Us to Glory, v. 9-18.

9) God subjected all things to man (v. 8); not to angels did he subject the earth that is to come, it, too, is to be subject to man (v. 5); yet we do not

see that even this earth is as yet subject to man. How, then, is this to be explained? Answer: **But him who has been made a little lower than angels, him we do see, Jesus, because of the suffering of the death** (he underwent) **crowned with glory and honor in order that by God's grace he should taste death for everyone.**

A masterly statement, indeed, masterly in covering every point with simple brevity. What we "observe" (ὁρῶμεν), what we have before our eyes wherever we look in this world, is by no means the whole of it, namely all things not yet subjected to man (v. 8); we Christians "glance at" (take a look at, βλέπομεν) "him who has been made a little lower than angels, at Jesus." And what do we see in him? A man like ourselves, "Jesus" being the name he bore here on earth, but now "crowned with glory and honor" (v. 7), which means "all things in subjection under his feet" (v. 8), this even in a higher sense than David predicated it of man, who spoke only of this present earth and did not speak of the fact that in our present sinful state this subjection of all things to man is not yet realized (v. 8).

How did this man Jesus come to be crowned thus? "Because of the suffering of the death," the articles to indicate "the particular suffering" and "the particular death" he underwent, a sacrificial, expiatory, substitutionary death which is known as such to the readers. Jesus did not suffer and die in a general way, merely die some kind of a death as all sinners suffer more or less and finally die. Of such suffering and death it could not be said that "because of it" a person is crowned with glory and honor. The soul that sinneth it shall die. It is sin that produces death. Jesus' death was a sweet-smelling savor to God, who therefore crowned him.

The weight of the statement lies in the purpose clause which, however, does not modify the participle

Hebrews 2:9 77

"crowned" but the phrase, the reference to Jesus' death. The construction is *ad sensum*: made lower than angels so as to suffer and to die had the purpose for Jesus that thereby he not only achieved crowning with glory and honor for himself but also the purpose "that by God's grace he should taste death (genitive after a verb of tasting) for everyone." The implication is that by virtue of this death of Jesus' everyone might attain glory and honor; this implication is reserved for actual statement in v. 10: "getting to bring many sons to glory."

"To taste death" = to undergo all its dread bitterness; it is not a softening but rather a strengthening of the simple verb "to die." Jesus tasted death, not by merely sipping, but by fully draining the cup. The emphasis is on ὑπὲρ παντός, masculine: "for the benefit of everyone." The fact that this includes universality as well as substitution is rather plain although neither idea is in the foreground, this being the idea of benefiting everyone by opening up to him the avenue to eternal glory and honor.

The writer of Hebrews does not make Psalm 8 Messianic, but he does read David's language in the Messianic light as all Scripture should ever be read. Two expressions are here read in that way. When Jesus became incarnate he, too, like all men, "was made a little lower than angels," certainly not according to his deity, which is immutable, but by assuming our human nature with its present earthly weakness. How completely he thus became one of us is plain. David's statement in v. 7 refers to man alone and is so used by the writer with reference to the God-man.

The perfect participle indicates a condition that endured and ended, its graph is ————• "A little lower" (degree) is unchanged from v. 7, and neither there nor here means "a little while." "Having been crowned with glory and honor" repeats this expression which was used in the psalm of David, who applied it to man's present state of superiority over all earthly creatures. Yet v. 8 points out that this really implies more, that all things without exception were to be beneath man's feet, a condition which man has not as yet reached. For it cannot be God's intention that man is to be over all things only in this transitory earthly life, that his superiority is to end with that. His present still imperfect superiority must be, as the writer of Hebrews says, the forerunner of a final complete superiority which is to be attained in the world to come (v. 5). This is already attained by Jesus whose human nature is now exalted, "having been crowned with glory and honor" after having been, like us, made lower than angels. This perfect is, however, the reverse of the former, its graph is •———, starting in the past, at his resurrection and exaltation, and extending to all eternity. In and through him we, too, are to attain what v. 5 implies of us.

The correct reading is χάριτι Θεοῦ: "by God's grace" Jesus tasted death's bitterness for the benefit of every one, "who died for our advantage on the cross." "By God's grace for everyone" is significantly adjoined, for this undeserved favor of God pertains to us guilty and doomed sinners and not to Jesus who died for our sins. Yet some interpreters prefer the variant χωρὶς Θεοῦ, "apart from God" Jesus tasted death, and then refer this to Mark 15:34 or state that Jesus suffered only according to his human nature and not according to the divine. "Apart from or without God" says too much, for God willed the death of Jesus, and Jesus drank the cup in obedience to God's will. The plea that the more difficult reading, the one that is textually least explainable, is probably the correct reading has only too often prolonged the life of even senseless readings.

The full and final glory, which is intended for man by God, is secured for him only through Jesus' suffering and death, who for this purpose, like us, was made lower than angels, tasted death's bitterness, was then exalted in eternal glory. Yet, remember that 1:1-14 precedes: this suffering, dying Jesus is the eternal Son. The writer presents the suffering Messiah who was such an offense to Jews, from whom the writer's converted Jewish readers were inclined to turn away. Himself a former Jew, the writer says to his readers: We see this Jesus crowned with glory and honor because of his death, that death which was intended for the benefit of every man. Jesus beckons us so that through his suffering and death we, too, enter into his glory.

10) So far should Jewish Christians be from taking the last offense at the suffering Messiah that they should rather see how it befitted God to make the Author of their salvation such an Author by means of suffering. **For it was fitting for him, on account of whom** (are) **all the** (existing) **things and through whom** (are) **all the** (existing) **things, that he as bringing many sons to glory make the Author of their salvation complete by means of suffering.**

In the case of the Messiah suffering is so far from being an outrageous idea that in the accomplishment of God's grace, that of bringing many sons to glory, it positively accorded with his own nature and his relation to all things to make the Author of their salvation the Author that he is by means of suffering. Nothing else would have befitted God, all Jewish and all human preconceptions to the contrary notwithstanding.

The writer does not speak of necessity although one might say that what is fitting and proper for God is, therefore, also necessary for him, for God cannot act in a manner that is unbefitting him. The fact that αὐτῷ refers to God and not to Jesus needs no proof.

God is the agent of the passive participles used in v. 9 as he is the agent also of this new sentence. To aid us in understanding his thought the writer does not merely say that "it is fitting for God" but that it is fitting "for him on account of whom all the (existing) things (are) and through whom all the (existing) things (are)," τὰ πάντα as in v. 8. The two διά clauses declare that all the things that exist and occur do so "because of him" and "through him"; they are on God's account, for his sake (i. e., for his glory), as they are also due to his agency (his hand being involved in them all.)

The question in regard to the origin and the existence of evil is not a part of τὰ πάντα, which τὰ ἔργα τῶν χειρῶν σου have already defined sufficiently in v. 7. Since everything centers in God's interest and his hands, everything that he does befits him; in fact, that is axiomatic for any normal thought about God. You and I may do things that are not fit and proper for whom and what we are and for our relation to the persons and the things dependent on us; such an action is unthinkable in regard to God. One must have an entirely perverted idea of God (such as paganism or the moderns have) in order to think that God could or would do what does not befit himself in regard to any single thing.

The object considered is God's leading or bringing many sons to glory. This is the glory of the earth to come which is mentioned in v. 5, our coming inheritance of salvation (1:14), our participation in the glory and honor with which Jesus has already been crowned (v. 9). As his "many sons" God wants to bring us from this sinful, unglorious earth to the everlasting glory of Christ in the earth to come. "Sons" is significant (Gal. 3:26, where the word is "sons" and not "children," A. V.). Sons are like their father.

Jesus tasted death "for everyone." While that point is not stressed, not all will be sons brought to glory — some refuse to be sons of God. The accusative ἀγαγόντα is this case because it serves as the subject of the infinitive τελειῶσαι; the attraction to the infinitive is stronger than that to the dative αὐτῷ would be, which also makes for clearness. It is not a lack of assimilation as R. 1039 regards it; it is quite classical. The aorist ἀγαγόντα is not due to a relation of the tense to the infinitive but is simply factual: as far as the fact of bringing many sons to glory is concerned.

To bring many sons to glory, to effect this, it was fitting "that God make the Author of their salvation complete by means of suffering." The verb means to make τέλειος, to bring to a certain τέλος or goal, the goal implied in the object of the verb and in the context. The sense is: "by means of suffering to make the Author of the salvation of the many sons, whom God intended to bring to glory, complete as this Author of their salvation." Expressed negatively: without suffering death as Jesus did he would not have been a complete Savior, could not have brought any men to glory as God's sons. He had to come as the High Priest with the blood of atonement even as this epistle in v. 17 of this chapter and in the following chapters unfolds at length. Only the suffering Savior could save, Isa. 53. It was the Father's will that he drink the cup (thus the prayers in Gethsemane). To be the Prophet and the King was not enough; to be the High Priest and to come with his blood and his death had to be added. So alone was he the Author of the salvation of the many sons of God, they were made such sons by him and by his salvation.

When Luther translates ἀρχηγός *Herzog* he follows the LXX's use of the word, which cannot apply here. Jesus is not the leader who enters salvation and glory with all these sons of God following him. The illustration given by Dods is inadequate: "He is the strong swimmer who carries the rope ashore, and so not only secures his own position but makes rescue for all who will follow." Jesus was not saved; he had no sins from which to be saved. He does not merely *help* us in saving ourselves. However well Dods intends his illustration, it is not in accord with the facts. Ἀρχηγός = αἴτιος of eternal salvation (5:9); the former is a personal term: "Author of their salvation," *Urheber;* the other an impersonal term: "cause of eternal salvation," *Ursache;* both state that Jesus caused and causes our salvation *in toto.* See C.-K. 179, etc.

It is a striking paradox to say that God's bringing us to *glory* should make it fitting for God to use the *suffering of death* for making the Author of our salvation the complete Author he had to be and, of course, is. Yet the fact stands, stands as a matter that is in every way befitting God who is back of all that this Author of salvation did, said, suffered, and obtained for us. This does not yet explain the whole matter, more must be said and is said in the following. Those who know God and his true relation to τὰ πάντα are put on the right track as to the connection existing between the suffering and the death of Jesus which crowned his human nature with glory and honor and enables God to lead so many to the same glory as his sons.

Weiss holds the view that God made Jesus morally perfect by means of suffering; that suffering was the opportunity which was arranged by God that enabled Jesus to rise to the height of moral perfection. But was Jesus ever morally imperfect, morally incomplete? Our versions with their translation "make perfect" might mislead their readers, but the Greek infinitive will never do so. Riggenbach is unclear when he speaks of *die Vollendung seines persoenlichen Lebensstandes.* This view is not made any clearer in his footnote: the old covenant institution of salvation is called faulty and incomplete, Jesus brought its completion, yet not by his suffering and death but only by his heavenly glorification. But the old covenant was complete at every stage; all the Old Testament sons of God were brought to glory through it just as the New Testament sons are. The *promise* (old covenant) was as complete as its *fulfillment* is (new covenant). The promise ever involved the fulfillment, and vice versa.

As far as Jesus himself is concerned, the writer of Hebrews declares him to be the Author of our salvation who is complete as such in every way by means of his suffering death for everyone, and he does not postpone this completeness to the ensuing glorification. The victor is merely crowned. His victory is complete *before* he is crowned (v. 9); only *"because* of the suffering of the death" (διά) was Jesus crowned, *because* his victory was complete, and certainly not in order to help to bring it to completion.

11) "For" carries the explanation a step farther. He who was made lower than angels and because of the suffering and the death on the cross was raised to glory; he for whom the Creator and Ruler of all things fittingly used suffering to make him complete as the Author of our salvation: he is our very brother. We should not forget that he is the *heir* of all things (1:2), and that to be brought to glory means that we *inherit* salvation, i. e., become *joint heirs* with him (Rom. 8:17). Is it not plain that he and we must thus be brothers? Also that the angels do not belong to this brotherhood? They are not to sit on his throne with Jesus and reign with him, only we are to do that. They never had "blood and flesh" (v. 14) which made it necessary that the Author of their glory state become incarnate. The heir, with whom we are to inherit, had to stoop down to become our brother. We should not, however, think of the modern way of

inheriting which puts all heirs on the same level, but of the old way where the first-born is the supreme heir, especially in the case of royal inheritance (1:6 and all of v. 5-14); our inheritance is wholly dependent on Jesus who is the heir, on him as our royal brother.

He stooped down to us in order to enable God to lead us, his many *sons*, to glory. He won the glory which we are to share with him. He won it by suffering death and thereby became the Author of our salvation, which is complete in every way. We shall not understand this properly unless we bear in mind all that precedes. Verse 10 itself and v. 9, too, rest on the basis that is laid in all that precedes.

For both the one sanctifying and the ones sanctified (are) all from one, for which cause he is not ashamed to call them brothers, saying:

I will announce thy name to my brothers;
In the midst of the assembly will I sing thy praise.

And again:
I myself will be trusting him.
And again:
Behold, I myself and the dear children whom God gave me.

"Jesus" (v. 9) and we are "brothers"; πάντες, which is placed emphatically at the end, includes him and us. He and we together with him are all "from one" as possessing "blood and flesh" (v. 14). This "one" is not God, the Creator, for then "all" could not exclude the angels who have been so clearly excluded although God created also them. This "one" cannot be Abraham, for "blood and flesh" are not restricted to him, nor did Jesus suffer death only for Abraham and for his physical descendants but "for everyone" (v. 9) although everyone does not obtain the salvation and the glory bought for them at so great a price. This "one" is Adam.

"Those sanctified" include also all the Old Testament saints, Adam himself and some in the Old Testament who were not of Abrahamitic descent, and then all those of the New Testament, so many of whom are Gentiles. Here we have the incarnation by which the Son (1:2) became man, our brother, like ourselves, "a little lower than angels" (2:7, 9).

Here we have an added point for explaining the suffering Messiah. By his death for everyone he won eternal glory and honor for his human nature as Jesus (v. 9); by his suffering death he was made completely the Author of our salvation so that God might lead many sons to glory, the glory which Jesus has won (v. 10); and now, an additional step and approaching the climax reached in v. 14, 15, Jesus, our brother, sanctifies and sets us apart for God as his sons, as no longer belonging to the world but to God (John 17:14-20), as sanctified by the suffering and the death of Jesus.

"The one sanctifying" is already a high-priestly term; "High Priest" follows in v. 17, and further on we shall hear all about this High Priest. Not merely because we are human beings with blood and flesh did our Sanctifier have to be our brother and also be derived from Adam, but because, in order to sanctify us, he had to offer better blood than that of animals, his own blood which alone cleanses us from all sin and thus makes us "the ones sanctified." We are beginning to enter the Holy of Holies of our faith. The great veil is being drawn back in these two terms: "the one sanctifying," "the ones sanctified," two substantivized timeless, characterizing present participles. Besides the expiation that sanctifies and washes away all sin and guilt we shall see in the brotherhood of Jesus with us, whom he thus sanctifies, also all else that draws him so closely to us as the High Priest in understanding our temptation and in sympathy with us.

Verily, God knew what he was doing when in bringing many sons to glory he made the Savior our brother!

12) The writer of Hebrews again lets the Old Testament speak to his Jewish Christian readers with its convincing power. This our sanctifier, who is one with us through Adam, is for this very reason "not ashamed to call us brothers," for instance in the great Messianic psalm (22:22): "I will announce thy name to my brothers." The point is in the words "my brothers." The quotation is the more effective because this is the psalm of the suffering Messiah and is so completely prophetic of the way in which Jesus died. By using ἀπαγγελῶ in place of the LXX's διηγήσομαι the writer proves that he is above mechanical quotation of minor words. "Thy name" is Yahweh's great name or revelation which centers in the Messiah, in his suffering and his exaltation for our salvation. His deity and also his exaltation might lead us to think that he would be ashamed to call us his "brothers"; but we are this. Jesus calls us that in John 20:17; his incarnation made him this, for by suffering as a man, by this alone could he be the complete Author of our salvation, our high-priestly sanctifier.

The second line is added: "In the midst of the assembly (ἐκκλησία) will I hymn thee," i. e., sing praiseful hymns to thee, Yahweh, as one among this assembly of my brethren. So Jesus went to the Temple in Jerusalem and sang the psalms of worship among his brother worshipers.

13) A second Old Testament word testifies: "I myself will be trusting him" (Isa. 8:17). The Hebrew: "I will look for (or to) him," means in trust and hence is the same as: "I will trust him" (Yahweh). The LXX does not have ἐγώ, but it appears in the next

verse. Hebrews adds it to the quotation from Isa. 8:17 in order to bring out the fact that the Messiah is referred to. Because it is added ἔσομαι is placed before its participle. The writer of Hebrews makes the prophet Isaiah a type of the Messiah in this utterance or conceives the Messiah as speaking these words. Although he was himself God and omnipotent, in his humiliation and in his human nature here on earth Jesus depended on God in complete trust. Remember all his prayers. On the cross he commended his human spirit into his Father's hands. In all this he was like all God's sons, living and then also dying in trust in God. The second perfect πεποιθώς is always used as a present so that it forms a periphrastic future form with ἔσομαι and not, as R. 375 says, a periphrastic future perfect.

The third Old Testament witness is taken from Isa. 8:18, and although it follows v. 17 it is introduced here as an independent witness by the preamble: "And again." "Behold, I myself and the dear children whom God gave me" is quoted because of the combination "I and the children." Both have the same human nature. That is why the quoted words include no more. Some would extend the meaning: "Behold, I myself" — ready for thy service, "and the dear children" — ready to aid me. But that is not the meaning in the original Hebrew or in Hebrews. "Behold" means: *wir stellen uns dir anheim* (Delitzsch): in the midst of Yahweh's judgments the prophet and his children place themselves into God's hands. Delitzsch adds that in Heb. 2:13 the words of Isaiah are made words of Jesus because the spirit of Jesus was in Isaiah; the family of Isaiah was a shadow of the reality, of Jesus and of the sanctified sons of God who are saved from the *massa perdita*.

The word used is not τέκνα but παιδία, the diminutive has the sense of "dear children," the word refers, not to birth, but to age, namely to littleness and dependence. The two points are these: 1) I and these children — human; 2) they are dependent on me as having been given to me by God. We have the same relation as that of sanctifier and sanctified in v. 11. "The dear children" means neither children of God nor children of the Messiah Jesus but children "from one" (Adam), v. 11. "Whom God gave to me" = John 10:29; 17:6, 9, 11, 12.

Deduction: How much the Suffering of Jesus Means, v. 14-18.

14) Since, then, the dear children have been in fellowship of blood and flesh, he, too, likewise shared the same in order that by means of the death he might put out of commission him who has the might of the death, that is, the devil, and free these, as many as by fear of death were their life long subject to slavery.

The first clause merely restates what the previous quotations contain although this is now put in a short and a direct way by taking over τὰ παιδία from the last quotation: these dear children, these brothers, these sanctified ones, these many sons of God, have ever had only human nature, "have been in fellowship of blood and flesh," are physical creatures. The perfect tense reaches back to Adam and continues on from that point; yet κοινωνέω, "to fellowship," implies that "blood and flesh" is not, as in the case of the brute creatures, the whole of their being; their soul or spirit, their real person exists only in fellowship with a physical body. The genitives of the thing after κοινωνέω are good classical Greek.

Thus "also he," the Author of this salvation, makes them his brothers: "he, too, shared the same" (blood and flesh) in order to accomplish their salvation. The order is "blood and flesh" probably because in Jewish literature the common expression "flesh and blood" designates the powerlessness of man over against God while "blood and flesh," as also in Eph. 6:12, states the physical substance of man. But we have the historical aorist (not the perfect) to mark the moment and the fact of the incarnation. This tense in no way implies that this sharing lasted only for a time and then ended. The incarnation is not indicated here for the first time; it is implied already in 1:2 and in all that follows, note especially "having been made a little lower than angels" in v. 9. Here, however, "he shared the same" is direct.

The adverb παραπλησίως does not reduce the sharing or indicate a difference between Jesus and these children of Adam, it rather enhances the verb: "likewise," "correspondingly" he shared our physical nature (10:5b). The fact that the eternal Son had no human father, that his incarnation was miraculous, is understood by all who know the eternity of his deity, which has also been fully indicated in the final clause of 1:2.

The point of the sentence is in the purpose clause: "in order that by means of the death he might put out of commission him who has the might of the death, that is, the devil, and free these, as many as (i. e., all these children) by fear of death were constantly living subject to slavery." In order to accomplish this purpose (actually to put out of commission, aorist) the Author of our salvation made himself one of us. As a man with blood and flesh he could and did die and by the death itself freed us from the death by which the devil held us. The statement is paradoxical: death freed from death; but it is the fact. One might think that Jesus' death wrecked him as death wrecks other men, but the extreme opposite is the fact — it saved us from death.

Καταργέω (one of Paul's favorite words) is to be translated according to the context. Here its object is the devil, "he who has the might of the death" and exercises this might, κράτος itself means might put forth. "Destroyed" (A. V.) is thus inexact; the murderous (John 8:44) devil still exists and murders. "Bring to nought" (R. V.) is better: the devil cannot murder us, we are freed by the death of Jesus; this murderer was put out of commission for us. The fact that Jesus tasted death "for everyone" is stated in v. 9 (no limited atonement); but so many prefer death to freedom from death and thus remain in the murderer's might: "Why will ye die, O house of Israel?" Jer. 18:31.

It is not necessary to say that διὰ τοῦ θανάτου, without αὐτοῦ, means "by means of *his* death," the article is used with the force of the pronoun. This same τοῦ θανάτου follows, but in this case the article cannot mean "*his* death." To be sure, "his" (Jesus') death freed us. By leaving out the pronoun αὐτοῦ the sense is "the death." As the means for putting out of commission "the thing properly called death" Jesus used "the very thing" that the devil's might wielded upon its helpless victims. By death Jesus smote death; both terms are objective.

There is no need to explain to these Jewish Christians how the devil got the might of death and its killing power into his hands; they know Gen. 3. In John 8:44 Jesus, too, needs to state no details regarding this matter. So also the manner in which "the death" that Jesus used struck from the devil's hand "the death" he was using is not elucidated although an elucidation follows. The point is the fact that Jesus became the Author of our salvation by tasting the bitterness of death, that God made him complete as this Author by means of suffering, and that this was fitting for God to arrange as being the One whose interest and governance are involved in everything, so that no Jewish Christian should ever again return to the Jewish dislike of the suffering Messiah and become offended at the cross. God thought this the fitting way to save us. Here there are no abstract reasoning and proof that this was fitting for God. Here are the facts themselves with their factual results. These are allowed to speak for themselves. These prove that God acted fitly in giving us the suffering Savior. No man who is saved from the devil and from death by means of this Savior's death will say that God used unfit means for saving him. The writer of Hebrews is truly Pauline in stating facts and the logic and the power of the facts as facts. Like Paul, he is a fact theologian. That is what makes these writers invincible.

15) Another aorist states still more of the blessed fact that was achieved by "the death" which Jesus used in accomplishing God's purpose: by means of this death, which robbed the devil of his might, Jesus "set free these, as many as by fear of death were their life long subject to slavery." Ἀπαλλάσσω = *durch Entfernung anders machen* (G. K. 253), "to make other by removal," hence "to free." We frequently find "all, as many as"; here we have "these, as many as" fear death, meaning all men. All are set free from the power of death, from the fear of death, although so many refuse this freedom. Τούτους does not restrict ὅσοι only to the saved.

The doomed are graphically described: "all who by fear of death (no article) were their life long subject to slavery." Pitiful indeed! From this fear Jesus' death set us free. This slavery his death broke. Διὰ παντὸς τοῦ ζῆν belong together, the infinitive is made a noun: "through the whole life (living)" = "their livelong lives," "all their lifetime" (our versions); it is found only here in the New Testament and is good Greek (Moulton, *Einleitung* 342; R. 1052). The genitive after ἔνοχοι is frequently found, its meaning is determined according to the context; here it means *der Sklaverei verfallen,* "subject to slavery." Men rightly fear death, for they are actually in its slavery because they are in the devil's might. Jesus' death changed this, it shattered the murderer's might; in the power of Jesus' death we escape.

16) For certainly (it needs hardly to be said) **not of angels does he take helpful hold, but of Abraham's seed he does take helpful hold.**

Although in the classics ἐπιλαμβάνομαι is not used in the sense of helpfully taking hold of someone, for which reason also the old Greek interpreters as well as the A. V. thought of the assumption of the nature, not of angels, but of Abraham's seed, yet that is the meaning here (C.-K. 659 and others). But why say that Jesus succors Abraham's seed? The answer is not that there is throughout a reference only to Jesus' descent from Abraham even in v. 11 (ἐξ ἑνός is then said to mean "from Abraham") and thus now to Abraham's seed, whether his physical or his spiritual seed. Both verbs are not historical aorists but present tenses to indicate the universal, enduring, helpful taking hold. Abraham's seed is referred to in order to show that even these, the chosen people, needed succor and not merely the Gentiles, a thing that Jews and Christian Jews who were inclined to revert to Judaism might think. To such Jewish Christians this epistle is addressed.

17) Hence he was obliged in all respects to be made like his brothers in order to be merciful and a faithful High Priest as to the things pertaining to God so as to expiate the sins of the people.

Ὅθεν occurs six times in Hebrews but never in Paul's writings; it is used like our "hence," not only in order to draw strictly logical conclusions but also to present natural results: "whence it comes that," "with which the result is connected." It is so used here; when he was taking helpful hold of the seed of

Abraham, Jesus, the Author of our salvation, "was obliged to be made like his brothers κατὰ πάντα, according to everything," i. e., in all respects. We now see why Abraham's seed is mentioned in v. 16, namely not in order to exclude the Gentiles or to leave them out of the present discussion. When the Author of our salvation assumed our human nature, "blood and flesh," he could not have become a Gentile in order to effect our salvation, he was obliged to become a Jew, one of the seed of Abraham.

The emphasis is on the phrase "in *all* respects," which, of course, has nothing to do with becoming a sinner like either the Gentile or the Jewish sinners. The phrase refers to the purpose clause: the likeness to the brothers had to extend far enough to enable Jesus to be the High Priest and to expiate the sins of the people of Israel. An incarnation in blood and flesh that did not take care of this essential purpose would have been in vain.

It was not necessary to explain either expiation or high priesthood to former Jews or to state what these are and what necessity there is for them. They knew all about the Old Testament Great Day of Atonement when the high priest killed the bullock and then the goat and brought their blood within the veil and sprinkled it upon the mercy seat to remove the sins, not of this or of that individual, but of the whole people; for despite all the individual sacrifices throughout the year so many sins remained that this comprehensive, annual expiation by the high priest had been arranged of God. Much more will be said in the following. All of it prefigured the great and final expiation of Jesus.

It is here connected with Jesus. For this he became incarnate, was "made a little lower than angels" (v. 9), was "not ashamed to call us brothers" (v. 11-13), he and we being "from one" (v. 11), he sharing our "blood and flesh" (v. 14). This explains how "he tasted death for everyone" (v. 9), was made a complete Savior "by means of suffering" (v. 10), "by means of the death" freed us from death (v. 14, 15). Thus he became "the Author of our salvation" (v. 10), "the one sanctifying" those who are truly sanctified, our "faithful High Priest" (v. 17) — these three terms are cumulative.

A wonderful developing and unfolding runs through this section; we are now at its climax. We also see why "it was fitting for God" to make Jesus what he is "by means of suffering" (v. 10), and why Jesus "was obliged to be like his brothers in all respects," also in his descent from "the seed of Abraham," because he took hold helpfully of this seed in the expiation of sins. Were not the Jews the only people to whom God had given the Old Testament high priesthood and the Great Day of Atonement, which prefigured the final expiation of the sins of the whole world? How can Jewish Christians think of disowning this their final High Priest? Some interpreters think that the term "High Priest" is introduced unexpectedly and without preparation on the part of the readers. Not at all. The whole of v. 9, etc., is the most adequate preparation. When the author called him "the Author of our salvation," "the one sanctifying," this demands that "High Priest" should now be added, which thus floods all that precedes with light.

Our versions have but one predicate: "in order that he might be a merciful and faithful High Priest"; yet "merciful" is placed before the verb and is thus made emphatic so that we evidently have two predications: "made merciful (toward his brothers) and a faithful High Priest" (toward God). Yet the two predications are not independent, for the one has no noun. This appears the more certain because the adverbial accusative belongs only to πιστός: "faithful as

Hebrews 2:17

to the things pertaining to God." As our High Priest Jesus was like the Old Testament high priests, and yet in one respect he was not like them, for these high priests only killed the sacrifice for the expiation while Jesus himself suffered the death. In this there was manifested his mercy toward us all: his own suffering and death freed us from the fear of the devil and of death. Ἔλεος, the adjective of which is used, is the feeling of pity for the wretched, their wretchedness being described in v. 15. On the other hand and joined with this is the faithfulness in regard to the things pertaining to God; for in order to rescue the wretched from their terrible state Jesus had to expiate their sins and omit nothing in restoring them to God.

We construe: "to be (aorist of actuality) . . . a faithful High Priest as to the things pertaining to God so as to expiate the sins of the people." This is not separated from his being merciful yet is itself a unit and is joined to his mercy. Εἰς τό indicates the purpose or the contemplated result of this High Priest's faithfulness in the things regarding God. Our versions' translations of ἱλάσκεσθαι do not sufficiently exclude the idea that *God* is reconciled or made propitious, which is a pagan notion. This word means *suehnen*, "to expiate." It is found only here and in Luke 18:13 (intransitive) in the New Testament and applies to "the *sins* of the people." C.-K. 519 says: "God's mind needs no alteration. But that he may not need to adopt a different procedure toward the sinner, an expiation of the sin is needed (a substitutionary intervention to obviate the penalty), and that an expiation, the institution and gift of which has gone out from himself and his love, whereas man in and for himself could not dare and could not find an expiation over against the wrath of God. . . . By the *institution* of the expiation God's love steps in in advance and meets his justice. By the *accomplishment* of the expiation man escapes the revelation of the wrath of God and remains in the bond of grace which does not withdraw itself from him. It is not that something happens to God as in the secular domain; the sacrifice is no tribute which is to satisfy or can satisfy God. Therefore we never read ἱλάσκεσθαι τὸν Θεόν. Rather something happens to man, who is removed from the wrath to come (Matt. 3:7; Rom. 5:9; I Thess. 5:9)." We need not discuss the LXX and the Hebrew *kipper*, on which see C.-K.

Note the present tense in εἰς τὸ ἱλάσκεσθαι: the one act of Jesus (10:12) is viewed in its continuous application to the sins of the people. There is no doubt that ὁ λαός refers to the people of Israel as does "seed of Abraham" in v. 16. Yet here, too, not as excluding the Gentiles but in the sense that, if Israel needed this High Priest's expiation, all other men needed it no less.

18) One additional point is added in order to describe the suffering Savior. Instead of turning from him the Jewish Christians ought to be drawn to him the more. This point, too, rests on the incarnation, on his being made like unto his brothers, and thus on his suffering. Γάρ does not introduce a proof; it only adds an elucidation. In v. 16 Jesus "takes helpful hold of" and in v. 17 he is "merciful." These expressions refer to his expiation of the sins, yet, as "for" now explains, this goes farther. **For in that he has suffered, he himself having come to be tempted, is able to help those who are tempted.**

The new point is the temptation; the verb is to be understood in the usual sinister sense. But αὐτὸς πειρασθείς should be construed together; not πέπονθεν αὐτός as our versions translate: "he himself has suffered." The fact that Jesus suffered and is the suffering Savior has been stated repeatedly; this needs no emphasis even as αὐτός is not placed before "he has suffered." The point is that "he himself was tempted."

We have a study in tenses here. The perfect includes the whole duration of the suffering which ended with the death; the graph is ─────── •
The aorist participle notes only the past fact that Jesus "was himself tempted" and connects this fact with his suffering. We may think of Gethsemane when Jesus wrestled with God in prayer. The present tense "he is able" = enduringly able. The present participle is iterative: "those being tempted from time to time." The final infinitive is an effective aorist: "actually and effectively to help."

One who suffered as Jesus did, being tempted as he was, is certainly able to help those who must ever and again undergo temptation. The fact that Jesus conquered the temptation is implied in the entire statement, especially also in the statement that "he has suffered," for the temptation consisted in this that he should evade this awful suffering and the death on the cross. His answer was: "Not my will be done, but thine!" and then he himself placed himself into the hands of his enemies (John 18:4-9).

The question regarding the temptation of Jesus is not acute here. Yet let us refer to *The Interpretation of St. Matthew's Gospel,* 155, etc., where it is shown that the temptation was real although Jesus could not fall — a point that confuses many. All of the preliminary temptations as they are recorded in Matt. 4:1, etc.; 16:21, etc., were only preludes to the final one in Gethsemane although the Gospels do not call Jesus' experience in Gethsemane a temptation. The victor is ever able to help those who are in the fight, to help them successfully (aorist).

Two questions have been raised: Was Jesus our faithful High Priest only when he entered heaven with his atoning blood or already when he entered his suffering; and was he perhaps High Priest in one way before and in another way after (Riehm)? As the

Jewish high priest was the same before he entered the Holy of Holies as he was afterward, so also was Jesus. Why make a distinction? Again: Did Jesus' suffering cause his temptation, or did his temptation cause his suffering? This alternative is misleading. The expiation of our sins made his suffering necessary; the devil caused his temptation as he does ours.

Verse 18 was so effective for the first readers of this epistle because they were compelled to suffer and were thus inclined to return to their old Judaism. Read the introduction. If they were the converted Jews in Rome, we can even visualize their situation. With v. 18 pointing to the suffering Savior and his temptation the way is open for the great admonition which brings his help effectively to the readers in their temptations.

CHAPTER III

The Sharp Warning:

Harden not Your Hearts, chapter 3

Consider Jesus in the Light of Moses, 3:1-6.

1) This is the preamble which resembles that found in 2:5-8. Moses is introduced because v. 7-19 cite the terrible unbelief that occurred on the journey through the desert under Moses. Let this story find no repetition under Jesus! We should not think that Jesus is put in contrast with Moses so that the readers are warned to forsake Moses for Jesus. They are paralleled — both Moses and Jesus are *faithful*. As Israel should have been faithful to Moses, so the readers should now be faithful to Jesus. In fact, the readers have a greater call to faithfulness than the unfaithful Israelites had as far as Moses was concerned because here is one greater than Moses. The two are alike, yet when they are paralleled, the greatness of Jesus must be kept in mind.

Verses 1-6 are thus important and necessary for a proper understanding of what follows. The placing of the two characters in juxtaposition, as is done here, is masterly indeed. The readers were tempted to forsake Jesus for Moses, but by doing this they would, despite their reverting to Moses, only repeat what the Israelites had done under Moses, repeat it in a way that is still worse because Jesus is greater than Moses. The writer makes the very inclination to turn back to Moses and to the old Judaism the basis of his warning not to forsake Jesus. This desire to turn from Jesus to Moses would be no more a turning back to Moses than was the action of the ancient Israelites, who had Moses and yet did not prove faithful to him.

If the writer had placed Moses in opposition to Jesus he would have aroused the antagonism of his readers. He proceeds as Jesus does in John 5:45-47. Yet, by being true to the facts when he places Jesus and Moses side by side and asks his readers to be faithful to both, the writer is able to bring out the fact that Jesus is far greater than Moses. And so both the similarity between the two and the fact that Jesus is the greater by far lend their powerful force to the warning appeal.

We now see why the appeal is ushered in by the preamble, v. 1-6, and why this opens with the call to consider thoroughly (κατανοέω) the Apostle and High Priest of our confession, Jesus. **Hence, holy brethren, sharers of a heavenly calling, consider thoroughly the Apostle and High Priest of our confession, Jesus, as being faithful to him who made him** (what he is) **even as also Moses** (was faithful) **in his whole house.**

Ὅθεν (see 2:17) refers back to 2:5-18; the careful consideration is to result from the previous presentation. The readers are directly addressed for the first time in order the more effectively to urge them to do what is asked. The common address "brethren" is enhanced by "holy"; ἅγιοι is often used as a designation for Christians: "saints." Here a brother is urging brothers. We do not think that the word alludes to "brothers" that occurs in 2:11, etc., and 2:17, where it is used with reference to Jesus; it is the standard address used when one Christian speaks to others. "Holy" adds the thought that they "have been sanctified by the sanctifier, Jesus" (2:11), their High Priest, who made expiation for them (2:17); in the present connection this adjective is the richer in meaning.

A second address: "sharers of a heavenly calling," adds still more in view of the following warning. They share alike in the calling they have received, one that is "heavenly," that emanates from God (I Cor. 1:2; Phil. 3:14). There is no need to put more into the adjective as some do. In the epistles κλῆσις always refers to the successful and accepted call. That thought is emphasized by the use of "sharers." Being such, the readers will certainly do what is asked of them since it belongs to their heavenly calling, namely "consider thoroughly (perfective κατά in the verb) the Apostle and High Priest of our confession, Jesus." "Apostle" is one who is commissioned as Jesus himself commissioned the Twelve and Paul. So God sent Jesus on his mission. Since it is here placed beside "High Priest," "Apostle" refers to 1:2: God spoke to us in the person of his Son whom he sent to be a Prophet like unto Moses (Deut. 18:15, 18). Jesus is at the same time our "High Priest" as already explained in 2:17. This term places Jesus above Moses who is never called a high priest.

The two designations of Jesus have but one article. The genitive "of our confession" is subjective: we confess Jesus as the Apostle and High Priest who has been provided for our salvation by God; it cannot be objective: the Apostle and High Priest who accepts our confession and brings it to him who has commissioned him. Our whole confession of Jesus is referred to and not some early, fixed formula of confession in which these designations for Jesus were employed. "Jesus" is added in order to bring out more fully his work for us on earth, and both titles speak of Jesus in his great office.

2) Πιστὸν ὄντα is predicative and states precisely what the readers are to consider well when they are thinking about Jesus whom they confess as God's supreme Apostle and High Priest. It is not well to

translate the participle as a relative clause: "who was faithful," etc.; we render "as being faithful," for his being faithful is the point to be considered. What a blessing for us, this faithfulness of Jesus! If Jesus had not been faithful, trustworthy, reliable in his great office despite all the suffering this involved (2:9-18), what would our condition be? Shall we lose all that his faithfulness has bestowed on us by giving up our faithfulness, our heavenly call, our confession of him?

Jesus is presented as our example, but only on the basis of his High-priestly expiation (2:17). Only those who are cleansed by his expiation can be faithful to God and to him. Faithfulness in us means above all faith in him as our Apostle and High Priest, unwavering and true confession of him as such. Jesus cannot be merely a moral example. The wording is again wonderful, for beside Jesus as our Apostle and High Priest are placed our heavenly calling (from God to us) and our confession (our response to God) — he in his saving office, we in our calling as saved — "faithful" being the great point now to be considered.

"As faithful to him who made him" means: God made Jesus the Apostle and High Priest, made him what we confess him to be. We may appeal to I Sam. 12:6 for this use of made (ποιεῖν) but not overlook Acts 2:36: "God made him both Lord and Christ (ἐποίησε), this Jesus whom you on your part did crucify." It is unfair to criticize the Greek fathers who understand these words in this way and to claim that they did it only in order to deprive the Arians of one of their proof passages against the deity of Jesus. Those Greek fathers were right, witness Acts 2:36. God "made" also the human nature of Jesus, wherefore Jesus also called him "my God"; but what are Arians able to make of this since they must show that Jesus did not possess the deity of the divine nature? The interpretation that God made "the historical personality of Jesus, i. e., not only created it but equipped and commissioned it as the task required for the accomplishment of which it was destined" (Riggenbach) is unclear and does not accept the simple meaning of the words.

Moses is placed alongside of Jesus, the Moses of whom these Jewish Christians think so highly, from whom also the writer detracts nothing: "even also as Moses (was faithful) in his whole house," meaning Israel. This is plainly a reference to Num. 12:7; it is almost a quotation. See the repetition of it below in v. 5. Some construe the ἐν phrase with πιστός, which would then mean that Jesus was faithful in *his* house (or in God's house). But such a construction does not follow the Greek order of the words. The use of the word "whole" is challenged, in part on textual grounds, but especially because no reason for its introduction is said to exist. But Num. 12:7 has "whole." The word is decidedly in place here, in v. 5, as well as in Numbers. In all three passages it states that Moses was faithful, not merely in a part of Israel, but in his management of the whole of it. Besides all this, some overlook the fact that Moses is an individual *"in"* the house while in marked difference to him Jesus is *"over"* the house (v. 6).

Here, then, are two individuals who are "faithful" in their high and most difficult offices; the one is even "the Apostle and High Priest" whom we confess. Dare we be faithless and recreant in our calling and our confession?

3) This application is as yet only implied, for the readers are left to ask why Jesus' faithfulness is made thus prominent. Before the answer is offered the point regarding Moses is more fully explained. While he and Jesus are examples in faithfulness, not he but Jesus is the greater. It may well be possible that the explanation is needed because the

Jews commonly placed Moses higher than even the angels. **For this One has been counted as worthy of more glory than** (παρά in comparison) **Moses by so much as he who constructed it has more honor than the house** (he constructed).

"For" does not indicate why the readers are to consider Jesus but elucidates what lies in the great double title of Jesus mentioned in v. 1, and what must be noted in an adequate consideration of the faithfulness he exhibited as compared with the faithfulness of Moses. The faithfulness of Moses is not *less* than that of Jesus, nor was Moses faulty in some way, nor did he neglect some part of his house and not attend to the whole of it. No; the relation of Moses to the house was less than the relation of Jesus to that house even as Jesus alone can be termed "the Apostle and High Priest of our confession," which it is impossible to predicate of Moses.

The writer points out what lies in the phrase that is used in Num. 12:7: "*in* my whole house." God, who made Jesus the Apostle, etc., "counted him worthy of more glory than Moses" (2:9: "having crowned him with glory and honor," in which we are to share). Of how much more glory? As much more honor as belongs to him who constructed the house than belongs to the house he has constructed. The verb has its advanced meaning; it does not mean "to furnish" the house with furniture and servants but "to construct," to build and also to furnish it completely (compare 11:7). One praises a grand house, yet praises far more him who planned and erected it (Ps. 19:1).

It is debated whether the relative clause is abstract and general or the spiritual house of God is referred to. We cannot press an "either — or" in this way; here the two go together, both are in the mind of the writer. "More than the house" has the genitive after the comparative. "He who constructed it" = Jesus.

We should not think of two houses, the Old Testament and the New Testament house; these are but one house that is composed of God's spiritual people. Note 11:26 where it is stated that Moses preferred "the reproach for Christ" as being a greater treasure than all the riches of Egypt. Note also John 8:56, 58. The power and the effect of the incarnation, the suffering, the death, the expiation (2:17), and the glorification of Jesus extend as far back as Adam just as they extend forward to the last day.

The relative clause includes far more than Moses. He was not "the house"; the true Israel was that, the Christian believers are that. Moses was only "in" this house, a part of it, although, to be sure, an important part. Glory and honor to him accordingly, but not as great as that of Jesus who built the whole house and made also Moses what he was in this house.

4) It is correct to judge glory and honor in this way from the relation of the persons to the house; even the glory and honor due to God are rightly judged in this way. **For every house is constructed by someone** (present tense in a general proposition) who, compared with anyone who is otherwise connected with the house, deserves the superior honor. This justifies the judgment expressed in v. 3a regarding Jesus and Moses. Although they were alike faithful they yet differ greatly in this other respect. **Moreover, he who constructed everything** (is) **God.** His being worthy of glory and honor is according. This statement seals the matter, for if even God is in this way rightly judged as to glory and honor, no one can possibly object when Jesus is honored by God above Moses.

If we translate δέ with adversative "but" (our versions, commentators) we encounter difficulty. It becomes difficult to find an acceptable meaning for the words. Riggenbach contents himself with the thought that, since God has constructed everything, it will depend on God as to what honor others receive.

Nor can we accept the idea that πάντα, "everything," includes the position which God gave to Jesus and to Moses regarding the house. Rendall says that Jesus was "the perfect representative of God" who constructed everything, Dods adds that Jesus is the Son, the idea being that Jesus thus obtained the more honor. This is but a variation of the idea of the early commentators that God in reality built the house, i. e., Jesus in his deity. An issue is made of Θεός as though this cannot be, or at least is not, the predicate. But what is gained by making it the subject? This confusion results when δέ is translated "but."

5) After the two explanations with γάρ "and" continues the thought of faithfulness. **And Moses (is) faithful in his whole house as a servant in regard to testimony of the things that were to be spoken, while Christ (is faithful) as Son over his house, whose house are we ourselves if we hold fast as firm to the end the assurance and the boast of the hope.**

Μέν and δέ balance the two statements, on the one hand Moses, on the other hand Christ. It is the relation to the house, as already explained, that causes the difference in regard to glory and honor where faithfulness is equal. Once more then: "Moses — faithful in his whole house" (v. 2; Num 12:7), yet we now have the significant addition: "as a servant" and no more. We are even told what his service was by an allusion to Num. 12:8: "with him will I speak mouth to mouth" so that he shall then tell the people. This is put into the condensed phrase: as servant εἰς μαρτύριον τῶν λαληθησομένων, future passive participle: that he may testify to the people the things God wants to have spoken to them from time to time, i. e., a servant to act as God's mouthpiece whenever God desired to speak.

This function Moses performed faithfully; his glory was according. Thus he was *in* the house. Θεράπων is frequently used in the Old Testament as a designation of Moses (Hebrew *'ebed*): *Diener*, a free servant who serves of his own accord and so carries out the wishes of his employer; it is in contrast with δοῦλος, "slave," who dare have no will of his own. In v. 5 and 6 the copula is absent, which means that nothing depends on it or on its tense. We, therefore, do not introduce it.

6) Now "Christ." The very change from "Jesus" marks his high office and dignity especially in this epistle where the simple "Jesus" is regularly used. Not only the copula is omitted, also πιστός is to be understood. "Christ — (faithful) as Son *over* his house" — not *in* — the opposite of "servant." "Over his house" is modifier enough of "Son" (just as the εἰς phrase modifies θεράπων: "servant for," etc.); there is no need to tell what this Son's functions are, he has the whole house *under* him. What about the Father? John 17:10 answers; also John 16:15; compare Luke 16:31. We are now told outright: "whose house are *we*" (the pronoun is emphatic), the New Testament Church which has followed the Old Testament Church, into which not Jewish physical birth places us but the "heavenly call" (v. 1). The fact that Jesus is over this house of his because he constructed it, and that his glory and honor are according, has already been mentioned.

Thomas Aquinas, Calvin, Delitzsch, Westcott, and others interpret the εἰς phrase in v. 5 as follows: "for a testimony of the things which should be spoken by God through the prophets and finally through Christ," i. e., Moses testified what these others should afterward speak. Our versions seem to have the same thought in mind. Yet the allusion to Num. 12:8 is rather strong, especially also the future tense of λαλεῖν: "With him *I will speak* mouth to mouth," etc. God is the speaker in the passive participle λαληθησομένων and not the prophets that were to come and Jesus. Moses was the faithful transmitter of God's words to Israel; his "testimony" as to what God said to him at any time was "faithful" and true.

When the writer says, *"We are Christ's house,"* he adds significantly *we* "if we hold fast as firm to the end the assurance and the boast of the hope." While he softens the force of these words by including himself and by using ἐάν, a condition of expectancy, this addition, nevertheless, indicates the state of his readers who had begun to waver and had thus caused the writing of this letter. It asks the readers: "Will you thus hold fast?" It calls on them to do so. The aorist subjunctive is properly used: κατάσχωμεν, "hold fast definitely." He likewise uses two nouns, each with its article because they differ in gender. The first is subjective: τὴν παρρησίαν, which does not mean "the boldness" (R. V.) but more correctly "the confidence" (A. V.), the advanced meaning of this word (M.-M. 497; C.-K. 451); when one feels bold and has no timidity in speaking to another he is perfectly confident and assured.

The second term, τὸ καύχημα, means neither "the rejoicing" (A. V.) nor "the glorying" (R. V.), which are activities, but "the cause of boasting," the thing about which one boasts, in this sense "the boast." Paul loves this word. It embraces all that we have in Christ as something of which we love to speak as our highest, richest possession so that it sounds as if we made it our boast. "Of the hope" is likewise objective, and since παρρησία never appears with a genitive, we connect "of the hope" only with "the boast" even as both are

Hebrews 3:6

objective: the great thing for which we hope is the thing that forms our boast.

This should not be overlooked, and we should not say that, because "assurance" is subjective, its companion term must also be subjective. If that were the case, we should undoubtedly have not καύχημα but καύχησις, the activity of "boasting." Then, however, this holding fast in firmness to the end would cling only to something that is subjective. Yes, we must hold fast our subjective assurance but equally the objective ground and basis on which it rests, namely Christ, the Author of our salvation (2:10), the Apostle and High Priest whom we confess (3:1), all that we have in him, the expiation (2:17), etc., all that forms and ever should form the objective content of our boast and our hope.

Our "hope" is the glory of which we are assured: God will bring "many sons to glory" (2:10), us among them. Jesus has already been crowned with "glory and honor" (2:9). He is the heir (1:2), and we are "about to inherit salvation" (1:14) as his co-heirs (Rom. 8:17). By his incarnation he joined us and made us "his brothers" (2:11-13), by his death and expiation he freed us from the devil, the might of death, the fear of death, and brings us the help we need in temptation (2:17, 18) and thus fills us with the assurance and boast of hope and glory that await us at the τέλος or end.

It is not enough to emphasize only our subjective holding fast; the objective realities must always be added even as these alone inspire us to cling fast subjectively. Many people feel firmly confident and assured and do a lot of hoping in their hearts but lack the actual divine realities; an awful disappointment awaits them in the end. Not so *we; we* have the realities if only, as one should expect (ἐάν), we hold them fast. "As firm" is the predicative adjective which modifies both nouns. The first is feminine, the second is neuter, so the adjective is feminine since this gender prevails over the neuter, and since, if it were made neuter, the adjective would appear to belong only to the second noun.

This "if" clause is an apt transition to the warning that follows, of which this entire paragraph (v. 1-6) is only the preamble. Indeed, if we thoroughly consider Jesus in his faithfulness, in the proper comparison with faithful Moses, we shall ever keep from the faithlessness which destroyed the Israelites in the very time of Moses.

Harden not Your Hearts! v. 7-14.

7) The unbelief and the hardening of the whole people of Israel during the forty years of their journey in the wilderness, not only as these are recorded by Moses but also as they are depicted anew by David in Ps. 95:7-11, are a mighty effective warning for us even today. They must have been an even more effective warning for the first readers of this epistle. They were of Jewish blood; are they going to repeat what happened to their ancestors in the desert? Faithful Moses has been placed before them beside faithful Jesus. Will they be faithful in their "heavenly calling" (v. 1) as Jesus and Moses were, or will they now prove faithless? This is what happened to their ancestors under Moses. Are they going to repeat this under Jesus who is so much greater than Moses?

They think of turning from Jesus to Moses. But Moses and Jesus belong together; both were equally faithful, Moses *in* the house as a servant, Jesus as the Son *over* the house (v. 5, 6). It is impossible to become faithless to the faithful Jesus who is the Son *over* the house without becoming equally faithless to Moses who is the servant in the house even as the house is one.

Moses would be the first to accuse them (John 5:45-47). All this lies in the use of this quotation, and it is brought to bear upon the readers with corresponding effect.

It is best to construe διό . . . βλέπετε (v. 12) and to regard the καθώς clause with its quotation as subordinate, a construction which the A. V. indicates by the use of a parenthesis. The writer does not adopt the language of the psalm as stating his own thought, for in v. 10 God speaks, and the writer cannot adopt the words of God as being spoken by himself. **Therefore, even as speaks the Holy Spirit:**

**Today if you shall hear his voice,
Do not harden your hearts as in the embitterment,
On the day of the temptation in the wilderness,
Where your fathers tempted me in a testing
And saw my works for forty years.
Wherefore I was disgusted with this generation
And said: Always they err with the heart.
Moreover, they did not know my ways
So that I swore in my wrath:
They shall not enter into my rest! —**
see to it, brethren, etc.

"Even as speaks the Holy Spirit" is not a formula of quotation which introduces Scripture. It is not a formula at all as witness 9:8 and 10:15 where we have a different wording; in Acts 21:15 Agabus says, "These things says the Holy Spirit," although he is not quoting Scripture. What David wrote about the old Israelites is attributed to the Holy Spirit as if the Spirit himself "says" it, still says it to us. David's words (see 4:7) are the Holy Spirit's words. This defines inspiration just as do Matt. 1:22; Heb. 10:15;

9:8; and many other statements. We do not talk about an "inspiration *theory*" but look at all these passages which present a clear *fact*: "the Holy Spirit says or declares" this and that which was written in the Old Testament.

The LXX is quoted with little change as being entirely sufficient for the writer's purpose. The Hebrew of Ps. 95:7b expresses a strong wish: "Today if you would only hear his voice!" although the LXX and the A. V., like Hebrews, translate the words as a conditional clause. In either case the psalmist expects that the Lord God, to whom he asks his people to return as the people of his pasture and the sheep of his hand, will again let these people hear his voice: "Today if you shall hear his voice," etc. Ἐάν is never used to express a wish; it denotes expectancy. Hence "today" is placed emphatically forward. The period of grace is not yet closed. When the genitive is used after ἀκούω, this case refers to the person who is heard; the accusative states what is heard. This difference holds good also in Acts 9:7; 22:7, 9; 26:14. Thus we have here: when you shall hear God speaking to you with his voice.

8) The subjunctive is used in negative commands with the aorist and not the imperative: "harden not your hearts." The aorist is peremptory: "When God in his grace shall at any time still let you hear his voice, do not by any means make your hearts stiff like a dried, hard branch that will not bend and yield to God!" It may be the last time he will speak thus to you. "My spirit will not always strive with man," Gen. 6:3. It is a serious mistake to think that God will go on offering his grace despite all our rejection so that we may yield when we please. "Too late! too late!" is written at various places in the history of the Jews. This psalm records one of these places: "as in the embitterment, on the day of the temptation

in the wilderness, when your fathers tempted me in a testing." We read the whole of this together.

The writer combines the accusative of the extent of time "for forty years" with the preceding clause whereas David has this phrase in the next clause: "for forty years was I disgusted," etc. This is not an inexact quotation but is intentional and interpretative. Κατὰ τὴν ἡμέραν means: "all along the day of the temptation in the wilderness," "day" denotes the whole forty years just as σήμερον, "today," in v. 7 does not refer merely to one day, i. e., the day on which David wrote and sang this psalm, but to the time (whatever its length) in which God would yet speak to Israel in grace. That is why the LXX's as well as our A. V.'s renderings of the psalm do not regard Massah and Meribah as proper names (Exod. 17:7). Even in the passage in Exodus the etymological meaning of the two terms is added: the one = "chiding or strife."

The Greek of the psalm (LXX and Hebrews) is: παραπικρασμός, "embitterment" of the people, *Widerspenstigkeit*, bitter rebellion (*meribah*); πειρασμός, "temptation," *Erprobung* or testing (*massah*). To be sure, David thought of Exod. 17:1-7, an incident that occurred in the second year of the exodus from Egypt, and by no means only of Num. 14 and 20:2-5. David refers to Exod. 17, 1-7 much as does Stephen when he in Acts 7:37-43 combines the story of the golden calf with the idolatries of Israel during the entire "forty years in the wilderness" (v. 42).

During the entire forty years the hearts of the Israelites under faithful Moses (v. 5) were hard, unyielding, embittered against God because of the hardships of the wilderness, and tempted and tried out God the whole time of "the day of the tempting in the wilderness."

9) We translate οὗ "where"; it is not "when" (A. V.); nor is it attracted from the dative: "wherewith"

(i. e., "the temptation," in attraction with the genitive of this word as its antecedent). "Where" = "in the desert." There during those forty years, David says to the Israelites of his time, "your fathers tempted me (God) in a testing"; the phrase emphasizes the trying-out to which they subjected God while they were debating whether they should accept him or not.

"And saw my works for forty years" refers to all the miracles which God did for them plus all of God's other manifestations in leading them. All these works the old Israelites "saw," but despite all that their hearts remained hard.

10) "Wherefore I was disgusted with this generation" (it is more than "displeased," R. V., or "grieved," A. V.); one may even translate, "I abhorred." Διό is used in place of καί in order to bring out more clearly the connection between the disgust and the sin; and instead of David's "that generation," which points away from his own, our writer, in quoting David, uses "this generation," i. e., not David's but the one to which David refers in this psalm. We quote in the same sensible way.

God expressed his disgust; he said: "Always they err with the heart," meaning that their case is hopeless. The LXX, too, has "always" (like Acts 7:51), yet not in order to add to the Hebrew but in order to render its meaning properly: "A people of erring heart are they," i. e., of one that is constantly erring. The emphasis is on "heart," which in the Hebrew and in the Greek is not the seat merely of the feelings but of the mind and the will and thus of the real personality. Their wandering in error like stars out of their orbit is due to their wicked will (Matt. 23:37: "ye would not"). People who have hearts like that are, indeed, hopeless.

Δέ is not adversative "but"; it states the matter in a different way: "Moreover, they did not know my ways." The verb used is γινώσκω. They knew God's ways intellectually (οἶδα) but refused to know them as their own, *cum affectu et effectu*, refused to know them so as to walk in them. "My ways" are the ones which God had mapped out for them to follow; the Old Testament frequently uses *derek*, singular and plural, in this sense. Δέ thus makes plain from what the Israelites wandered away. Αὐτοί is emphatic: "they on their part," over against *"my"* ways, which God, indeed "knows" (Ps. 1:6).

David is not quoting God in these two lines but is summing up all that God said of the Israelites at various times.

11) We regard ὡς as being consecutive (B.-P. 1431; R. 1000 wavers between "so" and "as"): "So that I swore in my wrath: They shall not enter into my rest!" This oath is found not only in Num. 14:21, etc.; v. 28, etc., for Num. 32:10-13 repeats it, and Deut. 1:34-36 records it anew; the psalmist summarizes. "In my wrath" is the inevitable reaction of God's holiness and righteousness to sin and ungodliness when the efforts of his grace are exhausted; see further Rom. 1:18. The form of the oath is: "As truly as I live," or, "As I live" (Num. 14:21, 28). God can swear by none that is higher than himself (Heb. 6:13). God's oath is irrevocable because he never swears, as men so often do, either foolishly or without knowing to what he swears (as is done in the case of all oaths that are asked by lodges, Lev. 5:4). His oath and its irrevocableness are due to the exhaustion of his grace when judgment must follow. In oaths εἰ = the Hebrew *'im;* it is only an apparent imitation of the Hebrew and is not un-Greek (R. 1024).

The rest into which those Israelites were not to enter was certainly that in the land of Canaan, but God's oath cannot be restricted to disbarment from only this rest on the strength of Deut. 12:9-11 or of any other passage. Our epistle could then not have used this psalm, as it does, against a wicked heart of unbelief; David could then not have written this psalm in order to warn his generation against the same thing. The unbelief here described excludes not only from typical earthly blessings but equally from the rest in the heavenly Canaan. We are not left to conclude this for ourselves; 4:8-11 states this outright. Those hardened Israelites who were perishing in the wilderness did not after all enter into heaven; they were damned in unbelief as obdurate resistance of the Holy Spirit always damns (Acts 7:51).

The mention of the forty years (v. 9) has been connected with the situation of the readers of the epistle, with the fact that they had seen the work of the Messiah these forty years since his death. Some rabbis spoke of the forty years of the Messiah; but the first of these rabbis did not live before the beginning of the second century; our writer could not have alluded to a thought expressed by them. To a Christian "the days of the Messiah" might refer to those that Jesus spent on earth or to those after his Parousia but never to those between these two events, to say nothing of only the forty years from the ascension to the fall of Jerusalem. To assume that our epistle was written after the fall of Jerusalem is not warranted. If this assumption were true, the writer would have referred to that terrible judgment, yet there is nothing in this epistle that even faintly alludes to this catastrophe.

Our writer does the very thing that David did: he uses the unbelief and the judgment of the Israelites in the wilderness as a warning for the Jewish believers of his time. By using David's psalm our writer is able to double the warning, for the psalm repeats Moses' account. The effect must have been strong indeed for Christian Jews.

12) **Therefore (v. 7) . . . see to it, brethren, perhaps there will be in someone of you a wicked heart of unbelief in apostatizing from the living God; yea, keep admonishing yourselves every day, as long as it is called today, lest someone of your number be hardened by means of the deceit of the sin, for we have become sharers of Christ if, indeed, we hold fast the beginning of the confidence firm to the end.**

On the connection see v. 7, διό. "See to it, perhaps there will be," has μή with the indicative after a verb of apprehension, not in the sense of "lest," but paratactically in the sense of "perhaps" (Moulton, *Einleitung* 304; also R. 1169). "Perhaps there will be" is a plain warning. "Brethren" indicates that the quotation is ended, that the writer is addressing the readers in his own person, and that the warning comes from a loving, fraternal heart. "In someone of you" aims to have not a single one lost, no matter who of the readers it may be.

"A wicked heart of unbelief in apostatizing from the living God" is plain language. That is the kind of heart the Israelites of the desert had, which brought on them the terrible oath, the kind of heart against which David warned his people in the psalm. The writer is expounding what is said of "the heart" in v. 10. The trouble of unbelief is always in the heart, the seat of the will. Both the adjective "wicked" and the stronger attributive genitive "of unbelief" characterize "heart." Note well that "a heart of unbelief" is ever wicked, for no greater wickedness exists than unbelief, a fact which so many fail to perceive. "See to it" = watch over each other; it would be terrible if someone among you should have such a heart.

The ἐν clause defines the unbelief as to its making the heart so wicked; it states wherein the wickedness of the heart consists: "in apostatizing from the living

God." That is what ἀποστῆναι means; the noun is ἀποστασία, "apostasy" (see II Thess. 2:3). The aorist infinitive expresses actuality, definiteness. "Unbelief" is thus understood in the sense of once having believed in the living God and then having turned away from him. The writer will have more to say on this.

"The living God" is a current designation among Jews, yet it has lost nothing of its force. It is here not in contrast with dead idols, for none of these Christian Jews were in danger of becoming pagans and idol worshipers. The name refers to the true God who as a living God keeps his promises and executes his threats. "It is a fearful thing to fall into the hands of the living God" (10:31). One may think that turning back to Judaism would not be apostasy from the living God; that is the opinion of modernists and their Unitarianism. But the writer calls that unbelief. See also Jesus' word in John 17:3 also in 5:23. Whoever apostatizes from the incarnate Son as he is depicted in chapters one and two thereby apostatizes from God himself; after rejecting the Son, no man can hold to the Father, the living God, the Son being "his glory's effulgence and his being's impress."

We may note that ἀπιστία is the opposite of πιστός which is used in v. 2, 5: "unfaith" and "faithful"— Jesus and Moses true and "faithful" to God in every respect in regard to the house (church)— an apostate member of that house faithless and casting away his faith in God. The Greek makes this contrast more effectively than the English which must use "faithful — unbelief."

13) We do not find an adverse idea in ἀλλά, adverse either to "see to it" or to "perhaps there will be"; neither can be followed by *"but* admonish yourselves." This is continuative ἀλλά, it is climacteric and not contradictory (R. 1185, etc.); we translate: "yea, keep on admonishing." The watchful eye is to see

whether there is "anyone"; the admonishing is to include "yourselves," namely all. We do not regard "yourselves" as the reciprocal "one another," for ἔν τινι and ἑαυτούς, "in someone" and "your own selves," are the proper balance. Κατά is distributive, and ἑκάστην means: "day by day" without exception; the phrase emphasizes the durative present imperative which is also the form of "see to it" in v. 12. "As long as it is called 'today' " once more quotes the emphatic "today" that occurs in the psalm (v. 5) and thus means "the today," not merely the present moment, but the still present grace; the article makes the adverb a noun. For the Israelites in the desert that today ended when God swore his oath of judgment; let the readers not compel the living God to repeat that oath in their case. Let them constantly admonish themselves.

Μή with the subjunctive expresses what is otherwise to be feared: "lest someone of your number be hardened by means of the deceit of the sin." The expression is varied: "in someone of you" (v. 12), now τις ἐξ ὑμῶν, "someone from you," we may say "of your number." The point is not merely that no single sheep of the flock is to be lost but that no start may be made with "someone," nobody knowing to what such a start may lead. The same verb is used here that was used in the psalm (v. 8), but it is now the passive. The following dative "deceit of the sin" can scarcely be the agent with the passive. This agent might be "the sin," which the article makes definite as the power that is called "sin"; yet "the sin" should then be in the dative. "Deceit" expresses the means; the agent by whom someone may be hardened is ominously left unnamed.

Some have identified "the sin" with "unbelief" (v. 12); yet "unbelief" is itself the hardening of the heart. The means by which both are caused is "deceit." We meet "sin" in 11:25 and especially in 12:1, 4, where its deceit also appears. "The sin" seems to mean the unwillingness to suffer for Christ's sake, the desire to enjoy the pleasures of this life; the sin's "deceit" is that forsaking Christ and returning to Judaism, it is not giving up God, but is the gain of escape from all the persecution and the dangers that are connected with faith in Christ. The details of this deceit are, of course, manifold. Each deceived individual has his own peculiar argument and plea to justify his folly.

14) The admonitions expressed in v. 12, 13 are strengthened: "for sharers of Christ have we become if we, indeed, hold fast the beginning of the confidence firm to the end." The present connotation of the perfect γεγόναμεν prevails even as what one "has become" he is now. We need not debate as to what is meant when the writer and the readers are now said to be "sharers of Christ." In v. 1 we have "sharers in a heavenly calling"; this calling joins us to Christ, he is the heir (1:2), we are "those about to inherit salvation" (1:14); or, since this verse vividly recalls 3:6, Christ over the house, we the house itself, we are, of course, ever to see to it and admonish ourselves that we may all continue in this blessed relation (v. 12, 13). This position of ours as sharers of Christ continues "if, indeed, we hold fast," etc.; πέρ is attached to ἐάν in order to make it intensive (R. 1154). "Hold fast as firm to the end" repeats this wording from v. 6. The thing to hold fast is "the beginning of the confidence" which made us and still makes us sharers with Christ.

Ὑπόστασις = "confidence in which one stands fast as well in doing as in bearing, in acting as in suffering," C.-K. 541. Schlatter's *Wagnis* and other conceptions of this widely used word do not commend themselves. No genitive is added as is done in 11:1. The word ὑπόστασις seems to have been chosen here because it is the verbal opposite of the preceding τὸ ἀποστῆναι, the one being a firm, confident stand, the other a standing away from, forsaking, apostatizing. "The beginning of the confidence" refers merely to time and not to a start that needs development, a thought that is not touched here. The idea is that of the true and noble beginning and of an equal end. If the end truly matches the beginning, we shall then be what we are now. Βεβαίαν is predicative to τὴν ἀρχήν: "the beginning . . . as firm." The saddest thing in the world is to see a noble beginning made in the Christian faith and then to have this lost before the end arrives.

Fail not to Enter into God's Rest!

15) In saying:
Today if you hear his voice
Do not harden your hearts in the embitterment,

who, pray, on having heard, made embitterment? Yea, did not all they who came out of Egypt through Moses? Moreover, with whom was he disgusted for forty years? Was it not with them who sinned, whose carcasses fell in the wilderness? Moreover, to whom did he swear that they should not enter into his rest but to them that disobeyed? And so we see that they could not enter in because of unbelief.

Our versions attach this verse to the preceding clause, which makes it a weak appendix that is incongruous when we note the clash in tenses: hold fast definitely to the end (aorist) while it is being said (durative present). The view that the γάρ occurring in the first question of v. 16 prevents us from construing v. 15 with v. 16 is due to a misunderstanding of γάρ.

Nor do we divide the quotation in the middle so as to obtain: "while it is said, 'Today if you shall hear his voice,' do not harden," etc.; for without the aid of our English quotation marks no one could surmise that the quotation is to be curtailed, and that the writer himself adds: "do not harden," etc., (the identical words used in the psalm, v. 8) as his own. We translate as above. The absence of a connective marks a new line of thought.

In connection with the two lines quoted from the psalm a series of dramatical, rhetorical questions is asked, which drives home to the Jewish Christian readers the fact that the people with whom David's psalm deals were Jews, obdurate unbelievers, all of whom perished miserably. Let the readers themselves answer these questions; the answers are self-evident. Do the readers want to join those wretched unbelievers? Ἐν τῷ with the infinitive is the idiom Luke loves; γάρ is not "for" (our versions) but deductive: "who, then," etc.; or: "who, pray (stop and think)," etc.

16) Γάρ is inserted for the very purpose of connecting all these questions with the preamble, v. 15. With the two lines of warning quoted from the psalm (v. 15, see v. 8) ringing in their ears, let the readers note who these people were that are referred to in the psalm. "Who, pray (γάρ), on having heard, made embitterment?" Why, those Jews in the wilderness. Not ignorantly did they make bitter rebellion but ἀκούσαντες, "having heard" or "after having heard," in spite of all that God told them. So the readers of this epistle now hear. Even David's psalm is made to sound in their ears. They are of the same nation as those who were under Moses and those mentioned in the psalm. Let them beware!

The ἀλλά is not adversative; read R. 1185, etc., and discard B.-D. 448, 4, which states that it intends to indicate that the τίνες in the first question is not τινές (not "some" but "who?"). This is the rhetorical, confirmatory ἀλλά: "yea," "indeed" ("nay," R. V.).

"Did not all they who came out of Egypt through Moses?" i. e., did they not *all* cause embitterment? Our A. V. translates these questions as declarative sentences and gets the idea that only some and not all made embitterment. This is apparently done in order to exempt Joshua and Caleb. But can two individuals convert a whole nation of over half a million into "some"? There need be no fear about two lone exceptions, especially in the case of readers who know their Old Testament. That wholesale unbelief in its frightful extent is the warning.

17) In v. 16 the questions drive home the bitter rebellion of those who heard, heard all that happened when they came out of Egypt under Moses. Now a parallel double question drives home the reaction of God and their miserable fate: "Moreover, with whom was he disgusted for forty years? Was it not with them who sinned, whose carcasses fell in the wilderness?" The question that has the negative οὐ each time contains the terrible answer to the "who" question. As v. 16 refers to the embitterment mentioned in the psalm so v. 17 adds God's disgust plus the forty years, which are also mentioned in the psalm.

In "they who sinned" there is repeated "the sin" mentioned in v. 13, which is so full of deceit. Sin and penalty are now combined: their κῶλα, "limbs" (a word that is taken from Num. 14:29, 32), i. e., their carcasses, fell in the wilderness. What a long, long line of graves — the saddest in the world! They came out of the bondage of Egypt under faithful Moses (v. 5), but they fell as corpses in the wilderness! What a dying for forty years; what deaths! Let your mind contemplate the whole tragedy. Read the lament of Moses in Ps. 90:5-9.

18) One more point referred to in the psalm: "Moreover, to whom did he swear that they should not enter into his rest (future infinitive in indirect dis-

course, R. 1032)?" Without a second question (and thus marking the end of the questions) the answer is added: "But to them who disobeyed." The doors of God's rest are closed to those who obdurately will not obey the voice of grace in the blessed "today" nor heed its warning. "Disobey" means refuse to believe.

19) Now the conclusion. At times καί has the force of "and so" (R. 1183). "And so we see that they could not enter because of unbelief" (repeating this fatal word from v. 12), the opposite of πιστός, believing and thus "faithful" (v. 5) and obedient. "We see" implies that the writer is confident of also his readers. Would that "we see" were true of us "today"! At one time they could, but soon they could not. When grace is exhausted, judgment descends. The cause (διά) was —"unbelief." Scoff at the idea that unbelief is so fatal, that faith should be so decisive. **Is it so easy to scoff at the thought of those graves?**

CHAPTER IV

The Attractive Promise:

*Those Who Believe Enter into God's Rest,
chapter 4*

The Rest Promised to Faith, v. 1-5.

The passage quoted from the psalm (3:7-11) is full of threatening and thus serves as a warning; but in this very threat there lies the most blessed promise, which the writer uses with equal effect to make his readers firm and to stop their wavering. He thus uses both law and gospel in the true, evangelical way and becomes a model that we may well follow.

Οὖν is merely transitional and not deductive. **Let us fear, then, lest perhaps, although there is (still) left a promise to enter into his rest, someone of your number imagine he has come to be behind. For also we have been told glad tidings just as also they; but the Word of the hearing** (the Word heard) **did not profit them, not having mixed itself by faith with those who heard.**

The imperative is an aorist which is perhaps ingressive: "let us get this fear"; it may also be constative: "let us fear," taking the whole course of fear together; in any case, the aorist is stronger than the present would be. Μήποτε is the literary expression that indicates anxiety (B-D. 370, 1). Verse 2 helps us to understand the force of the genitive absolute; it asserts the fact that "a promise of entering into God's rest is (still) left" to the readers, the glad tidings of it have been told them by the gospel preachers (v. 2). We translate this construction with "although"; our versions retain the genitive absolute of the Greek. The new and important word is "promise," to which v. 2 adds the equally sweet word "to bring good tidings," i. e., the gospel. After the warning voiced in chapter 3 we now have the drawing power of the promise.

We very properly have no article with ἐπαγγελίας: "promise of entering into his rest"; for while this repeats the psalmist's words about "entering into God's rest" (3:11) and "enter in" (v. 3, 19), in the case of the Israelites of the Exodus this included the earthly and the heavenly Canaan, but in the case of the readers of Hebrews it refers only to the heavenly Canaan. Those Israelites failed to enter into both because of unbelief (3:19); the promise of entering God's rest in heaven still remains to the readers of our epistle.

Yet someone may imagine that this is not the case. The writer again says only "someone," (3:12, 13), for he is reluctant to think that all or a large number of his readers could entertain such thoughts. How anyone might get such an idea is not stated. We have only the perfect infinitive ὑστερηκέναι, the subject of which is "someone of your number" (compare 3:13). Was the opinion held that by turning to Christianity this "someone" might think that he and his fellow Jews had made a great mistake, "had fallen behind"? Turning back to Judaism would then seem to be the way in which to regain this lost ground. Alas, this would be the very way in which to fall behind, to be debarred forever from entering into God's eternal rest; for this would repeat the unbelief of the Jews of the Exodus in the worst way. The μήποτε is here used with the infrequent present subjunctive, δοκῇ, "lest he continue to think or imagine."

This is the meaning. Our versions and some dictionaries like Thayer, B.-P., Abbott-Smith translate: "*seem* to have come short of it," and call this a polite form of expression that is used in place of the outright: "have actually come short of it," i. e., of God's rest. Some commentators say: "No one is even to *seem* to miss God's rest, to say nothing of actually missing it." But this cannot be the writer's meaning for the simple reason that both the writer and the readers were still in this life, had not as yet entered this heavenly rest; hence no one could "seem to have come short of it" (our versions). God's heavenly rest was still only "promise" in their case, was still awaiting fulfillment. No; someone could "think or imagine" that Judaism and not Christianity had the promise, and that turning from Judaism to Christianity was a mistake, a terrible falling behind and a losing of the promise. The genitive absolute assures the readers that the promise remains for all of us, and that for this very reason no Christian must imagine that he has lost it by becoming a Christian.

A few regard δοκέω as a technical legal term (a rare use); Riggenbach translates: *befunden werde*, "be found" in the finding of a judge as having fallen behind. The dictionaries have, however, not adopted this meaning. It is ruled out by the present tense of the subjunctive; a judge "finds" once and not continuously. This idea seems to be due to the effort to find something better than a polite statement or a statement that implies seeming.

2) "For" clears up the main point as to why nobody is to imagine that by having left Judaism and having become a Christian he has fallen behind: "For also we have been told glad tidings just as also those." The καί is not added for the sake of the pronoun "we" (there is no ἡμεῖs) but for the sake of the entire periphrastic perfect: "also we have been told glad tidings" (past action leading up to the present moment: ———— •). Gospel tidings are referred to. The verb defines "promise to enter into God's rest" (v. 1).

Note that this verb is to be construed with "we," Jewish Christians, and with ἐκεῖνοι, the Jews of the

Exodus. In their case the promise of God's rest was by no means only the earthly Canaan but also the heavenly Canaan, of which the land flowing with milk and honey was only the type. They also had the gospel tidings, of course in the Old Testament form (covenant with Abraham), while the writer and the readers have it in its New Testament form.

"But" the sad and tragic thing was that "the Word of the hearing (qualitative genitive: the Word they heard) did not profit them, not having mixed itself by faith with those who heard." They had it but did not believe it. "It did not profit" is the historical aorist and summarizes 3:7-19. The point stressed is the hearing: "the Word of the hearing," "they who heard," reverting to the psalm (3:8): "if you should hear his voice." We should note that "promise" and "telling good tidings" (v. 1, 2) certainly involve the thought that both be *heard*. But not only heard: the voice of his Word heard, the promise and good tidings heard, must also be *believed*. Therein the Jews of the Exodus failed so tragically: they *heard* the promise of God's rest, all that the glad tidings about this rest contained, but they hardened their hearts (3:8, etc.), they refused to *believe* and thus lost both the earthly and the heavenly Canaan.

The textual evidence for the accusative plural συγκεκερασμένους is very strong; it would modify ἐκείνους, but this would result in the strange meaning: "those (Jews of the Exodus) not having been mixed by faith with those who heard." Our versions have translated this accusative plural participle; R. V.: "they were not united by faith with them who heard." But who were those who heard and with whom those unbelievers were not united (mixed)? Joshua and Caleb; some unnamed people? If such were referred to, we should have: "have not been united by faith with them who did *believe*."

We give up this reading and prefer the one that has the nominative singular συγκεκερασμένος modifying ὁ λόγος: "the Word of the hearing (did not benefit those), not having mixed itself by faith (dative of means) with those who heard (that Word)," dative after σύν in the verb. Eberling: by faith *ist es (das Wort) ihnen nicht in Fleisch und Blut uebergegangen*.

The forms of the perfect passive and of the perfect middle participle are the same. The passive would here cause difficulty with the two datives. Shall we translate "not having been mixed *with* faith *for* those who heard," or, *"by* those who heard" (dative of agent)? Neither is likely. The middle is far better: "not having mixed itself by faith with those who heard." The Word did its utmost to accomplish this by beating constantly upon their ears so as to enter their hearts by faith. They, indeed, heard it but hardened their hearts, the very thing the Word warned them not to do (3:8, etc.). That is why they perished in the wilderness. Their tragedy was their unbelief (3:19). We, the writer says, have the same "promise to enter into God's rest," "we have been evangelized even also as they" (v. 1, 2); we see why the Word of hearing "did not benefit them." Are we going to repeat their folly and not let the Word mix itself by faith with us who also have this Word (promise, glad gospel tidings)?

3) "For" elucidates by carrying the positive thought a step farther: **For we are entering into the rest, (we) who have come to believe, even as he has said:**

So I swore in my wrath:

They shall not enter into my rest,

the works certainly existing since the foundation of the world, for he has said somewhere regarding the

seventh day thus: And God rested on the seventh day from all his works, and in this (place) **again:**

They shall not enter into my rest.

This positive part of Ps. 95:11 (Heb. 3:8) is the promise, the glad tidings of the Word of the hearing, that tell about "God's rest." Although it occurs in the dire oath which shut out those Israelites of the Exodus, what is stated in the psalm implies that there is this "rest," which is closed to unbelief but is sure and certain for all who believe.

"We are entering this rest, we who came to believe." This is not the present tense that is used in abstract statements, as some explain the tense, for it should then read: "they enter"; "we enter" is personal and refers to the writer and to his readers. The οἱ πιστεύσαντες is, of course, emphatic, being placed at the end; it is a historical aorist: "who did come to believe" as we did. This aorist stops with the past fact, and properly so; for the readers were wavering in their faith, and the writer warned them (chapter 3) and drew them with the Word and promise (chapter 4) to hold fast their faith. Will they do so? He hopes so and hence says, "We are entering into the rest." Like those desert pilgrims on the way to Canaan, we are plodding on through a harsh world. One by one, as we die, we enter into God's heavenly rest; all of us will soon get there, but as "those who came to believe," only as such and never as those who became apostate (3:12) and fell because of unbelief.

This our entering into the rest is "according as he has said" in his awful oath which we have explained in 3:11. The very fact that God swore that those unbelievers should not enter into his rest implies that God had wanted them to enter in, that he wants us to enter in even as he has left us the promise (v. 1), the glad tidings and the Word that seeks to mix itself by means of faith with those who hear. God calls it "my rest," and it is his indeed, established by him with all infinite blessedness, peace, and calm. The human mind is unable to fathom all that this word contains.

Κατάπαυσις is the human word that is chosen because of the unrest, the desert wandering of Israel, which in their case was to end in the "rest" of possession and enjoyment in Canaan, which was a prelude to the far higher "rest" in heaven with God. God's rest is not for himself alone; from the creation onward and despite man's fall God's rest is open to all men, his Word and promise produce the faith by which we all may enter it.

Note the perfect εἴρηκε; this tense denotes the permanence of the word he once spoke. His word does not pass away. Yet "has said" quotes written Scripture: in that *written* word God still *speaks* just as he did in the first utterance. This perfect is the companion to γέγραπται, "it has been written" and thus remains permanent forever. R. 132. Both terms combine revelation and inspiration.

Καίτοι and its genitive absolute have caused much *Kopfzerbrechen,* and various inadequate interpretations have resulted. It is not enough to state that καίτοι is concessive. It is concessive as a fact that is undisputed by the readers: "the works got to exist from the foundation of the world," i. e., they came into existence (γενηθέντων) *then* and not since then. Ἀπό is the Greek idiom: The works came into complete existence when God founded the κόσμος, the orderly universe, and "from" that time onward they "were" so for us who now look at them or speak of them. Ἐκ is used in the same way: from the distant object forward to the writer and not, as in English, from the writer back to the distant object. God's rest, which he intends that we shall enter, dates from the completion of the universe and will have no end. The κόσμος was made for us (2:1-8). Adam and Eve were to enter into the glory of God's rest. They sinned and did not believe God's word. Then came the gospel promise which they and all their descendants were to believe and thus, despite sin, to enter into God's rest.

This is the rest which Jesus promises, the beginning of peace in this life through pardon and sonship, the consummation to follow in glory. This is what the Spirit says in Rev. 14:13: "they shall rest from their labors." It is not allegory but a true parallel: God creates and thus establishes this rest; we, for whom it is intended, who are to be with Christ and God in glory, labor because we live amid sin, but we finally enter it by faith. God rested "from his works" (not "from his labors"). What this implies will never be understood by man because men cannot know what it means to create. Therefore they cannot comprehend what it means to cease creating.

4, 5) This genitive absolute is terse, and γάρ thus amplifies. It does not bring a proof; καίτοι concedes the fullest agreement on the part of the readers. We have a further statement that is taken from the Scriptures themselves, namely that God himself "has said somewhere — indefinite because it is said in three places: Gen. 2:2; Exod. 20:11; 31:17 — concerning the seventh day: 'And God rested on the seventh day.'" The writer combines this statement of God himself concerning himself with the one he has just used: "and in this place (v. 3) again (Ps. 95:11; see the exposition in 3:8): 'They shall not enter into my rest.'" The point lies in taking all these passages together. The rest from which the Jews of the Exodus were excluded, into which we are entering, is God's rest, the great Sabbath since the seventh day, of course not the earthly days and years that have rolled by since then and are still continuing but the timeless, heavenly state that has been established and intended for men in their glorious union with God.

These are not different kinds of rest: the rest of God since creation and a future rest for his people; or a rest into which men have already entered and one that has been established since the redemptive work of Jesus, into which they are yet to enter; or a rest "at the conclusion of the history of mankind." The seventh day after the six days of creation was a day of twenty-four hours. On this day God did not create. Thus God made the first seven-day week (Exod. 20:8-11; 31:12-17), and the Sabbath of rest was "a sign" (v. 17) so that at every recurrence of this seventh day Israel might note the significance of this sign, this seventh day of rest being a type and a promise of the rest instituted for man since the days of creation, the rest with God in eternal blessedness. Like Canaan, the Sabbath was a type and a promise of this rest.

The Admonition to Be Diligent to Enter into God's Rest, v. 6-11.

6) **Since, then, it remains for some to enter it, and those formerly given the glad tidings did not enter because of disobedience, he again fixes a day, Today, saying in the person of David after so long a time even as it has been said before:**

Today if you shall hear his voice,

Do not harden your hearts.

For if Joshua had given them rest he would not be speaking afterward about another day. Accordingly, there (still) **remains a Sabbath for the people of God.**

'Επεί draws the conclusion and sums up v. 3-5. The first point is the fact that God wants people to enter into his rest. That is why he made the original seventh day a day of rest even for himself, "a sign" (Exod. 31:17) of the blessed, eternal rest in which men were to be joined with him. B.-P. 148 renders aptly: "since, then, it abides by this that some," etc. Others: "it is a sure thing that some," etc.

"Some" is to be understood in the broadest sense: God wants men, as many as possible, to enter (actually, aorist) into his rest. Secondly, since "those who formerly were given the glad tidings (passive: were gospelized) did not enter because of disobedience," God once more fixes a day (τινά = our indefinite article, R. 743). It is always so: when some refuse to take the places that have been prepared for them, others will be offered these places (Matt. 22:8-10; Acts 13:46), and many of these will come.

7) From these premises the conclusion is drawn: "again he fixes a day, 'Today,' saying in the person of David after so long a time even as it has been said before: 'Today if you will hear,'" etc. God fixed a great day of grace for the Israel of the Exodus. This Israel is significantly called "they who were given the glad tidings"; this same participle was used in v. 2, but it is now the historical aorist. It was in vain. "Disobedience" would not accept these tidings (3:18: "they who disobeyed"). The word used might be "unbelief" as it is in 3:19. The way in which to disobey the gospel is not to believe its promise. God's grace might have stopped when those Israelites so completely rejected it, but God again "fixes a day," a signal "Today," a great day of grace. He does it by "speaking in the person of David" (ἐν as in 1:1, 2, R. 587), speaking to us "after so long a time even as he has spoken before" when David composed his psalm: "Today if you shall hear his voice, do not harden your hearts."

The first "Today" is a part of the quotation. This word is written twice and is thereby strongly emphasized: "Today, today if you shall hear," etc. On these lines from the psalm see the exposition of 3:8. The meaning is that "after so long a time" God is now, in this Messianic time, speaking to us in this call of David's. The writer is not concerned with the Israel of David's day; he says nothing about them and the following generations; he regards David as speaking to the generation of Jesus (1:2) and to the one following (2:3, 4). The warning feature in these lines of David has been used in 3:8, etc.; their gospel promise is now brought out in order to draw to faith and to bolster it up. The Exodus was a glorious day of grace; the day of Jesus and of his apostles was a still greater day of grace. Will the readers of this letter repeat the disobedience of the generation of the Exodus?

8) This γάρ intends merely that the word "rest" shall be properly understood. Joshua did bring the children of those whose carcasses fell in the wilderness (3:17) into the earthly Canaan. But when these attained the type they had not yet attained also the antitype, the heavenly Canaan. This is the point the writer wants the readers to note. He is not starting a discussion about the Israelites who did get to Canaan and about their descendants who lived there. What he wants noted is the fact that the rest of which God speaks in David's psalm is vastly more than anything earthly. Joshua did not bring those whom he led into this rest by merely bringing them into Canaan. The condition (εἰ with the aorist) is one of past unreality. Living in the Holy Land is not yet entering into God's rest.

The apodosis is one of present unreality (the imperfect with ἄν): "he would not be speaking afterward (μετὰ ταῦτα, 'after these things') about another day." There would be no need of this if living in Canaan secured the heavenly rest for every Israelite. So God speaks of another day "in the person of David" to both the Israelites of David's time and to us who now have this other day of grace. It is the day of Jesus and his salvation. David's generation and the generations that followed were to look forward to this blessed day by faith in the promise of its coming and thus to embrace its salvation by faith.

That was the object God wanted to attain by means of David's psalm. Whether God attained it, and to what extent he attained it during the time between David and Jesus is not discussed. The point is that God still speaks to us in David's psalm now that that day has come in Jesus so that we may believe and by believing be entering the heavenly rest (v. 3), the rest that is typified by the earthly Canaan, but only typified and not attained for Israel through Joshua. A greater "Joshua," namely "Jesus," brings us this rest, and he does that by faith alone.

Yeschuʻa is our English Joshua and Jesus; there is but one Hebrew word for both characters. In English we spell the two names differently in order to distinguish between the two persons. The older idea that Jesus is referred to in our passage need not be refuted.

9) Ἄρα (which is never the first word of a sentence in the classics) draws the main conclusion from what has been said regarding the promise that is contained in the two lines that are quoted from David's psalm (v. 3-8): "Accordingly, there (still) remains a Sabbath for the people of God." God calls it "my rest" in the psalm; the new designation is due to the elaboration that was added in v. 4 which explains this rest on the basis of Gen. 2:2; Exod. 20:11; 31:17, God's resting on the seventh day. The old Jewish Sabbath, which goes back to Gen. 2:2, is a type of heaven, the eternal Sabbath of peace, rest, enjoyment in communion with God.

Since the days of the apostles our day of worship is Sunday and no longer Saturday. This does not abolish the type which, like all other types, belongs to the Old Testament. The New Testament adds no types. It also continues none, for the antitypes begin in the New

Hebrews 4:9, 10 137

Testament. Our Sunday, the day of Christ's resurrection and of the outpouring of the Holy Spirit, is thus by no means the Jewish Sabbath which has been shifted to the first day of the week. It is far more, for by the power of Christ's resurrection and by his Spirit (Rom. 8:11) our mortal bodies shall be raised up to enter the blessed rest of the heavenly Sabbath, which the resting of God on that first seventh day only typified.

The statement is entirely general. All that is said in v. 6, 7 is that, although the Israelites of the Exodus failed to attain God's heavenly rest, God's promise still bids men to enter his rest, and v. 8 adds that this means far more than Joshua's bringing the Israelites into the earthly Canaan. It is God's eternal and heavenly Sabbath that is meant throughout. This is left, this remains as our great hope. Instead of again saying: "for those who believe" or "for those who do not disobey" (compare v. 3 and 3:18), we now have "for God's people." Λαός, which is so often used with reference to Israel, refers to the true Israel (compare Rom. 9:6) in this passage.

10) Γάρ adds the explanation which helps us to understand that this "Sabbath" is what God means by "my rest." **For he who did enter into his rest did rest** (or come to rest) **from all his works even as God from his.** The Greek uses the simple aorist tenses of fact whereas the English prefers the perfect: "he who has entered . . . has rested." This, too, is general, applying to any and to all time. When one, who as a believer belongs to God's people, dies he enters God's rest and, like God, rests from his works. It is true of all God's people who have already died and will be true of all his people who shall die at some future time. In v. 9 we have the collective "the people of God" and the present tense; we now very effectively have the singular and the aorist: "he who did enter," etc. We may think of Moses (3:5), of Joshua, of Caleb, of David,

who have been named thus far; but turn to chapter 11 and read all the great names that are mentioned there.

As to the "works" from which we rest, the similarity with God's works is simply this: as God set himself a task to perform during the six days of creation and, when he had finished it, rested in the contemplation of his work and its glorious perfection, so we have a task set for us, a vocation assigned us by God as his people, and when we complete it we are made partakers of his rest with all that this means of heavenly satisfaction and joy. In our case there are, of course, also much toil and pain (κόπος, Rev. 14:13, "labors"), it is not so in the case of God. God's rest is not idleness, nor shall ours be when we enter his rest. It is useless to speculate, for who can make plain what heaven is like? Scoffers mock at what the Scriptures reveal in figurative descriptions of heaven. The thought of a *dolce far niente* is unworthy, and that of an endless development both foolish and false. To carry ideas of time into the timelessness of eternity is misleading. Wait, be content, you shall soon see.

11) **Let us, then, be diligent to enter into that rest lest anyone in the same type of the disobedience get to fall.**

The admonition, in which the entire discussion culminates, goes together with the admonition voiced in v. 1. All of the intervening explanation justifies both. In v. 1 it is "let us fear"; in v. 11, "let us be diligent," both are strong aorists, decisive, effective. The latter strikes the positive note: "Let us exercise diligence to enter that rest" which awaits the people of God. God's grace alone can bring us into that glorious rest, but it does so by the objective means of his Word which we must diligently hear and receive, and by the subjective means of faith which the Word kindles and increases, which we must constantly exercise. To be diligent is not to grow cold, slack, or to give way to doubt. Diligence keeps to God's grace and Word and thus enters into the promised rest, its labors then being completed. The diligence referred to is the clinging to the Word in diligent faith; good works will, of course, follow, yet these are not discussed here.

The clause with "lest" again touches the negative side. We regard the verb as being complete in itself: "lest anyone fall," "anyone" as in 3:12, 13; 4:1. Ἐν is not "after" (our versions) nor "into," for one cannot fall *into* an example. The idea is that, if any one of the readers "falls," he will add the same kind of example of disobedience as the Israelites of the Exodus furnished in such great numbers long ago. The thought is not that he will fall into *their* example. The verb "fall" re-echoes 3:17: whose carcasses "fell." "Disobedience" is used as in v. 6 (3:18), and the word might again be "unbelief" (3:19), see v. 7. The aorist "get to fall" means no less than a fatal, final fall.

Do not Underestimate the Word of God, v. 12, 13.

12) This appendix is vital as the concluding word of both the warning voiced in chapter 3 and the promise given in 4:1-11. It is so essential because not only the warning and the promise are based on the Word of God as being "my voice," Ps. 95 (see 3:8-11), but also because all that this epistle contains from 1:1 onward ("God spoke") and will contain in the following chapters is based directly on God's Word. So the writer says: Let there be no illusion in you, my readers, regarding this Word of God and what it says about Jesus; let no one think that disbelieving or disobeying this Word is a light matter. The writer has dwelt especially on Ps. 95:11 (3:8, 11; 4:3, 4), God's oath, a most terrible Word of God. He now stresses the full power of the Word in its damning force. He has likewise dwelt on Ps. 95:7b plus 11: "Today" and "my rest," with all the promise that lies in this Word (3:8,-

15; 4:3-8). This, too, leads him to stress the power of the Word, the blessed promise of which is so mighty.

For living is the Word of God and effective and sharper than any two-edged sword and piercing as far as division of soul and spirit, of both joints and marrow, and keen to judge a heart's considerations and thoughts. And there is not a creature unexposed before him, but everything naked and laid open to the eyes of him facing whom this Word is for us.

The idea that ὁ λόγος τοῦ Θεοῦ refers to the Son, the personal Word, as it does in John 1:1, etc., is advocated by some of the Greek and also by a number of the Latin fathers. It is a fact that a person is referred to in v. 13 although he is not called "the Word"; ὁ λόγος at the end of the statement merely repeats this term from v. 12. It would not be out of harmony with the Christology of this epistle (note, for instance, 1:2) to have the Son called "the Word." When some, like Delitzsch, point us to the language of Philo, we note that this writer does not use the term "Word" in the sense of a divine person, and neither John nor the writer of Hebrews adopts the philosophizings of this Hellenized Jew.

This is rather certain in regard to the writer of Hebrews because of the date of the composition of this letter. The fact is patent that our writer does not speak of the Logos as John does. He does not employ this designation in passages where the term would be appropriate if he intended to use it. Its sudden introduction in the present connection would confuse the reader by taking him unawares. Moreover, what is said of "the Word of God" and the comparison with a sword do not fit a person.

This is the spoken and the written "Word of God," and not the word of the New Testament alone, or of the Ninety-fifth Psalm alone, but of the Scriptures which these former Jews had. This Word of God is not a mere sound that disappears and ceases when it is uttered, of which, at most, a record can be made in some book. That is what the word of man amounts to. The Word of God is as "living" as "the living God" (3:12) himself. God and his Word cannot be separated, which explains the pronouns that are used in v. 13, these denote God.

"Living" ("quick" in the older sense, A. V.) is "the Word of God." The participle is placed first for the sake of emphasis and dominates all that follows. It is "living" as being the Word of the "living" God, altogether like God in its power. It is an outflow of his life and therefore instinct with the same divine, imperishable, powerful life, either to kindle similar life in us or to react against all opposition. "God does not separate himself from his Word. He does not disown it as if it were a foreign thing to him. His it remains also when it comes into our ears, into our hearts, into our mouth, into our book. He knows it well as his own Word, as the expression of his own life. Therefore it is never dead matter, insensible to what is done with it; for it is a bond of union with the living God." Schlatter.

Four καί add further specifications. Ἐνεργής = full of living energy to carry out the will of God by either blessing or cursing as the case may be. What folly to treat the Word of God as though it is subject to our minds, our "views," our opinions! It is electric and smites him who tampers with it; it is electric to light him who bows beneath it. Who can escape its blasting power when he scorns its threats? Read, for example, Ps. 95:11 and look at the Jews of the Exodus. Read Matt. 23:38 and look at "the desolate house," desolate for almost 2,000 years. But the blessings of the Word are equally "effective" and energetic. Eternity rings with their praise.

The next "and" states this in figurative language, and the last "and" expounds this figurative language. The Word is not only like a sword, it is "sharper beyond any two-edged sword" (literally: two-mouthed, στόμα, mouth). Μάχαιρα was commonly used as a designation for the short, two-edged sword of the Roman hoplite or legionary (Eph. 6:17) although other types of swords could be called thus.

"Piercing," etc., makes a comparison with the penetrating power of the Word and thus uses an instrument which penetrates most quickly and effectually, the Word even exceeds any such instrument. The figurative sword is repeatedly used in this way: Isa. 49:2; Rev. 1:16; 2:12; 19:15. Some think only of the destructive power of the Word as it is exercised against "the disobedience" (v. 11). But while this is certainly included, all the other predications are indeterminate so that we must say that the figure brings out strikingly the ability of the Word to penetrate the innermost part of man, either to change him inwardly into a new man or, in case of self-hardening (3:8, 15; 4:7), to lay bare all his deadly guilt.

The statement is striking even in Scripture: "piercing as far as division of soul and spirit, of both joints and marrows" (we should not use the plural). The ψυχή, as distinguished from the πνεῦμα, is the life which the spirit gives to the body as long as the two are connected; hence the ψυχή is the seat of the thoughts, emotions, feelings, desires, volitions, and actions pertaining to our earthly and bodily existence; the πνεῦμα, which is the source of the ψυχή, is the immaterial part of our being that was created and breathed into us by the breath of God and is, therefore, the real seat of all his gracious operations in regenerating and renewing us.

In the unregenerate the *psyche* rules and the *pneuma* is enslaved; in the regenerate this is reversed, the *pneuma* is enthroned. Thus we are no longer ψυχικός (I Cor. 2:14), ruled by our earthly animated, sensual nature, but πνευματικός, "spiritual," ruled also in body and in bodily life by the spirit. "Piercing up to or as far as division of *psyche* and *pneuma*" is, therefore, not a sundering of the soul and of the spirit by the Word of God. The Word never does such a thing even also as the soul that animates our bodies and the spirit are not two entities which something may cut apart.

This applies also to the figurative terms which are added for the sake of illustration: "of both joints and marrow," for the joints, where the bones of the body articulate, and the marrow, which is inside the bones themselves, are not next to each other so that one could speak of cutting them apart. To pierce up to division of *psyche* and *pneuma* is that activity of the Word upon man by which it separates and shows up in its true nature all that inheres in his earthly, bodily life and in the condition of his spirit. This it does just as a piercing physical sword lays bare both the joints, where the bones meet, and even the bones themselves, where the marrow lies. Yet *psyche* and *pneuma* are not paralleled with joints and marrow or, assuming a chiasm, with marrow and joints, for these two are joined by τε καί so that the illustration "both joints and marrow" belongs as well to soul on the one hand as to spirit on the other. All the links of our soul life, of our thoughts, emotions, etc., as well as all the inner substance of them are penetrated, laid bare, exposed in their true nature by the Word. The same is true with regard to all that lies in, occurs in, and conditions the spirit, with all that God has wrought there or has been prevented from working there. The Word of God is the only power that can penetrate so deeply and expose so completely the inwardness of our being.

The practical side of this is apparent. In the light of the Word we recognize the vanity and the sinfulness of many of our earthly thoughts, strivings, purposes, and achievements, especially also our earthly, worldly, unspiritual opposings of the spirit. The world may laud many of these activities as being good, even praiseworthy; the Word pierces right through and shows what the soul is doing to the spirit. The Word likewise reveals the things of the spirit, its bondage under sin when the *psyche* rules, its liberation by grace and all that it receives in regeneration and renewal, in repentance, faith, and sanctification, which change the entire man. The Word makes us see the very joints and marrow of all these things.

The idea of Delitzsch that the Word exposes the corrupting power of sin in even our body ("joints and marrow" are taken in a physically literal sense as contrasted with *psyche* and *pneuma*) is rightly rejected by commentators as violating the language. Von Hofmann has the genitives "both of joints and marrow" depend on *"psyche* and *pneuma,"* but they evidently are a figurative and an elucidative addition. By combining the expression "up to division of soul and spirit" (as if these two could be cut apart) with I Thess. 5:23, "body, soul, and spirit" (as if these three could be cut apart) trichotomy is defended against dichotomy. But we are still waiting to see how soul and spirit are split into two entities.

In a consideration of this whole matter it should be remembered that our English word "soul" is not a true equivalent of the Greek ψυχή. In ordinary English "soul" is nearly the same as "spirit," but not so *psyche* and *pneuma* in the Greek. *Psyche* is often taken only in the sense of "life" because it animates the body. More than this, from ψυχή the Greek forms ψυκικός, an adjective that denotes a low condition that is due to nothing but the animation of the physical body and the resultant carnal appetites, desires, etc. We do not have such an adjective that is derived from "soul" because we think of "soul" as something that is far higher; hence arises our difficulty in translating a word such as *psychikos*. See I Cor. 2:14.

The illuminating addition "and keen to judge (κριτικός) a heart's considerations and thoughts" helps greatly in understanding the penetrating power of the Word. In place of "soul and spirit" we now have "heart," the center of our personal being, where the ἐνθυμήσεις arise, the "reflections" or the meditations, and the ἔννοιαι, the definite "thoughts or notions" that result. On these the Word as being *kritikos* passes true and genuine judgment as an infallible, unimpeachable, impartial judge. In order to escape the verdicts of the Word of God many try to dethrone this judge, to alter or in some way to evade his true verdicts. The readers of this epistle were starting on this course by shutting their eyes to what the Old Testament says about Jesus, to what, for instance, Ps. 95 says so plainly in warning and in promise as these are here set forth (3:8-4:11). But who can escape? Heaven and earth shall pass away but not the Word (Matt. 5:18); it shall judge us at the last day (John 12:48).

13) God and his Word are often identified as is done when the Word is said to foresee. In v. 12 it acts as a person, especially in its judging. Thus, without further indication, the two pronouns αὐτοῦ refer to God: "And there is not a creature unexposed before him, but everything is naked and laid open to the eyes of him," etc. Hide as a creature may, this Judge, God in his Word, sees him fully and completely exposed. "Not a creature unexposed (ἀφανής)" is strong because of the double negation; "creature" is a wide term which includes every person and everything that have been created by God. The singular "not a creature" is followed by the plural πάντα, "all things," and the negative statement "not one unexposed" by the positive "all things naked," etc. This is the height of emphasis.

Clothes hide, and men cover themselves with disguises, but they are "naked" in God's sight even as to their very inmost soul that animates their body and the spirit that forms their ego. The idea is intensified: "laid open to his eyes," omniscience penetrates utterly. The perfect passive participle is a form of τραχηλίζειν and has caused much linguistic discussion (see Riggenbach's long note). Men wonder how it comes to be employed in the way in which it is used here. The old Greek expositors had different opinions in regard to it, to which new ones have been added. The sense of the participle was, however, never in doubt, the companion term "naked" making it certain: "having been laid open and remaining so" in God's eyes. The best explanation of the figure seems to be: the neck of the victim is bent back in order to expose it to the eyes for the thrust of the knife. Like other terms, this one, too, seems to have lost much of its original literal meaning when it was applied generally. It is here used with the subject "all things."

The relative clause: πρὸς ὃν ἡμῖν ὁ λόγος also causes difficulty. Many understand the noun to mean "business," "reckoning," "account," and then translate: the eyes of him "with whom we have to do" (our versions), with whom we have to settle our account, to whom we are responsible. But this seems to be a rather weak ending of a strong sentence; it was self-evident to the readers that they had to account to God. Moreover, ὁ λόγος recalls the fact that this term is used in v. 12; here at the end just as at the beginning of v. 12 it ought to mean: "the Word." The dative ἡμῖν with the copula understood is a common Greek idiom: "facing whom this Word is for us," i. e., is ours. It is ours as putting us face to face (πρὸς, the face-to-face preposition) with God and his all-seeing eyes. C.-K. 679: *an den es uns weist*. This last clause thus most effectively connects God and the Word of God and justifies all that is said of both in connection with each other.

"The readers are to realize how closely what has just been said concerning God (3:8-4:11) touches them. They are not to imagine that they will be able to hide from God the real and inmost reasons of their discouragement and their unbelief or the slightest stirrings of their resistance against him and to present themselves before him as other than they are. The penetrating criticism which the divine Word exercises upon their entire being to the inmost parts illustrates to them the piercing sharpness of the divine vision and warns them not to subject themselves by indifference and disobedience to the judgment of God, whose verdict is proof against every bribe and unaffected by anything that would cloud or deceive it." Riggenbach. This is good as far as the warning is concerned (3:8-19). But 4:1-11 is promise and stimulates faith and obedience. These are equally exposed to the eyes of God, these are equally judged by the penetrating Word which sees through soul, spirit, and everything in the heart. This Word approves and thus upholds, strengthens, comforts all who believe and obey. Add this to Riggenbach's remarks and see how thus these two verses form the strong conclusion of chapters 3 and 4.

THE THIRD MAIN PART

Jesus, the Son of God, Our Compassionate High Priest, 4:14-6:20

The Son Touched with Our Infirmity because of His Suffering, 4:14-5:10

The Readers Aroused and then Assured, 5:11-6:20

The Son Touched with Our Infirmity because of His Own Suffering, 4:14-5:10

The Invitation to Come to This Our High Priest, 4:14-16.

14) All are agreed to make a division at this point. But where to stop is a question. To go on to 12:29 under the caption "Our Perfect High Priest" we consider impossible; chapter 11 which has no less than forty verses stops us. We should be compelled to make major divisions. We make them. One could combine 4:14-8:2 since 8:1 states the "sum." Yet 4:14-6:20 is a unit, and 7:1-28 is another; we keep them distinct, and 8:1, 2 sums them up before a new unit begins.

Having, then, a great High Priest who has gone through the heavens, Jesus, the Son of God, let us continue to hold fast to the confession! For we do not have a High Priest unable to sympathize with our weaknesses but having been tried in all respects in like manner (as we) except for sin. Let us, then, continue to approach with boldness the throne of the grace in order that we may receive mercy and find grace for timely help!

Hebrews 4:14

These verses form a compact unit in which the hortation is at once included. All that follows up to 6:20 is appended. Οὖν is again not *folgernd*, makes no deduction but merely proceeds to the new topic. True, the title High Priest has already been used (2:17; 3:1), so also "the Son of God" (1:2, etc.; 3:6), his suffering and temptation (2:9, etc.; 2:18), and "our confession" (3:1); but these are scattered and were used in other connections and thus cannot be resumed here with a mere οὖν.

On "High Priest" see 2:17 and 3:1; the addition "great" exalts his person and his office above all the Levitical high priests of the Jews and matches the fact that he "has gone through the heavens" in his high-priestly function, into the Holy of Holies of the very presence of God. "Passed *into* the heavens" (A. V.) is incorrect. In the Jewish Tabernacle the high priest passed from the altar that was outside through the Holy Place and so stepped behind the veil of the Holy of Holies. So our great High Priest, in a far more exalted manner, proceeded through what we call the created heavens into the presence of God. Only his greatness and this great act are now stressed and not the blood of expiation (2:17) and its effect although the title "High Priest" involves them; these points will be treated presently. As befits the new section of the letter together with the greatness of our High Priest, his name is added, "Jesus," which again calls to mind his incarnation, his life, sufferings, and death here on earth, but with the mighty apposition "the Son of God," which expresses his deity. Our High Priest is infinitely great in his person and his office.

"Having him, let us continue to hold fast to the confession!" We "have" him because of his having been made the great High Priest; God has given him to us as such. "The confession" recalls 3:1 where we are bidden "to consider thoroughly the Apostle and

High Priest of our confession." He, "our great High Priest, Jesus, the Son of God," and all that lies in this designation are the substance of the confession; κρατῶμεν means that we are to continue to hold him fast with all our "strength" by confessing our faith in him. The writer admonishes himself as well as his readers. Yet the present tense signifies that he and they have been doing this, it asks for steady continuation. The implication is that the readers have given evidence of wavering, of giving up this confession. "Keep on confessing him with heart and soul!" is the appeal.

15) We have the strongest motive for holding fast to him. The writer reverts to 2:17, 18 where he calls our High Priest "merciful," "himself tempted and thus able to help those being tempted," who calls us "brothers" (2:11, etc.). Our weaknesses dispose us to give up our confession instead of holding to it with strength; here is the answer that lifts up beyond any such weakness: "For we do not have a High Priest unable to sympathize with our weaknesses," the very contrary is the case; he knows all these weaknesses from his own experience, "having been tried in all respects in like manner (as we) except for sin." Is not his personal name "Jesus" which he bore here on earth when in his humiliation he took upon himself so many of our human weaknesses? How can we then think that he does not feel with us (συμπάσχω) in our weaknesses?

Already in 2:18 we have the aorist participle πειρασθείς which states the fact that he was tried. The perfect participle now says the same thing and adds only the full length of his trial and spreads it out in the past until it came to an end with his death (the graph would be ─────•). The emphasis is on the two κατά phrases: "in all respects" (literally, "along in everything"), "in like manner" (literally, "in accord with likeness" to us).

But this last has one limitation: χωρὶς ἁμαρτίας, "without, apart from, except for, sin." In all other respects there was ὁμοιότης but not in this respect. Luther translates: *doch ohne Suende;* our versions follow him: "yet without sin." But this "yet" is not in the text. To insert it means to construe the phrase with the participle whereas it belongs to the two κατά phrases. The difference is this: Luther and those who follow him take it that in all his temptations Jesus did not sin, did not yield to the tempter in committing a single sin, which is, of course, very true. The statement itself says more. Jesus' likeness to us, in which he was tempted, was total with one exception, namely sin. "Likeness without sin" resembles Rom. 8:3, "in likeness of sinful flesh." When temptation assailed Jesus it found no sin with which it could connect.

For this reason the temptations of Jesus were far more severe than ours ever are. The very first one was offered by the devil in person, continued for forty days (Luke 4:2), and ended with the devil's bringing all his cunning to bear upon him; but not the slightest yielding on Jesus' part was evident because there was not even the resemblance of sin in him. It is said that all that is necessary is to say that Jesus did not sin; more is in place after calling him "the Son of God," "the great High Priest who has passed through the heavens," namely that his likeness to us while he was on earth was "without sin." It has been well pointed out that the point is not the outcome of Jesus' temptation but the extent and the degree of his temptation. On the possibility of Jesus' falling, although that is not introduced here, see *The Interpretation of St. Matthew's Gospel*, 155, etc.

16) The γάρ used in v. 15 leads to the οὖν which occurs in v. 16. One who was so tempted, so able thus to feel for those who are tempted, is able to help us who are now being tempted (2:18), tempted even to fall

away from him as he was tempted to turn from his Father and that Father's will: "Let us, therefore, approach with boldness to the throne of the grace in order that we may receive mercy and find grace for timely need." Here, as in 3:6, we may translate "with confidence," namely with the confidence that fears not to lay all our weaknesses before the throne of the (divine) grace. The word "throne" is especially appropriate to the idea of "grace," for the King dispenses his unmerited favor ($\chi\acute{\alpha}\rho\iota\varsigma$) upon the guilty. 2:17 has already shown how he is able to do this: our High Priest has made expiation for our sins. The genitive is attributive. Jesus sits at God's right hand, and his expiation makes God's throne one of grace.

The fact that our approach will be made in contrition and in faith in our great High Priest and in corresponding prayer is self-evident. Ἵνα may express purpose: "in order to," etc., or contemplated result: "so that we may receive mercy and find grace," etc. The doubling emphasizes. The verbs and the objects are placed chiastically so that "mercy and grace" come together. "Mercy" is the love that helps the wretched, "grace" the love that pardons the guilty. "Mercy" is placed first because our weaknesses have been stressed. "For timely help" (in 2:18 the verb used is "to help") is help in good season, when we need it, before it is too late. How often we need such help of both pitying mercy and pardoning grace!

Luther very properly starts a new chapter with verse 14.

CHAPTER V

The Deep Humiliation of Jesus Shows Him to Be Our Great High Priest, v. 1-10.

1) The γάρ introduces this entire explanation (v. 1-10) which is an elucidation of 4:14-16, the essential point of which is found in 4:16: as our great High Priest Jesus is able to sympathize with our weaknesses, having been tried and tempted in every way in like manner as we are tried. We are now told that every Jewish high priest was a man who was taken from among men so as to be able to feel for them, he himself being beset with weakness. We are also told that this is not an office that anyone should take for his own glory. Since he was placed into this office by God, we see how deeply Christ was humiliated and by all that he suffered was made complete as our High Priest, one after the order of Melchizedek, no less than the cause of our salvation.

Once more, as in 2:9-18, but now from a new and a different angle the lowliness of Christ is presented in its true light for the Jewish Christian readers. Instead of being repelled by this lowliness it ought to be the very feature that should attract them. Instead of going back to the old Judaism with its high priests this Great High Priest should hold them. Although he was the very Son of God (4:14), the High Priest after the exalted order of Melchizedek, beyond all other high priests, he was yet brought down to the deepest suffering and a dependence on God in the days of his flesh, was drawn down completely to us in our weakness, was infinitely more than our brother and yet completely our brother (2:11, etc.), and was in every way the cause of our salvation (v. 9). Once more the Jewish objection to the lowly Jesus is not only removed, but the lowliness is again shown to be his High-priestly qualification, the one that brings him so exceedingly near to us in our weakness.

For every high priest, taken from among men for the benefit of men, is appointed with reference to the things pertaining to God to offer both gifts and sacrifices in behalf of sins, as able to be moderate with the ignorant and erring since also he himself is encompassed with weakness and for this reason is obliged, as for the people, so also for himself, to make offering for sins.

This is true with regard to every ordinary high priest among the Jews as the readers, who were formerly Jews, know full well. We read the whole section as a unit. The emphasis is on the participial clause used in v. 2: "as able to be moderate with the ignorant and erring." This is not the same as the ability of Jesus "to sympathize with our weakness" (4:15) but, while it is less, it is of the same order. There is here as throughout only likeness and not sameness. We note that every one of these high priests has sins like the people and must bring an offering for himself as well as for them; our High Priest is like us in every particular but one, he is "without sin" (4:15). His whole high-priestly function and his sacrifice are therefore vastly higher. Those high priests were only the type, Jesus is the antitype; yet the type does reflect the antitype.

The typical feature mentioned here is one that is frequently not noted: as every high priest was human and was related to those for whom he officiated in what pertained to God, so also Jesus stood in the same relation, as has already been developed in 2:9-18. Resting on this is the further and main point: as every high priest, because of his relation to the people, is able to have a feeling of moderation for them, so Jesus, be-

Hebrews 5:1

cause of his relation to us, is able to have even more, namely a feeling of fullest sympathy with us. Who, knowing and understanding this, could ever think of turning away from him?

The whole statement is worded perfectly, each brief item is expressed in just the proper terms, and each is found in just the proper place. Nothing is detracted from the Jewish high priests in order to magnify Jesus; yet by according them all that is theirs Jesus is magnified the more, and in a feature that is seldom noted, one that should win and hold every heart that has any knowledge of the Jewish high priesthood, and any feeling of need for sympathy in his weaknesses, and any longing for sympathetic genuine help (4:16). The present tenses are general as is customary in broad statements. Many a Jewish high priest, like Caiaphas and others of this last period of Judaism, was wicked and vicious and not at all like those mentioned. The writer makes no use of this widely known fact. Those of his readers who thought of it — and most of them surely did — were the more impressed. They are here told only about God's arrangement of giving his people of the old covenant high priests who were able to act with moderation for the ignorant and erring on the great Day of Atonement.

Unlike our versions, we construe: every high priest "taken from among men for the benefit of men"; the two phrases that have ἄνθρωποι are to be construed with the participle: God took every high priest from men to function for men. Each one was human and was to act for those who were human; each was one of their number. Every one "is appointed with reference to the things regarding God" (τὰ πρὸς τὸν Θεόν as in 2:17), an adverbial accusative and not an accusative with an intransitive verb (R. 486).

The ἵνα clause is appositional and states what things are especially referred to: "to offer both gifts and sacrifices in behalf of sins." We have the same statement in 8:3 and in 9:9 and thus do not cancel τε and make the "sacrifices" a part of the "gifts." It seems certain that this is a reference to the functions of the high priest on the great Day of Atonement and not to festivals and Sabbaths when the high priest also sacrificed. Leviticus 1, 2 speak only of "the priests, Aaron's sons"; Leviticus 16 speaks of Aaron and the Day of Atonement. The "gifts" may refer to the incense mentioned in Lev. 16:12, an accompaniment of the blood rite observed in the Holy of Holies. Προσφέρω is not commonly used in secular Greek with reference to bringing sacrifices. Ὑπὲρ ἁμαρτιῶν = "in behalf of sins," i. e., to remove them.

2) What the high priest does on the Day of Atonement is not the point, but how he does it: "as able to be moderate with the ignorant and erring," for whose sins of ignorance and erring he makes this atonement. Flagrant sinners, open violators were cut off from Israel without atonement and were cursed of God. Only those who erred in ignorance and thus had sins resting on them were freed on the Day of Atonement, for despite all the daily sacrifices such sins still remained, and the high priest acted for the people as a whole, for any and for all such sins. Although he had to deal with sins the high priest was not to be harsh and severe and act the part of a stern judge. He was "to be moderate." This term is carefully chosen. He was not to ignore the sins (for he was to make atonement for them as being sins), nor was he to condemn these sins to their proper punishment (for it was his part to make atonement for them).

"Since also he himself is encompassed with weakness" is the high priest's motive and reason for moderation toward all those for whom he officiates. Here, too, the moderate word "weakness" is in place; it is a companion to "ignorant and erring" and recalls.

"our weaknesses" (4:15) with which Jesus sympathizes. The intransitive περίκειμαι is used as the passive of περιτίθημι and thus has the accusative with passives, R. 815.

3) The ἐπεί clause continues the thought: "and for this reason is obliged, as for the people, so also for himself, to make offering for sins." Like the people, the high priest has sins so that he must make atonement in particular "for himself and for his household" (Lev. 16:17). We may have ὑπέρ or περὶ ἁμαρτιῶν as is the case in v. 1 and 2 of this chapter, with practically no difference in meaning. One who is thus bound together with the people in weakness and sins could, indeed, be moderate toward the ignorant and the erring; his very office involved as much and served as a constant reminder.

But this is typical of Jesus, yet it is so only as the partial and imperfect may reflect the complete and perfect. The link is the fact that Jesus, too, is one of the people and shares our weakness as a man; the thing typified is his sympathy with our weaknesses, which is imaged to a degree in the moderation of the high priest toward the weak. The type extends no farther, for the high priest has the weakness that produces sins while Jesus is wholly "without sin" (4:15). By how much more, then, ought the former Jews to be drawn to Jesus who, in this comparison, appears most truly as "the great High Priest," not another type, not a continuation of the type, but the great Antitype in his compassionate fellow feeling and sympathy for us?

A quiet appeal and an invitation to the readers seem to be implied. Have some doubted, wavered, thought of reverting to Judaism? Then they, too, are among "the ignorant and erring." Let them hasten to the throne of grace (4:16); their High Priest is full of sympathy for their weaknesses (4:15); they need his "timely help" (4:16). If, however, they remain obdurate, the writer has another word for them (6:4-8).

4) **And not for himself does anyone take the honor but as called by God even also as Aaron. Thus also Christ did not glorify himself to become High Priest but the One who said to him:**

**Son of mine art thou,
I myself have begotten thee!**

Even also in a different place he says:
**Thou a priest for the eon
According to the order of Melchizedek!**

To the first requirement of the high priesthood, the relation of the incumbent to those for whom he makes offering, there is naturally added the second, that no man can take this honor of the high priesthood for himself. Since he must function in "the things pertaining to God" and do that for all the people, it is God who must call him; God alone can say whose priestly function is acceptable to him. It was thus in the case of Aaron, the first high priest of the Israelites (Exod. 28:1).

5) So also Christ did not glorify himself in order to become High Priest; on the contrary (ἀλλά), he glorified him to become High Priest who spoke to him the words written in Ps. 2:7: "Son of mine art thou," etc. In v. 4 the high priesthood of Israel is called "the honor" which is bestowed upon the incumbents of this office by God; when reference is now made to Christ (the Messiah), the greater word "glorified" is properly used. See the exposition of Ps. 2:7 in 1:5. In that connection the supreme royal office of Christ is based on the statement which the King quotes from Jahweh as also the further quotations, especially 1:8, 9, show. Yet the office of the Messiah is *one* and has prophetic, high-priestly, and royal functions. Here the high-priestly are in the mind of the writer.

6) Hence a further quotation is added, one in which both the priestly and the royal features are com-

Hebrews 5:6

bined, namely Ps. 110:4: "Thou a priest for the eon according to the order of Melchizedek" and not merely according to the order of Aaron. The writer intends to elucidate the resemblance between Christ and Melchizedek in distinction from the Aaronitic priesthood (chapter 7). We may, therefore, be brief at this point. Psalm 110 has been quoted already in 1:13, but not the lines that are now cited. Melchizedek was both king and priest, but not so Aaron. When Kittel, *Die Psalmen*, tones this down by saying that Jewish kings exercised also priestly functions, the flinty fact remains that during the whole history of Israel the high priesthood was never combined with the kingship. No king ever entered into the Holy of Holies to offer the blood of atonement. In the whole Old Testament there appears only one character who is both king and priest, Melchizedek, king of Salem, whose priesthood no less a person than Abraham himself recognized. More about this in chapter 7.

Secondly, Melchizedek appears alone; no father or mother, no sons of his are mentioned in Scripture. He does not inherit his priesthood, nor does he transmit it to others. This strange figure, both priest and king, is the type of Christ who also stands alone, King and Priest in one, not by inheritance from predecessors, not transmitting his office to successors. The objection that Melchizedek is not called "high priest" is not valid, for any "priest" who is at the same time "king" is certainly the highest priest.

Thirdly, Melchizedek passed away, we hear no more of him; but he had no succession as Aaron had. In this feature he is the type of Christ whose priesthood is "for the eon," i. e., forever, with no successor in fact and none even possible. What the uniqueness of Melchizedek typified as best it could is the completeness of Christ's atonement: once accomplished, it stands forever. Aaron and his sons could typify some things in regard to Christ's High Priesthood, Melchizedek others. Ps. 110:4 thus sheds much light on Ps. 2:7; we see that Ps. 2:7 is properly used here. The writer does not want his readers to stop with the thought of Aaron when he calls Christ "the great High Priest" (4:14) and speaks of his priesthood. Melchizedek shows that here there is One who is greater than Aaron.

This must have had a tremendous effect on the readers who were former Jews. While they are thinking of going back to Judaism and its Aaronitic, Levitical high priesthood because they regarded it better than that of the lowly Jesus, these readers are startled to find one who is greater than Aaron in their Old Testament, one whom Abraham himself honored as being no less than a king-priest.

We should also see the wisdom of this writer; here and in v. 10 he does no more than to use the Old Testament phrase "according to the order of Melchizedek." *God* used this phrase with reference to the Messiah. Had the readers ever thought of that? Not at once and in one mass is the significance of this fact poured out upon the readers; they are to absorb its significance gradually. Thus the object of the writer will be the more completely attained. No mind will revert to Aaron; Melchizedek stands in the way. As sons of Abraham, who bowed before Melchizedek as the type of Christ (John 8:56), who never even knew the Aaronitic high priesthood, these Jewish Christian readers must surely follow Abraham. Or do they intend to harden their hearts (2:8, etc.)? David, too, Israel's great king who was in various ways a type of the Messiah, whose psalm is quoted, by revelation saw in Melchizedek the Royal Priest Christ and sang about him.

7) On the basis of the ordeal through which Christ passed the great relative clause (v. 7-10) establishes the fact that he accomplished his High-priestly

Hebrews 5:7

work only in obedience to God and was thus designated by God what the psalm calls him: High Priest according to the order of Melchizedek. What Jesus faced was that which was completely repugnant to flesh and blood, what he could undergo only by obedience and not by arrogant ambition. Some stop with this thought. But the description of the ordeal is surely to be combined with 4:15, 16 as well as with 5:2: the trial Jesus underwent in likeness to us, which caused him to be filled with sympathy for our weaknesses and gave him the moderation for the ignorant and erring that was so necessary for any high priest. The subject of v. 5, 6 is "Christ" and the pronouns "thou" in the quotations;. ὅς takes up Christ, and does this in a demonstrative way: **he who in the days of his flesh, having brought both petitions and supplications to him who is able to save him from death together with strong crying and tears, and having been heard for his godly fear, he, though being (the) Son, learned the obedience from what he suffered and, having been made complete, became for all those obeying him (the) cause of eternal salvation, designated by God (the) High Priest according to the order of Melchizedek.**

"In the days of his flesh" takes us back from the glorified, heavenly state of Jesus at God's right hand (1:8, 9, 13) to the time when he passed his days in the state of humiliation here on earth; he took our blood and flesh in order to die (2:14; compare 10:20). It is the night of Gethsemane, for there "he brought both petitions and supplications to him who is able to save him from death together with strong crying and tears." Note the strong doubling in "petitions (beggings) and supplications," which is intensified still more by the phrase "together with strong crying and tears." This was the agony endured in the Garden just before Jesus voluntarily delivered himself into the hands of his mortal enemies.

'Ικετηρία has become a noun although it was originally an adjective with ῥάβδος or ἐλαία to be supplied: "an olive branch bound round with wool, held forth by the suppliant in token of the character he bore" (Trench). It is found only here in the New Testament. The word means "humble, lowly pleading." The Gospels say nothing about the tears of Jesus during his agony of prayer in Gethsemane, but their accounts are brief, and this item may well have been reported by the three witnesses and have been preserved orally. We certainly do not say that the writer of Hebrews merely pictured the scene to himself and added the detail of the tears. The κραυγή or loud cry is derived from the Gospels, for the three disciples were a stone's throw away and yet heard all the words of Jesus' prayers.

In v. 2 προσφέρω is used with reference to priestly acts, and some think that this second aorist participle is used with the same force here. When offerings are brought, the dative and not πρός is regularly used. The fact that the πρός phrase is to be construed with the participle and not with "petitions and supplications" is evident on the basis of the participle itself, for it is a compound of πρός. The thought that the prayers, crying, and tears of Jesus were offerings brought to God is out of place, and doubly so in this description of Jesus' supreme ordeal. The great object of the writer is to describe the agony of Jesus in its full intensity. That is the depth of his humiliation. These are not "prayers" such as we read of at other times but literal beggings as well as pitiful pleadings of the man Christ Jesus in his utter dependence on God. Here there is all the weakness of the lowly flesh, the humble human nature which he bore, which accompanied his begging and pleading with (μετά) agonized crying and unrestrained tears.

The supreme moment had come for him as a man, and it had come of his own volition; he was now prepared to step into the death which was the curse of the world's sin in order to be made sin and a curse for us (Gal. 3:13; II Cor. 5:21). His entire human being recoiled from the horror of taking this step. Jesus knew all along that it would come to this and himself foretold his suffering and his death; yet already in John 12:27, 28 we see how his soul is troubled, and how already then he prays the Gethsemane prayer. When the actual hour came, then there occurred what is stated here. Our minds may ask all sorts of questions and seek explanations, but the facts stand: Jesus quivered in the depth of agonized suffering — and obeyed.

"To the One able to save him from death" he cried. This might mean that God should not let him enter death, or that, having entered death, God should raise him up again and thus take him out of death. It cannot be the latter because Jesus never prays to God regarding his resurrection. Already in John 12:27 and also in Gethsemane he prayed that, if it be possible, God might not make him drink the cup of death. Yet in John 12:28 this prayer ends: "Father, glorify thy name!" and in Gethsemane: "Not my will, but thine be done!" Some, like the A. V. with its references, introduce Golgotha and the cries on the cross (Matt. 27:46, 50), but these were neither beggings nor pleadings, nor were they accompanied by tears. The ultimate obedience was learned in Gethsemane, after Gethsemane and on the cross the obedience was only carried out.

The second participle elucidates the first: "and having been heard for his godly fear." Two facts are stated: that Jesus' begging and pleading was actually heard and fully granted by God, and that this granting was due to his εὐλάβεια. Superficial readers of the Gethsemane account take it that Jesus prayed not to die, that God, nevertheless, let him die, and that God did *not* grant his prayer, and then draw the conclusion that God at times does not grant our prayers, nor must we expect him to grant them. Yet we are told that "he was heard," which means that his pleadings were granted.

Some commentators start with the same opinion, namely that what Jesus really begged for was to be kept from death; they see, too, that it is here said that God granted this prayer. But in making these two statements agree they are satisfied with what is not really an agreement: they let the answer to the pleadings consist in God's freeing Jesus from the fear of death. It should be seen that the prayer was then really *not* answered, was at most answered only partially. Jesus did not ask to be saved from the fear of death; neither the Gospels nor our passage say this. To receive no more than deliverance from such fear is not a real hearing of his prayer, if what he prayed for was deliverance from death.

The mistake lies in this latter assumption. Jesus prayed for deliverance from death only with an "if": "if it be possible" (Matt. 26:39); "if this cup may not pass away from me, except I drink it" (v. 42). The real burden of his prayer was: "Nevertheless, not what I will, but what thou wilt" (Mark 14:36). So also Matt. 26:39, 42, "thy will be done," and this prayer of Jesus was fully and truly granted.

Jesus' prayer was heard and granted ἀπ' εὐλαβείας. We cannot separate this phrase from the participle and draw it forward to the main verb: "from his reverent fear Jesus learned his obedience"; we construe: "having been heard for his reverent fear." 'Από does not indicate cause (R. 580) but source or derivation; and the noun does not mean "the fear of death" but "the reverent fear of God" which shrinks from contravening God's will; "the fear of death" is the view of those who regard its removal as the answer to the prayer.

We see this εὐλάβεια manifested in the words: "Not my will be done, but thine," and in John 12:28: "Father, glorify thy name!" where also the same answer was given: "I have both glorified it, and will glorify it again." "From" (ἀπό) reverent fear of deviating from God's will as the proper answer to it came the granting of Jesus' prayer although it accepted his death on the cross as the final and complete execution of God's will. Both B.-D. 211 and Riggenbach are right: εἰσακούω cannot mean "to hear and free" or "by hearing to save" from the fear of death or from death. C.-K. 662 has the correct view of the noun but mars the interpretation of the whole clause by regarding the resurrection of Jesus as the answer to his reverent pleading.

8) By means of this ordeal of pleading and this answer on the part of God, Jesus, "though being (the) Son, learned the (full) obedience from what he suffered." The article is absent only because υἱός is the predicate; hence the translation "a Son" in our versions is incorrect. "The obedience," with the article, means the well-known complete obedience as distinguished from obedience in general. "Though being the Son, he learned the obedience" means that the Son, although he as such naturally obeyed the Father, "in the days of his flesh," when all his flesh and human nature recoiled as it could not but recoil from the terrible death for the sin and guilt of the world, learned "from what he suffered" the ultimate obedience, learned it as a man learns by actually undergoing that suffering in obedience.

Paul says the same thing in Phil. 2:6, 8: though in the form of God ("though being the Son") he lowered himself and became obedient unto death, even the death of the cross ("learned the obedience from what he suffered"), the cross involving the curse (Gal. 3:13) for the world's sin (II Cor. 5:21). All his begging and pleading in Gethsemane showed his willingness to obey, and the sufferings into which he then went obediently were the actual obedience he learned. He endured them all in perfect obedience until he expired on the cross.

We may distinguish between Jesus' active and his passive obedience when we analyze; but in reality the two are ever found together as one obedience. It is imperfect thinking to separate them so as to think that the active was for himself and only the passive for us, the active in order to make the passive perfect and without blemish as a pure and holy sacrifice to God. Note that καίπερ is always used with a participle; in ἔμαθεν — ἔπαθε we have an unsought but beautiful *parechesis*. We may recall 3:2: "the Apostle and High Priest of our confession, Jesus, being *faithful*," etc.

9) He learned the obedience "and, having (thus) been made complete, became for all those obeying him (the) cause of eternal salvation, designated by God (the) 'High Priest according to the order of Melchizedek.'" This is the same thought that was expressed in 2:10: "that God as bringing many sons to glory make the Author of their salvation complete by means of suffering." We have the same agent, namely God; the same means, namely suffering; the same verb τελειοῦν, to bring to a τέλος or goal, "to make complete"; the same object: "the Author of their salvation"—"the cause of eternal salvation"; finally, the same beneficiaries: many sons being brought to glory—all those obeying him, and 2:10 ends with 2:17, 18, the merciful and faithful High Priest who was tried and tempted. In the interpretation of 2:10 we have given that of 5:9.

In neither passage is there an idea of God's making Jesus *morally* complete. We refer the reader to what we have noted under 2:10. We reject the view that Jesus underwent a moral development and then attained completeness in his personal *Lebensstand*.

"Made complete" means complete as "the cause of eternal salvation." Without suffering the death which Jesus suffered he would not have been the complete Savior. To be Prophet and King would not have been enough; he had to be also High Priest and bring the blood of the all-sufficient atonement. Those who regard Jesus as being morally perfected go outside of the text in order to find the completeness referred to in τελειωθείς; but it always lies inside the text: "made complete as the cause of eternal salvation" — αἴτιος, "cause" = the personal term ὁ ἀρχηγός, "the Author," the one term elucidates the other.

"Many sons" in 2:10 = "all those obeying him," for true sons of God obey Jesus. The present participle describes their constant obedience. It is chosen in order to match the obedience of Jesus, for we are his brothers (2:11). We learn our obedience to him from him. He is our example. But it would be unwarranted to think that God made Jesus complete only as our example in obedience so that we may have him as our perfect model. Can *we* be the cause of anyone's eternal salvation? "Those who obey him" are denominated thus because they do vastly more than to copy his moral example of obedience to God. To obey him, namely Jesus, means above all to believe in him, to yield to him the obedience of faith, which then naturally results in doing his will by moral living, which is the fruit of such faith. The disobedience referred to in 3:18 is the unbelief mentioned in 3:19. We enter into God's rest (4:3) as "the believing ones." Note "the disobedience" in 4:11, which again means unbelief. Αἴτιος is the substantive, literally, "the One who causes," and is more appropriate than the abstract feminine αἰτία; since it is the predicate it does not have the article; in English the article is needed.

The discussion as to when Jesus became the cause of our eternal salvation is unnecessary. It occurred when he said on the cross: "It has been finished!" and yielded up the spirit. There is no need to postpone this until the time of the ascension and the *sessio ad dextram*. There is a significance in the writer's saying "the cause of eternal salvation for all those obeying him." Are the readers among this number? They have already been warned, notably in 3:11. Were some not thinking of disobeying in unbelief?

10) The last aorist participle rounds out the entire statement: "greeted or designated by God 'High Priest according to the order of Melchizedek,'" not by the writer on the basis of a deduction he has made but "by God" in the Davidic Psalm 110. This brings us to all that v. 6 has said and to the thought that Jesus certainly did not make himself High Priest. Here we have more than the antitype of Aaron, here is the type of Melchizedek, which was established already in Abraham's day. This High Priest was the cause of eternal salvation. We date the aorist passive participle back to David's psalm. That was prophecy, indeed, which was fulfilled when Jesus completed his High-priestly sacrifice on the cross.

A Humiliating Rebuke for the Readers, v. 11-14.

11) The writer is very frank with his readers. We have noted this in his admonitions, which are direct and do not mince words. He has touched upon the subject of Christ's High Priesthood which is not prefigured in Aaron but in the remarkable king-priest Melchizedek who, more than Aaron, reflects the greatness and the endlessness of Christ's High Priesthood. Shall the writer go on and say more on this subject even as there is much more of the highest value to be said? Something has come over his readers that makes him hesitate. They are no longer the people they once were. Their ears have become sluggish. The writer

tells them plainly what is the matter with them. Their sorry condition makes it hard for him to expound what God says in reference to Christ and Melchizedek. He intends to make the attempt in spite of this even as he has already begun to do (v. 4-10). His object in scoring his readers as he now does is to rouse them to use their ears as they formerly did; besides this he justifies himself for presenting the subject (7:1, etc.) in utmost simplicity as one feeds milk to babes. They themselves are the cause for his proceeding in ABC fashion.

This rebuke hurts. These readers were former Jews and were, therefore, thoroughly versed in the Old Testament. Now it, however, develops that they have been thinking of dropping back into the old Judaism and giving up Christ. Are they really such babes as not to know what God himself says about the supreme and eternal High Priesthood of Jesus in connection with Melchizedek to whom even Abraham bowed? Well, then the writer will put it in the form of milk for them so that as babes they may grow up anew. This rebuke is thoroughly deserved; it is at the same time administered so as to produce the fullest effect for the simple instruction that is now to follow.

The Greek phrasing is so idiomatic that a literal translation must be given up. **Regarding whom there is much for us to say, and it is made difficult to expound in saying it since you have become sluggish as regards hearing.** Περὶ οὗ is best regarded as a masculine because 7:1 begins with οὗτος, Melchizedek: In regard to Melchizedek as showing us the Priesthood of Jesus there is much for us to say, ὁ λόγος, the discourse required, is πολύς, considerable. There is much to be said about him, and all of it is most valuable. We supply ἐστί. The dative ἡμῖν with the copula is not the same as the genitive (v. 14). The latter = "belongs to"; the former = "one ought to." Here: "we ought to say a great deal about Melchizedek."

The plural is often regarded as an editorial plural: "I ought to say much," and we are referred to 2:5: "concerning which we are speaking." But the latter means "concerning which you and I are speaking"; so also our passage means "concerning whom there is much for you and me to say" in our λόγος or discussion. You will have questions to ask me, I will have answers, and both of us will discuss what God says. Although the sentence begins with a relative, this is only the Greek way of linking up; we should say: "Regarding him there is much," etc.

So much is there for us to discuss, and so hard is it to do it because of the condition of your ears! The verbal adjective is the second predicate with πολύς after the implied copula. It is passive in meaning: "made hard to expound or to interpret," and is modified by the infinitive "made hard to say in an expository way." The Greek matches ὁ λόγος and λέγειν, it is hard to duplicate this in English: *the discourse* required is considerable and is made difficult to *discourse on* so as to interpret since your ears have grown dull. The difficulty lies, not with what the Old Testament says about Melchizedek, not with the writer who knows what is said, but with the hearers and their sluggish ears. The sending station is in order, but the receiving radio set is out of order.

The perfect tense implies that the readers were once keen of hearing but have fallen into a dulled condition. This is now their state, and it is due to their inclination no longer to believe in Christ Jesus. Ταῖς ἀκοαῖς is the dative of relation which is used in the plural with reference to the organs or sense of hearing; we may say "sluggish as regards your ears." Unbelief closes the ears; incipient unbelief dulls them. These readers have made it difficult to interpret Melchizedek for them. By plainly telling them so the writer is trying to reopen those ears and to sharpen their hearing.

Hebrews 5:12

12) And, indeed, when, due to the length of time, you (now) ought to be teachers you again have need that someone teach you the elements of the beginning of the sayings of God and have come to have need of milk and not of solid food.

Γάρ is simply confirmatory, and καί adds this confirmation, which is really an intensification. Just look at yourselves, the writer says. Although you have been Christians for so long a time and ought to be teachers of other people you have dropped back so far that you need somebody again to teach you the very ABC of what God has said, you are like babes who need milk and have not yet advanced to solid food! This certainly hurts much more even than saying that their ears are sluggish. It is intended to hurt. Every presumption on the part of the readers must be destroyed so that they will hear.

Χρόνος is time in its length. The supposition that these were Palestinian Jews since they had been Christian for so long a time certainly makes the time long enough. But if they were Roman Jews who had been converted by Paul at the beginning of his first imprisonment they would by this time have been Christians long enough so that in view of their previous extensive knowledge of the Old Testament they should now, indeed, be teachers of others and certainly not need someone again to teach them the rudiments of the sayings of God (τὰ λόγια τοῦ Θεοῦ, Rom. 3:2). Στοιχεῖα is used in the sense of "rudiments," the ABC, and this meaning is assured by the genitive: "the rudiments of the beginning of the sayings of God," i. e., the ones with which a beginning is made when one is learning what God has said in the Old Testament. The problem is, the writer says, as to how we are going to discuss Melchizedek and what God has said about him, which is beyond the ABC, when you readers have to have the ABC taught you again. Your condition certainly makes such a discussion hard for me.

This literal statement is enhanced by the figurative addition "and have come to have need of milk and not of solid food." Χρείαν ἔχοντες is predicative to γεγόνατε, the perfect indicating the condition into which the readers have relapsed, one in which they are able to digest only milk and not solid food. The writer's problem is to reduce God's sayings about Melchizedek, which are really solid food, to milk for these readers who have reverted to babyhood. Well, this will explain the simplicity with which he proceeds in chapter 7.

13) For everyone partaking of milk is inexperienced in right discussion, for he is a child; but solid food belongs to mature persons, to those who by reason of their condition have their senses trained for discrimination of both what is excellent and what is bad.

"For" = "as I need hardly tell you," "as you all know." Everyone who is so young as to be on a diet of milk is incapable of doing anything in the way of λόγος δικαιοσύνης, he is still a child, anything that resembles proper discussion is beyond him. The genitive after the adjective is an ablative (R. 516), and δικαιοσύνης is adjectival: "right" discussion. A babe is not advanced enough in experience for such discussion; he is at best able to talk about childish things. On νήπιος compare I Cor. 13:11 as the best illustration of the meaning of the word. Some go too far when they think of a babe at its mother's breast that is able only to babble. As in v. 11 λόγος = discussion, *Eroerterung* (C.-K. 672). Although the statement is figurative it is worded so as to indicate what the figure signifies in the present connection.

Some, among them our versions, regard "the word of righteousness" as having an objective genitive: the word that treats of righteousness, the gospel about Christ's righteousness or about our imputed or acquired righteousness. Then, however, the article should be attached. The expression occurring in 7:2: "king of righteousness," is not pertinent. The context of our chapter contains no reference to righteousness.

14) The figure is continued: "but solid food belongs to mature persons," the predicate genitive with "is": "is of" = "belongs to." And τέλειοι is explained: "to those who by reason of their condition have their senses trained (or exercised) for discrimination of both what is excellent and what is bad," i. e., who are able to discriminate between the two. The figurative language is again so worded as to indicate the reality to which it applies. There is some uncertainty about ἕξις although it evidently refers to the maturity that is attained by the τέλειοι, thus their condition. The expression γεγυμνασμένα ἐχόντων is not a periphrastic perfect, for the perfect participle simply modifies τὰ αἰσθητήρια.

The reference to "both what is excellent and what is bad" does not drop the figure and now mean what is morally and spiritually excellent or, on the other hand, bad, for we read as one thought: "having their senses trained for discriminating between what is excellent and what is bad," namely in the way of solid food, which to eat, which to shun. There is only a contrast of maturity with childhood, of ability to discriminate and inability to do so. There is no thought of some special high development; the writer would be fully satisfied if his readers were the mature people they once were, and if they had not dropped back into a childhood that is lacking discrimination.

The rebuke is ended, and the writer counts on its effect, namely that his readers will shake off their sluggishness in hearing, will not compel him to begin their instruction over again but will rise to sufficient maturity to profit by what he will tell them as simply as he can regarding Melchizedek and Jesus.

CHAPTER VI

A Call to Christian Maturity, although It Is Impossible to Restore Those Who Commit the Sin against the Holy Spirit, v. 1-8.

1) The writer expects his rebuke to take proper effect. That is why Christian rebuke is administered, to be promptly effective. The writer tells his readers that they are again like children who need milk and the ABC of teaching instead of solid food. But he will not dismiss them as such children; this rebuke is to drive the sluggishness out of their ears (5:11) and to make them recover something of their maturity. Διό connects with the whole rebuke and not merely with 5:13 or 14.

Therefore, leaving the discussion of (what constitutes) **the beginning of** (the connection with) **Christ, let us bring ourselves** (in our discussion) **to** (what constitutes) **the** (proper) **maturity, not laying again a foundation of repentance from dead works and of faith toward God, of** (the) **doctrine concerning baptisms and laying on of hands, and concerning resurrection of** (the) **dead, and concerning eternal judgment. And this we will** (now) **do if God, indeed, permits.**

Λόγος is again "discussion," *Eroerterung*, as it was in 5:11, 13, the genitive τῆς ἀρχῆς names the contents, and the second genitive τοῦ Χριστοῦ him with whom the beginning of Christianity is connected. The participle is the aorist because leaving this discussion is a single act that is preliminary to turning to things that are more advanced. The Greek is compact but entirely clear; in English we must use more words in order to bring out the thought which the terse genitives convey.

Hebrews 6:1   175

The writer says: Let us turn from the ABC matters of Christianity, from what is milk for a child, and discuss matters that are more mature and advanced. He lifts his readers out of their low state for which he has scolded them in 5:11-14 so that they might at least in part attain the maturer state in which they ought to be. By expecting something better from them and even acting on that expectation he draws them to live up to that expectation. That is good spiritual psychology.

"Let us bring ourselves," namely in this our *logos* or discussion, "to the maturity," to what constitutes the proper maturity in this discussion in which this degree of maturity is needed. Again, as in 2:5; 5:11, this is by no means an editorial "we"; the very sense of the verb is against such a view. It is the middle voice and cannot mean: "Let me carry myself to the proper maturity." The writer includes his readers and wants them to betake themselves with him to the maturity of understanding and judgment that is needed for discussing what lies beyond the ABC of Christianity. This is his constantly fine attitude toward his readers; he lifts them up to his level wherever he can. While he, indeed, imparts he knows that they will the more readily receive when he draws them up to his own level. Τελειότης corresponds to τέλειοι used in 5:14 and signifies a "maturity" that is above the stage of a νήπιος or "child."

The participial clause explains: "not laying again (in our discussion with each other) a foundation of repentance from dead works," etc., not starting again from the very bottom like laying a foundation for a house. Surely, it will not be necessary to do this again. Surely, after the rebuke that has just been administered to them (5:11-14) the readers will be able to recover from the immature way in which they have been acting.

Three appositional genitives describe what is meant by "foundation." It would be one "of repentance from dead works — of faith toward God — of doctrine." The third needs objective genitives to explain with what such doctrine would have to deal: it would have to be "doctrine concerning baptisms and laying on of hands," etc. All these things are the elements, the ABC of Christianity. The readers can surely recall them without having them discussed anew; they can now surely advance with the writer to the further things such as solid food for adults to give them manhood strength.

All these genitives refer to basic Christian and not to the old Jewish teachings; yet they refer to what the readers as former Jews learned when they were brought to Christ. If this letter were intended for former Gentiles, some at least of these genitives would be different. The first two matters that grounded them in Christianity were "repentance and faith." As Jews they lived in "dead works," in outward observance of law. The Gospels and Paul's letters abundantly describe such "dead works." They were "dead" indeed, no spiritual life produced them, for this life produces fruit that is of an entirely different kind.

Of the many passages that might be cited here besides 9:14 let us mention only Matt. 7:16-20; 25:44,-45. On μετάνοια see the verb in Matt. 3:10: "to perceive or see afterward" thus "to change one's mind"; but this meaning is immensely deepened in the Scriptures and signifies the inner change of heart by turning from sin and guilt to cleansing and forgiveness by God's grace under the power of the law and the gospel. This word looks backward to guilt and forward to God's pardon. Here "from dead works" makes this word look back to these. Repentance frees from this millstone.

Coupled with this contrite repentance is "faith toward God," for the two always go together. "Repentance" sometimes includes "faith" without special mention of it; it is properly added here. If former

Gentiles were addressed, we should expect the mention of turning away from dumb idols to the living God (I Cor. 12:2). But why does the writer not say "faith in Christ" instead of "faith based on (ἐπί) God"? Because he refers to faith that is based on God who spoke concerning Christ in the Old Testament. The Jews did not need another god, they needed faith in the God whom they knew, genuine trust in him and in the revelation of his Word.

2) The third elementary characteristic of Christianity is "doctrine." This is added without a connective because it is an integral part of both repentance and faith without which neither can be laid down as a foundation. "Of doctrine" is also an appositional genitive to "foundation"; but the four modifying genitives are objective: doctrine "about baptisms," etc. These are connected by τε . . . τε . . . καί which join more closely than three καί would. These four form a closely connected whole. These Jews were taught what their baptisms meant for them (Titus 3:4-7). The plural is concrete to designate the actual baptisms the readers had received; the singular would be abstract to indicate what baptism as such means. We cancel the R. V.'s margin "washings" which is due to the supposition that the doctrine about Jewish lustrations is referred to. The Jews know all about them without Christian doctrine.

The governing genitive is generally placed before its dependent genitive, but even B.-D. 444, 4; 474, 4, registers an exception here. This placing does not seem to be due to mere rhythm but to a desire to weld this genitive more closely to its dependents. "Baptisms" and "laying on of hands" go together just as we still use the latter in our form of baptism. It is the old symbolic act that dates far back into Judaism and is benedictional by praying for God's blessing to descend upon the person indicated; it is at the same time symbolic of that very blessing. While it bestows nothing and, when it is joined to baptism, does not mediate the gift of the Holy Spirit, it does go with the words of prayer that accompany the act of the hands and ask that the Holy Spirit received in and through baptism continue to bless the person baptized. The other uses of the laying on of hands (Acts 6:6; 8:17; 13:3; I Tim. 4:14; 5:22; II Tim. 1:6) need not be discussed here.

Repentance, faith, baptism go together, which is another reason for placing "baptisms" forward. So also "resurrection of (the) dead" and "judgment eternal" (i. e., never to be altered) go together. Except for the Sadducees, the Jews, too, believed in these, but not as being connected with Jesus, who is the Resurrection and the Life and the Judge at the last day. The foundational doctrine of Christianity gave Jews what they could not attain in their work-righteousness and empty Judaism: the sure hope of a blessed resurrection in Jesus and the certainty that they would be justified in the eternal judgment.

Four items taken from the start of the Christian life and two from its consummation at the last day suffice for summarizing the foundation of Christianity, which it should not be necessary to lay again for the readers of this letter; they should stand on this foundation and permit this letter to discuss what will strengthen them and mightily further their Christianity. We note the reading διδαχήν, the accusative in place of the genitive. It is not well-attested textually and only confuses the wording and hence requires no further discussion.

3) Despite the handicap that exists in the readers the effort to which they are invited in v. 1 is now to be made: "And this we will accomplish if God, indeed, permits!" The reading varies between the future indicative (volitive) "we will," etc., and the aorist subjunctive (hortatory) "let us," etc. The latter seems to be a conformation with the subjunctive of v. 1 and unnecessarily repeats the hortation, whereas the for-

mer: "we will," etc., properly answers the "let us," etc., occurring in v. 1. What is being proposed (τοῦτο) is what is indicated in v. 1, namely to carry ourselves forward to the proper maturity. The proposal cannot be to lay the foundation anew, for this is negatived in v. 1, nor is it done in what follows. What is proposed is a mutual proceeding: *"we* will do or accomplish"; the writer cannot succeed unless his readers rouse themselves and cooperate, for the success of what is to be accomplished hinges also on them.

That is why the ἐάνπερ clause is added: "if God, indeed, permits (or: will permit)." In the case of the writer this means that God must aid him in the writing of what follows, and that God must aid the readers in overcoming the sluggishness and dullness of their hearing (5:11). On him depends the success of all our preaching and our hearing, which, like the writer, we feel especially when our hearers have begun to close their ears and need to be rebuked as is done in 5:11-14. On the part of the writer the clause implies the earnest prayer: "May God permit me to accomplish my part for the readers!" It implies likewise that the readers pray: "May God permit the accomplishment in us as far as our reading and our hearing of this letter are concerned!" There is no doubt regarding God, for the conditional clause is one of expectancy. This expectancy rests, as it should always also in our case, on humble dependence.

4) "For" explains that success might be impossible, that even God could not permit such a thing. **For those who were once enlightened and tasted the heavenly gift and became partakers of the Holy Spirit and tasted God's excellent utterance and (his) powers of the eon about to come and fell away, it is impossible again to renew them unto repentance since they are recrucifying the Son of God and exposing him to public ignominy.**

We note that this statement as well as the following one (v. 7, 8) are objective, are written in the third person. This statement presents the fact regarding what "is impossible" in the case of certain persons. The writer does not say that among his readers there actually are, or that he fears that there are, persons of this kind. His statement constitutes a warning: those once converted may fall so that it becomes "impossible to renew them to repentance." The readers are to apply that fact to themselves. One may go so far that even God's grace can no longer reach him; the judgment must then take him in hand and send him to his doom (10:26-31). What is said is not written in order that we may judge others as to their fall and pronounce it irreparable, but so that each of us may check himself lest he fall and be doomed.

In a study of what is said here and in 10:26-31 regarding the sin against the Holy Ghost we should begin with the passages found in the Gospels, namely Matt. 12:31, 32; Mark 3:28, 29; Luke 12:10, where Jesus warns the blasphemous Pharisees against committing this sin as they were beginning to do; we should also consult I John 5:16. Both those who were never converted and those who have been converted may fall into a state in which they make repentance impossible. They may already in this life reach a state that is similar to that of the damned in hell, yea, a state that is similar to that of the devils, for whom there is no repentance, no pardon. Although this is terrible beyond words, it is, nevertheless, true. Repentance may be lost and found again; it may also become impossible exactly as is here stated. God alone knows when the latter occurs; we can have only fears. The opposition of those who have never repented may grow so that they place themselves into a state where repentance and thus forgiveness become absolutely impossible.

Hebrews 6:4

This is rightly called the sin against the Holy Ghost, who is mentioned in this verse and in the three passages found in the Gospels. It is he who works repentance; to sin against him to such an extent that this is made impossible for him is to fall into the hands of the living God (10:31). Let us add that any person who *fears* that he has committed what has by another name been called "the unpardonable sin" by that very fear proves that he has *not* committed it, that the door to repentance has *not* been irrevocably closed against him by God. Those who have fallen as is here described never show such fears; their horrible fear sets in at death.

The Greek can separate ἀδύνατον from πάλιν ἀνακαινίζειν κτλ.; this cannot be done in English as our versions show. "Impossible again to renew" simply states the fearful fact; v. 8 indicates what alone remains. The four participles, all aorists of fact, have one article and thus describe the same persons; the accusative makes them the object of the verb "to renew again unto repentance." The descriptive participles furnish a complete picture. "They were once enlightened" by the Holy Spirit by means of the Word of the gospel; the aorist states the fact as an actual occurrence. The darkness was driven out, the Light, Jesus Christ, the light of his saving truth filled their souls.

Ἅπαξ, "once," is in contrast with πάλιν, "again" or a second time, v. 6. How one who has once been enlightened can deliberately return into darkness is beyond explanation, but only because an unreasonable act admits of no reasonable explanation, and all explanations which explain must of necessity be reasonable. In Matt. 22:12 the man who is confronted with his unreasonable act is speechless; no reasonable explanation is possible. In Luke 19:20, 21 the unreasonable act is defended by an attempt to make it appear reasonable; but this show of reason is at once blasted by the unreason it seeks to cover up.

The Novatians and the Montanists used this passage as Scripture proof for their penitential discipline, and they influenced many of the older writers. They had "to be enlightened" and also "to renew" and to "recrucify" (v. 6) refer to baptism and so claimed that the fallen could not be baptized a second time, but that they might obtain forgiveness by repentance. But "those once enlightened" never equals those once baptized. We need not, of course, separate the baptism of adults from their enlightenment, for all who come to true enlightening and faith themselves insist on being baptized as they also desire the Lord's Supper and all the other blessings of the church. "Light" and "to enlighten" are derived from the Old Testament and in the New Testament have no connection with the pagan mystery cults and the words that were used in their rituals or with the so-called "shock of enlightenment" that is found in the Masonic initiations of today. The aorist states the past fact that these persons were once enlightened; but this tense in no way denies the process involved, which leads up to faith and the adequate knowledge of Christ.

The connection by means of τε is close: "and have tasted the heavenly gift." To the sense of sight that of taste is added in order the more to describe the inner, personal experience of salvation. As to taste of death (2:9) means to experience its bittterness, so to taste of the heavenly gift means to experience the joy of receiving that gift and of being blessed by the unmerited grace which bestowed that gift, yea, as a sinner on this sinful earth to experience the heavenliness of it. Recall "heavenly calling" used in 3:1.

We confess that we are unable to see why "once" should not be construed with all the participles save the last, "fell away," which naturally needs no modifying adverb. To say that only the enlightenment is momentary while the other three are durative experiences is to have a wrong conception of the enlightenment. So we cannot restrict "the heavenly gift" to the Lord's Supper, the Holy Spirit, faith, regeneration, the gospel, Christ, the forgiveness of sins; nor can we exclude the latter as though it does not come from heaven when in fact our acquittal is pronounced by the Judge on his heavenly throne. "The heavenly gift" is comprehensive, one grand whole, entirely "heavenly" in its nature, far above anything earthly; in Eph. 1:3 Paul writes: "All spiritual blessings in heavenly places in Christ."

The third participle names the heavenly source: "and became partakers of the Holy Spirit" (no article is needed, this is a proper name). Καί is in place and not τε because the experience is now carried down to what these people themselves "became." "Partakers" places them among the rest, of whom the same thing can be said. They belonged to this heavenly company, the great *Una Sancta*. To be partakers or sharers of the Holy Spirit does not mean to divide the Spirit. He is a person, and those are partakers of him who with others receive him in their hearts with all that this saving, sanctifying presence means.

5) But this statement calls for amplification, for the Spirit does not descend from heaven and enter into our hearts. We need the statement "and tasted God's excellent utterance and his powers of the eon about to come." We get the Spirit by means of the ῥῆμα Θεοῦ which is thus defined by C.-K., 650: "What God has said or uttered without reference to its extent . . . yet according to the connection with special reference to the message of salvation," *dabar tob* (Hebrew), "excellent utterance." Λόγος Θεοῦ lays stress on the *thought* that is expressed in the Word, ῥῆμα on the *fact* that God spoke, although what he said is also included even as λόγος includes a λέγειν of some kind. We have, therefore, ῥηθέν, "uttered by the Lord" (Matt. 1:22), and λέγει, the Lord "says." The difference remains. In all of God's utterance his Spirit comes to enter our hearts

and to dwell there, nor is there an utterance that is as καλόν as this, which brings all God's heavenly gift to bless us for salvation.

That is why τε closely connects with God's utterance "(his) powers of the eon about to come." In Rom. 1:16 the gospel is called "God's power," not, indeed, his omnipotent power but his power "for salvation," his power of grace. What is said regarding "the living λόγος of God" in 4:12, 13 is equally true regarding his ῥῆμα. The plural "powers" is clearer than the singular "power" would be, for the plural leads us to think of the many blessed effects which these powers work in us. They are "powers" of a higher world than the earth and its powers of nature, which are able to produce only natural effects.

"The eon about to come" already exists and will take the place of "this eon" in which we now live on earth. Rev. 21:1-5. Although this eon still continues, that eternal eon in which God exists already sends its powers down into our present eon, sends them by God's utterance or Word and by the Holy Spirit who fills that utterance. Heavenly, eternal effects are thus wrought, which are to endure during the entire eternal eon to come: spiritual birth, renewal, sanctification, divine sonship, heirship, fear, joy, thanksgiving, glorying.

The writer again uses "tasted" but not because of a poverty of terms on his part — this epistle shows the very opposite of such poverty of expression — but because he intends to emphasize the experience of tasting and enjoying. We taste "the heavenly gift," and that includes the thought that we also taste "God's excellent Word and other-world powers" themselves by which the heavenly gift is made ours. Such a heavenly gift we already enjoy, but these powers that are operative in us promise far greater gifts to come (I Cor. 2:9). We taste the sweet presence and working of these powers which fit us more and more for this coming eon into which we shall be presently ushered. In Hellenistic Greek the verb "to taste" may govern either the genitive as it does in v. 4 or the accusative as it does in v. 5 without a difference in meaning; the classics use only the genitive. The writer intends to make no difference, nor should we seek one.

We note that the light implied in the first participle, the heavenly gift, the Holy Spirit, the utterance of God and the other-world powers are objective; but the participles are subjective to the highest degree, for they refer to the actual, personal, most intimate experience of these divine realities. Light and heavenly gift are not enough for the writer, he adds the Holy Spirit, the personal divine medium for this light and this gift, and the divine Word with its other-world powers, in and by which the Spirit comes and operates in us to produce this entire blessed experience. The writer thus describes Christians who became Christians in the fullest sense of the word. The aorists confine themselves to the fact without referring to the length of time the blessed fact continued.

6) Another καί is added and another aorist participle, and these complete the description of these Christians. We again have just one word as we had in the first participle used in v. 4. "And fell away," just this final fact. There is no need to say more, this one word tells the whole story. It is tragic to the highest degree. The following words describe how tragic it is. This is not a falling into some sin or error which is dangerous but not deadly; no denial like that of Peter in a panic of fear, like that of weak Christians who in order to save their lives were frightened by persecutions into sacrificing to pagan gods or to the emperor as a divine being. The church was inclined to consider the latter as being beyond hope, which was a mistake in many cases.

"And fell away" (literally "to the side," παρά) means to fall away utterly. They fell to such an extent that "it is impossible again to renew them unto repentance," i. e., again to produce repentance (see the word in v. 1) in their heart and so to change their state into one that is again καινός or "new" as they had once been made new. The subject of the infinitive is unexpressed; it need not be expressed, for no one, neither God himself, the Holy Spirit, nor his Word and the ministers of that Word are able to produce a renewal of the repentance that is gone.

It is the state into which they have fallen which makes renewal to repentance impossible. Two present durative participles describe this state, and we regard them as causal: "since they are recrucifying for themselves the Son of God and exposing him to public ignominy." As the tenses show, there is no cessation in this double act. The enormity of these acts is expressed by making "the Son of God" the object of them. They are repeating the awful act of the Jewish Sanhedrin, who crucified Jesus because he said he was the Son of God (Matt. 26:63-66). They are doing this "for themselves." They are not again actually nailing him to the cross as one who was accursed of God (Gal. 3:13), for he is now beyond human reach, in glory, but as far as his relation to them and theirs to him is concerned.

The second participle goes still farther, "exposing him to public ignominy" as the Sanhedrists did in Matt. 26:67, 68 when they spit in Jesus' face, knocked him about, and mocked him; when they brought him to the cross to hang there in public ignominy, and added to this outrage by their hideous mockery, Matt. 27:38-43. Those who fell from the Son of God openly denounce and revile him before the world, and, having once embraced him, they not only know how to do this most effectively like a friend turned traitor who viciously uses all that his former intimacy provides him, but do it so that men shall see what they as one-time converts of Jesus have now as disillusioned converts come to think of him. Outsiders may vilify the Son of God; they have never been personally in touch with him. What does that amount to? It is a different matter when his own converts eventually expose him to public shame. The word blasphemy is not used here as it is in the passages in the Gospels that speak about the sin against the Holy Ghost; but "exposing to public ignominy" is a full equivalent.

7) The illustration that is now added advances to the divine judgment which is necessarily involved. **For land that drank the rain often coming upon it and bearing plants suitable for those on whose account it is also being tilled partakes of blessing from God, but continuing to produce thorns and thistles it is rejected and nigh to a curse, whose end is for burning.**

When the author uses a piece of ground as an illustration, we feel that he is comparing the lesser with the greater: if this is undeniably true with regard to a piece of land, it will more assuredly be true with regard to men. In the reality (v. 4-6) we have men who did well and then went utterly bad; so in the illustration we have a piece of land which is first described as doing well and then as doing the opposite. This is the same piece of land; the article is to be construed with all three participles: γῆ ἡ πιοῦσα . . . καὶ τίκτουσα . . . ἐκφέρουσα δέ, "land that drank . . . and keeps bearing . . . but keeps producing." The fact that it drank the rain applies to both of the present participles; although the cultivation is not repeated in the case of the second (v. 8), such cultivation is, nevertheless, implied.

The tenses of the participles are used exactly. The rain keeps coming upon this piece of land (present, iterative); it drank all of this rain (aorist, fact). It continues to bear herbage that is suitable for those on whose account it is being cultivated, namely the owners who do the cultivating themselves or have their servants do it. While it is in this condition the land partakes of blessing from God as serving the purpose of God. Land is blessed when it does this. The illustration is so to the point because land could not do this on its own accord; it is like us who must receive God's light, gift, Spirit, etc., (v. 4, 5) and besides these the cultivating care of the church, its ministry, and its membership. So land must receive God's rain and the farmer's cultivating care. It is God's intent that such land produce what its cultivators need. So we should respond to all that is lavished upon us by God and by his church. Compare Ps. 65:10.

8) Yet land that is so well treated may be the opposite (δέ) and continue "to carry up" nothing but thorns and thistles. Was the writer perhaps thinking of Palestine with its 200 species of thistles which appear in 753 varieties (B.-P. 1320)? This would not necessarily locate the readers in Palestine, but it would remind them as former Jews of the kind of land that the Jewish nation had become, a people of thorns and thistles. That would be very much in point: receiving all God's bountiful rain plus all the diligent cultivation yet now allowing itself to be blown over with seed of all manner of thorns and thistles, carrying them up in noxious growth to the smothering out of all edible herbage (Matt. 13:7). Whatever a piece of land may have done before, it is now ἀδόκιμος, tested out and found to be no good for its purpose and thus "nigh to curse," so nigh that the curse will presently be carried into effect, its end for nothing but burning (10:27). This is not metonomy as though, while the burning sets fire to the thorns and thistles, the land itself is also burned like Sodom and Gomorrah. Only its end is burning; its product is not harvested for the cultivators but is set on fire, it is fit only for burning.

Here is the judgment with even the significant word "burning." The application to the people described in v. 6 is so clear that nothing needs to be added. The relative ἧς has its antecedent by way of the participles which modify γῆ, "land." Some regard "curse" as the antecedent, but the clause should then read: "a curse whose end is burning" and not "for burning"; it is the land that is destined "for a burning" of all its noxious product.

The Writer's Assurance and Desire, v. 9-12.

9) The idea that the writer "is almost startled by his own picture" in v. 4-8 or caught by its "alarm" and so hastens to tone it down, is not acceptable. He would then have cancelled v. 4-8 as any writer does who finds his words too strong for what he intends to say. Verses 4-8 are intended as a warning and are therefore written in the third person; and the readers need this warning, it is not retracted. While v. 4-8 hoist the danger signal v. 9-12 leave it hoisted but remind the readers of their past faithfulness and on this base the assurance that they will not fall and the desire that every one of them may continue in diligence to the glorious end.

But we are persuaded concerning you, beloved, things that are better and in keeping with salvation though we speak as we do. For God is not unrighteous to forget your work and the love you displayed for his name by your past ministering to the saints and your present ministering.

The perfect "we have been persuaded" has the force of the present "we still have the persuasion," we are still convinced. Some think that this "we" is editorial and equals "I," the writer alone. Although "we" and "you" are contrasted, the writer aims to say that many others, especially those that are with him as he writes, are convinced of better things in regard to the readers. They all realize that there has been a marked decline in the readers, but they are sure that this letter will effect complete recovery. This is not false optimism as v. 10 shows but one that is based on promising facts. The address "beloved," which occurs only here in this letter, indicates how dearly all these friends love the readers, and how all that this letter contains, even its severest warnings, is prompted solely by this love.

Τά is to be construed with both the adjective and the participle: "things better" than those described in v. 6-8, and those "in keeping with salvation," not tending to a curse (v. 8) and to damnation. The middle of ἔχω = holding themselves close to something, it is therefore followed by the genitive. Such better things and thus those that are in line with salvation the friends of the readers are sure they see in them to the present day. If this were not the case, it would be of no use to send this letter. On εἰ καί, "if also," R. 1026 notes that a protasis of this kind is made a matter of indifference. What the writer has said in v. 4-8 does not affect the confidence that is now expressed. It could do so only if it is misunderstood.

10) "For" explains the persuasion and confidence, yet not as being based on the readers themselves but on God and on his justness. He "is not unrighteous to forget your work," all that you have done and are still doing, "and the love" which prompted that work, "which you displayed for his name by your past ministering to the saints (aorist: completed) and your present ministering (present: incomplete, still going on)." If God should forget all this he would be unrighteous, unjust, in conflict with his own being as this is revealed by himself. "To forget" is followed by the genitive. God cannot possibly forget, i. e., cast aside and disregard what has been done and is being done because of love to his name. The "name" of God is God himself in his revelation. By his name he draws near

to us, and by it we know, trust, love, embrace him. That is why his "name" is used in so many connections.

Ἀγάπη is the love of intelligence and understanding that is always coupled with corresponding purpose. This love springs only from true faith. To be sure, this love produces work, but God ever looks for the love in the work, and it is this love that arises from faith that makes us and our work acceptable to him who is himself love. The thought is that in spite of the decline in the readers God has not cast them off as accursed; he will continue his grace to them in order to remove their incipient defection. So the persuasion expressed in v. 9 rests ultimately on God and on what he will surely do for the readers in his righteousness.

The readers have displayed their love "for God's name" (for God as revealed in Christ) in all their ministration "to the saints." Love to God and help to God's saints always go together. I John 3:16-18, 23, 24; 4:20, 21. "The saints" is one of the standard designations for true Christians whether they are of Jewish or of Gentile origin; we trace it back to Acts 9:13. "Saints" are those who are truly separated unto God. Some seem to think that whenever "ministering to the saints" is mentioned, this must refer to the saints in the motherland and in the mother church, to Palestine and to Jerusalem. So "the saints" is regarded as a special term which designates only these Jewish Christians of the homeland. But this is evidently an undue restriction of this term.

If the readers of this letter are themselves residents of Jerusalem and Palestine, this statement about having ministered and of still ministering to the saints becomes rather unintelligible, for this letter is addressed to *all* the Jewish Christians. The writer makes no division between them; he does not write a letter to the Jewish Christians of means in Palestine and not to the Jewish Christians who needed help. Consequently the readers cannot be located in Palestine. Furthermore, this ministering to the saints has nothing to do with the great collection which Paul gathered among all his Gentile congregations and carried to the saints in Jerusalem. That collection was made years before this letter was written.

The matter becomes clear when we regard the readers of our epistle to be the great body of Jews which Paul converted during his first Roman imprisonment (see the introduction). These converts did not give up their synagogue buildings in Rome. They retained several of the seven synagogues in Rome. They did not, as some suppose, join the old congregation in Rome, whose membership is mentioned in the greetings in Rom. 16. They remained distinct and had their own places of worship.

When in the year 64 Nero burned Rome, accused the Christians in Rome of this crime, and killed so many of them in the most horrible ways, by having remained distinct from the old congregation these Jewish converts escaped the worst. None had to suffer martyrdom. This came upon the membership of the old, original congregation in Rome. Having kept their old synagogues, Paul's Jewish converts were still regarded to be nothing but the Jews they had always been. But during those terrible days these converts did what they could for "the saints" of the old congregation, they "ministered" to them as much as was possible. They were doing this even at the time when this letter was written. Instead of disowning all connection with the old congregation and its membership Paul's Jewish converts helped and were still helping their fellow saints of that congregation, i. e., as many as were left.

We see how significant the statement is that God is not unrighteous to forget this work and the love for God's name which prompted this work of ministering in the year 64 and since then, which covers something like a period of three or four years. The readers had not escaped entirely as 10:32-34 shows, most likely because they helped those who bore the brunt of the awful persecution.

11) Δέ adds something different. Besides being persuaded regarding the readers the writer and those who are with him desire something from them that is in line with their persuasion regarding them. **Moreover, we desire that each one of you continue to display the same diligence unto the full assurance of the hope to the end so that you may not become sluggish but imitators of those who through faith and longsuffering are inheriting the promises.**

"We desire" means as loving brethren desire the best for their "beloved" ones (v. 9). This wording sounds weaker than a positive command and yet is for that very reason stronger, for it appeals to the beloved to show themselves worthy of being so beloved. Those who are beloved are by the very love that is bestowed on them drawn to satisfy the desires of their lovers.

In v. 9, 10 we have "you," the readers as a body; now the writer says "each one of you," every individual, not one excepted. This does not, of course, mean that some are to be examples to the rest, and that some are to copy others. "Each one of you" makes no distinction. It applies the loving desire to every one personally. Each is to keep on showing (durative present) the same diligence that all have shown and are still showing in their love for God's name and in ministering to the saints. And they are to show this same diligence in another direction, namely "toward the full assurance of the hope till the end," when that hope will be gloriously realized. The fact that the readers had been and still were diligent in one direction makes the writer confident that the readers will show themselves diligent also in this other direction in which they were beginning to be slack. He praises them for the one diligence in order to move them to the other.

Πληροφορία = full assurance; some, like the R. V., stop with the idea of "fulness." Yet when it comes to the thought, mere fulness of hope does not suffice; for this is the hope in the hearts of the readers, which is full only when it has fulness of personal assurance. It was this assurance that had begun to decline in the hearts of the readers; their hope thus grew less, it was like a flame that was burning lower and lower. "The hope" with its article is the true Christian hope of the coming glory promised by Christ. To exercise diligence in regard to the full assurance of that hope is with all diligence to examine the divine grounds on which our assurance rests. This will make us sure and certain, fully so in all respects, and will thus make our hope strong like a flame that blazes up steadily to full height. "Up to the end" the writer desires this diligence to be displayed, i. e., until the end of the life of each one of his readers.

12) Ἵνα expresses contemplated result, first a negative and then a positive result. "So that you may not become sluggish" in the diligence described. From 5:11 we know that the readers "have become sluggish as regards their hearing." While it is not said that they have become sluggish also as regards their hope, this is implied; for the diligence that is required to keep the full assurance of their hope is none other than diligent hearing and heeding the gospel with its assurance in regard to what Christ has done and will do. Thus the present reference to sluggishness is an advance on 5:11.

Not sluggish "but imitators of those who through faith and longsuffering are inheriting the promises." This unrolls before the eyes of the readers the example of their many fellow Christians who are faithful to the end. "Who are inheriting" is the iterative present participle, and to inherit a promise is not merely to get to us, and by it we know, trust, love, embrace him. That is why his "name" is used in so many connections.

'Αγάπη is the love of intelligence and understanding that is always coupled with corresponding purpose. This love springs only from true faith. To be sure, this love produces work, but God ever looks for the love in the work, and it is this love that arises from faith that makes us and our work acceptable to him who is himself love. The thought is that in spite of the decline in the readers God has not cast them off as accursed; he will continue his grace to them in order to remove their incipient defection. So the persuasion expressed in v. 9 rests ultimately on God and on what he will surely do for the readers in his righteousness.

The readers have displayed their love "for God's name" (for God as revealed in Christ) in all their ministration "to the saints." Love to God and help to God's saints always go together. I John 3:16-18, 23, 24; 4:20, 21. "The saints" is one of the standard designations for true Christians whether they are of Jewish or of Gentile origin; we trace it back to Acts 9:13. "Saints" are those who are truly separated unto God. Some seem to think that whenever "ministering to the saints" is mentioned, this must refer to the saints in the motherland and in the mother church, to Palestine and to Jerusalem. So "the saints" is regarded as a special term which designates only these Jewish Christians of the homeland. But this is evidently an undue restriction of this term.

If the readers of this letter are themselves residents of Jerusalem and Palestine, this statement about having ministered and of still ministering to the saints becomes rather unintelligible, for this letter is addressed to *all* the Jewish Christians. The writer makes no division between them; he does not write a letter to the Jewish Christians of means in Palestine and not to the Jewish Christians who needed help. Consequently the readers cannot be located in Palestine. Furthermore, this ministering to the saints has nothing to do with the great collection which Paul gathered among all his Gentile congregations and carried to the saints in Jerusalem. That collection was made years before this letter was written.

The matter becomes clear when we regard the readers of our epistle to be the great body of Jews which Paul converted during his first Roman imprisonment (see the introduction). These converts did not give up their synagogue buildings in Rome. They retained several of the seven synagogues in Rome. They did not, as some suppose, join the old congregation in Rome, whose membership is mentioned in the greetings in Rom. 16. They remained distinct and had their own places of worship.

When in the year 64 Nero burned Rome, accused the Christians in Rome of this crime, and killed so many of them in the most horrible ways, by having remained distinct from the old congregation these Jewish converts escaped the worst. None had to suffer martyrdom. This came upon the membership of the old, original congregation in Rome. Having kept their old synagogues, Paul's Jewish converts were still regarded to be nothing but the Jews they had always been. But during those terrible days these converts did what they could for "the saints" of the old congregation, they "ministered" to them as much as was possible. They were doing this even at the time when this letter was written. Instead of disowning all connection with the old congregation and its membership Paul's Jewish converts helped and were still helping their fellow saints of that congregation, i. e., as many as were left.

We see how significant the statement is that God is not unrighteous to forget this work and the love for God's name which prompted this work of ministering in the year 64 and since then, which covers something like a period of three or four years. The readers had

God could not, however, swear as men do, by one who is greater, for there is none greater than God. So the only way in which God could swear to Abraham was to swear by himself. Κατά is used with verbs of swearing, as R. 607 explains, because the hand is laid "down upon" the thing on which the oath is taken. This is true to this day. When the Bible is used, the person lays his hand upon the Bible when he is taking an oath. The Bible signifies God himself. Raising the hand points to God and has the same meaning. In order to do this more significantly three fingers are often held upright (for the Trinity), two are turned down (for body and soul), i. e., the person taking the oath indicates thereby that the Trinity may punish him in body and in soul if he perjures himself. The fact that all oaths, no matter what their form may be, are made κατά God, Jesus explains in Matt. 5:33-37 where he explodes the false notions of the Jews on this subject. The truth that oaths have their place and their legitimate use is attested by the fact that God himself takes an oath here, and that Jesus, too, took an oath before the proper human authorities (the government, the Sanhedrin), cf., Matt. 26:63, 64. Εἶχε is used with the infinitive in the sense of "could."

14) The oath is quoted: "Surely," etc., Gen. 22:17, but it is worded in direct discourse instead of in the original indirect form. It is also abbreviated because the oath is the main feature that is here emphasized. The promise was given to Abraham already in Gen. 12:7 whereas the oath was not added until Gen. 22:17; yet the promise was repeated in Gen. 22:17, and it was that whole promise which God sealed with his oath. The writer's statement is brief but entirely correct. We regard εἰ μήν as the correct reading; on ἦ and εἰ μήν note R. 192; 1024; 1150. All of these are particles that are used in oaths. The repetition of the participle with the verb: "blessing I will bless thee," imitates the He-

brew infinitive absolute (R. 1110) and strongly emphasizes the idea of the verb; it is like a superlative: "I will bless — multiply thee in the highest degree." Since the oath lies in the particles, this wording includes also the promise that is sealed by the oath.

15) And thus, having exercised longsuffering, he obtained the promise. This matches v. 12, "those who by means of longsuffering are inheriting the promises." So, in the same way, after exercising longsuffering, Abraham did obtain the promise. It ought not to be necessary to explain that this means that Abraham got what was promised and not that he got only the promise as a promise. Verse 12 likewise speaks of heirs who, one after another, actually get the inheritance, who are not merely made heirs that still have to wait for the inheritance.

An exaggerated literalism has the gift promised to Abraham consist of his multiplied descendants. But such an interpretation is untenable, for when Abraham died he saw only Isaac, his son, and Esau and Jacob, his grandsons. This interpretation is not improved by saying that Abraham saw the beginning of what was promised him in these three and so obtained the promise. Nor should it be said that what Abraham obtained was something that he lived to see and not something beyond this life, of which the readers could have no direct knowledge.

The sworn promise to Abraham centered in Christ. It was eternal salvation in Christ. Abraham obtained this at his death. Look at Matt. 8:11: Abraham is in the kingdom of heaven with Isaac and Jacob, and many are coming from the east and the west to sit down with him in that kingdom for the heavenly feast. The writer speaks of these many in 1:14 and 6:12, who inherit salvation one by one. They include both Jewish and Gentile believers, Abraham being the spiritual father of them all (Rom. 4:11-13); his seed is multiplied indeed.

Hebrews 6:15

How Zahn can place Abraham in the *Totenreich* and there let him get news of what happened 2,000 years after his death, is difficult to understand. Besides, this *Totenreich* is but extravagant fiction (see the author on John 8:56). Let no conceptions of earthly time disturb you; when Abraham died and entered the kingdom he beheld "the Lamb slain from the foundation of the world" (Rev. 13:8). He then obtained the promise (the verb takes the genitive) just as we do when at our death we go to recline with him at the feast in the heavenly kingdom.

Yet he obtained only "after having exercised longsuffering." In v. 12 we have the noun and here the aorist participle. In v. 12 faith and longsuffering are combined; here the latter is sufficient since the former has already been mentioned, and since longsuffering is never without faith. See v. 12 for the meaning of μακροθυμία, which is true also with regard to the verb. During his life Abraham had only the sworn promise of God; how he fared among men made no difference to him, note what is said in 11:8-10. Patiently, steadily he waited, "expecting the city having foundations, whose designer and maker is God." Abraham dismissed earth, men, and what men thought and did regarding him. It was "thus" that he obtained the promise.

We construe: "thus . . . he obtained," the adverb as a modifier of the main verb, i. e., "thus" as was promised with God's great, sure oath. He could not fail to obtain; assurance was actually doubled (v. 18), he had the promise and the oath in addition. Some construe: "having thus exercised longsuffering," the adverb as a modifier of the participle. It is found next to the participle, yet the participle and the main verb form a unit: "having exercised longsuffering he obtained," and the stress is on the main verb, on the great fact that he obtained. If "thus" is restricted to the participle, the implication would result that, save for

God's oath, Abraham might not have exercised longsuffering.

16) The explanation introduced by "for" extends to all that follows in v. 16-20 and not merely to v. 16. First, noting the effect of an oath among men generally, we are told that God swore his oath to Abraham, not for the sake of Abraham alone (which does not need to be said after v. 15), but especially on our account, so that we might have strong assurance and an anchor for the soul. We need but look at Abraham, at the way in which he obtained the promise, namely as sealed by God's oath, and then think a bit and remember how even among men an oath settles things, and how God's oath to Abraham refers directly to us. This would have a stronger force for the first readers since they were actually of Abraham's blood and already when they were Jews knew about the promise and the oath to Abraham and how one must ever be a true son of Abraham in order to inherit the promise that was made to him.

For men swear by the greater, and the oath (thus sworn) **is an end for them of all contrary statement, as far as making a thing firm is concerned.** This is the preliminary point which is made with a view to the main point that is about to be added. Men swear by the greater, namely by God, κατά as in v. 13. The result is that such an oath settles any matter to which such an oath is made: "it is an end (πέρας) for men of all contrary statement." They will no longer listen to any statement that contradicts the one that is sealed by such an oath. This is true when men take an oath, how much more, then, when God himself makes a sworn statement, in this case a promise, although he is compelled to swear by himself. Εἰs βεβαίωσιν is terse, and the noun is a word expressing an action: "for confirmation," which we expand in translation in order to bring out its meaning: "as far as making a thing firm is concerned." The Greek can place ὁ ὅρκος emphatically at the end; the article denotes "the oath" thus sworn by the greater who is God.

17) The sentence continues with a relative which connects God's oath with the effect of oaths in general: **wherein God, the more abundantly intending to show to the heirs of the promise the immutability of his counsel, interposed with an oath in order that by means of two immutable things, in which it is impossible for God to lie, we may have strong encouragement, who found refuge so as to hold fast to the proffered hope, which we have as an anchor of the soul, both sure and firm and extending into the inner part behind the veil, where as a forerunner there entered in in our behalf Jesus, become a High Priest forever according to the order of Melchizedek.**

The ἐν phrase = "wherein," namely "in connection with the fact just expressed about the value of oaths." God made use of the oath in order to shut out any doubt, question, or contradiction. He wanted the more abundantly to show forth the immutability of his counsel and so interposed with an oath (dative of means). The comparative means "more abundantly" than if he had used the promise alone. We construe it with the participle where it is placed: "more abundantly intending," etc. The R. V. combines it with the infinitive: "to show more abundantly." The participle and the infinitive "intending to show" form one idea, and the adverb thus affects both. The substantivized neuter adjective means "the immutable feature" of God's counsel, βουλή, as in Acts 20:27, that which God had resolved to do and thus promised. This "counsel" of God embraces the entire gospel plan regarding our salvation in Christ.

"By means of *two* immutable things" accords with the principle which runs throughout Scripture that at least two testimonies are legally necessary to establish a matter: Deut. 17:6; 19:15; Matt. 18:16; John 8:17, 18; II Cor. 13:1; Heb. 10:28. In John 6:31, 32 and 36, 37 Jesus himself complies with this necessity as he does also in 8:17, 18. Finally, two witnesses attest the whole of Revelation, the one witness in Rev. 22:16, the second in 22:18. We need not cite the passages that deal with the trial of Jesus and with that of Stephen. God himself complied with this principle, and since there is not a second person to testify, he interposed his oath "in order that by means of *two* immutable things, in which it is impossible for God to lie," the immutability of his counsel may be established, and we may be absolutely assured. Astounding condescension, yet a fact.

This "counsel" God wanted to show "to the heirs of the promise," of whom Abraham was one and all his multiplied spiritual children the rest. God's oath is for all of them by covering, as it does, the promise which pertains to all of them. The heirs are not Abraham's heirs but, including Abraham, the joint heirs of Christ (Rom. 8:17) who is the supreme Heir (1:2). The claim that these heirs are only those who are of Jewish descent is not tenable although this epistle is addressed to Hebrews and not also to Gentiles. The writer draws no distinction as Paul does in many places, note Rom. 4:10-13 (where Abraham himself is called an heir). "Heirs of the promise" recalls v. 12: "those inheriting the promise," and 1:14: "those about to inherit salvation." God intends this double assurance for all of them, namely that of his promise and that of his oath.

The discussion regarding the exact meaning of the intransitive ἐμεσίτευσεν is not serious. The R. V.'s "he interposed with an oath" is better than the A. V.'s margin: "he interposed himself by an oath," which some explain as meaning that God stepped in between himself as making the promise and the heirs to whom he made it, he, by swearing the oath, becoming not only the maker of the promise but also the witness—some say the *Buerge* or bondsman—guaranteeing the genuineness of the promise and thus its fulfillment. This would make God act in a double capacity, which is a complicated idea. It seems much simpler to make the oath itself the mediation between the promise and the heirs of that promise.

18) God used an oath "in order that by means of two immutable things, in which it is impossible for God to lie, we may have strong encouragement," etc. So much concerned was God to have all the heirs impressed with "the immutability of his counsel." To his immutable promise he added his immutable oath; thus there are two πράγματα or affairs in which it is absolutely impossible for God to lie. The writer uses the plain word "to lie." Any of his readers who would turn away from Christ and revert to Judaism would thereby charge God with a double lie: that his promise does not mean what it says; that his oath is perjury. That very idea would be blasphemy. The matter is put so bluntly because the writer fears lest there remain in any of his readers "a wicked heart of unbelief" (3:12).

From the generalizing third person, "the heirs of the promise," he now turns to the first person: "in order that . . . we may have strong encouragement," etc., for we surely intend to belong to these heirs. Παράκλησις has several meanings according to the context; "encouragement" (R. V.) is better here than "consolation" (A. V.). It is "encouragement" to hold out in sure faith and hope by relying on the immutable promise and on the immutable oath until we at last receive what is thus promised and sealed to us.

"We" in the verb receives a significant apposition: "who found refuge so as to hold fast to the proffered hope." The perfective κατά in the participle coincides with the effective aorist tense (R. 827), the verb itself means "to find refuge" (R. 828). Our versions translate with an infinitive of purpose: "who have fled for refuge to lay hold of the hope," etc. This is the accepted construction although Thayer is one of the few who call the infinitive one of purpose. While the infinitive belongs to the participle and not to παράκλησιν, we fail to see how the infinitive can signify purpose even when the participle is taken to mean "who fled for refuge," *die wir unsere Zuflucht dazu genommen haben, die Hoffnung zu ergreifen*. We prefer to regard it as an infinitive of result: "we who found refuge so as to hold fast to the proffered hope." The participle looks back to the mortal danger from which we escaped; the infinitive looks forward to the result achieved in this escape, laying hold of the sure and certain hope, and προκειμένη describes it as the hope "set before us," "proffered" by God's sworn promise.

Some interpreters regard this "hope" as subjective, the hope that animates our souls. But this view is not supported by the modifiers. The hope is "set before us," proffered to us by God, and we grasp firm hold of it. This surely means that it is objective, the thing for which we hope. The subjective feature is found in the infinitive, our fast hold on this hope proffered to us.

19) We now have this hope "as an anchor of the soul" to prevent our being swept away. Hope is often likened to an anchor, not to one that is lying in the ship, but to one that is gripping the bottom of the sea and holding the ship. The adjective plus the participle are predicative and belong to "anchor" and describe it as "sure" because it is "firm" and firm because "extending into the inner part of the veil," we should say, "behind the veil."

The καταπέτασμα τοῦ ναοῦ is the inner curtain or veil that hung between the Holy and the Holy of Holies as the readers, being Hebrews, well knew. In the Herodian Sanctuary a second curtain hung before the Holy. This, too, was at times called καταπέτασμα, and the plural was used as a designation for both curtains. But the regular term for the outer curtain was κάλυμμα, and only occasionally was the other term used. There is no reason to think of anything but the curtain before the Holy of Holies in this verse.

The writer says that the anchor of our soul extends into the inner part behind this curtain; it grips the Holy of Holies, the very ark of the covenant, the mercy seat where the atoning blood was sprinkled by the high priest. We know that he is not thinking of the physical Herodian Sanctuary in which the ark of the covenant no longer stood, nor even of the Tabernacle in the wilderness or of Solomon's Temple and Sanctuary. He has in mind the Holy of Holies in heaven, into which Jesus entered with his all-atoning blood.

For fear of mixing figures by placing an anchor in the Sanctuary behind the veil the R. V. connects all three modifiers with the relative; Riggenbach leaves the two adjectives with "an anchor" but has the participle modify the relative and thus "hope." The feared mixture of figures disappears when we note that "the inner part behind the veil" is not a figure but language that is taken from the earthly type in order to designate the reality of the heavenly antitype, which would at once be understood by the readers who were former Jews. As the anchor is out of sight, so the hope, promised and sworn to us, is out of sight. It is in the heavenly Sanctuary. It is the promised salvation through the all-atoning blood of Jesus.

20) It is "where as a forerunner there entered in in our behalf Jesus, become a High Priest forever according to the order of Melchizedek." "Jesus" is the proper name for him; it is the name that Pilate wrote on the superscription on his cross when he shed his blood "in our behalf" and then entered into the Holy

of Holies of heaven with that blood, there to make his sacrifice count "in our behalf." He acted as our High Priest in this, but did so in a high priesthood that was of a higher order than that of Aaron who never entered as our forerunner whom we are to follow, who always retained the veil in order to keep Israel out. Jesus removed the barrier of the veil. We see this typified in the case of the earthly Sanctuary when the veil was rent in twain (Matt. 27:51). Through the blood of Jesus we may now approach the mercy seat and live forever. Note that "Jesus" is placed emphatically at the end just as ὁ ὅρκος is in v. 16.

The writer has several times called Jesus "High Priest" and twice "High Priest according to the order of Melchizedek" (5:6, 10). This is now repeated for the third time with the addition of "forever" ("for the eon") as was done in v. 6 where it is quoted from Ps. 110:4. See 5:6 as to what this designation means. The writer is now ready and considers his readers ready for the full exposition which follows in chapter 7. Some take the aorist γενόμενος to mean that Jesus did not "become" our eternal High Priest until he entered heaven. That is the same as saying that the Jewish high priest became high priest only the moment he entered behind the veil. Jesus was High Priest during his entire office; when he shed his blood on the cross, and when he ascended to heaven forty days later, this office of his reached its climax.

CHAPTER VII

The Fourth Main Part

Jesus, the High Priest after the Order of Melchizedek, chapter 7

Introductory: The Scriptural Data Regarding Melchizedek, v. 1-3.

1) This strange person, who appears suddenly in and disappears as suddenly from the Scripture record (Gen. 14:18-20), who is in a remarkable way unexpectedly referred to by David in a quotation from God himself (Ps. 110:4), has given rise to still stranger speculation as to his identity. Rabbi Ismael, about 135 B. C., thought him to be Shem, Noah's son; this opinion has been accepted by Luther and by others. Philo saw in him a figure of the human soul, divine reason functioning in a priestly way as the ὀρθὸς λόγος (the upright word) that controlled the passions, delighted the soul and honored God with exalted thought; he did not regard Melchizedek as a historical person. Origen thought him to be an angel being; others specified this angel as Michael. Hierakas, at the end of the third century, made him a temporary incarnation of the Holy Spirit, others a similar incarnation of the Logos. Theodot, 200 B. C., and the sect of the Melchizedekites made him μεγάλην τινὰ δύναμιν, greater than Christ, the original of whom Christ was only a copy, through whom all prayers must be brought to God. There have been still other opinions.

There are three short verses in Genesis, one in the Psalms, nothing more in the rest of the Bible, yet here in Hebrews we have an elaborate exposition concerning Melchizedek and Christ. It is the statement made in the psalm that sheds the divine light on Melchizedek and those three verses of Genesis. Yet already this fact arrests attention, namely that God himself should so long a time after Abraham refer to Melchizedek in Genesis when he was speaking of David's son who was David's Lord. It was reserved for our epistle to add the complete light.

There was a call for it now. The readers, former Jews who were now thinking of returning to Judaism, are here confronted with their great forefather Abraham and are shown how he accepted the royal priest Melchizedek long before Levi and Aaron were born and the Aaronitic high priesthood came into existence. The readers want to be true sons of Abraham, yea, are thinking of returning to Judaism for that very reason. Well, let them look at Abraham and at the one priest to whom Abraham bowed. Let them consider what God said through David regarding this royal priest and regarding the Messiah-Christ who is typified by Melchizedek.

The very objection which the readers may raise against Jesus, the fact that he was not a son of Levi but descended from the tribe of Judah, was not in the Aaronic succession and thus not a legitimate priest and high priest, is made the most overwhelming proof for the absolutely exceptional, for the eternal High Priesthood of Jesus, which is, indeed, not according to the order of Aaron but, as God himself had declared by David, "according to the order of Melchizedek." Our High Priest must also be King eternal who has none to precede and none to succeed him, who is far beyond Aaron by being after the type of Melchizedek. All that God revealed about the significance of Melchizedek in David's time is thus brought to bear upon the readers of our epistle who need it. Although it appeared to lie dormant in those four Old Testament verses, it is "liv-

Hebrews 7:1

ing and powerful" (4:12) to save the readers from taking a fatal step.

The writer has used the most effective psychological method of approach. He has first prepared his readers. He has repeatedly presented Jesus as our High Priest, in fact, as our Great High Priest (4:14); he has twice quoted God's own statement in the psalm that Jesus was to be Priest and High Priest after the order of Melchizedek (5:6, 10). He has delayed until now to reveal in detail what this means. He has injected the strongest warnings against sluggishness of mind and the deadliness of unbelief. The preparation is complete; he now proceeds, and his exposition leaves nothing to be desired. The first step presents the main historical facts about Melchizedek. These are the data embodied in Genesis. Γάρ = in order that you may fully understand what God means by saying that Jesus is a High Priest forever after the order of Melchizedek (6:20).

For this Melchizedek, king of Salem, priest of God the Most High, the one who met Abraham returning from the slaughter of the kings and blessed him, he to whom Abraham parceled out also a tenth from everything, first, by interpretation, king of righteousness and then also king of Salem, which is king of peace, without father, without mother, without genealogical line, having neither beginning of days nor end of life, but having been made like the Son of God: remains a priest in perpetuity.

"This Melchizedek" = the man whom I have (6:20) so significantly brought to your attention for the third time (5:6, 10). There follows a series of appositions and nominative modifiers until the verb μένει is reached (v. 3). "King of Salem" and "priest of God the Most High" are quoted from Gen. 14:18. These are the significant features because this man was both king and priest and was unlike any other Old Testament personage. It is in vain to ask from what line this king-priest descended; he is "without genealogy" (v. 3), and speculation is useless.

But how could there be "a priest of God the Most High" in this idolatrous country of Canaan? The answer must be that the true religion of Noah had been fully conserved in Melchizedek. "The Most High" is not relative, not polytheistic: the highest of many gods as Zeus was called "the highest"; "Most High" is absolute, monotheistic: High beyond all other things. We now say "God Almighty" to express the same idea. "Most High" appears a number of times in the New Testament, being appropriated from the Old.

The textual evidence supports the reading ὅς instead of the article ὁ; the relative, however, produces a very awkward construction, one that it is impossible to attribute to a writer who is as masterly as our writer shows himself to be. The sigma with which the participle began was evidently written twice by some copyist so that ὁ became ὅς. We regard this expression as another apposition: "the one who met Abraham returning from the slaughter of the kings and blessed him," i. e., who on this occasion exercised his priestly function with regard to no less a person than Abraham. Note v. 7: only the less is blessed by another, who is thereby acknowledged as the greater. The kings that were defeated on this expedition of Abraham's are named in Gen. 14:1, 9: Amraphel, Arioch, Chedorlaomer, and Tidal, i. e., Khammurabi, Eriaku, Kudurlachgumal, and Tudchula as they are called in the inscriptions; yet the identification of Amraphel with Khammurabi is disputed. See Dodds who also notes that the monuments show us that these kings were contemporaries who lived 2,300 B. C.; they also furnish many interesting particulars regarding them.

2) We regard the relative clause as a further appositional statement: "he to whom Abraham parceled

out also a tenth from everything," i. e., a tenth part of all the spoils that were taken from the defeated kings. Καί states that besides receiving the blessing from Melchizedek, Abraham recognized and honored Melchizedek as a divine priest by presenting this notable and grand tithe, and v. 4 adds that it was taken from the finest part of the booty. Here was food for thought for the readers of this epistle: Abraham accepted a priest of the Highest who had no connection with the Aaronitic priesthood.

We do not adopt the parenthesis of the R. V.; we do not even need ἐστί which some supply, or "being" (A. V.). We regard the following as an apposition; ἑρμηνευόμενος is merely inserted in the sense of "by interpretation" or "when interpreted": "first, by interpretation, 'king of righteousness,' and then also king of Salem, which is 'king of peace.'" Blessing Abraham and receiving the tenth from Abraham in a double way emphasize the *priesthood* of Melchizedek; his *kingship* is made evident by his names: the Hebrew "Melchizedek" means "king of righteousness," and "king of Salem" means "king of peace."

The main point does not, however, lie in his being a king of some kind like the four kings Abraham had defeated but in his being king in harmony with his divine priesthood, a priest-king, who ought thus to be a king of "righteousness" and a king "of peace." This priest was the former by virtue of his very name and the latter by virtue of the name of the capital which he ruled. The point in noting the meaning of the names is the fact that they reflect the very attributes of Jesus, our royal High Priest, who in the very highest sense is the King of righteousness, the King of peace. The names of the type point to the far greater antitype. We may perhaps add that righteousness is the personal quality which shows itself in righteous ruling, while peace is the result for the capital that is ruled in righteousness, this capital being called "Salem" or "Peace."

It makes little difference whether we are able to identify the capital that was ruled by Melchizedek, to know whether this was, indeed, the later Jerusalem, which was in Melchizedek's time called "Salem," or some other city. Jerome favors a Salem (Salumias) that was located eight Roman miles from Scythopolis, eighty from Sodom. On the question of topography see Smith, *Dictionary of the Bible*, IV, 2788, etc. Some think that "king of peace" refers to no city at all but is a personal name like "king of righteousness"; but this is an untenable assumption. As in the case of ἑρμηνευόμενος, the Greek injects ὅ ἐστι, *id est*, almost anywhere in a sentence. Πρῶτον μέν and ἔπειτα δέ = "in the first place . . . in the second place."

3) The three adjectives and the two participles seem to be further appositions to the subject. The description advances beyond what is stated in Genesis in so many words to what appears in Genesis regarding this priest: he lacked everything that a Jewish priest had to have. He was "without father, without mother, without genealogical line, having neither beginning of days nor end of life." Every Aaronitic priest had to be able to trace and to establish his genealogy or be excluded from the priesthood (Ezra 7:63, 64); he was restricted even as to the wife he might marry, thus even the female line of descent (Ezek. 44:22; Lev. 21:7) was safeguarded.

All these regulations concerning parentage, genealogy, time of birth and time of death, and children born to continue the priestly line, all of which were so essential for the Aaronitic priests, were completely absent in the case of Melchizedek. The idea is not that he had no father and no mother, no ancestors and no descendants, no day of birth and no day of death. This is the extravagant supposition of those who made Melchizedek an angel, the Holy Spirit, etc., as noted above. The point is that, as far as the Scripture record is concerned, king-priest though this record makes him, it does so while omitting all these things because they are regarded as being wholly immaterial.

"Without father," etc., means that the Scriptures completely ignore his descent. Melchizedek did *not* inherit, nor did he transmit his priesthood, royal though it was. It depended on no connection backward or forward but inhered in his person alone; it was wholly independent of any connection save that with God. The old genealogical records were kept very meticulously, but Melchizedek's name and his line are found in none of them. He appears, he vanishes — that is all. Yet Abraham bows to his priesthood, Abraham, in whom all the nations were to be blessed (6:14). This fact must have been stunning to the first readers of our epistle who had in mind to leave Christianity for the old Jewish priesthood.

It is the second participle that caps the climax: because of all that v. 3 has said of him this Melchizedek is one who "has been made like the Son of God," the perfect tense indicating that he remains so. Not, indeed, as the church fathers thought, that as the Son of God Jesus had no human genealogy and no successor but that, like Melchizedek, nothing, absolutely nothing depended on the human genealogy of Jesus as far as his priesthood was concerned. The genealogies of Jesus, that of his legal father in Matthew, that of his physical mother in Luke, extend back to royal David and back of that, the former to Abraham, the latter to Adam, and nowhere are there any priestly ancestors; his tribe is that of Judah and not of Levi. The sudden way in which the Scriptures draw back and close the curtain on Melchizedek is the divine way of making him a type of Jesus, the King-Priest, who, like Melchizedek, stands alone and unique in his priesthood and is absolutely distinct from the long Aaronitic succession of priests.

"This Melchizedek" (v. 1), as he is described by all the appositions including the last participle which states his likeness to the Son of God, "remains a priest in perpetuity." How? He remains so because the type is perpetuated in the antitype Jesus. Thus "this Melchizedek remains in perpetuity." The difference between εἰς τὸν αἰῶνα, "for the eon," i. e., "forever" (5:6; 6:20) and εἰς τὸ διηνεκές is the fact that the former expresses eternity, the latter continuance or perpetuity. Jesus is eternal in his royal priesthood; Melchizedek is perpetual, his priesthood is perpetuated in Jesus. Jesus is independent, absolute; Melchizedek is dependent on the antitype Jesus, and his priesthood is thus relative.

Some would eliminate Melchizedek and have "remains a priest in perpetuity" refer only to Jesus. Others eliminate "the historic Melchizedek" and retain only an abstraction, "the typically prophetic Melchizedek picture." Some group together and let hang in the air all save the last participial modifier and then have "remains," etc., refer only to that. We do not, of course, share these views.

To be sure, Melchizedek died, and after his death he could neither bless as a priest as he once blessed Abraham, nor as a priest receive a tenth as he once did from Abraham; he ceased to function as a king-priest. Even if one should claim that, like Enoch, Melchizedek was transferred to heaven, he would have ceased to function. Only the Melchizedekites, who placed Jesus far below Melchizedek, could say that Melchizedek functioned and still functions and that all our prayers reach God through him. The text does not say that Melchizedek functions but that he "remains" in perpetuity. And it is *he*, "this Melchizedek," and not the mere Bible picture of him that remains; Ps. 110:4 states that this is due to the fact that David's Son and David's Lord is a Priest forever according to the order of Melchizedek. As real as is the antitype, so real remains and must remain his type, "this Melchizedek."

The Greatness of Melchizedek in Receiving a Tenth from Abraham, v. 4-10.

4) More must be said about Abraham's giving a tenth of the spoils of his victory over the kings to Melchizedek. This act of Abraham's is of the highest significance in regard to Melchizedek, the enduring type of Jesus, our King-Priest. Δέ takes up the new point. **Now behold how great this man is to whom Abraham gave a tenth out of the choice spoils, he, the patriarch!**

The readers are asked to look long and attentively at this point. Πηλίκος οὗτος is an indirect question, ἐστί being omitted. The relative clause is causal, for from Abraham's act one may judge how great he at least thought Melchizedek to be. A tenth he gave him (the emphasis is on the object) as priests receive a tenth, and that was selected out of the prime and most valuable pieces of the booty. Abraham did not make up a tenth out of the poorer articles but out of the most precious, and by this act showed his lofty estimate of Melchizedek. Gen. 14:20 says only "a tenth of all"; the fact that this consisted of the best parts must have been a point that had been conserved by oral tradition. "He, the patriarch," is placed significantly at the end in order to emphasize the greatness of Abraham and thus the more to enhance the greatness of Melchizedek.

5) Καί adds what Abraham's giving a tenth really involves when one considers the law of tithes; μέν and δέ balance the comparison between the Levitical priests and Melchizedek. **And, indeed, they from Levi's sons receiving the priesthood have commandment to tithe the people by the law, that is, their brethren, although having come out of the loins of Abraham; but he who does not reckon his genealogy**

from them has tithed Abraham and has blessed him who has the promises.

"Indeed" is too strong a translation for μέν, yet we need a word to translate this particle, and "indeed" is about the best we have. Ἐκ is not partitive; with οἱ it means "the descendants of Levi" and is modified by the participle "receiving the priesthood." We have already noted that some of Levi's descendants were excluded from the priesthood, those, namely, who married improperly or were unable to prove their descent. To the tribe of Levi there belonged the priesthood or the priestly service (Deut. 31:9; Josh. 18:7). They had received it through Aaron and Aaron's descendants. Levi is mentioned instead of Aaron in order to show the connection with Abraham more closely, for Levi himself was not a priest.

Thus they "have commandment to tithe the people by the law," the Mosaic law which embodied such a commandment and lent it divine sanction. This means that they had the legal right to tithe their own brethren, the point of which is made plainer by the addition "although (these brethren) have come out of the loins of Abraham." The circumstance that brethren should have the legal right and the divine sanction to tithe brethren, and brethren who had come from Abraham's loins, is remarkable but a fact; this is the force of καίπερ. Note how this tithing is related to Abraham himself through Levi. This is done because of what is said regarding Abraham in the comparison that is here made.

6) Something that is even more remarkable is now stated, something of which the readers had probably never thought: "but he who does not reckon his genealogy from them," who is not related to the sons of Levi or to Levi, who, in fact, has no recorded genealogy at all (v. 3), "has tithed" no less a person than "Abraham" himself, and has done that without apply-

ing a law—Abraham, who never before or after was tithed by anybody. "Has tithed" does not mean that Melchizedek demanded a tenth from Abraham but only that he received it when Abraham, recognizing the priestly greatness of Melchizedek, voluntarily brought him the tenth. "And," priest that he was, "has blessed him who has the promises," by this act, too, showing the kind of priest he is, one who was so high that, although Abraham had the promises of God (6:14), the very greatest of blessing, he could still bless Abraham. Note that "he has tithed and has blessed" are perfect tenses because of the lasting significance and effect of these priestly acts.

7) Δέ adds the principle which sheds the fullest light on these acts on the part of Melchizedek: **Now without dispute the less is blessed by the greater.** We should not separate the two acts, that of blessing and that of receiving the tenth, and think that something is now said only about the blessing. What receiving the tenth really means appears most clearly from the bestowing of the blessing. The two constitute a unit. In v. 6 blessing is mentioned in the second place only because blessing is used in v. 7; in v. 8-10 the tithe is further discussed, yet here, too, not apart from the blessing. It is a universally acknowledged fact that he who blesses is greater than he who is blessed. The Greek has the neuter singular in classic fashion and thereby brings out the idea of quality the more although this pertains to persons (B.-D. 138, 1), and R. 409, 763 add that this neuter singular is also used in a collective sense when a plurality of persons is involved. As far as bestowing and receiving blessing are concerned, the former quality makes this person greater than the one that has the latter quality.

Although he was blessed by God with the promises Abraham acknowledged himself as being less than Melchizedek when he bowed beneath Melchizedek's blessing. Abraham was right, for Abraham was not the king-priest, Melchizedek was; Abraham was not the royal-priestly type of Jesus, Melchizedek was. All the greatness of Abraham remains; by his very greatness he shows "how great" (v. 4) Melchizedek is. If someone should object that we bless God (James 3:9) and certainly are not greater than God, the answer is that we do so only with our tongue and not as was done here when Melchizedek acted for God by blessing Abraham.

8) Καί does not add a second and a separate item, nor does the καί used in v. 9 add a third. These verses complete the thought of the preceding so that we understand the whole of what is stated in v. 4-7. For the superiority of Melchizedek over Abraham includes his superiority over all the priests who were descended from Abraham through Levi. Although these, too, received tithes, this does not place them on an equality with Melchizedek; they actually paid a tithe to Melchizedek in Abraham. Μέν and δέ again balance the statements.

And here dying men are receiving tithes, but there one who has witness that he lives. And, to state it plainly, through Abraham even Levi, he who receives tithes, has been tithed, for he was yet in the loins of his father when Melchizedek met him. Verse 8 is preliminary; v. 9, 10 contain the main thought. "Here" points to the nearer fact, "there" to the one that is more remote.

Here "dying men are receiving tithes." One after another they die, and the tithes go to their successors in a continuous line. "There, however" (in the case of Melchizedek), we see nothing of the kind. Melchizedek has no successors to whom the high honor of receiving a tithe from anybody was or could be handed on. Melchizedek receives the one tithe from Abraham, Melchizedek who was "one given the testimony (passive) that he lives." It is certainly not the writer who at this late date and on the basis of conclusions at which his thinking has arrived gives Melchizedek this testimony. The testimony "that he lives" is given Melchizedek in the Scriptures.

Commentators are divided as to where this testimony is to be found: some think of Gen. 14, some prefer Ps. 110, while others appeal to both. The point is that the Scriptures deal only with the living Melchizedek and not with his having "an end of life" (v. 3). This is the fact, and he is said to live, not because he did not finally die, but because his royal priesthood was in no way affected by his death as was the priesthood of all the Levitical priests, which called for a continuous succession of priests, a constant transfer of office.

"He lives" does not mean that "Melchizedek still lives physically" but that "Melchizedek, as the typical king-priest lives in the antitypical King-Priest Jesus." His one act with regard to Abraham, royal and priestly as it was, stands irrespective of his physical death, stands in the King-Priest Jesus, who also by one act is what Melchizedek typifies.

There is no need to say that only "a Biblical *picture* of Melchizedek" lives as though the *reality* of Melchizedek is gone. Have we, then, also only a picture of the Levitical priests? No; we have also their reality. But even their picture would not be true to fact if it did not include their constant dying and succession, because this is the very feature which, in contrast with Melchizedek, marks *their* priesthood and any significance of it in connection with Jesus; for Jesus was not after their order but "after the order of Melchizedek." In the case of both Melchizedek and Jesus predecessors and successors cannot have a place.

9) The main statement follows. This is, however, misunderstood by some who take the parenthetical ὡς ἔπος εἰπεῖν to mean "as speaking loosely," i. e., not exact-

ly. Some say that what follows is not to be taken literally; but it is to be taken so. Others think the expression means that the following statement is bold and not unobjectionable, but that the writer ventures to make it nevertheless. Just about the opposite is true. This common phrase (although it is found only here in the New Testament) = "to use the right word," "to use a strong expression" (B.-P. 475), "to speak out freely" (Liddell and Scott, 589). Any one of these meanings is fitting, for this is exactly what the writer does when he says that Levi was still in the loins of Abraham when Abraham paid the tenth to Mechizedek; he uses the proper expression.

Stating it in a word, and that plainly: even Levi, the one who receives tithes, has himself been tithed through Abraham. To state it thus is telling in a double way. Levi never received tithes in person; he received them only through the Aaronitic priesthood which consisted of his descendants. So also, looking backward, Levi was not in person tithed by Melchizedek; he was tithed only through his great-grandfather Abraham at a time when that great-grandfather had not yet begotten Levi's grandfather Isaac. The former point helps to explain and to justify the latter.

Yes, Levi, the very receiver of tithes, "has been tithed" (perfect tense as in v. 6) and thus stands forever as one who was tithed. Abraham's act counts for all his descendants. Why speak of it as being "perhaps open to objection," as "loose" and not "literal" when countless acts of ancestors are regarded in the same way today? Did Adam's act not put death upon all of us (Rom. 5:12)? When a king abdicates, does that not count also for his sons and for their sons? When I squander my property, do my heirs still retain it? Why speak of Levi as not personally giving assent to what was done by Abraham before Levi was born? Although he was at that time unborn and gave no personal assent did Levi not share in Abraham's blessing, both that which was bestowed by God and that which was pronounced by Melchizedek?

10) The final "for" clause merely rounds out the whole statement that Levi and the entire priesthood that was descended from him bowed before Melchizedek in and through Abraham, their forefather. Can anything resembling that be said of Melchizedek? Thus the readers and all of us to this day behold how great this Melchizedek is (v. 4).

The Levitic Priesthood Brought no Completion and Itself Necessitated a Priest according to the Order of Melchizedek, v. 11-17.

11) The preceding section is built up on the very greatness of Abraham; but Melchizedek and the royal-kingly priesthood represented in him are shown to be even greater than Abraham. We have also seen that the priesthood that had its source in Abraham through Levi was beneath Melchizedek and the priesthood which he represents. Now we learn in what respect the Levitical priesthood is lacking and thus necessitated a greater priesthood, namely the one that is typified in Melchizedek and that is before us in Jesus, "a Priest forever according to the order of Melchizedek." Οὖν does not indicate a deduction but only a transition to this new side of the subject.

If, then, completion was by means of the Levitical priesthood (the people, indeed, have been subjected to laws on its score) what need yet that according to the order of Melchizedek there arise a different kind of priest and be designated as not according to the order of Aaron? For, with the priesthood undergoing a change, of necessity a change also of law occurs. For he of whom these things are said has belonged to a different tribe from which no one has (ever) attended the sacrificial altar. For it

is evident that our Lord has sprung out of Judah, a tribe in regard to which Moses uttered nothing pertaining to priests.

The condition is not one of unreality: "if there *were*" (A. V.), but of simple reality: "if there *was*" (R. V.); the writer assumes for the moment that completion actually *was* by way of the Levitical priesthood and on that assumption asks what is then an unanswerable question: "What need yet that according to the order of Melchizedek there arise a different kind of a priest," etc.? This could, of course, be expressed in the form of a present or of a past unreality: "If there were, or if there had been . . . what need would there be, or would there have been?" But either form of unreality would require a verb in the question, an imperfect or an aorist, preferably with ἄν.

Τελείωσις is a word expressing an action: "completing" or "completion by means of the Levitical priesthood," ἱερωσύνη, the institution: "priesthood" as distinguished from ἱερατεία in v. 5, "the priestly service." The thought is: "if the Levitical priesthood was the means of completing everything for which priesthood was designed," nothing more in the way of a priesthood was evidently needed. Yet God did not think so, for in Ps. 110 he speaks of an entirely different kind of priest (ἕτερον ἱερέα). The readers are confronted with the question: "What need yet that according to the order of Melchizedek there arise a different kind of priest, and (that he) be designated (λέγεσθαι) not according to the order of Aaron?" This is not a case of οὐ with the infinitive; the negative negates the phrase and makes the opposition sharp; a Melchizedek kind of a priest and *not* an Aaronitic kind.

The question is made acute by the insertion of the parenthesis: "the people, indeed, have been subjected to laws on its score," ἐπ' αὐτῆς (note the genitive!). The λαός are the Jewish people who not only had the Levitical priesthood as nations have certain institutions that have grown up in their midst but had been put under law by God on the score of this priesthood. God gave the Levitical priesthood to the Jews and then imposed a number of laws upon them with regard to this priesthood. The perfect tense "have been lawed," i. e., "have been subjected to law," stresses the condition as continuing thus under the laws imposed. So far removed is the writer from in any way detracting from the Levitical priesthood, so far from trying even covertly to make it appear inferior, that he himself brings out as fully as any Jew possibly could the high standing of this priesthood which was fortified by a whole system of divine laws as if this priesthood was the final thing to produce completion, to bring the Jewish people to the τέλος or goal, as far as expiation, salvation, and all else in their relation to God are concerned.

So a Jew might in truth exalt the Jewish priesthood. Where in all the world was there a priesthood that was graced thus, fortified thus by a system of legal enactments that had been made by God himself? The readers of our epistle seem to have had such thoughts when they were inclined toward Judaism. Here is their answer: if this Levitical priesthood, which is supported by all this law, was, indeed, the means for completion so that nothing more needed to be provided for, what need was there for God to arrange for an altogether different kind of priest as he did in Ps. 110?

'Επ' αὐτῆς is misunderstood by some, including our versions, which translate *"under it* the people received the law." But this is not the force of ἐπί. Some render "on the basis of it," etc. (B.-P. 445), which is also not the sense of the author. The phrase means *"on top of it"* the people have received law in order to keep this priesthood intact, to regulate it, to maintain its authority. What law is referred to is evident: it is not the whole Mosaic law but the laws that pertain to this priesthood; γάρ is added in the confirmatory sense of "indeed."

12) But was this volume of law supporting the Levitical, Aaronitic priesthood not unalterable? "For" explains: "For with the priesthood undergoing a change, of necessity a change also of law occurs." God, making a change or a transfer in the priesthood, namely from that "according to the order of Aaron" to that "according to the order of Melchizedek" as we see this in Ps. 110, necessarily changes also any "law" (no article) that supports the Aaronitic priesthood. The statement is couched in present tenses (participle in the genitive absolute and the main verb) as being a self-evident proposition which holds good irrespective of the time when the change is made. Μετατιθεμένης and μετάθεσις are mild terms that refer only to a change; the change was a complete termination of the Aaronitic priesthood, which was superseded by the Melchizedekian priesthood of Jesus, the Son of God.

The Jews as well as any other readers of this epistle were mistaken if they believed that the laws regarding the Aaronitic priesthood were unalterable and thus also made that priesthood unalterable. These laws rested only on the priesthood. When this priesthood was set aside, the laws of necessity went with it. "Completion" had to be attained; God could not permit inadequate means and laws concerning such means to stand in the way. These means and these laws served their temporary purpose; and when the time came, they had to be changed for something that would be permanent, complete, eternal.

13) Another "for" takes us a step farther: "For he of whom these things are said" in Ps. 110 by God himself and restated in detail right here by the writer "has belonged to a different tribe from which no one

has (ever) attended the sacrificial altar." These things are said about Jesus who is not of the tribe of Levi but of a different tribe, no member of which was ever a priest, ever like the Levitical priests functioned at the great altar outside of the Sanctuary where all sacrifices were burnt; for this is the meaning of θυσιαστήριον. A mighty change, indeed, a change to an entirely different tribe which ignored all laws that had confined the former priesthood to Levi and to Aaron!

The antecedent is embedded in ἐφ' ὅν: "He of whom," etc. Note that this is a singular; the change was made from the many Levitical priests to just one Melchizedekian Great High Priest (4:14). This point is held in abeyance but will be emphasized in v. 23. Note the two perfect tenses; they are not aoristic but descriptive of length of time: having held a permanent place in a different tribe, not having a permanent office at the altar.

14) "For" completes what v. 13 says in an incomplete way: "For it is evident that our Lord has sprung out of Judah, a tribe in regard to which Moses uttered nothing pertaining to priests." Πρόδηλον = "it is perfectly clear or evident" (M.-M. 538), everybody knows. Jesus is named "our Lord"; the pronoun "our" is confessional on the part of the writer and the readers, and "Lord" recalls Ps. 110 where David calls his exalted son "my Lord" *(Adonai)*. "Our Lord" gently draws the readers back to their confession and their faith in him. He has sprung out of Judah, "concerning which tribe Moses said nothing pertaining to priests," namely in all the laws pertaining to priests, laws to which reference is made in v. 11, 12. Even in Gen. 14, in the account about Melchizedek, Judah is not named. The fact that "our Lord" did, indeed, bring the completion, which was not achieved by means of the Levitical priesthood (v. 11), need not be stated, for this is what constitutes him "our Lord." We again have two per-

fect tenses, and they are to be understood in the same sense as they were before; and ἀνατέλλω recalls ἀνατολή (LXX), "Branch," in Jer. 23:5; Zech, 3:8; 6:12.

15) And more abundantly still is it self-evident if in accord with the likeness of Melchizedek there is raised up a priest of a different kind, the one who has become (priest), not in accord with a law of fleshly commandment, but in accord with a power of life indissoluble, for he is attested:

Thou a Priest for the eon
According to the order of Melchizedek.

What is "still more abundantly evident" than the fact that Jesus has sprung out of the tribe of Judah? What has been said in the foregoing (v. 11-13). Some commentators select only one or the other point: that there was no completeness in the Levitical priesthood; that there is need of a different kind of priest; that the law regarding the Aaronitic priesthood had to be changed; that Jesus is not of the tribe of Levi. But all these belong together, and one item cannot be separated from the others. In fact, all this that is even more evident than that Jesus is from a tribe about which Moses says nothing in regard to priests is repeated in the "if" clause which is then brought to its climax in the relative clause (v. 16).

That Jesus sprang from Judah is evident because this is a verifiable historical fact. Matt. 1:3 *sqq.* and Luke 3:33 *sqq.* show that these evangelists verified this fact on the basis of the genealogical records. The standing of Jesus as a priest is far more evident when we note the norm according to which he has become a priest, a norm, ground, or principle that is vastly higher than that seen in the Aaronitic priests (v. 16), one that is attested already in Ps. 110 (v. 17).

All this about Jesus' priesthood is so entirely evident "if in accord with the likeness of Melchizedek there is raised up a priest of a different kind," of which fact there can be no doubt whatever since in Ps. 110 God himself raises him up, namely David's son and David's Lord, "our Lord" (v. 14), with David, the royal ancestor of Jesus, coming from the tribe of Judah. The condition is one of reality: "if" as no one will dare even to question. The writer now says "in accord with the *likeness* of Melchizedek" and thereby expounds what τάξις or "order" in the psalm means. This "if" is only preliminary, the reality to which it points is fully assured.

16) The main point is to be found in the relative clause, ὅς has demonstrative, even causal force: "the one who has become (priest, ever so to remain — perfect tense), not in accord with a law of fleshly commandment, on the contrary (ἀλλά), in accord with a power of life indissoluble." Nothing but "a law of fleshly commandment," an outward law that demanded a certain physical descent and ancestry which extended back to Aaron and thus to Levi, a law that demanded the absence of physical defects, physical purification, marriage with a reputable daughter of Aaron, and the like — nothing more than such a law made Aaronitic priests. In the case of Annas and Caiaphas we see what some of them were. Even when they were noble characters, it was nothing but this outward law that governed their being priests.

Some extend "law" so as to include all that these priests did: sacrifice of animals and of gifts, purifications, etc.; but these official acts are not considered here, we shall hear of them later (9:10, 13). The same is true with regard to the singular "the one who" as already noted in v. 13, "he of whom"; the setting of this one over against the many Aaronitic priests is reserved for v. 23. "A law of fleshly commandment" has the attributive or qualitative genitive. Instead of "a law of flesh" or "a fleshly law" we have the much clearer combination "a law of fleshly commandment," i. e., a law that gives fleshly orders such as pertain to the physical flesh.

In the case of Jesus there was nothing of this kind; "on the contrary, he has become priest in accord with a power of life indissoluble," a power that is inherent in himself. "Of life" is again qualitative, it enables Jesus to declare: "I am the Life" (John 14:6; compare 11:25; 1:4). "Indissoluble" is placed last for the sake of emphasis. No death could dissolve and destroy this life when this priest sacrificed himself as the Lamb of God. Those are right who find the deity of Jesus back of this "life"; the psalm itself declares it in its first verse. They are also right when they place this "life" in the human nature of Jesus, for it shares all his divine attributes. Finally, they are right who connect his "power of life indissoluble" with the priesthood of Jesus and say that it enables him to bestow life also upon us.

17) The writer once more stamps God's own testimony in the psalm on all that has been said: "for he is attested: 'Thou a Priest for the eon according to the order of Melchizedek!'" The power of his indissoluble life makes him a Priest forever, one who is totally different from the whole Aaronitic priesthood, who is comparable only to the one remarkable, typical king-priest Melchizedek as portrayed especially in v. 3. Ps. 110:4 has really been the writer's text, especially from v. 11 on; he thus concludes with it at this point.

Three Convincing Contrasts, v. 18-25.

18) "For" = to explain still more what is said in v. 15-17, and what is thus said also in v. 11-14. We take it that this "for" extends also to v. 20-22, the second contrast that is added to the first by καί, and to v. 23-25, which are added as the third contrast by another καί. All three contrasts are worded in balanced state-

ments; in the first and the third we have μέν and δέ, in the second καθ' ὅσον . . . κατὰ τοσοῦτον καί. This is stylistic excellence.

For on the one hand (μέν) a disannulling occurs of the preceding commandment because of its weakness and unprofitableness — for the law made nothing complete — on the other hand (δέ) a bringing in (occurs) of a better hope by which we draw nigh to God.

This is the first contrast. It carries the thought expressed in v. 12 to its climax, namely, that a change of law necessarily occurs with the change of priesthood. The change of law referred to is not an alteration into a new law regarding priesthood; it is vastly more, a complete "annulling" or cancellation of the whole "preceding commandment" that supported the Levitical priesthood until the time of Jesus. The writer properly says "commandment" (taking over that word from v. 16) because he has in mind that part of the ceremonial law which deals with the priesthood. The reason God makes this disannulling is clearly stated: "because of its weakness and unprofitableness." This carries out the thought begun in v. 11 where it is the Levitical priesthood that fails to bring completion. We see that the very commandment which supports that priesthood suffers from weakness and unprofitableness and is thus the cause of its own annulling.

19) The little parenthesis with its historical aorist of fact puts this cause for disannulling beyond question: "for the law made nothing complete," namely "the law" that is here thought of, the one that pertained to the Levitical priesthood and upheld it, to which the Jewish people were subjected (νενομοθέτηται, v. 11). As "commandment" takes over this word from v. 16, so "the law" takes over "law" from v. 16. In v. 11 it is stated that the Levitical priesthood lacks "completion" (noun), so we now hear that "the law,"

the whole of it, which was given to impose this priesthood on the people, "did not make a thing complete" (verb). All that both this priesthood and the law pertaining to it could do was to precede (note προαγούσης), to pave the way for something better, for something that would, indeed, bring completeness and thus be final. The writer nowhere says that the Levitical priesthood and its supporting law were valueless but quite the contrary. They were weak, and in this sense unprofitable; they could not and actually did not bring anything to completion; in all that they accomplished they left out the final thing that was necessary.

We know what the lack was to which the writer refers. He points to that shortcoming in this verse and explains at length in the three chapters that follow. The Levitical priesthood and its law constituted a shadow (8:5; 9:23; 10:1; Col. 2:17) that was cast by something which was about to follow and was far greater, a shadow of Christ, the Son of God (v. 3), our Great High Priest (4:14), who was so different from this entire multitude of priests (ἕτερος, v. 11), who even came from a different tribe (v. 13), who would and did bring the actual expiation (v. 17) which this Levitical priesthood could only foreshadow. The shadow pointed Israel forward to the substance and the reality and urged it to put faith in this coming substance and to be saved by faith in it.

No greater mistake could be made, either before our Great High Priest wrought the expiation or now after he has wrought it, than to think that the shadow is the substance and to cling to the shadow with its incompleteness and to reject the substance with its completeness. The value of the shadow lies in what it foreshadows; apart from this it would be empty, was empty for all Jews who imagined the shadow to be the eternal substance and rejected the substance as not being even a shadow but a grand delusion.

On the one hand there occurs this annulling for the reason stated; "on the other hand (there occurs) a bringing in of a better hope by means of which we draw near to God." We supply γίνεται from v. 18. The present tense leaves the double statement general, without reference to historical dates. The A. V. supplies an aorist and overlooks the parenthesis and the correlation of μέν and δέ. As the "disannulling" is made by God, so also is the "bringing in." God removed the shadow and substituted the substance. This fact alone ought to be enough to show that what God brought in is something objective: "a better hope by means of which we draw near to God" ("of a better hope," objective genitive). Here, as in 6:18, "hope" is objective and not subjective. The writer does not stop to say what this objective hope is, this thing on which God wants us all to rest our hope for eternal life; he will do this in the following.

It is the expiating blood of our Great High Priest Jesus. This is a "better" basis of hope than the blood offered by the Levitical priests. It is "better" because it actually takes away all sins (εἰς τὸ ἱλάσκεσθαι τὰς ἁμαρτίας, 2:17; I John 1:7), and because this blood lent its expiating power to the Levitically offered blood and enabled it, too, to expiate. So many speak as if the Old Testament sacrifices removed no sin whatever; if that were the case, no believer during Old Testament days was saved from sin. In and of itself the blood shed during the Old Testament could not remove sin, but in its connection with Christ's blood it did remove sin. Its weakness and unprofitableness, its lack of completion lay in the fact that in and of itself it could do nothing, that its entire efficacy depended on Christ's blood which was yet to be shed. When that blood was finally shed, the whole Levitical priesthood and all its sacrifices, having served their purpose, were automatically disannulled — the better hope had come.

While "a better hope" is objective, the subjective side is by no means forgotten, for "by means of this objective hope, Christ's blood and righteousness (define it in other terms if you wish), we draw nigh to God," enter into saving communion with him in this life and into glorious communion in the life to come. Here the confessional *we* again appears as in v. 14 we have the confessional *our* Lord. It is wrong to think that only we and not the Old Testament believers draw near to God. The comparative "a better hope" excludes that thought. Those believers also drew near to God, also were saved here and hereafter; but only by the Levitical blood and expiation which was far beneath that of Christ because it was wholly dependent on the efficacy of his sacrifice.

Thus from this angle the readers are again shown that the Levitical priesthood had to be abolished when "our Lord" came as the eternal High Priest, and they are shown what would result for them if they turned away from this High Priest in order again to put their hope in the disannulled Levitical priesthood.

20) Καί adds another point to the γάρ used in v. 18, 19, one that lies on the surface of Ps. 110:4: **And in so far as** (they occur, namely this disannulling and this bringing in, v. 18, 19) **not without a sworn statement, (for they without a sworn statement are priests** (simply) **having become** (such), **but he with a sworn statement by means of him who says regarding him:**

The Lord swore and will not repent:
Thou a Priest for the eon!)

by so much also of a better testament has he become a surety, (namely) **Jesus.**

The ellipsis must be completed from v. 18, 19 as we have indicated (not from v. 19 alone). Some, like the A. V., complete it from the general connection, from the parenthesis used in v. 21, or from the thought expressed in v. 22: "And in so far as (he has become priest) not without a sworn statement"; or: "As not without an oath, so of a better testament has Jesus become surety" (Dods). But the parenthesis expresses its own thought and cannot thus supply something for the main sentence; the material between v. 21 and v. 23 is so extensive that v. 23 can scarcely round out v. 21 without an ellipsis as Dods proposes. It is more natural to connect with the preceding verses as we have indicated.

The annulment and the bringing in (v. 18, 19) occur "not without a sworn statement" (ὁρκωμοσία), which is a litotes, stating in negative form what is intended positively in a decided way. This negation applies to the whole Levitical priesthood. Most certainly, no such sworn statement could ever be made concerning it as is made concerning Jesus.

21) The parenthesis explains without delay: "for they without a sworn statement are priests" as the readers know full well, and γεγονότες adds that they simply "have become" such. There was a law back of them, and this only a temporary law, but never an oath, a sworn statement with irrevocable force. Those who regard εἰσιν . . . γεγονότες as a periphrastic perfect seem to be at a loss to explain the participle; yet they do not say why the writer should use the periphrastic and not, as he does so often in this whole connection, the simple participial form. They must then also supply the periphrastic in the next clause, where it is still more uncalled for, where ἐστί alone is in place.

"But he with a sworn statement (is priest) by means of him who says regarding him: 'The Lord swore,'" etc. Πρὸς αὐτόν is not "unto him" (A. V.) but "of him" (R. V.), better "regarding him," for Ps. 110:4 is not addressed to Jesus. "By him who says," etc. = by God, whose declaration in Ps. 110 still says what it has ever said. The oath proper is not recorded in the psalm but only the statement to which God declares that he has sworn. Hence it is inadequate to translate ὀρκωμοσία "oath" (A. V.; the R. V. translates "taking of an oath" and then just "oath"); the word means precisely what the psalm presents: "a sworn statement."

On the votive formula with εἰ see the oath quoted in 3:11; 4:3, 5. The doubling "swore and will not repent" is strong emphasis. The passive future form μεταμεληθήσεται, as R. 819, 334 explains, might have a passive meaning: "the Lord will not be made to repent," but it is most likely only the passive form doing duty for the middle: "will not repent himself."

The point is the statement itself that is sworn to by God, and this is not that David's son and Lord is only to be Priest but "Priest for the eon," forever (see 5:6), "his priesthood unchangeable" (v. 24), the opposite of the Levitical priesthood which according to God's intention was to be only temporary.

22) By as much as the sworn statement regarding the priesthood of Jesus involves compared with the unsworn Levitical priesthood, "by so much also of a better testament has he become a surety, (namely) Jesus." His name is emphatically at the end.

Monographs have been written on the term διαθήκη and its connection with the Hebrew b^{e}rith, "covenant." Our versions waver between the translations "covenant" and "testament." We give the sum of the matter. The Old Testament dealt with the promises of God to the chosen people. By means of these God placed himself in "covenant" relation to Israel (b^{e}rith). This relation, like the promises and the gifts of God to Israel, is always one-sided. It is always God's covenant and not Israel's and not a mutual agreement, not a συνθήκη. This promise and covenant obligate Israel, and Israel assumes these obligations, but the covenant emanates entirely from God.

The LXX translated *bᵉrith*, "covenant" in this sense, with διαθήκη, "testament," since this term has the same one-sided connotation; a will or testament emanates only from the testator. Christ brought about the fulfillment of the Old Testament promises. The result is that God's people now have the inheritance and are God's heirs: "If children, then heirs; heirs of God, and joint-heirs of Christ," Rom. 8:17. Thus by way of the LXX we have διαθήκη used in the sense of "will or testament" in the New Testament.

Riggenbach defines διαθήκη as the divine institution of grace which has these features in common with a human testament: 1) it rests solely on the determination of its author; 2) it aims to bestow treasure; 3) it connects the bestowal with certain conditions on the part of the recipients. The last point is not well worded; it should be: designates certain persons as the recipients.

Hebrews does not deal with the testament that was made to Abraham. It would be a serious error to think that in Hebrews the new testament is placed in opposition to that which was given to Abraham. As far as Abraham's testament is concerned, Jesus fulfilled the promises constituting this testament. Hebrews deals with Moses, Sinai, the Levitical ritual, all of which came in 430 years *after* Abraham, and in contrast with which Jesus brings in "a better testament" which is called "new" because the Mosaic testament was only to endure for a definite period of time (καινή, 8:8, the old, worn-out, to be replaced; νέα, 12:24, totally new, totally different, not even to be compared with the Mosaic testament). Abraham's testament never grew old, it stands today, its promise has been fulfilled in Christ. We are sons of Abraham, in possession of the promised inheritance.

When it came, the "better testament" had a wonderful Priest as its "surety," but more of this in 8:6, etc. The ἔγγυος of a testament is not its *Ausrichter*, "administrator" (Luther); nor is this a technical term; it simply means *Buerge*, "surety," "guarantor." Since a "testament" is entirely one-sided, it is impossible to think of a surety for men to God; Jesus is a surety for God to us. Nor should we try to include both of these ideas. It may well be possible that ἔγγυος is chosen to form a paronomasia with ἐγγίζομεν, for both are derived from ἐγγύς. Yet the two thoughts would be opposites: we draw near to God; Jesus stands near God's better testament in order to guarantee all its provisions for us.

We should not avoid the question as to how Jesus is "surety" of the better testament, for it will be asked, in fact, belongs to the interpretation of the word. One is "surety for a testament" (objective genitive) when he is at hand to insure to those named in it the reception of all that it is intended to convey. Jesus does this by being "a Priest forever" according to the sworn declaration of God (v. 21).

But we should unfold what lies in this expression. Some, like C.-K. 378, emphasize only "forever" and point to the exalted life of Jesus, to the fact that he is our "forerunner" (6:20), crowned with glory and honor (2:9), our King-Priest, etc.; but they do not mention his death. But we should surely also include "Priest" mentioned in v. 21 (his unchangeable priesthood, v. 24) and everything to which his human name "Jesus" points so emphatically; in other words, his life, his death, and his resurrection as well as his eternal glorification. For everything that makes him our High Priest, everything that he achieved here on earth in his human nature stands forever, and it is this by which "he has become" and ever continues to be (perfect tense) the surety who guarantees that our hope is sure (v. 19) and will be made our possession in due time.

23) Another καί adds a further item to the γάρ statement made in v. 18: **And they are more (in number), having become priests in consequence of being prevented by death from continuing to remain; but he, in consequence of his remaining forever, has an unchangeable priesthood; whence also he is able to save to the utmost those who come through him to God, ever living to intercede for them.**

We have noted that the writer repeatedly speaks of *many* Levitical priests and of only *one* Priest when he refers to Jesus. The significance of this vital difference is now strikingly revealed as far as both the cause involved and the effect are concerned. Οἱ μέν and ὁ δέ are the demonstrative opposites; the present tenses state the facts without reference to time.

Some regard εἰσι γεγονότες as a periphrastic perfect just as they do in v. 21, cf., R. 1119. But we say that, just as v. 21 has no periphrastic perfect, so also v. 23 has none. A strongly attested reading places the words exactly as they are found in v. 21: εἰσὶν ἱερεῖς γεγονότες; which may, indeed, be the original although it is difficult to decide this point. Either reading is *not* periphrastic. For one thing, we have the plain correlation: "they on their part *are* . . . he on his part *has*," two present tenses. For another thing, those who prefer this construction in v. 21 and here do not explain why, if the writer desires to use a perfect tense, he employs the periphrastic perfect when the simple perfect form would be sufficient. There is really no reason for the periphrastic form. The simple fact is that "they on their part *are* more numerous," we may say, "many" although the word that is used is not πολλοί. The comparative means: "more (in number)" than they would be if it were not for the fact that they have become priests because of their being prevented by death from continuing to remain in their office.

We construe γεγονότες διὰ τό κτλ., which states why they are so many. All of them have become priests, i. e., have at the very start become priests because of their being prevented by death from continuing to remain on in their office (note the iterative present infinitives). They are one by one stopped by death. At the time of the appointment of Aaron his sons, too, were appointed because Aaron would presently die; and so the number is a constant "more"; upon entering the priesthood everyone knows that death will end it for him.

24) There now follows the mighty contrast: "but he, because he remains forever, εἰς τὸν αἰῶνα," as God himself declares in his sworn statement in Ps. 110:4, "has an unchangeable priesthood." The διά phrases with the substantivized present infinitives are placed chiastically, thus close together, which heightens the contrast: they are prevented from remaining on — he remains forever. God says this regarding him under oath. He thus has a priesthood that is ἀπαράβατον; this word always has the sense of "unchangeable," *unwandelbar*, and does not mean, as some suppose, "untransferable" (C.-K. 184, etc.; B.-P. 126). Because he remains forever he has an unchangeable priesthood.

25) Ὅθεν is a favorite expression of the writer's and states a summary deduction as the result of this unchangeable priesthood of Jesus: "whence (or hence) also he is able to save to the utmost those who come through him to God," etc. The present tenses are continued, and relations of time are thereby omitted. It is debated as to whether εἰς τὸ παντελές has temporal force or not. M.-M. 477 thinks it has: "to save *finally*: so long as our Intercessor lives our σωτηρία is assured." Others think of degree: *ganz und gar*, "completely." The temporal idea, we think, need not be excluded, but it is not that proposed by M.-M., "so long as." The thought is not that by living forever and being priest

forever Jesus saves forever. The idea is more profound. It is expressed already in v. 11.

By the very fact that they continue in a succession the Levitical priests demonstrate that their ministration is incomplete as far as saving is concerned, that it is in reality ever dependent on the eternal Priest to come and on his ministration, and that their ministration is able to save only by making their work point to that Great High Priest. So they, indeed, saved men during Old Testament times, but never by their ministration alone, never as if their priesthood was complete, but ever only as pointing forward to the Messiah-High Priest and drawing the saving power from him. It is he and his priesthood that save "to the utmost," so that there is nothing to draw on in order to make up the whole that is necessary to attain the goal of salvation — πᾶν plus τέλος. This is necessarily the case, for he is the final Priest, the Priest forever, who has an unchangeable priesthood. We may state it in this way: only as proxies of Christ do those priests save; he saves as having everything (degree) forever (time).

We note that ζῶν is construed as were the two γεγονότες in v. 21 and 23. It lifts out one grand feature of Jesus' priestly work: "ever living to intercede for them" or "in their behalf." The writer does not say "in our behalf" because he couches the whole of v. 23-25 in present tenses so that the entire statement is kept general and thus general also in this last phrase ὑπὲρ αὐτῶν, "in their behalf." We should not separate this intercession of Jesus from his other priestly work as some would do, for it crowns his priestly life, death, resurrection, and exaltation. The proper conception is that he bases all his intercession on this other work. It is correct to say that in interceding he makes his whole mediatorial work count for our benefit with God.

No man may know how he intercedes. This is a matter between him and the Father. Yet we rightly put away all thought of humbly pleading, all thought of lowering himself in the act. Although he is exalted at God's right hand (1:13), Jesus, the Son of God incarnate, is still our Priest, living ever, active in the presence of God for us. We call this his *intercessio specialis* because it is made for "those coming to God" as is done in the High-priestly Prayer (John 17) and distinguish this from the *intercessio generalis* which is made for all men in order to extend their time of grace (Isa. 53:12; Luke 23:34). There is no intercession for the damned.

The High Priest That Became Us, v. 26-28.

26) In a summary statement which gathers up the main points discussed and combines the difference between Jesus and the Aaronic high priests with his likeness to Melchizedek and Ps. 110:4 the writer shows us the kind of High Priest that it became us to have. "For" connects with v. 25 and thus elucidates his power to save to the uttermost as ever living and now doing no more than interceding for us.

For such a High Priest was becoming to us, holy, without anything bad, without a stain, withdrawn from the sinners, and become higher than the heavens, who does not day by day have the necessity, like the high priests, first for his own sins to offer up sacrifices, then (for) those of the people; for this he did once for all by offering up himself. For the law establishes men as high priests who have weakness, but the word of the sworn statement, subsequent to the law, a Son who has forever been made complete.

In 2:10 we heard what was becoming to God, namely to make the Author of our salvation complete by means of sufferings. We now hear the counterpart, that it was becoming to us to have such a High Priest, who has all the basic requisites and thus has also been made complete forever. We see at once that τελειῶσαι used in 2:10 and τετελειωμένον correspond, and that thus the τελείωσις that was lacking in what the Levitical priesthood was able to provide (v. 11) is provided to the uttermost in this High Priest of ours. We have the same imperfect "was becoming" that was used in 2:10, but it now has a personal and not, as in 2:10, an impersonal subject. One might say "such a High Priest was necessary for us," which would also be true.

"Was becoming," fitting, appropriate, meet, does not put the matter on a lower plane; it deals only with another side, that of providing us with the proper High Priest, one who is this in a way that is complete in every respect, is fully fitted for his task. We may say that stating it thus leaves room for the temporary and incomplete work of the Levitical priests (v. 11), which was also fitting and proper in a way because it was preparatory for Christ and with its incompleteness pointed to the completeness of Christ, with its incompleteness depended on Christ's completeness and thus achieved its results through him.

The very fact that by means of the Levitical priesthood completeness was not attained (v. 11) together with all that is added in v. 11-25 show how it became us to have a High Priest of a different kind, one who is, indeed, absolutely complete as a High Priest. The imperfect tense is in place, for this propriety existed at all times from the very beginning of the priestly idea and the priestly expiation of our sins — completeness both in the personal qualification and in the work of the Priest who would, of course, be a high priest. If καί is retained, its force would be: was "precisely" becoming for us (R. 1181).

The matter is presented in an objective way: this objectivity is more convincing for the readers than if Jesus were actually named in this paragraph. Yet a little thought shows that all that is here said about the kind of High Priest that is proper for us is found in Jesus, in him alone. This form of presentation practically asks the readers to take these objective specifications and to find the High Priest in whom they appear. There is none other than Jesus despite the host of priests and of high priests the Jews have had. What a fatal mistake, then, for the readers to think of forsaking "such a High Priest" and turning back to Judaism, to the Levitical priests whose function had long been superseded as God himself declares in his sworn statement (v. 20-22, 28).

First, the character of the High Priest who is becoming for us is stated in five items, all five being appositions to τοιοῦτος: "such a one . . . holy," etc.; we do not have a relative clause: "who is holy," etc. (A. V.). Note that all five terms, like the very word "High Priest," refer to the human nature of this objectively presented High Priest. It would be utterly inappropriate for him to be anything but ὅσιος, "holy." This word takes us back to Ps. 16:10 (LXX) which is quoted in Acts 2:27 and 13:35: "thy Holy One," Hebrew *chasid*. This word for "holy" appears often in the LXX but infrequently in the New Testament, where it is not the same as ἅγιος, "holy" as separated unto God. Ὅσιος, as Trench shows well, is the opposite of polluted; in I Tim. 2:8, when the men are praying, they are to lift up hands that are "holy" in this sense, otherwise God will see their pollution and turn away from them. Our High Priest is such a completely "holy personality" who never deviates in the least from all God's ordinances and commandments, he is without a speck of pollution.

The next three terms are little more than synonymous elaborations. Thus ἄκακος, with not a thing that is κακόν, bad, base, or even morally inferior attaching to him. We unfortunately have no exact English equivalent for this word, hence we have the poor renderings "harmless" (A. V.) and "guileless" (R. V.). Ἀμίαντος

= "without a stain." Some have differentiated these three: the first relating to God, the second to men, the third to the world. We take them to be synonymous, all three, each in its way, emphasizing the one supreme quality of sinlessness: "without sin" (4:15); all three are the more weighty because the writer has already stated how Jesus was tempted and tried by suffering and death (2:9, 10, 18; 4:15; 5:7-9) without even the least fault appearing in him.

Some regard "withdrawn from the sinners" as a local withdrawing, as the negative to the positive "become higher than the heavens," both being the result of Christ's ascension. But why is the first participle a perfect tense of condition, the second an aorist? And why should the significance of the ascension be found in a separation and withdrawal of Christ from the sinners here on earth? "Having been withdrawn or separated from the sinners" completes the thought of the three preceding adjectives. Jesus lived his entire life among the sinners, but his whole life long he was "holy, without anything bad, without a stain," was ever in his whole person and character separated from them. Then finally: "become (by the one act of his ascension) higher than the heavens"; 4:14: "having gone through the heavens," 1:13 to sit at God's right hand, 2:9, "crowned with glory and honor."

That is the kind of High Priest that is proper for us if we are to have one such as we really need. The fact that only Jesus is such a High Priest need not be stated; the readers see that themselves. But if any of them have a lower conception of the proper High Priest who is such completely, the writer revises their idea and elevates it to what it ought to be. He is not offering only his own personal conception; he is offering God's own conception as it is contained already in Ps. 110 and then in all that God made Jesus to be.

27) One might regard τοιοῦτος . . . ὅς as correlative, and ὅσιος κτλ., as being parenthetical. We pre-

fer to regard this relative clause as another apposition. First three adjectives; then two participles; now a relative clause. Καί is placed between the participles to mark the fact that the appositions which are descriptive of the person and the character are not to be continued; the relative intends to deal with the work which such a High Priest as is proper for us should do. A relative clause affords room for inserting the necessary modifiers. It is also good style to make the last member of a coordinate series the longest.

The High Priest we should have is one who is not constantly under necessity of offering up sacrifices but one who once for all completes the sacrificial work by one all-sufficient sacrifice. That will, of course, make this High Priest entirely different from all the Aaronitic high priests who had to offer up constantly repeated sacrifices even for their own sins and in addition to that repeated sacrifices for the people. This is the thought of v. 27. Here, however, the aorist: "this he did once for all by offering up himself," breaks through the objectivity of the presentation and speaks directly of the historical fact of what Jesus did.

Some critics think that the writer of Hebrews betrays the fact that he does not know that the Jewish high priests offered sacrifices first for themselves and then for the people only once a year, on the Great Day of Atonement, that the writer imagined that the high priest did this καθ' ἡμέραν, "daily." These critics do not have much ground to stand on, for it can be readily observed that the writer says "once a year" in 9:7 and "year by year" in 10:1, and that he knows Lev. 16:2: "not at all times," as well as Lev. 16:29, etc., and v. 34: "once a year."

Commentators, nevertheless, wrestle with the sentence as it stands. Some think that the writer combines the daily sacrifices of the ordinary priests with the annual sacrifice of the high priest in an inexact way. They refer to Josephus for the information that the high priests offered sacrifices on special festival days. Or they cite the Mishna which says that on any day when the high priest so desired he performed the sacrifices. Philo even attributes to the high priest a daily sacrifice for his own sins which some other priest, however, usually brought for him. Others let καθ' ἡμέραν mean "yearly on a definite day" or explain the phrase in some other way. But what is here said about the high priests refers solely to what they did on one day in the year: offer a sacrifice (first for their own sins and then for those of the people, Lev. 16:6, 9).

We are unable to see why Riggenbach cites Lev. 6:12-16 in order to establish the fact of a daily sacrifice on the part of the high priest when Aaron and not his sons was the high priest. When he quotes Sirach 45:17 to prove that the high priest's sacrifice was made "daily twice" he contradicts his own claim that the writer of Hebrews deals, not with things as they may have been in later days, but only with things as they were instituted by God in the wilderness, in the Tabernacle, in the Mosaic record.

Καθ' ἡμέραν belongs where it is placed, ὃς οὐκ ἔχει καθ' ἡμέραν ἀνάγκην; it does *not* belong to "like the high priests." Trouble arises only when this is not kept in mind. Also when the sentence is read without reference to what precedes in v. 25, 26. Being sinless (v. 26), the High Priest befitting us certainly has no sins of his own for which to offer sacrifices; if he were not sinless, then, in order to intercede *daily* for us, *he* would most certainly have to interrupt his interceding and would *"day by day"* have to have his own sins removed first of all.

The same is true of such a High Priest's constant interceding for the people. Being sinless (v. 26), offering up himself once for all (as "a lamb without blemish and without spot," I Pet. 1:19) is sufficient ground for his "ever living to intercede for them" who come to God through him (v. 25). If he were not sinless and could not make such a sacrifice once for all, then he would, indeed, constantly have to interrupt his interceding and "day by day" repeat the sacrifice for the people as also for himself. In other words, this necessity would make him "like the high priests" of the Levitical priesthood, Aaron and his successors, who never got through, who never attained "completeness" (v. 11). Another *such* a high priest does not become us, who gets no farther, who also leaves the goal (τέλος in τελείωσις) still unattained. Then, too, why change from the Aaronitic to the Melchizedekian type, change even the entire law regarding the priesthood as is pointed out in v. 11-17? "Like the high priests" is an independent insertion and not an incomplete sentence which is to be completed from the following words. Τῶν ἰδίων ἁμαρτιῶν is not "*their* own sins" but "*his* own sins"; ἰδίων is plural only because of the noun.

Such a necessity must properly be absent in the case of the High Priest who is befitting us and our need. We might translate τοῦτο "the latter": "for the latter," the offering up of sacrifices for the people, "he did once for all by offering up himself" as the complete and all-sufficient sacrifice, which it was impossible as well as unnecessary to repeat. The very idea that τοῦτο can refer to both: offering up of sacrifices for his own sins and for those of the people, is, as Delitzsch says, blasphemous. No man can offer up himself for his own sins; the blasphemy, however, lies in ascribing sins to Jesus. Delitzsch takes von Hofmann to task for ascribing *quasi* sins to Jesus on the basis of 5:7, 8 and thus claiming that what Jesus did in Gethsemane is analogous to what the high priests did when they made sacrifice for their own sins. Ἐφάπαξ is far stronger than ἅπαξ. We have already noted that the aorist verb and participle now speak directly of Jesus although the subject is still "such a High Priest." The writer has Jesus in mind even in his general statements.

28) The writer closes by summarily bringing into opposition the Levitical, Aaronitic priesthood and that of Jesus which is like to Melchizedek and thus reverts to v. 11-25. "For the law establishes (appoints, places in office) men (mere men) as high priests who have weakness (sins of their own that require sacrifices); but the word of the sworn statement (of the ὁρκωμοσία mentioned in Ps. 110:4, see v. 21), subsequent to the law (and thus altering that law about the Aaronitic priests), establishes (by something that is far greater, a far greater High Priest) a Son who has forever been made complete (thus by his one sacrifice of himself bringing to completeness forever all things that God intended the whole priestly institution to complete)." Little more is needed by way of comment. The statement is again general and uses a present tense and has "a Son" and not the definite "the Son." All that precedes deals with the human nature of Jesus, but "a Son" shows that this is in union with his divine nature as we have already been abundantly told.

One new point appears in this paragraph, this that he offered up "himself" as the all-complete sacrifice. Nothing further is said here on this point; it will be fully elaborated in the following and is introduced here for that purpose.

Can the readers still think of renouncing such a High Priest, of turning back to the high priesthood that was long ago discarded by God? Can they forsake the efficacy of the Son's sacrifice of himself in order to fall back upon the merely human high priests who need sacrifices as much as the readers themselves do? Can they abandon the intercession of this everliving High Priest who is higher than the heavens and resort to the high priests who must die just as the readers themselves die (v. 23-25)?

CHAPTER VIII

THE FIFTH MAIN PART

**The Sacrificial Work of Jesus:
In Six Great Comparisons, 8:1-10:18**

The Preamble: the Main Point, v. 1, 2.

1) It is interesting to note how different men divide this epistle. There is but little divergence of viewpoint. This is due to the fact that the writer steadily elaborates his rather closely linked line of thought and inserts scarcely any marks of division. One might make 8:1, 2 the end of the previous section instead of the preamble of the new section. These matters are formal to a large extent, and we moderns like them because we are scholastics in this respect. Let us, then, say that we think that our division into chapters is properly made at this point and that v. 1, 2 form the preamble to what follows until 10:18. We add that this material seems to divide itself into six minor parts, in each of which a comparison is drawn.

    1) The two Ministries Compared;
    2) The two Testaments Compared;
    3) The two Tabernacles Compared;
    4) The two Kinds of Blood Compared;
    5) The Two Kinds of Sacrifice Compared;
    6) The Final Comparison regarding the Removal of Sins.

We trust that this outline of the thought will serve our purpose in understanding this section.

Now the main point in the discussion (is this): Such a High Priest we have as sat down at the right

Hebrews 8:1

hand of the throne of the Majesty in the heavens, as a ministrant of the Holy Place and of the true Tabernacle, which the Lord erected, not man.

We regard δέ as transitional as is done in our versions. As for κεφάλαιον, it makes no difference whether we call it a nominative or an accusative absolute, an adverbial absolute (R. 705), or even an apposition to what follows; for this is only a question of what one's grammatical sense prefers. The word may mean a sum or summary. The ancients added a column by starting at the bottom and writing the sum at the top whereas we place the sum at the bottom. A few writers think that the word is used in this sense, and that the writer is now summarizing what has been discussed thus far. Then, it seems, he should have used the perfect participle in the ἐπί phrase and not the present, "on what has been discussed" and not "on what is being discussed." Moreover, *is* v. 1, 2 really a summation of what has been discussed so far? Most writers do not think so but agree with the R. V. rather than with the A. V.

Κεφάλαιον also = "the chief point" (R. V.) and does not need the article; thus not "*a* chief point." The Germans can use *bei* as a translation for ἐπί; we shall have to say "*in* the things being said," i. e., "in the present discussion." This is the discussion that is now beginning, the main point of which the writer states at once so that the readers may keep it in mind, for he will elaborate it with many details among which this main and vital point might be lost sight of. It is not necessary to say that this main point has not as yet been touched upon, for it has in fact. We have been told of the ascent of Jesus to God's right hand, of his going through the heavens, of his being a Priest forever, ever living to intercede for us (7:25). Now, however, the discussion goes beyond this, as the outline given above shows, and centers on the heavenly

Tabernacle in which this our exalted High Priest officiates for us. This is the great point to be borne in mind as we read on. All that has touched upon it in the previous chapters is an aid, yet it has not quite come to the point that is now named.

Τοιοῦτον . . . ὅς resembles τοιοῦτος . . . ὅς used in 7:26, 27, and the two constructions have been considered identical. Yet in 7:26, 27 the intervening appositions make the ὅς clause another apposition as we have indicated, while the ὅς is now a correlative: "such a High Priest as," etc. The High Priest we now have is one that has been exalted to heaven in order to officiate in the Holy of Holies above and not in the Holy of Holies in a mere earthly Tabernacle. The main point is not the exaltation of Jesus; this is subsidiary. The main point is his exalted ministration in the heavenly Holy of Holies. For this High-priestly work of his "he sat down at the right hand of the throne of the Majesty in the heavens as a ministrant of the Holy Place," etc. The emphasis is on the predicative nominative "as a ministrant," etc. On the *sessio* review what is said under 1:3. "Of the throne" of the Majesty is added in order to bring out the royalty which lies already in the word "Majesty." Ours is a King-Priest like Melchizedek (7:1, etc., also 5:6; 6:20). His entire kingship appears in his *sessio* at the right hand of the throne of the Majesty in the heavens (1:13; 2:9; 4:14).

2) No Jewish high priest ever *sat* when he was executing his office. He was not a king who may sit in state, and his office permitted no sitting. Our exalted High Priest is both King and Priest and thus sits at the right of the throne of Majesty "as ministrant of the Holy Place and of the true Tabernacle." Throne and Sanctuary are not in conflict, nor is sitting as a ministrant. Λειτουργός is used in the LXX to designate the incumbent of a public office of various kinds; com-

pare our remarks on this word in Phil. 2:25. Some think that because it is here and elsewhere used as a designation for priests that therefore the word itself has a priestly meaning; but the priestly meaning is derived only from the context.

Τὰ ἅγια is a technical term and = "the Holy Place"; its use is similar to that of ἡ σκηνή, "the Tabernacle," which constitutes "the Sanctuary" where the presence of God dwells. In 9:3, etc., the Tabernacle of Moses is described with its two places, the Holy and the Holy of Holies. In heaven the two are one, and there is no veil between them; and it is of the heavenly "Holy" that our passage speaks. We may accept the translation "Sanctuary" in our versions as being correct in substance although the word used is not ὁ ναός; but we cancel the marginal rendering of both: "holy things."

"Of the true Tabernacle" is added because the writer, as already noted, has in mind only the Tabernacle that was built by Moses in the wilderness and not the later Temples of Solomon, Ezra, Herod; the writer deals only with the original and with what Moses says about that. Here he speaks of the heavenly architype: "the Holy Place and the true Tabernacle, which the Lord (Yahweh) erected, not man." The word "true" modifies only "the Tabernacle" and not also "the Holy Place."

The relative clause indicates in what sense ἀληθινή, "true," is to be understood, namely, "erected by the Lord." The earthly counterpart or copy was not "true," for it was erected only by man, namely by Moses (v. 5). The latter is only a copy (representation) and a shadow; the former is the genuine original which is indescribable in its holiness and heavenliness with its eternal presence of God.

We dismiss all our earthly conceptions of space when we are thinking of heaven as if God's throne of majesty stands somewhere in the space of heaven, as if this true Tabernacle also stands in some part of this space. Time and space do not exist in the other world. Only because we are unable to think and to speak of heaven in terms other than those of time and of space do the Scriptures condescend to do the same. But note what Rev. 21:16 says of heaven when it calls heaven the city of God and describes it as a cube! Read all of Rev. 21:9-27 and note that there is no Temple in this city (v. 22). In our verse we are facing what is infinite, and to reason finitely with finite ideas of time or of space is folly. Yes, God built heaven which is his throne, which is this Tabernacle where Christ is, where we are to be with him. Like the word "Tabernacle," so also the word "erected" is human language because the very idea of a heavenly "Tabernacle" (literally, "tent") is not that God should dwell there alone, but that it should open the fullest communion and union with him to his people.

In his *Parables of our Lord,* chapter II, Trench says of the lovers of truth: "To them the things on earth are copies of the things in heaven. They know that the earthly Tabernacle is made after the pattern of the things seen in the Mount (Exod. 25:40; I Chron. 28:11, 12), and the question suggested by the angel in Milton is often forced upon their meditations —

'What if earth
Be but the shadow of heaven, and things therein
Each to other like, more than on earth is thought?' "

The idea that the earth should be anthropocentric staggers many. What will they say when they find that heaven itself is so? Delitzsch defines τὰ ἅγια thus: "in brief the uncreated heaven of the divine glory," "above all space and time and filling all things is not comprehended by any." It is called both "the Holy Place" and "the Tabernacle" for our sakes; wherefore also Jesus is the High Priest and λειτουργός of this Sanctuary.

Philo indulged in the speculation that the world is the Holy and heaven the Holy of Holies, and that both are symbolized in the Jewish Tabernacle; but this view does not aid us in understanding our epistle. Even in their religious poetry the later Jews have the Old Testament idea of a connection between the Jerusalem above and that below. They are not thinking of God, the Messiah, or the church when they speak of the heavenly Temple but rather of the place of the blessed spirits. The writer of Hebrews says far more.

Some of the ancient commentators refer to ἐσκήνωσεν, "he tented among us," in John 1:14 and other passages and thus think of the heavenly Σκηνή or "Tabernacle" as being Christ's body. Verse 5 eliminates this idea: Moses did not see the body of Jesus on the Mount as the pattern according to which he was to construct the Tabernacle in the wilderness. In 9:12 "he entered in once for all into the Holy Place," certainly not into his body. When the Jewish ναός or "Sanctuary" appears as a type of Jesus' body in John 2:19-21, this does not make the body of Jesus identical with heaven as the heavenly Tabernacle.

The Two Ministries Compared, v. 3-6.

3) With γάρ the writer introduces the first explanatory elaboration of "the main thing" (v. 1) which he intends to present fully to his readers. If we compare the ministry of Jesus with that of the Jewish high priests and note the vast superiority of his ministry we shall see at once that it cannot be exercised in the earthly Tabernacle or Sanctuary as that of the Jewish priests was. Only this much is offered to begin with; more will follow at length.

For every high priest is appointed for the offering of both gifts and sacrifices; hence it is necessary that also this One have something which he may offer.

This general statement is basic for what follows and should, of course, not be separated from it and read by itself. It will then not be regarded as superfluous or as a digression. What pertains to every high priest because of the very nature of his office of necessity pertains also to "this One." If any high priest, including Jesus, has no offering to bring to God he is no high priest. To bring an offering is the very object (εἰς τό) of his appointment to his office.

On ὃ προσενέγκῃ (subjunctive whereas the classics use the future) see B.-D. 368; it is a mixture of a relative and an indirect deliberative question: "what he has to offer" and "what has he to offer?" This aorist subjunctive is as future in meaning as a present subjunctive would be. The only difference is this: the aorist is punctiliar and thus fits the *one* act of offering on Jesus' part; a present subjunctive would be iterative and would refer to repeated offerings. But repeated offerings cannot be ascribed to Jesus.

In the first clause εἰς τὸ προσφέρειν is properly an iterative present infinitive, for every ordinary Jewish high priest brought offerings annually and never finished this task as the years went on. The change to the aorist in the case of "this One" excludes such iteration on the part of Jesus. So also τι ὅ marks a difference. The ordinary Jewish high priest iteratively offers "gifts as well as sacrifices," two plurals; "this One" must, indeed, bring an offering, but only "something which," for the present leaving unsaid what this may be; we shall hear all about it in due time. In fact, this *one* offering of Jesus, made "once for all," has been mentioned already in 7:27: "this he made once for all by offering up *himself*" (aorist).

This ought to show that the discussion as to whether to supply ἐστί or ἦν in the second clause has no justification. The whole of v. 3 is general; the second clause is a deduction from the first, both have no particular reference to time.

Hebrews 8:4, 5

4) There is an implication in this necessity that every high priest must bring an offering, namely that he must also have the proper sanctuary for bringing such an offering. This is the point to be noted here, as v. 2 already shows. Jesus cannot, however, bring his offering in the sanctuary here on earth; it debars him from being even a priest, to say nothing of a high priest. **Now if he were on earth he would not (even) be a priest** — εἰ with the imperfect, then the imperfect with ἄν; both protasis and apodosis make this sentence one of present unreality. The μὲν οὖν merely advances to a point that is quite obvious: **there being** (= since there are) **those who offer the gifts according to law**, a law which debars Jesus because he is descended from the tribe of Judah (7:13,-14), to say nothing of the kind of δῶρον or "gift" that Jesus has to offer ("himself," 7:27). The wording is most exact: it keeps the general form in the condition of present unreality, the iterative offering of the priests (προσφερόντων), the general idea of "gifts (shortened from "both gifts and sacrifices" in v. 3), and again does not mention what "gift" Jesus may have to offer. The writer's thought is straight and exact: Jesus cannot be regarded as a priest among these priests.

5) The main point is introduced by the qualitative, half-causal οἵτινες: **they (being) such as serve a sketch and shadow of the heavenly (originals) even as Moses, when about to construct the Tabernacle, received divine direction, namely** (γάρ): **See to it, says he, thou shalt make everything according to the type shown to thee in the Mount!**

This is the main feature of the reason as to why Jesus cannot be regarded as one among the Jewish priests and high priests who do their service according to a certain "law" (v. 4), who are thus bound by such "law" to do their service in a sanctuary that is not "the true Tabernacle" (v. 1) but only "a sketch and shadow" of it as we see so plainly from Exod. 25:40 (Acts 7:44), the divine direction given to Moses when he was about to construct the Tabernacle (ἐπιτελεῖν, *herrichten*). If Jesus were to join the Jewish high priests in such a sanctuary and under such a law pertaining to such a sanctuary, it would mean that he, too, never gets beyond "sketch and shadow," never rises to "the true or real Tabernacle" (v. 2), to the completeness and the finality (τελείωσις, 7:11) without which he cannot actually save us (σώζειν εἰς τὸ παντελές, 7:25), without which even all that the sketch and shadow promised as to the substance and reality cannot be attained.

What is said about the Tabernacle as being the place for priestly service is auxiliary to the priestly service and no more. The full contrast regarding this place is reserved for 9:1-15. The point is here the ministry or service, that of the Jewish high priests being as inferior as their sanctuary, that of Jesus as superior as the heavenly sanctuary and all that is connected with it.

A ὑπόδειγμα is a sketch, tracing, outline, or adumbration; hence "shadow" is added in order to bring out the full idea. The ἐπουράνια are the heavenly original which Moses was shown in the Mount. It is asked whether this original is the actuality, "the Holy Place and Tabernacle" where Jesus is the ministrant (v. 2), or a representation of it which was offered to Moses on the Mount, such as he could more easily see and comprehend and thus copy in earthly material. Who can tell? We regard the perfect κεχρημάτισται as aoristic (see R. 898, etc.). Others take the perfect to mean that we still have the divine directions in the Pentateuch. The passive of this verb means "to be given a divine oracle." Ὅρα, in asyndeton with the imperative future ποιήσεις, is thus used only to make the command stronger (R. 949).

6) The logical νυνὶ δέ draws the conclusion. **Now, however, he has obtained a more excellent ministration by as much as he is Mediator also of a better testament, one of a kind that has been given legal force on the score of better promises.**

Why should any of the readers turn from Jesus for the mere reason that he is not and can never be a high priest like those of their nation who served only in the sketch and shadow of the true Tabernacle and not perceive that this inability means that "he has obtained a more excellent ministration (λειτουργία matches λειτουργός used in v. 2, which see) by so much (more excellent) as he is a Mediator also of a better testament," this being so much better "as being one that has been given legal force on the score of better promises"?

"He has obtained" and ever holds this more excellent ministration; τέτυχε is the Hellenistic form of the perfect when it is followed by a genitive, B.-D. 101. In 7:22 we have "surety of a better testament," God's guarantor to us that the testamentary promises will be duly bestowed upon us, the heirs; here we have "Mediator of a better testament," God's agent who "by offering up himself once for all" (7:27) actually makes the testament and all its testamentary promises effective. "Mediator," μεσίτης from μέσος, appears in our epistle for the first time. This term means "middleman," one who steps or stands in the middle between two; the context always indicates in what capacity or for what purpose he does this. Comparing 9:15; 12:24, we see at once that in this passage the word cannot signify "umpire" as it does in Job 9:33 (A. V. margin, also papyri); nor "peacemaker," one who helps two hostile parties to make up their difference and establish peace as when some neutral government (king or president) offers its good offices to bring two warring nations back to peace by the signing of a peace treaty. We doubt that the word was ever used in the sense of

Buerge, ἔγγυος, "surety," although 7:22 states that Jesus is also this for the better testament.

In Gal. 3:19 "mediator" is used with reference to Moses, but he is such in the sense of being Israel's representative who receives the law from God and brings it to Israel; he is a mediator only in this way (see the author's exposition of Gal. 3:19, 20). Some think that in our passage Jesus is presented as being such a mediator as Moses was and not such as the Jewish high priests were. But Jesus is not our representative to bring God's testament and its promises down to us. This "better testament" is the old testament which God made with Abraham, which is now carried into execution because it is now sealed with Jesus' blood. The law brought to Israel by Moses is also called a testament and as such is also sealed with blood (9:15-20), but only with the blood of calves and goats. This law-testament was temporal and came to an end. The law came in 430 years after the testament that was made for Abraham (Gal. 3:17); and Israel lost its promises because of transgression so that this law-testament came to an end.

Jesus is the Mediator of a better testament in a far higher and different sense than Moses was a mediator, the law was given to Israel only ἐν χειρὶ μεσίτου, "at the *hand* of a mediator" (Israel's representative). The mediatorship of Jesus consists in this that he offered up *"himself* once for all" (v. 27). He is the one Mediator "who gave himself as a ransom for all" (I Tim. 2:5, 6). He stepped in the middle and by his blood made the better testament better indeed and effective according to this testament's own provisions. The testamentary promises could not be fulfilled without his blood.

Since the testament is entirely one-sided, made for us by God, when Jesus serves as the Mediator he acts for God. We only receive the testament and the blood

Hebrews 8:6

that seals it and makes it effective. Only in this sense is he "our" Mediator. We may say that all of the prophetic work of Jesus belongs to his mediatorship (1:1, etc.; 2:3), for the preaching of Jesus reveals him as the Mediator. So also the active obedience of Jesus, which is inseparable from the passive, belongs to his mediation. But the supreme point is the High-priestly sacrifice of himself by which he entered into the Holy of Holies in heaven to become our Mediator forever. Moses was not a high priest; Moses did not go behind the veil with blood on the Day of Atonement. This Aaron and his successors did so that they are the types of Jesus in this his mediatorship.

Note that we have νενομοθέτηται ἐπί exactly as we did in 7:11, and there is a difference only in the subjects: in 7:11 the people are subjected to law on the score of the Levitical priesthood, here the better testament which is "of a kind (ἥτις) that has been subjected to law, i. e., has been legalized and given legal force on the score of better promises." It is the sacrifice of Jesus that gave the testament legal force "on the score of better promises" as is explained in 9:16, 17.

One might think that a testament needs no mediator, that it and the promises it contains are automatically in force. Yet this view forgets the fact that death alone puts a testament into force. God cannot die, but Jesus, God's Son, can and did, and thus the testament of God stands legally in force (perfect tense to indicate continuance) "on the score of (ἐπί as in 7:11) its better promises," nothing stands in the way of fulfilling every one of them for us in this life and in the life to come. The promises are not better in substance compared with the promises that were made to Abraham but in the fact that we no longer need to wait for the Mediator as Abraham had to wait for him. They are, of course, better than the promises that were attached to the law-testament which was brought in

430 years after Abraham as is now shown at length in v. 7-13.

The Two Testaments Compared, v. 7-13.

7) The Mosaic testament is compared with the better testament of which Jesus is the Mediator and not the testament which God gave to Abraham; v. 9 states this. Since we have a quotation from Jer. 31:31-34 we might, according to the original Hebrew *berith*, translate διαθήκη, "covenant" instead of "testament"; we should, however, keep in mind the reason the LXX chose διαθήκη when they were making their Greek translation (see 7:22), it will then make little difference as to how we translate into English. The point is to be remembered throughout that, like a testament, the covenant is wholly one-sided, is only bestowed on Israel, is only received. The readers must not for one moment imagine that what God gave to Moses is final and thus turn back from Jesus to Moses. "For" takes up the matter of the testament and explains how God himself supplanted that which had been given to Israel by the hand of Moses.

For if that first one (i. e., testament) were faultless, a place would not be sought for a second one. For faulting them he says:

Lo, days are coming, says the Lord
And I will consummate a new testament in regard to the house of Israel and in regard to the house of Judah,
Not like the testament which I made for their fathers
In the day of my taking them by their hand to lead them out of the land of Egypt,
Seeing that they themselves did not remain in my testament,
And I myself neglected them, says the Lord, etc.

We have a present unreality in both the protasis and the apodosis exactly as we did in v. 4; present because the matter is stated in the form of a general, timeless proposition. Our versions translate this sentence as a past unreality because they apparently thought that the statement should be historical. The present unreality is most pertinent for the readers, some of whom were at that very time thinking of returning to that former testament which they regarded as faultless and final, were thinking that their having accepted Christianity was a mistake. The reverse is true. It is not true that that testament is faultless, otherwise a place would not be sought for a new one (objective genitive).

8) The fact that a new one is in place is not the writer's deduction or claim but God's own assertion which was made already in the days of Jeremiah. "Faulting them" for whom that first testament was made, God himself says that he will make a new one. Whether we prefer the reading αὐτούς or αὐτοῖς, the pronoun is to be construed with the participle; the dative could not be construed with λέγει: "he says to them," because its position before the verb would give it excessive emphasis. We see that the fault does not lie in some imperfection in this old testament but in the people for whom it was made. Although it was good and holy in itself it could not and did not bring life to its recipients as Paul explains so lucidly in Rom. 7:7-12. The idea is not that God did not know this when he gave Moses that testament; Rom. 3:20b and Gal. 3:19 show why this law-testament was made for Israel; the latter passage states how long it was to stand. Thus it comes about that God made his statement already through Jeremiah.

The writer himself uses λέγει, a common way of introducing God as the speaker, and retains "says the Lord (Yahweh)" in v. 8-10 just as Jeremiah declares that he is repeating Yahweh's own words. This is both revelation and inspiration, and verbal at that. The prophet speaks as though he is repeating a dictation. If you were in his place would you dare to do anything else? Call this being "mechanical" if you will and repudiate verbal inspiration; such a view changes nothing regarding the genuine transmission which is four times vouched for: "λέγει, (God) says — the Lord says — the Lord says — the Lord says."

"Lo!" calls for attention to the Lord's communication. Hear and believe! Jeremiah writes "days are coming" four times (30:3; 31:27; 31:31; 7:32). Daechsel and others find chiliasm in these "days" and make Christ's mediatorial work preliminary to these millennial "days" of which the Lord speaks. But this view is untenable, for the final testament is made and consummated in Jesus and his mediatorial work, these "days" refer to the time of that work so that there cannot be a testament that is to come during a millennial era.

Now there follows the great promise which is to claim our attention: "And I will consummate a new testament in regard to (ἐπί, upon) the house of Israel and in regard to the house of Judah," etc. Hear Jesus as he institutes the Lord's Supper: "This cup is the new testament in my blood," Luke 22:20. For some reason the writer of Hebrews changes the LXX's διαθήσομαι διαθήκην with its two datives, which is an exact translation of the Hebrew, to συντελέσω διαθήκην with two ἐπί phrases. This is not inadvertence; there must be a reason. "I will consummate a new testament," i. e., bring it to its goal or finality, seems to revert to the τελείωσις (7:11) and τετελειωμένον (7:28) as if to interpret what the Lord means, namely not only to issue a new testament but to issue one with finality, one in the issuing of which its consummation will be included. For this consummation crowned the issuing when with his blood, shed on Calvary, Jesus entered into the Holy of Holies in heaven as our eternal High Priest (see v. 1, 2).

The prophecy speaks of the new testament as being for "the house of Israel and the house of Judah," yet we know that it is not intended for Jews only. Being intended for them, it is most certainly intended for all men. The writer is dealing with former Jews and thus does not stop to bring out the universality of this final testament. "House" pictures both kingdoms, Israel and Judah, as families, each dwelling in its house. The two ἐπί distinguish Israel, the northern kingdom, from Judah, the southern, although the former had already been swept away when Jeremiah received the Lord's message.

Chiliasts stress this double mention which runs through all the prophecies of the Messianic deliverance and make it a national conversion of Jews at the dawn of their millennium or during the millennium. But what about the northern kingdom, the lost ten tribes? Swept into exile, they disappeared and were amalgamated with the Gentiles. Right here we have the universality of the new testament. Lost among the Gentiles and turned Gentile, the gospel goes out to all nations to bring the new testament in Christ's blood to all.

9) The comparison is now made: "not like (according to) the testament which I made for their fathers (not with, our versions) in the day of my taking them by their hand to lead them out of the land of Egypt," etc. This dates the former testament, but it does much more: it indicates its promise. God led those fathers out of Egypt, willed them Canaan as a national home where they were to live as God's people. As a father takes a son by his hand in order to support and to hold him in difficult places, so God did with these fathers when he led them out of Egypt. We have a genitive absolute modifying a noun, a problem to the

grammarians since genitive absolutes regularly stand by themselves (B.-D. 423, 5); R. 1123 offers a different construction, one that is rather questionable.

We regard ὅτι as *consecutivum*: "not according . . . seeing that" or "inasmuch as that" (R. 1001); the ὅτι clause states the outcome of this testamentary promise as the reason for making the new testament entirely different. The A. V. has ὅτι = "because"; the R. V., "for." Ὅτι is neither; it is clearly consecutive. "They themselves did not remain in my testament," did not prove to be true heirs of what God intended that they should inherit, namely the land of Canaan flowing with milk and honey, where they were to live in perpetuity under God's richest blessings.

We have been told how they acted in the wilderness (3:7-11), and the writer makes that a warning for his readers. Here there is a still more earnest warning although it is not a formal warning. They acted thus, God says: "and I myself (strong ἐγώ) neglected or ceased my care for them." What else could God do? He cannot carry out testamentary provisions and bestow testamentary promises on heirs who repudiate the testament. The Hebrew seems to signify: "although I was a husband to them" (Luther: *und ich sie zwingen musste*); how the LXX render as they do has not been made clear.

Why the Israelites did not remain in the Lord's testament is not told here. It was because of their wicked heart of unbelief (3:12). This became so bad already in the wilderness that God swore his judgment oath (3:11; 4:3, 5); again so bad that the northern kingdom was entirely wiped out, that also Judah was sent into seventy years of exile in Babylonia. We know what was impending at the time when this epistle was being written: the Jews were losing Palestine and their national existence forever.

The forfeiting of the testament does not mean that the Jews were unable to fulfill the laws of Moses, and that only by perfectly fulfilling them could they be saved, that, therefore, God substituted the gospel for the law in the new testament. The Sinaitic testament was full of gospel, full of Levitical sacrifices to remove sins. In its new testament form the gospel still binds us to live a holy life. The fault of the Jews under that old testament was their hardness of heart (3:8, etc.; Acts 7:51-53; Isa. 5:1-7), it was thus that, as Acts 7:53 says, they kept not the law. In Matt. 5:20, etc., Jesus makes this plain; read his denunciations in Matt. 23:13-39 which plainly end with the final, permanent loss of the testamentary promise: "Behold your house is left unto you desolate" — land, nation, Temple, everything are gone going on 2,000 years.

10) We again have consecutive ὅτι to indicate the result of the previous result:

So that this (is) the testament which I will draw up for the house of Israel
After those days, says the Lord:
I will give my laws upon their mind,
And on their heart will I inscribe them;
And I will be their God,
And they shall be my people.
And they shall not each one teach his fellow citizen,
And each one his brother, saying: Know the Lord!
Because all shall be acquainted with me,
From their small to (their) great;
Because I will be merciful to their unrighteousness,
And their sins will I not remember any longer.

Here we have the inwardness of the new testament which God promised to draw up for the house of Israel (dative of advantage; not "with the house" as in our versions). Only Israel needs to be mentioned when the author repeats God's statement. It will be a testament without ceremonial, ritual, civil, and formal laws. All outward regulations will be discarded. "After those days" refers to the day promised in v. 8 and means after they set in.

The lone participle διδούς disturbs the grammarians. The most instructive discussion on this point is found in Moulton, *Einleitung* 352, etc. The participle is used as a finite verb and is not to be construed with what precedes but is parallel to "I will inscribe." The LXX has διδούς δώσω, some LXX copies omit δώσω. A large number of papyri use the participle in place of a finite verb in the same way. So we translate: "I will give my laws into their mind, and on their heart will I inscribe them." These are two synonymous lines, and the phrases are placed chiastically.

The διάνοια is the whole thinking power of man which directs his acts from inside of him and not from outside like some imposed code or legal force. The καρδία is the very seat of the personality with all its power of thinking, feeling, and willing, where all thoughts, words, and deeds have their secret origin. God's testament promise is that he will give as a gift to our mind and engrave as this gift on our heart his laws which will no longer be "set before" us (Jer. 9:13; Deut. 4:8; 11:32; etc.) as the engraved tables of stone and other Mosaic legal codes were.

The result is expressed by means of two additional lines: "And I will be their God, and they shall be my people," the two εἰς with predicates (R. 481, etc.) and λαός as a designation of God's chosen nation or people.

This is the beautiful ideal of sanctification which God will realize. It is the fruit of justification as v. 12

does not fail to state. It is mediated by true enlightenment as v. 11 states. No longer does the law hedge in one particular nation and shut it off from others with a high wall of legal restrictions. The law is no longer the stern παιδαγωγός to watch the boy on his way to and from school. All scaffolding is removed. In the Christian Church the unchanging moral features of God's law which define the holiness without which no man shall see God are directly implanted in the hearts of believers by the Spirit and the Word and thus constrain them to walk in God's ways.

We use the law as our *Regel* or rule, yet not in its multifarious legislative details that have temporary use and purpose only but as an aid to guide and to express our will to do God's will for Jesus' sake. God's true children of the Old Testament experienced the same thing but were ever weighted down with regulations and restrictions which the Pharisees even multiplied by adding their "commandments of men" with the result that on the whole the people "did not remain in God's testament" (v. 9).

11) The second superior mark of the new testament is the fact that in it "they shall not each one teach his fellow citizen, and each one his brother, saying: 'Know the Lord!'" This teaching is evidently regarded as a mark of inferiority of the old testament. In the new "all shall be acquainted with me, from their small to their great," i. e., this constant dependence for information shall cease. The form εἰδήσουσι is future (B.-D. 101) and not future perfect (R. 906).

It is open to question whether the difference between the two verbs γνῶθι and εἰδήσουσι should be stressed. The former indicates the relation of the subject to the object: *Erkenne den Herrn!* the latter only the relation of the object to the subject: *sie werden mich kennen;* the one stresses personal, appropriating knowledge *cum affectu et effectu,* the latter the knowledge which may not go to that length. The verb seems to be changed in these two poetical lines only for the sake of variation: all will have the right, appropriative knowledge of Yahweh. This *knowledge* is the basis of the *holiness* in their hearts (v. 10).

The difference between the two testaments that is here brought out seems unclear to some interpreters. Some think that in the New Testament times the Old Testament prophets and priests will have disappeared; but "each one his fellow citizen" and "each one his brother" say nothing about prophets and priests teaching the people, and to this day we still have preachers and teachers for the members of the church.

Others tread upon questionable ground. Langsdorff states: "Each person comes to the right knowledge by his own efforts, from within." This is, however, the claim of fanatics who repudiate the written Word as God's means of enlightenment and imagine that the Spirit speaks to their hearts immediately, without, beyond, above the Word of Scripture. Still others think that the Israelites had no personal experience of the Lord while we Christians have this experience. But the whole Book of Psalms, to mention only this, is full of the truest, deepest spiritual experience, cf. Ps. 23; Ps. 32; Ps. 103.

The difference lies in the revelation itself. Revelation was incomplete throughout the days of that old testament. From the time of Moses prophet after prophet appeared who brought message after message. Jeremiah, who is quoted, is one of them. This explains why one citizen and brother had to inform another. A prophet appeared, perhaps in the Temple, and before a smaller or a larger company spoke the Lord's message which he had received. Then those who heard it passed it on to others, one taught another. Take the message quoted. When Jeremiah first uttered it, when he also used symbolic acts as he did in 19:1; 24:1;

Hebrews 8:11, 12

27:2, how did all the people learn what he said and what he did? One had to tell another. Even the words and the deeds of Jesus were at first communicated in this manner. To be sure, there were also written records in the Old Testament times, yet overlook not II Chron. 34:14; and, in the case of Jeremiah's time, Jer. 36:32. After the return from Babylon there was the compilation of the whole Old Testament canon and the reading of these Old Testament Scriptures in the synagogues which then sprang up everywhere. But all this written revelation was still far from being in the state in which it is today.

Note what our writer says in 1:1, 2. The complete revelation came in Jesus, God's Son. After Pentecost the Spirit spread it far and wide. Although it was at first transmitted in the old, imperfect way this complete revelation was soon fixed for all time in a final canon to which all have full and free access. We are no longer dependent on merely what one may hear from another. No new prophets appear with new messages. We have all of God's Word; and each has it in his own hand. We can by it even test those who stand up to preach and to teach it. "From their small up to their great" is correct: from our children and our catechumens up to our great theologians; God's saving revelation, complete at last, is accessible to all alike. It is the fulfillment of the prophecy of Jeremiah and of Isa. 54:13; 11:9; Hab. 2:14; Joel 2:28; cf., John 6:45; I John 2:20, 27.

12) The third great mark of the new testament is the *forgiveness* it bestows on all who are placed under it: "Because I will be merciful to their unrighteousness, and their sins will I not remember any longer." The Hebrew word which is translated "unrighteousness" signifies "guilt," "guiltiness." This deserves full punishment, yet God says that he will be ἵλεως, "merciful," and will thus not punish. The synonymous line says

still more, namely that God will no longer remember the sins. They will be blotted from his mind and his memory as if he had never known them. The idea is not that God arbitrarily forgives and forgets any man's sins. "Blessed is he . . . whose sin is covered," Ps. 32:1. "As far as the east is from the west, so far hath he removed our transgressions from us," Ps. 103:12. "Thou wilt cast all our sins into the depths of the sea," Micah 7:19. It is the expiating power of Jesus' blood that covers, removes, and casts into the depths our sins; then they are, indeed, erased from the memory of God. This is divine forgiveness, the greatest mark of the new testament.

The Sinaitic testament should not be conceived as a mere set of laws that resulted in transgressions while the new testament is gospel and thus filled with pardon. Then the old would really be no testament at all. If it is claimed that the Jews had to keep the law in order to be saved, then none were saved before Jesus came. The Sinaitic laws of ritual are full of forgiveness. "Thou forgavest the iniquity of my sin. Selah," Ps. 32:5. "Who forgiveth all thine iniquities," Ps. 103:3. "If thou, Lord, shouldest mark iniquities, O Lord, who shall stand? But there is forgiveness with thee, that thou mayest be feared," Ps. 130:3, 4. The difference does not lie along this line. Christ's expiation on the cross was just as effective for contrite sinners who lived before Calvary as it is for those who live after Calvary, before Christ entered the Holy of Holies in heaven as well as after he entered it (v. 1, 2).

The difference lies in this fact: the old testament was given to a nation. It was thus that the bulk of this nation ever and again proved obdurate; "they did not remain in my testament" (v. 9). When this old Mosaic testament was brought to them because of their transgressions (Gal. 3:17, 19), they did not let even its threats and its judgments halt them and keep them true. The new testament is not intended for a nation. All that is national, temporal, preparatory, as far as preserving one nation as God's people is concerned, has disappeared. The new testament is intended for all men, no matter in what nation they may be found, who by contrition, repentance, faith, and holy obedience do remain in this testament and thus do obtain all that its testamentary provisions convey: enlightenment (v. 11), holiness (v. 10), and above all forgiveness (v. 12). As v. 8 states it with the word συντελεῖν, the new testament is actually consummated or accomplished, brought to its goal.

13) Yet it is not the universality or any other of the many great things contained in the word of God quoted from Jeremiah that the writer wishes to stress. For his readers, who are thinking of throwing away the new testament and its Mediator in the heavenly Holy of Holies and going back to the old national testament, the writer selects only this one decisive point from the quotation: **In saying a new one he has declared the first one old. Now the thing declared old and becoming aged (is) near to vanishing away.**

Do the readers intend to go back to such a thing? The writer lays his finger on just the one word "καινήν" which was used in v. 8. This one word is all-decisive for his readers: God himself has declared the first testament old when about 600 B. C. he said "a new one." Jesus did not make it old. It was old when God spoke centuries ago and certainly has not grown younger during all the following centuries.

Δέ is not "but" (adversative); it merely adds the point of God's having declared the first testament old centuries ago: "Now the thing declared old and becoming aged is near to vanishing away." This is a self-evident general statement; it is, therefore, worded with the neuter: τό with participles; not with the feminine, not following the gender of τὴν πρώτην. We regard παλαιούμενον as a passive and thus matching the active "God has declared." Some prefer to regard it as the middle: "the thing becoming old," because the next participle γηράσκον is not a passive. Both participles follow one article, both are also in the present tense which describes the thing, but that fact does not make both participles intransitive. The first: "the thing declared old," is not declared only so by God; it is secondly "becoming aged," actually weak, tottering with senility. Thus it is "near to vanishing away" like an old, old man who is sinking into his grave. To such a thing the readers would go back if they again became Jews.

"Near to vanishing away," like the descriptive present participles, does not refer merely to the present time of writing but to anything that at any time is in such a condition of decrepitude. When it is applied to the old testament this decrepit condition and the imminence of fading out completely existed already in Jeremiah's time. There is thus no particular reference to the condition of Judaism at the time of the writing of this epistle, the imminence of the destruction of the nation, Jerusalem, and the Temple. We cannot refer to this verse when dating the epistle. It contains nothing to warrant the assumption that the Temple was already destroyed. This vanishing away pertains only to the old testament of Moses. Whether the Temple and its rituals continue or not is in no way pertinent to what the writer says. We know that at the time of the death of Jesus its inner veil was rent from top to bottom (Matt. 27:51), a fact which leaves little to be desired.

CHAPTER IX

The Two Tabernacles Compared, v. 1-12

1) As in 7:11, μὲν οὖν is merely transitional, and μέν has no correlative δέ, and needs none. This δέ need not be found in v. 5 or even in v. 11. Nor is this mere transition concessive: *nun freilich, nun zwar,* "now indeed," "then verily" (A. V.), "now even" (R. V.). The writer simply passes on from a comparison of the two testaments to a comparison of the two Tabernacles. He first describes the Tabernacle in the wilderness and relates what the common priests did daily in the Holy and the high priest once a year in the Holy of Holies.

He wisely describes only the Tabernacle and not the Temple of Solomon, of Ezra, of Herod, least of all that of Leontopolis in Egypt; for it was the Tabernacle that Moses constructed according to the very pattern shown to him in the Mount (8:5). The Temples that were later built were only copies of this Tabernacle; our writer confines himself to the divine original. His description is in no way a *detraction,* for this would be a mistake as far as his readers are concerned. He does not merely *concede* the greatness of the Tabernacle which Moses built. Quite the contrary. The very greatness of that Tabernacle sets into true relief the Holy of Holies in heaven into which Jesus, our High Priest, enters.

Now, then, also the first (testament) **had ordinances about** (divine) **service and** (had) **the Holy Place in the world.**

The following "for" describes the essential details of this ἅγιον with reference to the divine λατρεία or "service" for which God ordered its construction (v. 5). Neither the "service" nor the "Holy Place" in which it took place were without δικαιώματα, divine righteous pronouncements or "ordinances" given by God himself. The verb used is an imperfect: "had," and takes us into the past, and does no more. There are two objects: the first testament (πρώτη, the same as τὴν πρώτην in 8:13) had such righteous ordinances and together with them had the necessary Holy Place, and the close connection between them is marked by τε. The ordinances dealt with the "service" (objective genitive), which is described for the readers in v. 6, 7. With the singular τὸ ἅγιον the writer refers to the entire Sanctuary or Tabernacle.

The fact that the adjective κοσμικόν is added predicatively puzzles the grammarians (R. 777); but the predicative idea is exactly what the writer wants, for this Holy Place as well as the service for which it was constructed were κοσμικόν; the word is used in the sense of "belonging to this world." By adding this adjective in a quiet way the writer does not wish to minimize the Tabernacle and leave the impression that it is less than "the greater and more complete Tabernacle, not made with hands, that is, not of this creation" (v. 11).

Kosmikon, "in the world," is used only for the sake of precision: the place where, under the divine ordinances, the divinely appointed priests and the high priest were to officiate as v. 6, 7 describe; they had to have "the Holy Place" in which they could do this. The emphasis is on the divine ordinances regarding service, to which the second object, "the Holy Place in the world," is only attached with the close connective. These are God's ordinances, and the readers may think that they are therefore final. The truth that they are not the complete and final thing will appear in due time. The one object of the writer in this connection is to express the greatness of the service and its sanctuary as being divinely ordered by God.

2) "For" initiates the description: **For a Tabernacle was fitted up, the first, in which** (were) **the**

Hebrews 9:2

candelabrum and the table and the showbread, which is called Holy Place.

The verb (now a historical aorist) applies to both the σκηνή, "tent or tabernacle," and its ritualistic utensils although these are mentioned in a special relative clause. The apposition ἡ πρώτη does not, of course, mean that there were two tents as the readers well know. The tent was double, a great curtain divided the two compartments.

Ἡ λυχνία is the golden candelabrum (not "candlestick," our versions) with its upright shaft and its six branching arms (three on each side) bearing seven lamps, adorned with almond blossoms, pomegranates, and lilies. The Tabernacle and Herod's Temple had one candelabrum, Solomon's had ten and also ten tables, II Chron. 4:8; compare 4:19 and I Chron. 26:16.

"The table" was for the showbread of twelve loaves, one for each of the twelve tribes, which were baked of fine, unleavened flour and were changed every Sabbath; the old loaves were eaten by the priests only. We follow neither B.-P. 1132 who makes ἡ πρόθεσις too concrete: *das Geraet fuer die Auslegung der Brote,* nor Riggenbach who combines the *prothesis* with "the table." Tholuck's *strues panum* is correct, "the lot of bread"; πρόθεσις merely states that the bread was set forth in order, thus making it what we call "the showbread." This bread is named as the third thing in the Holy Place. It was baked of unleavened flour and consisted of twelve thin, flat cakes and not large, round "loaves." The Greek pluralizes ἄρτος since it has no word for "loaves."

The front part of the Tabernacle (tent) is called ἅγια, "Holy Place," in distinction from the rear part which was ἅγια ἁγίων, "Holy of Holies," a superlative, "Most Holy Place," (v. 3). No articles are needed although they may be used in other connections. In v. 1 τὸ ἅγιον = the whole sanctuary; in 8:2 τὰ ἅγια =

the heavenly sanctuary. The neuter plural is idiomatic; such plurals appear also in σάββατα and in the names for some of the festivals.

3) And after the second veil a Tabernacle called Holy of Holies, having a golden altar of incense and the ark of the testament, overlaid entirely with gold, in which (there was) **a golden pot containing the manna, and the rod of Aaron that budded, and the tables of the testament, and above it cherubim of glory, overshadowing the mercy seat; concerning which it is not** (in order) **now to speak.**

Some think that this is the only local use of μετά in the New Testament: "behind the second veil"; but if we think of someone entering or looking into the tent from the front veil, "after" is quite sufficient. One would see the things named in v. 2 and "after" that what is now mentioned in v. 3, etc. On καταπέτασμα see 6:19.

This inner veil or curtain was woven of blue, purple, and scarlet wool and fine, twined linen (byssus), was adorned with the figures of cherubim and was hung on four gilded pillars of acacia wood that rested in silver sockets; it shut off the Holy of Holies from the rest of the tent. Behind this curtain only the high priest entered on the Great Day of Atonement. Note that the two designations: "which is called 'Holy'" and "called 'Holy of Holies'" are placed chiastically.

4) There is a crux in ἔχουσα θυμιατήριον. What was this, and where was it placed? Our versions think of "a golden censer." Riggenbach has the best defense of this opinion, and the word does mean anything that is used for burning incense, an altar or merely a vessel ("censer"). This, too, is true, that on entering the Holy of Holies the high priest carried a censer full of live coals upon which he sprinkled incense, that had been beaten small, so as to make a cloud to hide the

mercy seat lest he die; this was his first act on entering, Lev. 16:12, 13.

We do not think that this censer is referred to here. In the first place, it was not kept in the Holy of Holies, nor do we know that it was made of gold although it may have been. It was kept in a sideroom. The article is absent, but it is also absent from "a golden pot." The article may be absent because there was more than one instrument for burning incense. In the second place, it is inexplicable that the writer should fail to mention the fact that there was also a golden altar of incense which was permanently located in the sanctuary and was in daily use.

If the writer refers to this altar of incense, how can he connect it with the Holy of Holies when this altar stood in the Holy Place? Meyer says that the writer made a mistake and thought that this golden altar was behind the veil. The writer does not, however, say that this golden altar was "in" the Holy of Holies; he uses ἔχουσα. Although he uses the same word in connection with the golden pot, we nevertheless note a difference: a pot "contains" something, a great room "has" certain things pertaining to it. The difficulty is cleared up by I Kings 6:22: this golden altar was *"by* the oracle," stood near the veil, pertained to the Holy of Holies, and is so considered here. Exod. 30:1-6 (see also 40:5) describes this altar and then connects it with the ark of the testimony: "Put it *before* the veil that is by the ark of the testimony, *before* the mercy seat that is over the testimony"—"set the altar of gold for the incense *before* the ark of the testimony." This is conclusive for us. The golden altar of incense stood in the Holy Place close to the veil; when he was offering the incense the priest faced the mercy seat behind the veil; the incense was offered to God as being present on the mercy seat. Compare Zahn, *Introduction* II, 363, etc.

Thus we see how ἔχουσα can include both "an altar of incense" *in front* of the veil and "the ark of the testament" (see διαθήκη in 7:22) *behind* the veil. This altar is thus of greater importance than the candelabrum, the table, and the showbread. The ark is described as "having been overlaid all over (πάντοθεν) with gold." Exod. 25:11 says "within and without," it also had "a crown of gold round about." That is why the word which is used here is not χρυσός, gold as material, but χρυσίον, the diminutive, wrought gold, gold work in designs.

Κιβωτόν = box, chest, or ark; this sacred ark is called the ark of the testament because it contained "the tables of the testament" that had been brought down from the Mount by Moses. Exod. 16:32-34 does not say that the vessel which contained the manna was made of gold; the writer has probably obtained this information from reliable Jewish tradition. This golden pot and "the rod of Aaron that had budded" and bloomed and yielded almonds were in the ark besides the stone tables that were inscribed with the law (Exod. 17:6-11). Exod. 25:16 says in so many words that the testimony was to be placed in the ark (Deut. 10:1, 2). Concerning the omer of manna Exod. 16:33 says: "Lay it up before the Lord"; concerning Aaron's rod Num. 17:10: "Bring it . . . before the testimony to be kept for a token," etc. Yet when I Kings 8:9 (II Chron. 5:10) states that in Solomon's time there was nothing in the ark save the two tables of stone, the implication is that there had originally been more in the ark, namely the pot of manna and Aaron's rod just as our writer says. No one knows what had become of the manna and the rod.

5) The mercy seat and the two cherubim are described in Exod. 25:17-22, which see. The former was made of pure gold and served as the lid of the ark.

The cherubim stood on this golden lid, facing each other, their wings were stretched forward and thus overshadowed the mercy seat. They are called "cherubim of glory." The genitive is not an attributive genitive: "glorious cherubim," but a possessive genitive: "cherubim belonging to God's glory," for God was present in his glory between these cherubim (Exod. 25:22; 40:38). The Greek word "cherubim" is neuter and only occasionally masculine.

The Hebrew *Kapporeth*, from *kipper*, equals "cover," and from its use on the sacred ark "a means of propitiation." Combining this with the idea of covering, one may call it *Suehndeckel*, "propitiatory cover." Ed. Koenig, *Hebraeisches und aramaeisches Woerterbuch*. In his masterly rendering Luther uses the interpretative *Gnadenstuhl*, which our versions adopt when they translate "mercy seat." The LXX rendered the Hebrew word used in Exod. 25:17 ἱλαστήριον ἐπίθεμα and after that used simply ἱλαστήριον. Both the Hebrew and the Greek words became technical terms and remained so; the R. V.'s margin: "the propitiatory," both in our passage and in Rom. 3:25, seeks to convert the Greek term into a common noun and thus ought to be canceled. It was the sacrificial blood which was sprinkled on the cover that made it the *Suehndeckel* or mercy seat. See Rom. 3:25.

The writer only names these most sacred objects. Much might be said about their significance, but this is not the place for such instruction. So he adds: "concerning which it is not (in order) now to speak."

6) **Now these things having been thus fitted up, into the first Tabernacle the priests go constantly, attending to the services, while into the second only once during the year the high priest alone, not without blood which he offers for himself and the ignorances of the people.**

From the description of the Tabernacle and its fittings the writer advances to the functions of the priests. Δέ is transitional and is not to be connected with μὲν οὖν in v. 1. The description is worded in present tenses, which, referring, as they do, to the Tabernacle that is now long lost, are nothing but historical narration and contain no reference to what was done in Herod's Temple at the writer's time. The writer confines himself throughout to God's original Tabernacle as this is described in the Pentateuch. The perfect participle in the genitive absolute harmonizes with the present tenses of the main verbs: these things, so fitted up and in this condition, the priests use.

The priests enter the first Tabernacle daily without interruption and carry out the services by twice daily offering incense on the golden altar before the inner veil, daily attending to the lamps of the candelabrum, weekly changing the showbread. This is said about the common priests only in order to bring out more clearly what the high priest does. Μέν and δέ balance only the phrases into which these particles are inserted.

7) Into the second Tabernacle there goes only "once during the year the high priest alone," namely on the Great Day of Atonement. The genitive τοῦ ἐνιαυτοῦ is not distributive (R. 769), for this thought would require κατά with the accusative; nor is the genitive dependent on the adverb (R. 637). Since it has the article it is the genitive of the time within which: "during the year," and the adverb states how often: "once." This is in contrast with the priests who enter the Holy Place daily. "Only the high priest" is in contrast with the priests who take turns in daily officiating in the Holy Place. "Not without blood" is again in contrast with the priests who never use blood in the Holy Place. These points of contrast are brought out here because they are pertinent to what follows in regard to Christ.

From Lev. 16 it appears that the high priest entered the Holy of Holies twice on the Day of Atonement, once with the bullock's blood for himself and once with the goat's blood for the people. Late accounts speak of four times: first with the censer; next with the bullock's blood; then with that of the goat; finally to carry away the coal pan and the censer. "Once during the year" does not concern itself with such details since it excludes "more times during the year," more than this one day.

The blood "he offers for himself and for the ignorances (sins of ignorance) of the people." The fact that the blood was taken from two animals, each of which was offered in its own way, need not be introduced here. The offering of blood for the high priest himself has been touched upon already in 5:3. By writing "for himself and the ignorances of the people" instead of "for himself and the people" or "for the ignorance of himself and of the people," the difference is indicated: the blood that was offered for himself was for himself as high priest in order to enable him to act for the people. Ἀγνοήματα are sins of ignorance such as the people did not know about when they sinned and thus had not removed by sacrifices during the year as they did the sins which they knew about.

8) The sentence continues with a genitive absolute and now comes to the main feature of the entire description: **the Holy Spirit indicating this fact, that not yet has there been made manifest the way to the Holy Place, the first Tabernacle still having its position; which (is) a figure regarding the present period, in accord with which (figure) both gifts and sacrifices are offered, unable to bring to the goal, as far as conscience is concerned, him who renders the worship,** (these gifts and sacrifices being) **only, in addition to foods and drinks and various baptisms, ordinances about flesh, obligatory up to** (the) **period of** (the) **right order.**

During the whole period in which the Tabernacle has the Holy Place in front of the Holy of Holies the Holy Spirit himself shows that the way to the Holy Place in heaven, i.e., to "the Holy Place and the true Tabernacle" where Jesus is the High Priest and the ministrant (8:1, 2), has not yet been made evident. That arrangement of τὸ ἅγιον κοσμικόν, of the sanctuary here in the world (9:1), in two compartments shows that it is only a παραβολή, a parable or figure regarding the present time when Jesus has entered into the Sanctuary of heaven with his blood. In the figure the gifts as well as the sacrifices of blood, both those offered in the Holy Place of the earthly Tabernacle and those offered by the high priests in the Holy of Holies, are unable to accomplish the whole thing, being no more than divine ordinances about the flesh or human body and obligatory until the period when the right and final arrangement is instituted by God in the Highpriestly ministration of Jesus.

It would be the greatest mistake for the readers to think that the Tabernacle which God made Moses construct in the wilderness and fit up for the service by the priests and the high priest is the final thing and intended by him to remain for all time and only to be advanced from the Tabernacle to the Temple building in Jerusalem, when the Holy Spirit himself shows so clearly, by both the division of the Tabernacle into a Holy and a Holy of Holies and the nature of the ordinances that were prescribed for the whole Tabernacle services, that all this is only a temporary thing, a figure and parable of the time when God brings the right arrangement. This time is now here. We now have the final High Priest and the ministrant in the heavenly Sanctuary (8:1, 2). Can the readers now think of turning back to what was only a parable? Let them think of the old Tabernacle as highly as they will, what has now come in our High Priest Jesus appears only so much the higher as it also indeed is.

This is the thought of these verses, which should not be confused when one is studying the various details of the wording.

Τοῦτο is emphatic: "this" is what the Holy Spirit indicates by the arrangement of the old Tabernacle and the priestly services for which it was designed, "this," namely "that not yet (at that time) has there been made manifest the way to the (final) Holy Place" in heaven; we have the infinitive in indirect discourse (R. 1048) in apposition with τοῦτο (R. 1078). God ordered the whole construction, arrangement, and services of the Tabernacle (8:5); since all of this was for the sanctification of Israel, the writer now says that "the Holy Spirit" indicates what this Tabernacle, etc., really signifies regarding the heavenly Sanctuary and the High-priestly ministration of Jesus, the Spirit being the Sanctifier. The perfect tense of the infinitive extends over the whole time during which the Tabernacle arrangement stood as a figure; during all of that time the Spirit said: The way to the heavenly Sanctuary "has not yet been made manifest" by me, the real High Priest has not yet come.

The verb is most exact, for the way to the heavenly Sanctuary had been foreshadowed (v. 5, "sketch and shadow of the heavenly" originals), prefigured but was not yet made manifest as it now is since Jesus has as our High Priest gone into the heavenly Sanctuary. In τὴν τῶν ἁγίων ὁδόν the genitive is objective: "the way to the Holy Place," τῶν ἁγίων, as in 8:2, indicates the heavenly Sanctuary.

The genitive absolute: "the first Tabernacle still having its position," points out the significant feature that the way to the heavenly Sanctuary remains unmanifested while the division between the first and the second Tabernacle, i.e., between the Holy and the Holy of Holies, still stands (see v. 1-3). There is no reference to Solomon's, Ezra's, and Herod's Temples. There is no need for such a reference. The readers are acquainted with Matt. 27:51, know that by rending the inner veil the Spirit himself indicated the end of what the Tabernacle in the wilderness prefigured. When the sacrifice of Jesus on Calvary was complete, when he entered the heavenly Sanctuary with his expiating blood, all that the figure foreshadowed had come, the way to the heavenly Sanctuary was manifest at last. In the heavenly Sanctuary there is no longer a Holy Place and a Holy of Holies with a veil between them.

9) Ἥτις = "the first Tabernacle," the Holy Place before the Holy of Holies, and παραβολή is the predicate; the copula is omitted as being unnecessary: "which (first Tabernacle) a figure regarding the present period." In what respect is it such "a figure"? The entire καθ' ἥν clause explains. The qualitative relative says that this first Tabernacle is only a "parable." "The true Tabernacle" (8:2), the heavenly one, cannot have a division, a Holy and a Holy of Holies, it can consist only of a unit Sanctuary for the High-priestly act of our "great High Priest" (4:14). This earthly Holy Place has only a parabolic significance, one that is effective only for the time that it is needed. As a parable or figure it points forward to the time when it will be no longer needed, when the one heavenly Sanctuary will be manifested, when all parabolic pointers will be forever superseded.

The writer says that the first Tabernacle is of a kind or quality (ἥτις) that makes it such a parable "regarding (εἰς) the present period" in which Jesus has gone into the heavenly Sanctuary with his blood. The perfect ἐνεστηκότα is always used in the sense of the present; even in II Thess. 2:2 ἐνέστηκεν = "is present" (see the discussion of this passage where this meaning is vital). This period should be dated only in the present in which Jesus has entered the heavenly Sanctuary. The parable points to this present time, for its significance is now realized in this act of Jesus'.

The variant καθ' ὅν alters only the form of the thought: "in accord with this that," etc. The reading καθ' ἥν is textually preferable and connects with παραβολή. Some connect it with σκηνῆς, which is only a matter of formal grammar since "the first Tabernacle" is "a parable" so that connecting it with either takes in the other. Yet the writer explains in what way this parable *is* a parable: "according to it as a parable (i.e., as signifying something regarding the present time) both gifts and sacrifices are offered, unable" to bring anybody to the real goal. The parable thus points to the present time in which this goal is attained in the sacrifice that was presented to God in a better Sanctuary, in one that was without such a Holy Place before the Holy of Holies. As matching (κατά) the "parable" or figurative quality of the Holy Place in the tent in the wilderness, all the gifts (incense, showbread, lights on the candelabrum) and sacrifices (blood sprinkled on the altar of incense, Lev. 1:5; 16:18, 19) are offered, "unable to bring to the goal, as far as conscience is concerned, him who renders the worship," τὸν λατρεύοντα, "the worshipper" (R. V.) among the people, and not τὸν λειτουργοῦντα, the officiating person, the priest or high priest.

Μή is the regular negative with participles and needs no explanation as though it were "subjective" (the older view). The statement refers to every Israelite including, of course, also the priests, for all the gifts and sacrifices were offered for all of them. Yet of themselves none of these gifts and sacrifices, "as far as conscience is concerned," brought completeness (10:1-4). All they could do was to point to the one sacrifice of Jesus which would, indeed, bring completeness, actually attain the goal, and thus lead the Israelites to believe in that coming sacrifice in order by such faith to obtain pardon and free the conscience of sin and guilt. Without this coming sacrifice and faith in its efficacy no worshipper could have a conscience that was truly cleansed. Τελειῶσαι repeats the idea of the noun used in 7:11 and of the verb occurring in 7:19; 10:1, 14. See how this word runs through this letter in speaking of both Jesus and us (2:10; 5:9; 6:1; 7:28; 11:40; 12:23); this is quite essential.

10) Μόνον δικαιώματα (not the dative which a few texts have) is an apposition to δῶρά τε καὶ θυσίαι: these gifts and sacrifices "only, in addition to (ἐπί) foods and drinks and various baptisms, ordinances about flesh, obligatory up to (the) period of (the) right order," up to the time when the Spirit would institute the right and final order in Christ. All of this ritual and worship of the Tabernacle was only preliminary, temporal, transient. It was preparatory and not the right arrangement itself.

The readers should see this when they note that the gifts and sacrifices were "only ordinances about flesh" (objective genitive), regulated the worshipper's "flesh" or body, "rites" (A. V. margin) that were ordered by the divine Judge for the body—δικαιώματα also in v. 1. They were given only in addition to all the other ceremonial regulations about what foods to eat and to avoid, what drinks were to be used, and the baptisms (lustrations or washings) that were to be performed. It may be noted that these "baptisms" of the Jewish ritual were not immersions. "Carnal ordinances" (our versions) is an unsatisfactory rendering, the more so because the genitive is not adjectival. "Flesh," the outward body, is the opposite of "conscience." Ceremonial rites that pertain to the body only certainly cannot put the conscience into the full and complete condition in which it should be.

The εἰς phrase occurring in v. 9: "regarding the present time," is now followed by a phrase that says much more: these ordinances are "imposed and thus obligatory only up to the period of the right order," διόρθωσις, *rechte, richtige Ordnung* (C.-K. 818), when all the old imperfections of the Levitical and preparatory period would be discarded, when Jesus would bring everything to completeness (compare 7:11). "The time of reformation" (our versions) is not a satisfactory English rendering.

The parabolic nature of the Holy Place in the Tabernacle of the wilderness is thus fully shown. All the services for which it was designed were not the completeness which the Spirit intended for the conscience. This very incompleteness pointed forward to the time when all would be complete and right according to the Spirit's design. This blessed period had now come since Jesus had shed and offered his blood to God in the divine Sanctuary. No one must now forsake Jesus and imagine that he will find rest for his conscience in the old ordinances of the Tabernacle. The old Israelites had their conscience cleansed only by faith in the completeness which the coming High Priest would bring.

It is a bit surprising to note that the writer uses "the Holy Place" and not the Holy of Holies and what the high priest did there when he is bringing out the inadequacy of the Tabernacle and its function. He is wise in this procedure. The very fact that the Tabernacle has this anterior chamber shows that this could not be the final Sanctuary that had been designed by the Spirit for the expiation of our sins. As long as the Holy Place stood before the Holy of Holies, the latter was marked as not being the final Sanctuary. Yet the Spirit had never ordered Israel to have a Tabernacle that had only one room, only a Holy of Holies. The one final Sanctuary is not made with hands (v. 11) or by man (8:2); it is heaven itself, where the eternal God dwells, where Jesus appeared with his blood (9:24).

11) So much for *the earthly Tabernacle;* now, in comparison, *the heavenly Tabernacle.*

Christ, however, arrived as High Priest of the good things about to come by means of the greater and more complete Tabernacle, not handmade, that is, not of this creation, nor by means of blood of goats and calves but by means of his own blood went in once for all into the Holy Place, obtaining an eternal ransoming.

Although the writer often uses the name "Jesus," the name "Christ," which points to our Savior's office, is in place here, for his great High-priestly act is to be described. On the relation of the three aorists: participle, main verb, participle, little needs to be said. They present three closely connected historical facts like Caesar's famous dictum: *Veni, vidi, vici,* "I came, I saw, I conquered." Only the relation of the facts is involved in the tenses. The writer has the choice as to which of the three he wishes to make a participle, which the main verb, or whether he wants to use participles at all. The writer's choice is certainly a good one: arrived, he entered, obtaining. There is no thought of intervals of time in these aorists but only the thought of natural relation, and this is not expressed by the tenses as tenses but by the sequence of the statements. So we do not ask: "How long before he entered did he arrive, and how long after he entered did he obtain?" We may even leave out the participles and say: "As High Priest he entered for eternal ransoming," and we have the writer's meaning. We therefore disregard the dating of the first participle as if this goes back to the incarnation or to the assumption of Christ's office three years before his death.

Thus it also makes little difference whether we combine the two διά phrases with the first participle or with the main verb although the latter is generally done. Since παραγίνομαι is only a synonym of ἔρχομαι, we find no special significance in the choice of this word save that παραγενόμενος naturally fits εἰσῆλθεν and is used for this reason (see M.-M. 481 on the word). Γενόμενος would bring in an entirely different thought, one that the writer certainly does not want when he speaks of Christ's entering in, as if he entered in by becoming High Priest. The main point is the predication: "as High Priest of the good things about to come." As such he arrived, was at hand, and entered in. The writer tells us of the High-priestly act of Christ and at once names him as the High Priest.

It goes without saying that "High Priest of the good things about to come" aims to exalt Christ above all the common Jewish high priests, none of whom could be so designated. All that follows clearly shows this fact. Shall we read μελλόντων or γενομένων: of the good things "about to come" or "having come" (aorist)? We have "the good things about to come" in the undisputed reading of 10:1, which fact cannot be lightly brushed aside when the reading of our passage is to be determined. To say that Christ came as High Priest of the good things that have already come cannot be understood to mean that these things have come *since* Christ arrived; the aorist could only mean that, when Christ came, these good things were already here. This was the point that vexed the old Greek exegetes when they attempted to interpret this aorist.

The correct reading is τῶν μελλόντων. Our writer uses μέλλω repeatedly: in 2:5, "the world to come"; 6:5, "the powers of the eon to come"; 1:14, "those about to inherit salvation." In 9:15 this is called the eternal inheritance. The good things referred to belong to the world to come, they constitute our hope. By faith and hope we embrace them already in this life and taste the good Word of God and the powers of the world to come (6:5). As High Priest Christ entered heaven; the good things to come are heavenly. In "High Priest of the good things about to come" the genitive is possessive and connects Christ with these good things.

In a number of commentaries the first διά is regarded as being *local:* Christ went in *through* the greater and more complete Tabernacle; the second and third διά are *instrumental:* "went in, not *by means of* blood of goats and calves, but *by means of* his own blood." Even if we disregard οὐδέ, "nor," which seems out of place when the διά are taken in different senses, we hesitate to adopt the view of these commentators. They suppose that Christ went into the Holy of Holies in heaven (εἰς τὰ ἅγια, v. 12) by first going *through* something that corresponds to the Holy of the earthly Tabernacle of Moses. This anteroom they find in "the greater and more complete σκηνή or Tabernacle, not handmade, that is, not of this creation."

But what can this anteroom be? The idea that it is the body or the human nature of Christ is now commonly rejected and certainly has no support in 10:20. Since this σκηνή is "not of this creation" as the writer himself says, the created heavens cannot be referred to as they are referred to in 4:14: "having passed through the (created) heavens" in his ascension. So these commentators think that heaven itself, the uncreated place where God dwells, is divided into two parts that correspond to the Holy Place and the Holy of Holies of the Tabernacle of the wilderness. They think that the writer is exalting this heavenly anteroom "through" which Jesus passed in order to reach the heavenly Holy of Holies that was above the anteroom of Moses' Tabernacle.

We decline to follow them. In v. 8 the very fact that in the earthly Tabernacle the Holy Place still has its position before the Holy of Holies is pointed out as evidence that the way into the heavenly Holy of Holies has not yet been made manifest. Are we now to believe

that such an anteroom still has its position, an eternal
position, in front of the Holy of Holies of heaven, and
that despite this fact this anteroom is now *not* the
evidence that it is in v. 8 but rather the opposite, evidence that the way into the heavenly Sanctuary has
been made manifest? This surely cannot be the case.
If there is an anteroom in heaven as there is in Moses'
Tabernacle, the two anterooms cannot have an opposite
significance, to say nothing of this division of heaven
apart from any significance regarding the way to the
heavenly Holy of Holies.

The A. V. is correct. The three διά have the same
force: "by," i.e., "by means of"; the first is not
"through" (local), R. V. "Handmade" recalls the whole
Mosaic Tabernacle which was made by hand; the
heavenly σκηνή is not "handmade," is not even made by
God's creative hand as the elucidation "not of this
creation" adds. Christ needs *two* means for his High-
priestly act just as the Jewish high priests did: one is
the proper σκηνή or Tabernacle into which to enter with
the blood; the other is the blood which he may offer.
Then, it is objected, "the greater and more complete
σκηνή" would be the same as τὰ ἅγια. Why not? Are the
two terms not used in 8:2 to designate the identical
place as they are here in 9:11, 12? The one, namely the
σκηνή, names it as a tent; the other, τὰ ἅγια, names it
from the viewpoint of its sacredness. "The tent" serves
Christ as a means; "the sacred place" (τὰ ἅγια) he
enters. "The tent" does not mean the anteroom, and
"the sacred place" the inner room—two. The tent
includes the sacred place—one. Both terms are, of
course, appropriated from the Tabernacle of Moses
just as they are in 8:2 where the writer combines
them as they are in heaven.

Yes, this heavenly "tent" is far greater than that
which housed the earthly Holy of Holies. Epexegetical

καί adds the thought that it is far greater because it is "more complete," for this tent does bring to the goal. Here we again have this significant term to which we have drawn attention in v. 9; see the references cited there.

12) As the one means is greater, so is also the other, namely the blood. "neither by means of blood of goats (for the sins of the people, v. 7; Lev. 16:9) and of calves (for the high priest himself, v. 7; Lev. 16: 11)." See also 7:27. Christ does not need two kinds of blood as the Jewish high priest did who was himself a sinner: "but by means of his own blood," this one most holy and precious blood that atoned with eternal completeness for all the sins of all sinners from Adam on to the last one who shall be born. Christ's own blood is called that of the Lamb of God; all the τράγοι, μόσχοι, and ταῦροι, he-goats, young bulls (bullocks), and bulls are superseded. See Rev. 5:9, 12, 13; 14:8.

We keep the participle, the verb, and the participle in their close relation as together expressing a unit thought: "Christ arrived, did enter, obtaining." Then the difficulty regarding the means that were used by Christ in this act will disappear. When you separate the verb form, it will sound strange to say that Christ "entered by means" of something even if you make the means only his blood. "Once for all" is repeated from 7:27, in our study of which it has already been shown why no repetition is necessary or even possible. In 7:27 Christ offered up "himself"; here we have "by means of his own blood" instead of "himself," in John 10:17, 18 it is his "life."

"The blood of Jesus" is a subject that deserves an entire dissertation, especially since "the old blood theology" is so often attacked, called "gory," counted unholy and not sanctifying (10:29). The connotation of the term "blood" is that of sacrifice, the expiation of the sacrifice that covers and removes sin; thus "blood" is more precise than "death" since many deaths are bloodless. In a sacrifice the blood is shed or poured out so that the life goes out in death. The expiation is thus connected with substitution. The life of the sacrificial victim goes out in death so that the life of the beneficiary of the sacrifice is spared. This is by far not all; the blood comes to the altar, the sanctuary, the mercy seat, i.e., before God, in the way indicated by him so that he may accept it. Only *this* blood expiates and cleanses. Much more may be said. The one fact to be noted is that it is not the blood as a substance, nor the blood that is made to flow by mortal wounds that is involved in substitutionary sacrifice but the blood that is shed for the specific expiatory purpose. "Blood" thus = the completed sacrifice as it is brought to God.

The blood sacrifices of the Old Testament expiatory and cleansing rituals possessed efficacy only because God connected them with the eternally efficacious blood of his own Son (Rev. 13:8). That is the τελείωσις, the completion that reached the goal and came about only when our High Priest, Christ, offered "his own blood" in sacrifice once for all.

We discard the idea that at the time of his death Jesus took his blood into the heavenly Sanctuary before God. One is disturbed to read what Bengel, Stier, Delitzsch, and others say about Christ's blood; such things as that the blood Christ shed was received back into his body, that it was received into heaven, or that the blood which was left in Christ's dead body was increased and renewed. These distressing conceptions center particularly on the Lord's Supper, in connection with which some speak of "the *glorified* blood" that is now given us to drink in the Sacrament. Where does Scripture speak of Christ's "glorified blood"? The words that are used in connection with the Sacrament are: "my blood in the act of being shed for you" just as: "my body in the act of being given for you." When

Riggenbach regards "blood" as it is used in our epistle *bildlich,* "figurative," signifying "death," he surely does not fully understand the implication of his words. What Christ shed was "his own blood" and not something that pictures his death. Instead of saying that Christ's blood = his death, the reverse is true: where the Scriptures speak of his death they refer to his bloody death, his expiatory, sacrificial blood.*

The second aorist middle εὑράμενος has the first aorist a (R. 339). This is not an indirect middle (R. 809); it is the Attic use of the middle when the meaning is *erlangen,* "obtain" (B.-D. 310, 1; B.-P. 508); the middle of this verb is found only here in the New Testament. What Christ obtained is "eternal ransoming," λύτρωσις. The simplex is used here, in v. 15 the compound ἀπολύτρωσις with a genitive is found. The blood is the λύτρον or ransom that was paid by Christ in order to effect release from sin and guilt. Expiation and ransoming are the same in substance and closely akin in connotation so that "blood" is said to be the means of ransoming. This word and the one used in v. 15 are treated more fully in connection with our exegesis of Rom. 3:24 to which the reader is referred.

The Two Kinds of Blood Compared, v. 13-28.

13) In v. 12 the writer introduces the subject of the blood, which is now discussed at length so that we make a division at this point. **For if the blood of goats and of bulls and a heifer's ashes sprinkling**

---

* One of my students collected and studied all the passages that treat of the blood. It is most illuminating to read all that the Scriptures say in regard to Christ's blood (and death). Our devotional and our confessional literature is filled with statements regarding Christ's blood. Many hymns in particular mention the blood; this student also collected all the pertinent hymn lines. The "blood theology" is the faith of the church and will ever be.

those defiled sanctifies as regards the cleanness of the flesh, by how much more shall the blood of Christ, who by the eternal spirit offered himself blemishless to God, cleanse your conscience from dead works for serving the living God?

In v. 12 the contrast is: not by means of animal blood but by means of Christ's own blood. The blood of sacrifice is evaluated according to the victim that is slain, and the effect of the value is according; Christ's blood ransoms. "For" restates and thus elucidates the comparative value and the comparative effect, but it does so in a broader way as far as the animal sacrifices are concerned, in a fuller way as far as Christ's sacrifice is concerned, and in a personal way as far as the worshipper is concerned who receives the effect and the benefit of the sacrificial blood. "For" does not prove anything that is said in v. 11, 12, it unfolds more fully and advances the thought and thereby makes it entirely clear. The writer puts this elucidation in the form of a question and thus in a personal way calls upon the readers to answer from their own experience since they personally felt both the limited effect of the animal sacrifice and the completed effect of Christ's sacrifice. The readers themselves are asked to tell themselves the tremendous difference, and by this question the writer offers them the pertinent data that should prompt the correct answer.

The protasis is a statement of reality and as such presents the simple fact that animal sacrifices do, indeed, sanctify to a certain extent; the apodosis follows with its self-evident deduction regarding Christ's sacrifice, a deduction which is true in the case of those who have come into contact with Christ and his sacrifice even as the question is asked regarding these alone. In v. 12 "blood of goats and calves" refers only to the Day of Atonement, to what the Jewish high priest does on that day in the Holy of Holies for himself and for the people. In v. 12 there is a comparison only with what Christ did in the heavenly Sanctuary before God, namely pay the ransom of his blood and obtain the objective ransoming from God. In v. 13 "the blood of goats" still reminds the readers of the Jewish Day of Atonement and of the Jewish high priest's work, but "bulls" goes beyond this to other sacrifices of blood, and "a heifer's ashes sprinkling those having been defiled" shows how far beyond the Day of Atonement the writer now proceeds. The blood of all animals that were slain is now referred to, and this is considered not merely as being offered to God but also as affecting the individual persons by removing their defilement and sanctifying them.

The writer chooses the heifer's ashes because they illustrate best this personal effect on the individual, for the heifer's blood was used for the Tabernacle and for the whole congregation, and then the ashes of the entire animal, skin, flesh, blood, and even dung, plus cedar wood, hyssop, scarlet (Num. 19:4-6) were used, not only for the Tabernacle, but also for the individual persons who might be ceremonially defiled and unclean in order to cleanse these persons individually (Num. 19:18-22). The point of v. 13 is thus the effect of the blood upon an individual when it is applied to him according to the δικαιώματα or "ordinances" that are laid down in the ceremonial law (v. 1, 10).

This "sanctifies as regards the cleanness of the flesh," the present tense in a general statement without reference to a particular time. The person is again set apart for God as being clean and undefiled. But this cleanness pertains only to "the flesh," to the body of the person, even as the ordinances deal only with "flesh" or body (v. 10). The illustration of the heifer's ashes is exceedingly plain on this point because these ashes were used to remove the defilement that had been incurred by touching a dead bone, one slain, one dead, or a grave. This is bodily touching, bodily defilement, and thus to be cleaned by a bodily cleansing.

Yet we should not view this cleansing in a superficial way as if conscience is not at all involved. Although the cleansing of the conscience by means of Christ's blood which is referred to in v. 14 constitutes the opposite of all cleansing by animal blood, it still leaves a field for conscience in connection with these bodily, ceremonial cleansings, for a physically defiled Israelite had a bad conscience until he had secured bodily cleansing as this was prescribed for him in God's ceremonial ordinances. This is plain from Num. 19:20. The point of difference between the two cleansings lies in the fact that the ceremonial cleansing satisfies the Israelite's conscience only as regards his flesh and body and causes him to rest easy when that is again ceremonially clean; but the expiatory cleansing by means of Christ's blood frees the conscience "from dead works," from the deadly guilt of all evil deeds, which is a far more serious thing than any ceremonial defilement.

Nicodemus and Joseph of Arimathaea helped to bury the dead body of Jesus, which made them ceremonially unclean; being conscientious Jews, they would have themselves ceremonially cleansed. Peter denied Christ. He wept bitterly. His conscience required a different and a far greater cleansing to put it at rest. The Lord absolved him of this dead work; the Lord died to provide this cleansing absolution for him. So much here regarding conscience. Much more follows in 10:1, etc., on the matter of freeing from sins, which we need not anticipate here.

14) "By how much more shall the blood of Christ cleanse your conscience," etc., asks the readers to contemplate the efficacy of this blood. On "the blood of Christ" see the pertinent paragraph under v. 12. The fact that it is Christ's own blood (v. 12) lifts it

infinitely above all animal blood that is demanded by the ordinances of God to Israel. It is

> "A sacrifice of nobler name
> And richer blood than they."

The relative clause brings this value of Christ's blood to full view: "who by the eternal spirit offered himself blemishless to God." No animal ever offered itself in sacrifice; when it was offered it did not even know what was being done. Christ offered himself, being High Priest and Sacrifice in one. He willed to do this as the High Priest, to have it done to him as the Sacrifice. Those who shed Christ's blood, they were the ones who knew not what was being done. Christ entered the Sanctuary "by means of his own blood" (v. 12); the high priests used the blood of others (v. 25), namely of animals. As was the value of the blood, so was the value of its power and its efficacy.

The position of the phrase assures its emphasis: "who *by the eternal spirit* offered himself," etc. Our versions capitalize "Spirit," which is immaterial as long as we do not regard this as a reference to "the Holy Spirit" as some texts do which substitute "Holy Spirit" for "eternal Spirit." To say that the Holy Spirit was a means or a mediate agent in the offering which Christ made of himself to God is to invent and to inject a strange idea which is foreign to Scripture. The absence of the articles in the Greek intends to stress the qualitative idea of "eternal spirit."

"Christ" showed himself to be Christ indeed, our Great High Priest (4:14), by offering himself "by the eternal spirit," his own spirit brought himself as the offering to God. The idea that his act was ethical to the highest degree, voluntary, not only on his part as being the sacrificing Priest, but also as being the sacrificed Lamb, is the gist of what is conveyed. We see this at once when we note that the writer emphasizes the eternal nature of Christ's spirit.

The eternal spirit by which Christ acted as our High Priest when he was offering himself in sacrifice to God is his divine ἐγώ or person. No man could take his life from him; he laid it down of himself in sacrifice even as he then also took it up again (John 10:16). Being deathless because he was "blemishless" and God's own Son without sin, he yet died for us: his own eternal spirit gave his human body and nature up to death so that his blood might obtain an eternal redemption and salvation for us (2:14, 15). It was for this reason that his eternal spirit assumed flesh and blood which could die.

But we should not confine our thought to what happened on Calvary when Christ's blood was shed and when he gave up his spirit in death (John 19:30); we should include the entrance into the heavenly Sanctuary "by means of his own blood" (v. 12), where the High-priestly act was completed, and he was thus "offering himself blemishless to God." The victim which the Jewish high priests offered as a type was not merely slain outside of the Holy of Holies, but the high priest brought the blood of the victim into the Holy of Holies before God. The antitype, Christ, did not carry his poured-out blood up into heaven but used it in an infinitely more exalted way as the means (διά, v. 12) of expiation and ransoming. The typical victims had to be "blemishless," which prefigured the sinlessness of the Lamb of God. In allusion to this the writer adds: himself, "blemishless" to God.

"Eternal spirit" is by no means in contrast with the perishable ψυχή or πνεῦμα of animal sacrifices. Have animals a πνεῦμα or "spirit"? There is a contrast with Christ's own flesh and blood; and the thought that, because they are like our flesh and blood (2:14), Christ might by means of his blood be able to do no more than we can when our blood is shed should not be entertained. The idea is also advanced by some that at death our spirit passes into a *Totenreich* and remains there inactive and in a shadowy existence until judgment day; and, we are told, in contrast to our spirits, which are subject to this fate, Christ's spirit is called "eternal" because it is not doomed to such inactivity. Yet most of these believers in "the realm of the dead" hold that Christ's spirit did enter this place at death; but they are then interpreting other passages and not our present passage.

How much more, then, "shall the blood of Christ . . . cleanse your conscience from dead works for serving the living God?" The tense of the verb used is the common logical future; it is the more in place here because the writer now speaks of the subjective, personal effect of Christ's blood on his readers, which extends into the future. On "dead works" compare 6:1. The expression is still more apt here, for no one can serve "the *living* God" with "*dead* works." Dead works are the fruit of spiritual deadness, they have no spiritual life in them, no life through Christ from the living God. Some think that "dead" means "sinful" works in general. These certainly would be a dead weight on the conscience. Yet here, as well as in 6:1, "dead works" are scarcely crimes and flagrant breaches of law but rather all formal, empty, false legal observances and self-invented works whereby men would seek to stand before God (Matt. 7:16-20, 22; 15:9; other passages).

As far as the relation to conscience is concerned, all sins and these dead works, too, disturb the conscience only when Christ reveals what deadliness lurks in them. The writer perhaps uses "dead works" here in allusion to the defilement which was ceremonially removed by the heifer's ashes, for this defilement was caused by touching something that was dead. The fact that cleansing the conscience by Christ's blood includes μετάνοια or repentance, 6:1, has already been stated. The word λατρεύειν refers to the service that is due to

Hebrews 9:15

God on the part of all of us (so also v. 9) and not merely to the official service of priests (λειτουργεῖν).

15) To the value of Christ's blood as being his own, and to its value as this is shown in its complete efficacy, there is added (καί) also its necessity. The readers are to understand that, far from being strange and a reason for turning away from him and back to Judaism, Christ's death is the very opposite. By it Jesus went into the heavenly Sanctuary and effected what has been stated in the preceding verses. Is this not vastly more than Judaism ever had? So v. 14 ends with a convincing question. Now the very necessity of his death is shown by the fact that we are heirs who are named in a testament, and that what is willed to us in this testament cannot be paid out to us unless the necessary death to put this testament into force has occurred. Instead of being offended by Christ's death the readers as the heirs, who because of Christ's death receive what the testament provides in its promissory stipulations, ought to accept their inheritance most gratefully.

And because of this is he Mediator of a new testament in order that, since a death has occurred for ransoming from the transgressions at the time of the first testament, they who have been called may receive the promise of the eternal inheritance.

It is the very death of Christ that enables us to receive our eternal inheritance. Some think that διὰ τοῦτο refers to something that has been said and then point to this or to that preceding clause. The phrase faces forward: "Because of this is he Mediator of a new testament," namely this that the called may now receive the promise of the eternal inheritance. The whole statement is a unit, the whole of it turns on the idea of a testament and takes up and advances what has been presented in 8:6-13. We construe: διὰ τοῦτο ... ὅπως ... λάβωσιν κτλ. The preceding verses contain nothing that would lead us to think of a testament; the writer himself presents this new and additional thought and views the bloody death of Christ from this angle, which is so important for his readers because a dead Messiah was beginning to appear like no Messiah to them. The answer to them is that without his death he would be no Messiah. His death is necessary. No death, no testament in force!

We ask the reader to turn to 8:6 and to all that we have there said on Christ as the "Mediator" of the better testament which is now called "new," namely the old Abrahamitic testament in the newness which Christ gave it. The abolished testament, which is here called "the first," is that which was brought down from the Mount by Moses 430 years after Abraham; under this Mosaic testament Israel failed to inherit. This testament promised Canaan, but Israel lost it forever because of transgressions. In what way Christ is the "Mediator" of this renewed Abrahamitic and thus "new" testament, which is so much better than the one Moses brought, is stated in the genitive absolute: "a death having occurred for ransoming from the transgressions at the time of the first testament." Christ's *death* made him "Mediator of a new testament." The mediation consisted in this, that his death put the testament in force; it was the medium for that. After he had died, the testamentary inheritance could be paid out to the heirs. The genitive absolute has causal force: "since his death occurred" (historical aorist).

This was not an ordinary death as we have seen in connection with v. 12 and elsewhere in this epistle. Christ did not merely die of this or of that, in an ordinary way. This was an expiatory death for the object (εἰς) of ransoming (ἀπολύτρωσις) from the transgressions (objective genitive) at the time (ἐπί, temporal, B.-P. 447, item 2) of the first testament. We have the same objective genitive in καθαρισμὸν τῶν ἁμαρτιῶν, "cleansing *from* the sins" (1:3). On ransoming note what is said about λύτρωσις in v. 12.

Christ's death put the testament in force because his death paid the full and complete ransom. It canceled even all the sins that had been committed by Israel in the past, the very sins which lost Israel the Mosaic testamentary promises and its land of Canaan. These old transgressions, which accumulated throughout the entire period of the Mosaic testament, are mentioned because the two testaments and the two kinds of death and of blood are contrasted. There is no thought of limiting the sins for which Christ died. The writer is addressing former Jews and is indicating to them what the Mosaic testament failed to accomplish for them, and what the new testament and its Mediator did accomplish for them.

Much of the exposition of 8:6-13 applies also here, in particular what we have said on v. 12, as to how during the period of the old testament the true believers were saved from their sins. The Old Testament believers were saved by means of the Abrahamitic testament and by means of all that was typical of Christ in the Mosaic testament; but, of course, only on the strength of this death of Christ, which had to occur in the fulness of time as it did occur. The Mosaic testament and all its law came in "because of transgression" (Gal. 3:19) in order the more to drive Israel to the promise that had been given to Abraham in the testament and had been conserved in all the types of Christ in the ceremonial features of the Mosaic testament.

The entire past, the entire present, the entire future thus rest on the death that occurred on Calvary, on the Lamb slain from the foundation of the world. Rev. 13:8. The Messiah who died is the absolute necessity no matter in which direction we look. Without him as "Mediator of a new testament" all that God gave to

Abraham and then to Moses and Israel would be a hollow mockery. Without him there would be no "eternal inheritance," no people called to receive it. Absolutely everything hinges on this Mediator and the mediation of his bloody, sacrificial, expiatory death.

"Because of this is he Mediator, etc., that they who have been called may receive the promise of the eternal inheritance," may indeed and in fact receive it (not "might," A. V.). The aorist denotes actuality and does not refer to a certain time; it applies to all time. The perfect tense οἱ κεκλημένοι, "those having been called," denotes state, an enduring condition and no more. It, too, applies to all time; it should not be dated in the past and referred only to the Israelites who were called during past ages. Nor does the writer intend to say that those who were called in *past* ages shall *now* receive the eternal inheritance; that they have been dead for a long time and have been without the inheritance during that entire time. The tenses will not permit this interpretation.

"The promise of the eternal inheritance" is the actual fulfillment, the substance promised. The genitive is appositional: the inheritance is the thing promised, i.e., "the good things" mentioned in v. 11. The writer uses "eternal" three times and in a way that is marked: "*eternal* ransoming" obtained by Christ (v. 12), "by means of (his) *eternal* spirit" (v. 14), we are to receive "the promise of the *eternal* inheritance." This is intentional on the part of the writer and should not be regarded as an accidental use of the same word "eternal."

The call is always extended by God's gospel grace, and throughout the epistles, whether it is expressed by a noun, a verb, a participle, or a verbal adjective, the writers invariably have in mind the successful call. The perfect participle here describes the called as being in an enduring state. They are the heirs named in the testament. Whether they lived in the past, are living now, or shall live in future ages is not indicated by the tense. One by one, as they leave this life, they receive the eternal inheritance of which the call makes them the heirs. In this life they have the earnest or pledge of their inheritance, namely the Holy Spirit of the promise (Eph. 1:13, 14), and thus taste of the powers of the world to come already in this life (Heb. 6:5), and then, if they remain true to their call by faith, at death receive the inheritance in heaven. Note how "testament" and "inheritance" correspond.

16, 17) The writer puts into v. 15 all the terms and modifications that are necessary to express his full thought; yet his main point is the *necessity* of the Messiah's death since his readers are objecting to a Messiah who died as Jesus did (I Cor. 1:18, 23). This necessity the writer proves from the very nature of a testament, which comes into force only upon the testator's death. Thus already in v. 15 we have: testament —a death having occurred—the inheritance is received.

For where (there is) **a testament** (there is the) **necessity that the testator's death be brought in** (*muss notwendigerweise beigebracht werden*). **For a testament is in force** (only) **in case of dead persons, since it is not ever in effect when the testator is** (still) **living.**

These propositions are entirely general and are true to this day. This explains the absence of the copula in the two statements, the present tenses φέρεσθαι and ἰσχύει, and the generalizing plural "in case of dead persons." No testament is in force until the testator is dead, as far as paying out or turning over the inheritance is concerned.

The reading τότε in place of ποτέ is a copyist's error, who omitted one of the downward strokes of the letter π. R. 1159 thinks μή ποτε may indicate a question; B.-D. 428, 5 thinks it does; our R. V. translates so simply because μή and not οὐ is used with an indicative. The fact is that the use of μή is considerably extended in the Koine; see Moulton, *Einleitung*, 270, especially note 3 which cites all manner of examples, among them a papyrus which has ἐπεὶ μή and the indicative, which is not a question. The verb φέρεσθαι is a technical or a legal expression: a death must be brought in to put a testament into effect.

As far as Christ's being the testator is concerned, there is no difficulty whatever when we remember 1:2, where he is called the Heir of all things, the Heir promised to Abraham, the owner of all the good things (v. 11) of the whole inheritance. We thus inherit only from him. He is thus the testator as far as we are concerned, and the testament is his which names the called as the heirs. It is thus that we are joint heirs with him (Rom. 8:17). His death makes the inheritance accessible to all who are his heirs, and does that irrespective of time.

Some advance the idea that διαθήκη means "covenant" or at least a "disposition" which one makes of his own accord. But neither a "covenant" nor a "disposition" of property calls for the death of the author; but if either is made contingent on the author's death, then it would *eo ipso* be a testament. We cannot translate the word διαθήκη "testament" in these two verses when we translate the same word "covenant" elsewhere. For the writer would then be playing with a double meaning and would thereby destroy all real proof and all pertinency of what he is saying. Our inheritance does not rest on a play of words. See 7:22 on διαθήκη.

It becomes still clearer here why Christ is called "Mediator" of a testament. God made him the Heir, and thus through him alone who owns everything, through him and through his death as the testator, do we inherit as heirs. Although all comes from God, none of it reaches us save through Christ who serves as the medium (Mediator), the middle link, the testator for us, whose death gives to us, his heirs, the great eternal inheritance. Nevertheless, testament, testator, inheritance, present only one side of the vast matter, and it is misleading to press these human terms, which convey the divine facts, so that these facts become blurred and distorted. The human testator dies and remains dead, his property is conveyed to heirs who in turn die, successive generations of heirs step into the shoes of their predecessors. Our Mediator-Testator died and thereby made us heirs; yet he lives and makes us joint heirs with him, heirs who never die so that their inheritance might be lost to them. The word "eternal," which is used in v. 12, 14, 15, is not repeated and emphasized for naught.

18) A new light is thus cast upon the Mosaic testament itself, transient though it was, and upon so many of its features, a light that is most significant for the readers who are inclined to find fault with the death and the blood of Christ. The Mosaic testament was itself inaugurated with the death and the blood of sacrificial victims.

Hence neither has the first (testament) been inaugurated without blood. For when every commandment was uttered according to the Law by Moses to all the people, having taken the blood of the calves and of the goats together with water and scarlet wool and hyssop, he sprinkled both the book itself and all the people, saying: This (is) the blood of the testament which God designed for you. Moreover, also the Tabernacle and all the utensils for the official service he likewise sprinkled with blood.

Since there was so much use of blood in connection with the Mosaic testament and all that pertained to that testament, how can any of the readers find fault with Christ's death and blood in connection with the new testament? They should do the very opposite:

appreciate the fact that Christ's death and blood are infinitely more precious than all the Mosaic sacrifices.

What God gave to Israel by the hand of Moses can also be called a διαθήκη or "testament." The writer calls it so here in the sense explained in 7:22. But we should not say that the first or Mosaic testament "has been dedicated" (our versions). This Greek verb is used in that sense but also in the sense of bringing in something new, and here it means "has been inaugurated," and the perfect tense indicates the enduring condition which the blood effected for the testament. By that blood the Mosaic testament was put in force just as Christ's blood put in force the new testament.

When the writer now uses "blood" whereas in **v. 16** he speaks of the testator's "death" as a necessity for putting a testament in force, this does not mean that "blood" and "death" are only equivalents to the writer, "blood" being a figurative term for "death." An ordinary testament calls for a death, but not necessarily a bloody death or blood. We should understand that, whereas the writer uses the idea of διαθήκη or "testament" and its connection with death, he and his readers are well aware of the fact that the testaments discussed here go beyond ordinary human testaments with their necessity of human death, that these divine testaments require death indeed, but, being what they are, a sacrificial death, a death that yields sacrificial blood. It is thus that the writer now says "inaugurated with blood." The fact that all this blood entails the death of slain sacrificial victims is understood. These victims foreshadowed Christ and his blood, and they and he thus reflect in a higher way what even a human testament must have, an eventual death.

19) Γάρ specifies and states the facts; it refers to Exod. 24:1-8 but goes beyond this. Some think only of a dedicatory ritual such as we use when we dedicate a church; but the writer is describing how God *in-*

augurated that first testament with blood; from its very beginning the whole testament operated with sacrificial blood. "When every commandment was uttered by Moses to all the people" = when the whole testament of law was given to Israel, the sacrifices of blood were added in order to put that testament and all that pertained to its provisions in force. All that the Mosaic testament offered was mediated by blood.

The phrase κατὰ τὸν νόμον appears again in v. 22. It is commonly connected with the participle: "having according to the Law uttered" every commandment, but the phrase then seems superfluous. Did the Law demand this utterance? We thus ask whether these two phrases do not mean: "according to the Law or Torah," i.e., "as the record in the Torah shows"? This rendering makes the phrase parenthetical in both verses. What the writer states about blood is, he says, "in accord with the Torah"; it is Moses' own record and not merely the writer's idea.

Exodus 24 mentions no goats nor the circumstance that water, scarlet wool, and hyssop were used, nor that "the book of the testament" was itself sprinkled with blood. As far as goats are concerned, these may, perhaps, be included in the "burnt offerings" mentioned in Exod. 24:5, in which goats would likely be included. When sprinkling with blood was performed, the water diluted the blood and made a sufficient quantity; and a hyssop (wild marjoram) stalk, which was wound around with scarlet wool to act as a sponge, would be used as passages like Lev. 14:4, 6, 49, 51, 52, etc., indicate. Κόκκινος, "scarlet," is derived from κόκκος, the scarlet berry that was used for making dye (*coccus ilicis*), B.-P. 689. The circumstance that the blood was sprinkled on "the book" is not stated in Exod. 24 but may, nevertheless, well be the fact; since it was a book that had been made and written by human hands it, too, would need the cleansing of blood.

20) Moses accompanied the sprinkling with blood with the significant words: "This (is) the blood of the testament which God designed for you." The Torah itself speaks of *"the blood* of the testament." Since this is the author's point in quoting Exod. 24:8, the slight changes in the wording and the abbreviation are perfectly justifiable; it would, therefore, be unfair to charge the writer with a faulty memory.

21) Δέ = moreover and cites the sprinkling of blood also on the Tabernacle and on all the sacred vessels or utensils that were used for the official priestly service. This happened later than the event that is recorded in v. 19, 20; it is mentioned in Exod. 40, where, however, only "oil" and not blood is referred to. Josephus, *Ant.* 3, 8, 6, retells Exod. 40 and, like our writer, says: "The same (namely purify) he did to the Tabernacle and the vessels thereto belonging, both with oil first incensed, as I said, and with the blood of bulls and of rams, slain day by day one according to its kind." The sprinkling of the Tabernacle with blood appears as a correct Jewish tradition and is thus freely used by our writer.

22) **And almost all things are cleansed in connection with blood according to the Law,** i. e., to go by what the Torah says (as in v. 19); **and apart from blood-shedding there occurs no remission.**

To such a degree, the Torah itself says, blood is used for cleansing that it extends to almost all things that are cleansed. The adverb σχεδόν is to be construed only with πάντα as the A. V. rightly translates. The R. V. has the adverb modify both sentences and translates this simple little word: "I may almost say," as though it has all the emphasis. What the writer says is that just about all of the Old Testament cleansings are ἐν αἵματι, "in connection with blood"; almost always blood is used in one way or in another; and when it comes to remitting of sins, there is no remission "apart from blood-shedding," χωρὶς αἱματεκχυσίας, there is no exception at all here. The two statements, the first positive, the second negative, hinge on the phrases "in connection with blood" (ἐν) and "apart from blood-shedding" (χωρίς). Yet the first is broader, for it refers to πάντα, "all things," even as the writer has referred to certain things like the book of the testament, the Tabernacle, and its various utensils. These things and the people, too, were rendered ceremonially clean, but even that required the use of blood.

The ἄφεσις is even more; it is not intended for things but for persons. Although it is used here in an unmodified form it, nevertheless, means the remission of sins, literally, "the sending away." The thought is that expressed in 8:12. To send away the sins from a sinner as far as the east is from the west (Ps. 103:12), to the bottom of the sea (Micah 7:19), thus blotting out the sins even from memory (Isa. 43:25) as a cloud is blotted out (Isa. 44:22) and vanishes, this absolutely requires "blood-shedding," a word that is found nowhere else and is apparently the writer's own coinage.

This "remission" is the greatest cleansing of all. Nothing clings and sticks so frightfully close to the sinner as his sin, guilt, and just punishment. Blood, shed in substitution for him, this alone is able to free him. I John 1:7. In fact, only the blood of Christ so shed effects remission, all the blood of the Mosaic testament is only typical of Christ's blood and thus by divine arrangement draws its power to cleanse away sin from his holy, precious, all-sufficient blood.

Our passage has been extensively used against the supposed "unbloody" sacrifice which the Romish priest offers in the Mass. But no unbloody sacrifice is able to remove sins. The fact that the remission requires the application of the expiatory blood to the individual sinner by contrition and faith need not be developed at this point.

The great point is the truth that a Messiah who died, who shed his blood is the only possible Messiah; his blood, which is infinitely more precious, valuable, expiatory than all the other blood of Moses' testament, the readers ought to prize and not turn from as an offense. Was that old testament not inaugurated with blood? Does the Torah not tell all about it? Is every testament not put in force by the testator's death? Well, then, so Christ died, so he shed his blood, so this new testament in his blood (Matt. 26:28) is inaugurated as a testament, indeed, in all its features and especially in its blood, the completion of which was foreshadowed in the Mosaic testament with all its animal blood.

Some commentators find an exception to the requirement of blood for remission in Lev. 5:11-12. This leads some to ignore the difference between cleansing things ($πάντα$) and cleansing persons and the fact that only the latter require "remission." So they construe "almost" with the second clause, but this is unwarranted since this second clause is negative. Leviticus 5 presents no exception; it corroborates the fact that blood is needed for remission, for this passage permits only the very poor person, who is unable to provide the blood of even two cheap doves, to substitute a bit of flour and oil. Leviticus 5 allows the substitute only as a substitute for blood and thereby maintains the necessity of blood.

23) This necessity and this use of blood and sacrificial blood-shedding are found *on earth,* for Moses' Tabernacle and everything that was connected with it, including the people of Israel who worshipped at this Tabernacle, are on earth, and (most important of all) there is no remission of sins for any of them without blood. And this necessity of blood extends even to *heaven.* The readers would, indeed, be blind to see all this blood connected with the Tabernacle which God himself ordered Moses to construct and yet not to see

that this Tabernacle and all its blood are the copy of the heavenly Sanctuary, which they could not be if that heavenly Sanctuary required no blood. Nay, they require blood, far better blood, that of Christ himself. To take offense at his bloody death would be fatal indeed.

There is then necessity on the one hand that the copies of the things in the heavens be cleansed by these means, on the other hand the heavenly things themselves with sacrifices better than these.

Μέν and δέ balance the two matters about which the necessity is asserted. We unfortunately have no neat particles like these and thus use the heavy phrases "on the one hand—on the other." Our writer uses οὖν with a force that is little more than transitional. So he passes on to the new statement, which, although it rests on what precedes, is not a deduction from it. This is not a Pauline οὖν. It simply takes us a step farther.

Since these earthly things are copies of heavenly originals, it lies on the surface that they must reflect the heavenly originals in this most important matter of blood. Being only copies in earthly material and therefore inferior, mere earthly blood may serve for them; but certainly, since blood is so essential for these copies as the Torah itself says, the heavenly originals not only cannot be without blood they must, in fact, have far better blood even as they also actually have, Christ's "own blood" (v. 12) which needs to be shed but once.

The statement is cast in a general form. Ὑποδείγματα (the singular is used in 8:5) are adumbrations, sketches, we may say "copies." The necessity of the copies is such only because of the originals. The necessity lies in the fact that sanctification takes place "by these means" (τούτοις), the use of blood as described in v. 19-22. God ordered blood for the copies, his own Torah or Law says so; regarding that there can be no question in the minds of the readers.

We can say what causes the necessity of blood sacrifices: it is sin, the defilement of which must be removed, the means being sacrificial blood, nothing less. This necessity of blood could not exist for "the copies of the things in the heavens" if it does not exist for "the heavenly things themselves." And this means that the heavenly things must have "better sacrifices than these" (i.e., than these sacrifices) which serve for the inferior earthly copies. "Better sacrifices" is plural only because the statement is general in form; in reality the heavenly Sanctuary, of which the Tabernacle is only a copy, needs only the one sacrifice of Christ.

The entire cleansing power of "sacrifices" lies in the blood so that the writer now uses this word "sacrifices" whereas in v. 19-22 he uses blood; note "his sacrifice" in v. 26. The explanation that the Tabernacle and its furnishings were made by human hands and thus needed cleansing is not satisfactory, for the Sanctuary in heaven is not made by sinful human hands (v. 11, 24) and yet needs even better sacrificial blood than the earthly copy. Because both the copy and the original are to serve *sinners* they require blood. The cleansing does not remove defilement from the sanctuaries themselves. This is too apparent in the case of the heavenly Sanctuary; the blood-cleansing of these sanctuaries enables them to serve *sinners* without thereby becoming defiled. Thus blood is necessary for both the earthly and the heavenly. The very term *Hagia* (used again in v. 24) indicates this. When the readers see blood and sacrifice in the earthly Tabernacle as a divine necessity they must not find fault when they see Christ on the cross, which is a sacrifice that has far better blood and makes the true expiation for us in the heavenly *Hagia*.

24) Since sacrificial blood is a necessity for both earthly and heavenly sanctuaries and a better sacrifice for the latter, γάρ starts to say what this

means in regard to Christ. **For Christ did not enter into a handmade sanctuary, a (mere) type of the true one, but into heaven itself, now to appear before the face of God in our behalf.**

Let the readers think as highly as they wish about the sanctuary, the *Hagia,* which God ordered Moses to build; it is only "handmade," made by men out of earthly material, "of this creation"; only ἀντίτυπα (plural to match the plural ἅγια), mere type of the true *Hagia* ("the true Tabernacle," 8:2). Not into this mere copy did Christ enter but into the very original of which this handmade *Hagia* was the copy, "into heaven itself," to do there what could not be done, save only in a typical way, in the earthly Tabernacle, namely "to appear (actually) before the face of God in our behalf." All appearing in the copy, in the handmade sanctuary, could not be final although it was accompanied by ever so much sacrificial blood that was applied all around in all manner of ways even by God's own order (v. 19-22). Enough had been done on the part of all the Jewish high priests when they entered this handmade type-sanctuary. Christ did not repeat what the high priests had done sufficiently.

Christ entered into τὰ ἀληθινά, "the true *Hagia*," into "heaven itself." What was prefigured by the earthly copy had finally to be done in the heavenly original. For this reason God had given the copy, and without this the copy and all that was done in it would have been no copy but mere deception and pretense. The writer calls the genuine, original Sanctuary "heaven itself." This does not seem to agree with those who assume the existence of two heavens, an inner one for God's actual presence, which is like the Holy of Holies in the Tabernacle, and an outer one for the saints and the angels, which is like the Holy Place in the Tabernacle. The writer does not make such a division as has already been discussed under v. 11.

Into heaven itself Christ entered, "now to appear before the face of God in our behalf." See v. 11, 12; also 4:14 and 6:20. Only this much is said here, more will follow regarding what Jesus did when he appeared before the very face of God in heaven itself. The passive of the verb is used in the sense of "to appear" and is construed with the dative. The aorist tense denotes actuality and no more. There are no clocks and no calendars in heaven, no time but only timelessness, therefore the adverb "now" refers only to the actuality that is expressed by the aorist. This aorist is not constative. Our minds are tied to ideas of time; and we should respect this our mental limitation and from our ideas of time not draw conclusions regarding heaven and Christ's heavenly acts.

25) Οὐ and now οὐδέ: Christ did "not . . . nor," etc. Christ did not enter into a mere earthly sanctuary; **nor** (did he enter heaven) **in order to be offering himself often like as the high priest enters into the sanctuary year by year in connection with blood not his own, since (then) it would have been necessary that he suffer often from the foundation of the world on, but now once, at the consummation of the eons, he has appeared for putting away sin by means of his sacrifice.**

Not into an earthly sanctuary did Christ enter; nor into the heavenly one for an oft-repeated sacrifice of blood. Despite Christ's correspondence to the earthly high priests this double difference appears; it must appear, otherwise even the earthly sanctuary and the acts of the Jewish high priests would have no meaning. The readers would be absurd if they demanded in the case of the heavenly act of Jesus the constant repetition they see in the case of the earthly high priests.

No; Jesus entered to offer "himself," which is a sacrifice that cannot be offered "often." The Jewish high priest entered "year by year" (distributive κατά),

Hebrews 9:26

coming, as he did, "in connection with (ἐν) blood not his own," blood that was taken from other victims and already for this reason needed the constant repetition not to mention still other reasons that have been already indicated.

26) If any reader has the idea that Christ, too, should keep repeating his sacrifice of himself because the Jewish high priests did this, and that unless Christ made such a repetition he would not be the true High Priest, such an objector receives this answer: then from the foundation of the world onward, through all the past ages of the world, it would have been necessary for Christ to suffer again and again and never get through with such repetition, never get the real expiation completed.

'Επεί is a condensed, elliptical protasis like our word "else" or "otherwise." But it is a condition of reality and may thus be followed in the apodosis by any tense. This means that we do not regard the imperfect ἔδει as expressing unreality with ἄν omitted as R. 965 does or as "practically" such an apodosis (R. 920). This is the imperfect which the Greek uses to express present necessity, obligation, etc., which allows the reader to infer that it has not been met. This construction seems awkward only to the English and the German mind which do not have this idiom and thus use a condition of reality as R. 919, etc., properly explains. Our versions succeed quite well in conserving the Greek idiom in the English translation. See also B.-D. 358, 1, who indicates how the German renders this idiom.

A silent implication is involved in saying that Christ is then under obligation to have repeated his suffering "from the foundation of the world on," namely the implication that his suffering, now that he has endured it, affects all men who existed since the beginning of the world. The universality of Christ's expiation underlies all that is said in this epistle about

Christ's death for the Jews. We note, too, how the writer varies his terms: blood—death—sacrifice—and now suffer. They are the same in substance, but by varying the terms the author keeps all the angles of the substance before his readers. So the writer does not here say that Jesus should then have entered heaven often, should have shed his blood, should have died, should have offered his sacrifice often, but should have suffered often (παθεῖν, aorist, effective). If one cares to pursue this thought farther he might add that Jesus would then also have had to have been incarnate often, betrayed often, etc., etc., the whole of which is absurd.

The clear, sane fact is: "but now once, at the consummation (or end) of the eons, he has appeared for putting away sin by means of *his* sacrifice." This "once" is the "once for all" stated in v. 12 (7:27; 10:10), which is now even dated: "at (ἐπί, at the time of; cf., v. 15, 17) the consummation of the eons," i.e., at the time when all the past ages of the world have come to their joint goal, the great goal to which God intended them to come, namely this great new testament time (8:8-12). "Now," at this time, Christ "has appeared" here on earth (the perfect covers the whole time that he was here) and has suffered to accomplish his great object (εἰς), namely "putting away (the same word is used in 7:18) of sin by means of *his* sacrifice." Our versions translate as though αὐτοῦ were αὑτοῦ, the reflexive: "the sacrifice of himself," but it is merely "his," the simple pronoun which is emphatic only because of the contrast with v. 25, the high priest's coming with blood that is not his own. Since this object has been attained by this great and all-sufficient means, the idea of a repetition is impossible.

27) By the way in which the writer pursues the subject, this "once" that excludes even the thought of repetition, he seems to indicate that the readers made an issue of it and preferred the annual expia-

tion of the Jewish high priests to this one expiation of Christ. So once more (καί) and from another angle the one sacrifice of Christ is illumined. **And in accord with the way it is reserved for men to die (but) once and after that judgment, so also Christ, offered once to bear the sins of many, shall be seen a second time apart from sin by those expecting him for salvation.**

Καθ' ὅσον is not causal (R. 963), does not = "inasmuch" (R. V.), which seems to be regarded as causal. The fact that men die once is not the cause of what Christ did. The phrase expresses only correspondence: in harmony with the way in which it happens in the case of men generally, so it happened in the case of Christ. It is laid away or reserved for them to die but once, and after that each receives judgment, κρίσις, the pronouncement of a verdict by the heavenly Judge. After life is done, there is no living it over again a few more times; what awaits each one at death is God's verdict, either acquittal or condemnation; κρίσις is a *vox media*.

To say that this pronouncement of judgment comes only at the time of the final judgment at the end of the world contradicts Scripture. No one needs to wait until the last day to know God's verdict; he receives it at the instant of death. Death also at once places his soul into either heaven or hell; the verdict is executed at once. To think of anything else erases the correspondence with Christ's death, for he does not wait until the last day to learn God's judgment regarding his sacrifice. There is no *Totenreich* where the souls of the dead lie inert, in a shadowy existence until the last day; there is no probation after death although some would insert it here: "to die but once, and (after a probation when necessary) after that judgment."

28) Could it be different in the case of Christ? Would he have to die over and over again, repeat his sacrifice ever anew? Yes, endless repetition is in place

in the case of the Jewish high priests who never offer themselves, who come only with blood of animals, who are mere types and copies like their sanctuary, etc. "Christ, offered once to bear (aorist to express actuality) the sins of many," by his death accomplished everything, "obtaining eternal ransoming" (v. 12). The idea of a repetition is impossible just as is the idea that men should die again and again in order to attain judgment from God.

The passive participle προσενεχθείς is only a variation for saying, "having offered himself," and holds fast to the truth that Christ was himself offered in his death. We have the clear statement that Christ "bore the sins of many," which runs through so many passages: Matt. 26:28; John 1:29; I Pet. 2:24; I John 3:5, to mention only these. "The sins of many" is not a limited atonement, not a contradiction of all the passages that speak of a universal atonement such as II Cor. 5:14, 15: "If one died for all, then all died. And he died for all." "Many" is in contrast only with the One who bore the sins. The writer may well be thinking of "many" as a reference to Israel, for he is dealing with former Jews. Christ accomplished this purpose: he bore "sins of many," i.e., the entire penalty for their guilt; in this way the "putting away of sin" (v. 26) was achieved.

Instead of making the statement about Christ a mechanical parallel to the one about men the writer does far more. Men die once; but Christ did not merely die, he was offered, was made a sacrifice so as to bear the sins of many; that was the manner in which *he* died. At death men get the judgment that is due them, but Christ did not get merely such a judgment; the writer says vastly more: Christ "shall be seen a second time (ἐκ idiomatic) apart from sin by those earnestly expecting him for salvation," the same beautiful word that is used in Rom. 8:19, 23, 25: ἀπό plus ἐκ plus δέχομαι, the second preposition making the verb mean "to wait it out" (Thayer), i.e., to keep waiting until the expected actually appears. "A second time" refers to Christ's Parousia when all those who are expecting him shall be raised from the dead or shall be transformed (I Cor. 15:51, 52; I Thess. 4:17), when "salvation" shall be forever complete.

We retain the passive "shall be seen" with the agent in the dative although we may translate "shall appear to those expecting him." This, we may say, shows the judgment which Christ received for shedding his blood in death as the saving sacrifice for us all. "Apart from sin" refers to the sin for which Christ was offered, which is put away entirely by his sacrifice. After he is done with this sin of many, has removed it forever, Christ shall be seen by those who are expecting him.

The idea of Christ's ever repeating his sacrifice is absolutely excluded by the incomparable nature of the blood which he shed for us. Yes, he shall be seen here on earth once more, but only as the glorious Giver of the eternal salvation which the one shedding of his blood obtained for us.

CHAPTER X

The Two Sacrifices Compared, v. 1-10.

1) This section might have begun at 9:23. Moreover, the comparison of the blood and the comparison of the sacrifice are closely allied; "blood" occurs in verse 4 of this chapter. The main terms of this paragraph speak of sacrifices; that is why we combine these verses into one section. "For" = in order to explain the matter further. The writer reverts to 8:5: "sketch and shadow of the heavenly things" and develops the sacrifice of Christ in contrast with this shadow. **For the law, having (only) a shadow of the good things about to come, not the image itself of the things, year by year with the same sacrifices which they are offering in perpetuity is never able to bring to completion those who draw near.** Repeat year by year what is only a shadow, as many years as you will, this will bring no one to the τέλος, the goal, to the τελείωσις (7:11), the completeness that God intends for all of us.

We prefer the singular δύναται as does the A. V.: "the law . . . is never able," and not the plural δύνανται which the R. V. has translated. Although the plural has the greater textual support, it is easy to see that the singular was made a plural because the preceding relative clause has the plural προσφέρουσιν. It has been well observed that the plural of this minor clause is merely an indefinite plural: "which they are offering." There is no need to specify who "they" are; everybody understands that the high priests are referred to. Besides, the writer never thinks of saying that the high priests bring to completeness; he always

Hebrews 10:1

speaks of sacrifices doing or not doing such a thing. The writer here speaks of the law not doing this, of its inability to do it "with the sacrifices" which this law prescribes.

The reason the law is "never able" to effect completeness for those who draw near lies in the fact that it has only a "shadow" and not the real thing itself. "Shadow" recalls 8:2; also Col. 2:17, where, however, the reference is broader. "A shadow (and no more) of the good things about to come" makes these coming things the great realities, which are so near as to cast their shadow by means of what the law about the Jewish sacrifices contains. A shadow is not valueless, for it is cast by a substance. Where the shadow falls, the substance itself will presently appear. A shadow thus promises the substance. It would be wrong to hold only to the shadow as if it were the substance when the shadow bids everyone to look to the substance so that he may attain that.

"The good things about to come" are the same as those mentioned in 9:11. The view that they are not the eternal good things of the completed salvation but only the cleansing, sanctification, and completion bestowed by Christ in our present life has been answered in 9:11. Even the copies mentioned in 9:23 are copies of the "the things in the heavens" and are called "the heavenly things." Only so much is true: the heavenly good things to come, which have their significant shadow in the law and in what it prescribed for Israel, reach down to us in Christ during this life so that we now taste the powers of the world to come (6:5). But full salvation in final completeness is, after all, to be realized only in heaven.

"Not the image itself of the (actual) things πράγματα)" does the law possess. The word εἰκών is "image," not, however, the reflected image, the *Abbild* which is taken from the *Vorbild*, the copy made from the original, the image which actual things bear. The genitive is possessive and not appositional. The πράγματα are the same in substance as "the good things to come," the shadow of which alone is seen in what the law possesses. Having no more than the shadow, the law cannot bring us to the eventual goal, it can only point us to that goal, to a better sacrifice than the typical ones it possesses (9:23).

The phrase "year by year" cannot be transferred beyond the dative "with the same sacrifices" and connected with the relative clause although our versions do this. What the writer says is that the law "by means of the same sacrifices" which are the same "year by year," which they, the high priests, offer in perpetuity is never able to effect completion. Year by year the same sacrifices are offered perpetually on the great Day of Atonement. This ceaseless repetition, which is prescribed by the law itself, is the plainest sort of evidence for the fact that the goal is never reached thereby. "Year by year," which is repeated from v. 25, shows that the writer is speaking of the sacrifices which the high priests brought on the Day of Atonement and not of all the sacrifices that were offered throughout one year after another as some have thought. A far different and a vastly superior sacrifice is needed in order to achieve the completeness which we need to attain the good things about to come.

2) A pertinent question establishes this inability of the law and its sacrifices: **Else would they not have ceased being offered because the worshippers, once having been cleansed, have no more conscience in regard to sins?**

Let the readers themselves answer this question. Οὐ is merely the interrogatory particle which indicates that the only proper answer is "yes." Ἐπεί is the abbreviated protasis as it was in 9:26: "else," "otherwise." It is here followed by an apodosis of past unreality (aorist with ἄν): "would they not have ceased being offered," and done that for the reason (διά) that in some year these sacrifices had finally achieved the goal? The verb "to cease" is construed with the participle "being offered." The legal sacrifices would then most certainly have ceased. Once cleansed with enduring permanence (perfect participle), the worshippers have literally "not a single conscience any longer of sins," objective genitive, "in regard to sins." All of the sins would be cleansed away, the goal of a sacrifice that possessed finality for all sinners been attained as we see that it is now attained by the sacrifice of Christ.

To have no more conscience of sin is to be understood objectively: no more sins would disturb and harass conscience. Subjectively, if any person should sin and be disturbed in conscience, all he would need to do would be to return in repentance to that final sacrifice as we now return to Christ's sacrifice. A final sacrifice would not need to be repeated for any person's sin. But all these annual Jewish sacrifices are "the same," the one offered in any particular year never gets any farther than all the others that were offered in all the other years; completeness and finality are not in them, cannot be; they are never found in a mere shadow.

3) Ἀλλά is in contrast with the whole of v. 1, 2: **But in connection with them** (these annual sacrifices, there is) **a remembrance of sins year by year, for** (it is) **impossible for blood of bulls and goats to be taking away sins.**

Ἐν states what is connected with these solemn annual sacrifices when the Jewish high priest goes into the Holy of Holies to make atonement for the whole people. The whole institution of this sacrifice is a grand reminder of sins, which in the most serious way brings them to the conscience and always does that in the same way "year by year."

4) For most certainly — need the writer still argue? — none of his readers will believe that such a thing as "blood of bulls and goats" is ever able, no matter when it is sacrificed, to take away as serious and deadly a thing as sins. The writer needs only to say that such a thing is "impossible." The nouns have no articles, which brings out their qualitative force. The infinitive is durative: "ever to take away." This verb is most expressive: the sins are taken away from the sinner, this frees him from their hold of guilt and punishment, the sacrifice and its blood pick them up and take them away completely. Animal blood cannot do this. All it can do is to act as a shadow of this taking away by means of better blood and in this way connect the worshipper with the Messiah's blood through faith in him. Compare 8:12: "their sins I will not remember any more" in the new testament. These legal sacrifices keep up "remembrance of sins."

5) After the inability of the animal sacrifices that were ordered by the law has been thus pointed out, the writer turns to Christ and to what the sacrifice of his body was able to effect and uses Ps. 40:6-8 in its Messianic sense. **Therefore, coming into the world, he says:**

**Sacrifice and offering thou dost not want,
But a body didst thou fit for me;
Whole burnt offerings and sin offerings thou
      didst no approve.
Then I said: Lo, I am here;
In the bookroll it has been written concerning
      me —
To do, God, thy will.**

The writer puts the words of the psalmist into Christ's mouth when the latter comes into the world. Some deny the Davidic authorship of this psalm, but David's authorship needs little defense. The remarkable fact is that a passage like this should occur in any psalm. Delitzsch is right: "It is not as if Christ and *not* David speaks; but Christ, whose spirit already dwells and works in David, and who will hereafter receive from David his human nature, now already speaks in him."

The discussion regarding "coming into the world" is unnecessary. This expression is used in various connections, and these connections indicate whether an entrance into the world by birth or by office in the world of men is meant. In rabbinic language this expression is common for being born (Schlatter). The expression has that sense here, but, as Riggenbach rightly adds, not as though it were spoken at Christ's birth but as being the motto and mind of Christ from the time of his birth; David, the type, speaks in words that may be placed into the mouth of Christ, the antitype. The writer reads this passage from the psalm in the light that is shed upon it by the New Testament and thus hears in these lines of David the voice of Christ himself.

This is a clear statement that says frankly that all the animal sacrifices ($\theta\upsilon\sigma\iota\alpha\iota$) and the offerings ($\pi\rho\sigma\sigma\phi\rho\alpha\iota$, meat and drink offerings in the narrow sense, *minchah* in the Hebrew) are not what God wants. It repeats Samuel's word to Saul in a new way: "Hath the Lord delight in burnt offerings and sacrifices as in obeying the voice of the Lord? Behold, to obey is better than sacrifice, and to hearken better than the fat of rams," I Sam. 15:22. God appointed all these different sacrifices, and they all had their purpose, but the thought was never that God wanted such things from us for their own sake; what he wants is ourselves in the whole obedience of our being. The sacrifices had their typical importance. They pointed to the Messiah's sacrifice, and Israel rendered them in true obedience. When the Messiah came, his obedience was everything.

The Hebrew: "Mine ears hast thou opened for me," literally, "digged" so as to open a free channel into them, is rendered as follows by the LXX, which our writer follows: "But a body didst thou fit (or shape) for me," καταρτίσω, first aorist middle, second person, a translation *ad sensum*. The explanation that the LXX's σῶμα is somehow a fault in transcribing ὠτία ("body" in place of "ears") is untenable, likewise the view that the writer of Hebrews changed the LXX to suit his present purpose. "To do, God, thy will" in holy obedience (v. 7) remains the contrast to the earthly sacrifices, whether we have the Hebrew's "ears" opened to hear God's will or the LXX's "body" to respond to that will. Delitzsch is probably right: the LXX sought to make "digged my ears for me" more intelligible to their Greek readers by translating "shaped a body for me" by which to obey.

6) What the two lines quoted from the psalm say is repeated in a different form by the next four synonymous lines. "Sacrifice and offering thou dost not want" is repeated by: "Whole burnt offerings and sin offerings thou didst not approve," εὐδόκησας, *billigen*, B.-P. 498. Here and in v. 8 περὶ ἁμαρτίας is used as a noun; it = τὸ περὶ τῆς ἁμαρτίας προσφερόμενον: "sin offering."

7) "But a body didst thou fit for me" receives a fuller elaboration in three lines: "Then I said: 'Lo, I am here (ἥκω, have come, am here); in the bookroll it has been written concerning me — to do, God, thy will.'" What the bookroll of the sacred record has recorded regarding David, what he should do as God's will, that he is present to do and will do implicitly. He offers himself in voluntary obedience. In this regard he is the type of Christ. The sacred Old Testament bookroll contains much more concerning him than it does concerning David, and he is here to do God's will concerning him in a more exalted way.

Hebrews 10:7, 8 329

Κεφαλίς, "little head," is the knob (often very ornamental) of the round rod on which the parchment was rolled and is thus used as a designation for the roll itself; the word does not mean "head chapter" of a book (Liddell and Scott). The writer abbreviates the LXX; he adds "to do thy will" to what precedes but does not quote the whole sentence from the LXX. So he also writes only "God" instead of "my God," and the nominative ὁ Θεός is used as vocative. A few other very minor changes in the quotation call for no special attention in our interpretation.

8) The writer brings out the main point which he wants his readers to see in this significant quotation. **Saying up at the head** (in the quoted lines): **Sacrifices and offerings and whole burnt offerings and sin offerings thou didst not want nor didst approve, such as are offered according to law, he then has said: Lo, I am here to do thy will. He takes away the first in order to establish the second.**

The writer shows how the lines of the psalm are to be understood. Lines 1 and 3 go together, being synonymous. These two lines say the same thing and are thus placed ἀνώτερον in the quotation, "higher up" than the other lines. The adverb does not mean "above" as we refer to something we have written "above" what we are now writing (our versions), for in this sense the whole quotation is written above while the adverb refers only to lines 1 and 3 and presents David and the Messiah as saying them "in front of" the other lines. In the psalm these two lines say the first thing which is also negative, the thing that God does not want and does not approve. The writer is analyzing the six lines according to their content.

The qualitative relative clause introduced by αἵτινες is concessive: "although such as are offered according to law," i. e., in a legal way; nevertheless, God does not really want and approve sacrifices of this kind. The antecedents of "such as" are of two genders, feminine and neuter; in such cases the pronoun has the superior, here the feminine, gender. We have already explained how it happened that God, although he had by law ordered these sacrifices for Israel, did not do so as the final thing and in this sense could not be satisfied with them. They were a shadow, God must have the substance as the shadow itself shows.

9) After saying this "higher up" in his statement David (the Messiah) "then has said" as the second thing, the positive one, in lines 2, 4, 5, and 6: "Lo," etc. The author then summarizes these lines briefly as to the main thought which they contain, namely that the Messiah, without being ordered to do so by a law, of his own volition presents himself to God to do (aorist, with finality) the thing that God has willed, his θέλημα. The perfect tense "has said" is punctiliar-durative: •———▶, i. e., once said, the statement is to stand. The participle λέγων makes lines 1 and 3 subsidiary, the finite verb makes the sum of the other lines the main thought. What God does not want, etc., is wholly secondary to what he does want and what the Messiah, therefore, says he will do completely (aorist). Both the present participle and the main verb in the perfect intend only to analyze the quotation and no more.

Without a connective the analysis is completed with the succinct statement: "He takes away (annuls) the first thing in order to establish (aorist, effective) the second thing." The neuters put the two things abstractly, each in unit form: "the first thing," this entire offering of animal and vegetable sacrifices; "the second," this voluntary doing of God's will. The great force which these lines of the psalm and this true analysis of what they say have for the readers lies in the fact that David has written these lines in his psalm; they are in the Holy Scriptures, are a part of all that

Hebrews 10:10

David, the type, says for the antitype, the Messiah. The lines are the voice of the Messiah himself speaking to God hundreds of years before this Messiah "appeared" (v. 26) and did God's will. The writer treats this passage cited from the psalm in the same simple and lucid way in which he treats the passage quoted from Jeremiah in 8:8-14. The first testament yields to the second, God himself has said so (8:14); the old sacrifices disappear before what God has willed as the final thing, which the Messiah comes to do.

10) In connection with which will we have been sanctified by means of the offering of the body of Jesus Christ once for all. The relative has demonstrative force so that we may translate "in connection with *this* will." The preposition ἐν = "in connection with"; this is its first meaning; the context always indicates what the connection is. This is not "instrumental ἐν" and should not be translated "by" or "in." The statement is concentrated and masterly indeed. It proceeds at once to state the fulness of God's will and refers to both Christ's supreme act in doing this will as the Messiah by making himself the all-effective sacrifice and the application of this sacrifice to us in our sanctification once for all. Much is stated by these few words, but so much can be stated because of all that the writer has said in this epistle.

The periphrastic perfect "we have been sanctified" is modified by the adverb "once for all," which is placed emphatically at the end. The strong form ἐφάπαξ is applied to Christ's offering up himself "once for all" in 7:27, and its common form ἅπαξ is used in 9:28: Christ offered "once." It is now applied to us: "we have been sanctified once for all." The act of Christ was done "once for all" and needed no repetition or addition because of its finality and absolute completeness, and it produces an effect "once for all" and also needs no repetition or addition because of this finality and completeness. We see at once that this sanctification = our permanent justification which "once for all" sets us apart for God.

We are the ἅγιοι, "the saints," who are named so in scores of places, the ἡγιασμένοι, "those who have been sanctified" and remain so. The two terms are combined in Col. 3:12. Add such passages as 2:11; 10:14; 13:12; also Acts 20:32; 26:18, our inheritance and lot among "those who have been sanctified." It is a reduction in their meaning when G. K. regards these expressions as "cultus terms." It is a matter of course that, "having been sanctified," we also live a holy life. All that we still need to keep us free from the stain of sins that are still committed day by day Jesus himself states in John 13:10; his "clean every whit" = "once for all."

Διά states the objective means: "by means of the offering of the body of Jesus Christ." The writer now names Jesus as the Messiah who is indicated as speaking in the psalm (v. 5-7). As God willed the end, our sanctification once for all, so he also willed the means to this end, the offering of Jesus' body on the altar of the cross. In previous connections the writer has said that Christ offered up "himself," even that "Christ was offered" (9:28), and has repeatedly named his "blood" as the sacrifice. When he now writes "the body of Jesus Christ" he has the same thought in mind. Those who would make a distinction that is analogous to the Jewish sacrifices: blood = expiation; "body" = communion, parts of the animal sacrifices to be eaten, overlook the Lord's Supper where Christ gives us both his body and his blood to eat and to drink. The body became an offering by the shedding of its blood, both body and blood thus became the expiating sacrifice.

"The body" is mentioned in conformity with v. 5: "a body didst thou fit for me." The psalm does not have this word in the Hebrew, it is found only in the translation of the LXX; but that is not a reason the writer should not use the LXX's translation or that he should not again refer to the body as he now does when we know that he has used "Christ," "himself," "his blood," "his death," as equivalents and varied the terms only according to the context. More important is the relation between the type David and the antitype Jesus Christ as this is indicated in the words of the psalm. "To do, God, thy will" includes both of them. When David as the type was to do the will of God he volunteered to offer himself with all his bodily life to live as God willed; in this regard he foreshadowed the Messiah who bowed to God's will even unto death and gave his body in voluntary obedience even to the death on the cross (Phil. 2:8). Need we yet say that the type, because it is only a type, ever falls far short of the antitype, which rises to absolute fulness and perfection? David could not become an expiatory offering to God, which is saying only that the type cannot be its own antitype.

The Final Comparison regarding the Removal of Sins, v. 11-18.

11) This is the climax. The whole will of God, the whole sacrifice of death center in the removal of our sins. Freed of these, heaven is ours. Without Christ's expiation there are no remission and deliverance from sin. This is the heart of all Scripture. Those who remove this heart because they regard it as "the old blood theology" have left only a hopeless corpse. Καί adds the final elaboration.

And every priest stands day by day doing official service and offering many times the same sacrifices, such as are never able all around to remove sins; this One, however, having offered a single sacrifice for sins, sat down in perpetuity at the right (hand) of God, henceforth waiting until his enemies be placed as a footstool for his feet. For by means of a single offering he has brought to completion in perpetuity those who are being sanctified.

The reading "every high priest" is a faulty correction which does not accord with the obvious meaning. While the common priests stand on a lower level than the high priest, the mention of the common priests at this point intensifies the climax which is reached in Christ.

To be sure, not every priest stood ready to do his official service day by day. These priests were divided into twenty-four courses which served in turns, and in each course each priest had his particular service assigned to him by lot. The fact that each priest stands day by day doing official service when his group has its turn of duty is precisely what the writer wishes to state and puts in brief form because the point of the statement is found in the next participle: stands serving "and offering *many* times the *same* sacrifices."

This is significant, indeed. The sacrifice of the high priest on the Great Day of Atonement did not keep the people in a sanctified state until even the next year when that day returned. "Day by day" the common priests had to serve; "often," many, many times they had to offer the same sacrifices, which means not only the same daily morning and evening sacrifices over and over again, but also the same sacrifice for each type of sin over and over again for the stream of endless individual cases day after day. Always and always *the same* sacrifices, these never reached an end. Λειτουργέω = to do any official, public service, and is here thus applied to priests; the word itself does not contain the idea of priestly service.

The qualitative relative brings out the point of this endless repetition of the same sacrifices: "such as are never able to remove all around, i. e., in a complete

Hebrews 10:11, 12

all-around way (περί with αἱρέω perfective, R. 617), sins." Each of these same, repeated sacrifices offered day after day takes away only the single sin for which it is offered, every new sin requires another offering; in fact, as we have already seen in connection with the annual sacrifice of the high priest, these daily sacrifices, like the high priest's sacrifice, never expiated and thus removed sins; they merely pointed to Christ's expiating sacrifice which the sinner was to embrace by faith and by that have his soul and conscience freed. For that reason these many same sacrifices had to be constantly repeated, ever and ever anew and in the same way pointing to the final, all-sufficient sacrifice of Christ. The daily, many repetitions by the common priests only magnify what we have already been shown regarding the annual repetitions performed by the high priests.

12) The Greek has its μέν . . . δέ to balance the two statements; we cannot duplicate this but can only put "however" into the second: "this One, however, after having offered a single sacrifice for sins, sat down in perpetuity (the same phrase that occurs in 7:3 and 10:1) at the right hand of God," etc. What this single sacrifice was has been said a number of times, last of all in v. 10 where we are told that it was offered "once for all." Only this single sacrifice *he* brought; it did the work, it is all-sufficient "for sins," for all sins, any and every one, past, present, future. To this single, final, complete sacrifice all the Jewish ritual sacrifices pointed; this they foreshadowed, from this they drew their virtue until the day when "this One" offered it on the altar of the cross.

Then, having offered it, this One had concluded his sacrificing, "having obtained an eternal ransoming" (9:12). He did not then cease to be our Great High Priest (4:14); he remains our High Priest by virtue of this his single sacrifice. What ceased was the need of a further sacrifice on his part, what remains is his High-priestly intercession for us (7:25), his High-priestly help for us (2:18; 4:16), which is now extended to us from his seat at the right hand of God, where he is now enthroned in perpetuity, "crowned with glory and honor."

The writer reverts to the beginning of his great discussion in 1:3 (compare 8:1; also 12:2), namely to Christ's exaltation at God's right hand (see 1:3, which takes up Ps. 110:1). Some point to the wording which states that every priest "stands" while of Christ it is said that he "sat down." But standing was the natural way in which the priests performed their service; they could not perform it while sitting down. Christ sat down when he had completed his sacrifice, when he was about to render his further priestly service for us, which was the outflow of his single sacrifice.

13) Yet the writer does not repeat what he has said about this heavenly priesthood of Christ; he repeats what he has said in 1:13 regarding the supreme exaltation of Christ: "henceforth (τὸ λοιπόν is temporal) waiting until his enemies be placed as a footstool for his feet," see the exposition in 1:13. These enemies are the devil, his power of death (2:14), and all those who reject Christ. By the power of Christ's single sacrifice all believers of all time are rescued from these enemies who will lie powerless under his feet. That will occur at the end of the world, in the final judgment (I Cor. 15:24-26). This "until" clause indicates how far the single sacrifice of Christ reaches.

The contrast between the sacrifices of all Jewish priests and the single sacrifice of Christ is shown in an overwhelming way. It climaxes all that precedes. How can any of the readers possibly think of turning away from this sacrifice of Christ to the endless, ineffective sacrifices of the Jewish priests? For myself let me say that this entire stunning presentation makes me think of just one man as being the writer of this epistle, he of whom Luke writes: "He mightily convinced the Jews, and that publicly, showing by the Scriptures that Jesus is the Christ," Acts 18:28.

14) A simple explanatory clause is added: "For by means of a single sacrifice he has brought to completion in perpetuity those being sanctified." This connects with all that has been said regarding the τελείωσις which the whole Jewish system lacked and could never achieve but which Christ's single sacrifice did achieve at one stroke. To see to what extent the writer uses the idea of completeness, of reaching the τέλος or goal, follow this verb as it runs through this epistle in 2:10; 5:9; 7:19, 28; 10:14; 11:40; 12:23; then the three nouns in 6:1; 7:11; 12:2, and the comparative adjective in 9:11. It is God who sets the goal; this goal is our complete restoration. All that is contained in the law-testament that was given through Moses is preliminary to that goal, could not be any more. Christ brings completely to the goal yet is himself made complete by suffering in order to do this. His complete sacrifice attains the goal. By his sacrifice we become complete, are at the goal which God set for us. This is one of the golden threads that is woven into the wonderful pattern of this epistle. It combines with all the others.

This is what Christ has done "by means of one offering": "he has brought to completion those being sanctified." The completeness has been achieved and thus stands "in perpetuity" and affects "those being sanctified" (the same designation of them that was used in 2:11). The best grammatical note on this present participle is that found in Moulton, *Einleitung* 206, which places the tense of τοὺς ἁγιαζομένους in relation to the tense of τετελείωκεν (we have the same construction in 2:11): what is a completed fact for Christ in regard to us is in progressing relation to us, the objects concerned. If no relation of tense is intended, why did the writer not use a noun, say τοὺς ἁγίους or some other? We also note that the perfect used in v. 10, "we have been sanctified," is now repeated, but it is not restricted to "we" (writer and readers) but includes all who at any time experience the sanctifying power of Christ's completed offering and its completed effect on them.

The participle might be timeless: "the objects of sanctification," which is the view of R. 1111; others call it the equivalent of a noun, which is a solution that does not explain the tense involved; or the tense form might be iterative: "those from time to time receiving sanctification," which may then be descriptive of these persons, which is probably meant by R. 891: "descriptive durative." While the saints of all ages are referred to, we believe that in οἱ ἁγιαζόμενοι, "the ones being sanctified," we have the idea of the entire course of their sainthood; from its beginning to its consummation it appropriates the one offering of Christ as the means by which he has brought them to completeness, to the great goal set by God. All Jewish sacrifices are not a means that achieves this. The main point is that we should not think merely of being sanctified in the narrow sense of the term, sanctified in holy living, but in the wide sense, namely being cleansed from sin by justification through Christ's sacrifice, a justification that is entirely complete and abides forever, of which holy living is only the fruit.

15) Moreover, also the Holy Spirit bears witness for us. We have his own testimony to what has just been said, namely that Christ has achieved total completeness by his one offering, has brought those being sanctified to full completeness. The Holy Spirit is called the witness to this fact because he has left this testimony for us in the Sacred Scriptures, where it ever continues to testify.

Hebrews 10:16

16) For after having said:

**This (is) the testament which I will draw up
in regard to them
After those days —**
	the Lord says:
**I will give my laws upon their heart,
And on their mind will I inscribe them;
And their sins and their lawlessnesses I will
not remember any longer.**

This is the Spirit's testimony as he has recorded it for us through Jeremiah (31:33, 34) and preserved this testimony just as the Lord (Yahweh) uttered it. In 8:8-12 the writer has used the whole of this testimony, Jer. 31:31-34, for establishing another point, namely that God intended to abrogate the Mosaic law-testament by substituting an entirely different testament for it. The writer uses only a part of the full quotation here, the part that establishes what he says in v. 12-14. He is not pedantic or mechanical in the way in which he quotes but modifies the wording so as to bring out the main point of proof the more clearly for his readers.

It is unfair to the writer to say that he now quotes only from memory and thus does not get the wording as exact as he did in 8:8-12 where he consulted the LXX. The writer is just as free as we are when we are quoting for a purpose; the fact is that we often go beyond this and state only the gist of the statement made by some other writer. Our procedure is determined by the extent to which we wish to use the *ipsissima verba* of the other writer. Sometimes just the general sense is enough, sometimes certain words or phrases, sometimes more of the original wording, sometimes insertions or clarifying, interpretative paraphrasing. We should not expect the writers of Scripture to quote verbatim while we allow ourselves and others freedom according to the purpose in hand.

The writer divides the quotation because the second half of it is the essential part in this connection where he speaks of the completeness of "those being sanctified." So he writes: "After he (Yahweh) has said: 'This is the testament which I will draw up in regard to them after those days.'" He uses this part to show the connection in which God spoke the following: it was when God spoke about the wonderful coming testament (see 8:10). "In regard to them" will suffice here whereas "for the house of Israel" is the original as his readers know.

While "the Lord says" is a part of the original, the writer adopts it as his own statement in order to divide the quotation and to introduce the three essential lines that follow. The R. V. and others think that the division is to occur before the very last line and thus insert at the end of v. 16: "then saith he." They think that the readers could surmise this because the writer leaves out the six lines which Jeremiah has written between v. 16 and 17. We do not think so. The division occurs at "the Lord says." The fact that the three lines belong together agrees with this division, namely God's giving his laws into the mind and heart and not remembering sins and transgressions of law, for both acts form a unit and together constitute what the writer states in v. 14: "Christ with a single offering has brought to completion in perpetuity those who are being sanctified." We see here what it means to be sanctified, namely that God no longer remembers our sins (justification) and that he puts his laws into our hearts (so that we live a holy life, sanctification in the narrow sense), and both acts of God rest on Christ's one sacrifice.

The verbal changes from 8:10b and 12 are freely made by the writer and are not faults of memory. He thus places "heart" before "mind" because he wants to mention the organ of the inner personality first. On the participle διδούς see the explanation given in 8:10; see also the details of the exposition in 8:10, 12.

17) The two poetic lines quoted in 8:12 the writer welds into one and omits "I will be merciful." He does this in order the more to concentrate on "I will not remember any longer," the act of justification. For the volitive passive aorist subjunctive μνησθῶ he substitutes the volitive passive future μνησθήσομαι, but the meaning of both remains the same. He places "sins" first, and for "unrighteousness" he substitutes "lawlessnesses" (law violations) as an interpretative synonym.

18) **Now where** (there is) **remission of these** (there is) **no longer offering for sin,** i. e., there is no longer room for any such thing. That is the point here. It is vital for the readers who have been thinking of going back to Judaism and all its sacrifices. Since the sacrifice of Christ has been made for sin, all other sacrifice for sin is utterly without function or meaning. The statement is entirely general; while it is intended to apply to the Mosaic sacrifices for sin, any other such sacrifices are included. Like 9:22, this passage also excludes the Romish sacrifice of the Mass, the supposed unbloody recrucifixion of Christ by the priest.

On the great word ἄφεσις see 9:22. When God sends away "these," namely our sins and our violations of his law, so that even his memory does not recall them, they are gone indeed. But the Spirit himself testifies that God actually does this. We know what enables him to do so: Christ's full expiation of all sins. Ergo, drawing the conclusion from these premises: all sacrificing for sin is forever done with. Have you sin, no matter of what kind, here is its expiation, on the cross, in Christ's blood and sacrifice, and **here is its remission on the basis of that sacrifice.**

The Sixth Main Part

The Hortations to Faith and Faithfulness, 10:19-13:17

Hortations have been appended to several expositions in earlier sections of the epistle; from chapter 7 onward we have a grand series of uninterrupted exposition, and now there follows an equally grand series of hortations. This arrangement is obvious, also highly effective.

The Call to Draw Near, v. 19-25.

19) This first hortatory section is comprehensive, one grand sentence with three hortative subjunctives: "let us draw near—let us hold fast—and let us consider each other." These hortations are preceded by a participial statement that summarizes the preceding chapters by showing what we have to induce us to heed these hortations.

Having, then, brethren, assurance in regard to the entrance of the Sanctuary in connection with the blood of Jesus, which (entrance) he inaugurated for us as a way newly made and living by means of the veil, that is, of his flesh; and (having) a great Priest over the house of God, let us draw near, etc.

Οὖν is not merely transitional in this connection, for it indicates that ἔχοντες intends to state what the preceding chapters have set forth so fully. The whole high priesthood of Christ, the sacrifice of himself which achieved the final completeness, puts us into personal possession of assurance regarding entering the Sanctuary and into possession of a Priest who is great indeed, on whom this assurance rests. The address "brethren" marks the beginning of the new section of the epistle and at the same time intensifies the personal appeal of this threefold hortation.

Παρρησία, etymologically "openness and boldness in speech," readily passes into the meaning "confidence" (M.-M. 497), *die unverzagte, furcht- und zweifellose Zuversicht des Glaubens* (C.-K. 551). We have such assurance as a most valuable gift from Christ who obtained it for us by his blood. For this is "an assurance in regard to (εἰς) the entrance of the Sanctuary in connection with (ἐν) the blood of Jesus." The phrase εἰς τὴν εἴσοδον should not be stressed to mean an action: "to enter into the Sanctuary" (our versions). The action of entering in is not mentioned until v. 22: "let us draw near." When one is asked to draw near, he must first be confident in regard to the entrance he is to make, in regard to the "way" (ὁδός). Is the entrance open, open for him? It is indeed, right into the heavenly Sanctuary (τὰ ἅγια); we are freed from all hesitation, need not hold back for any reason.

This is "the entrance of the Sanctuary in connection with the blood of Jesus"; the phrase modifies "the entrance of the Sanctuary" and needs no article because only this one entrance exists. There is not an entrance connected with Jesus' blood and one or more others apart from his blood. The thought is changed when the expression is regarded as referring to the action of entering; or when it is thought that we, like high priests, may now enter with Jesus' blood. This sets aside all that the writer has said about Jesus when he stated that he entered the heavenly Sanctuary with his blood "once for all." What the writer says is that the entrance is open for us in connection with Jesus' blood; his blood has opened it for us so that it shall never be closed. Any uncertainty, doubt, or hesitation on our part on that score are removed.

20) The relative clause justifies such confident assurance on our part regarding this entrance into the

heavenly Sanctuary, for this entrance Jesus "inaugurated for us as a way newly made and living by means of the veil, that is, of his flesh." The relative ἥν does not refer to παρρησίαν because the predicative ὁδόν takes up εἴσοδον; nor can one say that "assurance was inaugurated," the verb and the object would not fit each other as little as they would if one should call "assurance" "a way or road." No; this entrance into the Sanctuary is "a way newly made and living." This way Jesus "inaugurated for us as a way new and living." The aorist states the historical fact, an act done "once for all." On "inaugurate" see 9:10, literally, "to bring in as new" (the word does not here mean "dedicate," which meaning would leave a wrong impression). Jesus opened or inaugurated this entrance as a way for us when as our High Priest he entered the heavenly Sanctuary as the writer has so fully explained. Thus it is rightly termed "the entrance of the Sanctuary in connection with the blood of Jesus" and is now elucidated as "a way newly made and living," inaugurated "by means of the veil, that is, of his flesh."

The language is exceedingly rich. This entrance or way is "for us"; we are to use it when we are confidently approaching God. Πρόσφατος, literally, "freshly killed," has lost its etymological meaning and is used in the sense of "recent," "fresh," "new." But a few years had passed since Jesus opened the way by means of his sacrificial death. More striking is the word "living." This does not = "a way of life," i.e., leading to life, ὁδὸς τῆς ζωῆς (Jer. 21:8); the participle is not an objective genitive noun. "Living way" is also not "life-giving way"; nor does "living"="abiding" or permanent way. All ways or roads that we know are lifeless; this way is "living" because it consists of Christ himself who is "the Way and the Life" (John 14:6), a way that is itself active and bears those who step upon it. We go farther than to say that it is "living" because of its *connection* with the living Christ; the living Christ *is himself* the living way.

Still more striking is the statement that Jesus "inaugurated" the entrance of the Sanctuary for us, opened it for the first time for our use as a new and living way, "by means of the veil, that is, of his flesh." On the Greek word for veil or curtain see 9:3. The meaning is simple. The means for entrance into the Holy of Holies in the Tabernacle was the great curtain that hung before it; the means for entrance into the heavenly Sanctuary is Jesus' flesh. Thus the writer says that the entrance into the heavenly Sanctuary was inaugurated or opened for us as a new and living way "by means of his flesh." As the veil in the Tabernacle was the only means of entrance to the inner sanctuary, so Jesus' flesh is the only means of entrance to the Sanctuary of heaven. In other words, without Jesus' flesh, apart from that, there exists no means by which we may go into the heavenly Sanctuary, may get into saving communion with God.

Note well "for us." In the case of the Tabernacle only the high priest dared to use the veil as a means of entry. This new way is for all of us; all of us are to use Jesus' flesh as the great means of entry. Yet we should not extend into an allegory the simple metaphor here used by going beyond its *tertium comparationis* of a means of entry: making ourselves high priests who, like the Jewish high priests, had to come with blood, who officiated for others, etc. There is no longer an offering for sins, no longer blood to offer (v. 18).

Note again that "his flesh" follows the designation the entrance of the Sanctuary "in connection with the blood of Jesus." "Flesh" and "blood" go together as far as this entrance is concerned. It is the slain flesh or body of Jesus that, like a veil, hangs before the heavenly Sanctuary and is the one means of entry. All that the writer has said on the suffering, the death, the blood, the offering of himself, the sacrifice of himself, is here brought to mind. The crucified Christ is the entrance, the entrance veil. "No man cometh to the Father but *by me*," John 14:6, by my blood, by my flesh, by this veil. This veil shuts out and forever hides the Father from all those who spurn it as the means of entry.

The διά is here not local: "through the veil," etc., (our versions, commentators). An entrance is not "inaugurated" (not even "dedicated" as our versions have it) "through" anything in a local sense but only "by means" of something. An incongruity results when we combine "new and living through (locally) the veil." It is eisegesis to insert the participle ἄγουσαν or some other participle: "leading through the veil." "His flesh" is also not "his human nature," for what about "the blood"? "His flesh" denotes the body of Jesus as it was sacrificed for us.

This whole statement aims to strike the readers squarely. No Jew, except the high priest, ever got to enter the Holy of Holies of the Tabernacle; the people had no way to the actual mercy seat. But these readers now have the actual entrance into the heavenly Sanctuary; they may pass in with joyful confidence. Yet they are thinking of turning from this entrance, turning back to Judaism, where even the earthly Holy of Holies is closed to them. How can they think of doing such a thing? Is it because Jesus was crucified, because this is an offense to them? But the very connection with Jesus' blood opens this entrance into the heavenly Sanctuary for them; his blood-stained flesh constitutes the very veil, the means of entrance, for them; to despise it means never to enter at all. The convincing force of this is tremendous, indeed. To this day it strikes all who spurn "the blood theology." This theology fills our epistle.

Some find an allusion to the rent veil in these words (Matt. 27:51). The writer, however, as not a few have observed, never goes beyond the original Tabernacle, never refers to Solomon's Temple, and certainly not to Herod's. The thought of the rent veil may occur to us, yet the writer makes no use of it.

21) Besides such "assurance" regarding this wonderful entrance we also possess "a great Priest over the house of God." The assurance is God's gift for our own hearts; this great Priest is placed over us as being the house in which God dwells. "Great Priest" recalls "great High Priest" used in 4:14 and all that has been said about his exaltation at God's right hand (last in v. 12). "Priest" is the proper word here instead of "High Priest" when we recall 7:1-25, Christ's likeness to Melchizedek, the king-priest. Jesus is still our Priest who is "able to save to the utmost those who come to God through him, ever living to intercede for them" (7:25). Has Judaism a priest like this? The writer does not say "over the house of Israel" (8:8) but "over the house of God," "whose house we ourselves are if we hold fast as firm to the end the assurance and the boast of the hope" (3:6).

22) So, then, **let us continue to draw near with a true heart in full assurance of faith, having been sprinkled as to our hearts** (to free them) **from a wicked conscience, and having been washed as to body with pure water; etc.**

The present tense means "let us continue to draw near, let us not cease for any reason." It is the same admonition that was given in 4:16: "Let us draw near with assurance to the throne of the grace in order that we may receive mercy and find grace for timely help." The Sanctuary (τὰ ἅγια) referred to in v. 19 is heaven itself, the eternal abode of God (not some inner place in heaven to which God has retired). Christ, by means of his flesh, is the entrance, our living way to this Sanctuary, our great Priest, by whom we have access to this Sanctuary, its throne of grace, and God himself.

We now draw near in worship, in prayer, and receive all the grace. At death the soul draws near, at the time of the resurrection also the body.

Προσερχώμεθα is a ritual or liturgical term that harmonizes with ἐρραντισμένοι and λελουμένοι as also with "the Sanctuary" and "the veil." "Let us draw near" or "go to" means actual entrance into this Sanctuary although in this life it is as yet only in spirit (John 4:24) or with our hearts. Endless blessings are thus to be ours. The call is given to those who are "brethren," who have already been going to this Sanctuary and need only to be urged never to cease going; it is not intended to exclude others who are not yet brethren; they, too, are still bidden to come, i.e., to become "brethren" with us and thus to come.

God always looks at the heart, our inner self, the seat of the mind and the will; his eyes penetrate through and through it. Hence we have the admonition to come "with a true heart," one that is ἀληθινή, not false, hypocritical, merely pretending and making a profession that is not warranted by sincere intentions. "A true heart" goes "in full assurance of faith," πληροφορία as in 6:3, which means more than "fulness" (R. V.), it is rather "full assurance" (A. V.), i.e., full certainty and that in full measure, and thus matches παρρησία that was used in v. 19. So great and glorious is what we have that nothing less than full assurance of faith should move us to draw near, a faith that is fully certain of its ground, not ignorant, doubting, or moved by human argument or objection. Many a heart needs the admonition voiced in this phrase. James 1:6, etc.

The subjective conditions for drawing near, namely a true heart and full assurance of faith, are the more to be expected because of the objective blessings the readers have received, the continuous effects of which are indicated by the perfect tenses of the participles and the divine agency in the passive voice. We do not separate these participles and begin the second admonition "and having been washed as to the body with pure water, let us hold fast," etc., (R. V. margin and others). This destroys the symmetry of the sentence. How are we to draw near? First μετά ... ἐν, two prepositions with their objects, and each object with one modifier; secondly, two perfect passive participles, each with its accusative after a passive, each with one additional modifier. This symmetry should not be marred by cutting off the last participle. Moreover, the two participles denote lustrations and are thus tied together also in meaning.

"Heart" and "body" correspond. The "heart" is properly mentioned where the "conscience" is concerned. The thought is not, however, that either "heart" or "body" is cleansed without the other; cleansing affects the whole man. The "body" is properly mentioned where the sacramental washing of baptism is concerned since the baptismal water touches the body. In adults the cleansing of the heart precedes the cleansing by baptism although baptism soon follows, must follow if the heart is, indeed, cleansed; in infants both occur together in baptism.

Both ῥαντίζω and λούω recall the Old Testament cleansing of the high priest before performing his great duty: he was sprinkled with blood, Exod. 29:21; Lev. 8:30; and was to wash with water, Exod. 40:12; 30:19; Lev. 8:6; 16:4, 24. The implication is not that we are high priests who are to be similarly cleansed, for we serve no high-priestly function in drawing near to God. The implication goes no farther than the fact that, like those Jewish high priests, we must be completely cleansed before we draw near to God and his heavenly Sanctuary. The fluid for sprinkling the hearts, which is not named here, is named in 12:24: "the blood of sprinkling that speaketh better than that of Abel"; also in I Pet. 1:2: "sprinkling of the blood of Jesus Christ"; also in I John 1:7. Christ shed his blood for all men, but now every individual has this blood applied to his inner personality, the heart, the seat of the ἐγώ. This inward sprinkling = justification through the ransoming that is in Christ Jesus, Rom. 3:24.

"To sprinkle from a wicked conscience" is a pregnant expression and equals to sprinkle and thus to free from a wicked conscience. A wicked conscience is one that has wickedness lying upon it. Even if such a conscience is lulled asleep, even if it is actually seared, it will in the end fill the sinner with utter condemnation. Only one thing can free us from the charges of such a conscience, can restore us to a "good conscience" that is able to approach God uncondemned, and that is Christ's blood. I John 1:7. How can one think of drawing near to the holy God in his holy Sanctuary with a wicked conscience? That will drive him into outer darkness.

The New Testament knows of only one washing, namely baptism. In Eph. 5:25-27 it is called "the washing of water in connection with uttered Word"; in Titus 3:5, "a washing of regeneration and renewing of the Holy Spirit"; in Acts 22:16 Paul is bidden: "Be baptized and wash away thy sins." Because baptism cleanses, the writer says washed by means of "clean" water, which certainly does not mean only physically clean as opposed to dirty water. Baptism is always applied to the body, but as the sprinkling of the heart affects the whole person, so also does this sacred washing of the body.

This is not a strong allusion to Jewish lustrations, for all these required repetition while no true baptism can be repeated, its effect is permanent. Baptism is the sacrament for all who are children of "God's house," even for infants and children who cannot as yet be reached by the Word that is preached and taught and by the Lord's Supper. "All you are sons of God through faith in Christ Jesus; for as many as were baptized in connection with Christ (εἰς = ἐν) did put on Christ."

23) Since the writer uses three subjunctives, the second needs no connective: **let us continue to hold fast the confession of the hope unbent, for faithful (is) the One who made the promise.**

In 4:15 we have the same admonition to hold fast the confession, but the word used in that passage is κρατέω, to use our strength in holding it; the word used here is κατέχω, simply to hold fast. The full assurance of faith (v. 24) is bound to confess aloud before the church and the world. See how faith and confession are welded together in Rom. 10:9, 10. As fire has heat and light, so faith has confession. But this "confession" is not merely subjective so that the writer says only: "Keep on confessing that you are hoping!" One holds fast something objective, here the *words* which form the confession of the church, which embody *what* we hope for, and not only the admission *that* we are hoping. The subjective feature lies in the holding fast. Seeberg is nearer to the facts than those who find fault with him when he thinks that the church had a kind of fixed catechism as its confession. There may not have been a regular catechism, but there were surely acknowledged ways of confessing both in what Christians believed and for what they hoped.

The predicate adjective has the emphasis: ἀκλινῆ: Keep holding fast the confession "unbent," i.e., never letting it be bent so as to droop, to lose its contents. Hold the confession firmly like a banner that is flying high and never drooping to the ground. Ever confess all your Christian hope fearlessly, courageously; never grow silent, never deny. In 4:15 and here the implication is that assaults will have to be faced; v. 32-38 speak of "a great conflict of sufferings," of being made "a gazingstock both by reproaches and affliction," of "spoiling the confessors of their possessions," etc. "Cast not away your assurance, which has great recompense of reward" (v. 35).

The present results of confession are often painful to bear. That is why the writer says "the confession of the hope": "knowing that you yourselves have a better possession and an abiding one" (v. 34). Whatever pain and distress our confession brings upon us must not darken the vision of the great hope that is awaiting us in the end. "For faithful (trustworthy, reliable) is the One who made the promise," who promised all that we hope for in the end. This faithfulness of God is expressed in I Cor. 1:9: "God is faithful, through whom ye were called into the fellowship of his Son, Jesus Christ our Lord"; I Thess. 5:24: "Faithful is that calleth you, who will also do it"; I Cor. 10:13 faithful also in not letting you be tried beyond strength. We may let go, he is unwavering and does not let go. If any confessor denies, loses the heavenly hope, the fault is his own and not God's. Here, however, God's faithfulness and sure promise are used as the great motive that should stir us ever to hold fast the confession of the hope; he will fulfill every promise, bestow help in our trials and the crown of glory at the end.

24, 25) The first admonition deals with the heart, the second with the mouth (confession), the third with conduct. The first with God, the second with the world, the third with the church: **and let us continue to consider each other as regards provocation to love and good works, not abandoning the assembly of ourselves as some have a custom** (of doing), **but offering encouragement, and by so much the more by how much you see the day drawing near.**

Let us put our mind down on each other. Each is to continue to think of what his own attitude and conduct mean in their effect upon his brethren. Remissness

Hebrews 10:24

causes double damage, to ourselves and to all the rest; our faithfulness produces double fruit, our own good deeds and a stimulation of others to like good deeds.

Παροξυσμός, when it is used in a bad sense, means excitation to anger, bitterness, an inflammation; it is here used in the good sense and means "an incitement to love and good works" (objective genitives). Ἀγάπη is the love of intelligent comprehension coupled with corresponding purpose, the root of good works, the love itself being the fruit of faith.

Luther writes on this faith that is active in love: "Oh, it is a living, busy, active, powerful thing that we have in faith so that it is impossible for it not to do good without ceasing. Nor does it ask whether good works are to be done; but before the question is asked, it has wrought them and is always engaged in doing them." *C. Tr.* 941, 10. Love and good works always go together; it is love that makes the works good in God's sight, who ever looks beyond what is outward to the inner motive of every deed.

Essential to such incitement to love and good works is the fact that we do not keep abandoning the assembly of our own selves. True, we need to have the Word preached and taught so as to keep our faith, confession, and love active and strong, and some have thought that this is the point; yet the writer thinks rather of the fellowship in the ἐπισυναγωγή, the gathering together of the church members, ἐπί adding only the idea of assembling together at a certain place.

"The assembly of your own selves" seems to imply a contrast with the gatherings of others who are hostile to the Christians, whether secret or open. So the Sanhedrin gathered to plot against Jesus. The verb means "to abandon," "to desert," as in Matt. 27:41: "My God, my God, why didst thou abandon me?" Acts 2:27: "Thou wilt not abandon my soul unto hell." II Tim. 4:10, 16; II Cor. 4:9. Zahn, *Introduction* II,

348, thinks that some of the readers merely attended other church meetings. The dative with the copula (which is omitted) is a common idiom for "have": "as some have a custom (of doing)," i.e., as some are doing. This is more than just carelessness; it is the beginning of apostasy.

The aim of the whole epistle is to counteract the defection from Christianity which had set in among the Jewish Christian readers. They had begun to revert to Judaism, to think the Jewish priesthood, Temple, sacrifices, etc., the real thing, to turn from this crucified Christ, etc. We see here that "some" were giving up their fellowship with the church. We conclude that they were going back to the Jewish synagogues in Rome. See the introduction, also v. 32, etc., for the reason of this defection: the burning of Rome, the horrible persecution which Nero visited upon the old congregation in Rome to avert suspicion from himself as having set fire to the city, the execution of Paul, the Christian religion being now treated by the authorities as a *religio illicita*. These Jewish Christians had not joined the old congregation, had kept to themselves in their synagogue houses of worship, had thus not been wholly identified with the Christians of the old congregations, and had suffered to a far less extent. Thus some were abandoning the meetings, were afraid to be seen attending them, were just remaining away, or, as is more probable judging from the aim of the whole epistle, were going back to the synagogues of the Jews in Rome to be Jews again.

What a dangerous example (see v. 26, etc.)! Instead of following it, let the readers keep "encouraging." Παρακαλεῖν always gets its meaning from the context; it may mean to admonish, comfort, encourage. The last meaning is best here, and certainly better than "to exhort" which is used in our versions. No object is needed in the Greek, the context shows what encouragement is referred to, namely the same that the writer is offering here. "And by so much the more by how much you see the day drawing near"; all these persecutions are signs of the end. Instead of letting such things move you to turn away from Christ they should move you to do the very opposite, for the great Day is near.

There is no question that ἡ ἡμέρα is the day of final judgment which is also called "that day." It needs no further modifier in the New Testament. To say that any day of judgment is referred to is an effort to evade a difficulty, namely that the writer thought that the end of the world would come in a very short time, that thus, since it did *not* come and has not come to this day, he was mistaken; all of which disappears when we interpret "the day drawing near" as a reference to some preliminary judgment day. This fear is groundless as is every charge that the New Testament writers were mistaken as to the day of judgment. Jesus told the apostles that no man is to know even "times or periods" (Acts 1:7) to say nothing of the exact day; that he himself (in his state of humiliation) did not know the day; but that we must ever see the signs of its approach, ever be ready for its arrival, in constant expectation of it. All the New Testament writers speak accordingly; we do the same today.

The correlative datives express degree: the readers will the more encourage each other the more they see the day drawing near, i.e., see these plain signs of its approach as foretold by Jesus. This is itself an encouragement, for on that day all our hope will be realized and crowned. Rom. 8:18.

The Warning against Apostasy, v. 26-31.

26) Hortation merges into sharpest warning, yet it does so in a natural way. Some are abandoning the Christian Church (v. 25). There is danger of apostasy and of what has been called "the sin against the Holy

Ghost" or "the unpardonable sin." It is the second time that the writer issues this warning; we should combine 6:4-8 with 10:26-31. The purpose of both passages is the same: to warn the readers by showing them what this sin is into which they are inclined to fall and by revealing to them that this sin is absolutely fatal. Riggenbach has understood the difference between these two passages correctly: the one is psychological, it stresses the fact that repentance and renewal are impossible; the other is soteriological, it points out that there is no sacrifice to wipe out this sin. In 6:4-8 the writer stirs up his readers to heed aright what he is about to tell them about the great High Priesthood of Christ; here he confronts his readers with the full consequence that must descend on them if they nullify the experience they have had of the High Priesthood of Christ.

For when willingly we go on sinning after receiving the realization of the truth, no longer is there left a sacrifice for sins but (only) **some frightful expectation of judgment and an eagerness of fire about to eat those hostile.**

"For" is not *begruendend;* it does not offer proof or reasons. "For" = so that you may understand this matter about withdrawing from the Christian assembly and the reference to the last day in regard to such as withdraw; understand what this really means. The genitive absolute and its modifier define the act; the main clause states the consequence.

"We" means any of us; "willingly" has the emphasis. We construe: "Willingly we sinning after receiving (aorist, actually having received) the realization of the truth." Sinning in ignorance or in weakness is not referred to but the deliberate, voluntary sinning of one who has really received the knowledge which is realization (ἐπίγνωσις, not mere *Kenntnis* but *Erkenntnis*) of the divine, saving truth, the actual reality of the

Hebrews 10:26, 27

gospel contents. In v. 27 such are called the ὑπεναντίοι, "the antagonists," those who have turned opposite, hostile. Add v. 29 with its further description. Compare what we have said regarding this sin in connection with 6:4.

It is, of course, not merely one deed but a continuous sinning, a *habitus*. 6:4 has stated that there is no halting of it by repentance. Its deliberateness, its being done against better knowledge, are added here. When some think that "willing" means without inducement or pressure from outside they might note that the devil operates with both, and that bringing us into this sin is not an exception. No man can explain how anyone can fall in this way unless he can offer reasonable explanations for the climax of unreason.

It is after the whole exposition about Christ's sacrifice that the writer can now say of this sin: "no longer is there left a sacrifice for sins," i.e., any sacrifice for sins that would have any effect on sinners of this kind. Since they permanently repudiate the one, final, supreme sacrifice of Christ, what is there left that might be brought to bear on these sinners? The thought is not that we must necessarily say that Christ did not expiate also their sin, but that repudiation of him and his sacrifice leaves them nothing. Since the readers are Jewish Christians, such a sinner may think that by his repudiation of Christ he will find safety in the sacrifices of Judaism when he again becomes a Jew. The writer has shown the vanity of such an escape, for all Jewish sacrifices helped sinners only by adumbrating Christ's final sacrifice.

27) What remains for such sinners is only "some frightful expectation of judgment," etc. Τις is rhetorical and belongs to the adjective (R. 743) and not to the noun or to its genitive. Such a τις sometimes minimizes, but sometimes, as here, by minimizing it intensifies the adjective: "some frightful" = a very frightful. Φοβερά

may be subjective or objective: the judgment that is frightful in itself, which meaning it has here; or the frightfulness of it that is felt by the sinner. This sinner may scoff at and blaspheme the judgment that is awaiting him, its frightful character remains the same.

Ἐκδοχή is found only here in the New Testament and is used in a sense that is not found elsewhere, not even in the papyri. It has the meaning "expectation," which corresponds to the verb used in 10:11 and is one of the interesting New Testament words on which more light is sought. The writer does not say "some frightful judgment" remains for such sinners but more impressively "some frightful expectation (looking for, A. V.) of judgment," i.e., all that is left is so frightful a wait although the sinners themselves do not realize it.

Explicative καί brings out what is meant: "and an eagerness or zeal of fire about to eat those hostile," those contrary or opposed. He again does not say merely "and a fire" but "a zeal of fire" as if the judgment fire were a living thing, its flames seething to devour these adversaries of Christ (B.-P. 527). Nothing can be more "frightful."

28) In 6:7, 8 an illustration follows; an illustration is introduced also here but one that also draws a comparison. In 6:7,8 nature is used as an illustration; here it is history. **One having defied Moses' law dies without compassion before two or three witnesses.** The participle means "to set at naught, to act as if it were not there," thus "to defy." The readers are former Jews and are acquainted with Deut. 17:2-7 and the rest of the crimes for which the Mosaic code decreed death. Is there any "compassion" (idiomatic plural in the Greek) for such defiance of law? No; the person dies "before two or three witnesses." R. 604 is right: ἐπί = "before," "in the presence of." Deut. 17:7 says that the witnesses are to start the stoning (cf., also Acts 7:58). This is the juridical ἐπί. There is no

thought of the trial but of the execution when the criminal dies, with nothing, absolutely nothing to remove the penalty.

29) We now have the comparison with an argument from the less to the greater in the form of a question which lets the readers themselves supply the inevitable answer. If this happens to a defier of Moses' law, what must then happen to a renegade who outrages the Son of God? **Of how much worse punishment do you think he will be counted worthy who trampled under foot the Son of God and counted as common the blood of the testament in connection with which he was** (once) **sanctified and insulted the Spirit of the** (divine) **grace?**

The comparison is drawn, not between a sin against Moses and this one against God's Son and the Holy Spirit, but between a sin against the divine law, the agent for the transmission of which needed to be only a man (Moses), and this sin against the supreme institution of grace, the agents of which are the two divine persons themselves. So the one sin is a setting aside of some portion of the divine law as if it were nothing, but this sin is the ultimate insult against these divine persons and what they have done for and in this unspeakably heinous sinner. Crime suffices to designate the one sin; but what word is there to designate the other? One participial designation is enough to describe the one sin; three are required to set forth the other.

"To count worthy of" is used when honor is the object; to use it with the opposite, with τιμωρία or "punishment" in the sense of vindication, makes the verb more striking. "To trample under foot" is illustrated by Matt. 7:6 where the hogs trample pearls into the mire. To do this to "the Son of God" brings to mind all that this epistle has said of his infinite exaltation from 1:2 onward. The writer does not say trample down some gift the Son of God brought as he says

"Moses' law" but trample down this infinitely exalted Son who is very God himself.

More must be said about him: "and counted as common the blood of the testament in connection with which (ἐν) he was (once) sanctified." It is the holy blood of the incarnate Son, and the readers will be compelled to think of all that this epistle has said about this blood of the new testament which it established. See διαθήκη in 7:22; and fail not to remember Matt. 26:28. To former Jews κοινόν means "without sacredness," like any common blood, and in this case, since Christ was crucified and executed, no better than the blood of the two malefactors who were crucified with him. And yet at one time this man had his heart sprinkled with this blood from a wicked conscience (v. 22), had experienced its sacred, sanctifying power, "had been sanctified in connection with it." The blood that once *sanctified* him so that he experienced its sanctifying power fully he finally counts as common, as not even being *sacred*. The enormity of sacrilege can go no farther.

It should, however, be added that this sinner "insulted the Spirit of the (divine) grace," for his is all the sanctifying work in our hearts, his the entire application of the divine grace to us, χάρις, the unmerited *favor Dei* extended to the guilty who deserve the damnation of justice (while ἔλεος is the "mercy" that is extended to the wretched). It is on the basis of this mention of the Spirit, to which are added Matt. 12:31, 32; Mark 3:28, 29; Luke 12:10, that this sin is called the sin against the Holy Ghost and the unpardonable sin. As there is no more "sacrifice for sins" (v. 26) that could reach this sinner, so after all his grace is insulted the Spirit cannot longer reach him.

30) What the writer says about the judgment that is awaiting such a sinner is not an empty threat on his part. **For we know** (you as well as I) **him who said:**

To me (belongs) **vengeance** (the act of exacting justice)! **I, I will give back due return!** Deut. 32:35 (Rom. 12:19). God will certainly carry out his threat. In ἀνταποδώσω, ἀπό has the force of "due" as it has also in various other compounds: what is due "from" me to give. This sinner will get full justice, *all* that is due him from God. The Hebrew has: "To me vengeance and recompense"; the LXX: "In the day of vengeance I will give due return." The writer quotes neither passage exactly but rather combines the two just as Paul does in Rom. 12:19. It seems that this Greek rendering was current in the early church.

The writer adds a second testimony (Deut. 32:36; Ps. 135:14): **and again: The Lord will judge his people.** Let no reader imagine that, because he is of Jewish extraction when he turns from Christ to Judaism, he will escape. Scripture names "his people" as the very ones on whom the Lord will pass judgment. The verb has the emphasis, and while κρίνειν is a *vox media* and means favorable as well as adverse judging, it is the latter in regard to which the writer warns the readers.

31) All he adds is: **Frightful to fall into the hands of the living God!** Φοβερόν repeats this adjective from v. 27. "To fall into someone's hands" (aorist, effective) is used with reference to an enemy or a criminal who at last drops helplessly into the power that finally settles with him. Four times the writer uses Θεὸς ζῶν, twice when warning, here and in 3:12, "to apostatize from the living God"; twice when inviting, in 9:14, "to serve the living God," and in 12:22, "the city of the living God." As One who is "living" and not a dead idol, not a fictitious god who is merely imagined God keeps his promises and executes his threats. Blessed are they who trust and obey him; frightful the fate of those who scorn his Son and insult his Spirit.

So much preaching is weak and flabby because it fails to sound the stern warning which the writer, like Jesus and the rest of Scripture, uses again and again. Preachers think it wise not to appeal to the motive of fear. But by not frightening men into heaven they fail to frighten them away from hell. The ζῆλος πυρός, "the seething zeal of fire" ready to devour, *is* frightful; to fall into the hands of the living God whom one has outraged *is* frightful. It is folly to hush this fact. So perverse are men's hearts, so dull their consciences, that when one is drawing them to the grace of the living God there is need, because of their perversity, that the fear of God be aroused in them lest they after all fall into the hands of the living God for judgment.

The Remembrance of the Former Days,
v. 32-34

32) As the writer turns from loving hortation (v. 19-25) to sternest warning (v. 26-31), so he now turns to remembrance of the noblest deeds of the readers which occurred in their recent past. Shall all that they have suffered be in vain? **Now call to remembrance the former days in which, after having been enlightened, you endured a great contest of sufferings, partly being made a theatrical show by means of reproaches and afflictions, partly by having gotten to be in the fellowship of those faring thus. For you both sympathized with the prisoners and accepted with joy the snatching of your properties, knowing that you yourselves have property better and abiding.**

This glimpse of "the former days" of the persons to whom this epistle is addressed is of the greatest value for identifying and locating them as we have pointed out in the introduction. They are a unit group of Jewish Christians who are unmixed with Gentile Christians. They underwent a period of persecution not long after their enlightenment. Yet none of their number lost his life by martyrdom, and none fled for his life. They suffered only public disgrace and afflictions and snatching of property. None of them were thrown into prison. But there were others, not of their number, not members of this purely Jewish group of Christians, who were imprisoned; the readers sympathized with these and thus brought upon themselves the measure of persecution that is described here. These are the data that are provided. Where do these data place the readers?

Only two places deserve consideration: Palestine and the city of Rome. In only these two places were there compact, purely Jewish bodies who were involved in persecution. Palestine does not fit. The Palestinian persecutions lie too far in the past; they occurred before the year 35, thus at least thirty years before the writing of this epistle. During that persecution the Jewish Christians involved were haled to prison, some were executed, and the great body of them fled the country. The picture drawn in our text is *not* one that fits Palestine.

Every item fits Rome. Between the years 61-63, during Paul's first imprisonment in Rome, this apostle converted a host of Jews in Rome. By his first day's work he converted some fifty per cent of all the leading rabbis and chief men of the seven Roman synagogues (Acts 28:24), the most successful single day's work Paul ever had. We scarcely need to say what this meant for those seven synagogues. Paul continued this work for two years. To get this story see the writer's *Interpretation of Acts*, 28:17-31.

Some think that all these converted Jews joined the original Christian congregation in Rome. They did not. This congregation, which was then some twenty years old, had never had contact with the Jews in Rome. No hostility had ever been aroused. That is why all those

Jewish rabbis and chief men came to Paul so freely on his invitation (Acts 28:17, 22, 23), is why Paul's success with regard to them proved so great on even the first day. This great body of Jewish converts remained intact in some of their own seven synagogues which now became their places of Christian worship.

In 64 Rome was burned, Peter was executed. In October, 64, the Christians were blamed for the fire and were imprisoned and brought to horrible death. These were the Christians of the old, original congregations, who were long known to all Romans as Christians, many of whom belonged to Nero's household (see the author on Rom. 16:10, 11, also on v. 3-16, which reveal the entire membership of the old congregation). Paul's great body of newly converted Jews, who had kept to synagogues of their own, escaped the horrible onslaught. Many of these recent Jewish converts became involved only because of their sympathy with the members of the old congregation who were imprisoned and then made martyrs. Of these days and of this measure of persecution that had been joyfully undergone by the readers our writer speaks. This epistle was written some time between the year 65 and 70, thus two, three, or four years after the events recorded in the verses before us. Every word fits the place, the time, and the events in Rome as described.

We take it that also Paul had most likely been executed in Rome before this epistle was written. This would make the date of the epistle the year 66 or somewhat later and would add to the situation of the readers the grave fact that at the time of the writing of this epistle they were adherents of a *religio illicita*, which was a serious crime. On this point, the martyrdom of Peter and of Paul, compare the remarks in connection with 13:7.

"The former days" are as recent as two to four years ago and are luridly vivid in the memory of all the readers. "After having been enlightened" means by Paul's work, who began this enlightenment (Acts 28:23) and continued it for two years, and the converted rabbis and leaders themselves won more and more converts. Yes, then the readers "were enlightened" (II Cor. 4:6); it is the proper word, and there is no reason to take it in the late sense of having been baptized (see 6:4). Only a short time after their conversion the readers "endured a great contest of sufferings," ἄθλησις, athlete's struggle. Still young in their faith, their spiritual muscles not hardened by long training, the readers successfully endured (aorist) this severe test of suffering. This is the summary statement; the specifications follow.

33) Τοῦτο μέν . . . τοῦτο δέ, "partly . . . partly" is elegant Greek. "Partly being made a theatrical show or spectacle by means of reproaches and afflictions" is a significant wording, indeed. The Christians of the old congregation were made a theatrical show by being sent into the arena to be torn to pieces by lions, wild dogs, etc., while Nero and all Rome enjoyed the spectacle, and by being tied to stakes, being smeared with inflammable material, made living torches in Nero's gardens so that he and his court might ride through and view the spectacle. All these perished horribly. The readers shared this show business to the extent of "reproaches and afflictions," the populace of Rome hooted and reviled them and inflicted all manner of indignity upon them.

The second "partly" completes this picture by adding how the readers became involved, namely "by having gotten to be (aorist ingressive participle while the first verb is a descriptive present) in the fellowship (adjective in the Greek) of those faring thus," the Christians of the old congregation, who were reviled and abused when they were hunted, caught, imprisoned, and then sent to death.

34) This still leaves the picture incomplete. How was this fellowship manifested? "For" explains and at the same time adds the limit of what the readers suffered during those days. "You sympathized with the prisoners"; that was a crime in the eyes of the populace. The readers might have played safe. Having kept their own organization in their synagogues separate from the old congregation, they might have kept entirely aloof when the storm broke, might have suppressed all feeling as if they had no connection whatever with the poor prisoners who were led away to the dungeons and to death. They, however, showed their sympathy with the consequence that in addition to suffering "reproaches" they had their homes invaded and plundered by rowdies. Καί . . . καί connect these two statements but do so in a way that is different from "partly . . . partly" in v. 3. "You both sympathized, etc., and accepted with joy the snatching of your properties," suffered your homes to be looted by the rabble. This is what Christian sympathy cost the readers.

They took it "with joy," gladly, "knowing that you yourselves have property better and abiding," ὕπαρξις, the singular to designate the spiritual and heavenly property in order to match ὑπάρχοντα, the neuter plural which designates the earthly items of property that were snatched away by the hoodlums. It was God's mercy that the readers did not have to suffer more. The writer does not say that any of them were imprisoned, still less that any suffered bloody martyrdom. If this had been the case, the writer would certainly have added these facts. Γινώσκειν is regularly construed with ὅτι and is in the classics followed by the accusative with the infinitive only when it means *ein Urteil faellen*, "to pronounce sentence" (B.-D. 397, 1), which is suitable here and accords with the writer's Greek: "you as judges pronouncing the sentence that you for yourselves have property better and abiding," better because it is abiding, which no one is able to snatch from you. The participle is iterative: making this judicial pronouncement every time any of your homes were looted.

The correct reading is τοῖς δεσμίοις, "the prisoners," and not τοῖς δεσμοῖς, "the prisons" (a meaningless variant), nor τοῖς δεσμοῖς μου, "my imprisonment," which the A. V. translates "me in my bonds." Although the latter is wholly untenable, it has caused some to think of Paul and to make him the writer of this epistle. Some copyist left out the iota in the word δεσμίοις and thus made it δεσμοῖς, and then in order to make sense some other copyist, who regarded Paul as the writer, added "my." Incidentally it is well to note that both the neuter plural δεσμά and the masculine δεσμοί are regularly used in the sense of "imprisonment" and not of "bonds" in the sense of fetters or chains.

The writer accords his readers the highest praise. Will they now, after all, prove false? The tribulations which now trouble them are not as bad as were those of a few years ago. Will they break under a strain that is less?

The Appeal not to Shrink Back, v. 35-39.

35) The readers did not shrink back during that severe trial of "former days"; they will surely not do so now. Οὖν rests this appeal on their former steadfastness. **Do not, then, throw away your assurance,** (it being) **such as has a pay-gift due** (you)! Παρρησία is used in the same sense as it was in v. 19, "assurance"; it is almost objective, the assurance given to us, which we must not despise and throw away. The litotes means: "By all means hold fast your assurance no matter what comes!" The relative is at once qualitative and causal and thus adds the great reason for not casting away our assurance: "it is of a kind that has a great μισθαποδοσία," pay-gift due you ($μισθός =$ pay$+δίδωμι =$ to give$+ἀπό$ in the sense of "due" or "in

full") ; our versions' "recompense of reward" is less clear. To throw away our assurance is to throw away the great, heavenly gift of pay in full which God intends presently duly to give us; the same word is used in 2:2 and 12:26.

36) For of perseverance you have need so that, by having done the will of God, you may carry off the promise.

Ὑπομονή is bravely remaining under a load and holding out. That is exactly what the readers need; having this virtue, they will not let continued affliction induce them to throw away their assurance and to think of turning from Christ because of persecution in order to seek ease and safety in the old Judaism. They need this perseverance "so that (ἵνα, contemplated result), by having done (effective aorist) the will of God (his good and gracious, saving will, John 6:40), you may carry off the promise," objective, what God has promised, namely everlasting life. This promise is the great pay-gift referred to in v. 35; κομίζεσθαι, middle voice, means to bring or carry away something as one's own and thus to have and enjoy it.

37) The writer continues with language that is taken from Scripture and uses it to express his own thought. He has no formula of quotation; he merely adapts Hab. 2:3, 4, transposes the clauses he wants, and uses them in a free way. The "for" does not offer proof, it merely advances the thought and lets the advanced thought elucidate the preceding thought. We ought to hold fast our confidence, it would be folly to throw it away; all we need is perseverance so that, having done God's will, his great promise will fall into our lap (v. 35, 36) ; for Christ is on the way without delay, but only faith will obtain life; God's soul rejects him who shrinks back in cowardice. The writer could have expressed this in his own words just as he does the thought of v. 35, 36; saturated as he is with

Scripture, he adopts Scripture, which his readers who are also versed in Scripture will note. We often do the same today. We thus pass by the discussion about the Hebrew and the LXX original and the minute comparisons which are made since the writer is only adopting and adapting the thought and the wording as he as well as you and I have a perfect right to do.

For yet a little, how very, very (little)! **The One coming will** (indeed) **come and will not delay. But the righteous one shall live as a result of faith; and if he shall shrink back, my soul takes no pleasure in him.** The advance of the thought is clear. Only a little while — then Christ comes to bestow the promised gift — but only on faith and not on him who shrinks back.

Ἔτι is found in Habakkuk, and μικρὸν ὅσον ὅσον is an expression that is found in Isa. 26:20. When R. 733 calls ὅσον ὅσον a LXX imitation of the Hebrew and in 978 a duplication that is found also in the papyri (it occurs also elsewhere), the two statements do not agree; for the papyri and other secular Greek writings have no imitations of the Hebrew. So it is doubtful whether the writer thought of Isa. 26:20 when he used this little preamble. We supply the copula: "There is as yet a little (μικρόν, sc. χρόνον) time, how very, how very (little)!" This, too, is an independent statement. What a little time is this in which we are called upon to persevere, to hold out under affliction! Why grow cowardly about it?

"The coming One will (indeed) come and will not delay," Christ will appear soon in order to bestow the promised glory. This repeats Hab. 2:3 with a personal subject and thus only adopts some of the prophet's language to express the writer's great New Testament thought, namely our certainty of Christ's second coming. He will most certainly come; his very name is still "the coming One." He has received that name because of his first coming but also because of his second coming. The thought is put positively and secondly negatively: "he will not spend time," χρονιεῖ (Attic future), i.e., will not linger or delay; the double statement is emphatic.

38) Since the time is short and Christ is coming without delay, the thing for us to do is to have faith and not to cast it away and to shrink back. This is the simple sense which should not be confused by the exegetical discussion about the LXX's rendering of Hab. 2:4 which is used also by Paul in Rom. 1:17 and Gal. 3:11. On the details see Rom. 1:17; these need not be repeated here. It is enough to say that the LXX misunderstood Hab. 2:4 on only one point: they inserted μου because they thought that the prophet meant "my" (God's) πίστις, "faith" or "faithfulness," *Treue*. The Hebrew has "his (the righteous one's) faith," *fiducia*. Like Paul, our writer leaves out "my" and the Hebrew "his"; like Paul, he deems the latter unnecessary. Some texts have "my" in our passage, and some commentators support it on the basis of the claim that its cancellation aimed at conformity with the reading found in Rom. 1:17 and Gal. 3:11. But "my" plainly bears the mark of being an insertion; those texts that have "my" are uncertain as to where it should be placed and apparently attempt to harmonize the reading with the LXX's rendering of Hab. 2:4.

In Rom. 1:17 and Gal. 3:11 this word of the prophet is quoted in the interest of justifying faith; our writer uses it as stating the necessity of faith for spiritual life. All three, Romans, Galatians, Hebrews, construe alike: "The righteous—*from faith* shall he live," i.e., his spiritual life has gone if faith is gone. Woe to us if Christ finds us so at his coming! The future tense is not to be referred to a future life that is yet to be received but to the spiritual life that is now rooted in faith, that springs from faith and will continue throughout the future. Here, as always, ὁ δίκαιος has the forensic sense: "the righteous one" who has this quality by virtue of God's forensic verdict, "the one declared righteous by God."

"And if he shall shrink back, my soul takes no pleasure in him" is the negative side. The verb means to turn oneself back secretly or in cowardly fashion, i.e., to give up one's faith, the very thing some of the readers are inclined to do. It is a mild expression to say "my soul has no pleasure in him," yet it is the more ominous for that very reason. The renegade shall not carry off the promise and pay-gift.

39) As he did in 6:9 but only stronger the writer inspires his readers to join him in the declaration when he says: **But to us on our part does not belong turning back to perdition; on the contrary, faith for soul preservation!**

The two genitives found with ἐσμέν are predicative (R. 497), in our idiom they mean "to us does not belong," i.e., "we are not of such a character but of the opposite character." The negative and the positive again emphasize. "Turning back" repeats the idea of the verb in the form of a noun, and "faith" is the opposite. But two phrases now bring out fully what is involved: any cowardly turning back leads "to perdition," ἀπώλεια, utter and eternal perishing (the word is regularly used in this awful sense); faith, on the other hand, is "for preservation of soul," περιποίησις is used in this sense also in the papyri. The two alternatives are presented plainly to the readers, and the writer has full confidence that they will recoil from the one and embrace the other. This use of ψυχή recalls Matt. 10:39; 16:25, 26.

CHAPTER XI

The Galaxy of the Men and the Women of Faith in Inspiring Array, chapter 11

1) This is one of the grand chapters of the Bible, a gallery of notable portraits of ancient great believers, each drawn with a master hand. They all believed the unseen, they all trusted a promise, things for which they had to wait and hope. One grand characteristic makes them all kin—faith. Things adverse, matters contradictory, painful, long, they refused to permit to quench their faith. Their names are here inscribed on an immortal scroll. So great is their number that all cannot be named, the full list is recorded in heaven.

This is a list the readers should contemplate. They are growing faint and cowardly, are thinking of shrinking back, of returning to Judaism. Let them consider that all these heroes of faith are named in the Old Testament. If they desert they do not desert *to* but *from* these men and these women and thereby place their names on that horrible list marked "Perdition" (10:39). Their names are still on the golden list; they surely aim to keep them there.

The opening statement defines what "faith" really is, this great term that was used by the writer in 10:38, 39 as well as by Habakkuk. Why quibble about the question as to whether this verse is a definition of faith or not? Why deny it even the character of a description (C.-K. 420)? We certainly agree with Delitzsch: "It seems to us that a more complete and accurate definition of faith and one that is more generally applicable could not be devised than that which is given here." "At the commencement of such a historical summary a comprehensive and general definition

Hebrews 11:1 373

of what faith is in itself . . . was the only definition suitable and possible." If this is not a definition of faith, pray, what is it? Delitzsch calls it generic and not specific; it is more exact to say that we have the *essence* of true religious faith, the heart of what the Scriptures call saving faith. Because one can define faith in other ways (for instance as knowledge, assent, and confidence) is not a reason for saying that this is not a definition.

Δέ is transitional. **Now faith is firm confidence in things hoped for, conviction regarding things not seen.** Although it is placed first, ἔστι is still only the copula. There is not the least reason for translating: "There is (exists) such a thing as faith, namely a firm confidence," etc. By placing πίστις after the copula it is brought next to its predicate, which is just what the writer wants.

Our versions and their margins suffice to show how translators and commentators and even dictionaries have wrestled with the meaning of ὑπόστασις in this passage, which is due in part to the various ways in which this word is used in Greek literature. M.-M. and R., W. P., propose "title-deed," but the word used in the papyrus which they cite means only something like "inventory." The word has the same meaning here that it has in 3:14 and clearly not the same as in 1:3. It signifies "firm, solid confidence" with the objective genitive "confidence in things hoped for." All the terms used in this verse are anarthrous and thus qualitative.

The A. V.'s "the substance of things hoped for" goes back to Aquinas and to others who rendered it *substantia* and to the idea of Chrysostom: faith, for instance, takes the resurrection, which is not yet a reality, and "substantiates" it in our soul. The A. V.'s margin "ground" is due to the older idea that ὑπόστασις means *fundamentum* (Calvin, Stier, and others): each in his way connects the things hoped for with faith as a foundation. The R. V.'s "giving substance to" tries to improve the A. V.'s "substance." It is not necessary for our purpose to take account of the various commentators and to discuss their various views.

The reason the writer makes "things hoped for" the object of the confidence in which faith consists is found in 10:35-39 where he deals with the future reward, the promise, the second coming of Christ, all of which are "things hoped for" and as such require persevering confidence and firm, solid trust that they will come to pass in due time. This is not confusing "faith" and "hope" or defining "faith" as "hope." The two are, indeed, closely related, hope being the resultant of faith. The definition is perfectly correct: "Faith is sure and firm confidence (ὑπόστασις) in things hoped for," the confidence that underlies these things as being certainly expected and awaited by us.

Because of 10:35-39 speaking of these things makes necessary an apposition that goes farther and includes not only future things for which we hope but also present, yea, past things. Note that this is an apposition, a wider circle that is drawn completely around the narrower one, and not an addition with καί. "Conviction regarding things not seen" is faith in its essence. The genitive is again objective: we have the conviction in regard to the unseen things that they exist in spite of our not seeing them. Riggenbach calls it *eine unwiderlegliche Ueberzeugung von unsichtbaren Dingen*, "an irrefutable conviction," etc. Ὑπόστασις and ἔλεγχος are synonymous, and each has its objective genitive, these genitives being neuter plural participles.

Both "confidence" and "conviction" are subjective, necessarily subjective because they define "faith," which is subjective. But all three imply something objective; they invariably do this. Confidence is inspired in us; conviction is wrought in us; faith (trust) is produced in us. Religious, Biblical, Chris-

Hebrews 11:1

tian faith is not different from faith in secular life in this respect; nor is true faith different from false faith in this respect. Satan produced faith in Eve by his lies which he dressed up as truth. Always, always someone or something impresses us as being genuine, true, right, reliable, in a word, as being trustworthy and so produces confidence, conviction; these are the essence of faith. Any so-called synergism is never a fact but only a fiction in regard to how faith—any kind of faith—is wrought in us. All synergistic notions regarding the origin of faith are specimens of shallow, false thinking, which is dangerous on that account.

Because ἔλεγχος is used also in the sense of "proof" some prefer this meaning in the present connection. Thus the A. V. translates *"evidence* of things unseen," which the R. V. seeks to improve by translating the word as a term expressing an action: "the *proving* of things not seen." The A. V. perpetuates the idea of the Vulgate which has rendered the word *argumentum,* Calvin translates it *evidentia,* others *demonstratio.* But we cannot conceive of faith as proof, evidence, an action of proving something unseen or as an argument for unseen things. Delitzsch supports this idea by saying: "Faith is its own certification, its own proof or evidence of divine realities." My faith is nothing of this kind. Faith is never its own basis. "Faith," "confidence," "conviction" are correlative terms; faith rests on somebody or on something outside of itself and *not* on itself. Somebody, something outside of me inspires faith or trust in me, otherwise I have no faith. It is this outside ground that shows whether faith is true, i.e., justified, or false, i.e., unjustified. Truth alone justifies me for believing or trusting; no lie ever does that; a lie succeeds in producing faith only when it masks itself as truth.

Only the essence of faith is defined in this passage and not the way in which it originates although any adequate definition of its essence naturally leads us to think also of the way in which faith is produced in us. As to the latter, true faith is produced by God, Christ, the Spirit, who come to us in and by the Word of Truth. Not to trust them and the Word is the crime of unbelief, the height of abnormality, of unreason. "Evidence," "proof," etc., is the objective contents of the Word, the ground, basis, productive power of faith. We note that ἔλεγχος never means "test," R. V. margin. B.-P. 387 has "proof for things that one does not see."

Schlatter, *Der Glaube im Neuen Testament*, 3, defends the active sense of ἔλεγχος, *Ueberfuehrung*, by making the genitive subjective: "The unseen things convince a man of their existence and of their saving power and make him certain concerning them." Schlatter's view is correct enough that faith is *ein Erlebnis*, an experience, "that one does not produce but experience faith as a gift of God and not as a human act." True as the latter is, and glad as we are to note the fact, the genitive cannot be subjective, nor need it be in order to regard faith as an *Erlebnis*. The two genitives are not diverse: "of things hoped for," objective, "of things not seen," subjective. If agency *were* intended by the second genitive it would be expressed in the form of a phrase in order to put this beyond question, and that the more because an objective genitive precedes. But a subjective genitive of agency is untenable because "the things not seen," by not being seen, do not convince us of their existence, are not the agent producing the experience of faith; this agent is the Word, the means of grace. This reveals the things not seen, all their reality, greatness, blessedness. As already stated, the writer presents only what faith is and not how, by what agent, or by what means it comes into existence.

Faith is confidence in regard to all the glorious "things hoped for," which, as far as we and our experience of them are concerned, lie in the future. These are, however, only a part of a far wider mass of things, the mark of all of which is the fact that they are "not seen" by us. Faith is a sure and certain conviction regarding all of them. All the past events recorded in the Old Testament, beginning with the creation of the world, are in this list; the life, death, resurrection, ascension, heavenly *sessio* of Christ, as these were at the writer's time recorded by Matthew, Mark, and Luke and preached everywhere by the Twelve and by Paul; all the future events such as our resurrection, the final judgment, the new heaven and the new earth. "Not seen, not seen," all of them; οὐ with the participle make the negation the more clearcut and decisive (R. 1138); yet we are as certain of these unseen things as if we saw them, even more so, for here on earth our eyes often deceive us.

Do you ask whether this faith, confidence, conviction may not be mistaken as is the faith of so many in earthly affairs, as is the faith of so many also in religious things? Strenuous though their faith is, they after all find themselves—mistaken. The answer is easy although the writer does not deal with it. If our faith were its own basis it would, indeed, hang in the air. Our faith rests on the Word of God. Matt. 5:18; Luke 16:17; I Pet. 1:25. Only if this Word is false is our faith in all the unseen things of this Word mistaken. They whose faith rests on something else, they are indeed lost. Let us add that the best translation to date is Luther's *eine gewisse Zuversicht dess, das man hoffet und nicht zweifelt an dem, das man nicht siehet.*

2) That this definition of faith as confidence in things hoped for, as conviction in regard to things unseen, is, indeed, the true definition is established by ("for") a fact that is known to all the readers: **For in connection with this** (faith) **the ancients were approved** (of God), i. e., received God's approving

testimony which is recorded throughout the Old Testament. The writer will now unroll the list of these ancients, will show that "this" was the faith they had, confidence and conviction in regard to the unseen, the hoped-for, and will note the divine approval they received. Do the readers want to be found in this glorious company with God's approval resting on them? Let them then heed 10:39!

Πρεσβύτεροι is not used as a title but in the ordinary sense and should not be translated "elders"; it is our "ancients," people who lived in olden times no matter how many years old each of them may have been. Ἐν is not *auf Grund* but "in connection with this (faith)," the context indicates the connection referred to, which is obvious here: when God saw this faith he openly gave it his testimonial of approval. Blessed the ancients who received this testimonial; blessed the readers and we today when we receive it!

3) Πίστει — Πίστει — Πίστει marches through the rest of this great chapter: "By means of faith—By means of faith—By means of faith." These datives are like flying banners that are borne in a great parade. On one golden cord all these names are strung together with the deeds that proved the faith in which they lived and died, the faith that God approved, his testimony being immortalized in Scripture. Always, always it was "this" faith as defined by the writer.

At the head of the galaxy of believers, ushering in the series of statements that begin with πίστει, the writer places one that is drawn from the first page of the Bible: **By means of faith we understand that the eons have been framed by means of God's uttered word so that what is seen has come to be not** (as derived) **out of things that appear.**

The criticism that, after mentioning "the ancients" in v. 2, the writer should continue with Abel in v. 4 and not insert this statement about what "by means of faith we understand," is not well taken. The reply that the writer naturally thinks of the first page of the Bible when he starts as far back as possible, is well enough; for he surely does this. But the reply should be made stronger. All that these heroes of faith are, and all that God's Word reports concerning them, is intended for us so that we may see the essential thing in their faith (v. 1). It is thus that the writer starts with "we" and, when he introduces this long history of faith in all these other persons, notes, first of all, that the first page of the Bible is simply believed by us. "By means of faith," the essence of which is confidence and assurance in regard to unseen things, by this means alone we understand how the world came to be.

We read that first page and believe it; we have nothing else to go by. The writer is, of course, addressing readers who join him in this faith regarding the creation of the world; he is not speaking to the pagans of his day, nor to the skeptics of our day. He says to his readers: "In this our faith about the creation of the world we ourselves illustrate what faith really is." It is a telling thing for the writer to begin this way. To have at once continued with v. 4 would have been a loss.

Moreover, he is taking his readers into the pages of the Bible in order to review what the Bible says about all these historical characters. He and they believe what the Bible says about these men and these women and the testimony God gives them in the Bible (v. 2) although neither he nor his readers have seen one of these illustrious persons. It would be of no use to name a single one of them if the readers do not believe what God testifies regarding them. That is why faith in what God says about creation on the very first page of the Bible is so pertinent here. It constitutes a grand sample of confidence in things unseen, a sample in the very readers themselves who believe also all else that is now to be presented to them from the same Bible about all these other believers, none of whom they have ever seen.

"By means of faith (and in no other way) we understand that the eons have been framed by means of God's uttered word." We were not there to see even the least thing, i.e., to hear God speak and then to see what happened. We take it all on trust. All else is excluded. He who refuses to have faith is left at sea; he cannot "understand," have in his νοῦς or mind, a single true thing about the whole matter. How can he know, when he is left to his own guessing in a matter so stupendous, that all guessing (hypotheses, theories, speculations) is utterly vain? He can fill his mind with rubbish, which is worse than nothing, and the mind is surely not intended for that. The mind simply has to have faith. Oh, no, not faith in what other men may please to say, who themselves were not there to see; but faith in him who *was* there, faith in what *he* is pleased to tell us about it, namely that *he* framed the whole world and set it on its course "by means of his ῥῆμα, his uttered word." He called all things into being.

In 1:2 we have "he made the eons"; καταρτίζω is a choicer term. Also ῥῆμα is most exact, "the word uttered," *vayomer*, "and God said." The idea is not that we now understand *all* about it, that *all* the questions of our finite minds are answered. Creation is beyond human comprehension. But we do understand the main thing, namely that God called the world into being. On τοὺς αἰῶνας see 1:2; it includes the cosmos in its extent of time and all that fills and forms one eon after another; heaven and earth and all that has its being in them. God created the light ever to shine, the firmament, land, and sea ever to stand, the heavenly bodies to move in their orbits, etc., etc. — eons, ages and ages thus filled, which is a grander concept than τὰ πάντα or πάντα (John 1:2), which views all the objects only as objects.

The view that εἰς τό with the infinitive always denotes purpose is untenable; it often denotes contemplated and also actual result. Here there is "a clear example of result" (R. 1003): "so that what is seen has come to be not (as derived) out of things that appear," so that this is the result, one that we by faith understand as being the result. The singular τὸ βλεπόμενον is collective and sums up as a unit all that we constantly see. It has come to be, come into existence, "not from things that appear," plural, taking in every last one of them that has in any way the quality of appearing.

Note the difference: "what is seen" *by us* with our eyes; "things that appear," show themselves *to us,* to our eyes and our senses. We do the seeing, such things do the appearing. What men see has not come into existence from prior things that might in some way make an appearance to our senses; what men see has come to be "by means of God's spoken word," it has received its existence in this way alone. Those are right who say that this means creation *ex nihilo.* Ps. 33:6, 9. But the writer's point is that we understand this fact as a fact only "by means of faith."

To regard the εἰς τό clause as expressing a purpose is untenable because of the tense of γεγονέναι. To translate: "in order that . . . has come to be," makes no sense; hence those who regard this as a purpose clause generally tell us what *they* think the purpose is, namely that God created the world by means of his uttered word "in order that" none of us should think that anything has come into existence from what already existed. This is substitution, not translation, not paraphrase.

There is some dispute about μή. It modifies the phrase; we translate "not out of things that appear." It negatives the phrase (R. 423). B.-D. 433,3 applies the rule that participles and adjectives that occur after a preposition have the negative particle *before* the preposition so that here μὴ ἐκ = ἐκ μή: "have come to be out of things that do not appear." This rule is to be applied only when the participle or the adjective is to be negatived. This rule cannot be applied here despite the fact that the Greek commentators did apply it. Those commentators understood "things not appearing" as equal to "nothing." They had the correct thought. Yet "things not appearing" might be equal to "invisible things," "things that do not show." The writer does not intend to say that the visible things have been derived from invisible things. Whence were these invisible, nonapparent things derived? The writer does not leave us with such a question. Nor with the question as to what these "nonappearing things" may signify. Those who negative the participle feel obliged to say what "nonappearing things" means. Some refer to *tohu vabohu*, chaos, as if this had no appearance; some to "images or architypes in the mind of God" (Delitzsch) akin to Plato's and Philo's "ideas," this is philosophic speculation; some, like Riggenbach, to ῥῆμα Θεοῦ, "God's utterance," as if this could be called "things (plural) nonappearing." If we leave the negative where the writer has written it, all is in order. Still other constructions are advocated such as construing μή with the infinitive or with the whole clause in a general way.

Abel, Enoch, Noah

4) By means of faith Abel offered to God a superior sacrifice than Cain, by means of which testimony was given to him that he was righteous, God giving him testimony on the basis of his gifts; and by means of it, though having died, he still continues to speak.

The writer starts with Abel and not with Adam because Genesis offers an example of God's approving testimony in the case of Abel and not in the case of Adam or of Eve. What made Abel's sacrifice to God πλείων, "more" in the sense of "superior," than the sacrifice of Cain? Abel's faith. That is stressed and not the fact that Abel offered a bloody and Cain a vegetable sacrifice, or that Abel offered firstlings and Cain not first fruits, on which some have laid stress by emphasizing these differences. The writer centers everything on Abel's faith in contrast with Cain's lack of faith.

Since the emphasis is placed on πίστει, "by means of which" has "faith" and not "sacrifice" as its antecedent. Abel's faith gained for him the approving testimony of God that is recorded in Gen. 4:4: "And the Lord had respect unto Abel and to his offering" while he had no respect unto Cain and his offering (v. 5). Abel is thus the first of "the ancients" who were given God's approving testimony in Scripture (v. 2). The matter is emphasized by the repetition of ἐμαρτυρήθη in the participle μαρτυροῦντος: "Abel was given testimony . . . God testifying." The writer sums up the testimony stated in Gen. 4:4 with εἶναι δίκαιος: "him to be righteous." This is indirect discourse, in our idiom it would be "that he was righteous" (direct discourse: "Thou art righteous").

The meaning of δίκαιος should not be reduced. To be sure, this is not the first verdict God pronounced on Abel's faith, but it is the one recorded in Gen. 4:4 in connection with his sacrifice shortly before his brother murdered him; but that fact does not change the forensic meaning of "righteous" nor the connection of faith with the verdict of God regarding Abel. Only by reason of God's verdict did Abel have the quality and the standing of being "righteous" in God's sight. The reason the writer sums up Gen. 4:4 in the statement "that he was righteous" appears in 10:38:

"The righteous, as the result of faith shall he live." The two decisive words "faith" and "righteous" are thus repeated. The LXX render Gen. 4:4: Καὶ ἐπεῖδεν ὁ Θεὸς ἐπὶ Ἀβελ καὶ ἐπὶ τοῖς δώροις αὐτοῦ (the Hebrew has "his offering"). The writer retains the LXX's phrase ἐπὶ τοῖς δώροις αὐτοῦ just as he generally adheres to the LXX. Abel's sacrificial "gifts" were the marked evidence of his faith that called out a renewed verdict from God which declared him righteous, not in words that God spoke to Abel, but by an act of God's regarding Abel. That act is here called "testifying."

God never looks only at our "gifts," he looks at what is back of them in the heart, whether there is faith, the confidence in things hoped for from him and his promises of grace, the conviction in regard to things unseen (v. 1). But when God pronounces his verdicts in public, testifies in public to men about any person who has faith, he stresses that person's works, in this case Abel's gifts. Jesus will do the same in the final, public judgment (Matt. 25:34, etc.).

"By means of it (i.e., faith), though having died (aorist to express the simple fact), he still continues to speak." The current idea is that the writer refers to Gen. 4:10, Abel's blood crying to God from the ground (compare 12:24), that from the fact that it cried thus after death we see the high value faith lent to Abel, God being still concerned about him after his death. Ps. 116:15 is adduced to prove this view: "Precious in the sight of the Lord is the death of his saints"; also Ps. 9:12.

We confess that we are unable to find this in our passage. The writer says that, although he had been dead for millenniums, Abel (not his blood) speaks (not cries) to us (not to God), speaks in the Scripture record by means of his faith as to how in the Scriptures God gave him approving testimony on the basis of his sacrificial gifts as evidence of his faith. So far, even

Hebrews 11:5

down to us, the voice of Abel's faith reaches despite his death. Chrysostom and others have Abel's voice urge us to like faith, a thought that is in line with the text.

5) By means of faith Enoch was translated so as not to see death and was not being found because God translated him, for he has received the testimony to have been before his translation well-pleasing to God. Now without faith it is impossible to be well-pleasing, for it is necessary that he who comes to God believe that he exists and becomes a giver of due pay to those seeking after him.

But for his faith Enoch would not have been taken to heaven without dying. The verb means "to transfer"; by using it twice and by adding the noun the author emphasizes Enoch's miraculous removal to heaven. As far as one is able to judge, this was instantaneous; Elijah was taken up visibly. Glorified in body and in soul like Elijah, Enoch is now in Paradise.

These two men did not undergo death; the infinitive with τοῦ denotes result, and "to see death" = to undergo or experience it ("to see" is similarly used in John 3:3). The transformation of Enoch resembles that promised in I Cor. 15:52 and in I Thess. 4:17. Delitzsch thinks that Enoch's translation occurred in the year 987 after Adam's creation. Adam had died, but Seth, Enos, Kenan, Mahalaleel, and Jared were still living, and Methuselah and Lamech were also living, but Noah had not yet been born. Being only sixty-five years old at the time of his translation, Enoch was young according to the ages which men reached at that time of the world's history when God so signally distinguished his faith. "He was not being found (imperfect) because God translated him" repeats the LXX's rendering of Gen. 5:24.

We construe the πρό phrase with the infinitive: "to have been before his translation well-pleasing to God," and the phrase is placed forward for the sake of emphasis. The Hebrew, "he walked with God," the LXX rendered "he was well-pleasing to God," which our writer retains. Some construe the πρό phrase with the main verb and then regard the phrase as local rather than as temporal and say that it indicates the order of the statements of Scripture: the saying that Enoch was well-pleasing to God (Hebrew, walked with God) is placed before the statement that he was translated to heaven. But look at Gen. 5:22-24 and see that in v. 24 everything is compressed into *one* very brief verse. It is a rather unimportant remark to point out that in Gen. 5:24 Enoch's being well-pleasing to God is recorded "before" his translation is recorded.

Furthermore, this idea does not agree with the perfect tense "he has received the testimony" (the significant verb being repeated from v. 2 and v. 4), the tense signifying that this testimony stands to this day and continues indefinitely. The πρό phrase is added so that we are not to think that God's testimony consisted in his miraculously translating Enoch and thereby testifying what he thought of Enoch. If this were intended, we should have the aorist. What the writer says is that the permanent testimony Enoch has received from God consists of what the Scriptures permanently record about his having lived for a long time in a way that was well-pleasing to God prior to his translation. The author therefore also uses the perfect infinitive which expresses past duration. The graph for μεμαρτύρηται is ⎯⎯⎯⎯⎯⎯→ ; that for εὐαρεστηκέναι ▶⎯⎯⎯⎯⎯●

6) Since Gen. 5:22-24 does not employ the word "faith" but only the expression "to be well-pleasing" (LXX), the writer expounds: "Now without faith (it is) impossible to be well-pleasing" (actually well-pleasing, effective aorist). In other words, what makes any man well-pleasing to God is faith; without it there is no possibility of pleasing God.

Hebrews 11:6, 7 387

Even this is elucidated ("for"). The man who comes to God in order to be well-pleasing to him *must* believe two things: first, that God "is," i.e., exists; secondly, that he becomes a giver of due pay to those seeking after him; the two statements after one ὅτι ever constitute a unit. Verse 1 underlies this statement; God and his heavenly reward of grace to believers are "not seen," yet faith is confident and convinced that God exists, that he is what he says he is, and that the heavenly reward promised by him and hoped for by the believer is a certainty although it is now unseen.

Δεῖ may express any kind of necessity; it is here the necessity that is involved in any actual pleasing of God. Μισθαποδότης, which is found only in one papyrus and in later ecclesiastical Greek, continues the expression that was used in 10:35 (see 11:26; also 2:2, where, however, the pay is punishment). Enoch is, indeed, a glorious example of how God approves faith, the faith that genuinely trusts the unseen, the unseen God, his unseen reward of grace, the faith that the readers must not throw away (10:35).

7) **By means of faith Noah, having received divine communication concerning things not yet seen, filled with godly fear, constructed an ark for saving his family; by means of which (faith) he condemned the world and became heir of the righteousness of faith.**

We need not translate "warned," which does not fit 8:5; "received a divine communication" is more exact. We connect this first participle with the περί phrase because the reader would do this. The divine communication certainly also concerned things that were not yet seen, namely the rain, the flood, the devastation of the world, about which the readers also know (hence the article). The second participle, "filled with godly fear," needs no modifier because it states the subjective effect of the objective reception of a divine communication concerning the things not yet seen; in fact, this relation of the participles, which is so immediately obvious, precludes any idea of separating the phrase from the first participle. We decline to make εὐλαβηθείς mean only "having become cautious or careful"; this reduced meaning is certainly not in place where a divine communication immediately precedes.

The older idea that when οὐ is used with a participle it is objective (v. 1) while μή is subjective must be discarded as well as all deductions that are based on this distinction. The common negation used with participles is μή (here μηδέπω, "not yet") ; οὐ is infrequent and is used only to make the negation more clear-cut. Beyond this there is no difference between v. 1 and v. 7. The negation used in v. 7 indicates in no way that the phrase is to be construed with the second participle. "The things not yet seen" takes up "things not seen" which occurs in v. 1. Noah believed what God told him, his "conviction" (ἔλεγχος) was complete although he as yet saw nothing.

Let us not lose the force of what this means in the case of Noah. The idea that the world should perish in a flood that was mountain high seems preposterous, fantastic, impossible. When God told Noah that he would send such a flood, Noah believed God without question. He had absolutely nothing visible to go by yet trusted God's word with full conviction. His is, indeed, a perfect example of faith as it is defined in v. 1. The great evidence of his faith is the fact that "he constructed an ark for saving his family" as God had told him (οἶκος is used in the sense of "family").

As it did in v. 4, δι' ἧς refers to faith: "by which faith he condemned the world." The view that Noah did not condemn the world of men because of their unbelief is untenable. The statement that the writer never uses κόσμος to designate the world of men is answered by 11:8. The brevity of the expression is misunderstood when this is said to exclude the fact of Noah's preaching to men ("preacher of righteousness," II Pet. 2:5), and that God demanded no such act of faith as Noah's from the rest of men. God delayed the flood for 120 years for the very purpose of giving the world of men time to repent and to believe Noah's preaching. The thought was not that they, too, might build arks, but that God might withhold the flood. This sketch of what Noah did intends to recall to the readers the whole story of Noah and not a mere fragment of this story. Noah's condemnation of the world is not so much Noah's as it is God's through Noah and his faith. So the Ninevites, so the Queen of Sheba shall condemn the Jews of Jesus' generation for their unbelief.

The fact that Noah was saved in the flood is implied; what the writer says is far greater, namely that by means of his faith he condemned the unbelieving world (a negative act) and (a positive act) "became heir of the righteousness of faith." The attributive phrase κατὰ πίστιν is a substitute for the genitive "of faith" (B.-P. 637); which fact should settle the discussion as to just what κατά means, whether "according to faith" or something else. We do not regard καί as introducing an independent sentence although it would still contain the word "faith." Everything is made dependent on πίστει at the head of the sentence, the relative δι' ἧς resumes the dative and governs to the end. As faith was the means for Noah's condemning the world that refused faith, so it was the means for his becoming heir of the faith-righteousness.

But "became heir" is not to be referred to his being designated as an heir whose inheritance was still in the far future but should be referred to his entrance upon the inheritance; we say "fell heir to." The genitive states what Noah fell heir to: "the righteousness of faith," the quality that is produced by God's verdict which pronounces a man righteous in his judgment.

The κατά phrase adds the thought that this quality belongs, always goes "along with" faith; hence also Noah obtained it "by means of faith" (δι' ἧς). Thus faith—faith—is again emphasized, the faith that is defined in verse 1.

It has been noted that these expressions are Pauline; they are indeed. The readers were even converts of Paul's; if, as we take it, the writer was Apollos, he was an associate of Paul (I Cor. 16:12; Titus 3:13). The sense, too, is Pauline. There is only one righteousness of faith all efforts to find another to the contrary notwithstanding. Noah's case is similar to Abraham's: both were righteous the moment they believed, yet after signal tests of their faith they are just as signally declared to be in possession of the great quality of righteousness which ever belongs to faith. The fact that righteousness *ever* goes with faith lies in the attributive phrase: τῆς κατὰ πίστιν δικαιοσύνης.

Abraham and Sarah

8) By means of faith, being called, Abraham became obedient to go out into a place which he was to receive for an inheritance, and he went out, not knowing where he was going. By means of faith he lived as an outsider in the land of the promise as not his own together with Isaac and Jacob, the fellow heirs of the same promise.

The first great evidence of Abraham's faith is his obedience. Being called to do so, he went out to a place which he was eventually to receive as an inheritance, and this he did, not knowing where he was going. The two points that belong to the essence of faith (v. 1) are apparent: Abraham believed God's promise about the land he was to have as his heritage (Gen. 12:1, etc.), which = "things hoped for"; Abraham did not know the land to which he was going, which = "things not seen." He went wholly and completely on trust.

In ἤμελλε λαμβάνειν we have the compound imperfect, which is descriptive of what in Abraham's life is past for us but was at the time future to him: "which he was about to be receiving." Κληρονομία = what falls to one's lot, thus "allotment" from God, or, taking God's promise as a testament, "inheritance." The Greek retains the present tense of the direct discourse when this is restated in the indirect: "where he is going"; the English changes to "where he was going."

9) Much more must be said about Abraham's faith as a pure trust in things hoped for and not seen (v. 1). He maintained this trust throughout his life. All his life long "by means of faith he dwelt as an outsider in the land of the promise (static εἰς R. 593) as (a land) ἀλλοτρίαν," belonging to others and not to him; he never owned it. He remained a πάροικος, a foreigner, who was permitted to remain in the land as an alien by those who as citizens owned and controlled it. Thus he lived only "in tents" and not in a city and its permanent houses. How long this continued we see from the μετά phrase: "together with Isaac and Jacob, the fellow heirs of the same promise." Even these never received the land as their own. They died, having nothing but faith in the promise—a grand exhibition of faith as it is described in v. 1.

10) "For" explains by telling us that this faith looked far beyond all earthly things: **For he kept awaiting the city which has the foundations, of which God is architect and erecter.**

The earthly land of promise is only the earthly type and symbol of the heavenly Canaan. The type is advanced from the idea of a land or country to the antitype of the heavenly city, the New Jerusalem. This brings out the idea of permanency, which is made still stronger by saying that this city of God "has the foundations," the foundations that Abraham's tents never had or could have even as a "city" is more than "tents." Rev. 21:10-27 describes John's vision of this city, v. 19, etc., dwells on its "foundations." The relative clause augments the idea of permanency. Cities that are built by men are strong and last long; but the technician (τεχνίτης) and public worker (δῆμιος+ἔργον), the architect and erecter, of this city is God (ὁ Θεός is marked as the subject by means of the article, the anarthrous nouns are predicates). Built by God, this city stands forever.

Abraham understood the whole promise that was made to him by God. It was by no means the truth that his descendants would possess Palestine as their national home at some future time; this earthly possession foreshadowed the Eternal City which Abraham and his spiritual descendants would possess as their inheritance forever. The imperfect tense states that Abraham's expectation ever went out toward this city; so also, we may add, did Isaac's and Jacob's. This was Abraham's faith in things hoped for and not seen. In this faith he lived and died. In this faith it made little difference to him when the promise regarding the earthly Canaan was fulfilled. What if he himself never lived to see this fulfillment? He expected a far greater, an eternal fulfillment.

11) There is a crux in v. 11. The reading καὶ αὐτὴ Σάρρα makes Sarah the subject, but the predicate does not fit her. Despite this disagreement many retain Sarah as the subject and make the predicate agree. There is something wrong with the text; this is also shown by the variant readings which copyists introduced in order to help out the idea that Sarah is the subject. No Greek text and no ancient version assist us in locating the trouble. Verses 8-12 deal with Abraham; Isaac and Jacob are only associated with him (μετά), and this must also be the case with regard to Sarah. The word αυτη was most likely originally intended as a dative, not as the nominative

αὐτή but as αὐτῇ, and indeclinable Σάρρα was thus also a dative. This is Riggenbach's solution, who regards αὐτῇ as the Greek idiom that expresses close connection (Kuehner — Gerth 425, 4). We thus translate: **By means of faith also with Sarah he received ability for projecting seed even contrary to (his) age-period since he considered him faithful who made the promise; wherefore also from one, and that — (one) that had become dead, there were begotten (as many) even as the stars of the heaven in multitude and as the sand of the shore of the sea unnumbered.**

Καταβολὴ σπέρματος, the standard and technical term for the projection or deposition of the *semen virile* into the womb by the male organ, is even combined with δύναμις: "ability" for such an action. This makes it impossible to say that Sarah received such ability, καὶ αὐτή, "even herself." Only by putting a different meaning into the expression, a meaning that is not found anywhere, can a female be made the subject. C.-K. 190 takes the expression to mean: "Even Sarah herself received ability for *Begruendung der Nachkommenschaft*," Thayer 330, "to found a posterity." But this meaning is incongruous. Since Abraham is so markedly the subject, why should not he but Sarah be made the founder of a posterity?

"Received strength (power) to *conceive* seed," in our versions, is a mistranslation. The A. V. adopts also the supplement, which a few texts add to the original: "and was delivered of a child" (εἰς τὸ τεκνῶσαι: so as to give birth), which does not, however, aid matters. Some note that καταβολὴ σπέρματος undoubtedly refers to the act of the male; so, in order to retain Sarah as the subject, they let εἰς mean "in respect to": she received ability "in respect to" Abraham's injection of semen into her womb, and then add the argument that "even she" had to be miraculously enabled for the sexual act and not only Abraham. This effort breaks down on the meaning of καταβολή, which ought to be the reverse, not Abraham's *injection* of σπέρμα, but her *reception*.

All these interpretations have trouble also with καὶ αὐτή as the renderings show: "Sarah herself also"— why "herself" when no one is compared with her? "Sarah in her place"—yet the word does not mean "in her place." Sarah "the sterile," στεῖρα — a textual addition that would help to make Sarah the subject. Sarah as *vas infirmius*—an interpretative rendering that is unsatisfactory. Sarah "likewise"—which needs no refutation. Sarah, "though at first unbelieving," yet "by faith" received ability to conceive. All these efforts try to solve the crux, which refuses to yield as long as Sarah is retained as the subject.

The great point is Abraham, and Sarah is only an adjunct (dative of association, R. 528-530) as being naturally required for the sexual act. The greatness of Abraham's faith in God's promise about inheriting Canaan, inheriting it as the type of the heavenly city, lies in trusting this promise despite the fact that he had no son by Sarah while the promise of God depended on such a son and heir. He actually believed what seemed to be an utter impossibility: "even contrary to (παρά, completely *gegen*, *wider*, B.-P. 975) his period of life," aged as he was. Yet the miracle happened: he received the necessary ability "since he considered him faithful who did make (English: has made) the promise." His faith secured what he hoped for (v. 1). So all else that God promised him would come to pass in due time.

12) The writer dwells on the result: "Wherefore also from one (masculine, Abraham) there were begotten (our versions: sprang from one) as many even as the stars," etc. This adopts the comparison used in Gen. 22:17 and adds "unnumbered" at the end. The articles bid us note each item separately: "as the sand—that by the shore of the sea—that (which is)

unnumbered" (without number). The doubling stars —sand intensifies the simile immensely. The texts vary between ἐγεννήθησαν and ἐγενήθησαν ("there came to be"); they do this also in other passages since both generally fit the context. Yet one should not say that γεννάω properly fits only a woman; Thayer: "properly of men begetting children." The object is implied in the verb itself and hence needs none in the Greek.

In order to bring out the miracle for which Abraham's faith was the means the writer inserts: καὶ ταῦτα, κτλ., (a classical concessive idiom in the Greek), "and that—(one) that has become dead," i.e., "him as good as dead" (our versions), and the perfect indicates a permanent condition that had set in.

The Patriarchs and the Heavenly City

13) In v. 10 the writer says that Abraham kept awaiting *a city* that has foundations, a city whose builder is God, and in v. 9 that Isaac and Jacob were in Abraham's company, all of them being tent-dwellers. This statement about "a city" is not the language used in Genesis as the readers will most likely note. Thus the writer inserts the little paragraph (v. 13-16) in which he explains about the heavenly "fatherland" and the "city" and sets forth more fully the faith of these "ancients" (v. 2) as trusting in things hoped for and not seen (v. 1).

In keeping with faith they all died, not having carried off the promises but (only) having seen them afar off and having saluted them and having confessed that they were strangers and pilgrims on the earth.

It was entirely in keeping or in accord and harmony with faith, κατὰ πίστιν as this is defined in v. 1 that these patriarchs died without having brought away the promises (i.e., the things promised them) in this life;

the expression is the same as that used in 10:36 and 11:39. To reject this meaning on the score of μή, which is then regarded as being subjective, and to suppose that οὐ would be required for this meaning is to operate with the older idea that μή is subjective whereas in the Koine it is the regular negation with participles. Since faith is confidence in things hoped for, conviction in regard to things not seen, it was altogether in line with faith that these patriarchs died as they did, having seen only afar off with the eyes of faith the great things promised them. "These all" refers only to "Abraham, Isaac, and Jacob" because, for one thing, Enoch did not die, and, for another, the writer has mentioned the "city" only in connection with Abraham who had Isaac and Jacob with him. In 10:36 and 11:39 we have "the promise" and in this verse the plural, but these are used in the same sense; all that lies in the plural is the thought that each of the patriarchs personally heard God's promise, or that the one promise contained various items.

The writer says beautifully: "having seen them only from afar and having saluted them" while in this life. They were like pilgrims to the Holy City who see its towers and spires on the horizon, ecstatically point to the vision and shout their acclaim. This is all they had during their earthly lives. The aorist participles are antecedent to the main verb. "And having confessed that they were strangers and pilgrims on the earth" and never anything more (see Abraham's confession in Gen. 23:4: "a stranger and sojourner"; also 24:37; 28:4), they spoke the true confession of faith. The statement that their confessions referred only to Canaan and not to "the earth," does not take into account the facts that Canaan was the land that had been promised to them, and that when we speak of staying "on earth" we, too, refer only to some one place and not to the whole earth. The indirect discourse retains εἰσίν whereas we change to "were" after a past tense.

14) With "for" the writer points out the fact that this negative confession of being nothing but strangers and pilgrims involves a great positive thought: **For they saying such things keep indicating that they are earnestly seeking a fatherland,** πατρίς, not just "country" (A.V.), nor "a country of their own," but "fatherland," where one's native home is, where one really belongs and is entirely happy. There is much more in this word than is generally noted. Unlike children of this world, these persons cannot settle down in some earthly place as their "fatherland" and feel fully satisfied and content there. They are born of God, they are children of God, this earth is not their home, and, although they are compelled to stay here, they constantly speak only as strangers and pilgrims speak and always show by this, show even unconsciously, that they are seeking for a fatherland in which they really belong.

It should be noted that the present tenses are not historical but present the thought as such irrespective of time. This point is important in regard to v. 15, 16. In v. 16 the present tense continues exactly as it was in v. 14. Between these two verses we have a condition of unreality. Since the thought before and after is cast in present tenses, this conditional statement cannot be a past unreality, it must match what preceded and what follows and be the same present unreality.

15) **And if they were remembering that one from which they went out they would have opportunity to return; now, however, they aspire to a better one, that is, to a heavenly one; wherefore God is not ashamed of them to be called their God, for he prepared for them a city.**

One wonders why this εἰ with the imperfect (protasis) and the imperfect with ἄν (apodosis), a perfectly regular *present* condition of unreality, should be made a *past* unreality (which ought to have εἰ with the aorist and be followed by the aorist with ἄν). The grammarians apparently think that this ought to be a case of past unreality and therefore regard it as past. B.-D. 360, 3 has only the unsupported remark regarding the use of imperfects in unreal conditions: *zeitlich ist das Imperfect zweideutig,* and then mentions John 18:36, ἠγωνίζοντο, which is clearly present unreality; he does not consider our passage.

R. 1015 as well as *W. P.* state that in our passage the imperfect tenses are *past* unreality but intend to stress *duration* in the past. These imperfects certainly convey the idea of duration, but as *present* unreality, as they always do, duration being quite proper in such present conditions. R. 922 lists some examples of conditions of unreality in which the imperfect "might denote a past condition." The list is unsatisfactory and contains only eight examples, including our passage which we do not regard as past unreality. Nor is Matt. 23:30; just because Matthew *might* have used a past condition does not make the present one he did use a past. Matt. 24:43 and Luke 12:39 are of the same nature; they are like John 4:10; all three are mixed conditions, the protases being present unreality, the apodoses past (ᾔδει is always used as an imperfect). John 11:21 and I John 2:19 are past unreality, the imperfect of εἶναι, as Robertson himself states elsewhere, doing duty for the seldom-used aorist.

This clears up the two variants. Some copyists changed the first imperfect into a present tense (reality), a few made it an aorist (past reality or past unreality) and thus made this condition a mixed condition. The writer generalizes the past facts regarding the patriarchs by speaking of them as though they were facts that were happening *now*. This is perfectly plain in v. 14 and 16 and thus ought to be equally plain in v. 15 where he uses the regular form for a present condition of reality. As though the writer has the patriarchs right before him he says that, if they were to remember the fatherland (Mesopotamia) from which they came out, they would have καιρόν, plenty of time or opportunity, to return to Mesopotamia. We see them doing nothing of the kind; they have no earthly fatherland. God's promises to them give them a fatherland that is infinitely more glorious than any earthly one whether it be the old Mesopotamia or the new Palestine.

16) Μέν and δέ balance: on the one hand no thought of an earthly fatherland, on the other, aspiration only for a heavenly fatherland. "Now, however," is logical and not temporal, for it states the reality regarding the patriarchs. As if he has them before his eyes the writer says that "they aspire to a better one, that is, to a heavenly one," one that is as much better as a heavenly fatherland is compared with any mere earthly one.

The present tenses continue: "wherefore God is not ashamed of them to be called their God," i.e., "the God of Abraham, of Isaac, and of Jacob" (Gen. 28:13; Exod. 3:6, 15; cf., Gen. 32:9; also Matt. 22:32). What this means is explained: God "prepared for them a city." These patriarchs God acknowledges as his children, and so he prepared a city for them, this heavenly city being their true, eternal fatherland. The final word "a city" takes us back to v. 10 where we are told that Abraham kept waiting for this wonderful city. It is now entirely clear from the explanation given in v. 13-16.

The writer could have placed all this into the simple historical past: "When they said such things they indicated, etc. And if they had remembered they would have had opportunity, etc. They, however, aspired, etc." He places all of this into the present and ignores differences in time, which enables the readers to think of themselves in the most direct way as having these patriarchs, as it were, right in their midst to show them what to think, to say, to expect.

Yes, the readers have tasted a measure of persecution (10:32, 33), have seen the members of the old congregation in Rome and also Peter and Paul brought to martyrdom. What if such things should recur? As former Jews Abraham, Isaac, and Jacob are their great examples of faith. See these patriarchs disregard everything in the way of an earthly fatherland, pass through life and die as nothing but aliens among men, aliens in fact, yea, aliens because they are ever aspiring to a better, a heavenly fatherland, the City of God, prepared for them by God. Will the readers do less?

These Old Testament men of faith are the models for all New Testament believers when it comes to what faith is and ever must be (v. 1).

Abraham, Isaac, Jacob, Joseph

17) The examples continue after the digression (v. 13-16), but whereas those cited in v. 4-12 refer to faith in the blessed hereafter, which we all should share, this group of four are individual illustrations of a faith that is not to be duplicated in us but is intended to inspire us to show our faith in the individual situations that come to us.

By means of faith Abraham, when being tried, has offered Isaac. Even his only-begotten he was offering, he who had accepted the promises, to whom it was said: In connection with Isaac shall seed be called for thee — having drawn the conclusion that even from the dead God is able to raise up; hence he also brought him away in the way of a parable. This presents briefly the greatest act of Abraham's faith, his trusting in the absolutely unseen, and that at a time when he was bidden to do what seemed to conflict directly with God's own promise.

The present participle πειραζόμενος harmonizes with the perfect προσενήνοχεν. In the course of being tried Abraham "has offered" Isaac; the tense emphasizes the permanent effect of the act as the writer and the readers still feel it. Πειράζω means simply "to try," and this word receives its sinister meaning "to tempt" only when somebody tries to make us do evil. After the great fact has been stated, καί restates it so as to bring out its inwardness. Abraham was offering no less than his "only-begotten." The imperfect tense of the verb asks the readers to dwell on Abraham's astonishing procedure.

R. 885 calls this "an interrupted imperfect," but imperfects and open tenses are never "interrupted," they hold the reader in suspense as to the outcome of an action; an aorist generally follows which states the outcome. So we here have ἐκομίσατο, "he carried him off." In Acts 7:57, 58 the two imperfects show how they were stoning—stoning Stephen; then in v. 60 the aorist states the outcome: "he fell asleep." "Only-begotten" = the one real heir who was born by his wife Sarah. Him Abraham was offering, "he who had accepted the promises" of God in regard to this son with such joy and such faith.

18) An appositional relative specifies the sum of these promises: "he to whom it was said (by God himself in Gen. 21:12) : 'In connection with Isaac shall seed be called for thee,' " i.e., shalt thou have seed that will be called seed indeed, called so and acknowledged as thy seed by me. Think of it — this son Abraham was now engaged in offering as a sacrifice! Who does not feel the tragedy that is being enacted? A father ordered by God to slay his own son, and such a son! God asking a human sacrifice, and such a victim as a sacrifice! We ourselves must feel that it is incredible; how much more did Abraham, the father, feel thus! Yet marvel of obedient, unquestioning faith:

Abraham is going forward with the offering! In Rom. 9:7 Paul, too, cites Gen. 21:12, and in this passage the full meaning of "seed" for Abraham in Isaac is the great point, namely spiritual seed through Christ, who, as far as his humanity was concerned, descended from the line of Isaac (not of Ishmael); all believers in Christ constitute this seed (see the elaboration of Rom. 9:7).

19) Yet Abraham's faith was not a blind faith: "having come to conclude that even from the dead God is able to raise up." We do not insert "him" (A. V.). Abraham concluded the full truth, not only that God is able to raise this one dead lad, his son, but is able to raise the dead. Abraham believed the doctrine of the resurrection, no less. By means of this doctrine Abraham harmonized all God's promises as they were centered in Isaac with this command of God's to offer Isaac in sacrificial death. To God he was offering this son (not merely killing him), and God could not cancel or deny the promises he had made with regard to this son; God's power to raise from the dead upheld Abraham's faith. He had never seen this power raise a dead person; here, too, Abraham believed the unseen (v. 1). The participle is to be construed with the imperfect: having this conviction, Abraham was offering Isaac. The whole sentence, beginning with καί, is perfect in construction and in wording.

Abraham's sacrifice of Isaac has been used to illustrate the fact that our faith must believe things that are contradictory in the Word of God; for does God not say two things to Abraham that are absolutely contradictory? This is shown to be an imperfect deduction, one that is made by faulty reasoning on our part. Abraham harmonized the *apparent* contradiction and thus removed the contradiction; he did not do this by means of his own reason or on the basis of human ideas but by means of the doctrine of the resurrection

Hebrews 11:19

and the infinite power of God. When we are then told not to combine one doctrine with another, not to let the light of one doctrine fall upon another in aid of faith, but to accept each separately, the example of Abraham directly upsets such derogatory ideas about the teachings of God's Word, none of which are contradictory.

Critics assert that even Job did not as yet know anything about the resurrection, that Job 19:25-27 does not speak of the resurrection of the body, that this doctrine arose much later and was probably due to Persian influence. This contention is answered by Abraham: "God is able to raise up from the dead." Abraham precedes Job; so does Genesis. The phrase ἐκ νεκρῶν is discussed in connection with Matt. 17:10; Mark 9:9; Luke 9:7; John 2:22; Acts 3:16. It is stated that this verse is a reference to v. 12, the miraculous birth of Isaac from parents who were as good as dead; but few will think of such a thing in a connection that deals with something that is so entirely different.

Ὅθεν = "whence," "hence," i.e., as a result, in reward for his faith. Abraham "even bore him off in the way of (ἐν) a parable." Κομίζω is the verb that is used in 10:36; 11:13, 39, where it refers to bringing off or carrying away for oneself the promise or the promises; so Abraham now brought away his son alive as a reward of his faith although because of absolute trust in God he was willing to offer him up to God in death.

But this is the least of it; he brought him away καὶ ἐν παραβολῇ. Alford's long note shows how this simple phrase has been thought to say a great number of things. Abraham brought Isaac away "in a parable," in a way which, like a parable, showed the power of God to raise up from the dead. II Cor. 1:8-10 is analogous. B.-P. 976: *als ein Sinnbild des gewaltsamen Todes und der Auferweckung Christi*. Some hesitate to regard this as a parable regarding Christ, Riggenbach specifically excludes all reference to Christ's death or to his resurrection; C.-K. 194 tone down the parabolic idea to an indication that God's promises would be fulfilled in Isaac. But our resurrection is impossible without Christ's resurrection; thus Job 19:25, etc., also contains both. See *The Eisenach Old Testament Selections* on this text from Job.

The fact that Isaac is a type of Christ should not be denied. What was nearly done in his case was actually done by God when he offered up his Son and then raised him from the dead. The parabolic features presented are too marked to be ignored; "to raise up from the dead" is too plain when it is combined with "carrying Isaac off in the way of a parable."

20) **By means of faith also concerning things to come did Isaac bless Jacob and Esau.** Isaac, Jacob, and Joseph are characterized by acts of faith that occurred near the close of their lives, faith thus summing up the life of each one; note v. 13 where we are told that the patriarchs died, not having seen the promised things. "The things to come" with which Isaac blessed his sons were to occur long after the lives of these sons had been closed; yet distant though they were, matters that were wholly unseen, matters only of hope (v. 1), Isaac "by means of faith" trusted with fullest certainty in their coming to pass and so blessed Jacob and Esau. The details of the blessing of these two as they are recorded in Gen. 27 and 28 do not matter as far as the faith of Isaac is concerned and are touched upon only by reason of the fact that Jacob's name is mentioned before that of Esau. How far into the future the blessing reached we see in Gen. 27:40, which refers to the time of Christ when an Idumean (Herod) ruled over Jacob's descendants.

21) **By means of faith Jacob, when dying, blessed each of the sons of Joseph and bowed in worship over the top of his staff.** The writer does not mention the blessing of Jacob's own sons or of any

one of them, not even that of Joseph but only the blessing of Joseph's two sons. Why are only Joseph's sons mentioned? Because they were born in Egypt, and Jacob adopted them as his own sons (Gen. 48:5); it was thus that he blessed them. That blessing was, indeed, a notable act of faith. Jacob was near his death and would not see the realization of his blessing, but Manasseh and Ephraim and especially their descendants would not remain in Egypt as Egyptians but would as sons of Jacob found two tribes that would live in Canaan. Jacob believed all that God revealed to him regarding the future, which was in line with the Messianic promise made to Abraham. This act of his so near his death attests his great faith.

The whole story is told in Gen. 48. Here the writer is again not concerned with the details although they are most interesting; he does not state how Joseph wanted the greater blessing for Manasseh, the older son, while Jacob insisted on bestowing it on Ephraim, the younger son. It is the fact itself that Jacob blessed them before dying that underlines his faith.

The clause introduced with καί intends to add only one more mark of Jacob's faith, namely his reverent bowing in worship to God. While this is recorded in Gen. 47:31 and thus just before chapter 48 and the blessing of Joseph's sons, it is well to remember that Gen. 47:27-49:33 belong together. In Gen. 47:29 Jacob feels that death is near; in Gen. 48:1 he becomes ill; in Gen. 49:33 he dies. So he also arranges with Joseph (Gen. 47:29-31) and with all his sons (Gen. 49:29-31) that they bury his body in Machpelah near Mamre in Canaan. This reverent bowing in worship is thus connected with Jacob as a dying man who in faith trusts all the promises of God to his very end.

The Hebrew, pointed as we have it in our Hebrew Bible, reads "upon the bed's head" (Gen. 47:31), which the LXX translate as if it were pointed to mean "upon his staff," and our writer follows the LXX's rendering. Gen. 32:10 does mention the staff that Jacob had carried ever since he left Canaan in flight. Many feel certain that the Hebrew means "bed," but does it? Horne, *Introduction*, II, 320 is much to the point when he says that the Hebrew must be read as "staff," for Jacob was at that time not confined to his bed, and those who take the Hebrew to mean that Jacob "bowed himself upon his bed's head" have difficulty in explaining just what this may mean; Delitzsch, who adopts the view of von Hofmann, offers this interpretation: "Jacob turned around on his bed with his face toward the head of it; turning his face to his pillow, he stretched himself out in the attitude of prostrate devotion." This is a case where the LXX seem to read their unpointed Hebrew more correctly than do the Hebraists of the present day. The older view that Jacob bowed before the staff of Joseph is unsupported; neither Joseph nor his staff is mentioned in the clause.

22) By means of faith Joseph, when finishing his life, remembered regarding the exodus of the sons of Israel and gave orders concerning his bones.

Like his father Jacob, Joseph ordered that his body be taken to Palestine; Jacob was at once taken there for burial, Joseph at the time of the exodus. From his youth until his death Joseph lived as an Egyptian, the vice-ruler of the land. Mummified, his body would lie in some grand Egyptian tomb. What more could Joseph wish for? Ah, much more! He took an oath from the descendants of Jacob to carry his body to Canaan when God should remove them from Egypt (Gen. 50:25). His bones were taken along (Exod. 13:19) on that long, long journey and were finally buried in Shechem (Josh. 24:32).

That was faith, indeed! Joseph believed all the Abrahamitic promises, believed that they would all be fulfilled in Canaan although this would occur years and years after his death; he believed so fully and strongly that he wanted his remains to rest in the land where the promise of salvation would be fulfilled. Like his own people, he considered his body to be in exile in Egypt; he believed the exodus would follow and said, "God will surely visit you" (Exod. 13:19); he believed that all the rest would follow. His, too, in so clear a way was faith in the sense of confidence in things hoped for, conviction in regard to things not seen (verse 1).

Moses

23) By means of faith Moses, when born, was hid for three months by his parents because they saw the child was fair; and they feared not the mandate of the king. By means of faith Moses, having grown up, refused to be called son of Pharaoh's daughter, rather having chosen to be basely treated together with the people of God than to have enjoyment of sin lasting for a period, having come to esteem as greater riches than the treasures of Egypt the reproach of the Christ; for he kept looking away to the due pay-gift.

From Genesis the writer proceeds to Exodus and dwells at length on Moses, not only because so much of faith appears in his life, but also because his readers esteem Moses so highly. They are thinking of forsaking Christ for Judaism because Judaism had Moses and all the ritual commandments given through Moses. Well, Moses himself is one of the greatest examples of faith in Christ. Let the readers, therefore, follow Moses, namely this faith of his. They will then cling to Christ as Moses did and have both Christ and Moses; otherwise they will lose both. John 5:45-47.

A great act of faith is connected with the babyhood of Moses when his parents (πατέρες is to be understood in this sense) hid him for three months (accusative of duration) because the child was ἀστεῖος (the same word is used by Stephen regarding Moses, Acts 7:20), really "citified" (not rustic, boorish) but constantly used as a designation for exceptional beauty. This the parents did "and feared not the mandate of the king," i.e., did not let this fear deter them. Neither Exodus 2 nor our passage implies that the parents of Moses kept the child because in its beauty they saw an indication that God would do great things through this child. The act of faith was the fact that the parents trusted that God would preserve this baby boy despite Pharaoh's mandate. They had no idea as to how it could be done and were not certain that hiding the child as long as they could would not be in vain in the end; they simply trusted in God for the unseen for which they hoped (v. 1); nor did they trust in vain.

24) Faith appeared again in a most marked way when Moses reached manhood and "refused to be spoken of as son of Pharaoh's daughter" (all three nouns are anarthrous because they are qualitative). The verb means "to say no, to deny, thus to refuse." What high position and honor to live at the royal court in all splendor, to be the adopted son of a royal princess, to enjoy all the exalted prerogatives of a member of Pharaoh's family! What prospects for a man's life!

Moses could also entertain the thought that in such a lofty position he might be able to do very much for his native people who were now sorely oppressed by the all-powerful Pharaoh. He turned his back on it all "by making the choice to be basely treated with the people of God"; ἑλόμενος (from αἱρέω) indicates action that is simultaneous with that of ἠρνήσατο. The Egyptians were not "the people of God"; these enslaved, crushed, cruelly maltreated Israelites were. Everything earthly invited Moses to refuse and to deny them; faith bade him to refuse and to deny the Egyptians and to choose to share the base treatment accorded to God's people because they were God's. In the infinitive there lies the idea of κακόν, a mean, base, disgraceful lot (this verb is found only here); compare the compounds with κακόν in II Tim. 1:8; 2:3, 9; 4:5, "suffering disgrace" and not ashamed of it.

25) Moses chose this lot "rather than (μᾶλλον ἤ) to have enjoyment of sin lasting for a period," the sin consisting not in sinful deeds in his court life but in disowning his people in order to enjoy the earthly grandeur at Pharaoh's palaces and court. One feels the temptation with which Moses was confronted.

26) A second aorist participle, which is in simple apposition, adds the thought which determined Moses to make his choice of faith: "having come to esteem as greater riches than the treasures of Egypt (genitive after a comparative) the reproach of the Christ" (objective genitive, R. 500), the reproach suffered for the sake of the Christ. One ought not to underestimate "the treasures of Egypt" as though they amounted to nothing, for they are to be regarded as being exceedingly great; but when they were placed beside all the loss suffered in reproach for Christ's sake, this loss, in the estimation of Moses, constituted an infinitely greater treasure. The expression is paradoxical and thus highly effective. This reproach was priceless honor for Moses.

The thought should not be reduced to a mere similarity between the reproach which Christ suffered and the reproach which Moses chose to suffer. The reproach of Christ is all the shame that was heaped on Christ, which culminated in his dying outside of the camp (13:13) as a crucified criminal; and whoever comes into contact with Christ by true faith must bear his part of that reproach or opprobrium. Whether the contact of faith is made before Christ actually died on the cross or since he died makes no difference whatever.

Because some interpreters are not satisfied with this simple connection by means of faith, deeper meanings have been sought in this "reproach of Christ." Christ is thought to have made Israel a *type* of himself in regard to reproach, and Moses is thought to have esteemed this type beyond price. Or Israel suffered as the *mystical* body of Christ. Others say that Christ as the *Logos* is seen in the old Israel, and that he suffered the reproach in his people. The matter is carried to an extreme point when the whole history of Israel is viewed as a preparation for Christ's incarnation, when Christ is regarded as being already incarnate in Israel after a fashion. These views bring Christ down to Israel whereas "faith," all this faith the writer is speaking about, brings Israel, Moses, and all believers of every time up to Christ and the reproach he suffered.

As for Moses' knowing about the Christ, in John 5:46 Jesus says that Moses wrote about him, and not merely in a sentence or two as in Deut. 18:15-19 (Acts 3:21-23; 7:37), but in all his writing. Even at the time when he made his decision Moses knew all about the reproach of the Christ and its heavenly value. His was the faith of Abraham, Isaac, Jacob, Joseph. Note v. 22 and what he did with Joseph's bones.

How he came to think as he did is explained: "for he kept looking away to the μισθαποδοσίαν," the same word that was used in 10:35: the full or due pay-gift (our versions, "recompense of reward") that awaits all true believers in the Christ. Moses ever kept his eyes on the things not seen (v. 1). "We not keeping an eye on the things seen but on the things not seen; for the things seen are for a season (only), but the things not seen are eternal," I Cor. 4:18.

27) Still more. **By means of faith he left Egypt behind, not fearing the anger of the king; for he was steadfast as seeing the Invisible One. By means of faith he has attended to the Passover and the splashing of the blood in order that the one destroying the first-born should not touch them. By means of faith**

they walked through the Red Sea as through dry land; which having undertaken to try, the Egyptians were swallowed up.

Patristic exegesis thinks of the flight to Midian, and it has some following. But this was a flight; and it was due to fear; and there was no steadfastness about it. To say that Moses went to Midian in order to bide his time until Israel's deliverance, is to controvert the facts; for Moses fled in discouragement, and when the time of deliverance came, God had to compel him to return as the deliverer. Vaughan, Delitzsch, and others who think of this flight reason away the fear recorded in Exod. 2:14, 15.

Κατέλιπεν means that Moses left Egypt behind never to return. This did not occur when he fled to Midian but when he led the children of Israel out of Egypt. "Not fearing the anger of the king" means that this time he did not fear as he did when he fled to Midian full of fear. Moses fearlessly confronted the Pharaoh again and again and demanded Israel's release. Read about this fearlessness in Exod. 10:28, 29. When Pharaoh was at last compelled to assent, Moses knew that this assent would not endure for long, but he left without fear of anything that the anger of the king might attempt to do before the Israelites escaped, and we know what Pharaoh did attempt.

The statement that Moses alone is here referred to, that elsewhere the exodus is always ascribed to him and to the people together, is pointless since Moses is the one who inspired the people to leave with him, Moses the one who "was steadfast" when the people wavered, Moses who ever saw the Invisible One with the eyes of faith, which kept all fear away. Ἐκαρτέρησε does not mean that Moses "endured" (our versions) in the sense that he suffered but that he stood firm in his strength, steadfast and fearless "as seeing the Invisible One" who was infinitely mightier than the little visible

Pharaoh. "The Invisible One" takes us back to v. 1, faith trusting "things not seen." He who at one time fled like a coward in fear of Pharaoh returned and left as a fearless hero of faith.

28) Two more marks of faith are noted in connection with his leaving Egypt behind. The view that v. 27 precedes v. 28 chronologically and must thus refer to the flight to Midian, is not supportable. In v. 13 it is stated that the patriarchs "all died," yet in v. 17-21 more acts of faith are recorded as being done by them. The aorist "he left Egypt behind" includes the whole grand act of leaving, parts of which were the Passover and the slaying of the first-born when the actual leaving started and the crossing through the Red Sea when the leaving was completed.

It was a great act of faith when, after all the plagues had failed to move Pharaoh, and when he had ordered Moses never to show his face before him again, Moses proceeded with the "Passover and the splashing of the blood ($\pi\rho\acute{o}\sigma\chi\nu\sigma\iota\varsigma$)" on the lintels and the doorposts so that the destroyer of the first-born in all of Egypt would not touch the Israelites on that fateful night, and that the Israelites would at last be able to get away. Remember how that Passover was to be eaten (Exod. 12:11); every person was to be ready to march away.

Πεποίηκε fits both τὸ πάσχα and τὴν πρόσχυσιν, the latter being found here in the Greek for the first time. It is hard for us to find a good equivalent English verb, the Germans have *veranstalten, vornehmen*. "Kept" in our versions does not fit the second noun. Some prefer "celebrated" because it is regularly used with reference to the Passover and to other festivals; but what about the second noun? Moreover, this was the inauguration by God, in which Moses served only as God's servant. Hence we also have the perfect tense amid plain aorists. What was done in Egypt was to be repeated in a certain way as an annual memorial. Moses thus "has done" (Greek), i.e., attended to the Passover and the splashing of the blood. "The one destroying" (participle) has the object "the first-born" while "should not touch" has the genitive αὐτῶν as its object, wherefore also the two objects are separated. Ὁ ὀλοθρεύων is cited from Exod. 12:23; and this destroyer is thought to be an angel in conformity with I Chron. 21:12, 15, ἄγγελος ὁ ἐξολεθρεύων, cf. Ps. 78:49; I Cor. 10:10, and Jewish tradition.

29) This verse presents the completion of the exodus as far as leaving Egypt is concerned and the walking through the Red Sea as through dry land (not "by" as in our versions, διά, "through," repeats the preposition that is used in the verb). Exod. 14:29 has διὰ ξηρᾶς, and Exod. 15:4 κατεπόθησαν. A relative clause is sufficient to describe the fate of the Egyptians: "which (genitive attracted from the accusative) having undertaken to try, the Egyptians were swallowed up" (the Greek has κατά, "down"), literally, "were drunk down," i.e., "were drowned" (A. V.); λαμβάνω with an infinitive is a classical idiom (it is used again in v. 36). The Egyptians had no promise and hence could have no faith; Moses and Israel had both. The promise produced the faith, and God kept his promise.

Jericho, Rahab

30) **By means of faith the walls of Jericho fell, having been circled for seven days.** Marching around and around Jericho seven days, seven times on the seventh day, then blowing the trumpets and making a great shout—how could such a procedure make massive fortifications fall? Who had ever heard of such a thing? How the soldiers and the commanders on those walls must have cast jibes and derision at the silent marchers as they were going around day after day! How safe they felt if the Israelite soldiers did

no more than this! Yes, it took faith to carry out this mode of attack which seemed to be no attack at all; it took faith in things not seen as v. 1 describes faith. Then suddenly there came sight. Incredible sight—all the walls fell! Josh. 6:1, etc.

31) **By means of faith Rahab, the harlot, did not perish with the disobedient ones, having received the spies with peace.** Josh. 2:1, etc.; 6:22, etc. This pagan woman who had sunk to harlotry believed the report about the God of Israel that filled the city. She alone believed and in her still pagan way obeyed that faith and received the Israelite spies "with peace," as friends to be protected and not as enemies of war to be delivered up. She believed that the city would fall; on that belief she acted. All the rest who lived in Jericho were disobedient; the aorist ἀπειθήσαντες states the historical fact. Unbelief is at times called disobedience because it is nothing less and is also the source of disobedient conduct. The people of Jericho laughed at the idea of surrendering their city, which was so mightily fortified, to soldiers who did not have even a ladder to scale the walls; they mocked at the very idea and perished. James 2:25 praises Rahab for her works, which were an evidence of her justification. See the exposition of James. Rahab became the wife of Booz, one of the ancestors of Jesus; see Matt. 1:5.

Still more Heroes of Faith and
Their Achievements of Faith

32) **And what shall I yet say? The time will fail me recounting about Gideon, Barak, Samson, Jephthah, both David and Samuel and the prophets, who through faith subdued kingdoms, worked righteousness, obtained promises, locked the mouths of lions, quenched power of fire, escaped sword's mouths, were brought to power from weakness, became strong in war, turned to flight the battle lines of aliens.**

Hebrews 11:32, 33

The list is altogether too long for the writer to give an account of the great evidence of faith in the lives of all the great personages in the past history of Israel, all of whom would deserve to be considered, about whom all the readers know. The writer has kept down to great brevity what he has thus far said about "the ancients" (v. 2); he must now abbreviate still more. In doing so he records a few more notable names to which the readers may add more. Then he adds a list of achievements and a list of sufferings and lets his readers exercise their historical knowledge in placing these terse items.

In the rhetorical question of deliberation: "And what shall I yet say?" λέγω is the deliberative subjunctive. "The time will fail me recounting about Gideon," etc. = it will take too much time to recount. The present participle is construed with με by a fine Greek idiom. The six names that are now added are not placed in chronological order with evident purpose. The reason for this does not seem to be an effort to list them in the order of importance. Samuel is placed last so as to be able to add "the prophets." While the four judges precede the one king, Samuel, too, was a judge and preceded David. All six ruled Israel, but this cannot be said of the prophets. The best we are able to say is that these names are only suggestive. The readers will be struck by this or by that name in the great history of faith; the writer indicates that the sequence of time is immaterial, that faith is the main thing.

33) The relative clause lists the achievements which the writer has in mind when he pens his list of notable names. Because of their contents the nine items can be divided into three groups of three. R., W. P., calls the asyndeton "sledge-hammer style." Each item is thrown on the screen by itself. As one succeeds the other, the effect increases. Chronology does not count, only the contents do. All the tenses are aorists to ex-

press historical facts. It is left to the readers to locate the terse references at the proper place in history. Each achievement was accomplished by means of faith, διά being now used and not the dative as was done before.

"Subdued kingdoms" as an athlete wrestles down his antagonist may well apply to David and to II Sam. 8. "Worked righteousness" applies to II Sam. 8:15; I Chron. 18:14, and to the righteous rule of any of the judges. "Obtained promises," as in 6:15, means the fulfillment of special promises that were given to individuals and not the supreme fulfillment of the final promise (v. 13, 39).

34) "Locked the mouths of lions" = Dan. 6:22 (scarcely Judges 14:6, or I Sam. 17:34, etc.). "Quenched power of fire" = Dan. 3:27 (cf. v. 19, 22). "Escaped sword's mouths" may apply to any escape in battle but also to Elijah's escape from the sword of Jezebel (I Kings 19:1-3, 10), perhaps also to the escape of Elisha (II Kings 6:14, etc., 31, etc.). "Were brought to power from weakness" refers, it seems, to Samson (Judges 16:28), perhaps also to the courage inspired by David's victory over Goliath which enabled Israel to triumph (I Sam. 17:26, etc.). "Became strong in war" as well as "turned to flight (ἔκλιναν) the battle lines of aliens" would apply also to David's victory over Goliath and to the resultant defeat of the Philistines, yet also to other victories that were accomplished by faith. The sword has two edges (4:12) which are called "mouths" because of their devouring or biting power. Παρεμβολή = camp, fortified camp, and then also "battle line."

Faith Triumphant in Suffering

35) It is less the change in construction (now a series of independent sentences) than the change of subject that marks the advance to the achievements of faith in suffering. **Women received their dead as a result of resurrection; but others were tortured,**

not accepting the ransoming in order to obtain a better resurrection. Yet others undertook to try mockings and scourgings besides even confinement and prison. They were stoned; they were sawn asunder; they died in murder of (the) sword. They wandered about in sheep pelts, in goat skins, being destitute, being afflicted, being basely treated — of whom the world was not worthy — erring about in deserts and mountains and caves and holes of the earth.

We at once think of the widow of Sarepta (I Kings 17:17-24) and of the Shunamite (II Kings 4:18-37), the one having her child raised from death by Elijah, the other by Elisha. These "women" are introduced because the grief they suffered through the death of their children was already in this life turned into joy when they received their children back "as a result of resurrection" (ἐκ) while others died "in order to obtain a better resurrection" at the end of time. The two statements belong together. We do not always need to wait for the unseen (v. 1) beyond; there are cases of believers whose faith has been rewarded already in this life, and that "as a result of resurrection": the children of these two women of the Old Testament and in the New Testament Jairus' daughter, the widow's son at Nain, Martha's and Mary's brother at Bethany.

Δέ is adversative because the writer intends to introduce a contrast. This contrast is an extreme contrast: "but others were tortured, not accepting ransoming in order to obtain a better resurrection" than one that would return them to this life. The readers who are conversant with their LXX will at once recall II Macc. 6:20, 29 (LXX, v. 19, 28). They will do this because of τὸ τύμπανον (the drum) which is used in that passage (here ἐτυμπανίσθησαν) and because of the remark that these others did not accept the ransoming by which they might have had their lives spared. So died

Eleazar, one of the most prominent scribes, who was already ninety years of age. II Macc. 6:18-30 recounts that he might have saved his life but refused to do so; ἀπολύτρωσις is the proper word, "ransoming," the ransom for his life being that he eat pork to please the king Entiochus Epiphanes.

The verb means to stretch upon a wheel-like frame, the body becoming taut like a drum, which is then beaten until the victim yields or slowly dies in agony. In IV Macc. 5:32 the instrument used for this torture is called τροχός, "wheel." The Vulgate translates our passage *distenti sunt*. Our writer uses the plural "others" and thus refers to the mother and to her seven sons who are mentioned in II Macc. 7, who, however, were tortured in various ways. They were mutilated, flayed, roasted. According to IV Maccabees the mother perished by fire. By using the verb with regard to others besides Eleazar the writer probably uses the word in a general sense so as to apply it to different modes of torture.

36) Ἕτεροι refers to others who were different from the ἄλλοι spoken of in v. 35. These "undertook to make trial" (the same idiom that was used in v. 29) of mockings and scourgings and on top of that (ἔτι δέ) of confinement and of prison. They undertook tryings of this kind. They were not killed like the ἄλλοι. A number of illustrations for these types of sufferings may be found in the persecutions which the prophets had to suffer; consider I Kings 22:27; II Chron. 16:10; 36:16; Jer. 20:2; 37:15; 38:6. The common idea regarding δεσμά is that this word means "fetters" (so the dictionaries), some translate "chains"; our finding in Acts and elsewhere is that the word means holding someone prisoner whether he is bound with fetters or not; hence also φυλακή, the actual prison house, follows here.

37) The subject is still the ἕτεροι used in v. 36; now, however, the author reports how some of them

ended in martyrdom. "They were stoned"—thus Zechariah (II Chron. 24:20, 21; Matt. 21:35; 23:35), according to tradition also Jeremiah while he was living in Tahpanhes, Egypt. This manner of execution is typically Jewish. "They were sawn asunder"—thus Isaiah according to Jewish tradition and also according to the apocryphal records and the Palestinian Targum on II Kings 21:16. This death was inflicted on captives of war, II Sam. 12:31; I Chron. 20:3.

There is much uncertainty regarding the next word ἐπειράσθησαν, even as to its place textually. The main trouble is with its meaning, "they were tempted," which does not fit in a series of verbs that denotes death. A few retain it; others assume an early corruption for either "they were burned" or "they were mutilated," or regard it as a mere insertion. There is nothing one can do but to pass the matter by; no acceptable solution has been discovered. "They died in sword slaughter" (an expression that is repeatedly used in the Old Testament)—examples are found in I Kings 19:10; Jer. 26:23.

It is by no means an anticlimax when the wretched life of fugitives is now described. Some fled from death and escaped, but what an existence they led! "They wandered around in sheep pelts (μηλωταί, found only here in the New Testament), in goat skins" (αἴγειος, adjective: "from goats"), having nothing better to clothe them. "Destitute" is a participle: in constant lack of food and drink. Another participle: "afflicted" or hard-pressed. A third: "basely treated." The three participles are significantly durative.

38) What a sad, sad lot all endured because they would not give up their faith. Here, however, the point is that amid all these terrible sufferings their faith ever trusted the things not seen, held to the things hoped for (v. 1). The writer, filled with admiration, exclaims in a parenthesis: "Of whom the world was not worthy!"

The world thought they were not worthy of it (Acts 22:22); the opposite was true: the world was not worthy to have such noble men and such women living in its midst.

Another participle concludes the sad spectacle: "erring about in deserts (uninhabited, wild places) and mountains and caves and holes of the earth" like wild animals. They were even worse, for these animals have their homes, but the fugitives had to keep on the move.

Summation

39) **And these all, although having received testimony by means of their faith, did not bring off the promise since God had in view as pertaining to us something better, (namely) that not apart from us should they be brought to completeness.**

The first participle is concessive and harks back to v. 2 where it is stated that the ancient believers had God's own approving testimony in Holy Writ which expresses God's pleasure in their faith (v. 5). Although this is undoubtedly true of all these believers who are mentioned by name or indicated by their deeds of faith, they did not, in spite of this divine approval, bring off the promise. "The promise" is properly the singular, for it designates the fulfillment of the great Messianic promise; the verb κομίζω is found also in 10:36; 11:13, 19. Verse 13 makes the same statement regarding the patriarchs, namely that they all died without having brought away the promises (the plural is used in this case since the promise was renewed to each of them). In 10:36 it is stated that we are to bring away the promise after we have done the will of God. These passages belong together.

In this life both the ancient believers and we of a later time bring or carry off some individual promises of God, i.e., we carry away the fulfillment of certain things which God has promised us: we have and enjoy the forgiveness of our sins, the gifts of his Spirit, the answers to prayer, God's comfort, help, support, etc. All this is blessed indeed. But carrying off "the promise" is a far more exalted thing. It is the final and supreme fulfillment, the consummation at the last day, the ultimate of all that we are hoping for, of all that is not seen (v. 1). It is the final approving testimony of Christ before the whole universe (Matt. 25:34-40), when Christ shall confess us, who have confessed him before men, before his Father (Matt. 10:32) and before the angels (Rev. 3:5). It includes the resurrection and the glorification of our bodies ("a better resurrection," v. 35), when Christ shall appear in his second epiphany to those who are expecting him for salvation. Thrice Jesus promised: "And I will raise him up at the last day," John 6:40, 44, 54 (Phil. 3:21). All that this promise contains = "the things hoped for, the things not seen" (v. 1), to be apprehended until they arrive only by faith pure and simple. It is the city that has foundations (v. 10), the new heaven and new earth, when the holy city, the new Jerusalem, comes down from God out of heaven (Rev. 21:1, 2), which event is described at length in Rev. 21:10-27.

40) The genitive absolute is causal: "since God had in view (looked forward to) as pertaining to us something better." What this "something better" is ἵνα states by means of an object clause that is in apposition with τι: "that not apart from us should they be brought to completeness." By letting all the Old Testament believers wait as he does despite the grand testimony with which he voiced his approval of their faith God had in view something that was far better than not letting them wait thus, than letting the consummation, Christ's second epiphany, at once follow his first epiphany.

The phrase περὶ ἡμῶν has the emphasis because of its position. It does not modify the object: "something better concerning us" (R. V.). The phrase modifies the participle plus its object: God's having in view something better for all the Old Testament believers was an act that pertained to us. As far as those Old Testament believers are concerned, the consummation could have come immediately after Christ's redemptive work had been completed. But, then, what about us? There would then have been no New Testament era; the completion would have been reached "without us." The writer stops with "us," himself and his readers, Jewish Christians, since his epistle is intended especially for them. We, however, think also of ourselves. There would have been no New Testament era, no world-wide reach of the gospel, no hosts of New Testament believers.

I Cor. 15:6 speaks about the existence of only 500 believers when redemption was complete. Would it have been a better thing to bring in the consummation soon after this? God is still delaying its coming; faith is still spreading to millions. Not without all these will the noble Old Testament believers be brought to completeness but will share this blessing in company with us. Many are coming from the east and the west to sit down with Abraham, Isaac, and Jacob in the kingdom, Matt. 8:11. What joy when the last day comes with its τελείωσις! We again have this term (now a verb) which was used repeatedly before, and it is now used in its most exalted meaning.

CHAPTER XII

The Author and Completer of the Faith, v. 1-3

1) While τοιγαροῦν builds on chapter 11, it is an admonition that is built on the host of examples. We should note that Jesus is not added as another, say the supreme example, but as something that is far greater. Τοι affirms, γάρ establishes, οὖν deduces: *ja denn doch* in German. **So, then, we, too, on our part, having so great a cloud of witnesses all about us, by having put away every weight and the easily hampering sin, let us by means of perseverance go on running the contest lying before us, looking away to the author and completer of the faith, who for the joy lying before him perseveringly endured (the) cross, despising (the) shame, and has sat down at the right (hand) of the throne of God.**

Καὶ ἡμεῖς is emphatic: "we, too, on our part," and intends to range us alongside of all the glorious believers mentioned in chapter 11, our faith, our strength, our conflict, our crown being the same as theirs. We should not get the impression from the A. V. that the Old Testament believers were also surrounded by a great cloud of witnesses. The first participle advances a motive: "having so great a cloud of witnesses all about us," namely all the believers mentioned in chapter 11. The figure of a cloud is not unusual to designate a great multitude, but νέφος is a mass of cloud that covers the heavens and differs from νεφέλη, a detached, single cloud. The figure is the grander because the former word is used. God's believers here on earth are but a "little flock," but the believers of past ages are a great host indeed. Their number has greatly increased since this epistle was written.

It is very dramatic to make these μάρτυρες spectators who are lining the ramparts of heaven, leaning over to watch us in the running of the race like the crowds in a great stadium who are watching the athletic events. The unsatisfactory feature about this idea is its spiritualistic touch: the spirits of the dead are still hovering over and around us. The souls of the saints are at rest, they are no longer concerned about the trials that occur on earth. The Scriptures teach that they behold the heavenly glories and say nothing about their beholding and watching earthly events. These saints are not "witnesses" that see our faith and testify about us; God does not ask them to testify about us. They are witnesses whose life, works, sufferings, death attest their own faith, testify to us through the pages of Holy Writ and in other history that they were true men of faith indeed (the faith defined in 11:1). Περικείμενον ἡμῖν, "lying around us," or adverbially simply "all about us" does not refer to an earthly presence of this cloud of witnesses, which gazes down on us from every angle. Like Abel, though dead (11:2) and long ago gone to their heavenly rest (4:9), their past life and their death still speak to us about what faith really is (11:1). They have left their multitudinous testimony which speaks to us from all sides and in countless ways.

The second participle is an aorist middle that states what must first be done by us in order to run properly: "having put away from ourselves every weight or encumbrance" that would act as a handicap in our running. Καί is explicative: "in particular the easily hampering sin," εὐπερίστατος; this word is found only here in Greek literature and is hence interpreted variously: C.-K. 1169, easy to avoid, easily surrounding or *bestrickend* = R. V.'s margin, "closely clinging to us," and our versions', "that doth so easily beset us." Luther combines weight and sin: *Suende, so uns immer anklebt und traege macht*, which is an interpretative rendering. Because the figure is that of a runner in the main clause, some carry this figure back into the participial clause: the runner runs practically naked, every weight is discarded, especially robes that cling to the limbs when one is running. The fact is that the figurative sense of the participial clause comes from the main clause: "let us go on running the ἀγών."

From our versions there comes the idea of "besetting sin": forms and types of sin to which an individual is personally inclined because of temperament, weakness, environment, etc. There are sins of this kind; here, however, sin as such and sin in all its forms and kinds is referred to, sin as such ever hampers us unless it is put away from us. To restrict this to the sin of apostasy, to which the readers were now inclining, narrows the words down too much.

The figure bursts upon us in the wording: "let us go on running the contest lying before us." The present imperative implies that the readers have been and are now running and calls on them to keep on more strenuously than ever. The preceding participle is involved in the imperatival idea, and we may follow our English idiom which would use two imperatives: "put away and run" and disregard the more exact thought of the Greek that 1) the putting away is one act (aorist), the running is continuous 2) the putting away subsidiary, the running is the main thing. Ἀγών = an athletic event; this may also refer to a "race," but it is also used with reference to other events. While running implies that the event referred to is a race, it is well to remember that races were not always run with other runners so that only one could be the victor (as in I Cor. 9:24); many were only tests of speed which were run to see whether the runner could equal a certain record of speed. The latter is the figurative idea employed here.

The durative idea of the present imperative is enhanced by the emphatically placed phrase: "by means of ὑπομονή," which is not "patience," which makes us think of quietness, nonresistance, and the like, but "perseverance" (remaining under and holding out under a severe strain). See Trench. The runners are not to let down under the strain, to slow up, or even to stop for any reason. The writer includes himself in his admonition. R., W. P., regards the subjunctive as volitive: "we will go on running"; it is hortative: "let us go on," etc. In 10:39 we have positive assertion; here hortation. Many start well in the race of faith "lying before us," which is like the track laid out for runners, but they do not hold out to the end, they fail in regard to perseverance.

2) The third participle adds the supreme motive for running with unfaltering perseverance, supreme because it involves the certainty of attaining the goal: "ever looking away (durative present) to the author and completer of the faith who," etc. We may see many things to dishearten us to continue the running, even to halt us entirely, but by ever keeping our eyes upon the originator and completer of the faith our speed will increase rather than lessen, our stamina will grow rather than fade out.

When Moffatt, like Delitzsch, makes ἀρχηγός "the pioneer of personal faith," he disagrees with 2:10 and 5:9; with all the Greek exegetes who regard ἀρχηγός = αἴτιος; with the fact that Scripture nowhere speaks of Christ as a believer (Delitzsch states that this is the only place); with the second term τελειωτής which cannot mean that Christ is the completer of his own faith, an example for us likewise to complete our faith.

"The *archegos* of their salvation" (2:10) = the "αἴτιος, cause of eternal salvation" (5:9); in the same sense we now again have "the *archegos* and completer of the faith," i. e., the originator and completer. C.-K. 179 presents the linguistic evidence to prove that only in certain connections does *archegos* mean an originator who himself first partakes of what he originates, and that this sense does not apply to 2:10 and 12:2. It is, therefore, unconvincing to quote irrelevant connections. The R. V. margin offers "captain," a meaning that might fit Acts 5:31 ("prince," *Herzog*) but does not fit here. Luther is right: "the beginner and completer of faith" (A. V. margin: "beginner"). Christ starts our faith and leads it to its consummation.

"The faith" (article) is not "our faith" (the article used as the possessive pronoun) but the faith defined in 11:1; hence it is specific (confidence and conviction in regard to things hoped for, things not seen) but as any and every believer has this faith and not only the writer and the reader. "Author and completer" (A. V., "finisher" — good; R. V., "perfecter" — not nearly so good) apply equally to "the faith" (objective genitive); the completing takes place when Christ gives to faith and to the believer "the things hoped for," "the things not seen." Τελειωτής repeats the τελειωθῶσι used in 11:40: all the Old Testament believers together with all the New Testament believers "shall be brought to completion" at Christ's Parousia (see 10:40); and as Christ is the beginner, so he is also the completer. The writer once more uses this significant derivative of τέλειος, "complete." Compare Phil. 1:6.

The statement that Christ did not originate the faith of the Old Testament believers is specious. Moses wrote of Christ (John 5:46), Abraham saw Christ's day (John 8:56), all the Old Testament believers believed in the promised Messiah. As the object of faith Christ is the cause of faith; even secular faith is kindled by its object. The statement that chapter 11 names nothing but examples of faith, and that thus Christ, too, is such an example, is more specious. Christ should then be mentioned in chapter 11, but without the designation τελειωτής, this second designation being here even connected with the first by one article.

Rationalism and modernism rob Christ of his deity, reduce him to a mere man, and thus depict him as being no more than a perfect example for us to follow. But what good does a perfect example do us who cannot possibly achieve perfection? We need vastly more than a perfect example, which by its very perfection may well cause us to cry in despair: "We cannot hope even to approach such an example!" From start to finish we need the divine Christ as the One who can fill us with faith, keep us in faith, and finally crown our faith.

The relative clause states what makes Christ the One who causes and completes the faith of believers: he is the One "who for the joy lying before him perseveringly endured (the) cross, despising (the) shame, and has sat down at the right (hand) of the throne of God." "The joy lying before him" is the glorification that followed the sufferings plus his kingship over all believers. As it did in v. 16, ἀντί expresses exchange: in order to get this joy Christ paid the price of the cross with its shame (in order to get the food Esau paid the price of his birthright). Some reverse this by making the joy the one Christ left behind in heaven, which he exchanged for the cross; or the joy he might have claimed as his while he was on earth, which he exchanged for the cross. But as it did in v. 1, προκειμένης means "lying before" or ahead and not somewhere else. During his entire humiliation, especially when he was foretelling the cross, Jesus referred to his resurrection and the enthronement with his Father.

For this "he perseveringly endured (the) cross," ὑπέμεινε repeats the ὑπομονή used in v. 1 so that we should retain the same word in English and translate either "by means of endurance" — "he endured" or "by perseverance" — "perseveringly endured." The passion history reveals how much lies in this brief expression. Σταυρός is a post that was driven into the ground as a means for executing a criminal and thus comes to mean a cross. The word has no article as also αἰσχύνη has none and thus stresses the quality of the nouns. "Despising (the) shame" is significantly added, which should be read with a Jewish eye as "cross" itself is. This is not the shame of dying a criminal's death but the shame of dying the death of a criminal who was accounted as accursed by God by his executioners (Gal. 3:13); so also Phil. 2:8. "Despising (the) shame" does not mean that the shame was a small thing, but that, in comparison with the joy, Christ scorned to consider it.

Τε connects most closely: Christ took the cross and the shame and with it the *sessio* in glory, this second being "the joy." We lose the main thought when we overlook the fact that this seating himself at the right hand of the throne of God (see the exposition in 1:3; cf., 1:13; 8:1) is the infinite exaltation of the human nature of Christ and thus the crowning of all his saving work for all eternity. This is the Savior, crucified, glorified, who is the originator and the completer of faith, also of ours. When the writer and the readers had him brought to them by the gospel they believed, he filled them with faith; when they shall see him at the right hand of the throne of God, he shall complete their faith by bestowing upon them the glory hoped for and not seen for so long (11:1).

This is again reduced to an example by some: as Christ was crucified, so we should suffer; as he looked beyond the cross, so we should; as he sat at God's right hand, so we shall receive glory. Such are "the lessons" we should learn from Christ. We refuse to accept such a reduction. We constantly look away to the Crucified and infinitely Glorified One as the Author and Completer (Rewarder) of the faith that trusts him as 11:1 states; we thus join and remain among the men and the women of faith mentioned in chapter 11. The last verb is the perfect tense: κεκάθικεν: once seated, Christ remains so forever.

3) From the present hortative the writer turns to the aorist imperative and thus completes his admonition. Γάρ is confirmatory: after saying, "Let us go on running, looking away" to Christ, the writer addresses his readers directly and emphasizes this looking at Christ. **Yea, take into consideration him who has perseveringly endured such opposition by the sinners against himself in order that you may not grow tired by relaxing in your souls!**

The pivotal word is ὑπομεμενηκότα which takes up the ὑπέμεινε used in v. 2 and most of all the δι' ὑπομονῆς occurring in v. 1. Now at last the example of Jesus is touched upon in one point, and that is perseverance. In v. 1, 2 we are to keep our eye on the beginner and finisher of the faith, on what he did to make him this. Now we are to take him into consideration as the One who has perseveringly endured in order that we may not grow tired and relax. Yet the imperative does not mean "compare" (R., W. P.), nor is any comparing to be done such as that he endured more than we are asked to endure. The verb means "to consider thoughtfully," and the aorist imperative calls for an effective, thoughtful consideration.

"Such opposition by the sinners" means the cross and the shame mentioned in v. 2. By calling this ἀντιλογία the author by no means makes it merely verbal "gainsaying" or "contradiction," for the word is also used to designate a rebellion. One reading has the singular "against him or himself," and another the plural "against themselves." Since no one has been able to make acceptable sense of the latter, we abide by the former (A. V., and R. V. American committee). R., W. P., says the plural may mean "against their better selves," which is von Soden's idea; against their better self and their own true interest. Even if one could find this in the reflexive ἑαυτούς, it would be a thought that is out of line. The readers are to put thoughtful consideration on "him who has been perseveringly enduring" such opposition. The perfect participle indicates the enduring, permanent character stamped upon Christ; in II Cor. 2:2 the perfect "having been crucified" indicates the same permanent character.

"By the sinners against himself." These contrasting phrases are abutted in order to let us feel the contrast: sinners — against the Sinless One. He who as the sinless One should have merited the highest praise from all men, who were not sinless, received the most terrible opposition at the hands of "the sinners," whom the readers well know. As he has *persevered* through it all, the readers surely ought to consider him well now when they, who are saved from sin by him, are asked to put away the hampering sin and to manifest *perseverance* in running their race to a successful issue. What Christ did for them is to inspire them "in order that you may not grow tired (aorist, ingressive: get to the point of tiredness) by relaxing in your souls" (present participle, probably middle, picturing the gradual letting down of effort). The imagery of the ἵνα clause appears to be that of the runner letting himself get tired of the effort and thus quitting.

The Sons Chastised by the Father,
v. 4-13

4) The asyndeton indicates a new paragraph and a new thought, which is chastisement. This casts a new and a wonderful light on all the persecutions and the hardships the readers are to endure perseveringly,

for these inflictions are plain evidence of the sonship
of the readers: only a father who is deeply concerned
for his sons chastises them. Bastards, who have no
loving father, are left without—do the readers want to
be bastards? However painful it may be at the time,
chastisement is necessary in order to rid us of the
hampering sin (v. 1) and to produce the fruit of righteousness so that we may be true sons.

Not up to the point of blood did you (as yet)
**resist in contending against the sin; and you have
been forgetting the encouragement which reasons
with you as with sons:**

> **My son, be not treating lightly the Lord's
> chastisements,**
> **Nor be relaxing when reproved by him;**
> **For whom the Lord loveth he chastises;**
> **Moreover, he scourges every son whom he
> takes over** (as a son).

Bengel thinks that v. 4 is still figurative, *a cursu
venit ad pugilatum,* pugilism is added to racing. This
is due to the fact that v. 4 is regarded as belonging to
v. 1-3 despite the lack of a connective and despite the
connective which draws v. 4 to v. 5. Commentators
then explain that the boxing matches generally drew
blood. This verse is literal. "Up to the point of
blood" is far more than a reference to a boxer's bloody
nose, mouth, etc.; it refers to a bloody death. The
aorist states the historical fact that the readers have
not had to resist to the point of bloody martyrdom in
their athletic contest with "the sin," being face to face
with it as the antagonist. Only the last participle continues the figurative touch. We have "the hampering
sin" in v. 1 and "the sinners" in v. 3 and now again
"the sin," but it is now almost personified as a power
that may bring the readers to martyrdom. This sin
would win if in fear of blood the readers would relin-

quish their faith; it would be vanquished if the readers, unafraid of a bloody death, held fast to their faith. The reason the writer notes the fact that the readers have as yet not had to face bloody martyrdom is to clear the way for what this paragraph says about chastisements, for chastisements do not kill, they only correct. The death of martyrs belongs to a different class; it is a high, glorious distinction that is reserved for only a few while chastisements are applied to all God's sons with distinctions also but only as marks of sonship.

The readers were shrinking from further inflictions such as those mentioned in 10:32-34, which they gladly endured while they now thought to escape them by turning back and again becoming Jews. They had forgotten what God says about chastisement. God might have had the higher distinction of martyrdom in mind for them as he had for other believers, and now these readers foolishly shrink from even this lower and universal distinction which God finds necessary in the case of all his sons. The implication is that certain other believers had, indeed, been called to bloody martyrdom. Who these others were we have attempted to show in the introduction: they were the believers in the old congregation in Rome. As far as the martyrs referred to in 10:35b are concerned, we need not exclude them although they belong to the Old Testament period; Jesus is, however, in a class by himself as we see from the expression "contending against the sin," nor is Jesus ever regarded as a martyr in Scripture.

5) What has come upon the readers up to this time is only chastisement such as is common to all God's sons, and in recent days the readers have been altogether (ἐκ in the verb) forgetting the παράκλησις or "encouragement" (better than "exhortation" in this connection), the character of which (ἥτις, qualitative) is

to reason, to talk things through with us as with sons. Wisdom is personified in Proverbs just as *paraklesis* is here; her word is quoted from Prov. 3:11, 12. To treat the Lord's chastisements lightly, as something that is little, and the synonymous expression to relax (the same verb is used in v. 3) when reproved by the Lord, means to fail in appreciating what the Lord thus does for his sons, to desire to be rid of his chastisement and his reproof: the very thing the readers were thinking of doing. In the classics and in the papyri παιδεία = "education" in general; in the New Testament (see Eph. 6:4) the word means "discipline," and in the present connection painful discipline, so that we translate "chastisement," for it includes "scourging."

6) The main point of the quotation lies in the reason that prompts chastisement and reproof; the Lord administers this only to those whom he loves; all chastisements are the plainest kind of proof that he loves those who are chastised. Ἀγαπάω, however, denotes the highest type of love, the love that is full of complete understanding and of corresponding lofty purpose and not the shallow, weak, grandfatherly love (seen in Eli) which lets sons go unchastised and uncorrected.

The last line says still more: the Lord lashes or scourges *every* son whom he accepts as a son in his family. Chastisement in its severest form is thus strong evidence of one's sonship. This casts the clearest light on all persecution that God lets us bear in this life for Christ's sake. It does correct us, drive out the sin that is still in us, but only in order that we may be more truly the sons that God would have us be. The last line follows the LXX which read the Hebrew with a different and, as Delitzsch thinks, a more correct vowel pointing than appears in our Masoretic pointing; the case is like that of 10:21 where the LXX reads vowels that have the word mean "staff" while the present pointing in our Hebrew Bibles has it read "bed."

7) The writer expounds. Only a few minuscules have εἰ in place of εἰς although some of the old versions follow this reading as does the A. V.; it seems to be modeled after v. 8. Since the thought of the attested reading is very acceptable, we follow this. **For chastisement you perseveringly endure; as with sons is God dealing with you.**

The phrase and the datives have the emphasis. The two terse statements point to the main things in the quotation: 1) the aim or object of the persevering endurance (the same word that occurs in v. 1, 2, 3) is "chastisement"; 2) this is treatment of the readers "as sons" (προσφέρεται, "he is treating you," M.-M. 552). These are the things the readers have been forgetting entirely. They are emphatically pointed out here. The two statements are now combined in the self-answering question: **For what son** (is there) **whom a father does not chastise?** Sonship and fatherly chastisement invariably go together.

8) This involves a negative deduction. **Now if you are without chastisement, of which all have become partakers, then are you bastards and not sons.** This is a regular negative syllogism. Major premise: All sons are partakers of chastisement. Minor premise: You are without chastisement. Conclusion: You are bastards and not sons. "If" in the condition of reality states that this conclusion inevitably follows with its judgment on the readers the moment they are no more chastised by their heavenly Father. This deduction is effective for the readers because they were growing weary of God's chastisement and were thinking of getting away from it.

Νόθος, here an adjective used as a noun, is one who has no known father, a bastard. Thayer and von Hofmann narrow the word down to mean the son of a concubine or a slave, and the latter then argues that God cannot have sons of this kind. Esau would be a case in point. Such an idea is not indicated in the words of the writer.

9) The negative syllogism is followed by an argument from the less to the greater which pursues the matter of chastisement a step farther and still keeps the human analogy. **Furthermore, we had the fathers of our flesh as chastisers and kept respecting them; shall we not much rather be subject to the Father of the spirits and live?**

The imperfects refer to an indefinite past duration of time, indefinite because it varies with the individual readers. We all, who are grown up, had earthly fathers who chastised us, and yet despite their chastising us we ever respected them (the middle "turn oneself to" is used in this sense). Shall we not much rather be in subjection to our heavenly Father and not only "respect him," give him honor, but far more "live," ever receive true spiritual life from him? The question again answers itself.

The comparison covers three points: 1) the kinds of fathers 2) the time of their fatherhood 3) our relation to them. The one kind were "the fathers of our flesh," the other is "the Father of the spirits." These genitives have been referred to when we were discussing the question of creationism and traducianism, a question that is not even touched here much less decided in favor of the conception that our flesh or body is procreated by the earthly father while our immortal spirit is created by God in the instant of our bodily procreation and in that instant joined to our body. Both body and spirit are derived from our parents, and God is the creator of both. "He has given me my body and soul, eyes, ears, and all my members, my reason and all my senses, and still preserves them," a simple Catechism truth on which no erudite, speculative commentator shall confuse us. These genitives do not elucidate the questions as to from whom and in what way we originate; they are genitives of relation and no more: the fathers who have to do with our bodily nature and themselves have this nature; the Father who has to do with far more than our flesh, with the spirits, both the bodiless, angelic spirits and the embodied human spirits, ourselves, all human spirits. This one divine Father is thus infinitely above all human fathers.

Hence we only "had" the latter fathers; in the case of most of us they are dead and gone, their whole father activity is ended. While the writer naturally says "fathers," the word by no means intends to exclude mothers who also certainly were our "chastisers." In v. 8 "son" and "sons" in no way exclude daughters — or is this writer speaking only *to* males and *of* males? This other Father is spoken of with a future tense which reaches from the present into the indefinite future: "shall we not much rather be in subjection" to him? His is to be an eternal fatherhood for us. But this is a question that is directed to our volition and not one about a fatherhood (creatorship) that simply exists but about a filial relation and attitude that we should assume, acknowledge and assume gladly. The question does not deal with a parallel: "We *had* earthly fathers; shall we not *have* a heavenly Father?" The question goes beyond that: "We *respected* our *earthly* chastisers; shall we not *be subject* to our heavenly Father?"

The point dwells on our relation, which our will may alter to our terrible detriment or may retain in the normal way to our great advantage. We should not be misled by the verbal correspondence: καὶ ἐνετρεπόμεθα — καὶ ζήσομεν. The tenses warn against making these two parallel: an imperfect that lies wholly in the past, a future that continues into eternity.

Much more should the meaning of the verbs prevent such a paralleling. Our having *respected* the earthly fathers is greatly advanced by asking about *being subject* to the heavenly Father. While being subject to him includes our willing acceptance of his chastisements it means far more, namely willing acceptance of our entire relation to him as our Father, we being his sons. It is thus that "we shall live"; the verb is used as it was in 10:38. This is a question, and hence the two future tenses are deliberative (see R. 875 on this use of the future): "Do the readers want this result of their relation to the heavenly Father?" Surely, they do. The verb means "to possess the true ζωή," the life that makes us true sons of this Father (John 3:15, 16). The future tense is not to be referred only to the hereafter, it begins now and extends into eternity. Blessed relation, indeed, that assures our possessing this life forever, and that not in spite of the chastisements it entails but as making these chastisements an aid for ever remaining in this spiritual life.

10) "For" explains the matter a little more fully and retains the comparison of the less and the greater: **For they kept chastising for a few days according to what seemed good to them; but he for what** (really) **profits so that we partake of his holiness;** οἱ μέν and ὁ δέ contrast the two. The imperfect "kept chastising" is the same as that used in v. 9. These earthly fathers did the best they could for the short time during which they had their children as minors. "According to what appeared good to them" (τὸ δοκοῦν, the present neuter participle) passes no judgment on the fathers but only marks their natural limitation just as "for a few days" indicates the limitation regarding the time at their disposal.

The chastising of our heavenly Father is a far greater thing, which we are to appreciate accordingly. Instead of mechanically contrasting the time: "for all the days of our earthly life" and the insight: "according to what seems good to him," the writer at once reaches much farther: "but he for what (really) profits" (again a neuter present participle). Those earthly fathers could do only what seemed good to *them* when they were chastising; all chastising of the heavenly Father rests on (ἐπί) what is actually profitable for us. There is never a mistake either subjectively or objectively on his part; the only question is: "Shall we subject ourselves and receive this blessed profit?" What this profit is, is made plain by the added clause. This is generally regarded as expressing purpose or intent under the impression that εἰς τό must mean purpose if at all possible. By ridding ourselves of this restriction we are free to find purpose, contemplated result, or actual result, according to which fits best. Contemplated result is surely correct here: "so that we partake of his holiness," an aorist to express actuality.

Like all derivatives of ἅγιος, ἁγιότης is not found in secular Greek and, with the exception of II Macc. 15:2, appears only here. It is an essential attribute of God. Absolutely holy himself, not only separated from sin but reacting against all sin, God is the source of holiness for all who are holy. Those who are holy are so only because they partake of his holiness. Our partaking of God's holiness is often taken to mean no more than similarity to God in moral character, his chastisements producing this character in us. In G. K. 115 this is narrowed down to our final perfect holiness in heaven. We agree with C.-K. 55 that the thought can here scarcely be only ethical and moral but must be soteriological and refer to the saving gift offered to us, in which we share, for the acceptance of which chastisement is to make us more and more ready. We may add that all holiness and Godlikeness in us has the whole of soteriology back of it and cannot be separated from this its source. Since we are to be ἅγιοι and ἡγιασμένοι already in this life we are partakers of God's holiness now although it is true that perfect holiness is ours only at the end.

11) The better reading is δέ. The writer takes up the last point in regard to our chastisement. **Now every chastisement for the present does not seem to be (a matter) of joy but of grief; yet later on it yields for those who have been exercised by means of it peaceful fruit of righteousness.**

Μέν and δέ contrast only the expressions of time: "for the present" (present neuter participle) — "later on." The two genitives are not ablatives: springing from joy — from grief (R., W. P. and *Grammar*), for this would be a strange thought; they are either predicative (our versions thus translate by means of adjectives) or the Greek idiom "to be of" which equals "to belong to." Those who expand "all chastisement" so as to include all chastisement by human fathers must, after all, in the second clause think only of chastisement by the heavenly Father. Every time God chastises us it does not seem to us to be a matter of joy but only a matter of grief. The writer does not deny this but indicates that this seeming is due only to our shortsightedness. Chastisement seems to be a matter to grieve over "for the time being"; "afterward," when we have its valuable fruit, it seems the reverse. Matt. 5:10-12.

The statement is the more effective because it is worded objectively. This objectiveness takes care also of the fact that some believers are not shortsighted but are like the Twelve who bore all chastisement and persecution with rejoicing (Acts 5:41). Not all who receive God's chastisement obtain its blessed fruit but only "they who have been exercised by its means" (the perfect tense to indicate the enduring effect). While the figure of the athlete is found at the beginning of the chapter it still lingers in the reader's mind and is thus revived by the verb γυμνάζω. When the strain and struggle of the spiritual athlete are over, he receives the reward. This is "peaceful fruit of righteousness," a compact expression in which the genitive is appositional: fruit = righteousness, the idea of peace is added by the adjective. This is the so-called acquired righteousness, yet it is forensic since God is the judge who passes his verdict on this fruit. Its peacefulness is the taste of sweetness which we experience when all is well between us and God. Chastisement tries us out; persecution reveals whether we shall be true to God, and when it does this it reveals that we are righteous, and that our soul may rest in peace.

12) Admonition rounds out this section: **Wherefore straighten out the limp hands and the paralyzed knees and make straight paths for your feet in order that the lame thing may not get turned off wrong but rather be cured.**

In v. 12 the wording alludes to Old Testament language such as that found in Isa. 35:3, and v. 13 alludes to Prov. 4:26. Allusion is not quotation. The figurative language cannot be made physical, for a man who has paralyzed knees cannot straighten them up so as to bear him. The readers are allowing themselves to grow disheartened amid the persecutions that have been coming upon them. This laming, paralyzing discouragement they are fully able to shake off and so are able to straighten themselves up again in the full strength of faith. In the preceding verses the writer furnishes them full power to do this, and we may add all that this epistle has presented as the basis for these verses. He, therefore, now issues the peremptory (aorist) call: "Brace up!"

13) With this goes the allied call to make straight tracks for their feet (not "with" their feet). These tracks or paths are the thoughts of the readers, which are to be true, straight, leading directly to their spiritual goal. All false and even inadequate thoughts

about persecution are like twisted paths that run off in all directions so that the feet do not know where they are going. To the order: "Brace up!" there is added the second: "Go straight!" Both apply to the heart and to the mind.

The neuter τὸ χωλόν is "the lame thing" and may refer to whatever is still lame in any individual after these orders have been obeyed; or more likely to the lame part of the body of the readers, the spiritual cripples among them. If there were a mass of crooked, twisted thoughts in the hearts of the membership generally, this lame contingent would get turned off completely (passive and also aorist). Instead of that this lame part is to get cured (again passive and aorist). The readers who brace up and go straight will thereby not only carry the lame along, they will thereby effect a cure of the lame. The first part of v. 13 is a perfect hexameter; the variant reading which spoils it is textually too weak to be allowed to do this (R. 421).

The Warning Found in Esau, v. 14-17

14) The writer has more to say regarding what the readers must do to prevent anyone of their members from going wrong and perhaps contaminating many others. His admonition turns to warning and offers the sad example of Esau. Verses 14-17 should be read as a unit; when this is not done, parts of the whole are misunderstood.

Peace continue to pursue with all, and the sanctification without which no one shall see the Lord! If this were a general admonition in a series of similar admonitions, we might translate "with all men," i. e., both inside and outside of the church (our versions). It would then be a parallel to Rom. 12:18; however, in the present context which centers on "the lame thing" (v. 13) and on any individual who may go wrong the parallel is Rom. 14:19: peace with all the members of the church so that no dissension may afford anyone cause for turning from Christ. This pursuit of peace is a part of the wider obligation of the whole membership with reference to its individuals, namely all that is comprised in "the sanctification, without which no one shall get to see (ingressive future) the Lord" (Matt. 5:8).

Ἁγιασμός is a word that expresses an action. It is not *Heiligkeit* but *Heiligung*, which is well described in G. K. 115 as always proceeding from a holy person, and thus in the case of self-sanctification (as here) always presupposing the holiness that is obtained by Christ's reconciliation in justification. The word denotes a process by which we become separated unto God in our entire life and conduct. We, who are already ἅγιοι by faith, are ever to continue in pursuit of ἁγιασμός, a life that is more and more sanctified to God. It is true that peace thus refers to every one of our fellow members, and sanctification to the Lord.

15) Verse 14 is only the preamble, the main concern is stated in the participle used in v. 15 with its three object clauses of warning: **continuing to exercise oversight lest anyone be dropping away from the grace of God; lest any root of bitterness springing up be causing trouble and by means of it many get to be contaminated; lest there be any fornicator or profane one like Esau, who for one meal gave away his own primogeniture. For you know that even when afterward wanting to inherit the blessing he was rejected, for he did not find a place for repentance although having sought it (the blessing) with tears.**

Episkopos is a bishop; the participle bids all the readers act the part of *episkopoi*, overseers, by exercising continuous oversight over each other. The three μή clauses merely unfold the ἵνα μή clause used in v. 13, "that the lame thing may not turn off in the wrong direction." The three sides of such an act are now unfolded: 1) loss of God's grace for the person himself 2) damage to many others 3) inability to make the loss good as shown by the example of Esau. The three clauses refer to the same person. The copula is to be supplied in the first and the third clause; it is omitted in the first for a special reason: the predicate is a participle, and the omission of the copula avoids the appearance of a periphrastic tense form, which is not intended by the writer. After the copula is omitted in the first clause it is omitted also in the third although the predicate of this clause consists of two nouns. We have two perfect trimeters in v. 14, 15: οὗ χωρὶς οὐδεὶς ὄψεται τὸν Κύριον; and: ἐπισκοποῦντες μή τις ὑστερῶν ἀπό. B.-D. 487.

The calamity ever to be guarded against is first of all "that anyone may drop away from the grace of God," literally, "fall behind" and thus be separated "from the saving grace of God." We should say "lose the grace of God." The picture is that of believers being carried forward to eternal salvation by God's grace, and instead of being carried forward to heaven like the rest this individual is left standing behind and is thus lost.

"Grace" is the unmerited *favor Dei* that comes to the guilty sinner in the gospel to free him from his guilt and sin, to make him a child of God, to keep and to bless him as such. To have that grace and then to drop away from it is calamity indeed. Yet the readers were in danger of doing this very thing by shrinking from persecution and thus being inclined to think less and less of Christ and again falling in love with their former Judaism.

If anyone among the readers thus loses the grace of God, it is not merely a loss for himself, it is also a danger for many others: "lest any root of bitterness springing up be causing trouble." The wording is adopted from the LXX of Deut. 29:18 (it is an allusion and not a quotation): μή τίς ἐστι ἐν ὑμῖν ῥίζα ἄνω φύουσα ἐν χολῇ καὶ πικρίᾳ. Little is gained by referring to the Hebrew of Deuteronomy and by discussing the text of the LXX which the writer may have had, for he is not quoting.

We all use allusion, i. e., borrow some word, some expression, some turn of phrase from well-known writers and modify these to fit our purpose. This is done to embellish our writing; it is sometimes done almost unconsciously. Anyone who is steeped in Scripture language will thus keep using allusion to its language; this will sometimes be faint, sometimes plain and strong as it is in the present instance. Peter uses "gall of bitterness" in Acts 8:23, a fainter allusion to Deuteronomy. In I Macc. 1:11 Antiochus Epiphanes is called ῥίζα ἁμαρτωλός, "a sinful root"; so here, too, "any root of bitterness" denotes a person, one such as the writer has just described as having left the grace of God. "A root springing up" to strong growth is a figure that is used repeatedly in Scripture to designate a person who develops a certain quality and thus affects others.

The attributive genitive describes the root or person. Some take "bitterness" in the sense of poisonous, which may pass. The point is the effect this person has upon the rest of the readers with whom he comes into contact: he "troubles or perturbs" them with his bitterness. Himself bitter against Christ, he embitters others against Christ, poisons them if you will. The verb is derived from ὄχλος. The writer's verb ἐνοχλῇ is not even in sound due to the phrase ἐν χολῇ which is used in Deut. 29:18.

A second clause completes the thought: "and by means of it (such a root of bitterness, i. e., such a person) many get to be defiled or contaminated" (ingressive aorist). It is bad enough when one loses the grace of God by becoming bitter against Christ; it is much worse when such a man spreads his bitterness so as to defile (μιαίνω) many in addition to himself. This verb would have a ritual meaning to readers of the LXX (cf., John 18:28): those defiled and made unclean would be debarred from every approach to God.

The thought is greatly reduced when it is referred only to the moral life, to sins of various kinds. It goes far deeper, it denotes the defilement that is due to the loss of God's grace, to sinking back into the filth and the guilt of sin, to the bitterness which scorns Christ and his blood and his righteousness. The writer is in no way blind to the danger which would ensue for the mass of his readers if even a single one of them should fall away from Christ and return to Judaism. We may say that the danger was the greater because the readers were a compact body, all of them Jewish Christians, all worshiping in their old synagogues in Rome, which had now become Christian churches. By returning to Judaism some influential former rabbi among them might draw a large number with him. In fact, as these synagogues had become Christian, so they might again become Jewish. *Obsta principiis!* Resist the beginnings!

16) The third clause warns against the inability of escaping from irreparable loss and damage after these are once incurred: "lest there be any fornicator or profane one like Esau, who for one meal gave away his own primogeniture." Some commentators seriously discuss whether sexual fornication is referred to or not and then often conclude that it is and charge the writer with adopting the Jewish notion that Esau was a fornicator (of which Scripture says nothing).

Others separate "fornicator" and "profane one" and then disregard this sexual fornicator and attach all that is said about Esau only to βέβηλος. Why should this one sin of sexual fornication be mentioned in this context when the writer discusses this sin where it properly belongs, in 13:4, in the section that deals with sins and virtues? The inadequate interpretation is not made right by setting up the claim that spiritual fornication is never predicated of an individual. Let us look at the text. This does not deal with a lone individual, with a lone moral lapse of one person, but with irreparable damage that may result for οἱ πολλοί as the result of one man's losing the grace of God, especially when he is one of the leaders who turns back to Judaism.

The writer at once explains πόρνος by adding ἢ βέβηλος and by explaining what he means by this by giving an example, "as (for instance) Esau." We often use "or" in the same way for the very purpose of excluding misunderstanding. "Or" means that "fornicator" is not to be understood in the physical but in the spiritual sense, i. e., as the sin of "a profane one," an "unhallowed one." Both terms carry forward the ritual connotation of contamination which is so abominable to Jewish ears. "Fornicator" emphasizes all the implied vileness from which the readers would recoil; and "profane one," which is made alternative by "or," brings out the idea that the person referred to is a fornicator in the sense of caring for nothing that is sacred or holy, treating it as secular or common.

Even this is not enough for the writer. An example very often elucidates a definition more than the addition of other terms would. We have such an example in Esau and in the way in which he traded away his own right of being the first-born for one βρῶσις or meal (one satisfaction of his appetite) as if that sacred right were a common thing to be used in trade for another common thing. The reflexive "his own" helps to bring out the distinctness of Esau's great right; he did not have it in common with his own twin brother.

'Απέδοτο, which is also written ἀπέδετο, is the second aorist middle.

17) "For" shows from the sequel of Esau's history that his birthright was anything but a common thing, and how fateful it was for him to act the πόρνος or βέβηλος by treating it so. Esau's birthright did not involve only headship of the family and great property rights as it did in the case of the first-born in Oriental lands and as it still does in royal families of our own time; it involved the inheritance of "the blessing," i. e., the Abrahamitic blessing, the bloodline of the Messiah. What Esau threw away for one meal was the ancestorship of the Messiah and the prerogatives which went with this. Moreover, this was one of those rights which, once lost, could not be recovered no matter what the effort put forth. Once gone, forever gone! After that: Too late, too late! There are acts that, once done, can never be undone. That is what Esau illustrates in the way of warning.

We regard ἴστε as the indicative: "You know that," etc., as the readers know; not as the imperative since the readers did not need to be told: "Know that," etc. They know "that even when he afterward wanted to inherit the blessing" by getting back his right of primogeniture "he was rejected" as one who had been tested out and found wanting and was thus cast aside. God is the agent of the passive. After the attitude which Esau had assumed toward the inheritance, which came to a climax in his cheap trading away the inheritance, God refused to have him as the heir.

"For he did not find a place for repentance although having sought it (the blessing) with tears" = he had repentance enough for his act, but there was no place where he might put it in order to make it restore the inheritance to him although he most earnestly (ἐκ in the participle) sought this inheritance. It is sometimes asked whether μετανοίας or τὴν εὐλογίαν is the antecedent of αὐτήν so that the R. V. and others insure the latter by placing "for he found no place of repentance" in parentheses. The A. V. chooses the other antecedent. There is no ambiguity in the Greek. The antecedent cannot be the genitive that is dependent on the other noun, for the two form one concept and are in this case even articulated; it must be the independent articulated noun τὴν εὐλογίαν. Our English "it" as a translation of αὐτήν leaves us at sea and would refer to τόπον (a masculine in the Greek). The English must thus use some device to convey what the Greek intends to say. Transposition would do it: "even when afterward wanting to inherit the blessing although having sought it with tears, he was rejected, for he did not find a place for repentance."

It is unnecessary to say that Esau sought *repentance* with tears; tears are themselves evidence of repentance. This leads Riggenbach to seek for some other meaning for μετάνοια, but this word is not the antecedent. Even the καίπερ clause is participial and, like θέλων, modifies the main verb "was rejected." Gen. 27:30, etc., shows plainly that Esau *did* repent, strong man that he was, "with a great and exceeding bitter cry." Μετάνοια = a change of mind, and this fits exactly. But the damage had been done, it was impossible for him to find "a place" where any repentance of his would do any good for recovering his birthright and thus "the blessing" of being the heir who was to continue the Messianic bloodline. Certain types of damage are irrevocable.

All this has nothing to do with Esau's eternal salvation or predestination. Our passage as well as Rom. 9:10-13 are misinterpreted by Calvinists (see the author on Rom. 9). "The blessing" is not Esau's salvation, which was sold to Jacob. Nor does the writer make the application that, if any of his readers goes wrong, he will irrevocably lose his salvation. It is inadequate to point to 6:6, for the *impossibility* of repentance is asserted there; but Esau *did* repent. What is taught by the example of Esau is the fact that, if one becomes a root of bitterness and defiles many others, although he repent, no repentance of his will ever revoke the damage he will have done to others. A terrible thing for anyone who is still Christian as the readers are to contemplate! It should be the final dread that would make every reader shrink back from returning to Judaism and leaving Christ.

The Holy City and the Assembly to Which You Have Come, v. 18-24

18) In one grand sentence (v. 18-24) in which the writer draws a comparison with Judaism he presents to his readers to what they have come as Christians. In the preceding admonition he asks that no one drop away from the grace of God and do irreparable damage to others; with "for" he explains what this grace really is, or rather to what it has brought them.

Some commentators leave us under a wrong impression, namely that as Jews the readers had had only Moses and the law while they now have Christ and the gospel. This view is unhistorical. Chapter 11 corrects it. The Jews had Abraham and the Abrahamitic covenant with all the Messianic promises, and we are told in 11:39, 40 that, although God fully attested their faith in his Messianic promises, all the Old Testament saints died without seeing these promises fulfilled in Jesus (Matt. 13:16, 17). In the development of God's plans, when the children of Abraham became a nation and were brought out of Egypt under Moses (11:27, etc.), the Jews had come only as far as Sinai and the giving of the law 430 years after Abraham (Gal. 3:17), this law being given to them because of transgression in order to keep them in the knowledge of sin (Rom. 3:20).

Hebrews 12:18 451

But the readers have come to the actual fulfillment of the promise made to Abraham, to Jesus Christ and to all that he has actually brought. This is the history of grace. The present paragraph must be read in the light of this history. The tragic mistake of the Jews was the fact that they clung to Sinai and Moses, to the law, and were blind to the covenant of Abraham with its promise of the Messiah and thus blind also to the fulfillment of this promise in Jesus. The readers who had made this mistake and had been rescued from this mistake were inclined to fall back into it in order to escape the persecutions that were connected with their faith in Jesus. This entire epistle seeks to keep them from taking this fatal step.

For you have not come to what is touched and to fire having been set ablaze and to murk and to blackness and to tempest and to trumpet's blast and to sound of utterances, which those who heard made entreaty that there be not added for them (any more) word, for they were not bearing (i. e., not able to bear) **the thing being enjoined: And if a beast (even) touch the Mount it shall be stoned! and — so frightful was the appearance — Moses said: I am terrified and quaking; on the contrary,** etc.

The writer's skillful Greek seems awkward even when parts of it are rendered only *ad sensum* as is done in our versions, and still more awkward when we seek to conserve something of the Greek idiom; it is actually masterly and rich in meaning. Note all the anarthrous nouns, to say nothing of the Greek tenses and what each conveys. By omitting the articles the author makes all the nouns strongly qualitative although the whole description is strictly historical.

The very first tense, a perfect, is significant: "you have not come" to what is here described = to remain with this as the final thing, the τελείωσις. All that transpired at Sinai to which God brought Israel was not the completion of the Abrahamitic testament and promise. It was added only because of the transgression (Gal. 3:19; Rom. 5:20) until Christ should come. The law made nothing complete (7:19), it came in only on the side. It was temporary, intended only for Israel. With this perfect tense the writer says: "You have not come to Sinai as the destination where you are to remain." With the same perfect tense he says in v. 22: "You have come ever to remain to Mount Zion." Bengel and then Delitzsch find seven items to which the readers have not come in v. 18-21 and again seven to which they have come in v. 22-24; but only for the first two and the last two items in these two sevens is correspondence claimed, and hence the two sevens would be merely formal for us.

The addition of ὄρει is so poorly attested that it can scarcely be admitted into the text on the plea of a very early omission in transcription. Yet it might just as well be there as "Mount" is certainly used in v. 20 and in the opposite "Mount Zion" in v. 22. Its omission by no means makes one item of ψηλαφωμένῳ καὶ κεκαυμένῳ πυρί whether we translate "to what may be touched and is kindled with fire" (i. e., the Mount, regarding πυρί as instrumental, R., W. P.), or "to fire that may be touched and has been kindled." Fire is certainly not something to be touched. The difference in the tenses of the two participles causes us to regard them as two items: "to what is touched," i. e., the Mount (R. 1118, and B.-D. 65, 3 have this mean what is "touchable" like a verbal in -τος), "and the fire having been set ablaze."

The present participle is simply descriptive: the Mount is touched (or "touchable") at any time (present participle), even now; unlike Mount Zion, Sinai is earthly, a mass of rock that any person may touch. The absence of the article describes it as being such a thing. The perfect participle that is used with "fire" is entirely different: fire, once set to blazing and continuing to blaze for a certain length of time, is then extinguished. This participle lies wholly in the past and denotes only a certain length of time during that past. The fact that two items are intended is evident also from the observation that the writer would not begin with fire and say nothing about *where* such fire was located. The place is earthly and still remains; the fire is unearthly and blazed for a time.

The next five items are also qualitative (minus articles): γνόφος, "murk," an impenetrable black pall. Then ζόφος, "blackness," which is stronger than "darkness." Then θύελλα, "tempest" or "whirlwind." All is unearthly at this earthly Mount. Compare Deut. 4:11 and 5:22.

19) The "trumpet's blast" which made all the people in the camp tremble is quoted from Exod. 19:16; the "sound of utterances," from Deut. 4:12, when, according to Exod. 20:1, etc., God spoke the Ten Commandments from the Mount; and the petition that no more should be spoken in this way from Deut. 5:25 and 18:16. The genitive ἧς, the object of οἱ ἀκούσαντες, refers to "voice" as belonging to a speaker, the accusative would refer to what the voice says; the speaker's very voice terrified. Λόγον refers to contents. This clause can be translated smoothly only *ad sensum*. The remark made in G. K. 195 to the effect that the request, which was originally made in humble fear of God and was acknowledged by God, is in Hebrews treated "as sinful declination of divine revelation" is unjustifiable, for the very next clause explains and justifies this request.

20) The Israelites "were not bearing the rigor" of an injunction that was as severe as this one (τὸν διαστελλόμενον, note the article): "And if a beast (even) touch the Mount it shall be stoned!" In Exod. 19, 10-13 this command which was given in regard to men is extended also to beasts; it is thus cited here (not verb-

ally) as an indication of the awfulness of all the manifestations. "The thing being enjoined" is not the Decalogue but, as the article indicates, the command regarding a beast.

21) Moses' own exclamation is added as being corroborative and still stronger: "I am terrified and quaking!" In Deut. 9:14 the LXX has καὶ ἔκφοβός εἰμι διὰ τὸν θυμὸν καὶ τὴν ὀργήν. While this occurred when Moses was coming down from the Mount (Deut. 9:19), there is no reason for saying that the writer of Hebrews was inexact in reporting Moses or for surmising that the writer is merely following a Jewish tradition. As to the wording, the previous quotation already shows that the author is citing only the substance without attention to verbal exactness. He is doing the same with the words of Moses. As to the situation, Moses was just coming down out of the thick darkness and was thus under the impression of the terrors of the law against all violators. The construction is perfectly in order when we read as parenthetical: "so frightful was the appearance" (present passive participle = the whole thing made apparent to the senses). Thus καί introduces εἶπεν.

22) **You have not come, etc., on the contrary, you have come to Mount Zion and to the living God's city, heavenly Jerusalem; and to myriads of angels in festal assembly; and to a church of first-born enrolled in (the) heavens; and to a Judge, God of all; and to spirits of righteous ones who have been brought to completion; and to a new testament's Mediator, Jesus; and to blood of sprinkling speaking something better than Abel.**

On the perfect tense see v. 18: "you have come," i. e., are still there ever to remain. When Israel came to Sinai, Israel had reached only a way station. Sinai was not to be the completion of the testament and the promise given to Abraham. Sinai was necessary only because of transgression. The completion is Mount Zion and all that goes with Mount Zion.

We have used the semicolon to separate the items. We find that there are eight and not seven. As in v. 18, 19 each new item was added by καί, this is again done in v. 22-24. Since the writer uses καί thus in two lists, it is unwarranted to assume that he should use two καί in different ways, namely in v. 18 only to connect two modifying participles as one item and in v. 22 to connect only πόλει and ὄρει as one item: Zion, "mount and city" of the living God, with "heavenly Jerusalem" as an apposition to both.

Delitzsch has Mount Zion = τὰ ἅγια, the Holy of Holies in heaven, and the city = ἡ σκηνή, the Tabernacle (8:1, 2; 9:11, 12), the former being the place where the divine *doxa* "dwells in sacred seclusion from the world of his creatures." But that is rather fanciful. "Zion" is the name of the highest elevation on which Jerusalem is built; the Temple hill Moriah is of a lower elevation. This seems to be the reason the term "Zion" or "Mount Zion" and not Moriah (although this bore the Temple, the earthly place of God's presence, where Abraham built the altar to offer Isaac) came to be idealized to denote the sacred city, the land, or the people, and then also heaven, the home of the blessed with God. The term "Zion" excludes the idea of God's dwelling alone "in sacred seclusion"; "Zion" never connotes the Holy of Holies. "Mount" is added because Sinai, too, was a mount. Israel came to the physical mountain; this Zion is heavenly. Both are called Mount, but what a vast difference!

This first item takes us only a little of the way, and hence the second is necessary: "and to the living God's city, heavenly Jerusalem." Sinai has no city; none could be built upon its crags or its pinnacle. While "Mount" marks the resemblance between Zion and Sinai, "city" adds the vast difference between them, and "city of the living God," like "heavenly Jerusalem," removes us from earth altogether. God only came down to Sinai accompanied by the phenomena mentioned in v. 18, 19 and not in order to remain there but only to remain a short time, only to communicate with Israel while this people stood afar off. The city of the living God, the heavenly Jerusalem, is the home and dwelling place of God and of all his people forever; the earthly city of Jerusalem is its faint shadow.

How far removed is the idea that God reserves Zion for himself while Jerusalem is reserved for his people we see at once when we note the earthly city in which the Temple with its Holy of Holies stood on Moriah and not on Zion. The idea that "Mount Zion" and "city of the living God, heavenly Jerusalem," constitute only a verbal difference is nullified the moment we think of Sinai and of the kind of a mount that it is. This is the city referred to in 11:10, 16, also in 13:14 (Rev. 21:2; especially 21:10, etc.). "The living God" is repeatedly used by the writer (3:12; 9:14; 10:31), each time according to the context; thus he is here the founder and the king of this city, which is, therefore, eternal and blessed forever.

Since καί separates these items, we construe: καὶ μυριάσιν ἀγγέλων πανηγύρει: "and to myriads of angels in festal assembly," the latter being a dative of manner. Some may prefer to make this an apposition to the first dative. Sinai, too, had its angels, but they did not appear in festal assembly, see Acts 7:53 and Gal. 3:19. The word "myriads" or ten thousands is repeatedly used with reference to angels (Dan. 7:10; Jude 14; Rev. 5:11). Since Christ has entered heaven after his work of redemption, the whole angel world rings with festal panegyrics (Rev. 5:1-12). Πανήγυρις is a general festal assembly and not merely a "general assembly" (our versions), and for this reason also it cannot be joined to ἐκκλησία. The church on earth is not as yet a festal assembly.

23) The fourth item reads: "and to a church of first-born enrolled in (the) heavens." This is the church on earth, for its members are enrolled in heaven, are thus not as yet there. "First-born" denotes rank and not precedence in time. Some recall Esau (v. 16), but his was physical and temporal precedence. The word is not elsewhere used with reference to believers, and it seems to denote the fact that as first-born the heavenly inheritance, the city of God, belongs to them as the heirs. All other men receive only a share of earthly gifts which they so often fail to appreciate. The perfect participle indicates that a permanent record has been made of their names in heaven.

The expression goes back to Jesus' word spoken in Luke 10:20, but this itself goes far back into the Old Testament. Exod. 32:32 speaks of blotting out Moses' name "from thy book which thou hast written"; cf. Ps. 69:28. Isa. 4:3: "everyone that is written among the living in Jerusalem." Paul writes of his "fellow laborers whose names are in the book of life" (Phil. 4:3). Daniel does the same: In the great tribulation "thy people shall be delivered, every one that shall be found written in the book" (Dan. 12:1). The passages found in Revelation (3:5; 13:8; 20:12) are familiar, especially 21:27: through the portals of the new Jerusalem (into the eternal communion with God) none shall enter "but they which are written in the Lamb's book of life."

This figure is most probably derived from the genealogical records that were kept by the Jews. To be recorded in heaven = to be counted among the justified. The moment a man is pronounced righteous by God (i. e., is justified), his name stands recorded in heaven. If his faith ceases, his name is blotted out. "They that depart from thee shall be written in the earth because they have forsaken the Lord, the fountain of living waters," Jer. 17:13. See also *C. Tr.* 1071, 25, etc.; 1085, 66 and 70.

"And to a Judge, God of all" (not neuter: "of all things") should not be reversed: "to God as Judge of all." This Judge has no limited view so that, when he judges some one person or a group, he may err; he is God of all. The idea of "Judge" is the fact that he will avenge any and all wrongs done to the righteous who may ever appeal to him for vindication against their oppressors; his court is ever open. So he is "Judge of the widows" (Ps. 68:5) and also "Father of the fatherless" who sees to it that their rights are not violated and punishes those who abuse these helpless ones. In v. 19 we are told that he proclaimed his holy law, and that those who heard shrank from the terror of his voice; here those whose names are recorded in heaven may freely place their sad case before him and be sure of vindication.

"And to spirits of righteous ones who have been brought to completion," i. e., brought to the final goal by a blessed death, the perfect participle stating that they remain there. The first of the great men listed in chapter 11, Abel, received God's testimony that he is "righteous." So we do not debate as to whether the Old Testament believers are included. The fact that πνεύματα means the spirits who have departed from their earthly bodies should not be doubted. God has judged them, pronounced them righteous (Rom. 3:24-26). Τετελειωμένοι, "having been brought to completion," will not be fully understood until we follow this word and its various forms through our epistle. Jesus is "the completer" of our faith as he is its author (v. 2). Not without us are the Old Testament believers brought to completion (11:40), for the completion of *all* believers in both Testaments is found in Christ. Study the nouns, the verbs, and the adjective in 2:10; 5:9; 6:1; 7:11, 19; 9:9, 11; 10:1, 14. The spirits of the blessed are now complete, their bodies will soon follow.

24) The list is continued with a consideration of him on whom all the foregoing depends: "and to a new testament's Mediator, Jesus," and then there is added wherewith he accomplishes his mediation: "and blood of sprinkling, speaking something better than Abel." The anarthrous nouns are qualitative. On "testament" review 7:22, on "Mediator" 8:6. Called καινή in 8:8, this testament is now said to be even νέα, not merely new as replacing the Mosaic testament which was old but as being totally different, beside which the Mosaic testament with what it had of promises concerning the earthly Canaan does not deserve serious consideration. The newness of this testament has nothing to do with the testament that was given to Abraham, for this stands forever and cannot be called old in any sense since Christ fulfilled its promise and sealed the inheritance to all the heirs.

Christ did this with his own blood (9:14) which is called "blood of sprinkling" (10:22) because it cleanses those who have it applied to them in faith. "Sprinkling" is derived from the Mosaic ritual (9:19-22). This blood makes the testament "eternal" (13:20). It speaks "something better than Abel"; κρεῖττον is scarcely an adverb: "better," i. e., in a better way; but a neuter noun. Abel, who was murdered by Cain, i. e., Abel's blood (Gen. 4:10), cried for vengeance. Christ, too, was murdered, but his blood speaks as we read in Luke 23:34. Christ's blood speaks of expiation, reconciliation, pardon even as it is intended for sprinkling and cleansing (I John 1:7). Παρά = "than."

How have we come to all that is here named and described? Not in a physical way as the Israelites once came to Sinai but spiritually by faith. As far as the church of first-born ones is concerned, we are in its blessed communion; as far as Jesus and his blood are concerned, we have the cleansing; as far as heaven, the angels, the glorified saints are concerned, we have come very near to them and will soon be in the Eternal City. How is any reader able to think of turning back after he has come thus?

Let Us Be Grateful, v. 25-29

25) The admonition is not presented as a deduction from the things to which we have come in Christ; no "therefore," οὖν, is inserted. The connection, however, becomes clear when we note that v. 18-24 state to what we have already come while this admonitory section tells us to what we are presently to come when God will again shake not only the earth but also the heaven. The τελείωσις, the completion, of which the writer has said so much, is in his mind; it shall extend to heaven and to earth (Rev. 21:1, 2). Instead of adding "the unshakable kingdom" to which we have almost come to the list given in v. 22-24 the writer reserves it (since we have not as yet actually come to it) for the admonition with which he desires to continue.

See lest you refuse him that speaks! It is God who speaks in all to which we have come. To refuse him = to say "no" to him and to what he says, to deny its reality. This would be unbelief, the very thing to which the readers were inclining. The negative admonition is a litotes, for the writer wants his readers to accept and to believe what God is speaking to them. He has just said regarding the blood of Jesus that it "*speaks* something better than Abel" and so repeats that word in the expression "him that speaks," namely God by means of this expiating blood which speaks of grace, pardon, eternal salvation. God spoke also on Sinai, there his voice struck terror into those who heard.

Let no reader think that because God now speaks pure grace he may refuse to hear in humble faith. **For if they did not escape when coming to refuse him making divine communication on earth, we on our part** (shall not escape) **when turning away from him** (making divine communication) **from** (the) **heavens; whose voice, etc.**

This is self-evident; it is impossible to assume the opposite. The Greek can condense the apodosis; the English must fill in the elision. The condition is one of reality even as the Israelites did not escape. The first participle has no article and is an aorist of fact: "when actually refusing," or ingressive: "when coming to refuse" by the disobedience of unbelief. Τὸν χρηματίζοντα is a timeless, descriptive, present participle with the article; they said "no" to the divine speaker, namely to God at Sinai. This word is used to designate any supernatural, divine communication.

We cannot refer this protasis to v. 19-21, namely to the request of the Israelites that God no longer speak with his terrifying voice from Sinai, but that he speak to them through Moses. This common interpretation states that by this request the Israelites refused God in unbelief, but this is not true; the request is also regarded as a sample of all future unbelief, but also this is not true. The Israelites refused God and his divine communication when they turned away from God and worshipped the golden calf. On that occasion they did not escape but suffered dire punishment.

Much more we on our part (emphatic ἡμεῖς) shall not escape when turning away (iterative present participle) from God who makes divine communication from heaven; in our idiom it would be "much less shall we escape." While God is the communicator in both clauses (and not Moses in the one, and Christ in the other), this does not conflict with the difference that at Sinai God makes his communication (the law) "on earth" while the communication we now hear (the gospel) is made "from (the) heavens." There is an intentional contrast in these directly opposite phrases, and no less a contrast than that God's present communication is far, far superior to the one he at one time made to the Israelites on Sinai. Although all those manifestations at Sinai were so stupendous they were, nevertheless, only "on earth," in that one locality. They magnified the law mightily indeed, yet this law came only because of transgression (Gal. 3:19), as an adjunct to the Abrahamitic testament and promise. Great as this communication was, its greatness only makes this other stand out as being vastly greater even as it comes to us "from heaven."

We see its exalted contents in v. 22-24, to which there must be added the consummation indicated in v. 26, 27. It is asked how this communication comes from heaven. We find the answer in John 15:26, 27; 16:7-15; Acts 2:11: "We hear them speak in our tongues the wonderful works of God." The Holy Spirit conveys the divine gospel communication which begins at Pentecost. As now being embodied in the New Testament writings this revelation speaks to us. These readers in Rome had heard Paul and then also Peter for a brief time (see the introduction); but the entire gospel is God's voice from heaven. The refusal to hear at Sinai was severely punished (Exod. 32:28, 35); the refusal to hear the gospel shall certainly not escape punishment. The trajection of ἐπὶ γῆς by separating it from τὸν χρηματίζοντα has been called unprecedented, but all efforts to connect it with the intervening participle cancel the contrast with ἀπ' οὐρανῶν; we shall have to learn that the Greek is flexible enough to do what it plainly does here.

26) The contrast, one communication made on earth, the other coming from heaven, is only preliminary; it is the relative clause that brings the main

contrast, which lies in what the voice did at Sinai and in what it declares it will yet do when bringing in the consummation of all that v. 22-24 contain: **whose voice shook the earth at that time but now has given promise, declaring: Yet once again I will rock not only the earth but also the heaven. Now this yet once again indicates the change of the things shaken as things that have been made in order that there may remain the things not shaken.**

The fact that the great rock-mass of Sinai shook and quaked is attested by Judges 5:4, 5; Ps. 68:8, 9; 77:18; 114:7. The writer combines this with Hag. 2:6, the promise which the same voice of God made and which, as the perfect tense implies, still stands: "Yet once again I will rock not only the earth but also the heaven." The writer quotes, not verbatim, but correctly, and inserts "not only but also" in order to emphasize the truth that this "once" will include also the visible heaven itself. To shake something is to show its instability and therefore its temporary nature. Sinai shook, it was not the final, unshakable place for Israel, who also left it behind soon enough. What happened through the voice of God at Sinai is only an advance sign of what, according to that voice, shall happen again, namely the whole earth and the very heaven about the earth shall be made to rock ($\sigma\epsilon\iota\omega$).

Although the earth and the firmament with its heavenly bodies seem so stable and permanent they are really transient; God founded the earth, and the heavens are the work of his hands, "they shall perish" (1:10). Being shakable and unstable, they cannot endure in this condition. When time ceases, when only eternity, which means timelessness, exists, no shakable things will remain. Thus, as far as the earth is concerned, the Scriptures point us to every earthquake that occurs as a sign of the transient condition of the earth, Matt. 24:29. We read still more in II Pet.

3:10-13. This is, however, promise: "the voice has promised" us this mighty coming change (v. 27). We are to look forward to it with joyful anticipation. We are to long for it as we long for the coming of the beautiful springtime when the fig tree buds and puts forth its leaves, Matt. 24:32, 33.

27) Expository δέ tells us what is contained in the prophecy and promise: when the voice says "yet once again," this indicates the μετάθεσις (the same word is used in 7:12) or "change of the things shaken as things that have been made" (the perfect describes them as being made or created by God and still existing as such). Τό makes a noun of ἔτι ἅπαξ; μετάθεσις = "change" or "removal" only in the sense of change. "As things having been made," these things are subject to the will of their Maker (Riggenbach) who might have made them to be unshakable and permanent; but God would then not have promised this final shaking and change.

Such permanency is promised in Isa. 66:22 in regard to the new heavens and the new earth: "For as the new heavens and the new earth, which I will make, shall remain before me (i. e., never to be shaken into a change), so shall your seed and your name remain." Add Isa. 65:17, etc.: "Behold, I create new heavens and a new earth; and the former shall not be remembered, nor come into mind. But be ye glad and rejoice forever in that which I create; for, behold, I create Jerusalem a rejoicing, and her people a joy. And I will rejoice in Jerusalem, and joy in my people; and the voice of weeping shall be no more heard in her, nor the voice of crying," etc.

When one is considering this subject, no single passage should be unduly stressed. If 1:10; II Pet. 3:10-12; the passages about "passing away" are so stressed they might lead us to conclude that the present heaven and the earth shall be totally annihilated in order to be replaced by a new heaven and an earth that are created *ex nihilo*. Our passage, Rom. 8:19, etc., and especially Rev. 21:1-5 reveal that annihilation will not occur but a complete change of rejuvenation, and this to the extent that the present separation of our heaven and our earth from the heaven of the blessed, glorious presence of God, the angels, and the saints will be abolished. So great shall be the "change" that is produced by this shaking which is promised by Haggai.

God's purpose or rather the result contemplated by this "yet once again" is "that there may remain (aorist, for good and all) the things not shaken" (present participle: not of a quality to be shaken), the things unshakable which Abraham expected when he lived and died in the faith of the hoped for and the unseen (11:1, 10), "the city having the foundations (hence never to be shaken), whose architect and constructor is God," "Mount Zion, a city of the living God, heavenly Jerusalem" (v. 22). This heavenly part is already existing and will at the last day come down and be joined to the transformed earthly part (Rev. 21:10-27).

The ὡς is not causal. R. 1140 says that ὡς may be causal, temporal, conditional, modal, etc., also concessive, yet he here regards the "as" as causal. The resultant sense is that *because* things have been made they are shakable and subject to change. But what about the new heaven and the new earth which are also to be made by God, the city having foundations whose architect and maker is God (11:10)? "As" denotes manner. As having been made by God = to be as he has wanted them to be, not at once of permanent and timeless but of transient form to await their final, permanent form. Although they were created in perfection (Gen. 1:31), even this perfection was not the final form. If Adam had not sinned, if he had resisted the tempter and been confirmed in holiness and righteousness like the good angels, the earth and the heavens would have become glorified; now they must wait.

We are told that ἵνα may be construed with τὴν μετάθεσιν or with τῶν πεποιημένων. But another construction may well be possible. The clause modifies the whole of what is indicated by the promise of Haggai, namely "the change of the things shaken as having been made" (this combination is not to be separated); in fact, "that there may remain the things not shaken" is the real point indicated by "yet once again," indicated so that we may know it. There is no reason for making "remain" signify "await" (a meaning that is foreign to this epistle; we have only one example of this meaning, Acts 20:23) especially in the face of Isa. 66:22: "The new heavens and the new earth, which I will make, shall *remain* before me."

28, 29) Wherefore, as receiving a kingdom unshakable, let us be grateful, whereby we serve God in a well-pleasing way together with reverence and awe, for our God is a consuming fire.

Warning against refusal (v. 25) and admonition to gratitude lie close together, in fact, are combined in these last two verses. The greater the promised consummation "when all things shake and fall" and the kingdom awaits us, the greater should be our gratitude to God, and yet, ever prone to sin as we are, the more should our gratitude be coupled with reverence and awe of God who is a consuming fire (Deut. 4:24) for those who reject him by unbelief in his Son.

The reading of the relative clause varies between the subjunctive "may serve" and the indicative "serve." Which to accept is a problem; we choose the latter because it is a little more simple. "Together with reverence and awe" should not be attached to the relative clause but to χάριν of the main clause, for the μετά phrase is too weighty to be a mere appendage to the relative clause, for it is substantiated by καὶ γάρ (= etenim).

"A kingdom unshakable" is the city which Abraham was expecting (11:10), Mount Zion, etc., (12:22), God's rule of glory in all eternity which is unshakable, final. We are now in the act of receiving it through God's grace. When we think of the poor sinners that we are, the thought of this kingdom should overwhelm us with gratitude. Ἔχω χάριν = "to be grateful, to exercise gratitude." Through this we certainly serve God in a way that pleases him. The verb "to serve" (λατρεύω) is used repeatedly in this epistle with reference to the service and the worship which are due to God from all of us. Much may be said about this gratitude, as to why it pleases God, and why it renders all our service so acceptable to him. Yet the fact that in his wrath against ungrateful unbelief God is a consuming fire is revealed already on Sinai (v. 18); cf., 10:31. Grace and blessing so infinite; judgment so fiery — how can the readers, how can we today, waver or hesitate?

CHAPTER XIII

Let Christian Virtues Continue, v. 1-6

1) In a brief paragraph the writer touches upon the Christian moral conduct of his readers at a few points that are especially necessary and important for them. The absence of a connective marks these injunctions as constituting a separate group; each injunction is also allowed to stand by itself. The first one is general. **Let fraternal affection continue to remain!** The present imperative acknowledges the past love and urges only its continuous remaining. It is never to grow cold.

The pertinency of this admonition is obvious. Anyone of the readers who would be inclined to give up Christ and to revert to Judaism would promptly show that decline in faith by coldness and indifference to his Christian brethren. Love to the brethren is one of the outstanding marks of Christian faith. It is the new commandment given us by Jesus in John 13:34 and repeated again and again: I Thess. 4:9; I Pet. 1:22; I John 2:10; 3:11, 23; 4:7, 11, 12, 21.

When ἀγαπᾶν is used it refers to the love of intelligence coupled with corresponding purpose; when φιλεῖν is used as it is here in φιλαδελφία it refers to affectionate love, showing kindness, sympathy, offering help, etc. In our times, when so many false brotherhoods are established that claim to be superior to our brotherhood in Christ and urge their claims and their benefits to the detriment and even the disruption of our spiritual brotherhood in the faith and the confession of Christ, it is especially necessary to emphasize the divine character of the bond of brotherly love which unites us as believers in Christ and to urge all our brethren ever to continue therein and to cut loose from every antagonistic tie.

2) One of the ways of showing this love is now adduced. **Be not forgetful of friendliness to strangers for thereby some have unawares entertained angels.**

This, too, is a present imperative. One form of φιλαδελφία is φιλοξενία. Not only the brethren whom we know personally in our own city but also brethren that are strangers to us are to receive our fraternal friendliness; the word employed is another compound of φίλος. They may be only traveling brethren; to open the home to them for lodging and for food, to give them information and help, will be a great aid. Some of them will be poor, especially in need of such help. Public hotels and lodging places were unknown at this time. In a large city like Rome any strange Christian was at a disadvantage. Such brethren had sometimes been compelled to leave home because of persecution and to wander among strangers; these especially would need Christian hospitality and help.

In Gen. 18:3, Abraham, and in Gen. 19:2, Lot actually entertained angels unawares. The construction ἔλαθον with the participle is classic; the main idea is found in the participle, the verb adds only the adverbial notion "unawares." The thought of the statement can hardly be that by entertaining strangers we, too, may have the good fortune of sometimes receiving angels into our homes. The Old Testament incidents are too exceptional to admit of such a generalization. It is sufficient to say that, as some were unexpectedly blessed by receiving strangers, so we, too, may be thus blessed. We may go a bit farther: Christ identifies himself with his saints so that what we do for them we do for him, Matt. 25:38, 40.

3) **Continue remembering the prisoners as having been made (their) fellow prisoners; them that**

are disgracefully treated as being yourselves also (still) in the body!

To keep remembering is not to be forgetting (v. 2); the writer only varies the expression. These prisoners were such because of their faith. See the introduction regarding what happened in Rome in the year 64 and compare the exposition of 10:32-34. "As having been made fellow prisoners" is not to be understood in a physical but in a spiritual sense: feeling their imprisonment as if it were your own. Although we are unable to effect their release we can do what the Christians did for Peter (Acts 12:5): pray for such prisoners. In Peter's case the prayers brought about even his release. "Whether one member suffer, all members suffer with it," I Cor. 12:26.

The writer leaves unsaid how the readers are to remember the prisoners. They can sometimes visit them (Matt. 25:39), do something toward obtaining their release, etc., at all events they can pray for them. In the ancient synagogue prisoners were remembered in the service; this was also done in the early Christian Church. We still pray: "Be thou the protector and defense of thy people in all times of tribulation and danger."

Without adding a connective the writer enlarges the circle: "them that are basely or disgracefully treated" (see the same participle in 11:37), i. e., in any way abused because of their Christian faith. Recall Moses in 11:25, 26: "having chosen to be basely treated together with the people of God rather than to have enjoyment of sin lasting for a period." "As being yourselves also in the body" refers to our susceptibility to the same sufferings. In addition to the inward, spiritual tie there is also the outward bond of the same bodily condition. The readers had already suffered in this way (10:32-34).

Hebrews 13:4

4) In v. 3 the writer expands, he now condenses. He has mentioned the fact that we are still in the body; he now takes up one bodily relation, that of marriage. This shows that the writer proceeds in an orderly way. To say that he proceeds merely theoretically is to deny what the entire epistle shows, namely that it fits the needs of his readers in every part, and it does so here. The Judaism of the day was very lax regarding marriage as the Gospels show in regard to Palestine; this laxity was certainly not less in great Gentile centers like Rome. The admonition given here was needed, it would otherwise not be found here. It aims at elevating marriage, the closest relation, which was sanctified by God himself at creation and is no less sacred in Christianity as Jesus himself shows.

Honorable let marriage be in all respects, and the bed undefiled; for fornicators and adulterers God will judge.

Shall we supply the indicative "is" (A. V.) or the imperative "let be" (R. V.)? The matter is not one of mere grammatical form. The patristic exegesis supplies "is" on the supposition that the writer defends marriage against a false asceticism which, because of the κοίτη (bed, marriage bed, copulation), considered marriage as being not really honorable but defiling or filthy. The writer is thought to contradict this error by saying that marriage *is* honorable, the bed *is* undefiled. This is the idea that underlies the translation of the A. V., and it has been introduced into our marriage ceremony, namely the stout assertion that there is nothing dishonorable in marriage or defiling in marital copulation. This view led to the alteration of the reading: since γάρ does not fit, δέ was substituted, and our A. V. consistently translates this altered reading: "*but* whoremongers," etc. It is a pity that the A. V., which so often follows Luther, disregards his correct translation: *Die Ehe soll ehrlich gehalten werden*, etc., although he has the inferior *aber* in the last clause.

Only the imperative is in place. Marriage is to be kept honorable, its honor is never to be defiled by sexual violation. The positive τίμιος is expounded by the negative ἀμίαντος, "honorable" = "undefiled"; and γάμος is defined by κοίτη, "marriage" meaning in particular "the marriage bed." The defilements that dishonor marriage are fornication, which dishonors marriage in advance, and adultery, which dishonors marriage after it has been entered into. It is pedantic to claim that γάμος means only wedding or nuptials; its second current Greek meaning is "marriage."

Ἐν πᾶσιν does not mean "in all persons" or "among all persons." This view is due to the supposition discussed above, namely that all Christians are to consider marriage honorable and undefiling. Here, in v. 18, in Eph. 1:23, etc., the phrase = "in all respects," *in allen Stuecken* (B.-P. 1012, lists the passages). Marriage is in no way to be disgraced by sexual unfaithfulness on the part of either spouse. "For God will judge fornicators and adulterers," he whom the writer has just called "a consuming fire."

5) The analogy of Scripture steadily joins the filthiness of fornication and adultery with the filthiness of avarice and covetousness. Even in the Decalogue the Sixth Commandment is followed by the Seventh. Yet in 10:34 we find another reason for this admonition. A good many of the readers had suffered severely by having their homes robbed and wrecked during the persecutions of the year 64 and were thus in a bad state financially. Hence the admonition offered here is coupled with the strongest comfort and assurance. We, of course, supply the imperative. **Without money-love the conduct, being**

contented with the things at hand! The force of the injunction is increased by its terseness. It reads like a general Christian motto: "Non-silver-loving the conduct!" Τρόπος is "turn" of mind, manner, or conduct. Not even a possessive pronoun is added. The readers once took joyfully the losses inflicted on them (10:34); let them keep that spirit: "contented with the things at hand."

We decline to regard ἀρκούμενοι as an anacoluthon, or as a participle used like a finite verb (R., W. P.), or to read it with Moulton's suggested refinements (*Einleitung*, 288); this participle is construed *ad sensum*. Since participles have case, number, and gender in the Greek they can be used with a perfect precision that is not possible in the case of either English or German participles. Contentment with whatever little God has given or left us is the cure for all money-love, all worry about money, and the like.

We have what is far better than all earthly wealth: **For he himself has said** (perfect tense as in 1:13: and what he has said still stands): **In no wise will I let go of thee, nor in any wise will I abandon thee! so that, being of good courage, we on our part say:**

**The Lord for me a helper; I will not fear.
What shall man do to me?**

The one thing is what God says to us, the other what we say to him in return. In God's statement we have two volitive subjunctives, aorists, decisive, with the usual double negative οὐ μή, and ἀνῶ is the second aorist of ἀνίημι. The Greek doubles the negative: οὐδ' οὐ μή, "nor in no wise," a construction which the English stylists avoid. The verbs are synonymous: to let go of someone is to abandon him; but the latter is the result of the former. Alas, we often think that God has let go, has abandoned. He never does. The citation is taken from Deut. 31:6, 8; I Chron. 28:20. It is not slavishly literal, for the third person is changed to the first, and the two significant verbs are juxtaposed. Philo does the same, but we have no reason to think that he is being quoted here. It is most natural to quote as something said by God what Moses says of him, whether this is done by our writer, by Philo, or by yourself. God's promise is better than any bond or note on any bank, financial institution, or most stable government, for all these may have to repudiate their bond; God never does so.

6) The result of God's sure promise (ὥστε with the infinitive to express result, R. 999, etc.) is our courageous reply by making Ps. 118:6 our own, which was Luther's favorite psalm, his *Confitemini*, the exposition of which gave him so much comfort during the trying days on the Coburg. The good courage recalls the joyfulness expressed in 10:34. By using the emphatic "we on our part" the writer makes himself the spokesman for his readers by voicing their united trust. When he uses words of Scripture in v. 5, 6, this is most effective for his readers, former Jews, who are now growing weak in their Christianity because of persecutions. They are not giving up Deuteronomy nor the Psalms but are only following Moses and the psalmist by relying on God and on his sure promises.

Let Us Go out to Him outside of the Camp! V. 7-17

7) In this paragraph the writer addresses to his readers the call to separate themselves completely from the camp of Judaism, to go out to Christ crucified, the changeless Christ, to be true to those who have preached and are now preaching this Christ, and to bring the offering of praise and obedience. The absence of a connective in v. 10 and in v. 17 might lead us to think that we have points of division in those

verses, yet the thought presents itself as a unit and should be left so.

It begins with the blessed memory of the departed leaders whose faith the readers ought to imitate. **Keep calling to mind your leaders who were such as spoke to you the Word of God, whose faith keep imitating, carefully viewing the issue of their manner of life.**

The readers have been shown the Old Testament heroes of faith in chapter 11; there are others that are closer to them, their own "leading ones" (substantivized descriptive present participle). Οἵτινες, which is both qualitative and causal, describes them: "such as (and because they were such as) spoke to you the Word of God." The second verb states why these leaders are to be kept in mind: "Whose faith keep imitating." The writer uses no official name but says only "leading ones" and in his description brings out the two facts that they spoke "the Word of God" and that they had "the faith." "Your leading ones" implies that the readers followed them when they spoke the Word of God, followed them in the same faith.

They were true leaders, indeed. All our church leaders may well look closely at this characterization: speaking the Word, the whole Word, and nothing but the Word (Acts 20:26, 27), and doing this with true personal faith; hence never once misleading the church. God, ever give us such leaders! All followers may well look at these words. Only such leaders are they to follow because they speak the Word of God. Such leaders they are to imitate in their own faith. God, ever give us followers of this kind!

The participle adds what the readers are especially to view most carefully in regard to the faith of their departed leaders, namely the ἔκβασις τῆς ἀναστροφῆς, an expression that it is hard to translate literally: "the end of their conversation" (A. V.), "the issue of their life" (R. V.). Take II Tim. 4:6-8 as a commentary and an illustration. There is the whole ἀναστροφή, the course of Christian life and conduct, and then its ἔκβασις, the act of going out of it by a blessed death. There is the whole work of these leaders to be kept in mind; there is their exemplary faith to be remembered; in particular, there is the conclusion of their life to be examined carefully. The latter is so important for the readers because they were thinking of a different conclusion for themselves, namely a going back to Judaism and a dying as Jews. After having had such leaders, how can the readers answer to God if they after all fall back and end their lives in a wholly different manner?

The fact that the leading ones referred to are now dead and gone is evident. Those who place the readers in Palestine or in Jerusalem identify these leaders with the apostles and mention especially the martyrs Stephen and James and call the readers the second generation. "*Your* leading ones, such as spoke *to you* the Word of God" does not fit this idea of a second generation. See the introduction regarding the identity of the readers. We take them to be the mass of Jews in Rome who were converted by Paul (Acts 28:17, etc.). We thus take "your leading ones" to be Paul and Peter, both of whom were martyrs when this epistle was written. Peter suffered martyrdom in 64, Paul probably late in 66 or very early in 67.

Since these were an unmixed body of Jewish Christians, we think that when Peter arrived in Rome he devoted himself also to them. The readers know how these two leaders ended their lives as the noblest examples of faith. Were there others? We can say only one thing, namely, that no elders of this body of Jewish Christians died as martyrs during the Neronic persecutions (10:32-34). Whether one or more of their elders had died otherwise and may thus be referred to along with Peter and Paul we cannot say. As to other opinions, we assign these to the judgment of our readers and are content to voice our own convictions.

8) In a most effective way, without a connective, the writer adds: **Jesus Christ, yesterday and today the same, and for the eons,** i. e., for eternity. Jesus Christ, changeless, immutable! Here there is the person and the office. "Yesterday" = when he was first preached to the readers by Paul and then by Peter. He has not changed. "Today" he sits at God's right hand as he did yesterday, our great High Priest (4:14); so he does to all eternity. Jesus Christ is the sum and substance of the Word of God that was spoken to the readers by those departed leaders, he upon whom alone they rested their faith, which the readers are ever to imitate. "Yesterday" should not be carried back to eternity although Rev. 13:8 is true. The writer is not speaking abstractly; his "yesterday" is historical because it follows verse seven as it does. Jesus Christ cannot be anything but "the same" in regard to all that this letter has said of him. The only question is whether the faith of the readers will also remain the same.

9) The admonition is added without a connective: **By varicolored and strange doctrines be not carried aside, for it is an excellent thing that by grace the hearts be made firm, not by meats in connection with which they were not benefited who walked about** (in life).

One doctrine must be ours, one changeless doctrine, that which presents the changeless "Jesus Christ." Whether we say "Jesus Christ" or "doctrine" makes no difference, for he is the sum and substance of the "doctrine," and the "doctrine" is the true, adequate presentation of him as this substance. So Paul offers nothing "save Jesus Christ and him crucified" (I Cor. 2:2), and he does this "not in words which man's wisdom teaches, but which the Holy Spirit teaches, combining spiritual things with spiritual word" (I Cor. 2:13). The words = the doctrine. The entire teaching of the Scriptures, the entire teaching of Jesus is doctrine. "My own doctrine (διδαχή) is not my own, but his that sent me," John 7:16. This divine "doctrine" cannot change because the saving facts it presents are changeless.

Hence we have the admonition: "By various and strange doctrines be not carried aside!" Their very variety (literally, "many colored") brands them as being false, for the truth is always one, unalterably one, lies are ever many and motley. They are also ξέναι, "strange," like strangers or foreigners; they are not the old, familiar faces but odd, alien, suspicious from the start. They are the inventions of men, manifold and strange like men, not the Rock of Ages, the eternal, immutable truth from the eternal God. All they do is "to carry aside" (παρά in the verb), off the true, safe course — whither, one can only guess, certainly not to God. "Be not carried aside" (present imperative: now or ever) applies to any and to all such doctrines. The injunction is comprehensive. Among such doctrines is the Jewish teaching which was threatening to mislead the readers at this time. It is here classified and branded with all the rest.

The present imperative implies that the readers had not yet been carried aside; yet the fact that they need this warning indicates that they were not in a state of firmness but were rather wavering and hesitating. Hence the reason for not being carried away is added: "for it is an excellent thing that by grace the heart be made firm" (present infinitive: as the writer is now making it firm). "By grace" is emphatic; its position makes it so just as the preceding dative is emphatic. Those doctrines carry away; grace ever makes firm. Instead of saying "by the one true doctrine" the writer at once names the divine power in this doctrine: χάρις, "grace," God's undeserved favor which

Hebrews 13:9

operates in and through his Word (doctrine) and roots and grounds the heart, the center of our being, in the saving truth (John 17:17; Eph. 4:14, 15).

A third dative follows and is also placed forward for the sake of emphasis: "not by meats in connection with which they were not benefited who walked about" (in life). With this dative the writer comes to the doctrine that was at that time threatening to carry aside his readers. It is summarized in the one word βρώματα, "meats," which is at once understood by the readers especially because of the added clause: that they who walked had no benefit or profit from these "meats."

The early Greek commentators and some since their day construe ἐν οἷς with οἱ περιπατήσαντες, but this construction is incongruous. The participle means "to walk about"; in its metaphorical sense as it is used in the papyri it means "to conduct one's life" (M.-M. 507) and never quite loses its etymological meaning. While it is often construed with ἐν: "to walk about (live) in sins — in good works — in the ways of righteousness" and the like, such phrases are always congruous. One does not "walk about (live) in meats" — that would be incongruous; but those who walk about (do their living) may be benefited ἐν βρώμασιν, "in connection with meats," i. e., by eating them; again they may not be profited in them.

B. Weiss attacks the grammar on the score that the article with the participle debars connection with the phrase since no other example of such a connection can be found. The incongruity alone is enough. The phrase goes so naturally with "were not benefited" that it seems gratuitous to give the participle meanings which it never has in order to make it fit the phrase: "they that have been *occupied* therein" (A. V.), "wherein they that *occupied* themselves" (R. V.), *die sich damit abgeben* (Riggenbach). Some change the phrase in order to gain the same end.

It lies on the surface that the clause refers to meats that were supposed to profit, i. e., strengthen spiritually, those who needed such benefit in the daily round of their lives. The writer says that they did not get benefit in such "meats." What does he mean by these βρώματα, *Speisen*, foods? Some think that kosher Jewish food is referred to. It is said that this word is used regularly with reference to such foods, which is, of course, true, for what other word could be used? But the benefit of kosher eating was not derived from the foods that were eaten but from the foods that were shunned. *Avoiding* foods that were regarded as unclean kept the Jews clean.

Moreover, this epistle nowhere touches upon the subject of kosher food, it deals throughout with far graver subjects. As far as kosher food was concerned, its use or nonuse was entirely a matter of liberty to Christians. The whole subject had been settled long ago. As far as these Jewish Christians are concerned, it is safe to assume that they never stopped eating kosher; it cannot be assumed that they had stopped eating kosher since their conversion and were now inclined to begin kosher eating again. The whole epistle, the present context, as well as what we know about the danger that was confronting the readers establish the fact that these profitless βρώματα were cultus meats.

This is a reference to the σύνδειπνα, joint feasts, which the Jews were permitted to have already in Caesar's time; these great joint meals were among the special concessions granted to the Jews of the Diaspora. Josephus, *Ant.*, 14, 10, 1-8, records Caesar's decrees in full, and in paragraph 8 has these particulars: "Now it does not please me that such decrees should be made against our friends and confederates, whereby they are forbidden to live according to their own customs, or to bring in contributions for common suppers and holy festivals, while they are not forbidden to do so even at Rome itself, for even Caius Caesar, our imperator and consul, in that decree wherein he forbade Bacchanal rioters to meet in the city, did yet permit these Jews, and these only, both to bring in their contributions and to make their common suppers. Accordingly, when I forbid other Bacchanal rioters I permit these Jews to gather themselves together according to the customs and laws of their forefathers and to persist therein. It will be, therefore, good for you [throughout the empire] that, if you have made any decree against these our friends and confederates, to abrogate the same by reason of their virtue and kind disposition toward us."

The readers of this epistle are living in Rome. The writer alludes to the celebrations of the Jews in Rome. Roman Jews would seldom be able to attend the celebrations in Jerusalem. Throughout the Diaspora the Jews made the more of their local "common suppers" as Caesar's decree calls them. They helped greatly to bind the Jews together. That was the profit the Jews had from them — not confirmation by divine grace for their hearts in the true faith, only confirmation in their bigoted Judaism and the doctrines supporting it.

10) **We have an altar of sacrifice from which (even) they have no authority to eat who serve the Tabernacle. For of what animals the blood is brought by the high priest into the Sanctuary for sin, of these the bodies are burned outside of the camp.**

The way in which the writer advances his thought by alluding to Jewish practices creates difficulties that are acknowledged by the best of the commentators. We agree with those who decline to find too much in these words. Allusions are never to be pressed, for we then get beyond the writer's meaning into thoughts of our own, which is no longer exegesis.

We have no contrasting ἡμεῖς and no δέ: "but *we on our part* have," etc. We have only the simple ἔχομεν and a relative clause which describes the altar we have as one that excludes all eating and hence also all βρώματα such as the Jews had, for which they had secured a Roman decree of permission throughout the empire, of which they were also very proud. This altar is one without meats and eating and is filled only with "grace." We see it typified by the Day of Atonement, by the sacrifice that already then excluded every idea of "foods" to be eaten (v. 11).

The mention of a θυσιαστήριον is an allusion to the Jewish sacrificial altar. We have what this Jewish altar typifies. Yet the writer again thinks of the Mosaic Tabernacle and not of the Temple, for he says that of the altar which we have even they have no authority to eat who serve the Tabernacle. These are the priests. The verb λατρεύω is used as it was in 8:5 and not λειτουργέω. The latter = official ministration; the writer aims to say more than the latter, namely the service of worship for one's own soul (λατρεύω). He is thinking of sacrifices that were made at the Tabernacle by the Levitical priests, not merely for other Israelites, but for the priests themselves, in particular of the great sacrifice on the Day of Atonement. The allusion is plain and readily caught by the readers who are former Jews. The Christian altar of sacrifice bears a sacrifice that is like that which was offered on the Jewish Day of Atonement, which admitted of no eating whatever.

There were sacrifices such as the thank offerings, the *scheˡlamin*, Lev. 19:5-8; 22:29, 30, of which only the people ate; the Passover is similar to these. Then there were sacrifices of which both the priest and the person bringing the sacrifice ate certain designated parts. Finally, there was this sacrifice on the Day of Atonement of which none had a right to eat. The writer alludes to this last type of sacrifice. Instead of saying we have "a sacrifice" the writer says we have "a sacrificial altar." The difference is most important. The altar that we have had only *one* sacrifice, the one that is typified by the sacrifice on the Day of Atonement; it is not like the Jewish altar on which *all kinds* of sacrifices were offered. Thus because our altar bears only *one* sacrifice, namely the one indicated, it admits of no eating by anybody (v. 11) ; it is unlike the Jewish altar save for one exceptional sacrifice.

11) It is this point that "for" explains. The bodies of the animals, whose blood the high priest brought into the Sanctuary of the Tabernacle "for sin" (his own sin first and then also that of the people), were not eaten, not even by any of the priests, not even when they were λατρεύοντες, serving the Tabernacle in the capacity of worshippers for their own soul's good; these bodies were burnt "outside of the camp," speaking in terms of the sojourn in the wilderness in the days of Moses. The *tertium comparationis* in the type and the antitype lies in the fact that the sacrifice was not to be eaten. To extend it beyond that point implies to misunderstand the writer's thought.

By abiding with this *tertium* we have the great fact of grace, the grace which Israel had in the sacrifice of the high priest on the Day of Atonement which cleansed away Israel's sins and received its cleansing power from the blood of Christ, the antitype, and the atonement he made. Type and antitype are marked by the fact that both exclude eating. This type is raised above all other types of sacrifice and offering by this outstanding mark. Since one altar with this sacrifice has come, the Jewish Day of Atonement is ended, its purpose is fully served. All God's grace is bestowed by Christ's atoning blood. All these Jewish βρώματα are profitless. The preceding chapters have developed and explained all this at length. In the light of these chapters the allusions now used are plain and most significant.

We add a few additional notes. It is not well to say that "we have an altar" = the cross on Calvary. Christ's cross stood "outside of the camp," "outside of the gate" (v. 12). An incongruity would thus result. In the Jewish type the altar before the Tabernacle, the Sanctuary within the Tabernacle, and the place outside of the camp for burning the bodies are distinct and separate; in the antitype nothing of this kind appears. We may speak of Christ's cross as an altar in a figure of our own making but not when the allusions in these verses are properly explained.

It is not in place to say that the altar we have is the Lord's Table. This is unwarranted because all eating is excluded. To speak of spiritual eating is not satisfactory. Moreover, the Lord's Table is not for children and babes; the malefactor on the cross did not partake of this table. Yet all these may say, "We have an altar." After what we have said regarding "those serving the Tabernacle" we pass by the efforts to regard these as anything but the priests of the Tabernacle.

12) A surprisingly new and yet perfectly true deduction is now made: **Wherefore also Jesus, in order that he might sanctify the people by means of his own blood, suffered outside of the gate. Now then, let us be going out to him outside of the camp, bearing his reproach! For we have here no continuing city, but we are seeking the one about to come.**

The significant point is the fact that the bodies of the animals, whose blood was used to cleanse and sanctify the people on the Day of the Atonement, were burned "outside of the camp." "Outside of the camp" is significant. The camp enclosed Israel; to be outside of it meant to be removed from Israel. So these animal bodies were taken outside, and this act symbolized the removal from Israel of the sin for which these animals had been slain. In order to show that Christ's blood was likewise to sanctify the people (as already stated in 9:12-14; 10:29) he, too, suffered "outside of the gate," on Calvary outside of Jerusalem. "Gate" is substituted for "camp" because the journey through the wilderness during which Israel pitched camp was long a matter of history when Jesus suffered. Jesus bore away the sins of the people, bore them outside of the gate in order to gain for them the sanctification of atonement by means of his own blood.

"His own blood," holy and precious, retains the idea of sacrifice, retains it better than the word "death." Without shedding of blood there is no forgiveness and hence no sanctification, 9:22. It is better to say "Jesus suffered" than to say he "died." The mention of Jesus' death would suggest the death of animals on the Day of Atonement, which took place at the side of the altar and not outside of the camp. Any suggestion that would parallel the deaths is avoided. Jesus "suffered" is preferable also because it brings out all that happened on Calvary; the animals died after a quick thrust of the knife and not after a long agony of pain.

13) The very significance of complete ejection from Israel, which lies in what is said of the animals in v. 11 and is then predicated of the suffering of Jesus, is now applied to the readers: "Now then, let us be going out to him outside the camp," etc. The present iterative imperative is in place because the writer and the readers must again and again repeat this act, namely every time they are called to bear "Jesus' reproach."

The Jews cast Jesus "outside the gate" like a criminal accursed (Lev. 24:14; Deut. 17:5). We see from Gal. 3:13 how the cross intensified the idea of being accursed. In 12:2 the cross and the shame are combined. In 11:26 Moses esteems "the reproach of Christ" above the treasures of Egypt. We have the same word here: τὸν ὀνειδισμὸν αὐτοῦ, "his reproach," all the vilification heaped on Jesus: the curse of the cross, the crown of thorns, and every other indignity. Here belong all such passages as Rom. 8:17; II Cor. 1:5; 4:10; Phil. 3:10; I Pet. 4:13. "Outside of the camp" adopts this phrase from v. 11. It is full of significance for Jewish Christians, for it denotes a complete and a continued break with the Jews and with all Judaism. From Jews, yea from the Jewish nation came and still comes "his reproach"; Jews have taught the world to despise Christ. They shouted that he should be crucified and now point at his cross in derision.

We have reached the climax of the epistle. From the start its aim has been to restore the wavering faith of the Jewish Christian readers in Jesus, to rid them of their recently conceived desire to go back to Judaism. To accomplish this effectively the break with their nation, with all Jews must be final, irrevocable, apparent at every turn. This is here told them in the most masterful way. The writer includes himself; he adopts a wording from the ritual of Moses for the Day of Atonement, and he does this after the fullest preparation. Who could do better? We are Gentile Christians who are less apt to catch all the implications in the allusions; it will be well to work ourselves into them. We must read with Jewish eyes. The personal gain for us will be a better application to ourselves who must bear the world's reproach of Jesus and not merely the Jewish reproach.

14) Why this going out loaded with the reproach of Jesus? In connection with 11:10, 14-16, coupled with 12:22, the answer is that here we do not have a continuing city, one that remains; we are only pilgrims and strangers (11:13), wayfarers for a few days. We are seeking the city that is about to come, the city

eternal, immutable. It is no loss to the writer and to the readers to be treated as outcasts by their Jewish nationals; as Christians they belong to a far more exalted nation (12:23, 24). We have no hint here that the year 70 is already past, that Jerusalem has fallen, and that the Jewish nation is wrecked forever. Judging from the way in which the writer words his hortation, these events had not yet transpired although it is true that he touches the late history only where he must (as in Jesus' suffering "outside of the gate" of Jerusalem) and otherwise reverts to the Tabernacle in the wilderness (v. 10).

15) Trusting solely in the sanctifying power of Jesus' blood and going out unto him from the Jews and from Judaism means turning away from Levitical sacrifices, none of which are any longer needed. In the case of Christians only the *sch^{e}lamin* (thankofferings) could be left, and these no longer in their old Jewish form but in a far higher form that corresponds to the Christian's relation to God through Jesus.

Through him, therefore, let us keep offering up sacrifice of praise constantly to God, that is, fruit of lips confessing his name. Moreover, the doing good and fellowship do not be forgetting, for with such sacrifices God is well pleased. These are ever to be our sacrifices, and we ourselves are to be the priests.

"Through him" means with his priestly mediation and without any other. "Through him" we may ever draw nigh to God, both ourselves to get help from the throne of grace for the time of need (4:14-16), to strengthen our faith and our hope, and to stimulate our love and our good works as we assemble jointly (10:19-25) and, as the writer now adds, "to offer up constantly to God sacrifice of praise," which is defined as "fruit of lips confessing his name," i. e., acknowledging his name or revelation by which he makes himself known to our hearts and by which we know him.

God's ὄνομα = his revelation of himself in Christ Jesus. To confess this "name" is the highest function of faith (Matt. 10:31, 32; Rom. 10:9, 10). The language recalls Ps. 54:6. So many think that works that are helpful to men are worth more than confession of the name; but without this confession all else is vain. The question is illy put: "Which is more important for a congregation, to maintain the confession or to save souls?" The more we confess, the more truly we confess, the more we help to save souls; and vice versa. The alternative with which the question confronts us is not an alternative; it is a fig leaf behind which to hide the shame of failure to confess (Matt. 10:33).

16) The direct praise of true confession, which is directed to God himself, must ever come first although it employs only the lips; yet these are to speak out of the abundance of the heart (Matt. 12:34). Next there comes "the doing good and fellowshiping," the two being combined under one article. "The doing well" is more than doing good to our neighbor in the sense of being kind and helping him. All our deeds must be well done, no matter whether they are done for others or not.

Some commentators and then also some of the dictionaries (Thayer and Abbott-Smith may serve as examples) think that in Rom. 15:26; II Cor. 8:4; 9:13; and in our passage κοινωνία means "communication, contribution," and that in Romans and in II Corinthians it may be translated "collection." Our versions adopt this idea: "to do good and to communicate"; Dods offers "charity" as a proper comment, and Delitzsch: "It means plainly the assistance rendered by charitable contributions." The word does *not* have this meaning. It means "fellowship." Here we have the combination doing well in all our deeds and acts and doing this in faithful fellowship by holding close together. Regarding the latter the writer has already said "not abandoning the assembly of your own selves as is the custom of some" (10:25). We cannot find the idea of charity in the word κοινωνία by making it mean a communion of earthly goods; it means communion of hearts, these being bound together by faith and then by love, all making the same noble confession.

The poor and needy are not mentioned in this epistle. Some of the members had lost their possessions (10:34); yet the writer tells them only to be content with the things at hand and comforts them with God's promise of help (13:5, 6). Charitable gifts are not mentioned, because this was evidently not necessary; the readers were already attending to this. We are pleased to note that C.-K. 612, etc., and B.-P. 687, etc., do not define κοινωνία as "contribution." "Do not be forgetting" is a litotes and equals always be remembering. Such are the sacrifices, the writer says, with which God is pleased; let the readers dismiss the thought of any other kind.

17) It seems best to add v. 17 to this paragraph instead of letting it start the next. It harks back to v. 7. Some of the leaders were dead, and although they are dead they still speak and are ever to be kept in mind; others have stepped into their place. What about these? **Be obedient to your leading ones and submit, for they are watching over your souls as having duly to give account, so that they may do this with joy and not as groaning, for this is unadvantageous for you.**

In the light of what this epistle reveals about the readers we conclude that the leaders among them were staunch and true at this time, and that the desire to turn away from Christ and back to Judaism was found only among the members. This prompts the writer to remind all the readers of the high responsibility that is resting upon the leaders — a good thing also for the leaders themselves to hear — and of the damage that disobedience to true leaders entails.

"Obey and yield." One obeys when one agrees with what he is told to do, is persuaded of its correctness and profitableness; one yields, gives up, when he has a contrary opinion. The pertinency of the latter is apparent. Any of the members that are inclined to leave Christ are to give up this notion and thus obey their faithful leaders. Αὐτοί is emphatic: "*they* are the ones who are watching over your souls" so that these may not be lost or even endangered. The verb recalls Jer. 6:17; Ezek. 3:17, etc.; 33:1, etc. God set the prophets of old as watchmen over Israel.

Not as being self-appointed and accountable only to themselves are the leaders doing this watching with such concern for your souls but "as having to render due account" to God. Ἀπιδίδωμι with λόγον = to render due account. The future participle is very rare and has a temporal meaning here: "shall render account" when their work is done. R. 1128 misunderstands ὡς when he says "as much cause as purpose"; it is neither. This word has its common meaning "as": the readers are to look upon their leaders, and these leaders, too, are to look upon themselves "as in due time to give account," B.-D. 425, 13: *als solche die; im Gedanken, dass sie, usw.*

Those who are called to watch are to give the alarm at the approach of danger; they are to give it early enough so that those who are watched over may meet the danger or may escape it. When an appointed watchman proves a dumb dog, calamity results. Woe to the people whose leaders are blind watchers, unable to distinguish foe from friend or to recognize danger before it is too late. Watching means warning at as early a time as possible, and the warned must heed — otherwise why set watchmen? Watching implies keeping oneself and others safe where danger is known to exist or where one fears its existence. Where no danger exists watching is not needed. But where safety is at stake no one but a fool takes chances. All this applies to the church in the highest degree where the safety of souls is to be guarded. Some watchmen in Israel take their accountability lightly, they will find their medicine in Ezek. 33:7, etc. Whoever assumes or is given responsibility over the souls of any others, even of only one other, is fully accountable.

Ἵνα introduces contemplated result. These leaders are to find their followers obedient and yielding so that they may do their work and bear their responsibility with joy and not with groaning. The participle is strong, cf. Rom. 8:23. This joy is found when all hear and heed, and none is either hurt or lost. The groaning comes when some will not hear and heed, and, still worse, when some are actually lost. Recall 6:4-8; 10:26-31.

A litotes concludes this part of the admonition: "for this is unadvantageous for you." While *they* groan, *you* would do worse than groan. All the advantage of having faithful leaders and watchmen would not only be lost but would turn into the opposite. It is bad when no one rings the alarm and warns, it is a thousand times worse for you and for me when we are deaf to a true warning. A litotes often sounds mild and becomes a meiosis, but it is in reality only the stronger because of that.

Conclusion, v. 18-25

18) Be praying for us! For we are persuaded that we have a good conscience in wanting to conduct ourselves well in every way. Moreover, I urge you the more to do this in order that I may the more quickly be restored to you.

The request for prayers needs no comment; but the plural "for us" does. It is not a literary plural, for no careful writer says "we" and "I" in the same sentence as is done here when he is referring only to himself in both instances. Nor does "we" refer to the writer and the leaders mentioned in v. 17. "We" = the writer and his companions. Like Paul, the writer had a few associates with him as the readers in Rome know. Even if he had only one, this "for us" is in place.

It is impossible for us to say what lies back of their conviction that they have a good conscience in wanting to conduct themselves well in every way. Various suggestions are offered, but they are, after all, only surmises. The view that the writer is speaking only of himself is unacceptable; his companion or his companions are included. If they had been imprisoned on some charge, the writer would have said so.

As always, ἐν πᾶσι means "in all respects," *in jeder Hinsicht*, as it does in v. 4; see B.-P. 1012. When we have the will to conduct ourselves well in every way we do, indeed, have a good conscience. This does not mean that conscience may not err; but if it should err with such a will, this would be due only to ignorance. Since this is written at the close of an epistle such as this, such an error is excluded. As far as we are able to say, this assurance about a good conscience bears on the contents of this epistle. Some of its warnings are sharp, plain language; the readers are to know that conscience compels the writer to speak to them in such a way. The men who are associated with him approve every word with a like good conscience.

19) When the writer now uses the singular without an emphatic, contrasting ἐγώ he speaks of his own return and not also of the return of such associates as he has with him. The explanation is simple: he has some time ago left his readers on some important mis-

sion and has taken one or more assistants along with him; he is anxious to return and expects to leave these helpers behind to attend to what may still need their attention. He counts on the earnest intercession of the readers to bring God's blessing on his present mission, which would enable him to leave it in the hands of his associates while he himself hastens back to his readers, who, as the entire letter has shown us, certainly need him. To go beyond this and to surmise that the writer was imprisoned is of little actual value.

20) As the writer asks for the prayers of his readers, so he offers prayer for them. **Now the God of peace, the One who brought again from the dead the great Shepherd of the sheep in connection with blood of an eternal testament, our Lord Jesus: may he fit you out in every good thing to do his will, he doing in you the thing well-pleasing in his sight through Jesus Christ: to whom the glory for the eons of the eons! Amen.**

In this one sentence the writer sums up all that his epistle contains and puts it into the form of a fervent prayer-wish. While it is addressed to the readers in form, the appeal is in reality made to God. "The God of the peace," peace with the article in the sense of "the divine peace," names him as the fountain of this *schalom* and conceives this εἰρήνη or peace objectively as the state or condition that is established by him, into which we enter, in which we dwell, which we are given to enjoy. It is "the peace" of God in the soteriological sense as the apposition shows.

This apposition presents the God of the (divine) peace as "the One who brought again from the dead the Shepherd of the sheep, the great one, in connection with blood of an eternal testament" and names this great Shepherd as "our Lord Jesus." While the wording "the God of peace" is Pauline (Rom. 15:33; I Thess.

5:23) and "the Shepherd of the sheep" is an Old Testament allusion (Isa. 40:11; Ezek. 34:23), which both Jesus and Peter adopted (John 10:11, I Pet. 2:25; 5:4), the main thing to note is the correspondence of "peace" with the imagery of "the great Shepherd of the sheep." Under this Shepherd's staff there is divine peace indeed.

Israel had other shepherds, but they died and passed on; this Shepherd is "the Great One" (note "Great High Priest" in 4:14) because God "brought him again from the dead" by a glorious resurrection and did this "in connection with blood of an eternal testament." The nouns are qualitative and thus without articles. No other shepherd like this one did Israel ever have. Perhaps there is an allusion to Zech. 9:11: "the blood of thy covenant (testament)"; but why not think of Jesus' own word "my blood of the new testament" (Matt. 26:28) and of all that this epistle has to say about this very testament and about the blood by which it is established? A new word, "eternal," is applied to "testament" (on διαθήκη see 7:22); yet all that has been said about this testament has fully shown it to be eternal indeed.

It is the covenant or testament that was received by Abraham. It was at first promised, but this promise was duly fulfilled by Jesus, namely "in connection with his blood," the expiatory power of which is permanent, eternal. The testament that was brought to Israel by Moses was only a temporary addition; Israel had lost its promises. The eternal seal upon the expiation of Jesus is his resurrection, when God brought him again "from the dead" (on this phrase see Matt. 17:10).

Ἐν puzzles some, but it means "in connection with blood," etc., and modifies ὁ ἀναγαγών. The phrase connects God's act of raising from the dead with the blood of Jesus as expiatory blood and thus blood of an eternal testament, blood that establishes eternal peace.

Jesus was the great Shepherd of the sheep before he died (John 10:11), but as the One who lays down his life for the sheep (v. 15) even as he in due time also laid it down. There is no mixture of incompatible terms: the peace — the Shepherd — blood — eternal testament — brought back from the dead. The moment one understands these terms, they harmonize and put into compact form what this epistle presents at length.

This Shepherd's name is effectively placed last: "our Lord Jesus." The possessive "our" is always strongly confessional; it voices the faith of the writer and of his readers. We generally have the fuller form: "our Lord Jesus Christ"; as we have noted, the writer loves the simple name "Jesus," but he now adds "our Lord" as the soteriological title. This Lord purchased and won us with his blood and made us his own, and he now rules us as his own with the rule of love and of grace; this is the meaning of "Lord."

21) Καταρτίσαι is the optative of wish: this God, "may he fit you out (effective aorist) in every good thing (good in the sense of being beneficial for you) to do his will, he doing in you the thing well-pleasing before him" or "in his sight" (Phil. 2:13), and do all this "through Jesus Christ." To do God's will should not be restricted to doing what are called good works; it includes, above all, faith in Christ (John 6:40). To do his will (effective aorist infinitive) is not a matter which we are able to accomplish. All the admonitions that are addressed to the readers in this epistle are not to be understood in this way. God must fit us out in an effective manner (aorist), in fact, he must then continue doing (present participle) in us the thing that is well-pleasing in his eyes. We are to do, yet all the while God is doing. This is the blessed concursus of grace. This very epistle exhibits it: through it God is doing his work in the readers; and so by doing it the

readers will do his will, and thus God will produce in them the thing that is pleasing before him. This phrase is Hebraistic but juridical, "well-pleasing" when we stand before him in order to be judged.

The διά phrase modifies the optative together with all its other modifiers: the whole wish, all that God is to do and thus the readers are to do, all of it is to be accomplished "through Jesus Christ" who is the Alpha and Omega of all God's saving work and of our work as this is wrought by God. The Savior is mentioned three times in this prayer-wish.

Is the doxology directed to God or to Jesus Christ? We cannot compare it with Rom. 16:25-27 because in that passage the relative is resumptive of the dative τῷ δυναμένῳ while the relative is not resumptive here since v. 20 begins with the nominative ὁ Θεός. Commentators are divided: some apply the doxology to God, others to "Jesus Christ." Read the whole prayer aloud and note the effect. We must say for ourself that we believe that the ascription of glory is made to Jesus Christ. The sonorous εἰς τοὺς αἰῶνας seems to crown the διαθήκης αἰωνίου that preceded. Still more important: this entire epistle intends to magnify Christ even as three designations for him appear in this prayer. He it is to whom "the glory," the glorification, the praise and honor, are ascribed at the end. The intent of the writer is manifest, namely to apply to him this doxology which Jews constantly apply to God. So Jesus is elevated in chapter 1, so he is now again elevated. It is not merely the grammar that decides, it is the weight of the thought.

We do not supply a copula, neither the optative: "to whom be," etc., nor the indicative: "to whom is" (i. e., belongs). This doxological ending is exclamatory and thus needs no copula; it is stronger without one. The phrase: εἰς τοὺς αἰῶνας τῶν αἰώνων = "to all eternity." "The eons of the eons" is really a superlative which is formed by adding the genitive to the accusative. While these expressions are terms that indicate time, the multiplication eons of eons is the Greek way of indicating "eternity," which is also a term that indicates time. Human language has no other kind of term or terms to express what is not time in any sense, what is in reality the opposite of all time and is, therefore, inconceivable to the human mind.

Like other such doxologies, this one, too, ends with "amen," the seal of verity, which is always intended as a confession of faith and of deepest conviction. "Amen" is only the Hebrew word for "truth." It has been taken over unchanged into other languages and is used as faith's solemn seal.

22) **Now I urge you, brethren, to bear with this word of urging, for I have written to you briefly.** "I urge" and this word "of urging" are a paronomasia. The writer confesses that he has been urging in his entire letter. He asks that the readers bear with him for doing so. Καὶ γάρ is *etenim*. When he says that he has written to them (epistolary aorist) only "briefly," this is said in view of the greatness of the subject and of the personal interests involved. The writer betrays a little of Paul's feeling who, too, wrote in order to keep congregations true and was anxious about the manner in which his urgings would be received by his readers.

23) **You know that our brother Timothy has left, in company with whom, as soon as he comes, I will see you.**

If this is an indicative, the writer refers to what the readers already know about Timothy; if it is an imperative, the writer offers this news to his readers. "Our brother" intends to say that he is a brother to the readers and to the writer. Timothy was well known to these readers in Rome, for he had been with Paul often during Paul's first imprisonment in Rome when Paul converted so many of the Jews of the seven synagogues of Rome. If, as we feel rather certain, Apollos was the writer, it seems entirely natural to find him waiting for Timothy in order to return to Rome with him. Paul was dead. Timothy needed no longer to supervise the churches in the province of Asia where Paul had placed him, for about this time, when the Jewish war began, the apostle John, a greater than Timothy, had come to Ephesus in order to remain there as the leader of the Asian churches.

The Greek commentators regard ἀπολελυμένον as a passive and then take it to mean that Timothy "has been released from prison," or they regard it as a middle, "has left and is now absent as this letter is being written." If the former were the meaning, we think that the aorist participle would have been used; the perfect is far more in place to indicate the latter idea, for this tense then explains that Timothy is still absent since he has gone on some mission for the time being, but that he will soon rejoin the writer by returning. Those who think that Paul is the writer of this letter regard the participle as a reference to a release from imprisonment. This idea also changes the time of the writing by dating it during Paul's imprisonment in Rome and presupposes that Timothy, too, had somehow been confined in prison. We cannot accept this view. The writer is separated from Timothy and is awaiting his return. The construction of γινώσκω with the participle is classic.

As soon as Timothy returns, the writer (Apollos) intends to go "in company with him" (μετά) to see the readers in Rome. He does not plan to go alone; the readers know Timothy so well that he will be a great help to the writer in holding the readers to their Christian faith. The expression ἐὰν τάχιον ἔρχηται = "as soon as he comes." Unlike v. 19, τάχιον does not have the comparative idea here, see B.-P. 1291 on ταχέως: *bald, alsbald*. See also Riggenbach on the meaning of the clause.

24) **Salute all your leading ones and all the saints.** On ἀσπάσασθε, the common imperative used with regard to those to be greeted, see Rom. 16:3-16, where it is used repeatedly. It asks the readers to express the salutation of the writer to each other. This was commonly done by kissing one another, by doing this in place of the absent writer as if the kiss came from him, and, of course, using appropriate words. The leaders are honored by a separate mention, which is in harmony with v. 17. "Saints" is the common term used in the early church to designate true believers, see Acts 9:13. As "saints" they are separated unto God, made holy by the blood of Christ through faith and through a holy life. The Old Testament Jewish conception has advanced to the great Christian conception as is seen for instance in Eph. 1:1: οἱ ἅγιοι καὶ πιστοί.

There salute you those from Italy = the Italians send their greetings. Much has been written about these Italians, about who they were, and especially about where they were, whether in Italy at the writer's side or outside of Italy with him. We do not care to review the different opinions; it is enough to offer our own. We take these Italians to be associates of Apollos, who were present with him outside of Italy. We have no idea where the epistle was written; the postscript in our A. V. and other postscripts are valueless. Several Italians traveled with Apollos and Timothy in the interest of the churches. Whether one or the other of them haled from Rome we are unable to say. Paul found brethren at Puteoli (Acts 28:14). At the time when this letter was written Italy had a number of churches. So these were Italian workers who were with Apollos and Timothy. These send their greetings. That is all. Is is asked why the congregation at the place where the epistle was written sent no greetings. If we knew where the letter was written we might be able to answer this question.

25) **The** (divine) **grace with you all. Amen.** See Titus 3:15.

Soli Deo Gloria

The Interpretation of the Epistle of St. James

INTRODUCTION

Sometime between the years 40 and 50 that James who was at the head of the mother church in Jerusalem wrote this epistle to the Jewish Christians of the neighboring provinces.

These findings rest on the evidence furnished by the epistle itself and on the historical data embodied in Acts, to which we may add a few items that are found in other writings. Tradition yields no additional information. It is also well to note that the Biblical evidence that is available on these important points may be reviewed and examined by us at this late day as directly as it was in the early centuries when the question concerning the admission of this epistle into the New Testament canon was first discussed and was finally unanimously answered in the affirmative.

* * *

The date of composition is determined by the epistle itself. It is addressed to purely Jewish Christians exclusively and speaks of the moral life which these Jewish Christians should lead in the midst of the unconverted Jews with whom they associated in the various cities in which they lived. Thus the period within which such an epistle could have been written lay between the general dispersion of the old mother congregation at Jerusalem after Stephen's martyrdom and Saul's violent persecution in the year 35 and the Apostolic Conference held in Jerusalem in the year 52 to settle the great question about the relation of the incoming Gentile Christians to Jewish Christians. The limits of this period may be reduced still more. Time enough elapsed after the year 35 to allow the Jewish Christians to settle in distant cities and to develop the faults which this epistle seeks to eradicate, yet not time enough to effect a complete separation from the

Jews in these cities. The date must be advanced a number of years beyond 35 and must be fixed a number of years prior to 52.

This choice of date may be elaborated at length by a detailed review of the contents of the epistle and of the pertinent data of Acts plus an examination of all other opinions down to those of the latest critics, who place the epistle into the second century and call it a forgery that is unworthy of any serious treatment. Such an elaboration is not in line with our present purpose.

* * *

Regarding the place of writing little needs to be said since this is determined by the person of the writer, the James who was the chief elder of the congregation at Jerusalem from the time when this congregation adopted an organization until his martyrdom in the sixties (dated by Josephus in the year 63, by Zahn in the year 66, by Hegesippus as late as 68). The reason for this identification of the writer lies in the fact that all we know about this James from the other New Testament writings, in particular from Acts, accords perfectly with the character and the contents of this epistle. Here we might again elaborate at length with a wealth of detail. We confine ourselves to a few important items.

Acts 15 shows the position James held in Jerusalem where the Apostolic Conference took place. James presided; he summed up the findings which were then embodied in a brief letter and sent to all the mixed congregations by duly appointed messengers. In Acts 13:17 Peter sends word to James of his escape from Herod. In Gal. 1:19 and 2:9-12 we note James in the same position of prominence in Jerusalem. We also note it in Acts 21:18. This is the James to whom the Lord granted a special appearance after his resurrection (I Cor. 15:7).

* * *

Introduction

We might precipitate the reader into the thorny brush from which very few have emerged without having had their exegetical robes badly torn, namely a complete discussion of the relationship of this James to Jesus. We propose to follow a safer way. In Gal. 1:19 Paul calls James "the Lord's *brother*," and in I Cor. 9:5 Paul speaks of the fact that "the *brothers* of the Lord" have wives. Recent scholars assert that this James was a uterine brother of Jesus, a son of Joseph and Mary who was born after Jesus, one of the four brothers and the several sisters mentioned as "brothers" and "sisters" of Jesus in Matt. 13:55 and Mark 6:3, one of the "brothers" mentioned in Matt. 12:46. The question is thought to be solved by the word ἀδελφός and its plural "brothers," argumentatively by the suggestion that all objections are due to Catholic reverence for Mary as *semper virgo*, whom Joseph never touched sexually, who bore Jesus only and no other children. Other argument is also used, but this consists of efforts to square all the other passages, in particular those that mention the sister of Mary and her sons, with the claim that the mother of Jesus had other children, those named in Matt. 13:55 and Mark 6:3.

As far as Protestant scholars are concerned, the suggestion that they are swayed by undue reverence for Mary is unfair. As far as they are concerned, Mary may have had these other children — why not? When we differ from this view we do so because the word ἀδελφοί does not solve the question at issue in the way in which the word is thought to do this. Examine the evidence and see for yourself.

Nowhere do we read: "the sons or the children of Mary or of Mary and Joseph." In Matt. 13:55, 56 and in Mark 6:3 the people of Nazareth ask: "Is not this the carpenter's son? is not his mother called Mary? and his brothers, James and Joses and Simeon and

Judas? And his sisters, are they not all with us?" We read "his brothers — his sisters" and not "their other children" (this carpenter's and Mary's). Matthew avoids this expression, and not only he; it is constantly avoided. The people of Nazareth speak. *They* regarded the carpenter Joseph as the physical father of Jesus, who had *not* been born in Nazareth; and so *they* speak of these others as Jesus' brothers and his sisters. This same avoidance appears in even a more striking way in Acts 1:14: "These (the eleven apostles) continued with one accord in prayer and supplication, *with* the women and Mary the mother of Jesus, and *with* his brothers." The two prepositions σύν (associative) mark two groups. The second group is not connected with Mary: "and with *her* other sons," but only with Jesus: "and with *his* brothers." Why? If here or anywhere the reading were *"her* sons," we should not hesitate for one moment to consider James (and then also Jude, Jude 1) the uterine brother of Jesus. But this is the very thing the Scriptures do *not* say and avoid saying in these notable passages.

It is said that these "brothers" always appear in the company of Mary and must therefore be her own sons. The fact is that they appear in Mary's company just once, in Matt. 12:46, etc., where they desire to remove Jesus from work. Once is not always, and here, too, they appear only as *"his* brothers."

We look also at John 19:25: Jesus commits his mother to John. If James and Jude, to say nothing of the other two brothers and of the several sisters, were uterine children of Mary, how could Jesus turn this mother over to John? It is said that they were not believers (John 7:5), and that this fact explains the action of Jesus on Calvary. Does it? James at least came to fullest faith immediately after the resurrection of Jesus, Jesus even appeared to him personally (I Cor. 15:7). We add to this the fact that James had his permanent residence in Jerusalem and, as far as we know, never traveled afar, while the apostle John had the call to travel, and we see him at least in Samaria (Acts 8:14) with Peter, these two being closely attached to each other. To say that *"his* brethren" = uterine sons of *Mary* is to beg the question.

All the efforts to arrive at certainty from the data at hand in the New Testament are unsatisfactory. Take the supposition that these brothers and sisters of Jesus were the children of Mary's sister. A plausible case can be made of this supposition. Why should two widowed sisters not live as one family and have one home, etc.? And why should the children not be considered brothers and sisters, the more so since there was only the one boy (Jesus) on the one side? We shall not go into this except to say that in John 19:25 three women are mentioned and not four (see the author on this passage). We consider finally the supposition that these were Joseph's children by a former marriage. But the data at hand do not furnish sufficient evidence to support this view.

Coming down from certainty to probability (ready to content ourselves with that), the least probability is on the side of the view of uterine children. A greater degree of probability exists for the assumption of cousinship, children of Mary's sister. Examine the evidence; do it with an unbiased, judicial mind. Since certainty eludes us, to speak positively is, in our opinion, a mistake.

* * *

Another question is asked: "Was James an apostle?" The claim that he was is based on the genitive that is used in Acts 1:13. He is regarded as the second James in this list that is offered by Luke because the last of the eleven is called "Judas (Jude) of James," i. e., of the James, the ninth in the list, "of

James" being translated *"brother* of James." The New Testament writers James and Jude are thus regarded as apostles and uterine brothers of Jesus. John 7:5, "did *not* believe," is said to mean "did *not fully* believe" or something to that effect. Luke's introduction of James in Acts 12:17 without further explanation as to his identity is explained as being due to Acts 1:13. The first apostle James (John's brother) was dead by Herod's sword (Acts 12:2), which left only the second apostle James mentioned Acts 1:13, whose brother was Judas. But in Acts 1:13 this genitive "of James" does not mean *"brother* of James" (A. V.) but *"son* of James" (R. V.) *because* immediately preceding we have the genitive "of Alpheus" in the sense of "son of Alpheus." If this last genitive were not to mean "son of" but "brother of," Luke would have had to write ἀδελφός before the genitive; there is no alternative. Whatever one may say about Luke's introducing James in Acts 12:17 without further note, it is unwarranted to regard him as an apostle in Acts 1:13. For that matter, Luke also fails to say in Peter's speech in Acts 12:17 how this James comes to hold a position such as Peter indicates; in fact, even in Acts 15:13 Luke offers no explanation whatever to inform us why this James should serve as president of the Apostolic Conference when Peter himself is present.

James is not regarded as an apostle in Gal. 1:19 as some assume. "But other of the apostles saw I none," means what it says. The addition "save (εἰ μή) James, the brother of the Lord," does not mean that after all Paul *did* see another apostle, but means that he saw one other man, a leading person who was so important that he feels he must be mentioned along with the apostle Peter. For the Galatians might accuse Paul of not telling the whole truth if he failed to name also James although James was not an apostle. Paul could not omit the name of James, for the Judaizers in Galatia certainly claimed to have this James on their side over against Paul. So Paul mentions James and distinguishes him from the apostles yet honors him highly as "the brother of the Lord," and in Gal. 2:9 he names him before Cephas and John as one of the "pillars." All of this is plain when we know what Acts tells us about this James, the head of the mother church in Jerusalem for years past.

* * *

The story of this James may be sketched in brief. He knew Jesus intimately from his youth. Like his brothers and his sisters, he did not believe in Jesus. This does not imply that he was averse to the Messiahship of Jesus, but his ideals regarding what such a Messiahship should be were earthly (John 7:3-5). On one occasion at least he and the rest of the family thought that Jesus had lost his mental balance and ought to be restrained (Matt. 12:46, etc.) and helped to make efforts to restrain him. Jesus was finally crucified, arose from the dead, and vouchsafed to appear to James (I Cor. 15:7). This wrought a mighty change, not only in him, but also in his three brothers. We now see them in the company of the eleven apostles and of the women saints, among the latter is also the mother of Jesus (Acts 1:14). James presently appears as the head of the Christian congregation at Jerusalem. It must have been his high character and his personal importance which made him the choice of the congregation and of the apostles for this important position. The apostles had to travel, James could and did remain permanently in Jerusalem, where he also finally suffered martyrdom.

Luke gives us a glimpse of his character. James presides at the Apostolic Conference. After speeches by Peter and by Paul, James makes his speech in which he supports these two apostles with Scripture and then with clear, balanced judgment offers the resolution which the conference adopts unanimously, embodies in a formal letter, and sends to all the congregations that have a mixed membership of former Jews and former Gentiles. This resolution was received with joy everywhere. It settled a most troublesome question in a considerate, just, and effective way. Not Peter, not Paul, not John, it was this nonapostle James who proposed the resolution and the plan of putting it into a brief encyclical. The way in which he proposed to help the congregation by means of this circular letter is identical with the way in which he a few years before this convention helped the Jewish churches by his own personal letter. Among the Jews in Jerusalem James came to be known also as "James the Just," a designation which certainly described his character.

* * *

Nowhere in the New Testament is there a trace of conflict between James and any of the apostles, including in particular Paul. James's is the oldest piece of writing in the New Testament. He himself lived in the old Jewish fashion. Hegesippus, who is quoted by Eusebius in his *Church History*, 2, 23, describes James as a Nazarite who drank no wine or strong drink, who ate no animal food, whose head was not touched by a razor, etc. He was not a Judaizer, nor did he lend support to the Judaizers. Acts 15 shows clearly what his position was; Galatians 2 corroborates Acts 15. Judaizers did attempt to hide behind his skirts when they were antagonizing Paul; they also misquoted Peter and, in fact, all of the Twelve in the same way.

James and Paul, like the Twelve, are in fullest agreement on the doctrine of justification. Those who assume a conflict between James and Paul regarding this doctrine do not properly understand James 2:14-26 and often also Paul's teaching. We might treat this entire subject at this place but prefer to leave it where it belongs, in connection with the exegesis of 2:14, etc. Living in the Jewish way was entirely a matter of liberty for the individual; Paul himself says: "Unto the Jews I became as a Jew," and in Acts 21:20, etc., willingly assents to observe a distinctive Jewish custom (see the author on this passage).

* * *

We read that it is surprising "that one recognized as such a thorough Jew as James, the brother of our Lord, and who used Aramaic, should have written in such idiomatic Greek" (R. 123, where the Greek of James is discussed). This surprise is due to preconceptions. The little country of Palestine was of necessity thoroughly bilingual. The French idea of knowing only French and our own inattention to anything but English are not found among the Jews in apostolic times, are not found today as the writer learned when he was traveling through Syria and Palestine. In fact, in these countries ordinary people today speak several languages. Reared in Galilee, James, like Jesus, learned Greek from boyhood and thus learned it idiomatically. As a collector of the port custom Matthew could not have held his post without proficiency in Greek; and thus he writes better Greek than Mark in his Gospel. Besides, there is always the native linguistic ability of a man with which we must reckon; James had it. So there is no reason whatever for surprise. The supposition that the epistle of James is a translation from the Aramaic is unwarranted. Peter (Matt. 26:73) and other native Galileans might betray their origin by the burr in their pronunciation; this does not appear when they write.

In his commentary Mayor has investigated the Greek of James exhaustively even in many points that need no investigation and that net us very little. The mode of thought found in James is more important.

He employs simple language to express his thought. This is thought to be due to his Jewish type of mind; yet there are good writers in all languages who express themselves in simple instead of in complex, involved sentences. Character and type of mind have not a little to do with one's form of language. James is forceful, direct, compact, avoids circumlocutions. He speaks like a prophet; he has many original, striking metaphors and similes; he has a poet's imagination. His scorn and his irony are devastating.

Mayor has not understood Paul well enough when he describes him as being "passionless and pale" in comparison with "the volcanic energy" of James. Paul is more tremendous than James in the use of many a figure and many a thought. Paul's sweep of mind is far greater; he always sees all sides of a subject, takes care of every angle of thought, fortifies it on every side. Paul's emotions play over the widest range and down to the deepest depth; he reaches into all the emotions of his readers in the same way. Paul gauges all the reactions of his readers and not only some or those of a few. James does not attain such heights. He moves in a much narrower groove; but in that groove he moves with power, deep insight, convincing conviction, certainty of result.

James is concrete and not abstract in thought. There is power in this although he is not alone in this respect. His figures and his illustrations are taken from rural life, from sea and sun, from domestic life and from public life, as Mayor groups them. James certainly loves *paronomasia;* he has an ear for alliteration, homœoteleuton, and rhythm. We expect a man of his type to draw on the Old Testament; he knows his LXX. Many of his statements sound like the words of the old prophets. Some of them have Hebraistic parallelism, which is always attractive. Mayor has gone to the trouble of comparing the language of

James with that of the canonical books of the Old Testament; of the Apocrypha (Wisdom of Jesus, Son of Sirach; Book of Wisdom); of Philo; of the early patristic writers; even with the language of the Greek philosophers. As far as the Apocrypha are concerned, at most only linguistic allusion appears and never a quotation. When, on the basis of this finding, some make the deduction that the epistle could not have been written by a Palestinian but only by a Hellenic Jew, this deduction is not warranted by the premise.

* * *

A great number of years passed before this epistle was placed permanently into the canon. It appears in the ancient Syriac version, the Peshito (dated in the second century); but in the West Eusebius (born about 270) still classes James among the antilegomena (*Church History*, 2, 23) although he himself quotes James in two of his other books (Mayor, page XLIX). An acquaintance with James may be noticed in the writers of the early church. The first authoritative insertion into the canon was decreed by the Council of Carthage in 397; the Eastern Church made the insertion at the Trullan or Quinisext Council in 672.

The explanation for this delay is not difficult to find. The epistle is addressed to Jewish Christians who were living in many different places at a time when the gospel had not yet made an appreciable impression on the Gentiles. This fact naturally restricted the circulation of the epistle when Gentile congregations were later established over the entire empire. The epistle deals with the moral life of Jewish Christians and does not treat any of the great gospel doctrines *in extenso*. Even now, since it is in the canon, it is of less importance than most of the other parts of the New Testament. The writer designates himself "God's and the Lord Jesus Christ's slave" and his readers "the twelve tribes, those in the Diaspora." While both designations were perfectly clear to the first readers, later generations did not find them so. Which James was this? There were questions and doubts. These arose anew among the Reformers of the sixteenth century and had the same effect on them.

When we today call the Epistle of James deuterocanonical, this is done in order to register these facts and not to cast aspersion upon the genuineness and the usefulness of the epistle. "Canon" means measuring rod. The church uses the deuterocanonical books as a measuring rod but regards them as "deutero," secondary, because it has rods that are "proto," which have become such because of their continued use in the church.

Luther's views regarding this epistle have never been adopted by his church. In his exposition of the First Epistle of St. Peter he writes in 1523: "If one wants to preach the gospel, it must, in short, be on the resurrection of Christ. He who does not do that is no apostle; for this is the main part of the gospel. And those are the right, noblest books, which teach and impress this, as stated above. Hence one can well feel that the Epistle of James is no right apostolic epistle, for there is hardly a thing of this in it." Erlangen ed., vol. 51, p. 337. In order to understand this note page 327: "Therefore St. Paul's Epistles are more a Gospel than Matthew, Mark, and Luke. For these describe little more than the history of the works and wonder signs of Christ; but the grace which we have through Christ, none expounds so energetically as St. Paul, especially in the Epistle to the Romans. Since now much more depends on the word than on the works and deeds of Christ; and where a person would have to do without the one, it would be better to lack the work and history than the word and doctrine: therefore, those books are properly to be praised highest, which treat

Introduction 515

the most the doctrine and word of the Lord." In 1522 (Erlangen ed., vol. 63, p. 115) Luther expressed the same opinions regarding the synoptists as compared with the epistles of Paul and of Peter and regarding Christ's word and works: "If ever I should be without the one, the works or the preaching of Christ, I would rather be without the works than without the preaching. For the works help me nothing, but his words, they bestow the life, as he himself says (John 5:51)." Concluding, Luther says: "Therefore St. James's Epistle is a right *strawy epistle (ein recht strohern Epistel)* compared with them (i. e., John's Gospel, Paul's Romans, Galatians, Ephesians, and First Peter), for it bears no evangelical character *(kein evangelisch Art)*." Erlangen ed., vol. 63, p. 157: "But this James does no more than drive to the law and its works, and in a disorderly way throws one thing into another, so that I imagine it was some good pious man or other who took up a few statements from the disciples of the apostles and so threw them on paper, or perhaps out of his sermon the thing was composed by another."

Much has been made of "a right strawy epistle," but the worst that Luther said is found in the last quotation, namely that the epistle comes from a third or perhaps even a fourth hand, that it is removed from the time of the apostles and thrown on paper in a disorderly jumble. He wrote marginal comments on many passages in his Bible, but only four brief remarks are found in the margin of James (Erlangen ed., vol. 64, p. 251, etc.). Since the great Church Councils had fixed the New Testament canon, it remained fixed until the whole subject was again reviewed during the period of the Reformation. Erasmus and Cajetan were in doubt about the apostolic authorship of James.

To what extent Luther went we have seen. In his first edition of the New Testament in German in 1522 Luther made a separate group of James, Jude, Hebrews, and Revelation and placed them at the end of the volume and assigned them no numbers in his table of contents. In the first complete German Bible issued in 1534 "a right strawy epistle" is omitted from the introduction to James. Since 1603 the disputed books have numbers in the table of contents. On April 8, 1546, the Council of Trent once more declared James canonical and pronounced its writer to be an apostle. The extreme was reached in the Wuerttemberg Confession of 1552, which declared that only those books of the Old and the New Testament are to be called canonical *de quorum auctoritate in ecclesia numquam dubitatum est*. In Wolder's Polyglot, Hamburg, 1596, the seven deuterocanonical books are pronounced "noncanonical" even as some had already called them "apocrypha of the New Testament."

Among the Calvinistic theologians the disturbance was of a very minor nature. Zwingli, Calvin, Beza accepted James as canonical although uncertainty regarding the identity of this James was admitted.

The agitation sketched above resulted from the necessity of translating the Bible and thus determining anew the bounds of the canon, the one source and norm of true Christian faith. At the Council of Trent Catholicism likewise pronounced anew on the canon. Many confessions of the sixteenth century did the same as also the constitution of church bodies still do. Since 1600 the questioning has ceased as far as the evangelical churches are concerned. Critical scholars still express their doubts. Modernists regard the whole Bible as outmoded Jewish literature and pick and choose from its contents what they need for their moralizing lectures. The divine inspiration of the Epistle of St. James and thus its canonicity are assured as far as the church is concerned. It is not disturbed even by Luther's peculiar opinions and much less by the hostile opinions of lesser men.

CHAPTER I

The Greeting, 1:1

1) James, God's and the Lord Jesus Christ's slave, to the twelve tribes in the Diaspora: be joyful! The nominative to indicate the writer; the dative the people addressed; the imperatival infinitive the greeting — all in regular ancient letter form. This document is a letter and not a diatribe as has been stated. The loving address "brethren," even "my brethren," "beloved brethren," appears again and again; James takes the readers to his heart with this and makes himself one of their number.

This is the James who heads the mother church at Jerusalem, is the chief of its elders, "the brother of the Lord," the associate of the Twelve apostles, is in dignity and standing almost apostolic, whom the Lord himself made a witness of his resurrection (I Cor. 15:7) by a special appearance to him alone, the man who presided at the Apostolic Conference a few years after he wrote this letter. He was so well known that in the early days of the church's history his name "James" was enough to identify him in Jerusalem (Acts 12:17); it is enough to enable the readers of this epistle to identify him.

We should remember the relation of the mother church to all the other churches in all other places. Even the Gentile churches that were later founded by Paul regarded the church at Jerusalem as the original church that had been gathered by the Twelve, as the mother of all other churches. All other churches must maintain fullest fellowship with this original church. In a deep, spiritual way all of Paul's churches were parts of the original church, extensions of her in other lands. This relation and connection with the mother church was especially strong in the case of the readers who were addressed by James.

They were not only Jewish Christians; many of them had come from Jerusalem, had been members of the mother church, had fled from Jerusalem because of Saul's persecution. They felt themselves most intimately connected with the mother church since so many of them knew James personally. When they were obliged to flee the fugitives preached the Word wherever they settled (Acts 8:4); they won new converts, but these also felt themselves in the same close relation to Jerusalem and thus in relation to James, who had become the chief elder from the time when the mother church had been organized under its own elders. This was due chiefly to the distinction that had been accorded him by the Lord and to the superiority of his personal character. In later ages and in distant lands the question arose as to who this "James" or Ἰάκωβος ("Jacob") was; this question did not exist for the persons who received his epistle.

The apposition "God's and the Lord Jesus Christ's slave" is not added for the purpose of identifying James; it would, in fact, not identify him for people who did not know him. The apposition states in what capacity and in what manner James intends to address his readers, namely as a slave. Some regard δοῦλος as official since this term is applied to Moses and the prophets. Paul uses it a few times in the captions of his letters. Others regard the word as meaning "worshipper" and fortify this view by a reference to pagan usage.

When James denominates himself a *doulos* of God and of Christ he wants his readers to consider him as one who belongs wholly to God and to Christ, yea, one whose whole will is wholly subservient to their will, who never questions it, never deviates from it (C.-K. 361). As such a slave James addresses his readers who are his "brethren," likewise slaves of these heavenly masters, likewise bowing their wills to these masters in all things. By the use of this term James places himself on the same level with his readers and them on the same level with himself. They are to hear what this fellow slave of theirs has to tell them about the obedience that they all owe their masters in heaven and especially also to point out to them where they have been remiss and have followed their own wrong and foolish wish.

This word thus fits this ethical and nondoctrinal letter in the closest way. Like his readers, James acknowledges two masters who own him and direct his will: "God and the Lord Jesus Christ." There are no articles in the Greek because these are proper nouns exactly like Ἰάκωβος which also has no article and should have none. The significant factor is the combination "God" and "Lord Jesus Christ." This does not intend to convey the thought that the God of the New Testament is the same as the God of the Old. When James combines "God" and "Lord Jesus Christ" when he is calling himself their slave he points to the divine grace, redemption, justification, sanctification, and salvation that have come to him as a slave of God and of Christ and have come equally to his readers as brethren in this slavery. This "Lord" is the one who bought them as his own by his blood (I Cor. 6:20; 7:23); by him they have come to the Father (John 14:6): "my Lord, who has redeemed me, a lost and condemned creature, purchased and won me from all sins, from death and from the power of the devil, not with silver or gold, but with his holy, precious blood, and with his innocent suffering and death, that I may be his own, and live under him in his kingdom, and serve him in everlasting righteousness, innocence, and blessedness, even as he is risen from the dead, lives and reigns to all eternity" (Luther).

"Lord Jesus Christ" is his full name; "our" is often added. Κύριος is to be understood in the full soteriological sense; it certainly also includes the deity of Jesus even as God and this Lord are here joined in a saving relation to James. The title "Lord" goes back to the days before the death and the resurrection of Jesus when the apostles saw their divine Lord and Savior in Jesus. When many Gentiles came to faith, "Lord" came to have an added significance in opposition to pagan divinities and the deification of the Roman emperors, which was expressed by calling them "Lord"; but this title does not have such significance for James. Jewish ears heard the LXX's meaning in Κύριος since *Yaweh* and *'Adon* were translated by the Greek word Κύριος. To Jewish Christians Χριστός, whether it is placed before or after "Jesus," meant "Messiah," the Anointed, who had been promised in the Old Testament.

Equally pertinent is the designation of the readers as "the twelve tribes in the Diaspora." The article is repeated with the phrase, and this fact places its connection with the noun beyond question. First Pet. 1:1 has a similar expression: "the elect strangers of the Diaspora" i. e., of a number of provinces, Pontus, etc.; yet this expression is only similar. James refers to all the Jewish Christians that are scattered in localities outside of Palestine. He does not refer to all the Jews of the far-flung Diaspora throughout the Roman Empire, for James is not addressing Jews as Jews. He is as a Christian Jew writing to Jewish Christians only in order to admonish them concerning their life as Christians. There could as yet have been no congregations that had a heavy contingent of Gentile converts; this designation would then not have been fitting, for it would apply to the Jewish portion of the readers in

James 1:1

one sense, to the Gentile portion in another. Moreover, the Gentile portion could not have understood this expression without a good deal of added explanation.

Although the ten tribes had been lost for a long time and, save for a few individuals (Anna, Luke 2:36, is one), had been absorbed in distant exile, in Matt. 19:28 Jesus speaks of the twelve tribes, and Paul does so in Acts 26:7. James speaks of the twelve tribes in an ideal way. At this time Judah and Benjamin were regarded as Israel. "In the Diaspora" means outside of the Holy Land, among Gentile people. The extent of the Diaspora is not further limited because this limitation lies in the Christian faith of the persons addressed. Applied to them, the designation becomes symbolical: the true people of God who, like James, were now slaves of God and of the Lord Jesus Christ, were Christians, some of them living in Jerusalem and the Holy Land, others, namely those addressed, in the Diaspora.

Still more is suggested by the thought of being "in the Diaspora." The Jews regarded it as ideal to reside in their own land within easy reach of Jerusalem and the Temple. Although so many of them voluntarily lived far away among pagans, this seemed to them like living in exile, their real fatherland and true earthly home being the land given them by God. This Jewish conception is applied to the readers in a symbolic or figurative way: they are far away from the mother church, the central seat of the gospel, from the watchful care of the apostles and the elders of the mother church; they are among Jews in pagan cities and are suffering trials and temptations accordingly and have all sorts of faults and sins growing up like weeds in their midst and all too few capable gardeners to do the weeding. As any Jew felt himself to be amid special dangers to his religion in the Diaspora, so these Jewish Christians are depicted by James as being in a similar condition regarding their Christian life. It is with this thought in mind that he pens this letter. "The twelve tribes" is to make them think of their high calling in Christ; "in the Diaspora" is to make them think of their condition.

One may debate about the extent of the Jewish Christian dispersion. Some have called it eastern and then regard First Peter as a corresponding letter that is addressed to the western dispersion; but this view is not universally accepted. We have only Acts as our guide. We cannot extend this dispersion beyond Syro-Phoenicia and Syria.

Another point that is discussed is whether these Jewish Christians were still members of the Jewish synagogues. The Christians in Jerusalem were certainly a separate group and were no longer members of the synagogues although they attended the services at the Temple (to judge from Acts 21:23, etc.). The Christians in the Diaspora had their own places of worship (2:2). They were, however, a part of the Jewish community of each city and thus had a good deal to suffer from their own nationalists. We know of little more that can be said. James writes with full knowledge of his readers' condition, which required, not doctrinal instruction to fortify against apostasy (as in Hebrews), but moral admonition. This lack of doctrinal instruction disappointed Luther when he read this epistle; but there is no reason for disappointment. An ethical epistle is as much in place as are the ethical portions of other epistles, and as is the ethical teaching of Jesus himself.

The greeting is χαίρειν, an imperatival infinitive like those that are used in laws and in maxims (Moulton, *Einleitung*, 283). This is the common greeting in secular letters; we have another sample in Acts 23:26. It is used in Acts 15:23, for James perhaps dictated the letter of the conference. This form of greeting is a part of the evidence for the early date of our epistle; a little later, when Paul writes his letters, the Christianized form χάρις, κτλ., appears, and the unmodified χαίρειν, "be joyful or happy," disappears.

Trials and Temptations, 1:2-18

How to Consider Trials, v. 2-4

2) What James thinks of his readers he shows by the way in which he designates them. He starts the body of his epistle without a preamble such as thanks to God for the good existing in his readers, a prayer for their need, a remark that information about the readers has reached him and the mother church. This directness we consider part of the character of James. It is a mark of the entire epistle. Sentence after sentence is short and direct; and when the last admonition is reached, he stops as he has begun. In all of this James resembles the old prophets, whose spirit fills him to a marked degree.

Consider it all joy, my brethren, when you fall foul of various kinds of trials, realizing that the testing out of your faith works out constancy.

The greeting is necessarily phrased in the third person. James at once begins the body of the epistle with a loving address in the second person, "my brethren." As a brother he asks his brethren to accept his admonition; as a brother he is concerned about his brethren and the trials with which they are beset. He and they are "brethren" in "the faith," slaves of God and of the Lord Jesus Christ. This should not be overlooked, and the epistle of James should not be regarded as lacking the gospel basis of saving, justifying, sanctifying faith. We have the whole basis in these first two verses. The readers are beset by many trials; they also show great faults in their lives. With a loving, sympathetic heart James takes up the trials first of all.

How should the readers consider their many trials? As "all joy." The participle states why: because their faith is thus developed into constancy, brave perseverance. It grows into strong manhood. It is tested out; the dross is removed. Christians ought to rejoice because of that and not pity themselves or grow sad.

One of the characteristics of James's style is to repeat a word he has just used. So χαράν here repeats χαίρειν: the greeting "be joyful" goes forward into "all joy." The thought is that, when trials come, a lot of joy comes to people of faith. There is no denial that trials also produce strain and pain; there is, however, the reminder that, when they come, and when we evaluate them aright, we ought to bear them with joy. The flesh will not like them, but the spirit will rejoice to prove itself and to gain from the trials what Christ intended should be gained. The aorist imperative is in place, for it is more decisive than the present and determines once for all that the readers are to consider it all joy whenever trials come, no matter when they come, or of what kind they may be.

James loves occasional, unsought alliteration: here πειρασμοῖς περιπέσητε ποικίλοις. The verb is used in the sense of "encounter" and refers to an unwelcome encounter (robbers in Luke 10:30, misfortune, and the like): one falls somewhere where trials are all around him, and he cannot get away, they pounce upon him. We translate this Greek word "trials" and not "temptations" (our versions) because the verb says that we fall foul of them; we encounter them from without. In v. 13, 14 James speaks of temptations and shows that these are due to a man's own inward lust. The adjective means "varicolored," "motley"; these are trials of various kinds, they are like Joseph's coat of many colors. The aorist expresses actuality: "whenever you actually fall foul of various kinds of trials."

3) Just as direct and to the point as is the admonition is its substantiation: "realizing that the testing out of your faith works out constancy." Γινώσκω is the proper verb, οἶδα would not be; the latter indicates only the relation of the object to the subject, the former the relation of the subject to the object. I "know" many things which do not affect me; I "realize" things that do affect me and cause a strong reaction in me. The ὅτι clause states what we are to realize in all our trials. The participle matches the imperative: realizing what trials really are and what they accomplish, we will consider them all joy. They constitute "the testing out of our faith," and this testing out produces constancy. Τὸ δοκίμιον, the substantivized neuter adjective, is the classic substitute for an abstract noun. James knows his Greek. Paul loves this verb "to test out" and its derivatives. Faith is a precious thing; it is like gold which should stand every test and, whenever it is tested, should be accepted as having full value. "Trials" and "testing out" match.

We should regard trials as tests of our Christian faith. If we have true faith we ought to be glad to have it tested out and proved to be genuine. If I have genuine gold coins I shall welcome any test to which they may be subjected. Faith is, however, not cold metal to be weighed and subjected to strong acids; it is a living, vital matter. Its testing out thus produces ὑπομονή, which is another word that is found in Paul's epistles, "remaining under," lasting because it is genuine, hence "constancy," "perseverance." Trench calls this a noble word which always has a background of manliness: "the *brave* patience with which the Christian contends against the various hindrances, persecutions, and temptations that befall him in conflict with the inward and outward world." It is never used with reference to God because it always refers to things: "The man ὑπομένει, who, under a great siege of trials, bears up and does not lose heart or courage." His faith is genuine and, because it is living, grows with every test. The companion word refers to persons and is thus used also with reference to God: "The man μακροθυμεῖ, who, having to do with injurious persons, does not suffer himself easily to be provoked by them or to blaze up into anger." In general propositions we have the present tense; in κατεργάζεται the preposition is perfective: the testing "works out" constancy.

4) **Now let this constancy have (its) work complete in order that you may be complete and entire, lacking in nothing.**

Δέ is neither "and" nor "but"; it is expository and brings out the point that is implied in v. 2, 3. With ἔργον τέλειον James repeats κατεργάζεται; τέλειον is also repeated by τέλειοι. This verbal linking is beautiful and links the thought as well. If the result of trials is so good, we should have this result in its entirety. Let this noble constancy of faith then have "its work complete," i. e., so that its goal is fully reached. Many trials may come upon us, but each carries our constancy nearer to the goal. Let it continue to do so (present imperative). Who wants to remain incomplete, immature?

Our aim must certainly be "that we may be complete and entire, lacking in nothing." Τέλειοι = having reached the goal of our faith by constancy; ὁλόκληροι adds the thought that all the parts of this completeness and this constancy are present. These positive adjectives are intensified by the addition of the negative "lacking in nothing," neither coming short of the goal nor having one part or the other still missing in us. The adjectives are finely discussed by Trench, *Synonyms*.

This is the proper way to look at all our trials: they help to do something that is most necessary and blessed for our faith, that brings it to constancy, and this constancy makes us complete and entire in our faith. It is certainly a matter of joy to see this work progressing more and more toward its end. It is not necessary to bring in the whole round of Christian virtues and of the moral life. James deals with our faith in Christ, with the constancy of this faith, its manly maturity that has no weak spots anywhere. Trials test it out for possible weak spots so as to make us genuine and solid all around. Trench is unclear regarding the word "entire": so that no *grace* is wanting. James is speaking of the root, which is faith, not of the fruits, which are Christian graces. James is not a moralist; he is a genuine apostolic preacher.

How to Use Prayer when Trials Come, v. 5-8

5) Now if anyone of you lacks wisdom, let him ask from God who gives to all without reservation and not as upbraiding; and it shall be given to him.

The fact that James should speak of "wisdom" in connection with trials is entirely natural. James knew Ps. 73 and the Book of Job, where men wrestle with the great problem of trials that overwhelm the godly and do not come upon the ungodly, and where the true solution of the problem is offered. In this verse James speaks of wisdom only in this connection; in 3:13, etc., there is a different connection. Σοφία is true knowledge that is applied in a practical way. There is a wide range of subjects to which the application of wisdom may be made. James here applies wisdom to faith as it benefits one under trials. We have a sample of this wisdom in v. 2-4; yet wisdom has a much wider application in connection with our faith.

We note that λείπεται repeats λειπόμενοι, that αἰτείτω is repeated in v. 6, and that διδόντος and δοθήσεται emphasize the idea of giving. A Christian may well feel himself in the dark in the midst of trials. A good degree of wisdom is required to see the good in trials. The Twelve had such wisdom when they rejoiced to suffer shame for Christ's name, Acts 5:41. It is not difficult to obtain: if anyone lacks it, let him pray for it, and it will be given to him. James re-echoes many sayings of Jesus, which is an indication that he heard them from Jesus' own lips. "Ask, and it shall be given you." (Matt. 7:7; 22:23; Mark 11:24; John 14:13; 15:7; 16:23).

The remarkable thing is the fact that James designates "the One giving," namely "God," as giving ἁπλῶς, which epexegetical καί expounds as meaning μὴ ὀνειδίζων. The adverb is never used in the sense of "liberally" (our versions); this meaning is given it only because it *seems* to fit the present context. The meaning is *rueckhaltslos* or *ohne Bedenken* (G. K. 385). When God gives he gives and has no secret, restraining thoughts. He gives "without reservation" and thus "not as upbraiding" the petitioner, not as scolding him for his lack of wisdom, i. e., for his foolish thoughts about God's sending perplexing trials.

This is said in order to encourage each of us to ask of such a kindly and true Giver. The middle voice of αἰτέω, as 4:3 shows, does not have the same force as the active although G. K. thinks so; but see Moulton, *Einleitung*, 251, etc.; R. 805. B.-D. 316, 2 thinks that in 4:3 the middle and the active are exchanged, and B.-P. 38 minimizes the difference between them. It is, however, acknowledged that the middle is used regarding asking in business relations, where a person has a certain right to ask for something. By his oath Herod had given Salome such a right (Mark 6:24, middle). By his promises to us God has given us such a right, and the middle imperative bids us use this right. The middle voice harmonizes perfectly with the way in which James designates the great Giver. Even the fact that he gives "to all" means much; for no matter who the poor, distracted person is, God does not intend to let him go away empty. Yet God has his means for giving the great gift of additional wisdom. This is his Word. Wisdom does not come down out of the sky. God's Spirit instructs, enlightens, makes us wise by means of his Word. This angle of the matter James takes up in v. 21, etc.

6) James speaks of faith: **But let him ask in faith, nothing doubting; for the one doubting is like a seawave wind-driven and tossed** (up and down). **Yea, let not that person think that he shall receive anything from the Lord — a man double-minded, unstable in all his ways!**

"Let him ask" takes up the preceding "let him ask"; the object to be asked for is wisdom as this is applied to the trials that come upon us Christians. We should confine ourselves to the closely connected thought of James and not think of some other object such as the cessation of the trials or benefactions apart from trials. The testing out of faith is to work out constancy, and this constancy is to have its work complete so as to make us ourselves complete and entire, lacking nothing. Such trials are, then, to continue. The great need of the believer is wisdom to understand all God's purposes in placing us amid these continuous trials.

When a believer asks for this wisdom he must do so "in faith," i. e., altogether "in connection with ($\dot{\epsilon}\nu$) his faith." This means not only that his prayer for wisdom must spring from true Christian faith, but also that it must be offered wholly in the interest of this faith, its complete constancy and our own becoming complete. This prayer, offered thus "in faith," has the direct and unqualified promise that it will be given what it asks, for the one thing that God wants to do is to bring the faith of every one of us to this completeness. "In faith" (positive) is made clear by the addition "nothing doubting" — μηδέν because of the participle, the natural negative of which is μή; and by διακρινόμενος, judging now in one way, now in another about our trials and hence "wavering" in judgment (A. V.) or "doubting" (R. V.).

James does not mean that we are not to doubt that our prayer will be granted by God. Nor does he mean that this prayer asks for the cessation of trials or for something that is not connected with trials and with our faith during these trials. Nor does James have in mind a faith in God in general and not a faith specifically in Christ. Nor is the truth here expressed altered by the fact that often God does not hear our prayers. James is writing to brethren who are one with him in confessing themselves as "slaves of God and of *the Lord Jesus Christ*," and "your faith" (v. 3) is faith in God and in the Lord Jesus Christ. The older commentators who understood "in faith" to mean faith "in Jesus Christ" are correct. This entire epistle deals with *Christian faith* and shows how this faith should be genuine, true, active, living, fruitful.

"In faith" implies prayer that comes to God and the Lord Jesus Christ with trust, simple trust, and in the interest of this its trust, that asks for wisdom to establish itself more and more, to be fully and in every respect the faith and trust it ought to be so that by it the petitioner is made the complete Christian he ought to be. Μηδὲν διακρινόμενος expounds this: when he asks wisdom of God and the Lord as a true slave of both (v. 1) he is to have no other thought, no other judgment in his mind, no indecision of any kind, half of the time deciding in his secret mind (the participle is middle: "for himself") that he wants this, half of the time that he wants that, neither one of which is in the interest of simple, genuine faith. As God is the One who gives ἁπλῶς, "without any secret reservation in his mind," so we must ask for wisdom for our faith without any secret contrary, vacillating notions in our minds. To put it in our own words: God is honest and frank in his giving and in his promise to give, and he wants every petitioner to be honest, frank, and true in his asking. Alas, too many speak proper words when they pray amid trials, but they do not mean them in the bottom of their hearts.

In a flash, by a striking figure, James exposes what "the one doubting" really is, i. e., what God sees him to be. Here the participle again repeats the preceding participle. "He is like a seawave wind-driven and tossed up and down." The second perfect ἔοικε is derived from εἴκω and is found only here and in v. 23. It always has a present meaning. The *tertium comparationis* is instability. A seawave is unstable; at one time the wind blows it one way, again another way. It is subject to the play of the wind, to all its vagaries. More than that, it is tossed, keeps going up and down, up and down. There is a double instability, a lateral and a perpendicular one: running in whatever direction the wind may take, bobbing up and down without cessation. A thought strikes the unstable mind from one direction and then from another, and the mind has no resistance, no ὑπομονή, constancy, it just yields. Yet even so it is inconstant, for it sinks and falls, sinks and falls. It takes up a thought and then drops it again; it rises in enthusiasm with a thought and then lets go of it in discouragement. Pitiful indeed! James had not lived in Capernaum beside the Sea of Galilee for nothing.

7) Γάρ is confirmatory: "Yea, let not that person think that he shall receive anything from the Lord." The apposition describes "that person" so as to show the reason that he certainly cannot expect to receive

anything: "a man double-minded, unstable in all his ways." Note how James uses ἄνθρωπος, "a person," and ἀνήρ, "a man"; he uses the latter when he attaches qualifiers. The usual comment has ὁ Κύριος equal God (Old Testament designation) and points to 4:10 and 5:4, 10. But what about 1:1; 3:9; 4:15; 5:8, 11, 14, to which 4:10 and 5:10 also belong? After James uses "Lord" with reference to Jesus in 1:1 and repeatedly in other chapters, we see no reason for making "the Lord" mean "God" in the present passage. The truth is that only in 5:4, in the combination "Lord Sabaoth," does James use "Lord" as a designation for "God"; elsewhere he writes "God" when he refers to God. Some commentators seem to think that the New Testament or at least James (who is regarded as being excessively Jewish) warrant no prayer to Jesus and thus no answer to prayers from Jesus (which has the appearance of subordinationism).

8) The A. V. translates v. 8 as a separate sentence by inserting a copula; others punctuate so as to make this "man" the subject of "shall receive." The R. V.'s translation is correct; we have a most effective apposition. The adjective "double-minded" ("double-souled") is a new Greek formation so that some think that it was coined by James; it is used often after the time of James as if it caught men's fancy. This word is certainly expressive of just what James means by the figure he used in v. 6: a ψυχή that seems like two by flying in opposite directions. This is enhanced by the verbal "unstable (not placed down to stand solidly) in all his ways." A weak wobbler does not wobble merely in one respect.

James broadens in his description of the man he has in mind and in what he says about the prayers of such a man: he need not think that he will receive "anything," to say nothing of so great a thing as wisdom. We need not discuss as to how far "all his ways" is Hebraic (the singular is used in 5:20); found frequently in the Old Testament *(derek)*, "way" and "ways" are also used repeatedly in the New Testament and are natural in all languages where, as in Greek, we also use the corresponding verbs "to go," ἔρχομαι, or "to walk," περιπατέω.

A Bit of the Wisdom That Is Good for the Christian amid Trials, v. 9-11

9) We have a piece of this wisdom in v. 2-4; this is another piece. It is wisdom, indeed! Δέ, which is omitted in the A. V., is translated "but" in the R. V. (as it is in v. 5); it is really the common transitional particle and is then not adversative. **Now let him boast, the brother, the lowly one, in his high position; on the other hand, the rich one in his lowly position!**

This is beautiful parallelism and antithesis. We keep the word order of the Greek and its emphatic position of the imperative, its emphasis on "lowly" (the article is repeated as if the adjective is an apposition in a climax; see R. 776 and the examples). "The brother," writes James, yours and mine, any one of "my brethren" (v. 2). But it is here "the lowly one," not the rich one (v. 10), the one who is poor in earthly wealth, lowly in his entire station in life. It makes no difference as to how this brother comes to be so lowly. Many poor Jews embraced Christianity; many had lost their property during the persecution that had been inaugurated by Saul. We take it that not a few of the readers who were addressed by James were lowly in regard to money and in regard to their social position.

That fact itself was a trial for them; it was so in ancient times, read Ps. 73:3-12. These lowly Christians see the earthly riches and prosperity of unbelieving Jews. They ask the question asked in Ps. 73:11. The worst feature is not their poverty but the "waters of the full cup wrung out to them," the maltreatment to which their lowly position subjects them. If they would give up their faith in Christ they might improve their earthly state; their refusal multiplies their trials in many ways (v. 2). Does James pity them and allow them to pity themselves? The very opposite: Let such a brother boast, yea, boast, no less, "in his high position!" Let wisdom open his eyes to see what "height" he has attained. He is a true child of God in Christ Jesus. Priceless spiritual blessings are his. Let him shout for joy (v. 2: "all joy") !

10) On the other hand (δέ is used in this sense), the brother who is rich as Abraham, David, Nicodemus, Joseph of Arimathaea, Barnabas (Acts 4:37) were rich — to mention only these — what about such a brother? Christ always found some true believers among the wealthy and those who were in high earthly positions, not so many, yet some (I Cor. 1:26). This brother has an equal reason for boasting, yet his boasting extends in the opposite direction: Let him ever keep boasting, yes, boasting, no less, "in his lowly position." Just as "the lowly one" and "the rich one" refer to earthly positions, so "in his height" (ὕψος) and "in his lowliness" (ταπείνωσις) refer to spiritual positions. The two statements balance perfectly; the imperative belongs to both. The beauty of thought and of expression is greatly increased when James has ταπείνωσις repeat ταπεινός. We have seen how James employed this literary device several times in the few preceding verses. Here, however, this verbal correspondence is far more effective because "the lowly one" is to be understood in the earthly while "his lowliness" is to be understood in the spiritual sense. We credit James with great mastery of thought and of expression.

Faith in Christ lifts the lowly brother beyond his trials to the great height of a position in the kingdom

James 1:10

of Christ, where as God's child he is rich and may rejoice and boast. Faith in Christ does an equally blessed thing for the rich brother: it fills him with the spirit of Christ, the spirit of lowliness and true Christian humility (Phil. 2:3-11: "with lowly-mindedness," v. 3). As the poor brother forgets all his earthly poverty, so the rich brother forgets all his earthly riches. The two are equals by faith in Christ.

But instead of using only this idea, which is rather common in Christian circles, the wisdom which James offers goes much farther. He puts his thought chiastically and flashes the chiasm upon his readers by means of the contrast between "height" and "lowliness" by making this "lowliness" (spiritual) the counterpart of "the lowly one" (in earthly life). This rich brother has lost all high-mindedness, he has gained the lowliness which is true Christian and spiritual wisdom. Earthly riches no longer affect him. He knows himself to be a poor sinner who is saved by grace alone, whose earthly life is only a poor, transient flower.

Other interpretations are offered. One regards this rich brother as a rich worldling and says that James treats him with sarcasm by telling him to glory, if he wants to glory, in being nothing. We pass this and other inadequate interpretations by.

James continues with ὅτι *consecutivum* (on which see R. 1001): **seeing that as herbage bloom he shall pass away, for the sun rises with the heat and withers the herbage, and its bloom falls off, and the beauty of its appearance perishes.**

Note the repetition of ἄνθος and χόρτος. Faith in Christ produces true humility in the rich brother by bringing him to the full realization of the fact that, rich as he may be, he shall presently pass away like the bloom on the herbage. It is the poet in James that leads him to expand the figure. Moreover, he wants its fulness to impress every wealthy believer the more with the wisdom (v. 5) which lies in the thought of the scorched bloom.

11) Γάρ makes it all plain. The aorists are gnomic (universal and timeless, R. 836, etc.), and we can translate them only with the English timeless present. The sun rises with the heat (καύσων with σύν). But this word does not refer to *Eurus*, the Sirocco or burning wind that blows from the east and the south, the hot desert region near Palestine, B.-P. 665, etc. Then the herbage dries up (ξηραίνω); its beautiful bloom falls off, and all the loveliness of its face (πρόσωπον) perishes. **Thus also shall the rich one fade in his goings** (μαραίνω, "to extinguish," the future passive is to be understood in the sense of the middle), hardly in his travels as a merchant who is buying and selling; or while he is still busy acquiring more wealth and before he feels satisfied to rest and to enjoy it; but in his activities in general. For we must note that the figure as it is expanded applies to the life of the wealthy man and not only to the withering away in death.

To be sure, the lowly, poor Christian will also die; but he never blooms like the one who has wealth. The figure is thus applied only to the latter. If he as a true Christian learns lowliness he loses nothing; Christ is his all in all. Would that every rich Christian might glory in his lowliness!

Blessed the Man Who Is Tested out by Trial,
v. 12

12) **Blessed a man who remains constant under trial, seeing that, having gotten to be tested out, he shall receive the crown of the (heavenly) life, which he promised to those who love him.**

Our versions seem to be under the impression that the turn from trials to temptations is made at this point and translate: "Blessed the man that endureth temptation." But this is not satisfactory, for πειρασμός was used in the plural in v. 2, and ὑπομένει has the same root as the twice repeated ὑπομονή occurring in v. 3, 4, and δόκιμος repeats the τὸ δοκίμιον that was used in v. 3. This causes it to appear certain that James is still speaking of trials. In addition, his calling the man who shows constancy under trial (trials working out constancy, v. 3) "blessed" completes the thought expressed in v. 2, that we must count it "all joy" when we fall in with all kinds of trials. In v. 2-4 the mediate cause for joy is brought forward: constancy is wrought out, and when it has done its work completely, we are ourselves complete, entire, lacking nothing. Now the ultimate effect of trial is brought forward, the reception of the crown of the heavenly life. Thus in every way, linguistically and in thought, v. 12 is to be associated with v. 2-4.

This is a beatitude like those that are found in the Psalms, like those spoken by Jesus (Matt. 5:3, etc.). Μακάριος is the Hebrew *'ashre,* which is used, for instance, in Ps. 1:1: "Blessed!" It is neither a wish: "May he be blessed!" nor a mere description, but a judgment, a verdict (like the opposite οὐαί: "Woe!") and thus exclamatory. There is no need for inserting a copula. Ἀνήρ is used as it was in v. 7.

What we have said regarding ὑπομονή applies also to the verb which means "to remain bravely constant under" something, thus to persevere, to hold out, and here to do this under "trial," which always intends to test out a man, to reveal whether he is genuine or not in his Christian faith. The singular "trial" is collective as befits the general statement.

Consecutive ὅτι, "seeing that," is like the one that was used in v. 10. This is what is consecutive, what follows such constancy under trial: "having gotten to be tested out" (like a genuine gold coin), found genuine and thus accepted as no less — such a man "shall receive the crown of the life" (appositional genitive: the crown = the life), the crown of which Paul speaks in II Tim. 4:8; and John in Rev. 2:10, where τὸν στέφανον τῆς ζωῆς appears exactly as it does in our passage. Trench states that στέφανος does not mean "crown" in the sense of a royal crown and advocates that διάδημα alone means the latter, "diadem," which consists of a fillet or ribbon that is bound about the head. But there are many instances in the LXX in which *stephanos* is used with reference to royalty: II Sam. 12:30; Ps. 21:1, 3; Zech. 6:11; Rev. 4:4; etc. The crown (*stephanos*) of thorns, like the reed (scepter) in Jesus' hands, was to mark him as King of the Jews. Christians are made *kings* and priests who are to sit with Christ in his throne, to reign with him (βασιλεύειν). While "crown" often designates the victor or is a mark of high honor, it has also a royal connotation, in fact, Isa. 63:3 combines crown and diadem. In 2:5 those who are rich in faith are called "heirs of the kingdom" and, as is done in our passage, are described as "those who love him," i. e., the Lord.

The context decides whether victory or kingship is the implication of the crown. Here, where trial is in the context, the former suggests itself, yet, in view of 2:5, not without the latter. One may wonder whether James thought of the victor's wreath which was bestowed after an athletic contest as Paul does in I Cor. 9:24, 25. This is unlikely in the case of James as well as in the case of his readers who, as former Jews that were confined to Jewish ideals, had the Old Testament imagery in mind. Paul wrote for Gentile Christians, and the pagan imagery of the great athletic contests, which formed such notable events in the great cities where he labored, would be recalled to their minds.

James does not need to name the Lord as being the one who promised this crown to those who love him; his readers know that it is the Lord. The Gospels have no promise that contains the word "crown"; Matt. 19:28a is the nearest approach to it. Yet life eternal is promised often, both as we have it now and as we shall have it in glory. So we take it that James refers to no special passage but to all the Lord's promises of heavenly glory. It is a supposition to think that James refers to an unwritten promise of Jesus in which the crown of life is promised to those who love him.

It is difficult to understand why some regard God and not the Lord Jesus as the subject. Some commentators of this epistle seem to ignore Jesus and to substitute God at other points (as in v. 8 in the case of "from the Lord") also as though James did not think of Jesus very often. In 2:5 James does speak of God's promise to those who love him, yet at the very beginning (1:1) God and the Lord Jesus Christ are combined as owners and masters of James, their slave.

It is worth noting that love is frequently emphasized in connections like the present one, here love to Christ (as in II Tim. 4:8) and in 2:5 love to God (as in Rom. 8:28). The fact that this love is the outcome of faith (v. 3) is self-evident to James and to his readers. The Lord's promise to those who love him stimulates their love; his love will fulfill this promise in the case of those who love him. He delights to crown them in the end. As our faith makes us constant under trials, so also does our love for him who first loved us and died to save us. This is, of course, ἀγαπᾶν, the noble love of understanding coupled with corresponding purpose. The substantivized present participle "those loving him" is qualitative in order to indicate their enduring love to him. Trial tests love as well as faith.

How Temptation Works in Us, v. 13-18

13) Let no one when tempted say: I am being tempted from God. For God cannot be tempted as regards things base; and he himself tempts no one.

James proceeds from trials to temptation. We may note that he does not use the noun πειρασμός as he did in v. 2 and 12 but verb forms. While this noun may mean "temptation," solicitation to commit sin, by combining the noun with δόκιμος, testing out as tried and true (cf., v. 2, 3, 12), James indicates that he uses the noun in the sense of "trial" and not in the sense of "temptation" with its evil connotation. Trench compares the two verbs: when they are used together (as the noun and the adjective are used in v. 2, 3, 12), the idea is that trial tests out so that the person tried is found genuine. In v. 13 there is a different thought: there is no δοκιμάζειν or δόκιμος, no testing out with the expectation of finding genuine. We here have the opposite, namely the evil sense of πειράζειν, for the context shows that solicitation to sin is meant. We should translate "tempt." The way in which James proceeds from trials to temptations shows that the former may turn into the latter, and that James has this in mind when he now deals with the latter. That is, however, all we may say. James does not confuse the two, nor should we when we are interpreting him.

No person, when he is tempted, is ever to say: "I am being tempted from God" and blame the solicitation to sin onto God. Ἀπό is not ὑπό: "by God," as if, like Satan, God were the actual tempter. Ἀπό has the idea of remoteness and suggests the thought that, while tempters are the direct agents who are trying to make us commit deadly sins, God is somehow to blame for the whole thing. If, then, we do fall because of temptation, the blame is not really ours.

We see a sample of this in the very first temptation. Adam says to God: "The woman whom *thou* gavest to be with me, she gave me of the tree, and I did eat." *God* was to blame, for did he not create Eve for Adam? Adam certainly did not create her for himself! There are all manner of ways in which the blame can be shifted to God. Did he not make us with these bodily appetites of ours? Did he not create sex, for instance? Did he not make so many things so attractive to us? Does he not place them so dangerously near to us? So the fallacious reasoning runs on.

An additional word may be in place. The Holy Spirit led Jesus into the wilderness in order that he might be tempted by the devil (Matt. 4:1). Jesus was to vanquish the devil. Heb. 2:18 and 4:15 add the thought that Jesus was tempted and tried for our sakes. In the Lord's Prayer we ask God so to lead us by his providence as to keep us out of temptation that is too strong for us and to strengthen us in the temptation we do have to face (see on Matt. 6:13). I Cor. 10:13 indicates how God answers this petition. When God sent Jesus to be tempted by Satan, and when he now lets Satan tempt us, we should not blame God but should remember that God's own Spirit helped Jesus to crush Satan, and that he now helps us to vanquish him. Thus we are to be made more and more proof against temptation. But there is another side to temptation, which v. 14 points out. *There* lies the real danger.

As for God, he is ἀπείραστος κακῶν, "untemptable as regards things base." The genitive indicates relation: *nicht versuchbar im Boesen, dem Boesen fremd,* C.-K. 918; this is not an ablative (R. 516). Κακά are things that are morally base and degrading; "evil" in our versions is not exact enough. The opposite is ἀγαθά, things beneficial, *heilbringend,* good for salvation. Δέ adds the other side. As nothing that is base in any way is able to tempt God, so he on his part (αὐτός) "tempts no one," never solicits a single believer to anything that is morally base. Ever and ever he warns against all moral baseness. We have his warning when we come in contact with baseness in this base world. God puts his Spirit into our hearts to strengthen us to repel all baseness like Joseph (Gen. 39:9) when we do come into outward contact with it. He even keeps from us any temptation that is beyond our strength.

14) Would that James could have stopped with v. 13! **But each one is tempted by his own lusts, being drawn out** (by them) **and allured with bait.**

We note that James does not say: "Each one is tempted by the devil or by wicked men who act as the devil's tools." That would go only halfway in refuting the charge against God; it would also fail to put the blame where it must eventually be put, namely on ourselves, for James has this in mind (v. 15). It is not well to punctuate as our versions do; the phrase is to be construed with the main verb, and since the modal participles are also passive, it is in effect to be construed also with these.

Each one "is tempted by his own lusts." Even innocent things often arouse these evil desires, and, of course, appeals that are made to them from wicked sources easily arouse them. We should look for the blame here. While it is a *vox media* for "desire," ἐπιθυμία, like πειράζω, has developed a bad meaning so that we translate "lust." Temptation draws it out and then lures it with bait; these participles are figurative: in this way the hunter and the fisherman draw the game or the fish out and get them to take the bait. An illustration has been found in Eve who was first moved from her secure trust in God by the words of the tempter and was then attracted by the fruit itself. As far as the temptation of one who is already a sinner is concerned, who is already subject to lusts, the difference between him and Eve should not be overlooked.

15) The matter is left incomplete in v. 14 where "by your own lusts" is the main point. A new figure completes the natural history of lust as it operates in temptation. **Then the lust, having conceived, gives**

birth to sin; and the sin, having been completed, brings forth death.

Note the perfect parallel in the wording. The metaphor resembles Ps. 7:14. The object is not to show the course of fatal temptation by tracing it from lust to death but by exhibiting its course and its outcome to show that it cannot possibly be "from God." Lust conceives (συλλαμβάνω in the sexual sense, sometimes with an added phrase, "to become pregnant") when it allows itself to be excited by its object; it becomes like a female that is hot for impregnation and then gives birth to sin. No article is used because the type or kind of sin is immaterial, actual sin of one kind or another is meant. Some think of sin in general, but lusts are many, and each gives birth to its own kind of sin.

Once the sin is born, it comes to completeness. This does not mean that, like a babe, it gradually grows to the adult stage. James is speaking of a Christian who loses his faith and spiritual life in some temptation. Unbelievers are in spiritual death from the start. When sin is born of the fleshly lust that is still lingering in the believer, the question still remains whether his faith, which is crushed down for the moment, will not again assert itself and rid itself of the deadly hold of sin by true repentance. Peter repented. Ananias and Sapphira carried their sin through to completion. David repented. Sin is brought to completion when repentance is blocked.

The two participles are quite different and are chosen because they are so exact; they could not be interchanged. Sin does not conceive, it is brought to completion and then brings forth death, i. e., spiritual death, separation from God and the life in God. Τίκτει and ἀποκυεῖ are synonyms; the compound is found only here and in v. 18. Sin is pregnant with death because of its very nature; in another figure, the shadow of sin is death.

It is an injustice to James to say that he is inferior to the Jew Philo in his spiritual insight into and his psychological tracing of temptation through lust to sin and to death. James uses less words, only a few lines. Try to put the whole matter into so few words and then compare your effort with the words of James. His are perfect and masterly; like Philo, you, too, will fall far behind him.

16) **Do not be deceived, my brethren beloved!** namely in this matter of temptation, as if you could in some way shift the blame onto God. The verb may be middle, and the present imperative with μή may give it the meaning: "Stop deceiving yourselves!" The loving address reveals the earnest solicitude of James.

17) This is the truth in regard to God: **All giving** (that is) **good and everything given** (that is) **complete is from above, descending from the Father of the** (heavenly) **lights, with whom there is no variation or shadow cast by change.**

Nothing except what is good and complete comes to us from God; all the bright heavenly bodies are his children, he can change even less than they. Because James has a hexameter in πᾶσα . . . τέλειον, some commentators deny that he wrote it and attribute it to somebody else and let James quote it. And the readers of James are to know the source of the quotation. Well, James is a fine writer and perfectly capable of drifting into metrical rhythm (R. 1200). It is not honorable to rob even a holy writer of his just due.

The words are beautifully chosen and are placed exactly right. Δόσις = the act of giving; δώρημα, a word expressing result = the thing given (δῶρον would be just "gift," and δωρεά a "present"). The two words that are chosen by James correspond: in everything that is given we see the giving, and the giving always has something it gives, and both of these are "from above," "descending" to us from God. The A. V. has both nouns mean "gift" and erases the richness of James; the R. V. has "gift" and "boon" and translates neither term exactly.

The adjectives are placed predicatively: "all giving (that is) good and everything given (that is) complete." All and every one of them (act as well as object) are from above, i. e., from heaven, God's throne, where alone goodness and completeness dwell. In regard to ἀγαθή both C.-K. and G. K. note the religious meaning that refers to salvation: all giving that is *heilbringend,* beneficial in a saving way. To which is to be added τέλειον; the thing given is "complete," not falling short of the goal. Seek not on earth among imperfect, faulty creatures such δόσις and such a δώρημα. Without exception they descend to us from above. Look upward for them!

In v. 5 James has already described the Giver as the One who gives without reservation, without upbraiding us who deserve nothing at all from him. After thus showing his character as a Giver he now describes his changelessness. "From above" points us to heaven, and "from the Father of the lights" places him above all the radiant heavenly bodies. We see them as "the lights" in the firmament. Well, they are great and wonderful, but they are only this far greater Father's children, who is the eternal, perfect light. We decline to allegorize these "lights" into shining spirits or into anything else. As James saw the sun, the moon, and the stars, they led him to see still more, namely their fatherly Creator himself.

These lights vary, they are sometimes brighter than they are at other times. They are only creatures. With God there is no variation whatever but only an unchanging refulgence of blessedness and of glorious goodness. Ἔνι = ἔνεστι, and παραλλαγή is not an astronomical term. These lights are subject to τροπῆς ἀποσκίασμα (another word in -μα expressing result), "a shadcw cast," the genitive is a genitive of cause: "due to turning" or "change" (M.-M. 642). In our opinion the comment that speaks of revolutions of the heavenly bodies, the waning moon, the eclipses, etc., leaves us quite at sea by introducing strange astronomical ideas. James is saying something that his readers, who are ordinary people, are able to understand at once. Many a night is entirely dark, and nothing is seen in the sky. A change has cast a great shadow. There are dark days when the sun is in shadow. "Change," τροπή, comes and goes. With God there is nothing of this kind. "I am the Lord: I change not," Mal. 3:6. "God is light, and in him is no darkness at all," I John 1:5.

Could temptation, i. e., solicitation to anything morally base, κακά, v. 13, come from him? It can come only from beneath, from the pit of hell, from the lusts that are still within us (v. 14).

18) James can say more. **Having willed it, he brought us forth by means of truth's word so that we are a kind of first fruits of his created things.**

God has regenerated us, has made us a kind of first fruits that are set peculiarly apart and sanctified unto him. Will he undo this by tempting us to sin? The participle is emphatic. It is not enough for James to say that God brought us forth, he adds that God willed to do this. The best distinction between βούλεσθαι and θέλειν is found in C.-K. 224, etc. These verbs are synonyms, both refer to the will willing something, the former being wider than the latter so that the latter may be substituted for the former but not vice versa. The former = to have in mind, to intend, to will in preference; it marks the chosen direction. Paul uses it when he is directing Timothy: "I intend" that this or that be done and not something else. Θέλειν expresses determination, the will energetically pressing for the deed. The former is in place here. While we were lost in sin, God resolved by free choice not to let us

James 1:18 547

perish in sin but to bring us forth as new creatures by means of his saving Word. And this will of his is without variation or change (v. 17) ; it is impossible to think that God should alter or modify it in any way.

James uses "brought forth," the same verb that he used in v. 15. We have seen that James loves to repeat a word instead of using a synonym and a different word. Sin brings forth death, that is its nature; with his Word of truth God brings forth a holy first fruits that are consecrated, freed from sin and death. This undoubtedly means regeneration. The dative of means "by truth's Word" places the matter beyond question; cf. I Pet. 1:23; I Cor. 4:15. Neither noun has the article because the quality of each is to be stressed. The absence of the article does not make the expression indefinite, for the genitive lends definiteness. There is only one "Word of truth," i. e., the gospel, the power of God unto salvation. "Thy Word is truth," John 17:17, and sanctifies. Whether the genitive is regarded as appositional: "Word consisting of truth," or as objective: "Word speaking truth," makes little difference; we might make the genitive qualitative as it is in a compound: *Wahrheitswort*, "Word marked by truth." As "Word" it reaches our heart, as "truth," ἀλήθεια, it brings us reality, the whole reality, the actual facts about ourselves, about God, about Christ, about the plan of salvation. "The Word" is often enough, so also is "the truth." Singly or combined they stand against falsehood, lies, delusions; in v. 16, "do not be deceived."

So strong is the older grammatical opinion that εἰς τό expresses only purpose that Mayor regards forty-one of the forty-two of these clauses that occur in Paul's writings as pure purpose clauses. Even the grammarians prefer to find a purpose wherever they can regard the thought as a purpose. Our versions find a purpose here: "that we *should* be a kind of first fruits of his creatures." How long do we have to wait after God has brought us forth by truth's Word until we get to be such first fruits? Are we not at once God's sons, children, heirs, saints, ἡγιασμένοι, those having been sanctified, etc., etc.? The εἰς τό states result here: God brought us forth "so that we *are* a kind of first fruits," etc. Our new birth from above (John 3:3: ἄνωθεν) is not incomplete, partial, incipient; this δώρημα from above (ἄνωθεν) is τέλειον, complete (v. 17).

First fruits (an idiomatic plural in the English, a collective singular in the Greek although it is used also in the plural) of the harvest and of the first-born belonged to God in a peculiar way; see the Bible Dictionaries. The figure is expressive in the case of readers who have come out of Judaism, C.-K. 180, *Deo sacrum.* Of all the created things we reborn children of God are his peculiar possession, sacred to him, not only created by him but also brought forth in a spiritual birth by means of his Word. Will he tempt us again to fall away? Nay, he will continue to shower perfect gifts upon us (v. 17). The addition of τινά, "a kind of first fruits" (R. 742), indicates that James applies the metaphor of first fruits in a special way. Also pagan writers use the plural of this word (Liddell and Scott), but they do so without the far richer connotation that is derived from the Old Testament.

Hearing and Doing the Word, v. 19-27

19, 20) James has mentioned "truth's Word" in v. 18 with a purpose in mind. Being brought forth by it, we are ever to hear and to do this Word. This admonition is set forth at some length.

Know it, my brethren beloved! Moreover, let every person be swift for the hearing, slow for the speaking, slow for wrath; for a man's wrath does not work God's righteousness.

James 1:19

The A. V. follows the inferior reading ὥστε in place of ἴστε. The latter may be either the indicative (R. V.) or the imperative of οἶδα, either an acknowledgment that the brethren do know or an admonition telling them to know. The address "my brethren beloved" (v. 16) again marks the earnestness and the loving concern of James and — we think — a new paragraph. Yet, whether it is appended to v. 18 or regarded as starting a new paragraph, the unexpressed object of what the brethren know or are to know (and thus to act on) is what James has been saying in the preceding verses; it cannot be what follows because this consists of more imperatives. James says only ἴστε, "know," and not γινώσκετε, "realize." He asks for the less, for what is easy, and is concerned that his readers get to know a few vital things about God and about what he has made of them. James will tell them what to do with this knowledge.

First of all and as a preliminary effect (specifying δέ introducing it), "let every person be swift for the hearing, slow for the speaking, slow for wrath." Ἄνθρωπος and ἀνήρ are used as they were in v. 7, 8. Infinitives with adjectives would be enough to express the idea, but εἰς (with the dative idea, R. 1052) is even more expressive. The aorists mean: the whole business of talking. James is clearing the way for the proper reception of the saving Word of God. A person who keeps up his own talking makes a bad hearer.

Like a flash there comes the second βραδύς, "slow to wrath." That is the trouble with lack of hearing and keenness for talking: not everybody will care to hear so much talk, other talkers will also talk, will contradict, hence there will arise a clash, the "wrath," the violent passion. One must have seen Orientals in action to get the full effect of what James forbids. While I was touring in the Orient I saw a slight difference of opinion argued with a violence that seemed to promise immediate blows if not murder. Intemperate talking leads to this sort of thing, and the bitter wrath thus engendered often rankles in the breast of someone for a long time.

James points out what such wrath is never able to produce, namely to work "God's righteousness." The verb "to work" shows that "righteousness" refers to conduct which is adjudged by God as righteous. The genitive is not subjective, for God prescribes this righteousness and right conduct, it comes from him. "The fruit of righteousness is sown in peace by them that make peace" (3:18).

It seems best to take this injunction in its full breadth, to regard it as a general principle of Christian conduct which includes also our meekness in hearing the Word but which goes farther as a general principle always does. So we should not restrict "wrath" and regard it as anger with God for sending us trials, angrily charging him with tempting us. Such implications do not lie in the injunction. C.-K. 312, etc., thinks of wrathful, passionate defense of God's honor as though God's righteous cause were dependent on our *Eifer* (bringing in also justifiable wrath by a reference to Eph. 4:26); but this seems rather far afield.

21) Wherefore, by putting away all shabbiness and what there is of a lot of baseness accept with meekness the implanted Word that is able to save your souls!

There is and will be discussion regarding what James wants his readers to put away. The questions involved are: what is the meaning of $\rho\upsilon\pi\alpha\rho\iota\alpha$; does $\pi\tilde{\alpha}\sigma\alpha\nu$ modify also $\pi\epsilon\rho\iota\sigma\sigma\epsilon\iota\alpha\nu$; what does $\pi\epsilon\rho\iota\sigma\sigma\epsilon\iota\alpha\nu\ \kappa\alpha\kappa\iota\alpha\varsigma$ mean? We can state only our opinion. In the first place, $\dot{\alpha}\pi o\theta\acute{\epsilon}\mu\epsilon\nu o\iota$ is to be understood literally, it is not a figure that is taken from removing clothes. The literal sense is entirely sufficient. In the second place, $\pi\tilde{\alpha}\sigma\alpha\nu$ has its mate in περισσείαν: the readers are to get rid of *all* ῥυπαρία and, as Oesterly puts it, of all the "manifold" baseness, or, as B.-P. 1041 has it, of *all die viele Schlechtigkeit*. Περισσείαν means that there is a whole lot of it, and all of it must be put away.

Κακία is not "wickedness" (R. V.), the word for this term would be πονηρία; nor "malice" (R. V. margin), a mistranslation that is found in a number of passages; it is *Schlechtigkeit*, "baseness," "meanness," "good-for-nothingness," and there is a lot of it of various kinds. We cannot translate περισσεία "superfluity" (A. V. although "superfluity of naughtiness" has caught the English ear), nor "overflowing" (R. V.). Everybody feels that James does not intend to say that we are to put away only the *excess* of baseness; *all* of it, whether it is excess or not, must go. Περισσεία indicates only that there is a great quantity of baseness just as πᾶς points to all of the ῥυπαρία. Luther is right when he translates simply: *alle Bosheit* (*Schlechtigkeit* would have been better).

If ῥυπαρία means "filthiness" as many translate this New Testament *hapax legomenon*, one wonders why "all filthiness" is brought into this connection unless all sinful conditions are to be referred to by filthiness and then by baseness. Taylor, in Mayor's *Commentary*, suggests that ῥυπαρία is to be regarded passively and base, κακία, actively; but who would sense such a distinction? Besides, the latter is a condition as is also the former. The best hint is found in Plutarch who uses this word in the sense of "shabbiness" in money matters (Mayor). Applied to the mind of a Christian, it would match "meanness" when describing the condition which prevents the accepting of the saving Word with meekness. Never ready to hear and to learn, always quick to talk a lot, even quick to flare up when others will not let him talk, or when they venture to contradict, this person shows himself cheap and shabby and also mean and inferior in his mind. He is not fit to accept the Word in that state.

The opposite of these hindering conditions and their outgrowths is "meekness," πραΰτης or πραότης (allied to ταπεινός, "lowly" and "lowliness," which are used in v. 9, 10; see Trench). The pagan world despised the lowly man and admired the bold, masterful man who made others bow to his arrogant will; but Christianity elevated "lowliness" or "lowly-mindedness" as being one of the great spiritual qualities to be sought and to be cultivated in the spirit of Christ. The pagan world, however, regarded "meekness" as a virtue, but only when it was understood in the sense of equanimity and composure; but Christianity placed meekness into its true relation to God and thus also to our fellow men. It is that inwrought grace of spirit which accepts God's Word without back talk, dispute, or questioning; it also accepts his providential dealings in the same spirit. Its root is the full realization of one's sinfulness and unworthiness and of the grace which God extends. Thus James writes: "in meekness accept the implanted Word as the one able to save your souls." Cf., 3:13.

Ἔμφυτον does not mean "engrafted" (A. V.), the word for this thought would be ἐμφύτευτον; nor is the Word a bud that is grafted into us. The adjective might mean "innate," something that is natural to us, but this would not be true. "Implanted" (R. V.) is correct, but it is not proleptic: implanted by being received. The readers are Christians, the Word has been implanted in them; James is not telling them to accept it for the first time. The acceptance referred to by this aorist imperative of actuality is made clear by v. 22: a full, actual, complete acceptance which does not only hear the Word and formally accept it but actually does the Word. To be sure, the readers are also to hear it again and again. In this epistle James himself continues this implanting. What he means is that they shall completely accept the Word which they have already heard and will continue to hear. James may, indeed, have in mind the parable of the Sower and the Seed and the good soil that produces a hundred fold.

"As able (or: as the one able) to save your souls" not only describes the Word but at the same time offers the supreme motive which ought to urge its eager acceptance. Paul calls it "the δύναμις or power of God for salvation" (Rom. 1:16), "by which also you are saved" (I Cor. 15:2), "the gospel of your salvation" (Eph. 1:13). The supposition that James refers only to the law cannot be entertained; the law is never able to save the soul but is able to show only how much the soul needs saving (Rom. 3:20). To save "your souls" by no means excludes the salvation of the body. No contrast between soul and body is implied. The soul is mentioned as that which animates the body and may thus be used as a designation for the entire person; Acts 2:41, "about 3,000 ψυχαί or souls."

22) The effective aorist imperative is followed by a durative, descriptive present imperative, and δέ specifies what effective acceptance of the saving word means. The German *aber* may particularize in the same way. **Now continue to be Word-doers and not only hearers, cheating your own selves by false reasoning.**

The present tense does not imply that the readers have never been doers or have ceased to be doers; some of them may have grown slack in doing, all of them are ever to continue being doers. To this day many are satisfied to be only hearers or little more than that. Too many are at least feeble doers. It has been correctly observed that this was the great fault of the Jews. They attended the synagogue diligently, again and again heard the lections that were read there in regular order like our Gospel and our Epistle lections; but the saving gospel that was contained in the Old Testament Word which they heard failed to produce saving faith and the fruits of that faith in them. They trusted in their hearing and in a measure of formal obedience to the ceremonial regulations of the Mosaic law. When their rabbis, scribes, and elders taught the Old Testament Word they went no farther.

James is misunderstood when he is regarded as an exponent of Jewish thought and teaching to the effect that one must not only hear the precepts of the divine law but also do them. James is regarded as insisting only on Christian ethics. Matt. 7:21; Luke 6:46; 11:48; Rom. 2:13; I John 3:7, and John 7:17 are interpreted in the same way. For this reason such injustice is done to James. He is regarded as a preacher of works and not a preacher of faith like Paul. Yet he has just said that we must "receive the Word" and that that Word has power "to save our souls." To be a doer of the Word is to do the will of God, and his Word and will are "that everyone which seeth the Son and believeth on him may have everlasting life" (John 6:40). To do the Word is *to believe* it for the saving of the soul. The Word ever asks for *faith* and intends to work faith. If it is thought that James had the Sermon on the Mount in mind, then one should not forget Matt. 6:12a, the prayer for forgiveness; 6:33, seeking first the kingdom of God and his righteousness; to say nothing of the Beatitudes, of first becoming a good tree, and of having the righteousness that is better than that of the Pharisees. He who neglects faith may stress works all he pleases he will get no genuine works at all.

To be only a hearer means more than to be lazy in doing; only a hearer means hearing without real faith. Like Paul, James knows that faith cometh by hearing, and hearing is by the Word of God (Rom. 10:18) which is to be heard in faith. Its first and foremost call is: "Believe!" That is why we do the Word by faith, and why this faith is called obeying the Word. Where true faith is found all else follows. The mere hearers are described as "cheating themselves by false reasoning" (M.-M. 487). They reason and argue παρά, beside the mark; their thinking is off the track. Hearing is a means, a very essential means and not an end.

23) James offers a convincing reason for his admonition. To make it more concrete and vivid he individualizes and shows us a sample of each kind of hearer and weaves in an expressive figure. **Because if one is (only) a Word-hearer and not a doer this one is like a man taking cognizance (only) of the countenance of his being in a mirror, for he took cognizance of himself and has gone away and straightway forgot what kind he was. But the one who looked closely into what is complete law, (namely) that of the (true) liberty, and remained so, having become not a forgetful hearer, on the contrary, a work-doer, this one shall be blessed in his doing.**

The description of each of the two individuals is elaborate. "If one," etc., thinks of a forgetful hearer; but "he that did," etc., presents the actual hearer who did not forget. The difference is not a mere variation in style; James only imagines the one while he offers the actual past and future history of the other.

A hearer and not a doer of the Word "is like (ἔοικεν, see v. 6) a man (ἀνήρ, see v. 7) taking cognizance of the countenance of his being in a mirror." The best translation of γένεσις is *Dasein,* C.-K. 234; it does not mean *Lebenslauf,* B.-P. 242. "Natural face" in our versions regards the expression as a part of the figure that is suggested by "in a mirror," but James says more than this; "the face of his birth," R. V. margin, is unsatisfactory. This man does take cognizance, he does it carefully; the supposition that he takes only a superficial look at his countenance is not correct. Of course, he looks only at the image of himself (ἑαυτόν in v. 24), at the outward side of his being (γένεσις); he does not get into the inwardness of the Word at all. We have these hearers to contend with in all our preaching; the real power of the Word does not penetrate them. In the day of Jesus and of James Judaism had many of them.

24) "For" explains by stating what happened in an actual case. This man "took cognizance of himself," which was well enough, and then "has gone away and immediately forgot what kind (of man) he was." This is what made him a hearer only: he saw, he went off, he forgot. His hearing netted him nothing as far as the real purpose and the power of the Word are concerned. The two aorists are usually called gnomic; the perfect between them then causes difficulty, and some call also it gnomic, and B.-D. even speaks of *Verdacht inkorrekter Mischung,* suspicion of an incorrect mixing of tenses. R. 844 and 897 are better: this is the dramatic, vivid perfect. The English mind should catch a little of the mental alertness of the Greek, which purposely changes the tenses; this is "a sort of moving picture arrangement." Instead of incorrectness we have something that is finer than mechanical correctness.

But we should drop the gnomic idea. James describes an actual case that occurred in the past. The man took cognizance; he actually did so; the aorist says so, but it does *not* say that anything of this cognizance remained with the man. He went away; the perfect implies that this being away continued. We then have another simple historical aorist: "he forgot what kind (of man) he was"; all of it just dropped out of his mind. It is the same picture that is drawn by Jesus in a different way in Matt. 13:4, 19: the little birds just carried away the good seed. "He has gone

James 1:25

away," and very soon while doing so "he forgot" while his going away continued. Yes, he came and heard again and again, but this was the story every time. The oftener he did this sort of thing, the more easily he was able to repeat it: to hear — to be going away — to forget.

25) On the other hand, here is one who looked closely into the Word itself. From the use of παρακύπτω in John 20:5, 11 the conclusion has been drawn that the verb always implies only a hasty look; but in I Pet. 1:12 this looking into by the angels is not hasty. In John 20:5 John, too, must have taken a most earnest and serious look into the tomb. Not only did this man look closely into the Word and what it really contains, he "remained" so. It gripped and held him; "remained" (παραμείνας, an aorist participle to indicate the fact) need not be a perfect tense (to match the perfect tense used in v. 24), for the verb itself expresses continuance. "Remained" = he did not forget but "became (got to be) not a forgetful hearer (like the other man), on the contrary, an (actual) work-doer," the objective genitive emphasizes the idea of "doer." We need not repeat that the doing and the work referred to are not mere good works but first and foremost true, living faith.

So "this man will be blessed in his doing." The future tense after the aorist participles surprises us. James does not say "was blessed"; he certainly "was," but he will also be blessed for evermore. Not the mere hearer but the actual doer, not he who forgets but he who remains will be blessed; the one remains empty, the other will be filled with divine blessing by the heavenly Giver (v. 5). Μακάριος (see v. 12) is used in the Beatitudes.

What does James mean by νόμος (no article is used either here or in 2:12) τέλειος ὁ τῆς ἐλευθερίας? In substance the same as "truth's Word" (v. 18) and "the implanted Word" (v. 21), the contents of which are both law and gospel, the doing of which = repentance and faith (in v. 18 regeneration) and a life of Christian obedience. James refers to the contents of the Old Testament plus the teaching of Jesus and his apostles. Here and in 2:12 and also in "royal law" in 2:8 we have designations that are borrowed from Jesus himself and reflect John 8:31, 32; Jer. 31:31-34 (not only v. 33), and the Sermon on the Mount, especially the failure of not doing and the blessedness of doing which are described at the end of this Sermon (Matt. 7:24-27).

Nothing is gained by referring to the term *Torah* when speaking of νόμος. To look eagerly into what is "law complete" is to study to do what Jesus expresses in John 5:39, what the Jews did not do, namely to see him in the Word and not merely the Mosaic ceremonial regulations, for which failure Moses himself would accuse the Jews (John 5:45-47). So to look into the Scriptures means to have saving faith: "the implanted Word, the one able to save your souls" (v. 21). "Complete" (τέλεως) = both law and gospel which constitute the *nomos;* James uses the word *nomos* so as to include both. He does not use εὐαγγέλιον in this letter. Those who eliminate the gospel from this expression of James's have difficulty in understanding his thought, cf. C.-K. 426, etc.

"Complete law," without the article and thus strongly qualitative, is made specific by the attributive genitive: "(namely) that of the (true) liberty." This is probably a genitive of relation although its relation to "the liberty" characterizes also this law, shows that it is "law complete." "The liberty" with its article is the one the readers know (John 8:31, 32). The legal injunctions with which alone the Jewish religion dealt were nothing but slavery; John 8:33, etc., makes this very plain. The gospel feature of the Word brings the real liberty, the freeing from the curse of sin and from the power of sin. Leave out the gospel from the *nomos* of James, and "the liberty" becomes an illusion, it is like the blessing in the verb "shall be blessed." No doing of any system of legalism ever brought true liberty or blessing to save the soul.

We might at this place compare in detail what Paul and James say regarding liberty and law. It will not be necessary, for nowhere does Paul say that our liberty allows us to transgress the moral law by sinning (James expresses the same thought in 2:10-12), and everywhere Paul says we are freely to slave for God. To have James disagree with Paul is an unsatisfactory undertaking. Rudolph Stier's commentary on James sermonizes, but its comments on this verse are worth reading.

26) James returns to v. 19, 20, his starting point: a lot of talk about religion and wrathful contention about it are anything but what God wants, who sends us the Word so that we may accept it in meekness, hear and do it, and thus be blessed and saved. **If one thinks to be religious while not bridling his tongue but deceiving his heart, this one's religion is vain. Religion pure and undefiled before God and the Father is this: to visit orphans and widows in their affliction, to guard oneself unspotted from the world.**

The A. V. has "among you," which is the translation of a spurious reading. We translate "thinks" and not "seems" (A. V.). James does not say that this person "seems to be religious" to others who see him; James says to this person himself that he "thinks he is religious." Θρησκός (accent thus), which is found only here in the New Testament = one who observes the *cultus exterior*. There is no doubt that the man does this, he is religious in this sense, James does not deny it.

James only adds the rest of it. This man thinks he is religious "while not bridling his tongue but deceiving his heart." The kind of religion which he practices allows him to let his tongue go like an unbridled horse, it is without inner religious control. This is another of the telling figures used by James. He returns to it in 3:3 where he has much more to say about the tongue of the teachers of the church. The indefinite τις makes the statement broad, it is like "quick to talk" which occurs in v. 19. This man is always voicing his own opinions and damaging people right and left like an unrestrained horse; he talks even religion in the same way and is not meek to hear the Word for his own soul's good. James adds "but deceiving his heart," fooling himself in his very religion. Well, this man has "religion," a *cultus exterior*, but it is μάταιος, i. e., it does not get him to the goal for which religion is intended. James does not say κενός, "empty," for this man's religion has a sort of religious content, but it is one that does not save his soul or make him μακάριος, "blessed."

27) While "religion pure and undefiled" is also a *cultus exterior* it shows its pureness and its undefiled state by proper fruits, two of which are named as samples. The first is "to look in upon, to visit with comfort and help, orphans and widows in their affliction," those who are most in need of help, who are mentioned so often in the Old Testament as being under God's special protection. It seems as though James has in mind Matt. 23:14 and Luke 20:47: the hypocritical Pharisees who devour widows' houses and for a pretense make long prayers. To visit the least of these brethren of Jesus is to prove oneself a true slave of the Lord Jesus Christ, Matt. 25:40. This is a sample of the love which is the true fruit of faith. As far as we are able to glean the circumstances of the readers from the epistle itself, there was much room for works of

James 1:27   561

this kind. Already in the old mother congregation there were many widows (Acts 6:1); these, too, had fled during the persecution under Saul, which fact certainly did not improve their circumstances.

With an arresting asyndeton James reaches into another side of the true Christian life which is an evidence of "religion pure and undefiled before God the Father," namely "to guard oneself unspotted from the world." James resembles John in this use of "the world" as a designation for the ungodly, unbelieving mass of men; we regularly use the word in this sense today (see also 4:4). The world is vile and foul; to guard oneself unspotted means that none of this uncleanness lodges permanently in our hearts and our souls. It means also that we attend to constant cleansing (John 13:10). If the other is a work of love, this is surely a work of faith.

The readings vary as to the use of the article or the articles or the absence of the article in the παρά phrase, but the sense remains practically the same. Some copyists seem to have tried their hand at altering the reading according to their ideas of Greek usage. "God the Father" requires an article in English. He judges as to what religion is pure and clean, undefiled and unspoiled. We learn his judgment from his Word.

Rationalists have pointed to this passage as being one that supports their idea of genuine religion: Just do works of charity and lead a clean moral life; all the rest does not matter! They do the same with Peter's statement: "In every nation he that feareth God and worketh righteousness is accepted with him" (Acts 10:35): Just so you believe that there is a God and try to do what is right! But it is not fair to select a single sentence out of an epistle or a discourse and to ignore the context.

CHAPTER II

Respect of Persons, 2:1-13

The Folly and the Sin of Toadying to the Rich, v. 1-7

1) My brethren, do not let the faith in our Lord Jesus Christ, (who is) the glory, be connected with respect to persons!

The friendly address "my brethren" introduces the new subject and bids the readers heed the admonition in a fraternal spirit. As believers in a Lord who is so glorious they ought not to make such improper distinctions among men; their faith ought to put them far beyond this common worldly practice. The ἐν phrase is adverbial; it should be noted that, when it is used with adverbs, ἔχω commonly means "to be." So we do not translate "do not have" or "do not hold" but "do not let faith be in connection with" or "connected with." The sense is: Keep it free from such a blemishing connection.

Προσωπολημψία is the act of being partial to a person when one sees who he is. A judge is guilty of this when he does not consider the just merits of a case but the standing of the man on trial. Men generally do this: if a friend does wrong, they close an eye and call it right; if a rich man or a powerful man comes along, they toady to him. Neither the plural nor the singular of this noun are Hebraic although the verb and its derivatives are Palestinian Greek, which is derived from the Hebrew *nasa' phanim*, to lift the face on a person in the sense of being favorable or partial to him (M.-M. 553). It is said of God that he is no respecter of persons but is always fair, just, righteous to all.

Τοῦ Κυρίου is the common objective genitive after πίστις: "faith in our Lord Jesus Christ." We have the same designation in 1:1. It here emphasizes his deity, his greatness, and his exaltation. The final genitive τῆς δόξης has caused much discussion, but most of it is regarding the construction, and less of it regarding the sense. It emphasizes the glory of the Savior in whom we believe, his exaltation in everlasting glory. We who believe in a Savior that is so infinitely glorious see the utter vanity of all earthly glory and rise above being impressed by it as worldly men are foolishly impressed. However it may be construed, this is the force of the last genitive. Our versions construe: "the Lord of glory." While this makes smooth English, the whole name and title, "our Lord Jesus Christ," is a standard unit, which means that one word in it cannot well be modified in this way. Bengel and others regard the genitive as an apposition: "our Lord Jesus Christ" is called "the glory" as he is called the Way, the Truth, the Life, the Light, etc. Others regard it as a qualitative genitive which is stronger than an adjective and translate "the faith in our glorious Lord Jesus Christ" or, "in the glory of our Lord Jesus Christ." The view that "the glory" refers to "the Shekinah" does not commend itself. It is based on the strong Jewish character of James. The fact, however, is that James exhibits the most marked Christian character, and his language is clear, idiomatic Greek.

It is worth noting that here and throughout this epistle James deals with Christian conduct, but ever does so on the basis of "the faith of our Lord Jesus Christ," in which James is one with his brethren. The entire substructure is soteriological, which also appears at every turn: the deity of Christ, his whole work as the Savior, our regeneration, our life in the gospel as the life of faith, etc. Stier exclaims: "Alas, this precious epistle has been in all ages too much misunderstood, and on that account too few have been found swift to hear it. . . . It is pre-eminently a New Testament writing and by no means a legal one." To read it as being altogether Jewish is to read it through a veil.

2) "For" specifies by showing to what James refers. **For if there comes into a synagogue of yours a man with a gold ring on his finger, in shining clothes, and, on the other hand, there comes in also a poor one in shabby clothes, and you look upon the one wearing the shining clothes and say: Thou, do thou sit here please! and to the poor one you say: Thou, do thou stand there! or: Sit thou on the floor by my footstool! did you not get into doubt in your own selves and get to be judges marked by wicked considerations?**

The condition of expectancy (ἐάν) simply visualizes a case which may occur at any time. We take συναγωγή to mean "a synagogue of yours," for James mentions the places in it: "here," a prominent place, "there," an obscure place. "Assembly" is not the meaning, for the fact that the congregation is assembled in its place of meeting is self-evident. The two contrasted visitors are outsiders; we take them to be Jews. The one is rich, high, ostentatious. The eye catches the costly ring on his finger and is struck by his brilliant clothing, very likely a flowing robe of pure white silk or of finest wool. The gentleman deigns to look in upon these Christians to see what their worship is like. Paul speaks of such visitors coming into the church of the Corinthians (I Cor. 14:23, 24).

Again, there comes in a poor man in a shabby garment. The eye at once notes his poverty, ῥυπαρά, compare the noun ῥυπαρία discussed in 1:21. He, too, has heard of these Jewish Christians and comes to see what their religion and their worship are like. The opinion that the Jewish Christians are still worshiping in the Jewish synagogue, and that what James depicts

takes place in a synagogue that is composed of Jews and
of Christians, cannot be accepted. Already in Jerusalem
and at the very beginning of their history the Christians had their own meeting places, in fact, had to have.

3) James describes how the one wearing the
garment, "the brilliant one" (the adjective is added by
a second article and is like an apposition or a climax,
R. 776), becomes the cynosure of all eyes and is
obsequiously invited to a prominent seat, everybody
being delighted at his condescension to visit them.
Ropes points out that καλῶς scarcely means "in a good
place" (our versions), but his view does not seem to be
based on facts. In various Greek liturgies the minister
directs the congregation: στῶμεν καλῶς, which seems to
mean: "Let us stand, please!" although the Spanish
liturgies translate: "Stand we all fairly!" The great
gentleman is given a prominent seat with great
deference. So much, James says, are you Christians
still impressed by a gold ring and a bright rag!

But to the poor man no deference whatever is
shown. He is told "to stand there" by the wall or
wherever he can be wedged in in the rear; or else he is
asked by someone to sit on the floor, close to the person's footstool, where there is just room enough for a
man to squat. We should remember that most people
sat cross-leggedly on the floor, only more important
persons had elevated seats, chairs, benches, etc. No one
would think of treating the rich visitor in this fashion,
oh, no! That is the point James makes. His readers are
still respecters of persons in the evil sense of the word.

4) James brings this home to them with a double
question: "Did you not get into doubt in your own
selves?" and then elucidates this by adding: "And get
to be judges marked by wicked thoughts?" Luther
gives only the general sense: *bedenket es nicht recht
und macht boesen Unterschied.* Some are puzzled by
the aorists and call them gnomic, our versions thus

translate them with present tenses. Gnomic aorists do not appear in specific, direct questions, they are universal and timeless. These aorists are quite regular: the readers got into doubt and became such judges *before* men such as the two described who came into their synagogue, consequently the readers act so when such men come in.

Διεκρίθητε and "became κριταί marked by wicked considerations" (the genitive is qualitative) are intended to match; hence the second half of the question illumines the first half. Among the various meanings that are possible for the first verb, "to doubt in yourselves" is after all the best. The faith of the readers should have taught them to show the same courtesy to all their visitors and not to make distinctions, not to judge according to considerations that are no less than πονηραί, not only "wrong" or "evil" but actively "wicked." Since when does "the faith in the Lord Jesus Christ, (who is) the glory," justify considerations which treat the man with a fine coat as being superior and the man with a shabby coat as being inferior? Is the soul of the one worth more than the soul of the other? Are not all men, rich and poor, equal in the house of God? Something is wrong with the faith of those who have not heard the Word of God sufficiently to learn this and to act on this elementary truth (1:22, etc.).

5) **Listen, my brethren beloved! Did God not choose for himself the poor as regards this world, rich in connection with faith and heirs of the kingdom which he promised to those loving him? You, however, did dishonor the poor one.**

The imperative requests attention to what follows and does it with the same loving concern that was manifested in 1:19. We note the vividness of the command, the question, and the assertion as if James had his readers before him. They certainly do not deny the outstanding fact that God chose for himself to be his chosen people "the poor as regards the world (dative of relation), rich in faith," etc. They are poor in one respect, namely in regard to the world; they have precious little money, etc. But in another respect they are rich indeed, namely, ἐν πίστει, "in connection with faith" (the faith already mentioned in v. 1). This does not mean that their faith constitutes their riches, for their riches are "the kingdom" of which their faith makes them heirs. This kingdom is "the crown of the (heavenly) life," for regarding both this crown and this kingdom James says: "which he promised to those loving him"; on the designation "lovers of God" see 1:12. Their wealth consists of the heavenly kingdom of which they are joint heirs with the supreme Heir Christ (Heb. 1:2). As kings they shall join Christ and sit in royal splendor on his heavenly throne (I John 3:2).

We do not regard the second and the third accusatives as predicative as the R. V. does: "to be rich in faith and heirs." It would then be necessary to supply εἶναι. Then, however, the statement would be strange indeed. It would leave the impression that the earthly poor as a class were chosen by God to be believers and heirs of heaven. James is not speaking of the earthly poor in general but, like Paul in I Cor. 1:26, of the membership of the church, where we find "not many wise men after the flesh, not many mighty, not many noble," but quite the contrary. Stier says: "Seek them in the cottages and under mean garments." James would not say that the earthly rich are *eo ipso* debarred from the kingdom; in I Tim. 6:17-19 Paul tells the rich Christians what kind of people they must be. Earthly riches are a handicap as far as true faith is concerned; many a word of Jesus was spoken to this effect, and James has these words of Jesus in mind.

The object which James has in view is quite plain. The poor visitor at the services is far more likely to become a believer than the rich one; yet the readers treat the former with churlishness, the latter with obsequity. They ought to treat both with the same honorable friendliness. "*You*," James says, "did dishonor the poor man" (representative singular, R. 408). You acted as if this were what your Christian faith had taught you whereas it taught you the very opposite. Look at your own numbers! How many of you would be heirs of the kingdom if God would act as you do?

Here James again operates with the great essentials, with faith, the kingdom, the promise or gospel, and with love as the fruit of faith. Those who regard him as a Jewish moralist apparently pass very rapidly over these great Christian fundamentals.

6) From the poor James turns to the rich. **Do the rich not tyrannize you and on their part hale you to courts? Do they on their part not blaspheme the noble name, the one called upon you?**

James is speaking of the rich Jews who were for the most part Sadducees and at this period (A. D. 35-65) were the tyrannous oppressors of the poorer Jews and thus also made a specialty of harassing Christian Jews. The Roman government allowed the Jews in the Diaspora a great deal of legal control over their own nationals. We see this when Saul carries letters to Damascus to arrest Christian Jews (Acts 9:2) and when he speaks of persecuting them "even unto foreign cities" (Acts 26:11). In Corinth the proconsul Gallio remands Paul's accusers to the Jewish tribunal to try him there if he has been guilty of an infraction of Jewish law. Rich and powerful Jews in the Diaspora were thus able to maltreat poor Jews and especially Christian Jews by dragging them before their synagogue κριτήρια, courts or judgment seats.

This fact, which is so clearly reflected in our epistle, is one of the evidences for its early date. After the Jewish war broke out in the year 66 all this underwent a radical change. Αὐτοί is emphatic. Are *they* not the ones who drag you before courts? It is not said that all rich Jews were so ruthless. The next question which has another αὐτοί shows of whom James is speaking.

7) "Do *they* not blaspheme the noble name, the one called upon you?" Καλόν = excellent, illustrious, noble. James refers to the name of Jesus which was used in the baptismal formula: "In the name of the Father, *and of the Son,* and of the Holy Spirit." This holy name, which makes the readers "heirs of the kingdom," so many of these rich Jews revile or blaspheme. We need not tone down the word "blaspheme." The expression "called upon you" occurs in the LXX (II Chron. 7:14; Jer. 14:9; 15:16; Amos 9:12) with reference to those who were marked by God's name as being his own (note: "God chose for himself" in v. 5). Plummer quotes Justin Martyr who lived at a later period: "That which is said in the law: 'Cursed is everyone that hangeth on a tree,' confirms our hope which is hung upon the crucified Christ, not as if God were cursing that crucified One, but because God foretold that which would be done by all of you (Jews) and those like you. . . . And you may see with your eyes this very thing coming to pass; for in your synagogues you curse all those who from him have become Christians" (*Trypho,* XCVI). The readers of James certainly have no reason for bowing and scraping obsequiously before some rich Jew when these rich Jews treat a poor Jew with disdain.

What One Transgression of Law Does, v. 8-13

8) James cuts off completely every evasion: **If, however, you are carrying out a law royal** (in its quality) **according to the Scripture: Thou shalt love thy neighbor as thyself! you are doing nobly; but if** (in doing so) **you have respect of persons you are committing sin, being convicted by this law as transgressors.**

If the claim is made by any of the readers that by treating a rich Jew with such solicitude they are carrying out "law royal" in quality according to the Scripture passage (Lev. 19:18, repeated by Jesus in Matt. 22:39): "Thou shalt love (future in legal commands) thy neighbor as thyself!" James answers: "You are doing excellently." There is no question about it; we should ever love our neighbor as ourself. Ἀγαπᾶν means to love with intelligent, purposeful love. James does not want his readers to mistreat a single rich Jew when he comes to their services or at any other time, no matter how vicious such a Jew may be.

A number of answers have been given to the questions as to why νόμος βασιλικός is anarthrous and as to what "royal law" means. The article is absent because the term is wholly qualitative; hence it does not mean "*the* royal law"; nor is "royal law" merely equal to "thou shalt love," etc., it is simply in accord with this Scripture, this Scripture being a formulation of "law" that is truly "royal" in its quality. It is "royal," kingly, not because it emanates from God or from Christ as King; not because it applies to kings, or because it makes kings of those who obey it. It is "royal law" because it is sovereign over all other laws, is a law of such a quality that on it "hang all the law (Torah, Instruction) and the prophets" (the whole Old Testament, Matt. 22:40). "The whole law is fulfilled in one word, even in this: 'Thou shalt love thy neighbor as thyself!'" Gal. 5:14. Cf., I John 4:20.

9) But the readers must carry out truly what they are pleased to call "royal law," an expression that is found only here in Scripture. Here is where their trouble lies: "Yet if (in your claim to carry out royal law as voiced, for instance, in this Scripture) you have respect to persons (treating one Jewish visitor in one way because his dress shows him to be rich, and another Jewish visitor far differently because his dress

shows him to be poor) you are committing what is sin" (again qualitative and hence anarthrous); and that not because James says so but as "being convicted by the law (article of previous reference: by this very law) as transgressors"; for royal law forbids this very thing, to treat one man in one way, another in the opposite way.

10) With γάρ James elucidates in a simple manner. **For whosoever guards the whole law but stumbles in one point, he has become guilty of all points. For he who said: Thou shalt not commit adultery! said also: Thou shalt not kill! Now if thou dost not commit adultery but dost kill thou hast become a law-transgressor.**

In the Koine we may have the indefinite relative and the subjunctive with or without ἄν; the sense is the same. We have the perfect twice in the main clause: γέγονε and γέγονας. The grammars seem to have some difficulty with this form. To call it "gnomic" (B.-D. 344; R. 897) does not explain the tense; it states only that the proposition is general; to call it a prophetic perfect (R. 898) does not explain it fully either. The case is one that is imagined: "Whosoever guards the whole law but stumbles in one point," i.e., whoever may do this at any time, no matter when; by that fact of stumbling in one point "he has become guilty of all points" and ever remains so. The imagined case is in imagination treated as one that is looked back upon, and the perfect states the abiding result.

The claim that by treating the rich visitor with such deference while giving scant attention to the poor visitor love to the rich visitor is being shown (v. 8), is one that is often put forward: by doing such legal things as these men would shield themselves and think that this will let them escape when they fail to do other things of the law. James might have shown that it was not at all love that prompted the deference to the rich visitor. He has in a way done this when he charges his readers with respect to persons, which is certainly not in accord with "royal law," with love. It is always a base thing, whether such respect is shown by a partial judge (a superior) or by poor people (inferiors) who cringe before the rich and the powerful. James takes up the deception at its very root, in its relation to the law itself. Since when is keeping a part of the law an excuse for transgressing some other part? The very opposite is true: "These ye ought to have done and not to leave the other undone," Matt. 23:23. To stumble in one point is to be guilty of all points.

James assumes an extreme case: that a man actually keeps the whole law and stumbles in only one point. He would not say that such cases actually occur: "For in many things we all stumble" (3:2). But assuming such a case, instead of the keeping of so much of the law covering up the one case of stumbling, the very opposite occurs; the one case of stumbling makes us guilty of transgressing the law in all points. A glass that is struck at only one point is nevertheless shattered. The law is not a set of ten pins, one of which may be knocked down while the others are left standing. The law is a unit, its unity is love; to violate it at one point is to violate love as such, the whole of it. We constantly tend to minimize our sins and thus to reduce our repentance and amendment of life; we need James to show us the whole damage of sin, the whole condemnation of the law, the full depth to which repentance must go.

11) James illustrates by using a simple example. It is the same God who said in his law: "Thou shalt not commit adultery!" and also: "Thou shalt not kill!" The aorist subjunctive and not the aorist imperative is used in negative commands; this aorist is peremptory. "Now if thou dost not commit adultery but dost kill thou hast become a law-transgressor." Vice versa

would also be true; likewise any other two specifications of the law. What is transgressed? Why, the law. The whole law condemns the transgressor of any part of it. Even in human courts no just judge will excuse one crime by referring to the noncommission of all other possible crimes. He does not say: "Here are one hundred laws which this man did not break; hence his breaking of only one law does not count." You need not touch an electric wire at a 1,000 points, you get the full shock of the current by touching just one point. To transgress one commandment reveals the fact that you are not true to the law. From the generalizing "whosoever" used in v. 10 James advances to the direct personal "thou" in v. 11.

12) Instead of trying a subterfuge in order to excuse ourselves as regards the law, and thus by even a single transgression bringing down upon ourselves, who have many transgressions (3:2), its whole condemnation, James bids his readers to give up everything of this sort. So (ever) **keep speaking and so (ever) keep acting as about to be judged by means of liberty's law. For the judgment is without mercy for him who did not exercise mercy; mercy boasts against judgment.**

Οὕτω . . . ὡς correspond. The former cannot refer to the preceding thought. James tells his readers ever to speak and ever to act (present, durative imperatives) as people who are about to be judged by God, not by means of the law, i.e., the Ten Commandments, two of which have just been quoted, nor by the summation of the second table (v. 8, 11), but by "liberty's law" (both anarthrous nouns are qualitative). The readers will then escape the condemnation of the law. "Liberty's law" will be their merciful salvation.

We see at once that everything depends on what James means by "liberty's law" which repeats "law complete (in quality), the one of the (true) liberty," occurring in 1:25—see the exposition already given. The Ten Commandments cannot be called "a law of liberty." We think the commentators are not clear when they eliminate the gospel from this "law of liberty" and yet place this law in the heart (Jer. 31:33) so that we do the law freely of our own selves. How can this be done save by the gospel alone? See how Jer. 31:34 adds the forgiveness of sins. Even then we still sin and need constant forgiveness and cleansing from all unrighteousness (3:2; I John 1:8-10). James undoubtedly refers to both law and gospel when he speaks of "liberty's law" which he also calls "the implanted Word, the one able to save your souls" (1:21), "truth's Word" (1:18) which contains the promise of the crown of the life for those loving God (1:12). That is why this paragraph begins with "the faith in our Lord Jesus Christ, (who is) the glory." He warns us not to let this our faith become damaged or destroyed by such a sin as respect to persons (v. 1) and by playing off our supposed obedience to some commandments of the law against transgressions of this or that other commandment.

Ever speak and ever act, James says, as people who embrace the Word of God truly by living faith, and who are to be judged by Christ at the last day by means of this Word: "The Word that I have spoken, the same shall judge him in the last day," John 12:48. This Word is not a law of liberty because it liberates us from obedience to God's holy commandments or even from a single point in any of them; the gospel itself and true faith impel us to this obedience. James twice calls us "those loving God" (1:12; 2:5); this love, the fruit of faith, does freely what God bids in the law; this is liberty indeed. Without it the law produces only slavery as Paul shows so completely. Our happiness is to be judged by means of the law of liberty. Blessed are we when we are doing the Word, doing it by believing and by loving (1:25). When Christ judges us by liberty's law he will do this as he himself has said in Matt. 25:34-40: he will treat all our good works as evidence of our faith, give us the promised crown (1:12) and the promised kingdom as those who love God (2:5). Though we have stumbled often, the repentance to which James continually urges his readers will liberate us from all guilt.

13) For, certainly, that last judgment is without mercy for him who did not exercise mercy. Has Jesus himself not said so in describing this judgment (Matt. 25:41-45)? What is all this about letting Jesus be hungry, thirsty, a stranger, naked, sick, in prison, and doing nothing for him, but failure to exercise mercy? The commentary on our passage which is found in Matthew 25 is too plain to be overlooked. Yes, these people will say what Jesus states in Matt. 7:22; but see what an answer they have already received. Even doing the greatest works without faith in the gospel will leave them guilty in all points of the law.

Ἔλεος is "mercy," the pity for those in distress. Read Hos. 6:6, and Matt. 9:13; 12:7. Glancing back at the poor man mentioned in v. 2, etc., we see that the readers should have been kind and merciful to him; but they were not. Where, then, were their faith and their love? James is not taking exception to a minor fault; he sees fully what is wrong and speaks plainly indeed. He continues to do so in the next section which has become famous although it is often misunderstood.

James closes most effectively: "Mercy boasts against judgment." The unmerciful shall not find mercy in the judgment; the merciful shall boast even in the face of judgment. This is not the language of legalism, which would be farcical in view of v. 9 plus 3:2; it is the language of Christ and of the gospel (Matt. 5:7; 25:40). "Mercy" is to be understood in the same sense as it was in the previous sentence, the mercy produced in the believer's heart and life by the mercy of God, the evidence of true faith. Jesus will publicly acknowledge this mercy as an evidence of faith, and so it may indeed "boast against judgment," no judgment condemns the man who has this evidence.

Barren Faith, v. 14-26

Lacking Its Works, Faith Is Dead, v. 14-17

14) As the right use of the law and the right trust in the gospel are associated in the mind of James, so true faith and works as fruit and evidence of faith naturally also are. This is the teaching of Jesus and of all his apostles. James presents it in a lucid and a simple way, and it is unfortunate that some do not understand James, which includes Luther (see the Introduction). **What the profit, my brethren, if one declares to have faith yet does not have works? Is that faith able to save him?**

Two self-answering questions penetrate to the bottom of the whole matter. The profit amounts to nothing. The faith which this man has is unable to save him. The second question which has the interrogative particle μή implies "no" as the proper answer. The address, "my brethren," urges the questions upon the readers, who are not to be like the person that is introduced. Ἐάν with its two subjunctives pictures a vivid case, that of a person who asserts that he has faith and yet does not have works. His assertion amounts to this, that faith can exist without works. He declares and yet has not. We have two coordinate verbs, hence they are of equal weight; the second is not a mere subordinate participle.

Faith itself cannot be seen; it makes its presence known by a proper confession and by its proper and natural works. A tree is known by its fruits (Matt.

James 2:14

7:16-20). Now here there is a man who declares that he has true and proper "faith," but everybody sees, and, in fact, he himself must admit, that he has not the "works" that belong to such a faith. He is like the man mentioned in 1:26 "who thinks that he is religious"; but this man says so and names faith as the ground of his claim. Yet he is one who has not works. To go back into the epistle: he, for instance, does not bridle his tongue (1:26), does not visit orphans and widows and keep himself unspotted from the world (1:27), and makes no true effort to carry out the royal law of love (2:8), has respect to persons such as rich worldly men (2:9), fails to show mercy (2:13).

The great question is: "Is that faith able to save him?" In the expression ἡ πίστις the article is that of previous reference, *"that* faith" which he says he has but fails to prove that he has no matter what faith he may actually have. James has used the expression "able to save your souls" in 1:21 and now refers to the same salvation. As far as James is concerned, there is no question that true faith "saves," but only true faith and not a fruitless thing that one may call faith. James has exactly the same conception of saving faith that Paul has when the latter declares that we are justified by faith without works of the law: a true and living trust in the Savior Jesus Christ (see v. 1). Paul does not have in mind one kind of faith when he says that faith without works saves while James has in mind another kind of a faith when he says that without works faith does not save. Both refer to identically the same kind of a faith, and both attribute to it regeneration (1:18), justification, and salvation.

Paul and James deal with different kinds of works. Paul deals with works of law which have nothing to do with true gospel faith, which are the boast of all Pharisees and all work-righteous men, who think that they are able to save themselves by such works, at least to aid Christ in saving them. Trust in works of law is the direct opposite of faith in Christ alone. James deals with gospel works, which ever evidence the presence of gospel faith, which, like this faith, glorify Christ alone, without which all claim of having true faith is spurious, a self-delusion. Both James and Paul attribute salvation to a living faith (Mark 16:16; John 3:16), but Paul lays stress on what must be removed if a man is to have and to retain this faith, James on what dare not be absent when a man has and wants to retain this faith. Paul roots out what destroys and excludes faith; James stimulates sluggish faith. The two are in perfect agreement; in the ethical parts of all his epistles Paul, too, calls for the fruits of faith.

We need not stop to figure out what kind of a faith this man has who lacks the true works of faith. It is certainly not a faith that saves him as James states. One of the strange phenomena is the fact that Luther, who had so little use for James, nevertheless writes in his famous preface to Paul's Romans as he might well have written in a preface to James: "Oh, it is a living, active, energetic, mighty thing, this faith, so that it is impossible that it should not work what is good without intermission. It does not even ask whether good works are to be done, but before one asks it has done them, and is ever doing. But he who does not do such works is a man without faith, is fumbling and looking about him for faith and good works, and knows neither the one nor the other yet chatters and babbles many words about both." If this is not the voice of James, whose is it—even down to the chatter and babble (1:19)?

15) James illustrates by referring to a case of charity that is not charity at all; the mercy that should reveal the presence of faith is absent, and this absence reveals the contrary. **If a brother or a sister are naked and lacking of daily food, yet one of you should say to them: Go in peace; be warmed**

and be filled! but (if) you do not give to them the necessities for the body, what (is) the profit? i. e., what good is it to you?

While a double subject is ordinarily followed by a singular verb in the Greek, the difference in gender (masculine and feminine) makes a plural necessary here because the adjective and the participle cannot be repeated in two genders and must be masculine plurals and thus be followed by a plural verb. Two common needs are mentioned, lack of clothing and lack of daily food.

16) James asks, if in a case of this kind one of you should say to these needy ones (aorist: finish it off with this) : "Go in peace; be warmed and be filled!" and yet give them nothing for their body, "what is the profit" (the same question as that asked in v. 14)? James means, what profit is there as far as proving real faith is concerned? Less than none. First, "one of you" and then the plural, "you should give," is a variation such as Paul loves.

James is an excellent teacher. He takes a most ordinary case of poverty, in connection with which it would be an elementary act of Christian faith and brotherly love to extend at least some help. None is extended. Only words: "Goodbye, goodbye, be warmed and be fed—only I can do nothing for you!" We regard the verbs as passives and not as middle imperatives. The passives imply: "Let somebody else warm and feed you!" What do you think of a faith that produces such evidence?

17) James tells us what he thinks: **So also this faith** (the one the person referred to in v. 14 claims to have), **if it have not works** (supposing that the illustration is true), **is dead according to itself,** which does not mean "dead in itself" (nothing is ever dead in any other way) but "according to its own showing." Having a special and an easy opportunity to show its life, it shows the very opposite. A dead

tree, a dead branch fails to show life by not bearing fruit.

James states with utmost plainness what sort of a faith this is that fails to produce the fruits of faith. It may be some sort of a faith: *fides generalis,* as the dogmaticians say, faith that believes in God and in Christianity in a general way; *fides historica,* a faith that knows the outward facts of the gospel history and would not deny them; a *fides dogmatica,* one that is posted regarding doctrines and is perhaps keen to argue about them like the faith of some scientific theologians. It cannot be more than a mere *notitia* and *assensus,* a matter that was in the head, that dried up there and did not enter and vivify the heart.

Yet James by no means makes works help to constitute faith as if works were the life of faith, so that, when works are added, we have *fides formata,* while without works *fides* would be *informata* (the Catholic conception of faith, which is rather plain work-righteousness).* True gospel works are the native and the necessary product of faith. This faith, which saves before it ever does a single work, saves by embracing Christ and reveals itself by producing love and works of love, which, wherever they appear, show that real, saving faith is present. It is also the faith that stands trials (1:2, etc.) and overcomes temptation (1:12, etc.). Note "faith" in 1:3, 6; 2:1.

---

* One should understand the Catholic conception. As far as the Catholic is concerned, *fides* does not consist of knowledge — assent — confidence. Knowledge is not necessary, which claim Bellarmin states even drastically: *Fides distinguitur contra scientiam, et melius per ignorantiam quam per notitiam definitur,* faith is defined *rather by ignorance* than by knowledge. The elimination of confidence from faith is authoritative, Council of Trent, sess. VI, can. XII: *Si quis dixerit, fidem justificantem nihil aliud esse quam fiduciam divinae misericordiae, peccata remittentis propter Christum, vel fiduciam solam esse, qua justificamur, anathema sit!* Whoever says that justifying faith is *fiducia,* confidence in divine mercy, or that it is confidence alone

The only Kind of a Faith without Works That One May Have Is like That of the Demons, v. 18-20

18) A variety of interpretations of this passage is offered in the commentaries. They discuss a number of points, among them the questions as to who is meant by τὶς—σύ—ἐγώ; whether an objector or a supporter of James is speaking; how far his address extends; what the point of it really is. Some mention an alteration of the text or speak of a possible serious omission from the text. A great number of pages would be required to present the many different views, many of which find a rather involved thought in the few, simple words of the text whereas James expected his readers to understand him without difficulty.

James has just demonstrated (v. 14-16) and then stated (v. 17) that on its own showing the faith that has no works is "dead," amounts to nothing (certainly cannot save). Somebody, it makes no difference who, will come and assure one or the other of the Christians to whom James is writing that what James tells them is a mistake: **But someone will say** (to one of you): **Thou hast faith** (real, live faith despite the lack of works and despite what I, James, say about this lack in v. 14-17), **and I** (James) **have works** (and only want to make them more important than they are).

---

by which we are justified, let him be accursed! Thus, according to the Catholic conception, faith is only assent to what the Catholic Church maintains and requires. This assent is naturally *informis* or *informata*, lacking form or content. This content is secured by adding the works which the Catholic Church prescribes to the assent. Thus the *fides informis* becomes more and more *fides charitate formata*, the works, as it were, give body to the assent. All that the Scriptures say regarding πίστις cries out against this Catholic conception. Πίστις is knowledge, assent, and confidence, and the Greek word contains especially the idea of trust, confidence, *fiducia*, which is anathematized by the Catholic decree.

This "someone" is any member of the church who himself has no works; he is the "someone of you" mentioned in v. 16 who, for instance, puts off the naked and hungry with nothing but empty words; he does not like what James is teaching, that faith such as this is dead. He thus assures the one and the other of the Christians who hears from James that such a man's faith is dead: "Thou, why thou hast faith! James is making too much of works; just rest easy with your faith."

Regarding me, James adds, this someone, of course, admits to thee: **and I have works,** and hence I make them so important for everybody. It is this ἐγώ that causes so many interpreters difficulty; they think that it must be identical with τὶς; it refers to the writer, to James himself. James could not use αὐτός, "he," and the third person of the verb ἔχει because this would leave the readers at sea as to who "he" might be. He uses the straightforward "I." When this someone actually spoke to a fellow member of the church, his words were: "and *James* (of course) has works." When James himself quotes the man he naturally does not quote his own name but substitutes "I." The thought of this "someone" is: "Let James have his works; they are not what he thinks they are. Do not thou, my friend, to whom I am speaking, worry about thy not having works!"

All pastors know that there is still many a "someone" about who tells his fellow church members the same comforting thing. Ever and ever it eases church members away from the noble and the ardent works of faith and of love of which they ought to have great sheaves to bring in on harvest day (Ps. 126:6). What such members do are not works of faith at all; what they do requires nothing as great and as vital as faith; it calls for only a little respectability, a little decency, and often only a little of this.

James now turns, not to this "someone" (as is often supposed), but to this "thou" whom "someone" seeks to mislead. In the simplest fashion James explodes the assurance which "someone" would offer to this "thou": **Show thou to me thy faith without the works!** Just show it! "Someone" tells thee: "Thou hast faith." If he is right, and if despite lack of works thou hast faith, go ahead and show that faith of thine without works! Thou wilt find it as I, James, tell thee, a dead thing. This "someone" says: "I (James) have works." I, indeed, have works: **and I will show thee from the works my faith;** thou wilt promptly see the difference. If thy faith is without works it is *dead;* as shown by the works, mine is *anything but dead.* The fact that both κἀγώ are identical should be obvious; the fact that the second = James and thus also the first is plain.

As far as ἀλλ' ἐρεῖ τις is concerned, this formula is not like those found in I Cor. 15:35; Rom. 9:19; 11:19, and in secular discussions. Look at the three passages themselves—even the form is different; but what is of more import—the use is different. In our passage "someone" is not contradicting James, and James is not then answering this "someone"; "someone" is quoted who will say what he does to one of the Christian readers of James, and James offers to make the test with this reader. This is a much finer thing than merely letting an objector contradict the writer, and letting the writer then meet the objector's objection. We have three persons and not merely two. We have two persons seeking to win a third.

It is also supposed that James imitates the moralistic diatribes of his times. I doubt that James ever heard or read one of them. James is a man of parts, direct in his thought, not a trained dialectician but practical in every way. He does independently just what such a practical man would do, and he does it by hitting the nail squarely on the head.

19) He delivers a second, still more stunning blow. "Someone" will tell this church member that he is right, that he has faith although it is a faith without works. If that is, indeed, the case, what sort of faith is it, what does it believe? James has called it a "dead" faith *(fides generalis, historica, dogmatica,* see v. 17). What is the content of such a faith? **Thou believest that One is God. Thou dost well! Even the demons believe it and — shudder!**

That is the kind of faith that this "someone" would persuade thee is a good enough faith for thee. Some think that James is asking a question: "Dost thou believe, etc.?" A rhetorical question is not out of place; but there is doubt on this point. We have several variant readings, but all of them have the same sense: "One is God." In the expression εἷς ἐστιν ὁ Θεός, εἷς is the subject and ὁ Θεός (although it has the article) is the predicate, and this expression should not be translated as it is in our versions: "there is one God," or: "God is one." The reason for this is the fact that this = Deut. 6:4, which since the exile formed the *shema'* that was prayed religiously morning and evening by every Jew; in later times the *shema'* was amplified by additions from Deuteronomy.

This summation of a faith that is dead is perfect in every way. James is writing to former Jews who certainly still prayed their *shema'* regularly. The use made of it here to describe the contents of a dead faith would strike every reader, for it would make him think of the Jews — he was at one time among their number — who continually pray thus, whose faith is a dead thing, the fruits of it (as Heb. 6:1 and 9:14 tell other Jewish Christians) are "dead works" from which we need to repent and have the conscience cleansed.

James 2:19, 20

There is no call for a discussion of Jewish and Christian monotheism at this place, or for Zahn (*Introduction* I, 97) to advance the conclusion that the "someone" referred to in v. 18 is a Jew. It is likewise not helpful to say that the *shema'* would not express the dead faith of a Jew who had become a member of the Christian Church because he would in his dead way add the name "the Lord Jesus Christ" (cf., 1:1). The demons' faith, as this was expressed by the demon spirits in the demoniacs, certainly acknowledged Jesus as the Son of God, but that did not improve their faith. Dead faith is ready to say "yes" to all the articles of faith. James is not listing *all* that such a faith accepts, for quantity is not the point.

"Thou dost well!" is certainly irony since it is followed by: "Even the demons believe it and—shudder!" The verb denotes terror which makes one's hair stand on end. This comes like a thunderclap. No more stunning illustration of dead faith has ever been presented. Yes, even the demons have faith. Will this "someone" tell them that that is enough? Will he intimate that the demons are saved by their faith; that the Christian to whom he says: "Thou hast faith," needs no better faith?

20) Δέ connects this verse with the foregoing. **Now wilt thou realize, O empty man, that the faith without the works is barren?** Is this not enough to make thee realize this and to stop listening to "someone" who would tell thee that this kind of a faith is enough? The infinitive means "to realize" and not merely "to know." "O" is used sparingly in the Greek and thus is emphatic when it is used.

It sounds severe to call this church member an "empty man," one who is hollow. Some have thought that κενός has the same force as ῥακά has in Matt. 5:22; we do not think so; the terms do not even resemble each other, to say no more. "Empty man" is the proper word. His head and his heart should have been filled with "the Word of truth" (1:18), with "the implanted Word" (1:21), so that he might know what true faith is, so that no "someone" could come and persuade him to be satisfied with a faith that is no better than that of demons.

The reading varies between ἀργή and νεκρά; we have "dead" in v. 17, and some scribe apparently inserted it here (A. V.). To call faith without works "barren" faith after calling it "dead" is certainly apt: dead things are barren. Even the wording ἔργων—ἀργή, "works—workless," matches. "What the profit?" which was asked in v. 14 expresses the same thought. There is no profit at all, such a faith is barren of salvation, of any saving power.

When G. K. has the word mean only *wertlos*, "worthless," its distinctiveness is erased. His added exegesis even Romanizes: "Faith (intellectually understood) is to a degree only the shell" and "attains its necessary fulness" by works, which would certainly be the *fides formata* of Romanism. The faith that is dead and barren is only intellectual or a mere sentiment; it never attains anything substantial. The faith that is not dead and barren, and that shows by its fruit of love and good works that it is not, is by no means merely intellectual; it is *fiducia*, the confidence of the heart, and hence moves our innermost being and thus saves. We have an illustration of what "barren" means when capital lies idle and draws no interest; but this is only one illustration.

Abraham's Faith Had Works, v. 21-24

21) **Abraham, our father, was not he declared righteous as a result of works when he brought up Isaac, his son, upon the altar of sacrifice? Thou seest that the faith was helping by means of his works; and as a result of the works the faith was**

brought to its goal, and the Scripture was fulfilled, the one stating: And Abraham believed God, and it was reckoned to him for righteousness, and he was called God's friend.

Abraham is venerated as "the father of believers" to this day. In Rom. 4:10-12 Paul shows in a most striking way that Abraham is the father of believers, of both the uncircumcised and the circumcised. Being Jewish Christians, the readers of James wanted to be true spiritual sons of Abraham and have a faith exactly like his. When James calls him "*our* father Abraham" he refers to him as the great national ancestor of himself and of his readers; what James has to say about the spiritual connection with Abraham appears in the predications. In Romans 4 Paul naturally presents also the spiritual connection of the Gentile believers with Abraham, a connection that is fully on a par with that of all Jewish believers. Since he is addressing only Jewish believers before the question regarding Gentiles arose, James naturally says nothing in regard to the latter; a short time after this epistle was written, at the conference in Jerusalem, James takes his stand with Peter and with Paul regarding the Gentile believers who were then coming into the church.

The readers were not using the example of Abraham as a proof that faith without works is enough for salvation. James is not controverting this idea; he does not mention it. To introduce this idea is to start an unnecessary controversy.

The negative particle οὐκ implies that all of the readers of James will promptly assent to the fact, will not regard it subject to doubt, that Abraham was declared righteous ἐξ ἔργων when he brought his son Isaac up upon the sacrificial altar. 'Ἐκ refers to source. "By" in our versions is unsatisfactory. The works did not declare Abraham righteous; God did this, for he is the agent implied in the passive. The English "by" might denote means; but the Greek ἐκ is not used to express means, this would be expressed by διά or by a simple dative. God's verdict on Abraham arose "out of" works: this verdict was the outcome, the result, of works. Although only the one great work is mentioned, the plural "out of works" is a plural of the category and is in place. To make one work the source of the verdict is to use works when doing so. The plural does not mean that this one work completed the line of Abraham's works and thus finally secured the great verdict for Abraham.

Ἐδικαιώθη is the historical aorist, and the verb is as completely forensic in James as it is in Paul, as it is everywhere in the Bible, as it is in the Hebrew and in the Greek even outside of the Bible. It implies that God is the Judge who pronounces the verdict "righteous!" This significance has been established from every angle. The passive is a true passive and is not to be understood in the sense of tne middle "became righteous"; it means "was declared righteous." *Ist* or *hat sich gerecht erwiesen* (Calvin, Philippi), and *dazu gelangen, dass man gerecht ist* (von Hofmann), are wrong translations linguistically as well as Scripturally. The one Judge regarding righteousness is God, which fact nothing will ever alter. Δικαιοῦν and σώζειν, "to declare righteous" and "to save," are not the same; to substitute the one for the other deflects us from the Judge, his judgment seat, his verdict, the relation into which this verdict places us. I may *save* a drowning man without pronouncing a *verdict* on him.

The participial addition is of the utmost importance. Since it is an aorist it may indicate an action that is simultaneous with or antecedent to the action of the main verb: "at the moment he brought up Isaac," or "having brought him up," "after he brought him up." This point is immaterial, for it is settled by ἐκ: the verdict resulted "out of" the works.

The essential point is the fact that James is not speaking of the *first* verdict which God pronounced on Abraham when Abraham was *first* brought to faith. That occurred before Abraham had done a single work. That was a verdict ἐκ πίστεως, out of faith alone. The content of this faith, which makes it the source of God's verdict, is Christ, the Christ of the promise of the Old Testament and of the fulfillment of the New Testament. Paul presents this first verdict of God's fully and with vigor in various portions of his epistles. James presents God's *subsequent* verdicts. The last *subsequent* verdict is the one which we all expect at the last day. We have it recorded in advance in full in Matt. 25:31-46. As James says, it will be rendered "not out of faith alone" (v. 23). Certainly not. If any *subsequent* verdict finds us without the works of faith it will find us with a faith that is at best dead and barren. The verdict on that faith is condemnation since such a faith could embrace Christ only outwardly. Every *subsequent* verdict that finds us with the works of faith acquits us, declares us righteous, for the works of faith attest the genuineness of the faith which inwardly and truly clings to Christ. The most notable of these subsequent verdicts is the final one at the last day.

Like James, Paul, too, refers to these subsequent verdicts. That is why he constantly urges his readers to do good works (I Cor. 15:58; II Cor. 9:8; Eph. 2:10; Col. 1:10; I Tim. 6:18, to mention only these). It is the preaching of the Sermon on the Mount over again. Like James, Paul presents the final subsequent verdict as being one that is based on the works of faith (II Cor. 5:10; Rom. 2:6; 14:12). This is again the preaching of Jesus in Matt. 16:27; John 5:29. Finally look at Rev. 2:23; 20:12; 22:12.

We have the *same doctrine throughout*. The supposed clash between James and Paul is not based on facts. As James, so Paul knows of no verdict of acquittal for a faith that is dead and barren. Every subsequent verdict must include the works of faith. From the time of its creation true faith must attest itself by corresponding works. "And thus it would really be time for theology to perceive as its own misunderstanding of James the misunderstanding about Paul which it saddles on James." Beyschlag. See also v. 1.

There is no difference between James and Paul in regard to faith, good works, and declaring righteous. The difference that is sought in these terms with the object of harmonizing James and Paul fails of its good intent. Paul goes farther than James, for he is compelled to do so; he deals with the sinner's *first* acquittal, which James has no occasion to do; he also deals with *works of law,* which James does not need to treat. The readers of James were inclined to evade good works and to rely on a dead faith; those of Paul to rely on works of law without Christ and true faith in him.

James selects the greatest work of Abraham's faith, the deed which Abraham performed when he placed Isaac, his son, on the sacrificial altar. Review *The Interpretation of Hebrews,* chapter 11, 17-19, in order to understand this work of faith fully. Ἀνενέγκας ἐπί = "brought up upon the altar"; at this point, when Isaac had been placed on the altar, God intervened. James might have referred to some other work of faith that was done by Abraham, or he might have mentioned more than one work as the writer of Hebrews (11:8-19) does. Since this greatest work was the crown of all others it serves the writer's purpose eminently. Abraham had already been declared righteous (Gen. 15:6, this, too, was a subsequent verdict); he was now again declared righteous by another subsequent verdict (Gen. 22:16-18). While the word "was declared righteous" does not occur in connection with the latter, no more decisive verdict was ever pronounced upon any man. It is well to bear in mind the fact that God has many ways of declaring righteous; note, for instance, how Jesus acquitted the malefactor, Luke 23:43.

22) While he still retains the singular "thou" James states what this act of faith on Abraham's part meant: "Thou seest that the faith was helping by means of his works." C.-K. 442, etc., is right: συνεργέω= "to help." It does not mean "to cooperate with" as some suppose. C.-K. says that the entire connection becomes incomprehensible, and the very point of proof is destroyed, when it is supposed that a cooperation or working together is spoken of so that the works, too, become the workers; on the contrary, it is faith through which the works have value in that they attest the genuineness and the living quality of the faith; faith proves itself in our life by the fact that it acts, loves, suffers, etc. "Everywhere where the word occurs it speaks of help, assistance." We add that only when the subject is plural does a cooperation occur, and it is then a cooperation of the parts of this plural subject alone (Rom. 8:28, πάντα).

The dative τοῖς ἔργοις is one of means and is not due to the σύν in the verb. It is a current error that faith and works (or faith and love) pull together like a team of horses. Works are not independent, they cannot cooperate or stand in an equal partnership with faith. They are produced by true faith, and faith uses them as its means. The sense is: "the faith was helping by means of the works." The imperfect tense leads us to expect a following aorist even as we are as yet not told to what Abraham's faith was helping by means of his works.

Three historical aorists tell us this fact: "and as a result of the works the faith *was brought to its goal*, and the Scripture *was fulfilled*, the one stating: 'And Abraham believed God, and it was reckoned to him for righteousness,' and he *was called* God's friend." To this outcome Abraham's faith helped "by means of his *works.*" We once more have the phrase "as a result of the *works,*" and it now occurs in the statement that the faith of Abraham was brought to its great goal.

We should not translate ἐτελειώθη Abraham's faith "was made perfect" (our versions), for this would leave a wrong impression. One might think that Abraham's faith had hitherto been imperfect, had not been sufficient for God to declare him righteous. And the translation Abraham's faith "was brought to completion" would leave the impression that Abraham's faith had been incomplete until the time of the offering of Isaac so that God could not really justify him until Abraham brought this offering. In Roman Catholic phraseology: until the time of the offering of Isaac Abraham would have had only a *fides informata;* his work of offering Isaac then converted this faith into a *fides formata,* which was at last perfected or made complete. Only a Romanist believes that.

'Ετελειώθη means that Abraham's faith "was brought to its goal." It is passive: *God* brought Abraham's faith to its goal. God did this ἐκ τῶν ἔργων, "from out of the works," i.e., these works that were involved in Abraham's offering of Isaac, "as the outcome or result" of these works. God called upon Abraham to do these works in faith; Abraham's faith helped by means of these works so that God brought Abraham's faith to its goal as the outcome of works. The verb συνήργει leaves unsaid *to what* Abraham's faith "was helping by means of his works"; we now learn to what it was, namely to the goal to which God wanted to bring his faith and did bring it. That, however, advances us only one step. We must now be told what this goal was to which God brought Abraham's faith while God let Abraham help by means of his works, God brought Abraham's faith to its goal as a result of these works.

23) We are now told this. The goal is the fulfillment of the Scripture passage concerning Abraham:

"And Abraham believed God, and it was reckoned to him for righteousness." We again have the passive ἐπληρώθη: "and the Scripture was fulfilled, the one stating, etc."; it was fulfilled *by God*. This reads like a reference to a prophecy or a promise, and such it is.

"Abraham believed God"; πιστεύω with the dative does not mean that Abraham believed *in* God, but that he believed what God said. Thirty years before God called for the works of Abraham's faith that were manifested in the offering up of Isaac, God spoke the great prophecy and promise that is recorded in Gen. 15:1-5, regarding which v. 6 states that Abraham believed it when he heard it, and that God reckoned his faith to him for righteousness. Scripture records this fact (Gen. 15:6). James says that thirty years later, when at God's command Abraham, who had believed that prophecy and promise, offered Isaac and thereby, as it seemed, was about to destroy that prophecy and promise, God fulfilled this Scripture which is set down for us in Gen. 15:6, this Scripture about Abraham's believing God, etc. The readers of James know how God fulfilled it. He did not overthrow that Scripture, did not cancel the prophecy and promise recorded in Gen. 15:1-5 and thereby make null and void the faith with which Abraham had for thirty years believed (Gen. 15:6), the faith which in this last supreme ordeal was ready to go as far as Heb. 11:17 indicates. Although the command to sacrifice Isaac seemed a nullification of Gen. 15:6 it proved a fulfillment. God preserved Isaac.

At the time of this offering up of his son Abraham's believing God thirty years before was vindicated. God maintained the prophecy and promise of thirty years before, which rested entirely on Isaac. Abraham laid Isaac on the altar, but God preserved Isaac without even raising him from the dead (Heb. 11:17). Abraham's faith of thirty years before, which he had kept alive for thirty years, "was reckoned to him for righteousness." God stood by that reckoning and that verdict of his when Abraham, still believing what God had said, laid Isaac on the altar. After his son had been preserved to him, Abraham heard the blessed words that are recorded Gen. 22:16-18, words which were even sealed with an oath. This was renewed assurance to Abraham's faith that what God had said thirty years before would be fulfilled to the uttermost. To this goal Abraham's faith was brought by God.

Yet—and this is the point which James would make —not without the works of Abraham but as a result of these works, i.e., as a result (ἐκ) of Abraham's deeds when he did with Isaac what he had been told to do by God. This is the value of Abraham's works of faith.

The subsequent verdicts of God, which declare a man righteous, have reference to a faith which produces these its proper fruits. Λογίζομαί τινι εἰς τι = "to reckon to somebody for something" and is the *terminus technicus* of Scripture for God's act of declaring righteous, which C.-K. 681 defines: "Something is transferred to the subject (person) in question and reckoned as his, which he for himself does not have . . . it is accounted to the person *per substitutionem;* the object present (faith) takes the place of what it counts for (righteousness), it is substituted for it." In these subsequent verdicts on Abraham his faith with all its works did not *make* him righteous, God merely acknowledged what Abraham had been *made*. Although he was not righteous but a sinner, God counted, reckoned, pronounced him righteous, and did that not because of the worth and merit of his *act* of believing but because of the value of *what* he embraced by believing. Abraham embraced the promised Messiah and the perfect righteousness of this Messiah (John 8:56) as it was offered to him in God's promise. That is the substitution which is involved in God's reckoning of faith **as right-**

eousness, acquitting the believer and pronouncing him righteous. See the further exposition in Rom. 4:3.

As a further result of the goal of Abraham's works of faith James adds the fact that "he was called God's friend." This title for Abraham became current among believers. The genitive "of God" is not objective: "friend to God," but subjective: God regarded and treated him as a friend. This statement does not occur in the Old Testament but is drawn from it. In II Chron. 20:7 Abraham is called "thy friend forever," LXX, ὁ ἠγαπημένος σου εἰς τὸν αἰῶνα; in Isa. 41:8 "my friend," LXX, ὃν ἠγάπησα. While φίλος does not occur, we find Philo using it, and the church fathers, of course, also employ it. The Arabs still use it frequently: "Khalil Allah" (Allah's friend), or simply "El Khalil" (the friend). Even Hebron, the city of Abraham, is termed "El Khalil." The thought of James is that God reckoned Abraham as his friend because of the way in which Abraham's faith showed itself *in the works* of faith.

24) From the facts regarding Abraham as they are recorded in this passage of Scripture (Gen. 15:6) and as they are amplified by Abraham's offering up of Isaac we are able to gather what applies to faith in every person's case. **You perceive that as a result of works a person is declared righteous, not as a result of faith alone.**

The rendering of the A. V. is more correct than that of the R. V., for μόνον must retain its emphasis. In the R. V. the emphasis is on "faith." We have shown that James is dealing with God's *subsequent* verdicts and not, as Paul, with God's *first* verdict, when, as Paul states it in Rom. 4:5, God "declares the ungodly man (ἀσεβῆ) righteous." Every subsequent verdict is drawn "out of works" and not "out of faith alone." A dead and barren faith does not secure the verdict, let "anyone" say what he will (τὶς in v. 18a). The fact that these are works of genuine faith is evident; dead and barren faith has no works, it is dead and barren for that very reason.

When in Rom. 3:28 Paul writes χωρὶς ἔργων νόμου, "without works of law," these works are entirely different from the works of faith of which James speaks. Whatever lies at their root, whether it is a dead faith or not, their very name "works of law" shows that they have nothing to do with the gospel, which produces true faith and true works of faith. To rely on "works of law" in order to procure God's favorable verdict, is to repudiate Christ and true faith in him. This is the truth that workers of law and Judaizers compelled Paul to set forth at length. James has people to contend with who imagine that they are able to retain God's favorable verdict without the works of faith, who fail to see that they would then have only a dead faith. After telling them that such a faith is dead, without profit, and barren as far as salvation is concerned, James says that in the case of Abraham they may see that a person is declared righteous by God "not out of (ἐκ, as a result of) faith alone." It is certainly true, as true as the fact that no person is declared righteous "as a result of works of law." The present tense is used in general propositions.

Rahab's Faith Had Works, v. 25, 26

25) James adds another illustration to the same effect. It is in contrast to Abraham in many respects. This is a woman, a pagan, who was a harlot during her life as a pagan. More noteworthy still. Abraham had believed for thirty years; but this pagan woman had recently come to faith when the Israelites were surrounding Jericho and sent their spies into the city. In Josh. 2:9-11 we have her confession of faith. Rahab is listed among the ancestors of Jesus, Matt. 1:5. **Likewise, moreover, also Rahab, the harlot, was she not declared righteous when**

she received the messengers and hurried them out by another way?

"Likewise" makes Rahab's a parallel case, and δέ adds it as one that has outwardly different features. James even has a parallel wording: the question, "was she not declared righteous?" Her name is placed forward with an apposition, her works are added by aorist participles. All this is exactly as it was in v. 21. R. 966 and 1128 let the participles state the reason or cause for which Rahab was declared righteous; see the identical construction of the participle in v. 21.

So young is this woman's faith; yet because it was a genuine faith it had corresponding works: she received the messengers, she protected them, she hurried them off (ἐκβάλλω). James does not need to narrate all the details, his readers know them. Heb. 11:31 reads: "By means of faith Rahab, the harlot, did not perish with the disobedient ones, having received the spies with peace." Throughout Hebrews 11, the great chapter on faith, each person's faith is exhibited by his works, Abraham's, for instance, at length. Like Heb. 11:31, James does not speak of Rahab's justification in the sense of saving her soul. Her faith saved her from perishing "with the disobedient." By God's verdict she was not condemned to perish as were the rest of the disobedient in Jericho. We leave it at that, for even in the verdict of God regarding the preservation of her life we see a faith that is alive with works. Her subsequent history shows further, saving verdicts of God.

26) James once more sums it all up as he does in v. 17: **For as the body without breath is dead, so also the faith without works is dead.** The emphasis is on "dead" which was the decisive word also in v. 17. One dead thing is likened to another, namely a physically dead thing and a spiritually dead thing. We are able to see the former: "the body without breath"; nobody doubts its deadness. Faith cannot be

seen because it is in the heart; but "the faith without works" is just as dead.

The *tertium comparationis* is found in the two χωρίς phrases: "without breath—without works." Fault is found with this comparison. Breath and works are called incongruous as far as their relation to the body and to the faith is concerned. But this implies extending the *tertium*. Only in one point need there be congruity, and James certainly names that point: absence proving deadness. Absence of breath, deadness of the body; absence of works, deadness of the faith.

Our versions and others think that πνεῦμα means "spirit." There is no reason for thinking that James intends to give πνεῦμα the meaning "spirit" and not "breath," for if he had intended to name the animating principle of the physical body he would most certainly have used ψυχή, the regular term for this very thought.

CHAPTER III

Teacher and Tongue, 3:1-12

1) James now takes up "swift to hear, slow to speak," which were mentioned in 1:19 and develops "slow to speak" as he developed "swift to hear" in 1:19-27. A general connection is obvious: proper hearing of the Word will not make us respecters of persons (2:1-13) nor people with dead faith (2:14-26); proper hearing will bridle the tongue (1:26) and will not put the needy off with mere words (2:15, etc.).

Be not many teachers, my brethren, knowing that we shall receive greater judgment! The admonition is again most fraternal. The wording is exact; μή does not precede the verb but precedes πολλοὶ διδάσκαλοι and thus shows that while some must of necessity assume the responsibility, many others should not do so. We should think of the early churches in which any members might speak in the meetings. First Corinthians 14:26-34 is instructive: any brother might contribute some word; yet Paul lays down restrictions: it must be for the purpose of edifying only, must occur in due order, two or three only are to speak, and the women must keep silent. James has the same ideas. "Teachers" does not mean "elders" in the pastoral office; it refers to members who arise in the meeting in order to instruct their fellow members.

The participle states the reason that many should not want to avail themselves of this privilege: "since you know that we shall receive greater judgment." James says that "we shall receive"; he includes himself. He is teaching in this epistle and is a teaching elder in the congregation at Jerusalem. He shows that he feels the weight of responsibility or rather his accountability because of thus teaching.

Everyone of us who assumes to teach, whether he is in office or not, shall receive greater or heavier (R. V.) judgment, namely from God. God will hold us the more answerable. This, of course, means in case we are faulty or wrong in what we teach or in the manner of our teaching. The claim that "to receive judgment" means "to receive condemnation" (A. V.) goes too far. James did not expect condemnation for his teaching, nor does he intend to say that all teachers will be condemned. Κρίμα is and remains a *vox media*. God will look more closely at all teachers when he judges them. Teachers undertake to convey God's Word in the way in which God wants it conveyed; God will judge them on that score. Those who do not teach will, of course, not be judged in this way.

The damage that wrong teaching, whether it be in substance or in manner, may cause is indicated by what James later says about the tongue. Untold damage may result; we see it everywhere to this day. This text about the judgment that teachers shall receive cannot be impressed too deeply upon all who teach today, whether they do it professionally or as volunteers.

2) Why this mention of judgment? **For in many things we stumble all.** Like I John 1:8, James makes no exception. Πολλά is an adverbial accusative: "as regards many things." "Stumble" recalls 2:10; James does not say "fall," for this connotes the fatal falling, and such a fall takes place only once. To stumble (iterative present) is figurative for sinning without falling from grace. One stumbles and yet goes forward on the road; when he falls fatally or, as the Greek may state it, falls to the side, his Christian career is ended. This is James's great confession of sin. It includes far more than sins of teaching or even sins of the tongue. James places these sins into

the class of the many sins which true Christians confess daily (Matt. 6:12).

If someone does not stumble in word, this one is a complete man, able to bridle also the whole body.

James loves to repeat a word and so again uses "stumble," but he now restricts it to speech, ἐν λόγῳ, to what a person says. James names the goal which we all should strive to attain. The member of the body that it is hardest to control is the tongue. The man who is able to control his tongue is able to bridle and to keep in control also the whole body and its desires. Loss of control of our other bodily members will show itself in lack of control of the tongue. It responds to sin most easily.

The man who does not stumble "in word" is τέλειος; he has reached the goal. This word does not mean that this man never sins again, is a sinless saint. The goal of perfect sinlessness is not reached in this life. What James says is similar to what Paul writes in I Cor. 9:27: this man is able "to keep under his body," make it behave itself, make it act like a horse that is under a stiff rein. "To bridle the whole body" means to restrain it and all its members including the tongue which is the hardest to restrain. "To bridle" then implies that, if it were not for the bridle, the body would run into sin; the sinful inclinations and desires are there and also the outward solicitations and incitements.

James has the same view of the body and its members that Paul has, namely the body is not the source but the territory of sin, the place where sin seeks to maintain itself even in the regenerate. Both Paul and James speak like Jesus who says that a man may do this or do that with his body or with some member of it in order to keep it in order (for instance Matt. 5:29, 30). It is the heart, the ἐγώ, that gives the tongue, the members, the body rein to run into sin or on in sin, and by God's grace this self is also able to bridle any and all members and, when the stirring to sin comes, draw the rein tight like a masterful rider.

How many men are there who have such control of the tongue? James does not imply that there are none but only that there are not many. He implies also that such men are the ones that are qualified to teach and not those who have as yet failed to control their *logos* or speech, i.e., their tongue. By stating this qualification of teachers James holds up to his readers the goal which they all should attain by bridling the whole body. He asks all who have been teaching and who ever think of teaching to apply this standard to themselves; nor does he except himself as the "we" used in v. 1 shows even as he himself is following this standard in the writing of this epistle by saying not a word too much or too little. James starts with teachers but broadens out so as to include all Christians. He uses ἀνήρ as he did in 1:7.

3) **Now if we put the horses' bits into their mouths so that they obey us we turn about also their whole body.**

The present tenses are general: we do this as a regular thing in order to get this result again and again (present infinitive). The point is that by means of putting bits only into their mouths we swing to the right or to the left as we desire, not only the horses' heads, but their entire bodies; we make the whole horse go where it should go.

The fully attested reading is εἰ δέ; it should not be replaced by the poorly attested ἴδε or ἰδού. In the translation of the A. V. James seems to be making an application to us in v. 3; but the application has been made already in v. 2 so that v. 3 brings only the illustration, the point of which is the fact that the bit in the *mouth* controls the horse's *whole body*. Δέ is the proper connective for adding this point. The illustration is so apt because in connection with v. 2

one might question as to whether a man's not stumbling in word proves ability to bridle his whole body. The horse is a perfect illustration.

James uses the plural "horses." Not simply one horse obeys now and then, his whole body being turned at will by the rider or the driver by means of only the bit in the mouth, all of them are so controlled. The illustration has argumentative force: if we do this with horses, strong, spirited animals, a mere touch of the rein swinging them around, shall we not do this with ourselves who are much more than horses? The εἰ of v. 3 agrees with that used in v. 2; χαλινούς repeats the χαλιναγωγῆσαι occurring in v. 2 in the way in which James likes to repeat.

4) We do not agree with those who say that at this point James begins to depict the *damage* which the tongue is able to do. The rudder of a ship is like a bridle and a bit in the case of a horse; both the horse and the ship are *controlled* by a little thing. The damage done by the tongue is referred to in the figure of the little fire that gets out of control. This corrects another view, namely that James had borrowed from a book which he had read, but that he confused these figures when he began to use them. These are figures that are independently arrived at by James himself, and they are used by him with keen insight and great skill, each being exactly to the point. He uses them in pairs, which fact you may call Jewish if you wish. Each time he offers, as it were, the minimum of two witnesses. We still demand at least two witnesses in every court.

Lo, also the ships, although being so great and driven by stiff winds, are turned by a very small rudder whither the push of the steersman intends.

This illustration is still more remarkable, hence we have the exclamation "lo." Ships are far larger than horses. While they have no will of their own as horses have they are driven by "stiff" winds, great gales, that neither they nor anything else can swerve from their course. Σκληρός is used with reference to a dead branch that no longer bends. Yet these great ships are controlled by a very small rudder and are directed "whither the push of the one steering intends" and not whither the mighty push of the wind would drive them. Ὁρμή is the impulse given the tiller by the hand of the helmsman. Βούλομαι often = to intend; in the Koine ὅπου = both "where" and "whither."

5) **Thus also the tongue is a little member and (yet) boasts great things.** James applies the two illustrations. The point is the smallness of the tongue and the greatness of its effect. It is said that μεγάλα αὐχεῖ, whether it is written as two words or as one, is used only in an evil sense, which fact is then stressed to imply that the damage done by the tongue is introduced by v. 4. But this expression only suggests the possibility of evil. The tongue may go wrong and, being like a bit or like a rudder, may do corresponding damage. James, however, reserves the damage done by it for a separate treatment. Note the alliteration: μικρὸν μέλος . . . μεγάλα; so also in the following the play on ἡλίκον . . . ἡλίκην.

The damage which the tongue does is now illustrated in a striking way. **Lo, what sized fire kindles what sized forest!** The fewest words, the mightiest picture. The play on ἡλίκος should not be lost as it is in our versions. "What sized" = a *tiny* spark when it is used with reference to fire; yet it = immense size when it is used with reference to woods or forests. The smallness and the greatness used in the previous illustrations remain; but whereas the horses and the ships are *controlled* by a slight instrument, the tiny fire operates in an *uncontrolled* way and produces a vast conflagration. To say that these figures **are** clumsily employed is to misunderstand James.

6) **And the tongue is a fire. As the world of iniquity the tongue is constituted among our members, which defiles the whole body, both setting aflame the wheel of existence and being set aflame by Gehenna.**

Nothing stronger was ever said about the tongue. Editors dispute about the punctuation. Shall we draw ὁ κόσμος τῆς ἀδικίας forward and then place a period after it; or shall we draw this expression to what follows? We incline toward the latter punctuation because of the article. There is no substantial difference between these constructions. In either case "the world of iniquity" refers to the tongue.

There is also a dispute about the sense of ὁ κόσμος. In this case there is little reason for hesitation as to the meaning. James has three times called the tongue little but most mighty; he now calls it a regular cosmos, "a world of iniquity," a vast organism that is composed of or marked by iniquity (according as the genitive is considered one of substance or one of quality). The tongue, we may say, is the embodiment of all wrong. It utters every wrong emotion and thought and puts every kind of a wrong deed into words. As such "it is constituted" (probably a passive as in 4:4) among the members of our body; no other member is like it or can be compared to it for range of evil influence.

The fact that what is thus said about the tongue does not apply to the tongue as such but to the uncontrolled wicked tongue is made plain by the attributive participle ἡ σπιλοῦσα, which is modified by two other participles: the tongue, "the one defiling the whole body, both setting aflame the wheel of existence and being set aflame by Gehenna"—this is the tongue that is set among our members "as a world of iniquity." James carries the figure of the fire through.

"Defiling" is thought to be a mixing of figures because it introduces a second and even an unallied figure. This is a hasty judgment which the last word of the sentence, "Gehenna," corrects — the fires of Gehenna are full of defilement. The wicked tongue defiles not merely itself with its fire but "the whole body," for there is no sin that is committed by any member of the body and no sin that requires the whole body for movement, attitude, etc., in which the tongue does not assume the control; and it does this by the way in which it speaks of the sin, helps to plan it, joins with what it says in carrying out the sin, defends, upholds, and continues the sin after it is done, etc. By means of a final modifier James explains how this one little member can thus control the whole body with defilement.

Since the active and the passive participle are so strongly matched, we translate καί . . . καί "both . . . and": "both setting aflame . . . and being set aflame." This means that these two participles are not continuations of ἡ σπιλοῦσα, that the three participles are not a unified description that is governed by the one article: the tongue "the one defiling . . . and setting aflame . . . and being set aflame." This is the thought of the R. V.; the A. V. separates the last participle from the other two by means of a semicolon. The two matched participles modify ἡ σπιλοῦσα, "the one defiling the whole body," by stating both how far this body defiler extends the reach of its inflammation, and whence this its terrible inflammatory power comes.

Because it is the defiler of the whole body the tongue reaches out, "setting aflame the wheel of existence." You and I do not exist merely as separate entities. Each of us is not a house that is set off by itself so that, if it were set afire, it alone would burn. James thinks of us as houses that are set together in a great city. A fire that is kindled in any one house will spread and become a great conflagration. Forget not the forest fire that was started by an uncontrolled spark. The whole body which is defiled in every member and part has a thousand contacts in all directions. Thus the body defiler "sets aflame the wheel of existence."

There is much discussion about ὁ τροχὸς τῆς γενέσεως. We note only the following. It is pretty well agreed that we should read τροχός, "wheel," and not τρόχος, "course" (A. V.; its margin has "wheel"); and as it did in 1:23, γένεσις should mean *Dasein*, "existence," and not "birth," "nature," or something else. It really makes little difference whether we have "wheel" or "course."

Where did James get this expression? It is said to be of non-Jewish origin but is here given a Jewish cast (C.-K. 234). It is thought to hail from the Orphic mystery cults and to have been adopted by James without being understood by him. This is elaborated by some to mean that the tongue = the axle of this wheel, that this axle is heated to a flame, that it then sets fire to all the spokes and to the whole wheel. C.-K. says that "the burning life wheel is the image of an instrument of torture that right drastically depicts the tortures of hell which a man may bring on himself by his unbridled tongue."

The meaning of this expression is not a question regarding James but one regarding his readers. James wrote "the wheel of existence" and expected his readers to understand him. His whole epistle is so sensible and practical that a man such as he is would not introduce a pagan term which he had picked up somewhere and had left undigested. The holy writers are not paupers and constant borrowers.

James wrote "the wheel of existence." And since this combination is not found elsewhere, James invented this figure: our existence moves as a wheel, and this firebrand of a tongue sets it entirely aflame. There is nothing occult, Jewish, or pagan about this thought or about the figure. The figure is not as bold as the one we have in the expression "the cosmos of iniquity." No ordinary reader should have difficulty in understanding it. The tongue does set fire to the whole round of our being or existence. Note how some bit of slander sets a whole village or a town afire. Or see what vicious propaganda does in a whole nation or in many nations. International hatreds are thus fanned into wars. Consider the moral and the spiritual field. Vicious moral teaching, popular religious and doctrinal errors, rage like vast conflagrations and leave countless victims in their wake. The whole round of existence is set aflame by the evil tongue.

Where does this devastating fire originate? The tongue that sets aflame thus is itself "set aflame by the Gehenna." James does not say "by hades," for this word means only "the unseen place" while "Gehenna," the vale of Hinnom, has the connotation of both defilement and fire. South of the walls of Jerusalem lay the valley that had been desecrated by the worship of Moloch, in which children were burned (Jer. 2:23; 7:31; II Chron. 28:3; 33:6). Josiah declared the place unclean (II Kings 23:10), and it was then used as a place for the disposal of offal (Jer. 7:32, etc.; 31:40). Thus *ge ben Hinnom*, "the valley of the Son of Hinnom," furnishes the Greek word γέεννα, "Gehenna," as a designation for hell, the place of the damned; in Matt. 5:22 it is called "the Gehenna of the fire." Some add to the story of the valley, but we have no evidence that the Jews ever burned criminals alive, or that bodies of dead criminals were dragged out to this valley, or that constant fires were kept burning there. "Gehenna" shows that James knew what he was doing when he combined defiling and burning.

Jesus carries the wickedness of the tongue back to the heart: "Out of the abundance of the heart the mouth speaketh," Matt. 12:34; he also said: "Out of the heart proceed evil thoughts, murders, adulteries, fornications, thefts, false witness, blasphemies; these are the things which defile a man," Matt. 15:19, etc. James goes farther, he traces the inflammatory power of the tongue back to Gehenna, to hell as the source of all defilement and moral burning. To know the devasting power of the tongue, and to know that Gehenna shoots its vile flames out through the human tongue, is to be warned so that every one of us may keep absolute control of his tongue, which is, however, done by grace alone.

7) Not only does the tongue do such a frightful amount of damage; man himself cannot tame it and check this damage. "For" adds this further point as an explanation of the extent of damage wrought by the tongue. **For every kind of beasts and birds, of creeping things and things in the sea, are subdued and have been subdued by mankind; but the tongue no one of men is able to subdue. An unstable base thing! Full of poison death-bearing!**

James uses a telling comparison. Some of these creatures are great and fierce, yet man subdues and has subdued them. James has two pairs and uses φύσις twice in the sense of the German *Art*, which we can duplicate by "kind": "kind of beasts," etc. — "human kind" (or "mankind"), the latter is the dative after passives. The one has brute nature, the other human nature (φύσις). The verbs, however, have a stronger meaning than "tame," for not all wild things have been tamed; they have been "subdued" by man's cunning and power. The verb = *baendigen*. The present passive makes the statement a general one; for the sake of emphasis James adds the perfect "have been subdued" to indicate the general past fact.

8) Although the tongue is so small and is caged in man's own mouth, which man needs only to shut in order to master the tongue completely, "no one of men"

is able to subdue it by any power belonging to his φύσις. There is no need to add "has been subdued."

The next words are not appositions to τὴν γλῶσσαν so that we must assume that the nominative μεστή is made an apposition to an accusative. These additions are exclamations, and no copula need be supplied: "An unstable base thing!" (nominative, there is even alliteration in the Greek). That is what the tongue is. The adjective is the same as that used in 1:8: a κακόν or "base thing" that cannot be made to stay down in its proper place. The noun ἀκαταστασία is the word for "tumult."

Another exclamation: "Full of death-dealing poison!" the feminine adjective is used because "tongue" is feminine. We recall Ps. 58:4 and 140:3, but these are not the source of the figure that is used by James. James needs no special source for calling the tongue poisonous with deadly poison; nor did the psalmist need a special source for his expressions. James is composing his own portrait of the tongue. The whole of v. 3-8 is written regarding the tongue as such and pictures it as it operates everywhere in the world with frightful damage.

9) Not until he reaches this point does James refer to his readers and thus applies what he says in a general way to Christian believers, among whom he includes himself. **In connection with it we bless the Lord and Father, and in connection with it we curse human beings who are after the likeness of God. Out of the same mouth there comes blessing and cursing. These things, my brethren, ought not so to be!**

Christians possess the grace of God, which is a divine power that is able to control the tongue; yet James has confessed in v. 1: "As regards many things we stumble all," his "we" being the same as it is in this new confession.

Christians certainly bless God, whom James designates "the Lord and Father"; the two terms have one article. Search is again made to find out where James procured this title for God. Well, he coined it, which is certainly as good as if some earlier writer had done so. The double term implies that as "the Lord and Father" he certainly deserves our ascriptions of blessing, i.e., doxology, praise, laudation. The readers, no doubt, still followed the Jewish custom of adding: "Blessed be he!" whenever they named God. That is what the tongue of every Christian ought to do.

Yet what happens? Provoked by anger, which does not work the righteousness of God (1:20), we forget the royal law of love (2:8) and curse the human beings who are in the likeness of God (the *imago generalis* and not the *imago specialis* in the narrow sense of holiness and righteousness). These human beings still bear much of the divine stamp with which God created man: each is an immortal spirit, a person who has will, self-consciousness, knowledge, dominion. These are damaged but not destroyed, conscience still binds man to the right and condemns the wrong. The point of this reference to the likeness of God is the close connection existing between God and men. This fact brings out the enormity of what the tongue does when it blesses the one and curses the other and imagines that it can do both.

The two statements are simply placed side by side with καί. The repetition of ἐν αὐτῇ is most effective. This is not "instrumental ἐν." It has its first meaning "in connection with." How blessing and cursing are connected with the tongue is obvious. The perfect γεγονότας = "have been and thus are" in accord with God's image. Hence we are to bless them as we do God and not to curse them.

10) James drives the point home: "Out of the same mouth there comes out blessing and cursing." What an enormity! "These things, my brethren, ought

not so to be!" Χρή is found only here in the New Testament, it was finally displaced by δεῖ. It is not difficult to answer the question as to whether a curse is ever justified on a Christian's tongue. No curse of his own is. The only curses his tongue may ever utter are those that have been pronounced by God on men whom God must curse; and then a Christian must be very sure that he is employing only God's imprecations. But how many succeed in controlling the tongue in this way? This is only one field in which the tongue gets out of control. Nor does James exclude himself. A mumbled imprecation, a hasty, suppressed one, is still a vitiation of our blessing God.

11) James again resorts to expressive figures to drive this thought home to the hearts of his readers as he has impressed it on his own heart. **Does the spring** (do you suppose) **gush forth out of the same cleft the sweet and the bitter? Is a fig tree** (do you suppose), **my brethren, able to yield olives, or a vine figs? Nor** (can) **salt water yield sweet.**

These things do not happen in nature. Therefore, if a similar thing happens in human life with regard to the tongue, this must be regarded as an enormity, a monstrosity. This is precisely what James wants us to think with regard to the Christian's tongue whenever, instead of blessing men, it is in danger of cursing some one or actually does so. Rom. 12:14; Matt. 5:44. The interrogative word μήτι (μή in v. 12) expects a strong "no" as an answer; its force is: "You certainly do not suppose do you, etc.?" Certainly, no one expects a spring to gush out (βρύει) "the sweet and the bitter," clear, drinkable water and brackish, saline, undrinkable water. No spring does that; only a Christian's tongue will do it when it is not watched closely and held in check firmly enough.

12) "Sweet and bitter" are opposites and contradictory; the one is good, the other bad, and both of

them do not come out of the same cleft and spring. But more must be said with reference to the tongue. James says this with another illustration. Certainly, a fig tree is not able to yield olives, nor a vine figs. While both olives and figs would be good, whether they came from their own trees or not, such a thing as bearing two different species of fruit is not possible for a tree or a vine. Οὔτε advances this thought of ability and returns to the two kinds of water; and since a spring consists of water, James now says: "Nor (can) salt water yield sweet," i.e., the salt water cannot stop being salt and all at once yield sweet water no more than a fig tree is able to yield olives, or a vine figs. The illustrations are thus carried to a complete climax.

The implied application to the tongue is the point that it will produce according to its *nature* and not otherwise, and that it can have only *one* nature and not two or more. If it then blesses and curses out of the same mouth, something is wrong. It cannot be possible that its cursing is untrue; thus it follows that its blessing must be untrue, be nothing but formality and hypocrisy. It is, indeed, water out of the cleft, but brackish, undrinkable water to God. Even a tree and a vine yield only the one kind of fruit.

The A. V. follows a poor, amplified reading which seems to be but an effort to understand the original one. The R. V. is correct, and its translation is good. Some regard ἁλυκόν as "a salt spring," but it is an adjective and modifies ὕδωρ just as does γλυκύ: "Salt water cannot yield sweet water." Especially the οὔτε is questioned as though it should be οὐδέ (as it is in the Sinaiticus). In our opinion οὔτε is correct, and it is not harsh or hard. It is correct because an οὔτε is implied in the previous questions; it is also correct because the οὔτε we have occurs in an assertion which ends the questions with a decisive "nor." Why this "nor" is assailed even to the point of casting suspicion on the correctness of the reading the objectors have failed to make clear.

The Two Kinds of Wisdom, v. 13-18

13) The preceding section deals with the tongue; in v. 6 it declares that the defiling tongue is set aflame by the Gehenna. Between Gehenna and the tongue there lies the territory of the heart, the passions, etc., which clamor for utterance by the tongue. The opposite is also true; a good heart has good desires, etc., and these, too, use the tongue. From the tongue James advances to the heart. Wisdom should dwell there in order to express itself by means of the tongue and the conduct. James lets the thought of wisdom dominate his admonition, but not in such a way that he speaks of its presence and its absence; in a more striking way he thinks of two kinds of wisdom, one from above, the other not from above, and shows us the products of the two.

Who (is) wise and understanding among you? To regard this as equivalent to an indefinite relative clause: "whoever is wise," etc., or to a conditional clause: "if one is wise," etc., is to lose the power of the question. "Who is wise," etc., asks every reader to examine himself: "Am I wise and understanding; do I lack wisdom?" The question at the same time bids the readers to examine each other and to note well those who are wise among their number, for these would be the models to follow. Moreover, the question indicates that *all* ought to be wise, yet that *all* are by no means wise as they ought to be. James has touched on wisdom in 1:5 and has shown how lack of it in understanding trials may be supplied by praying to God. The connection takes in the whole extent of wisdom in regard to true Christian conduct.

"Wise and understanding" indicate one and the same moral quality as the following "wisdom" shows. One is spiritually "wise" when he apprehends the divine truth and applies it; ἐπιστήμων adds the idea of being expert. The claim that James is thinking only of teachers (v. 1) is not supported by anything in the paragraph; all should be wise and understanding. **Let him show from his excellent conduct his works in connection with wisdom's meekness!**

The touchstone to be applied is "wisdom's meekness." Meekness is one of the great qualities which wisdom produces in a wise person. There are other qualities which will, of course, also be present. James singles out this one because he wants to deal with that side of the Christian life in which "meekness" is essential, πραΰτης as this is explained in 1:21, which is here the meekness in relation to our brethren and fellow men, which, of course, rests on our meek attitude toward God. It is that lowly attitude of heart which is full of gentleness and mildness toward others, the opposite of arrogant self-assertion and of ruthless domination. James loves to repeat a word and thus says not merely "in connection with meekness" but with "wisdom's meekness" and repeats the idea of "wise."

The thought is not merely that, if one claims to be wise, he is to prove it by his conduct; the thought is far more specific: let him take his conduct and show by his works that they are connected with wisdom's "meekness." The emphasis is on "meekness." Where this is absent from the conduct and cannot be shown to exist in the deeds, true wisdom is not present. A man may know much, may display great learning and other impressive qualities, "meekness" is the main thing, "wisdom's meekness." Ps. 25:9; 37:11; 147:6; 149:4 have been cited in this connection, but it is James who connects wisdom with meekness and thereby shows his depth of insight, which is not merely the fact that wisdom shows itself in conduct but shows itself in the meekness of that conduct.

14) James at once states what is wrong with so many. **But if you have bitter zeal and selfishness in your heart, do not be boasting and lying against the truth! This wisdom is not one coming down from above but is earthly, sensual, demoniacal. For where there is zeal and selfishness, there is disturbance and every bad thing.**

From the absence of meekness James goes back to what this absence reveals in regard to wisdom. If instead of meekness you have "bitter zeal," fanaticism, passionate determination in your heart and "selfishness," mercenary, selfish ambition, then do not be boasting and lying "against the truth," namely the gospel, as if such wisdom were its fruit.

Ζῆλος, a *vox media,* is here to be understood in the evil sense; it is not as narrow as our "jealousy" but as broad as overzealousness in any matter for which one contends; hence "bitter" is appended and is to be understood in the sense in which τὸ πικρόν is used in v. 11, offensive, unpalatable to all who come in contact with this fanatic zeal. "Bitter" indicates the effect produced on others. Ἐριθεία is not found in secular Hellenistic literature nor in earlier Greek; it occurs only in Aristotle. Some connect it with ἔρις, "strife," the German *Hader*. But it is derived from ἐριθεύειν, to work for wages as a mercenary, and hence = *Lohnsucht,* the selfish spirit that seeks its own will and advantage. "Selfishness" seems to be the best translation or "self-interest," which terms bring out the personal motive of the heart.

"Do not be boasting and lying" may mean: "Stop boasting," etc., (R. 851, etc.), for the readers would be doing no less than boasting and lying against the truth if they continued to have such bitter zeal and selfishness in their hearts. In G. K. ἀλήθεια is understood to mean *Rechtschaffenheit,* uprightness, honesty. But why do we then have "the truth" with the article? The lack of uprightness is contained in the verb "be not lying." "Against the truth" can scarcely mean "against the fact in your case," you pretending to be wise and understanding while you are anything but that in truth. We understand James to mean that the readers would be boasting of being wise exponents of the gospel truth but would by that boast be lying to the great injury of the gospel truth, and this they must stop. He certainly does not handle his readers with kid gloves.

15) If they think that this is wisdom, it is not one "coming down from above" where "the truth" has its source (the participle is used as an adjective, it is like the following adjectives and is not a part of the periphrastic tense as R. 881 supposes) but a wisdom that is "earthly," the cheap wisdom of worldly men who do not even know what spiritual, heavenly wisdom is: "sensual," ψυχική, of a type that goes with what animates only the body, our earthly life; still worse, "demoniacal," demon-like, note Gehenna in v. 6. All earthly wisdom is folly; it selfishly seeks its own advantage, and men call it wise, but it always defeats itself. We have no exact English word for ψυχική, a derivative of ψυχή. By *psyche* the Greek understands man's immaterial part as it animates his physical body; hence to be *psychikos* is to be devoted to nothing higher. The opposite is *pneumatikos,* spiritual, devoted to spiritual, divine, eternal interests.

This sham wisdom seeks the transient interests of the sensuous, bodily life, and even when it secures them it loses them. "Demoniacal" is not too strong, for, as was the case in v. 6, this traces the deceptive, lying wisdom back to its ultimate source. "These three words, 'earthly, sensual, devilish,' describe the so-called wisdom, which is not of divine origin, in an advancing series—as pertaining to the earth, not to the world above; to mere nature, not to the Spirit; to the hostile spirits of evil, instead of to God" (Ropes). In later years the church called the Gnostic "wisdom" Satanic, yet this was a reference to doctrine while James speaks of ethical wisdom.

16) The fruits of this wisdom show that it is just what James says it is: "For where there is zeal (which James has just called bitter) and selfishness, there is disturbance and every kind of wretched affair." The vices are "in your heart" (v. 14); these are their outward product. We have the adjective ἀκατάστατος in v. 8 and in 1:8 and now the noun ἀκαταστασία, "disturbance," disorder, confusion, even tumult. Is such a condition an evidence of wisdom? Is it from God, or is it from demons? Should such "wisdom" be found among Christians? To this James adds: "and every bad thing," φαῦλον πρᾶγμα; the adjective is a synonym of κακός, the German *schlecht* or *schlimm*, morally bad or base: "every kind of wretched πρᾶγμα or affair."

17) But the wisdom from above is first pure, then peaceable, yielding, obedient, full of mercy and good fruits, without vacillation, without dissimulation. Moreover, fruit of the (true) righteousness is sown in peace by those making peace.

This is the wisdom that James wants all his readers to have. Since it is the wisdom "from above," its source heavenly and divine, James divides its inner quality: "first pure," ἁγνή, the German *lauter;* this is the quality with which this wisdom affects others. Since it is "pure" it is wisdom throughout, clean in all respects, and thus graces the heart.

Then in its effect on others it is "peaceable"; it never starts quarrels, strife, dissension, and turbulence. With this goes ἐπιεικής, "yielding" toward inferiors, not insisting on strict rights. Trench cites the greatly forgiven retainer mentioned in Matt. 18:23, who experienced his lord's yieldingness, which was expected also of him. Matched with this is εὐπειθής, "obedient" where superiors are concerned. These first three belong together.

"Full of mercy and good fruits" means "mercy" toward any that are in distress, who have special need, and "good fruits" of all kinds for all with whom this wisdom may come in contact. "Good" is to be understood in the sense of morally and spiritually beneficial. This wisdom never dispenses anything that is harmful or something that is useless.

The next two are a pair: ἀδιάκριτος, ἀνυπόκριτος, "non-vacillating, non-hypocritical." It does not judge in one way now, in another way at another time. "Without partiality" in the A. V. is partially correct, "without doubtfulness" in the R. V. margin likewise; but "without vacillation" or wavering is nearer the meaning of the Greek word. We have the verb in 1:6 and 2:4. One can always count on this wisdom's deciding every case in the same true way. So it also never acts the hypocrite, never wears a mask. It never speaks in a fair manner when it secretly means otherwise; its words are never hollow.

18) Δέ adds still more; but this is not a further description of true wisdom. It is an elaboration of the fruit of peace, "peaceable" being the first great operative quality of true wisdom. Earthly wisdom and its bitter zeal and selfishness produce disturbance and every kind of bad thing (v. 16); "fruit of the (true) righteousness is sown in peace by those making peace." These have the true wisdom. They work to produce peace in the Christian sense, undisturbed spiritual wellbeing. The picture of sowing in peace is one of beautiful peace. The verb is passive, and hence the dative is naturally regarded as the dative of the agent as it is in the A. V.

The expression "fruit of righteousness is sown" is a pregnant expression which refers to the crop instead of to the seed and thus brings in the harvest. "The righteousness," with its article in the Greek, is the true righteousness which should grace the lives of all Christians; it is the *justitia acquisita* even as it is sown and develops from the sowing and not the *justitia imputata*. We do not regard the genitive as appositional so that "fruit" = "the righteousness"; we prefer to regard it as the genitive of origin: fruit produced by the true righteousness, meaning all the good things that this righteous condition of Christians lets them taste and enjoy. "Every bad thing" comes from worldly wisdom; wholesome "fruit" from this righteousness when it is sown in peace by those who love and labor for peace.

CHAPTER IV

Friend of the World, Enemy of God, v. 1-10

1) The readers have followed the earthly, unspiritual, devilish wisdom. James tells them plainly what kind of people they have become and calls on them in strong terms to repent. We see what impelled James to write this epistle. These Christians in the Diaspora were degenerating frightfully, were descending to the level of the Jews among whom they lived; somebody had to apply a stern hand in order to bring them to their senses, somebody to whom they would listen. James undertakes that task.

Whence wars and whence fightings among you? (Are they) not hence, (even) out of your pleasures that keep campaigning in your members?

Πόθεν . . . ἐντεῦθεν correspond. What is the source of all these wars, what the source of all these fights in your midst? James uncovers the source of these deplorable actions. "Wars" refer to wider dissensions; μάχαι to single and smaller conflicts. The connection with 3:17, 18, with what is there so emphatically said about peace and "those making peace" is obvious. These Christians are not devotees of Christian peace, they are chronic fighters. James does not pretend to prove it, for the matter is all too obvious. In order to bring these people to their Christian senses James points out to them the vicious spring (3:11) from which such bitter waters flow, the kind of a tree from which such fruits develop.

He lets the readers themselves say what that source is: their own pleasures that keep campaigning in their members. The ἡδοναί are "pleasures" in the sense of feelings that please themselves, selfish desires (ἐριθεία, "selfishness," in 3:14) that are pleased when they obtain what they want; see the word in Titus 3:3, "enslaved by lusts and manifold pleasures." James keeps the figure of war when he characterizes these pleasures as constantly "campaigning" in the members of his readers. They go on the warpath, keep up fights.

"In your members" does not mean that some of the bodily members of an individual Christian keep up a campaign against his other bodily members, but that the battling between the Christians is connected with their bodily members. This does not mean that hands, feet, tongue, etc., are merely used in these fights as soldiers use weapons, but that the fighting has its seat — its quarters and camp as one has put it — in the sensuous part of man.

Paul also speaks about the vicious law that still operates "in my members" (Rom. 7:23). Like James, he views the body and its members as territory in which the power of sin, after being ousted from its throne in the spirit, still maintains itself. Thus Paul often speaks about bringing the bodily members into proper subjection. But while Paul describes them as warring against the spirit, James deals with no inner conflict but with the wars that result between Christians, between individuals or between factions. There is no necessity for making James speak of the war between the members and the spirit by supplying something after the participle such as "campaigning against the soul" or "against the mind."

The idea that in the section about the tongue (3:1-12) and then also in the next one about the two kinds of wisdom and so also now in this one about the fights James is speaking only of religious teachers, of their jealousies, controversies, violences, etc., is without foundation. Homilies on the *odium theologicorum* and the virulent way of conducting theological controversies are not in the mind of James. The supposition that James is writing to Jews in the whole Diaspora generally, and that he is speaking of their wars with each other, wars between Pharisees, Sadducees, Herodians, Essenes, Zealots, Samaritans, is untenable. He is dealing with the personal animosities, quarrels, factions, etc., that disgrace the Jewish Christian membership itself. The possibility that this condition may have been inherited from their former Jewish passions may be admitted. Yet to this day and in our own experience, when passions are given free rein in Christian congregations, we see the members tearing each other in all manner of fights, each person or each faction seeking only its own ἡδοναί.

2) **You lust and do not have; you murder and use zeal and do not obtain — you fight and you war.**

This is the dreadful situation obtaining among you! Despite all your sinful desiring you do not obtain what you are after. This is repeated for the sake of greater emphasis by the use of stronger terms: "you murder and put forth zeal and (for all that) you do not obtain." We cannot assume that murders were literally committed. For such murders the criminals would have been executed by the secular government. The commentators note James's agreement with the Sermon on the Mount; here Matt. 5:22 is to the point; we also have I John 3:15 which speaks to the same effect. From ἐπιθυμεῖτε, the evil desire or lust in the heart, James proceeds to its manifestations: φονεύετε καὶ ζηλοῦτε, to actual efforts to obtain what is sinfully desired. "You murder" is to be understood in the ethical sense; "wars," "fights," "campaigning," and "you fight and you war" are to be similarly understood.

The terms used by James are purposely made strong in order that they may penetrate into the hearts of the readers. To say that "you murder and use zeal" is an intolerable anticlimax involves the far more intolerable supposition that James is addressing people, many of whom had committed and were committing physical murder. The two verbs are not arranged so as to form an anticlimax. The two verbs lie on the same plane, the second is only more comprehensive: hate and its manifestations are one form of sinful zeal to obtain a desire, and zeal includes all other manifestations of this kind and for this purpose.

The present tenses in this and in the next verse are not "gnomic"; these are iterative and descriptive presents. The idea is not conditional: "If you lust you do not have; if you murder," etc.; it is concessive: "although," etc., and it is thus much stronger than the use of concessive participles could have made it. In order to avoid the anticlimax it is proposed to punctuate: "you lust and do not have, (and being disappointed) you kill; you are jealous and do not obtain, (and being disappointed) you fight and war." Moreover, it is thought that this construction gives proper balance to all parts of the sentence besides removing the anticlimax. But it does not balance the verbs, for mere lust does not rise to murder, nor does jealousy advance to fights and wars.

James says that lusting does not get you what you want; acting vicious and with the zeal of heat is not able to make you attain your end. He then adds μάχεσθε καὶ πολεμεῖτε, "you fight and war," and repeats "wars" and "fights" from v. 1. James intends to say: "In this way wars and fights continue among you. When these wars arise, evil passions are their source; and since these passions remain unsatisfied, the fighting and the warring go on and on."

3) More must be said. Because they are in such a condition the readers either do not pray or pray in a base way. **You do not have for the reason that you do not ask for yourselves; and you ask and do not receive because you ask for yourselves in**

a base way, in order that you may waste (it) in your pleasures.

People who lust only for what gives them pleasure will fight and keep on fighting for satisfaction although they fail to get what they want. If they were to turn to God and to pray they would have to ask for something that presupposes a far different desire. So they do not ask for themselves at all and do not have the high and blessed things which God would gladly give them.

Again they do ask, but they receive nothing. God turns from them "because they ask in a base way, (only) in order to waste (what they would like to receive) in their (sinful) pleasures." No wonder God's ears are deaf to all such asking. Κακῶς is not as mild as "amiss" (our versions); it means "basely" or in a mean way. The purpose clause states what baseness is involved. Δαπανάω means "to spend" and then "to waste" or to squander.

James mentions no objects throughout these verses; he does not need to. He does not say for what they war and fight, for what they lust, for what they kill and use zeal, and what they fail to have and to obtain. So he also does not mention what they fail to ask, or what they do ask when they ask in their base way. James points only to "the pleasures" that cry for satisfaction and to what these cravings impel the readers to do. That is enough. Such craving, we need not be told, burns to get only base things. Anyone who comes to God in true prayer will come with motives of a far different kind, and what these will ask we again need not be told. Some supply the objects which James leaves out. With "you lust and do not have" they supply riches, money, etc.; with "you kill and use zeal," etc., they supply the thought that it is zeal for position, honor, and the like. But such efforts are unnecessary. The ἵνα clause intimates that what the readers want is only what they may consume in their pleasures and significantly repeats ἡδοναί from verse 1.

To read into these words the thought that Christians ought to pray for the satisfaction of their lusts, and that, if they did so in the right way, God would give them what they want, is imputing to James a sentiment that he never intended to express, and the matter is not made better by telling us that James is using "poetical form" in these verses; or that throughout the section v. 1-10 he may be putting together "not very skilfully" a number of quotations "taken from a variety of authorities in order to make this protest against a disgraceful state of affairs more emphatic and authoritative." We do not consider such comment seriously.

This is the passage in which the active and the middle are used side by side: αἰτεῖν and αἰτεῖσθαι. Is there a difference between them? In G. K. we are told: "A difference worth mentioning does not exist . . . yet the middle seems to be preferred in business relations or in official connections." Moulton, *Einleitung*, 251, etc., has already answered this as far as James is concerned. Business and official relations are, of course, not in place here so that the middle and the active would have equal force, and Blass would be right when he says that the change which James makes is "arbitrary." Moulton says rightly: "It is not easy to see that an author like James should have come to such a purposeless crotchet *(Schrulle)*." There is a difference, and it is one that is intended by James and is noted by his readers, yet it is not that thought of by Mayor and by R. 851 who say that the active implies asking without the spirit of prayer; the middle would then mean asking with this spirit. How can James then write κακῶς αἰτεῖσθε? Can one ask "basely" with the spirit of true prayer? The active = "you ask"; the middle = "you ask for your own selves." Moreover, the middle appears in the διά and the διότι clauses where asking for your own selves is the point; while the active "you ask and do not receive," αἰτεῖτε καὶ οὐ λαμβάνετε, plainly alludes to the αἰτεῖτε found in Matt. 7:7 where the active alone is in place.

4) In v. 1-3 James states what is wrong and where the root of it lies, namely in the ἡδοναί, the pleasure-cravings of his readers. He now adds rebuke, admonition, correction. **Adulteresses! do you not know that the friendship for the world is enmity against God? Whoever, then, has come to intend to be a friend of the world establishes himself as an enemy of God.**

"Adulteresses" is to be understood in the same ethical sense as "you murder" is in v. 2. The latter is a reference to the Fifth Commandment and points out what the readers do to men, the former refers to the Sixth Commandment and points to what they do to God. The variant that is translated in the A. V., "adulterers and adulteresses," is an attempt to improve on the feminine by referring to the two sexes of the readers, which is entirely out of place. The epithet is taken from the Old Testament where Israel is represented as the wife or the betrothed bride of God, and where her unfaithfulness is pictured as adultery: "They go a whoring from thee," Ps. 73:27. Jesus uses the same expression in Matt. 12:39; 16:4, "an adulterous generation"; it is also used in Rev. 2:22. In the New Testament the church is pictured as the wife and the bride.

"Adulteresses" is the stern but true verdict of James on his guilty readers and their shameful conduct. This one scathing word is enough. It should produce deep contrition and prompt, full amendment. The question justifies this address and the verdict it contains. If it is asked how James can call these people "my brethren" (1:2, etc.), "my brethren beloved" (1:19), the answer is that they are not yet apostates, that "brethren" appeals to the faith and the love that are still left in them, while "adulteresses" scores the sins into which they have fallen, which James would eradicate by God's grace and this letter.

"Do you not know?" expresses surprise and shock. They act as if they did not even know; οἶδα is the proper word. The implication is that they must certainly at least know. This question intends to revive this knowledge and thereby to make it effective in them. They are letting this knowledge lie dormant. James first states this as a question in order to shame these sinners and then as a strong assertion which admits of no evasion. They must certainly know "that the friendship for the world is enmity against God." Both genitives are objective, which means that both φιλία and ἔχθρα are active. This is also the case in the next clause. There is no reason for making the first genitive objective and the second subjective: "your friendship for the world — God's enmity against you."

"Friendship" and "enmity" are abstract and general. James keeps the general idea in ὃς ἄν but thereby makes it individual and thus personal: "Whoever, then, has come to intend to be a friend of the world is established as an enemy of God." This is true of any and of every such case which may occur at any time; hence we have the present tense καθίσταται. This verb means more than *werden* (B.-P. 608); "is" an enemy (A. V.) is too weak. The form is either passive (B.-P.) or middle (Thayer, C.-K. 534); it is probably the latter: "he takes his stand," is established in a position or establishes himself (R. V. "maketh himself"). "As an enemy of God" is a predicate nominative. We should note the aorist βουληθῇ which means whoever "has come to intend," has reached the fixed intention, actually reached it once for all. By this very fact that man is

James 4:4, 5

established as an enemy of God. βούλομαι often means "I intend." It has this meaning in I Tim. 2:8; 5:14; Titus 3:8.

Οὖν shows what is contained in the ὅτι clause. We see what adultery signifies. When people of God, who shoud be true to God as a wife should be to her husband, love the world they commit spiritual adultery, they are like a married woman who gives herself to other men. When James calls this "enmity against God" he shows fully that this adultery means turning from God to the world. One cannot embrace both God and the world. To embrace the one is to be an enemy of the other. James does not say that his readers have definitely broken with God but that they are in danger of doing so. Only in this indefinite clause does he use the aorist "whoever definitely intends to be a friend of the world." To each reader it suggests the question: "Is this really my fixed intention?" James confidently expects the answer "no."

In the expressions "the friendship of the world" and "to be a friend of the world" James uses "the world" as he did in 1:27 and much as John does in I John 2:15-17. Worldly men constitute "the world" which is at enmity with God, but I John 2:16 states what makes them "the world," and what attracts foolish and blind Christians: "the lust of the flesh, the lust of the eyes, and the vainglory of life." The world promises satisfaction to the ἡδοναί (v. 1, 3), the pleasure-cravings that are still left in the Christians. They foolishly imagine that they may obtain these while they remain friends of God.

5) "Do you not know, etc.?" means that the readers do know, and that this fact admits of only one alternative: **Or do you think that the Scripture speaks in an empty way?** κενῶς, in a hollow way, its words mean nothing. What James says about friendship for the world being enmity against God the read-

ers know from "the Scripture," and James interprets this for them and says that it means no less than that every friend of the world establishes himself, sets himself down, as the enemy of God. Is it the opinion of the readers that this is only empty talk?

Far from it. **Jealously yearns the Spirit whom he made to dwell in us; moreover, he gives greater grace** and tells us so himself, v. 6. God made his Spirit to dwell in us so that this Spirit may make and keep us true friends of his. That Spirit yearns jealously and is grieved when we become friends of the world and thus begin to be enemies of God. By this positive statement James shows that what God declares in the Scriptures is far from being empty. Paul, too, urges us not to grieve the Holy Spirit with whom God has sealed us. Πρὸς φθόνον is adverbial (R. 626) and = φθονερῶς (B.-P. 1140); it is like other πρός phrases with such nouns; in the New Testament ἐπιποθέω and its derivatives are always used in a good sense, "to yearn lovingly."

6) Δέ = "moreover." This, too, the readers are to note, namely that in consequence of this yearning God "gives greater grace," undeserved favor of all kinds. This is what his friendship to us means. Do the readers want to forfeit it? James quotes Prov. 3:34 as it is in the LXX and changes "Lord" to "God": **God resists the haughty but gives grace to the lowly.**

This substantiates what James has just said about God's giving grace. The haughty are the friends of the world, for the world promises to satisfy their pride, which God does not do. The lowly or humble realize that they have nothing, and they are happy to receive God's rich grace which satisfies their souls. They are like empty vessels which God can fill; the haughty are full — how can God fill them? Least of all do they desire "grace" which is intended only for the unworthy and the humble.

Many pages have been written regarding the different interpretations of v. 5 and the discussions of these interpretations. We confine ourselves to two points. We are not convinced that the question is a formula of quotation. Such a formula has never been used: "Do you think that the Scripture speaks in an empty way?" If a quotation *were* to follow, we should certainly expect the addition "saying that."

What follows has never been verified as being a quotation; nothing like it has been found in any writing as all admit. The fact that the Scripture does not speak in an empty way refers to v. 4 which presents as a teaching of Scripture the truth that friendship of the world is enmity against God, etc. The idea is not that this is a quotation, but that it is a teaching of Scripture and by no means empty. Τὸ πνεῦμα cannot refer to our human spirit (our versions), nor does ἐπιποθεῖ ever mean "lusts," for this word never has an evil meaning. It is also strange to think that envy of our spirit should suddenly be introduced at this point. We note that the attested reading is κατῴκισεν, "made to dwell," and not κατῴκησεν, "dwelleth," which is used by the A. V.

7) Because God gives grace to the lowly, James urges his readers to drop their haughtiness. The ten imperatives that follow are peremptory aorists that call for decisive action. **Accordingly, submit yourselves to God!** The second aorist passive ὑποτάγητε is to be understood in the middle sense and matches the preceding ἀντιτάσσεται; both are derived from τάσσω: God "ranges himself against" the proud — "you range yourselves under" God. The verb means: take your position in the τάξις, the rank and file, under God to do his will and to obey his Word alone; do this effectively, definitely, once for all.

But withstand the devil, and he will flee from you! Do this just as decisively and just as definitely. The one act involves the other. "To withstand" him involves an attack on his part. Eph. 6:10, etc., describes at length with what weapons we are to fight the attack. The tense as well as the verb imply that we can successfully withstand the devil although this will mean a fight. Success is also indicated by the addition: "and he will flee from you" like a defeated enemy. James has mentioned "demoniacal" wisdom and thus now mentions "the devil" himself, the head of the demon kingdom. Although he is great and mighty, we can put him to flight.

> "Deep guile and great might
> Are his dread arms in fight:
>   On earth is not his equal....
> Scowl fierce as he will;
>   He can harm us none,
>   For he is judged — undone;
> One little word o'erthrows him." (Luther)

Friendship of the world is friendship with the devil, supine submission to him. The world and the devil are always associated.

8) **Draw near to God, and he will draw near to you!** The aorist is again decisive and indicates that the readers are not to draw a step or two nearer to God but are to approach him completely. This is said to Christians who are to flee to God by repentance and faith, who will then always find him drawing near to them in grace, pardon, protection. The devil will flee from us, God will draw near to us. James intends to use this contrast. The parable of the Prodigal illustrates the returning to God in repentance and his drawing near to the repentant one.

Two additional imperatives state how we are to draw near to God, or, we may say, what a part of this act means. **Cleanse hands, sinners! and purify**

hearts, double-minded! Note the fine synonymous parallelism, yet "hands" and "hearts" combine outward and inward renewal. Both verbs are used to indicate ritual cleansing, "to cleanse" for the removal of the uncleanness, "to purify," more positively, to render pure. Here the words do not, however, have a ritual meaning but refer to true Christian moral cleansing and purification. They would, however, retain some of their ritual flavor for Jewish readers. The absence of the articles with "hands" and "hearts" stresses the qualities of the nouns. "Hands" makes us think of all our deeds, for they are so much employed for our deeds; while "hearts," the seat of the thoughts and of the will, constitute the inner source of all our actions.

"Brethren" will not serve here where James must indicate what is to be removed. "Sinners" is the proper form of address. The hands must cease from the sinning in which they have been engaged. Δίψυχοι (1:8), people with a double *psyche* — we call them "double-minded" — fittingly describes the bad condition of the heart; it is like "adulteresses" which was used in v. 4. They have a hankering after the world while they think that they are holding to God.

9) We again have three imperatives (v. 7), but they are now entirely unmodified and together demand true repentance but do so in a concrete way, for all three refer to the evidences of repentance, since where these truly appear, repentance will fill the heart. **Be wretched and mourn and sob!** So the readers are to feel because of their past worldly, sinful, double life. They are to be broken up about it; they are to mourn over it. This verb recalls Matt. 5:4 where Jesus calls such mourning ones blessed. In true sorrow of heart they are to sob at the thought of their sins as repentant Peter and the sinner mentioned in Luke 7:38 sobbed.

The next clause, which has only one imperative, brings out the change that is depicted by the three preceding imperatives. **Your laughter, let it be turned into mourning, and your joy into dejection!** These are the laughter and the joy of their past sinful ἡδοναί or "pleasures." Let true repentance turn them into "mourning" — James loves to repeat and to link together — and into dejection (the adjective κατηφής means to be "of a downcast look"); compare the publican in Luke 18:13. The supposition that James demands that the whole life of Christians is to be one of weeping, sadness, etc., is untenable. James describes what must take place when sinning Christians return to God on their knees in true repentance.

10) The last imperative is summary and, like the third, is followed by a glorious promise. **Humble yourselves in the sight of the Lord, and he will exalt you!** We may compare Matt. 23:12; Luke 14:11; and also I Pet. 5:6; yet James speaks of self-humiliation in repentance only, and we should not extend the force of his words beyond that. The passive is to be understood in the middle sense as was the one that was used in v. 7. "The Lord" probably refers to Christ; the term connotes his exalted lordship which is filled with grace toward us whom he has made his blessed slaves (δοῦλος in 1:1). The exaltation is thus that of pardoning grace (v. 5, 6); the penitent sinners are restored to their position in this Lord's kingdom.

Speaking Against a Brother, v. 11, 12

11) It is not exact to say that James now reverts to 1:26 and 3:1-10, namely to what he said about bridling the tongue and about the uncontrolled tongue. This is apparent from the way in which he corrects the sin to which he now draws attention; it is a usurpation of authority that conflicts with the authority

James 4:11 635

of God. This little piece as well as the next one (v. 13-17) are to be connected with the foregoing (v. 1-10), with the readers' turning away from God, no longer subjecting themselves to God, no longer being humble but haughty. This spirit always shows itself in the way in which it treats the brethren. In I John 4:20, 21 the same truth is expressed; James, however, scores a specific sin and not lack of love in general.

Stop talking against each other, brethren! After the ten preceding aorist imperatives, all of which are positive, the present and the negative imperative strikes a different note and itself already shows that James is taking up a new subject. The address, "brethren," substantiates this stern rebuke ("adulteresses," "sinners," in v. 4, 8) and then again turns to admonition. To talk against each other or about one another (genitive after the preposition in the verb) is unwarranted derogation, *afterreden* (Luther), it is our common expression "running each other down," which is still a frequently occurring sin. When the present imperative is negative it often means to stop something that is being done (see R. 851, etc.). The plural implies that this sin was rife among the readers.

He who talks against a brother or judges his brother talks against law and judges law. Now if thou judgest law thou art not a doer of law but a judge, i. e., thou art assuming a wholly unwarranted authoritative position that belongs not to thee but only to God. The first statement is objective: "The one talking against his brother," etc. The second is subjective: "Now if thou judgest," etc. The subjective rests on the objective. Together they form a syllogism which is compact and straight to the point. "Or" is conjunctive and not disjunctive. One may call this sinner a person who talks against his brother "or" one who judges his brother. The same person is referred to, and hence we have but the one article; two articles would denote two sinners and would imply that there is a difference in their sinning.

We usually expose this sin by showing that it reveals lack of love or a sinful condition in the heart. James exposes it in a more striking way, namely by placing this sin in relation to law and thus by way of law in relation to God. The basic proposition is that one who runs down a brother thereby judges his own brother. Both are protected by law; in fact, this equal protection makes them brothers. By first using "a brother" and then "*his* brother" James has the possessive pronoun emphasize this relation. Thus, since talking against a brother is judging one's own brother, this is no less than talking against law and judging law. It is attacking law as though it should not protect one's own brother; judging one's brother is *eo ipso* judging law itself.

The thought is completed by saying what this sinner really makes of himself. James now speaks personally. "If thou judgest law thou art not a doer of law but a judge," i. e., instead of together with thy brother remaining under law to be a humble doer of law and to have its protection thou art making thyself superior to law, art passing judgment on law itself, art saying that it has no business to protect thy brother, that it should leave thee free to attack him *ad libitum*. In short, no one can run down a brother without running down law; or, what amounts to the same, judging one's own brother is judging law, making oneself superior to it instead of remaining humbly under it simply to do what it orders. What James thus says is perfectly true; he looks at the vilifier and slanderer with a clear eye and sees him as a usurper who is in conflict with the position that is occupied by God alone.

Anarthrous νόμος does not = "the law"; James does not use the article of previous reference when he mentions "law" the second time, he keeps the word purely qualitative throughout. The reason is obvious. He is not writing to Jews but to Christians; hence he does not say "the law," i. e., the Mosaic code. He has already spoken of "law complete, the one (related to or marked by) the (true) liberty" (1:25), also of "royal law" (2:8); and so he now again writes simply "law — law." The idea that James refers to the *Torah*, and that he has in mind the old rabbinical controversies about "unnumbered differences of opinions with regard to legal observances" and disputes of his readers about "what was and what was not *Torah*-observance," each vilifying the other who differed from him, is unsupported by the context.

12) **One (only) is the lawgiver and judge, the One able to save and to destroy. But thou, who art thou as the one that judgest thy neighbor?** Who art thou to arrogate to thyself the position which belongs to God alone? Εἷς is the subject and not merely the numeral: "There is one lawgiver" (A. V.), and the sense is, "One only." "The lawgiver and judge" is the predicate (R. V.) and has the article because it is identical with and convertible with the subject (on this use of the article with the predicate see R. 768). This is an important point. Moreover, the one article combines the two nouns "the lawgiver and judge." Since God is the one he is also the other. The articulated participle ὁ δυνάμενος, κτλ., is an apposition: "the One able to save and to destroy." These two acts establish God's position (Matt. 25:46). This is a reference to God and not to Christ who is never called "the lawgiver." Christ executes God's judgment (John 5:27).

The final question is crushing. Thou, whose position is at the side of thy brother, at the side of thy neighbor, thou who shouldest be "a doer of law," whom makest thou thyself "as the one that judgest thy neighbor"? James uses the thought that Jesus expressed in Matt. 7:1; Luke 6:37; Paul uses it in Rom. 14:4, 13. This flagrant, arrogant judging usurps God's authority, sets aside his law and judgment, and presumes to set up law and judgment of its own. The articulated participle ὁ κρίνων is a predicate apposition to "thou": "as the one that judges."

James himself states the kind of judging he refers to, namely καταλαλεῖν, running down a brother. To think that this refers to all judging would destroy the entire epistle as well as all apostolic denunciation of the sins of the readers. Preachers are to voice God's law and God's judgment on evil conduct in no uncertain terms (II Tim. 4:2; II Sam. 12:7), and brethren must likewise correct each other. But the judging that goes beyond this and aims only at tearing down the good name of a brother by imputing to him false motives and intents is an entirely different matter. It is a flagrant usurpation as if we had the power to send to heaven or to hell according to any law which we may be pleased to set up.

Planning Business without Regard to God's Will, v. 13-17

13) Disregard of God is still the underlying thought; in v. 1-10 God is disregarded in preference to the world, in v. 11, 12 he is disregarded by judging a brother, he is now disregarded and ignored when one is planning business — something that is done constantly to this day.

Come now, you who say: Today or tomorrow we will go to this city and will spend there a year and will do business and will get gain — you such as do not know a thing of tomorrow!

Ἄγε is used like an interjection; νῦν is added in order to make it more pointed. In the classics it introduces an imperative as it does in 5:1. The fact that this expression is repeated in 5:1 is not sufficient reason for concluding that the same persons are referred to in both places. Οἱ λέγοντες is a vocative. Some texts have "today *and* tomorrow we will go"; but why James should be thinking only of a city that is two days' journey away is not apparent. The reading is "or." The distance to the city selected and the time needed to get there are wholly immaterial.

Nor is James thinking of only one case. The thing planned is sometimes to start today; it is sometimes to start tomorrow. What is true of the start is also true of the entire project; it is all fixed and settled: we will go to this city (the one we have selected), we will spend a year there, we will do business (we have the word "emporium"), we will get gain. The whole thing is settled, down even to the profits of the year's trade.

The Jews always loved trade and were shrewd in making it pay. Travel and trade were brisk during the days of the empire. The Jews had ready means of communicating business conditions and opportunities to their own people. Jewish Christians were of the same type and were posted on business conditions where they were still in contact with Jews. The future tenses are volitive: we will do so and so. The point is that those who speak as these people do — James is addressing these alone — add nothing concerning God. They act as though the course of a whole year were entirely in their own hands.

14) With a touch of irony James adds: "you such as do not know a thing of tomorrow" to say nothing of all the morrows of a whole year! R. 961 thinks of the English "whereas" used in our versions when he regards οἵτινες as concessive; it is qualitative: "you such as do not know." The texts vary between τὸ τῆς αὔριον and τά, the text B omitting the neuter article. We prefer the reading that has the genitive with τό. This preference disposes also of Westcott and Hort's punctuation which includes the following words: "such as

do not know of what sort your life of the morrow will be." The sense of such a construction would be wrong, for these people do not know whether they shall be alive tomorrow. Τῆς (supply ἡμέρας) αὔριον modifies τό: "the thing of the morrow." "Boast not thyself of tomorrow; for thou knowest not what a day may bring forth," Ps. 27:1. An example in point is the rich fool who planned to build his barns greater when that very night his soul was required of him.

James has this uncertainty of life in mind. **Of what sort is your life? A vapor, to tell the truth, you are one appearing for a little while, thereupon also vanishing away.** Ἀτμίς = *Dampf, Dunst,* "breath," or "vapor," of either steam or smoke; in 1:10 James uses a different figure. Instead of saying "is" James uses "you are," which is stronger. Γάρ = "to tell the truth" or "in fact." James himself brings out the point of the metaphor: "a vapor, one appearing for a little while, thereupon also (καί, just as it appears) vanishing away," now you see it curling up, now it is completely gone. Compare Ps. 39:4-6. How foolish to plan for a whole year as if we were sure of living out the year!

15) We construe: You that say, "Today or tomorrow we will, etc.," . . . **instead of your saying, If the Lord wills, we shall both live and do this or that.** Over against what these people actually say James places what they ought to say as Christians. Our life and our every movement depend on the Lord's will. Without his will not a sparrow falls to the ground, Matt. 10:29, 30. We are told that formulas like "if God wills," "with God," "the gods intending," "the gods willing," were common among pagan Greeks, and that "James is here recommending to Christians a Hellenistic pious formula of strictly heathen origin." In later centuries such a form was used also by Mohammedans: *inshallah,* "if God will," which is a com-

James 4:15

mon, colloquial expression in modern Arabic. Finally, we are told that the Jews borrowed it from the Mohammedans.

The Old Testament, it is true, does not use "if God will," "if ὁ Κύριος wills." The New Testament does. Paul makes his return to Ephesus contingent on "if God wills" (Acts 18:21); in I Cor. 4:19 and 16:7 we have "if the Lord permit," in Heb. 6:3 "if God permit." It is not at all a question regarding James alone. The apostles and the early church used these expressions and used them in a variety of forms. It has yet to be shown that they adopted them from Greek pagan sources. Simply to assert this is by no means to prove it. Was the apostolic dependence on God and the Lord incapable of producing its own expressions? Did it have to be taught by pagans and by their polytheism? Deissmann's assumption that we meet pagan words, expressions, and ideas at every turn in the New Testament, and his scorn of every effort to read the New Testament without the pagan spectacles which he offers us, should be firmly challenged. We challenge also those who find many Jewish apocalyptic citations, no matter how farfetched these may be. As for Mohammedanism, this drew on Christian sources and added its fatalistic conceptions while the Greeks always thought polytheistically.

"If the Lord wills" (either the aorist subjunctive θελήσῃ or the present θέλῃ, one act of will or God's willing in general) is the entire protasis of the conditional clause. "We shall both live and do this or that" (καί . . . καί) are plain future indicatives exactly like those used in v. 13 and are in the apodosis of the conditional clause. A few texts make the two future indicatives aorist subjunctives. We then translate: "If the Lord will and we live (condition doubled), let us do this or that" (hortative) or: "we will also do this or that" (volitive). As for the double condition, the

Lord's will controls not only our doing this or that but also our being alive or not.

Only "if the Lord wills," shall we live and do this or that. It is always *Deo volente* and never *nobis volentibus*. To forget this is serious indeed. *Gott macht dann einen Strich durch die Rechnung*. But when we say "God willing," this must not be an empty phrase on our lips. When James says that "we shall do this or that" he includes much more than business and getting gain; "this or that" covers everything that God may permit us to do. He may let us fail in business in order to keep us humble, to destroy our love of money, etc.

16) But now you are boasting in your pretensions; all such boasting is wicked. To one, then, knowing to do good and not doing it, to him it is sin.

The language used in v. 13 is a boast; it is only a sample, for those who think and speak thus, who disregard God in their lives, will do so many times and in many ways. It is worse than boasting, it is boasting "in your pretensions." The noun ἀλαζονεία and the adjective ἀλαζών = hollow pretense, making more of oneself than the facts warrant; in particular, acting as if one has more than he has when he perhaps has nothing, or pretending to do what is beyond him. Here the pretensions are the fact that these people act as if they could dispose of the future while it in reality rests solely in the will of God (G. K., 227, etc.). All such boasting is πονηρά, "wicked," actively wicked, no less, and in this sense "evil."

17) James states exactly where this wickedness lies; he does it by stating the general principle which takes in much more than is here discussed but certainly covers also this boasting in foolish pretensions. All the commandments of God, in fact, also all the gospel directions for the Christian life are broad and general and thus apply to individual situations and to specific

cases. If the readers did not know and thus failed to do what is καλόν, good in the sense of morally excellent, they would have some excuse. The readers cannot plead for mitigation. So in this their action the principle applies to them that to one knowing to do what is excellent and yet not doing it, to him this omission is plain, downright sin, ἁμαρτία, missing the mark. The two dative participles are without the article: "one knowing and not doing," and while they are indefinite and broad they are somewhat limited by the definite αὐτῷ, "to him."

The supposition that because this principle is so broad it applies to all that James has written in this epistle, cannot be correct; for it should then be placed at the end of the whole epistle. James intends to apply it to what he says in this paragraph. Jewish casuistry regarded many omissions as not really being sins; but this is not typically Jewish, it is the superficial judgment of thousands today, even of many who have been taught and should know better. James is, however, not combating Jewish casuistry here.

There is the similar Roman Catholic doctrine of probabilism, to which Plummer draws attention. Its greatest exponent is Liguori, the Jesuit. In the moral field this casuistry allows one, if he is able to raise some doubt about the full validity or extent of a moral law, to follow his own inclination, i. e., to do or to omit to do on the strength of such a doubt. With this doctrine goes its companion, probabiliorism. On the whole subject and also on the present stand of the Catholic Church, Meusel, *Kirchliches Handlexikon,* furnishes information. Not to do when one knows is *not* sin as long as one can on at least some father's say-so or on some apparent ground cast some doubt on what one knows one should do. How many Protestants follow the same principle in order to justify their own sins of omission or of commission!

CHAPTER V

The Impending Judgment of the Ungodly Rich, v. 1-6

1) The ungodly rich are here apostrophized as was done by the Old Testament prophets when they denounced foreign nations such as Babylon (Isa. 13:6), Moab (Isa. 15:3), and others. These "rich" are not Christians. James does not call them to repentance and amendment; judgment alone awaits them. In marked contrast to this terrible section is the next which is again addressed to the "brethren." In 2:2, etc., one of these haughty rich Jews deigns to visit the Christian congregation; in 2:6 James reminds the Christians of what such rich Jews make them suffer. James now predicts their judgment. If it be asked whether this denunciation applies to Christians, the answer is that it does if they are in this ungodly class, merely bearing the Christian name does not exempt them.

In 1:10, etc., James speaks of the rich Christian and states that he is to remain humble. James evidently makes a difference between rich men and by no means denounces all rich men indiscriminately. He follows the example of Jesus that is recorded in Luke 6:24-26 where woe is pronounced upon the rich in the same way. In this denunciation James is not concerned with the rich Jews who may never hear what he writes about them; his object is to warn the Christians lest they envy such rich Jews. Verse 4 recalls 2:6; some of the Christians work for such ungodly rich Jews, are oppressed and cheated by them, suffer even worse things at their hands while their oppressors live delicately. The humble, suffering Christians must see these ungodly rich in the true light. Read Ps. 73, which is an Old Testament parallel, which likewise comforts the poor child of God and keeps him from envying the ungodly rich.

This section very appropriately follows the preceding one which speaks of doing business and getting gain and planning it all without God. In fact, the whole of chapter 4, v. 1-10 regarding "pleasures" and "friendship for the world," v. 11, 12 regarding acting superior to law, v. 13-17 regarding forgetting God when making money, leads directly to this excoriation of the rich. Yet James is charged with patching heterogeneous pieces together. He found this paragraph somewhere and inserted it here; a "redactor" is also mentioned. Instead of recognizing that James follows the Old Testament and the preaching of Jesus, Jewish apocalyptic literature is cited in order to shed light on this paragraph and the next because the Parousia of the Lord and the last judgment are mentioned in them.

Come now, you rich, sob while howling in your wretched conditions that are coming! "Come now" is used as it was in 4:13, but, as is the case in the classics, it has an imperative here. Οἱ πλούσιοι is the vocative with the article and denotes a class. In 4:9 the sobbing is to be the evidence of repentance, it is here that of despair. The onomatopoetic ὀλολύζοντες recalls Isa. 13:6; 15:3; Philistia in 14:31; Moab in 16:7; Tyre and the ships of Tarshish (23:1, 14), to mention only the howling of these Old Testament nations when judgment descends upon them. This word came to be used only with reference to utter woe and no longer with reference to jubilation. Audible sobbing is to be pierced with agonized wailing.

Ἐπί is "over" and is best rendered into English by "in." "Wretchedness" is the noun that corresponds to the verb that is used in 4:9, but this wretchedness is now not the feeling of repentance but the effect of fatal judgment. The present participle "those coming" is a prospective present (R. 1116); James sees the wretchednesses "coming" and thus bids these ungodly rich to howl in advance of their coming.

2) **Your wealth has rotted, and your garments have become moth-eaten. Your gold and your silver has rusted; and their rust shall be for testimony to you and shall eat your flesh as fire. You laid up treasure in the Last Days!**

This is their treasure and their wealth; it is full of destruction for itself and for those who have given their hearts to it. The allusion to Matt. 6:20, 21 is plain; but James has pondered on this word of Jesus' and carries it much farther as his subject demands, namely the judgment on the ungodly rich.

"Your wealth" is a comprehensive designation for all the earthly riches on which these men have set their hearts, their very name οἱ πλούσιοι is derived from ὁ πλοῦτος; "your garments," "your gold and silver" are concrete specifications which let the readers dwell on separate items of wealth. This is the only wealth that these men have; they are not rich in God as James wants his brethren to be: "rich in faith and heirs of the kingdom" (2:5); they are not "rich toward God" (Luke 12:21). We recall Jesus' word about "the deceitfulness of riches" (Matt. 13:22); the rich young ruler who would not tear his heart from his riches, Luke 18:23; Matt. 19:23; Rev. 2:9, and other passages.

"Has rotted" is likewise comprehensive and is thus followed by "have become moth-eaten," "has rusted," in the specifications. These perfects (the first and second perfect) need not be called proleptic, propheticoperfects that are equal to future perfects (R. 898), for these riches have always been rotting, turning motheaten, rusting, they were never in any other condition. They appeared fine and grand but were the opposite for those who put their heart's desire on them. *"Your* wealth," "*your* garments," "*your* gold and silver" do not include all wealth, etc. Paul tells the godly rich how to treat and how to use their riches (I Tim. 6:17-19), they are to employ them for good works. Such wealth does not rot.

3) We need not make excuses for James when he speaks of gold and silver having rusted. These two metals never rust. The verbs James uses are figurative. Wealth does not rot; nor do fine garments actually become moth-eaten, rich people take good care of them. Besides, many of their garments are made of silk. As far as these rich are concerned, as far as these things are supposed to make them rich, these things are like a lot of rotten, moth-eaten, rusted stuff that deserves to be thrown out. People who have nothing better are the most wretched beggars. Their gold and their silver are like iron that is rusted through and through or rusted clean away (κατά in the verb). The whole passage is exalted and is worded in Hebraic parallelism. When James says that gold and silver rust he becomes purposely paradoxical when his words are understood literally; hence the real meaning of the metaphor strikes the mind forcibly.

In 3:8 ἰός (Latin *virus*) = poison; we here have its primary meaning "rust" (Liddell and Scott): "their rust shall be for testimony to you." This latter phrase is often used by Jesus, compare Matt. 8:4; 10:18; 25:14, etc. This rust shall eventually speak most mightily as a witness whose testimony cannot be contradicted. The very presence of rust is a testimony. There is no need to say what the testimony declares.

This rust, James adds, "shall eat your flesh parts like fire." This is even more striking than saying that gold and silver rust. The future tense places us at the time of the judgment. Rust eats iron slowly, fire eats fiercely. This rust affects not only the gold and silver but, when it appears "for testimony" in the judgment, shall act suddenly "as fire." The point of contact in "rust" and "fire" is the eating or destroying power; this reaches its full fierceness in fire, and therefore fire is the very word that is so constantly used with reference to judgment.

James does not say merely "shall eat you" but "your fleshes" (a plural we do not use). Some think of the well-fattened bodies of the rich although many a rich miser is thin. Some think of the burning of offal and refuse in the vale of Hinnom (Gehenna, 3:6). "Your fleshes" is not used as the opposite of "your bones" nor in contrast with "your souls." Riches furnish pleasure and pride for the flesh, for the bodily life while it lasts; this shall turn to fire in the judgment. James believes in the resurrection of the bodies of the damned (Dan. 12:2). "Your fleshes" = animated bodies. At one time these ungodly rich let their bodies revel in wealth while they were bedecked with fine garments and ornamented with gold, etc.; those bodies will suffer the pangs of hell-fire. Regarding these bodies James echoes statements made by Jesus: "the whole body cast into hell" (Matt. 5:29, 30), "the fire of the Gehenna" (Matt. 5:22); God "is able to destroy both soul and body in Gehenna" (Matt. 10:28).

"You laid up treasure in the Last Days," you certainly did! The "Last Days" (no article is needed) are the days of the Messiah, those that have passed since his first coming and that precede his second coming. How many such days there would be James did not know, nor does anyone else know. We have the advantage of knowing that they already run into centuries; but they may end tomorrow. We should not say that "the last days are the days of judgment, when punishment will be awarded"; judgment does not come in "days" but "in the last day." The "Last Days" are rich days of grace, the time to lay up "treasure in heaven, where neither moth nor rust doth corrupt" (Matt. 6:20), so that "thou shalt have treasure in heaven" (Matt. 19:21, spoken to a rich man). But look at the treasuring that these rich have done! They are like him who laid up treasure in Luke 12:21. The word is very ironical. *"For* the last days" (A. V.) is incorrect.

4) **Lo, the wages of the laborers that mowed your field, having been kept back by fraud by you, cry out; and the shouts of them that reaped have entered into the ears of the Lord of Sabaoth!**

Like a flash James reveals by a concrete example how the rich, whom he apostrophizes, obtained so much of their riches. The example is not cited from their business dealings with other rich men, from their investments, from their buying and their selling, where they overreach, cheat, and trick, but from their dealing with poor laboring men. James flashes on the screen a scene such as is presented in Matt. 20:8 where the laborers are paid off after they have done their work. They have mowed the fields, they have done the reaping. These rich men own lands and employ many hands. This scene is purposely placed in the harvest season when their wealth is greatly increased by the new crop and not in the sowing season when the crop is as yet a matter of the future.

Although so much is acquired by them through the abounding goodness of God, these rich men rob their helpless laborers who are poor and must hire themselves out to work in the harvest fields. The reading varies between ἀπεστερημένος, "having been robbed by you" (ἀπό to indicate the agents in the passive), and ἀφυστερημένος, "having been held out by you." Instead of paying the full amount to the laborers on some fraudulent pretext or other a part of the amount is held back, and the laborers are thus robbed. James uses Hebraic parallelism in the double statement, which thus sounds like the voice of the old Hebrew prophets.

The wage held out "cries" or "yells" to God for justice and vengeance, it is a *himmelschreiende Suende*. This thought is taken from the Old Testament: Abel's blood cries to God; the sin of Sodom (Gen. 18:20; 19:13) cries for punishment. Deut. 24:15 demands that the hire of the laborer be given him before the sun goes down, for he is poor and sets his heart on it, "lest he cry against thee unto the Lord, and it be a sin unto thee." These rich men do not only delay payment but trick the laborers out of a good part of it. James says first that "the wages fraudulently kept back yell" as if the wages that are thus retained had a loud voice. He then repeats by adding "the shouts of them that reaped," the loud complaints of the reapers when the shortened pay was handed to them. In Matt. 20:8, etc., the owner orders his manager to overpay most of the laborers; the order given here is to underpay them. But the thought advances: these shouts "have entered into the ears of the Lord of Sabaoth" who will, indeed, take vengeance.

The tenses are worth noting: two aorist participles indicate the completed mowing and reaping; a perfect participle the fact that the wages are held back permanently; a present tense to indicate the continuous crying of the wages held out; a perfect tense to express the shouts that "have entered" the Lord's ears to remain there until he responds to them. James calls God Κύριος Σαβαώθ, "Lord of hosts." In the New Testament this expression occurs again only in Rom. 9:29, and there only in a quotation; yet it is found frequently in the Old Testament although in the LXX it is not always rendered by the transliteration "Sabaoth." The term describes God according to his omnipotence and his majesty; his hosts are the stars of heaven and the angel armies. As Yahweh of hosts he leads the armies of Israel to wreak vengeance on their enemies. These pitiful cries of the helpless laborers have entered the ears of this almighty Lord, and what that implies need not be stated.

5) **You lived in high style on the earth and luxuriated: you fattened your hearts in connection with a day of slaughter.**

This is what these rich did with their ill-gotten gains; in this way they spent the money of which they robbed poor laborers. Τρυφᾶν = to live luxuriously or in high style; σπαταλᾶν, *schwelgen, ueppig leben* = to live in the same way but with the idea of wastefulness (I Tim. 5:6). In Luke 16:19 the heartless rich man was clothed in purple and fine linen and fared sumptuously every day. This tribe has never died out.

The second member of the parallelism states what these rich really did. In this connection τρέφω means *maesten*, to fatten as one fattens animals for butchering. James goes far beyond feeding and fattening the bodies; he says "you fattened your hearts," i. e., your hearts desired nothing but luxury on earth, and you fed them on this. Only a few interpreters seem to know what to do with ἐν. The A. V. follows the inferior reading "*as* in a day of slaughter," but the addition of "as" is out of place. Ἐν is not εἰς, "for a day," etc. To think of Luke 17:26-30 and to say that the high living continued even on the day of slaughter, is not satisfactory, for the preposition does not state the date of this fattening. Ἐν is used in its original meaning "in connection with a day of slaughter," and the context conveys what connection is meant. These rich did not know it, but it is, nevertheless, the fact that their high living was connected with a day of judgment which would arrive in due time.

Jeremiah 12:3 has "day of slaughter," and in 7:32 and 19:6 "Tophet" and "valley of the son of Hinnom"

(Gehenna) are changed into "valley of slaughter"; judgment is often conceived as a slaughter. It is not necessary to apply what James says of a slaughter of the rich who fatten their hearts to the rich Jews who were actually slaughtered during the siege of Jerusalem (Josephus, *Wars*, 5, 10, 2; also 5, 13, 4). We may translate "the day of slaughter," the genitive making "day" definite; yet we need not think only of the last day of judgment.

6) A third sin is added: **You condemned, you murdered the righteous one; he does not withstand you.**

Some have thought that this refers specifically to the murder of Christ because in Acts 3:14, 15 Peter calls him "the Holy and Righteous One," and in Acts 7:52 Stephen calls him "the Righteous One"; cf., 22:14; I Pet. 3:18. But the last statement and its present tense show that James refers "the righteous one" to any person whom the rich want condemned or even killed. Recall 2:6. Riches lend power. However innocent a man might be, these rich fellows found ways and means to condemn him when they so pleased, be it in their own Jewish courts or before pagan tribunals. This condemnation sometimes resulted in the execution of the innocent. To this limit these unscrupulous rich went. James no doubt writes as he does because he had Jesus in mind, whom the rich Sadducean members of the Sanhedrin killed.

When James now uses the present tense "he does not withstand you" he makes this scene as graphic as if it were transpiring before our very eyes. This shows us how the preceding aorists are to be understood. These are not merely historical with reference to the past but present an action irrespective of the time in which it may have occurred. Westcott and Hort regard this sentence as a question: "Does he not withstand you?" i. e., is this not enough to justify you?

James 5:6, 7 653

One may recall John the Baptist who had nothing but righteousness with which to withstand the adultery of a Herod. James may intend this as an ironical question. To change οὐκ into Κύριος is unwarranted: "The Lord does not withstand you," does not stop you. The verb is a middle and not an impersonal passive. We should not translate "resist you," for a righteous man is bound to resist. As we did in 4:7, we translate "withstand"; this the righteous man is unable to do, he must suffer what the unscrupulous inflict on him.

Patience until the Lord's Parousia, v. 7-11

7) Be patient then, brethren, until the Parousia of the Lord! Although unscrupulous men inflict all manner of wrongs on you (2:6; 5:4, 6) and prosper despite this their wickedness (Ps. 73:3, etc.), "be patient" under it all. The aorist imperative is strong and decisive. Mayor compares γλυκύθυμος, "sweet-tempered," ὀξύθυμος, "quick-tempered," and μακρόθυμος, "long-tempered," the opposite of "short-tempered." Trench has "longanimity," the long holding out of the mind before giving way to passion or action; it is ascribed to both God and men because the word refers to the wrongs that men do him and us while ὑπομονή refers to adverse things and thus cannot be used with reference to God. James means: "With steady, unwavering patience endure all the wrongs that men may inflict upon you." We remember that James suffered martyrdom with such patience. As one brother urges on another, so James urges on his "brethren."

"Until the Parousia of the Lord" = until the glorious second coming of Christ for the final deliverance of the believers and the final judgment on all the wicked. It is true that the Christians of apostolic times lived in constant expectation of the Parousia as we all ought still to live. It should not be said that they were certain that they would live to see the Parousia; they were no more certain of it than we are today. The trouble with us is that almost 2,000 years have passed, and we have come to think that the Parousia is still far off. The Old Testament does not use Παρουσία with reference to the coming and the presence of Christ; but it is so used already in the question which the disciples ask Jesus in Matt. 24:3: "thine own Parousia and the complete finish of the eon" (it occurs three more times in v. 27, 37, 39). Deissmann's idea that the word is of strictly pagan origin is contradicted by this early purely Jewish use in which the pagan conception of an emperor's visit does not appear. Ἕως is a preposition that governs the genitive.

Lo, the farmer waits for the precious fruit of the earth, being patient for its sake until it receive early and late rain. Do also you be patient and make firm your hearts because the Parousia of the Lord has come near!

The illustration is to be credited to James although the comparison of the end of the world with the time of harvest is used by Jesus in Matt. 13:30; in Matt. 24:32 Jesus uses the illustration of spring which shows the nearness of summer. The farmer has to wait for the precious grain, and he does so, "being patient for its sake (ἐπί, *wegen, um . . . willen*, B.-P. 446) until it receive the early and the late rain." The grain is planted in late fall and gets the early rain at that time and the last rain in early spring. During this entire time the farmer waits in patience. Whether the word "rain" is included in the text or not, this and not "fruit" is referred to; nor does the farmer receive the rain (R. V. margin and A. V.) but the fruit. The *tertium comparationis* is only this patient waiting for the sake of the fruit; we should not allegorize the early and the late rain.

8) James himself states the point when he once again calls for patience and for making our hearts firm while we wait because the Parousia of the Lord has come near, i. e., is near. Christians may expect it at any time.

9) Be patient, says James, and that means: **Do not keep groaning, brethren, against each other in order that you may not be judged. Lo, the Judge is standing before the door!**

The verb does not mean "to murmur" but "to groan" (Rom. 8:23); it is here used with κατά: to groan against each other as though one can blame his distress on another. When one is full of complaint he is ready to grumble against even his best friends in an unreasonable way. To give way to such feelings invites judgment from the Lord. And the readers must know that the Judge is already standing before the door. He has risen and has come near. What if he opens the door and steps in as suddenly and unexpectedly as he has said he will and finds us impatient, groaning at each other in dissatisfaction instead of being patient and firm?

10) **As an example of the suffering of what is bad and of this patience take, brethren, the prophets who spoke in the name of the Lord.**

Examples always encourage. James has in mind Jesus' word that was spoken in Matt. 5:12, perhaps also in 23:34 (cf., Acts 7:52); that is why he says, "we call blessed," we, like Jesus, pronounce a beatitude on the prophets who were such patient men. There is only one way in which we can join the glorious company of the prophets, and that is to bear with patience the sufferings that come upon us. Κακοπαθεία does not mean "hardships"; it means what the elements of the compound word signify: "suffering what is base, bad, mean." James says: Take "the prophets" as such an example; he implies that others who were not prophets might serve in like manner, in fact, he later mentions Job. The articles: *"the* suffering, etc., *the* patience" = the one we are discussing.

"Who spoke in the name of the Lord" = and yet had to suffer so much and be so patient. Although the Lord honored them by making them his mouthpieces, they were not spared. Note that James uses λαλεῖν and not λέγειν; they merely made utterance, the Lord used them. James indicates divine inspiration.

Some misunderstand the phrase "in the name of the Lord" because they misunderstand the force of ὄνομα. This phrase does not mean "as the Lord's representatives," "in the Lord's authority," or anything similar; but "in connection with the revelation of the Lord." Follow the phrase through the New Testament and note that we are baptized "in connection with the name," etc., believe in the name, etc. By his name the Lord reveals himself; by his name we apprehend what he reveals of himself. So we constantly hear of his ὄνομα, his name. The connection which ἐν implies is always shown in the context; it is here the connection of the prophets with the name, they were the recipients and the transmitters of the revelations.

11) James has thus far spoken of μακροθυμία to which he now adds ὑπομονή. The former is patience when persons abuse us, the latter is brave perseverance under things that distress us (Trench, also C.-K.). Job is mentioned as an example of the latter although he had to bear a good deal also from persons, from his wife and from his three sorry comforters. **Lo, we call blessed those who have bravely persevered!** who did remain under the things that were afflicting them without quailing, groaning, blaming, etc. We admire this brave perseverance in others; let us count ourselves among them when we are likewise distressed. **You heard about the brave**

perseverance of Job, and you know the goal of the Lord, how that the Lord is very pitiful and compassionate.

The readers have heard about Job; James wants them to recall Job's ὑπομονή and to remember how he held out under the severest afflictions. That is one thing; the other is τὸ τέλος Κυρίου, "the end, conclusion, or goal of the Lord," genitive of the author or a subjective genitive: the outcome to which Yahweh brought persevering Job when he cleared up the whole problem of the suffering of the righteous and gave Job double the amount he had before his affliction. James says: "You know his end" and what it means, namely "that (epexegetical ὅτι) the Lord is very pitiful and compassionate." These are two choice adjectives; the former is found only here, the latter is poetical.

James admonishes to patience and brave perseverance and does not fail to add the strongest comfort. He does not stop to make the application to his suffering readers and to tell them that the Lord has a goal set also for them, that his great pity and compassion are extended also to them, and that he will at last bring them out of all their suffering and to the blessed goal.

The Last Admonitions, v. 12-20

Regarding Swearing, v. 12

Now before all (else), my brethren, stop swearing, neither by the heaven nor by the earth or any other oath!

Δέ is only transitional. Πρὸ πάντων is temporal: before the readers do anything else they must cease using oaths and thereby taking God's name in vain. James aims to say that this is the first thing the readers must stop. The phrase does not denote superiority (R. 622) as our versions translate it: "above all," nor does it contain a comparison with the "stop groaning" used in v. 9, to stop swearing being even more necessary. The matter is simple: people who are given to the vice of swearing must stop that first of all, before they proceed to anything else.

A wrong turn is given to this injunction when swearing and cursing are combined, or when swearing is connected with the sufferings that are mentioned in the preceding section. This view confuses swearing and cursing. A man who is in distress utters no more oaths than one who is not in distress.

When James specifies: "neither by the heaven nor by the earth or any other oath," he simply restates what Jesus says in Matt. 5:34, 35. He is not quoting Jesus but is repeating the directions of Jesus more briefly. James does this also elsewhere. The supposition that Matt. 5:34, 35 was current in another form, and that James is writing this form, is gratuitous. The Jews avoided using God's name when they swore; the readers were guilty of the vice of swearing, which James tells them they must stop before all else. Jesus adds Jerusalem and one's own head to heaven and earth and states why reference to these objects in oaths is the same as swearing by God himself. James is content with two samples of this kind and adds no explanation. Yet he says "any other oath." The three accusatives are not accusatives of the same kind. The first two mean *"by* the heaven, *by* the earth," the third is not *"by* another oath," but is a cognate accusative: "stop swearing any other oath" (R. 471 and 484).

There is a good deal of discussion as to whether absolutely all oaths are forbidden by James; the same discussion is carried on in regard to Matt. 5:33-37. On this latter passage see *The Interpretation of St. Matthew's Gospel*, 233. God swore (Heb. 6:17), Jesus swore (Matt. 26:63, 64). Like Jesus, James forbids the taking of oaths in our ordinary conversation. **But let your yea be yea and your nay be nay lest you fall under judgment.**

James again repeats what Jesus said, but he does it in his own way. Jesus added "what is more than these is due to the wicked one"; James tells us what this means, namely falling under God's judgment. Oaths that dot our conversation are not a mild and excusable habit even when they do not name God outright. Since we are honest and truthful people, our "yes" ought to be a "yes," our "no" a "no."

Regarding Prayer in Distress and in Sickness, v. 13-18

13) It should not be difficult to see that v. 12, which is to stop this habit of swearing, is closely associated with the right use of God's name in prayer. How can a person who is constantly swearing meaningless oaths in his daily talk do any real praying or have the elders pray for him when he becomes ill? **Does anyone among you suffer ill,** i. e., something that is bad? Is he in any kind of distress or trouble? **Let him pray!** Let him cast his pain and his burden upon God. God is our refuge (Ps. 57:1). True prayer brings strength, comfort, help. We need not elaborate.

Is anyone in good spirits? Let him sing praise! This word is used with reference to playing a stringed instrument and then also with reference to singing with the voice and the heart, in the New Testament with reference to sacred music. (Eph. 5:19; I Cor. 14:15). As the sufferer turns to God, so does also the cheerful Christian who praises God for the happy days he enjoys.

14) **Is anyone sick among you? Let him call to him the elders of the church, and let them pray over** (B.-D. 449) **him, oiling him with oil in the name of the Lord; and the prayer of the faith** (i. e., of the

faith thus evidenced) **shall rescue the patient, and the Lord shall raise him up; and if he has been committing sins, it shall be remitted for him.**

James takes us into the sickroom. He wants "the elders of the church" called to the patient. We need to say little about these elders; James was one of them. From its earliest days each congregation had several "elders" to manage its affairs, to teach and to see to the teaching, etc. This arrangement was taken over from the synagogue. The elders functioned somewhat as our pastors do; they were usually older men who had sufficient experience for their tasks, and there was always more than one in each congregation. James uses ἐκκλησία, "church," in the sense of congregation. It is not necessary to assume that all the local elders came to every bedside or, that, if more than one came, all those present prayed in turn and all applied the oil. One or the other came and gave the necessary attention.

"Let them pray over him" is the main verb while "oiling him with oil" is a participle, which thus marks the minor and subsidiary act, a fact that should be noted. James uses ἀλείφω ἐλαίῳ and not χρίω. The difference is material; compare the use of the former in Luke 7:38, 46; John 11:2; 12:3; Mark 16:1; of the latter in Luke 4:8; Acts 4:27; 10:38; Heb. 1:9. The difference is lost when both verbs are translated "anoint"; only the second verb should be translated in this way, for it is used with reference to the *sacred* act while the first refers to the *common* use of oil. We do not "anoint" a piece of machinery, we "oil" it. This difference in Greek usage cannot be ignored, nor can χρίειν be used with reference to the preparation of a dead body or with reference to the perfume that was used at feasts; the word for this would be ἀλείφειν; nor can one use the latter word with reference to the sending of the Spirit upon Jesus or the ceremony of inaugurating a king, etc. Χριστός = the Anointed One. "Christian" is derived from this word, and both terms are forms of χρίω. The church had no terms that were derived from the verb ἀλείφειν. We make this plain by our translation "oiling with oil"; "anointing" in our versions leaves the wrong impression.

If what the elders are to do is what the Catholic priest does: put a bit of oil on the eyelids, the ears, the nostrils, the mouth, the hands, the kidneys, the feet, then James could not write ἀλείφω; for what the priest does is a sacred act. The participle which James uses means that the sick person's body is to be rubbed with oil just as the nurse now rubs a patient's body with alcohol. The ancients used olive oil in this way. There are plenty of illustrations that demonstrate this fact. Isa. 1:6 has the expression "mollified with oil"; the Good Samaritan applied oil and wine to wounds and bruises, wine to cleanse, oil to mollify them. A mixture of oil and wine was used in the case of the malady which attacked the army of Ælius Gallus, and it was applied both externally and internally (Dion Cassius 53, 39; Strabo 16). Herod the Great was bathed in a vessel full of oil when he was thought to be at death's door (Josephus, *Ant.* 17, 6, 5). Celsus recommends rubbing with oil in the case of fevers and other ailments. These are some examples; others have been collected.

This oiling with oil was to be done "in the name of the Lord," see v. 10 on this phrase. Praying was the main act, using oil in the name of the Lord was a second and a minor act. Both the imperative and the participle are aorists; but that means simply that single acts are referred to. The relation of the aorist participle to this aorist imperative might be that of coincidence: prayer and application of oil occur at the same time; but it is here antecedence: first "having oiled with oil," then let them pray. This order of the acts seems the proper one. After the body has been eased, the patient is able to attend to the prayer that is being offered for him.

The reason for summoning the elders of the church, one or more of whom answer the summons, is indicated in Matt. 18:19, more than one person is to pray. In Acts 12:5 the church prays for Peter. Paul asks for the intercessory prayers of his churches. As officers of the church the elders do not act merely on their own behalf but also on behalf of the church. Our pastors still attend the sick, read Scripture to them, offer prayer, cheer and strengthen them spiritually. The liturgies used in our German-speaking churches provide prayers that are to be offered up by the entire congregation for any member that is seriously ill. These special intercessions are incorporated into the general prayer. This is a practice that all our churches should follow.

It is said that this oiling with oil must be symbolical, sacramental in some way, ritual, at least an aid to the sick person's faith, it would otherwise be medical and would make the church elders physicians. This is setting up alternatives, using the one to force acceptance of the other, a rather common type of argumentation. But the use of olive oil upon the body was not restricted to physicians; the Good Samaritan was not a physician, nor did he administer a sacrament. To rub the body with oil was a common practice. Paul was not a doctor when he urged Timothy to use wine for his stomach's sake. Any member of the family could apply the oil and could do this as often as it seemed desirable. Why not? When James directs the elders to do it when they visit a patient, this means that the church, for which the elders act, is concerned about the body as well as about the soul. The fact that James writes ἀλείψαντες ἐλαίῳ is rather decisive. Acting as elders, they would use the oil "in the name of the

James 5:14, 15

Lord," for all bodily help comes only from the Lord, a fact which an act of the elders would properly emphasize.

Nor should we overlook the fact that also women and children were patients, for James writes "anyone." It is our opinion that when an elder or two came to a woman's or a child's bedside, some member of the family was asked to apply the oil before the prayers were offered. In this direction regarding the oil James seems to be following Mark 6:13. How the Twelve came to use oil when they were miraculously healing the sick, we are unable to say. In their case the act appears to have been symbolical. Jesus now and then used outward means in this way, note especially John 9:6. The word used in this passage is ἐπιχρίω, *aufschmieren, beschmieren*, C.-K. 1168, "to smear upon." Regarding χρίω C.-K. 1132 says: "In the New Testament it is used only in the sense, following the Old Testament anointing, of consecration and equipping for holy service," a sense that is never connected with ἀλείφω. The addition of "the name of the Lord" to the application of oil does not make this a sacrament or a ritual, for "we do in word or deed all in the name of the Lord Jesus" (Col. 3:17), and whether we eat or drink, or whatsoever we do, we do it all to the glory of God (I Cor. 10:31).

15) James says that "the prayer of the faith shall rescue the patient" (τὸν κάμνοντα, "the ailing one"), σώσει, rescue him from his illness. James does not say the prayer and the oil; still less, the oil used in the name of the Lord (as if this were a sacrament). James has more to say on the efficacy of prayer (v. 16b-18). James writes as Jesus himself speaks when he simply adds his great promises to prayer (Matt. 7:7, 8; 21:22; Mark 11:24; John 14:13; 15:7; 16:23). The fact that all true prayer for earthly blessings is based on the condition "if the Lord wills" (4:15) does not

need to be set forth here. That every patient for whom the elders prayed would promptly recover, and that none would die, is certainly not the meaning of James. To argue that prayer is therefore not effectual, is fallacious; for God does grant recovery in answer to prayer. Hezekiah may serve as an illustration, Isa. 38:1, etc. James says "the prayer of *the* faith," meaning the faith evidenced by the patient when he sends for the elders and by the elders when they pray as they do.

The prayer of such a faith does not act as a charm to produce the recovery. Nor does it act by way of autosuggestion like mental healing. The elders are not prayer-healers such as we have today. Nor are they miracle-workers. James writes to many churches, and it is preposterous to think that the elders of all these churches were able to work miracles. The New Testament tells us very much about the elders of the apostolic churches, but nowhere does it ascribe miraculous powers to them.

The application of oil soothes the body to a certain degree; the prayer comforts and strengthens the mind and the soul by placing the patient into the Lord's hand with faith and confidence in his gracious will. It is the Lord who raises up the patient to renewed health and strength. The prayer directed to him moves him even as he himself has promised. The elders do not bid the patients to rise up and walk. The Lord will raise them up in recovery. The fact that natural means are not to be discarded as some fanatics demand the mention of the oil sufficiently indicates, to say nothing about the further teaching of Scripture.

If the patient has been committing sins (periphrastic perfect), "it shall be remitted (impersonal verb) for him"; ἄφεσις, "remission," sending away his sins from him, shall be his. The plural "sins" as well as the perfect tense refer to repeated and continued

James 5:15, 16

sinning in the past. The thought is that the Lord will not withhold his answer to the prayers that are made in true faith, will not withhold recovery because of such sinning in the past. He will forgive and graciously heal.

Until the sixteenth century the church followed the practice outlined by James. Pope Innocent I is the first authority who spiritualized the whole procedure. But centuries elapsed before the sacramental idea emerged. In the twelfth century Petrus Lombardus named this as the fifth of the seven Catholic sacraments; three centuries later the Council of Trent established the Catholic sacrament as we know it today. Mark 6:13 is thought to indicate the institution of this sacrament. This is based on the assumption that the Lord ordered the Twelve to use oil sacramentally; the actual promulgation of this sacrament is ascribed to James.

In this Catholic sacrament the oil is applied by a priest who touches eyes, ears, nostrils, mouth, hands, kidneys, and feet with consecrated olive oil. Yet "Extreme Unction" is restricted to patients who are on the verge of death; should any recover, it may be applied again. Also the Greek Catholic Church has this sacrament, but it is not administered only to the dying. These data should be generally known. More than a millennium was required to develop the Catholic sacrament of Extreme Unction. One should also know the Catholic theory involved, namely that the Scriptures furnish only germs for many doctrines which the church then develops; one of these doctrines is purgatory.

16) Confess, then, your sins one to another and pray one for another that you may be healed.

Οὖν is important since it connects what is now said with the preceding. The sins referred to in v. 15, 16 are conscious sins which distress the conscience, fall heavily upon it especially when sickness sets in. James is not speaking of our general sinfulness as he does in 3:2. Such known sins would interfere with the prayer of faith and with our calling for the elders to pray for us. They must be removed. Yet James does not say: "Confess them to the elders whom you have called." He does not use the aorist imperative as he does in v. 14. He uses two present imperatives: "Make a practice of confessing your sins one to another, and make a practice of praying one for another" (reciprocal pronouns). This means that we are not to wait until sickness strikes us before we confess. Of course, if we have not confessed before, it is surely time we did so then. Confess "one to another" should not be restricted to sins and wrongs that are committed against each other. To be sure, also such wrongs are to be confessed and righted, but James makes no restrictions as to the kind of sins that are to be confessed.

One cannot restrict this confessing and say that it is to be made to the elders only (priests, pastors, clergy). One brother may confess to another whatever burdens his soul. This includes the fact that one brother may absolve another in the name of the Lord. We need not state that the pastor will often be chosen as father-confessor; and when a brother is chosen he will be one whom we can trust with our confession, one who will truly deal with us as in the presence of God. The great point to be noted is the fact that James does not say merely that we are to confess our sins to God as all Christians know that they should. Confessing to a brother has two well-known additional benefits when one has committed sins that distress the conscience: 1) to unbosom to a brother is itself a relief, 2) to hear the absolution pronounced in God's name affords additional peace. We are so constituted as to need both.

"In order that you may be healed," means when you get sick. To think of soul-healing, or of this in addition to body-healing, implies to overlook the connection that is made by means of οὖν as well as what follows in regard to prayer. Confession is certainly good for the soul. Here, however, confession is mentioned in connection with a person that is sick and wants prayer to the Lord for his recovery. Sins that burden the conscience would interfere with such a prayer, would prevent trustful reliance on God's gracious promises. Conscience would point accusingly to such sins as constituting a barrier between us and the grace of God. All that can be done to have such a barrier removed ought surely to be done.

Plummer furnishes a survey of the history of confession; see also Meusel, *Kirchliches Handlexikon*, the articles on "Beichte" and "Letzte Oelung."

James returns to prayer. **A righteous one's petition avails a great deal when putting forth its energy.** This is a fact. Even aside from sickness prayer is a strong power to move the Lord. James now uses the word δέησις, "petition," "begging," for he wants to bring this side of prayer to the fore; εὐχή includes all forms of prayer, praise, adoration, blessing as well as humble begging. Simple, straightforward begging avails a great deal, for it secures for us so much that we want and often brings us what is better than what we want, namely what we really need.

James says rightly "a righteous one's begging" and not the begging of an unrighteous one. James has in mind one who has truly confessed his sins and has been acquitted in God's judgment, one who is justified by God. We should not think of this δίκαιος as being one who has kept the commandments, who has the acquired righteousness. He may have this righteousness because he has lived in true Christian obedience and is rich in good works, but in God's sight these are only an evidence of faith. All our works, which are still so imperfect, need the atoning merits of Christ to make them acceptable to God. The righteous one is what he is because of the imputed righteousness. To him God's heart and hands are open. Dan. 9:18:

"We do not present our supplications before thee for our righteousness but for thy great mercies."

The discussion regarding ἐνεργουμένη, as to whether it is passive: "when made energetic" by the Spirit or middle: the petitioning "becoming or making itself energetic," is not clarified by Mayor's quotations and remarks. C.-K. 441, *sich kraeftig erweisen, sich mit kraeftiger Wirkung geltend machen;* B.-P. 412, *wirksam;* A. V.: "effectual fervent," are certainly right in regarding the form as a middle. Thayer's "solemn and earnest" is an unsatisfactory explanation of the middle; so is also the R. V.'s "in its working." The passive will not do because no agent is implied in the context. The participle is not = to the infinitive as a complement to ἰσχύει: "is able to work much." The participle becomes emphatic by being placed last in the sentence. A righteous man's begging does avail much when it is putting forth its energy, namely in most earnest, continuous, persevering pleading, *wenn es dem Herrn in den Ohren liegt.* Examples: the Canaanitish woman; the importunate widow (Luke 18:1-8).

17, 18) James himself offers an example which does not so much prove the energy but the sure confidence of prayer and the great deal which it accomplishes. **Elijah was a man of like sensations with us, and he prayed with a prayer that it rain not, and it did not rain on the earth for three years and six months. And again he prayed, and the heaven gave rain, and the earth sprouted up its fruit.**

It was necessary for James to say that Elijah was "a man of like sensations with us" (the same expression is found in Acts 14:15) because the Jews made so much of Elijah. The readers are not to attribute the great effect of Elijah's prayers to any exceptional qualities that were inherent in the person of this prophet himself. He was an ἄνθρωπος, a human being, just as we are. This fact is intensified by ὁμοιοπαθὴς ἡμῖν, which does not mean "of like passions or of like nature with us." The gods were considered ἀπαθεῖς, unlike human beings. The verb πάσχω that is found in these adjectives refers to suffering and vicissitudes that are incident to human existence. Elijah had to endure vicissitudes of all kinds just as we do. Although he was a great prophet he was a plagued human being and felt pain just as much as we do.

The readers know that this man prayed with a prayer that it should not rain, and it did not rain for three and one-half years; and again he prayed, and the heaven gave rain, and the earth produced its crop of grain. This is what one man's prayer did; it was πολύ, "much" indeed. "Prayed with a prayer" is not a Hebraism, nor is it equal to "prayed earnestly" (intensification); it is an intensification of the idea of prayer itself by means of the dative; it is somewhat like a cognate object which is used for the same purpose. The infinitive with τοῦ states the object for which Elijah prayed (Moulton, *Einleitung*, 334); many regard it as an infinitive of purpose, which does not fit this case. The verb "to rain" is impersonal.

First Kings 17:1 does not say that Elijah prayed that it should not rain. Elijah only declared that there should not be dew or rain during these years except according to his word. So also I Kings 18:1, 41, etc., report no prayer on the part of Elijah although v. 42 shows him in the attitude of prayer. To make an issue of the absence of the word "prayer" or "to pray" in First Kings is an unfair proceeding "inasmuch as also the prophets received the power for their work only by faith and communion with God, and faith receives power to remove mountains," Delitzsch. The very way in which Elijah swore that there should be no rain during these years except at his word indicates that he had communicated with God in prayer. As for prayer in bringing on the rain, I Kings 18:41, etc., leaves little to be desired save the actual word "he prayed." Instead of raising doubt about the accuracy of James, or letting him repeat unreliable Jewish tradition, it would be well to study the record of Elijah's action as this is recorded in First Kings more closely.

First Kings does not report the number three and one-half years; in 18:1 we have "in the third year." Thus another discrepancy is pointed out: First Kings says about two and one-half, and James says three and one-half years. Jesus, too, says three and one-half years in Luke 4:25, and old Jewish writers have the same number. The idea that three and one-half is symbolic because it is the half of seven, and that it came to be regarded as the length of time of the famine because it was such an ill-omened number, a number that indicated a long calamity, is not substantiated by a reference to Dan. 7:25 and 12:7. James and Jesus are not using symbolical numbers.

"In the third year" (I Kings 18:1) has long been understood correctly. It does not indicate the entire time of the drought but marks the time after the events that are recorded in chapter 17. Elijah spent over two years in Zarephath, and thus "in the third year" he was sent to confront Ahab. That the drought lasted three and one-half years is a well-known fact of history, one that was certainly not forgotten by the Jews who knew that history far better than we know that of our own nation.

Prayer has done mighty things; it still does them and always will. But why should commentators refer to such fictions as the story of how Rabbi Chaninah, on being caught in a shower of rain, prayed: "Master of the Universe, the whole world is pleased while Chaninah alone is annoyed"—this stopping the rain? On getting home he prayed: "Master of the Universe, shall all the world be grieved while Chaninah enjoys his comfort?"—and the rain came down again. This makes a farce of prayer and of Elijah's effectual prayer. But preachers still narrate rather astonishing stories about answers to prayers, and their hearers are left under the impression that they should duplicate such feats. Dangerous indeed—what if they should try?

19) The closing words of James are still connected with what he has just said, namely with confessing sins and praying for each other. **My brethren, if anyone among you shall err from the truth, and anyone shall turn him back, let him realize that he who turns a sinner back from (the) error of his way shall save a soul from death and shall hide a multitude of sins.**

A loving address prefaces this sweet gospel assurance with which James would stimulate every brother to restore every other brother who wanders from the saving truth into sin and spiritual death. The sentence is written in the spirit of Jesus, cf., Matt. 18:11-13; Luke 15:3-10. The construction is a perfectly regular condition of expectancy: ἐάν with subjunctives in the protasis, future indicatives in the apodosis. James is writing of cases which he expects to occur.

A brother of ours may not only sin and thus have sins to confess (v. 15, 16), he may even err or wander from the truth (1:18, "truth's Word"). How some can state that James does not refer to doctrinal error, that his whole letter does not touch doctrine, and that, therefore, one should not try to change another person's opinion or way of thinking, is difficult for us to understand. James touches doctrine at almost every turn; he is not a moralist but a true believer. To him "the truth" is the whole Word, the entire gospel and not an ethical abstract of it.

What was one of the great dangers that threatened his readers? Why, to revert to Judaism. To be sure, James also includes all mortal sins. But the most damnable and deadly sin is unbelief. Read what is written to other Jewish Christians who were thinking of going back to Judaism (Heb. 6:4-8; 10:25-31). Doctrine and faith are never mere "opinions" or just "ways of thinking." Behind and beneath all wrong morals is wrong doctrine, more or less of unbelief. What erring from the truth means to James is all too apparent from what he says about turning such an erring one back to the truth; such erring means that a soul is in death and in a multitude of sins.

Both subjunctives are aorists of actuality; they designate an actual erring from the truth so that it and its saving power are lost and an actual turning such a lost one back to this saving truth. The first is passive in form but probably middle in meaning. When a Christian loses the truth, it is notoriously difficult to turn him back to it. It is not easy to revive a lost faith. As the passages in Hebrews state, faith may be so completely lost that rekindling it may even become impossible. The heart of James goes out to all his brethren in the Diaspora; he is much concerned that none may ever be lost. He wants to make allies of all his readers so that they, too, will work to prevent such a calamity. They must keep on confessing to each other, praying for each other, and come to each other's rescue in the hour of mortal danger.

20) To be successful in such a rescue is, indeed, a glorious thing. The imperative is strong: "let him realize that he who turns a sinner back from (the) error of his way shall save (or rescue) a soul from death," etc. What a great thing it is to rescue a person from physical death! This is a greater thing, for spiritual death is far worse than physical death. James states this in the third person: "he that turns back." He thereby makes the statement objective and general for every case of this kind. How this turning back is accomplished is indicated by the means: the sinner is turned back to the truth by the truth.

There is only one objective means to save such a sinner, namely the truth; and only one subjective means, repentance (contrition for sin, faith in the Savior). We translate "shall turn back" and "he that turns back." Some translate this Greek word "convert," but the former seems more correct. Γινωσκέτω = let him realize, which is more than "let him know."

James doubles the statement. Death is produced by sins so that to save from death is to rid the sinner of his sins: "and shall hide (or cover) a multitude of sins." The expression "to hide" sins is taken from the Old Testament: Ps. 32:1; 85:2; cf., also I Pet. 4:8. "To hide sins" does not mean to keep them secret; the word is used in the intensified sense, to hide them from God, from whom nothing can be kept secret (Matt. 6:4, 6). There is only one way in which this hiding or covering can be done—under the blood of Christ. If sins are hidden, God will not see them, for they have actually disappeared. Blessed the man who can aid another in this way! The idea that by rescuing another the rescuer hides his own sins is contrary to Scripture, it should not be attributed to James as a piece of old Jewish teaching to which he still clung.

James closes with this statement about saving the sinner's soul and freeing him from his sins. It is a fitting close. We expect no greetings in this encyclical. He might have added a closing wish as Paul usually does, or as Peter does in his first epistle. James concludes as John does in his first epistle. His last "my brethren" is enough.

Soli Deo Gloria

www.ingramcontent.com/pod-product-compliance
Lightning Source LLC
Chambersburg PA
CBHW051414290426
44109CB00016B/1295